Creating the Productive Workplace

The built environment affects our physical, mental and social well-being. Here renowned professionals from practice and academia explore the evidence from basic research as well as case studies to test this belief. They show that many elements in the built environment contribute to establishing a milieu which helps people to be healthier and have the energy to concentrate while being free to be creative. The health and well-being agenda pervades society in many different ways but we spend much of our lives in buildings, so they have an important role to play within this total picture. This demands us to embrace change and think beyond the conventional wisdom while retaining our respect for it. *Creating the Productive Workplace* shows how we need to balance the needs of people and the ever-increasing enabling technologies but also to take advantage of the healing powers of Nature and let them be part of environmental design. This book aims to lead to more human-centred ways of designing the built environment with deeper meaning and achieve healthier and more creative, as well as more productive places to work.

Derek Clements-Croome is Professor Emeritus in architectural engineering in the School of the Built Environment at the University of Reading, UK, and Visiting Professor at Queen Mary University of London, UK. He worked in the building design and contracting industry for several years before entering university life. He has founded and directed courses including a BSc in building environmental engineering at Loughborough University in 1970 and an inter-disciplinary EPSRC-sponsored MSc in Intelligent Buildings at Reading University in 1996. He has also worked in architecture and building engineering at the University of Bath, UK (1978–1988).

He now offers strategic advice to clients, designers and facilities managers on attaining and managing healthy and sustainable environments in buildings of all types. He researches, writes and lectures on these issues for companies, universities and wider audiences nationally and internationally in China, Australia, New Zealand, South Africa, Poland and Finland particularly. Some of his books have been published in Chinese and Russian. He edits and founded the *Intelligent Buildings International* journal first published by Taylor and Francis in 2009.

Derek is a Commissioner on air quality and biodiversity for the boroughs of Hammersmith-Fulham and for the Zero-Fifty Commission for Haringey. He is also Building Environmental Expert for the CABE arm of the Design Council, and a Fellow of the Royal Society of Medicine and also the BRE Academy.

He was a member of the UK Green Building Council team that wrote the Report *Health and Wellbeing in Homes* July 2016, and the World Green Building Council Report 2014 on *Health, Wellbeing and Productivity in Offices*.

'A growing body of research demonstrates that our work environments can have a profound impact on our health, wellness, and productivity. Creating the Productive Workplace comes at an important moment as employers are increasingly recognizing that healthy offices not only help attract top talent and provide benefits to employees, but also create a valuable return on investment.'

Paul Scialla, Founder of the International WELL Building Institute

'Without productivity growth economies are reliant on employment growth. But as societies age this may disappoint. Productivity improvements can be achieved through innovation and as we transition further to a service economy the office workplace is a perfect place to find gains. Research into this field is advancing all the time and this book provides an excellent reference into how and why workplaces can boost the productivity of their inhabitants.'

Bill Page, Chair of British Council of Offices Research Committee and
Research Manager, Business Space, LGIM Real Assets

Creating the Productive Workplace

Places to Work Creatively

Third edition

Edited by Derek Clements-Croome

Routledge
Taylor & Francis Group

LONDON AND NEW YORK

Third edition published 2018
by Routledge
2 Park Square, Milton Park, Abingdon, Oxon, OX14 4RN

and by Routledge
711 Third Avenue, New York, NY 10017

Routledge is an imprint of the Taylor & Francis Group, an informa business

First edition published by E & FN Spon 2000

Second edition published by Taylor & Francis 2006

British Library Cataloguing-in-Publication Data
A catalogue record for this book is available from the British Library

Library of Congress Cataloging-in-Publication Data
Names: Clements-Croome, Derek, editor.
Title: Creating the productive workplace : places to work creatively / edited by
    Derek Clements-Croome.
Description: Third edition. | New York : Routledge, 2017. | "First edition published
    by E & FN Spon 2000. Second edition published by Taylor & Francis 2006." |
    Includes bibliographical references and index.
Identifiers: LCCN 2017007657 | ISBN 9781138963344 (hb : alk. paper) |
    ISBN 9781315658834 (ebook : alk. paper)
Subjects: LCSH: Industrial productivity—Congresses. | Environmental protection—
    Congresses. | Environmental policy—Congresses. | Work environment—Congresses.
Classification: LCC HC79.I52 C73 2017 | DDC 658.3/14—dc23
LC record available at https://lccn.loc.gov/2017007657

ISBN: 978-1-138-96334-4 (hbk)
ISBN: 978-1-315-65883-4 (ebk)

Typeset in Sabon
by Apex CoVantage, LLC

Contents

Figures

Tables

Contributors

Ann Marie Aguilar is Director of European Operations for the International WELL Building Institute™ (IWBI) – a public benefit corporation whose mission is to improve human health and well-being through the built environment. With a background in architectural design, she has extensive industry experience delivering environmental design, and worked for over 10 years at Arup delivering sustainability consultancy and new global health and wellbeing services.

Joseph Allen is the director of Healthy Buildings Program in the Center for Health and the Global Environment at Harvard T.H. Chan School of Public Health.

Francesco Anselmo, Lighting Design, Arup London.

Azizan Aziz is Assistant Research Professor at the Center for Building Performance & Diagnostics at Carnegie Mellon University, Pittsburgh, PA, USA. Aziz is a trained architect with extensive experience in sustainable design, the design of integrated systems for high performance buildings, post occupancy evaluation and building performance monitoring and analytics. With over 20 years of research and demonstration projects, Aziz has initiated innovative data analytics projects with federal, corporate, campus and municipal leaders.

Peter A. Bacevice is Director of Research for HLW International. In addition, he is a researcher with the University of Michigan's Ross School of Business where he has been involved in a long-term study of coworking and the growth of the mobile workforce. Pete divides his time professionally between New York and Ann Arbor, Michigan. He holds a PhD in Education from the University of Michigan.

Peter Barrett is a past President of the UN-established International Council for Research and Innovation in Building and Construction (CIB). He is Emeritus Professor of Management in Property and Construction at Salford University in the UK and Honorary Research Fellow in the Department of Education at Oxford University. He is an international advisor to the OECD and the US-based Academy of Neuroscience for Architecture and American Institute of Architects. He now carries out strategic consultancy on optimising the impact of buildings on learning, most recently for the World Bank in Romania.

Hannah Beveridge is a Senior Associate and Senior Design Strategist for HLW International where she works alongside the design team to align design strategy with clients' business strategies and real estate needs. Having worked in Australasia, the UK and Europe across a range of sectors, Hannah brings broad knowledge of workplace trends and industry benchmarks to her work. She holds a BA in Psychology and Anthropology from the University of Melbourne, a BA in Interior Architecture from Monash University, and a Masters of Innovation, Creativity and Leadership from Cass Business School.

Bill Bordass moved from science research to the multi-skilled design practice RMJM London, where he worked on building services, energy and environmental design. He then set up William Bordass Associates, which studies building performance in use. He was also co-founder of the Usable Buildings Trust (UBT) charity, which promotes better buildings through understanding how they actually work, how people get things done, and the relationships between users, management and technologies.

Stephen Bowden is a Chartered member of the Chartered Institute of Ergonomics and Human Factors (CIEHF) and is registered with the Centre for Registration of European Ergonomists (CREE). He is experienced in ergonomics and human factors ensuring and integrated approach between humans, machines and work systems within industrial, office, manufacturing, oil/gas, defence and aerospace. He has a specialist interest in an ergonomics approach to well-being and the association between ergonomics, well-being and productivity.

Liz Burow is Associate Principal and Director of Strategy and Discovery for HLW International where she leads a team of design strategists and workplace planners that service clients globally. Liz and her team work directly with clients to uncover needs and collectively build key programming, visioning and planning strategies. She has also developed and taught numerous courses at the intersection of design and business at Parsons The New School for Design in New York. Liz graduated from Washington University with a B.A. in Architecture and earned her Masters of Architecture from the Massachusetts Institute of Technology.

Michel Cabanac, Professor, Department of Psychiatry, Université Laval, Québec, Canada.

Kay Chaston joined Stanhope in 2001 as CEO to open Chiswick Park following a career in North America's premium hotel industry. A strong brand was created there which formed the backbone of the Chiswick Park development, emphasising the idea of place-making, community building and creating a destination. Kay directed the creation of an Estate Company that successfully redefined the value proposition to attract end users, sustain long-term attraction and deliver industry leading asset value. Kay rejoined Stanhope in 2014 to manage the Television Centre estate and to work with Alistair Shaw to deliver this pivotal part of the successful and exciting regeneration of the White City area. Kay is now a consultant.

Derek Clements-Croome is Professor Emeritus at Reading University and Visiting Professor at Queen Mary University London; a Commissioner on air quality and biodiversity for the London Boroughs of Hammersmith and Haringey. He is the editor of *Intelligent Buildings International* journal, and conducts health and well-being research with British Council for Offices and UK Green Building Council. He chairs the CIB Commission W098 on intelligent and responsive buildings and the CIBSE Intelligent Buildings Group. See www.derekcroome.com

Erica Cochran is Assistant Professor of Architecture at Carnegie Mellon University, Pittsburgh, PA, USA and Chair of the Architectural Engineering and Construction Management Program.

Dr. Cochran is active in building performance research and environmentally focused practice engaged in educational, residential, commercial, community and transportation facility projects.

Sarah Daly is Director, Strategic Sustainability & Partnerships, Sustainable Homes, London. She has been involved in regeneration and development for nearly 20 years with multiple perspectives from her own consultancies, as managing director of an architectural practice and European Head of Marketing for a global environmental consultancy. Her research interests include the business case for sustainability; health and well-being; skills for retrofit; and modular construction. She is currently working on a number of initiatives with BEIS, DCLG, the GLA and the private sector to drive up standards of sustainability in the built environment. Sarah holds an MSc Sustainable Development (Exeter University).

Mark Eltringham is the publisher of *Workplace Insight* and *Work&Place* and is a writer, speaker and commentator on workplace issues. He was the launch editor of *FMX*, *OnOffice* and *Workplace Law* and has written for numerous publications in the UK and overseas. He is a Fellow of the Royal Society of the Arts.

Adam Garnys, CETEC Pty Ltd, Melbourne, Australia and CETEC Foray Ltd, London.

Vyt Garnys is Managing Director and Principal Consultant at CETEC, a company he formed in Australia in 1987 with operations now in Europe. Vyt focuses on enhancing indoor environment quality and providing IEQ services that improve the health, wellbeing and productivity of building occupants. He is Chairman of the Standards Australia Committee for Indoor Air and is a National Association of Testing Authorities Laboratory Registration Assessor.

Ron German joined Stanhope in 1987. His main focus is predevelopment. He also takes a particular interest in design matters. Ron is responsible for ensuring that Stanhope's buildings are 'best in class' through research and best practice. He is also responsible for a portfolio of projects and has particular expertise in design, town planning and specification of developments. Ron sits on the Board of Management of the British Council for Offices.

Brian Gilligan, High-Performance Buildings Expert, Office of Federal High-Performance Buildings, US General Services Administration, Washington, DC, USA.

Travis Hale, CETEC Pty Ltd, Melbourne, Australia and CETEC Foray Ltd, London.

Volker Hartkopf is Professor of Architecture and Director of the Center for Building Performance & Diagnostics at Carnegie Mellon University in Pittsburgh, PA, USA. At CMU, Dr. Hartkopf co-founded the first multi-disciplinary graduate program on total building performance, and initiated the Advanced Building Systems Integration Consortium, a collaboration of industry, government and CMU disciplines dedicated to building science research, education, and demonstration. This National Science Foundation Industry/University Cooperative Research Center (NSF I/UCRC) was instrumental in the creation of the Intelligent Workplace.

Judith Heerwagen is an environmental psychologist whose work focuses on the behavioural, psychosocial and health impacts of buildings and on translating research evidence into policy and design practice. She is currently a Research Psychologist with the US General Services Administration, Office of Federal High-Performance Buildings Washington, DC, USA.

Veerle Hermans is a Professor at Vrije Universiteit Brussel, Faculty of Psychology and Educational Sciences (Work and Organisational Psychology Research Group), Brussels, Belgium. She also works for IDEWE, External prevention service for safety and health at work, Heverlee, Belgium.

Adam Jaworski, Buildings Engineering (Electrical), Arup London.

Kevin Kampschroer, Director, Office of Federal High-Performance Buildings, US General Services Administration, Washington, DC, USA.

Despina Katsikakis is an industry leader with an international reputation for thought leadership and innovation, on the impact of the workplace, on organisational transformation and business performance. She serves as an independent adviser to corporate occupiers, real estate developers and investment funds. A former Chairman of international consultancy DEGW, Despina has over 30 years' experience working with corporate clients including; Accenture, BBC, BP, Cisco, Deutsche Bank, GSK, Google, Microsoft, Morgan Stanley and Unilever, to develop ground-breaking workplace initiatives, and has an extensive track record of successfully implemented global workplace programmes that have delivered significant improvements to people and business performance.

Khee Poh Lam is Professor of Architecture at Carnegie Mellon University, Pittsburgh, PA, USA, on leave to serve as Dean of the College of at the National University of Singapore. Dr. Lam is an educator, researcher, architect and consultant who specializes in life-cycle building information modeling and computational design support systems for total building performance analysis and building diagnostics. Professor Lam is a member of the Board of Directorsof the Energy Foundation and the Global Buildings Performance Network (GBPN).

Bertrand Lasternas is Senior Research Scientist in the Center for Building Performance & Diagnostics (CBPD) at Carnegie Mellon University, Pittsburgh, PA, USA. Trained as a mechanical engineer at Paul Sabatier University, Lasternas is a leader in innovative building system design, controls and diagnostics, as well as data analytics for advancing the performance of buildings over time.

Adrian Leaman specialises in studying building performance from the users' point of view. He is mainly associated with his work with the consultancy Building Use Studies and the Usable Buildings Trust charity, which he co-founded with co-author Bill Bordass. Much of their work can be downloaded from www.usablebuildings.co.uk

Steve Lee is Professor and Head of Architecture, Carnegie Mellon University, Pittsburgh, PA, USA. Professor Lee's research and practice focus on advances in systems integration, material innovation, renewable energy and the integrated design process for high performance commercial and residential architecture. He is a LEED accredited professional and provides sustainable design consulting services for institutional and commercial clients in Europe, Asia, Canada and the United States.

Victoria Lockhart is among the first global cohort of Accredited Professional (AP) trained in the WELL Building Standard®, and provides support to the industry as a WELL Faculty member. Vicki brings expertise in sustainable green building practices alongside a passion for leveraging medical insights and new technologies to enhance human experience and well-being. She was part of the core team developing the new health and well-being consultancy service at global consulting engineering firm Arup, and in 2017, joined the International WELL Building Institute™ (IWBI) – a public benefit corporation whose mission is to improve human health and well-being through the built environment.

Vivian Loftness is University Professor and Paul Mellon Chair in Architecture at Carnegie Mellon University, Pittsburgh, PA, USA. A LEED Fellow, Fellow of the American Institute of Architects and Design Intelligence, Professor Loftness is an internationally renowned researcher, author and educator focussed on environmental design and sustainability, advanced building systems integration, climate and regionalism in architecture, and design for performance in the workplace of the future.

Piers MacNaughton is Associate Director, Healthy Buildings Program, the Center for Health and the Global Environment, Harvard T.H. Chan School of Public Health, MA, USA.

Jason Margrave, formerly Stanhope, now Quintain. His main focus is predevelopment activities including new opportunity identification. Jason's experience over the last 17 years has been in brownfield regeneration, bringing forward complex sites and undertaking predevelopment workstreams including briefing and appointing teams, assisting with land assembly negotiations, securing third party agreements, detailed design, construction procurement and enabling works. He is also involved in the company's research agenda and product design. Jason is an active committee member of both the BPF and BCO.

Jenn McArthur is Assistant Professor in Department of Architectural Science, Ryerson University, Canada. Her research investigates the relationship between workplace productivity enablers, building sustainability, and organizational performance. She is currently developing a tool to measure workplace productivity to quantify the impact of renovation and other interventions.

Jeremy Myerson is Director of the WORKTECH Academy, a global knowledge network exploring the future of work and workplace, and holds the Helen Hamlyn Chair of Design at the Royal College of Art. He co-founded the Helen Hamlyn Centre for Design – the Royal College of Art's largest centre for design research – in 1999, which he directed for 16 years. He is the author of several books in the workplace field and his most recent titles include *Time & Motion: Redefining Working Life* (2014) and *Life of Work* (2015).

Naoe Nishihara is an Associate Professor of Faculty of the Liberal Arts, Department of Education at University of the Sacred Heart, Tokyo, Japan. She has published articles on thermal environment and workplace productivity. Her current research interests include thermal comfort, sustainable lifestyles and home economics education.

Nigel Oseland is a workplace strategist, change manager, environmental psychologist, workplace psychophysicist, author and international speaker with 11 years' research and 19 years' consulting experience. He helps occupiers redefine their workstyles to create cost-effective workplaces that enhance well-being and performance. When not engaged in research and publications, Nigel runs his consultancy practice Workplace Unlimited and also organises the Workplace Trends series of conferences.

Kay Pallaris is the founding director of Mapping Futures. Her focus is on planning for environmental wellbeing, with 18 years of experience working in the development and regeneration sectors. She holds a masters in Environmental Monitoring, Modelling and Management, and in Urban Design in Development. As a Chartered Geographer, her work focuses on the applied science of geographic enquiry and spatial analysis to develop evidence-based, sustainable and heath-driven place strategies. Her practice is informed by her research interests in all aspects urban health and multi-sensory design.

Kevin Reader leads the Workplace Strategy team at Aberley, who are a leading independent workplace advisory organisation, specialising in the analysis, design, management and delivery of work environments that improve the individual's performance. He has over 25 years' experience providing thought leadership with a practical application, using analytics to develop a people-focused business-led approach. His role is assisting organisations to put its people at the core, by focusing on the connection between People, Place, Technology and Operations to improve outcomes for the organisation and its customers.

Richard Reid, Controls Engineer, Building Performance & Systems, Arup London.

James Richards, Senior Consultant, Digital, Arup London.

Usha Satish is Professor of Psychiatry and Behavioral Sciences at SUNY Upstate Medical Center.

Bryan C. Steverson, High-Performance Buildings Program Advisor, Office of Federal High-Performance Buildings, US General Services Administration, Washington, DC, USA.

Michael Stych is project leader and director for Arup's Digital Skills Network in UK, Middle East and Africa region. He has championed the development of IoT and 'smart' buildings skills and technologies in business. His focus is on the design of innovative, low-energy building services that are responsive to the needs of users. He works closely with clients, design teams and contractors to fully achieve early-stage ambitions.

Shin-ichi Tanabe is a Professor of Faculty of Science and Engineering, Department of Architecture at Waseda University, Tokyo, Japan. He is an expert in the fields of indoor air quality, thermal comfort, and energy. Zero Energy Building including houses and office workers' productivity. He is a Vice-President of Architectural Institute of Japan and the Society of Air-conditioning and Sanitary Engineers (SHASE).

Mallory Taub joined Arup in 2012 and has gained experience in the San Francisco, London, and Boston offices as a sustainability consultant working towards reducing environmental impacts of the built environment while maximizing opportunities for enhancing occupant health and well-being. She brings a holistic, interdisciplinary approach to developing sustainability strategies for high performance buildings and portfolios. She has experience in the application of LEED and WELL building rating systems and has also supported the delivery of projects against project-specific sustainability frameworks.

Michael Trousdell, Associate Director, Arup Building Engineering. Michael is a mechanical engineer with a passion for delivering sustainable and innovative building services solutions for diverse building projects. He has experience in medical product and manufacturing design; following a focus on that in his engineering degree, he worked on wind farm construction for a period of five years before joining Arup's building engineering division. At

Arup he is responsible for prompting the adoption of advanced Digital Design process and integration of Internet of Things solutions into buildings projects. His portfolio of projects includes buildings such as the Warner Stand at Lord's, an all-electric building which includes an innovative open loop combined heating and cooling system.

Briony Turner is Climate Services Development Manager, Institute for Environmental Analytics, University of Reading. Briony has over 12 years' experience of urban regeneration, housing research and knowledge exchange, working within and across public, private, academic and third sector organisations. Briony is an associate editor of *Intelligent Buildings International* journal. Her current research interests include multi-sensory built environment design, indoor environmental quality, socio-technical transitions, climate change adaptation and climate services.

Jennifer A. Veitch is Principal Research Officer, National Research Council of Canada; Adjunct Research Professor of Psychology and Neuroscience, Carleton University, Ottawa, Canada; Director of Division 3, Interior Environment and Lighting Design, Commission Internationale de l'Eclairage, and an editorial board member of *Intelligent Buildings International*, *Journal of Environmental Psychology*, *Environment and Behavior*, *Lighting Research & Technology*, *Leukos*, *Architectural Science Review*, and *Light & Engineering*.

Jacqueline C. Vischer is an Environmental Psychologist specialising in environments for work. She is a founder of the field known as workspace psychology. She has authored and edited several books, and contributed numerous chapters to volumes on facilities management, building performance, workplace psychology and building programming and evaluation. She has advised a wide range of organisations internationally on managing workspace comfort, designing innovative workspace, and planning workspace change. Dr Vischer is Professor Emeritus at the University of Montreal, where she founded the New Work Environments Research Group (Groupe de recherche sur les environnements de travail). Many of her writings are available at – and can be downloaded from – www.jacquelinevischerbiu.com

Pawel Wargocki is Associate Professor at the International Centre for Indoor Environment and Energy, Department of Civil Engineering, Technical University of Denmark, Copenhagen, Denmark.

Bernard Williams, a Chartered Surveyor by qualification (FRICS), has developed a career as a consultant specialising in building and facilities economics. He established Bernard Williams Associates (BWA) in 1970 to provide advice, economics and project management all around the development life-cycle. He lectures extensively and in 2010 took up a visiting chair at Sheffield Hallam University. His writings include *Facilities Economics*, *Whole-life Economics of Building Services* and *An Introduction to Benchmarking Facilities* (all from IFPI Ltd). He is the developer of the CombiCycle and EstatesMaster Whole-life Cost and Sustainability models and in 2005 led the ECDG research project 'Benchmarking the efficiency of the EU Construction Industries'.

David P. Wyon is Professor at the International Centre for Indoor Environment and Energy, Department of Civil Engineering, Technical University of Denmark, Copenhagen, Denmark.

Foreword to first edition

by Nick Raynsford MP, Parliamentary Under Secretary of State Minister for Construction and London

Buildings provide the environment in which the business community operates, and their procurement and operation represent a considerable business cost. Getting this environment right clearly holds the potential for better performance of both human and physical resources, and thus significant rewards to business and the wider economy. On an individual level, our working environment can have a major impact on our attitudes to our work, and in turn on our personal efficiency and productivity.

To realise this potential, we have to understand better the whole-life performance and economics of buildings. We must also gain a greater understanding of the potentially significant – but currently poorly understood – linkages between the productivity of building occupants and the operation of the internal building environment.

My Department has made improving the productivity of non-domestic buildings one of the four key themes of its new Sustainable Construction research and innovation programme. We have called for proposals to improve understanding of the business benefits of effective building design, and to generate more practical guidance and exemplars, so that clients and occupiers can make informed decisions about improved design and management of indoor environments. We are looking particularly at collaborative, multi-disciplinary, ways of tackling the issues. Our aim is to make sure that the overall performance of buildings is enhanced.

That is why this book is so timely and why I am delighted to be associated with it. The book highlights the issues employers and everyone who designs and commissions buildings need to address to create more productive and, above all, more *sustainable* workplaces. This will be good for individual employees, businesses, communities and the natural environment now and in the future. I very much hope that readers of the observations and suggestions contained in the following pages will be inspired to make or seek positive changes to their workplace.

Nick Raynsford MP

Foreword to second edition

I was delighted to provide a foreword for the first edition of this book seven years ago. It made an important contribution to our understanding of a range of factors which together go to make up a successful and productive building. Writing at the time I emphasised that:

> Getting this environment right clearly holds the potential for better performance of both human and physical resources, and thus significant rewards to business and the wider economy.

Since then the world has moved on in many significant respects. Issues of sustainability have rightly assumed greater importance in the way we approach new development decisions. We have also come to appreciate better the interaction of different influences which contribute towards the successful operation of buildings. We are more ready to consider in advance how a building will be managed and maintained over its lifetime. And of course the technology we use has also advanced significantly.

So I was very pleased to learn that a second edition was being planned which could both reinforce some of the important messages contained in its predecessor and reflect the progress that has been made in the intervening period. I congratulate Derek Clements-Croome on pulling together the existing and new contributions which make up this new edition, and wish it the success it deserves. It is in all our interests that we continue to strive to create inspiring and productive workplaces.

Nick Raynsford MP
November 2005

Foreword to third edition

In an era in which our homes are our pensions and iconic buildings are a wealth-generating commodity, it can be easy to forget first principles. Namely, our buildings are primarily there to serve their users – enabling shelter, quality of life, and providing the best possible environments to work, learn, heal or spend leisure time.

Our lives revolve around, and within, buildings. In fact, many of us spend 90 per cent of our time inside them. Yet we are only just collectively waking up to the fact that buildings have a major impact on our health, well-being and productivity – through indoor air quality, the chemicals given off by materials, the lighting, the views, and the extent to which they integrate nature.

Until recently, nobody in real estate has perceived much value from delivering anything different. The system is perceived to work by those with a vested interest in the status quo, even if it means as a species we are getting more sedentary, more stressed and less connected to a natural world which itself is under severe strain.

But things are changing, and quickly. Those who think the system will keep working in perpetuity are in for a nasty shock. I detect three, related, reasons

1   Our understanding of the human body is growing all the time, for instance, the importance of light on our circadian rhythm, or the importance of nature for our mental health.
2   Individuals are increasingly engaged in their own health and well-being, and taking personal responsibility for it, which is feeding a growing industry worldwide.
3   Technology is putting power in the hands of building users, providing real data in real time, at lower prices and in a format that everyone can understand.

The result? There is going to be value in, and demand for, buildings that enable their users to be happy, healthy and productive. Organisations that are ahead of the curve will prosper – whether they are in the business of providing space, or occupying it.

Of course, human health is inextricably linked with planetary health, given we depend on the Earth's ecosystems to meet our needs. It is vital, therefore, that human-centred design supports efficient resource use and regeneration of our natural environment, and it is heartening to see that in many cases there is a virtuous circle.

We cannot, however, take that for granted, and where there are tensions and trade-offs, we must continue to strive for solutions. Health is not 'the new carbon'. Our buildings must maximise benefits for people *and* support environmental restoration – it cannot and need not be one or the other.

That potentially symbiotic relationship between social and environmental imperatives is one of the reasons that I find this topic so fascinating. It is a compelling element of the business case for sustainability in our buildings and wider communities. It is also one of the reasons why the Green Building Council movement, in the UK and globally, has put such a significant amount of time and resources into the topic.

However, for those of us who are advocates for this agenda, the great challenge is translating the growing body of evidence into a change in day-to-day practice in the market. Or, to put it another way, moving from interest to action. There are companies leading the charge, but we haven't yet reached tipping point. This edition, therefore, is a timely update to a pioneering publication, bringing some of the best thinkers and practitioners together in a fascinating compendium of evidence and advice. It is a powerful resource, and should be mandatory reading for anybody with influence over the development, design, delivery and occupation of our workplaces.

John Alker
Campaign and Policy Director
UK Green Building Council and Board Director
World Green Building Council

Preface to first edition

The culture of living and working is undergoing accelerating social and technological changes. The release of creative energy in people is vital for them as individuals as well as for communities and society at large. Creative self-fulfilment leads to vitality in nations. There is recognition now that the daily rhythms of life need to be appreciated; there is also a need to understand how we think and concentrate and under what conditions our performance diminishes or improves. A high level of sustained focused concentration is necessary for a high level of productivity. Environments for working in are becoming more fluid to meet changing work patterns and to deal with all the different ways we need to think and communicate during any single working day. This book opens up some solutions but also poses many problems which, it is hoped, will provoke some thought and ideas for the future.

This book is partly based on the proceedings of a conference entitled 'Creating the Productive Workplace' held in London in October 1997. Over 200 people attended. Delegates came from a wide range of disciplines, including those who are interested in acquiring knowledge about human behaviour in buildings, and those who have to design and manage buildings in practice. I would like to thank the team that helped me to compose this conference, which included John Doggart from Energy Conscious Design (ECD), Nigel Oseland from British Research Establishment Ltd, and Aubrey Rogers from Bournemouth University. The administration was admirably executed by Peter Russell and Lilian Slowe, of Workplace Comfort Forum, together with their team of helpers. I would also like to pay tribute and give thanks to the sponsors and associates who have supported the event financially and with time and advice.

Sponsors: The Department of the Environment, Transport and the Regions (DETR); Energy Efficiency Best Practice programme; Clearvision Lighting Limited; RMC Group plc; Trigon Limited.

In Association with: Association of Consulting Engineers; British Council for Offices; British Institute of Facilities Management (BIFM); Building Research Establishment Limited (BRE); Building Services Research & Information Association (BSRIA); Construction Industry Council; Construction Industry Environmental Forum; De Montfort University (Department of Design Management); ECD Energy & Environment Limited; Ecological Design Association; Energy Design Advice Scheme (EDAS); European Intelligent Building Group; University of Bournemouth (Department of Product Design & Manufacture); University of Reading (Department of Construction Management & Engineering).

I would also like to thank Maureen Taylor and John Jewell for their usual diligence in helping to prepare the manuscript.

Derek Clements-Croome
Reading, October 1998

Preface to second edition

Society changes, technology advances and both affect why we work, how we work and where we work. Painters, writers, sculptors and composers usually work from home and create their own studio for creative activity. Nowadays a significant number of office workers use a home base. But there are many occupations requiring team work where the effectiveness of communication becomes critical. The flexible arrangement of space and responsible environmental control systems are all-important. At a basic level, the building enclosure is another layer of sensory clothing providing stimuli for our visual, aural, olfactory, tactile and gustatory senses. Bland architecture fails to provide those conditions of light, sound, indoor air quality, temperature and freshness which lift the spirits and which enable us to do better work. Human-oriented design means not only gains for individuals but for business organisations too. Workplace absence debits national economies with significant costs and a good proportion of these are due to poor environmental conditions.

Many say we are what we eat; actually we are what we *sense* as each experience, including eating, enhances our life pleasurably or otherwise. We live through our senses. Buildings and the environment they create provide many of the stimuli which enrich further those provided by people and our work.

The book has been extended to include more case studies as well as the latest research needed to guide building designers towards providing healthy, sustainable and effective conditions for work. Much remains to be done to translate this holistic integrated environmental concept into a message for clients to demonstrate how business value can be improved.

As we move towards a 24-hour society with many digital artefacts, but which is socially more open and demanding, the need for an integrated vision is becoming ever more evident. Research, practice and business are each vital entities which need to meld together to maximise value. The range of international experience recorded here is a step in this direction.

I am indebted to all the authors and to Gülay Özkan, Maureen Taylor and Nishita Goenka for their hard work and enthusiasm in preparing manuscripts and compiling references.

Derek Clements-Croome
University of Reading, May 2005

Preface to third edition

Since the previous editions in 2000 and 2006 the workplace has undergone many changes physically, technologically, socially and environmentally. Expectations of occupants have risen from ones of pure utility to higher levels of environmental awareness. Occupants desire flexible and expressive places to work which are conducive to creative thought.

Buildings, together with their surroundings, affect physical social and mental well-being. This has been reflected in various reports by the UK Green Building Council and British Council for Offices and detailed in various chapters. Companies are beginning to realise the business case proven by increased profitability when their staff are healthy and work with their best energy. Beyond this, lower absenteeism and presenteeism reduce medical costs nationally. The importance and value to the national productivity of all this were fully acknowledged in the House of Lords Paper 100 *Building better places* (Select Committee on National Policy for the Built Environment Report of Session 2015–16).

We must not remain insular in our quest to understand the links between the human, work and place. Other fields like neuroscience, occupational psychology, biomimetics and medicine can offer streams of knowledge that show how our minds and bodies react in different environments. Medical faculties contributed valuable peer-reviewed scientific data to the US WELL Standard, for example, and yet rarely if ever do medics attend any seminars or conferences held in our field.

Understanding how we think creatively needs us to unlock the secrets of consciousness and this still remains a challenge for neuroscience. The science of the brain is advancing rapidly, however, so this is a field that will affect our understanding of how we concentrate and think creatively. In another respect intelligent buildings can be modelled in a similar way to the brain where connectivity is one of the key features. When connectivity breaks down, our systems for operating buildings get confused and things do not work effectively; in a similar way with degenerative brain illnesses, the connectivity loses power, speed and disconnections occur.

The book is set out in four parts to reflect the landscape of knowledge; the scientific evidence; practical experience via case studies; and a look towards the future. The content is about 90 per cent different from the previous edition to reflect the vast changes in attitudes, knowledge and design of places for work. I would like to thank all the authors from practice and academia who are masters in their fields for contributing. In addition, many thanks to John Alker and his colleagues at UK Green Building Council; members of the CIBSE Intelligent Buildings Group; Francesca Ford and her team, including Trudy Varcianna, Grace Harrison at Taylor & Francis; Gülay Özkan in Turkey for editing assistance; Dr Tong Yang at Middlesex University; Ben Kirkpatrick for some of the graphics in Chapter 1; Dr Husam Alwaer at Dundee University; members of the British Council for Offices and the UK Green

Building Council; Ann Marie Aguilar and her team at Arup; and many more colleagues and friends for stimulating conversations about ideas and experiences relating to the changing workplace. My students from here in the UK and in many other countries are a constant source of inspiration.

Derek Clements-Croome
Professor Emeritus
School of the Built Environment
University of Reading
December 2016

Part I

Health, well-being and productivity landscape

Chapter 1

Effects of the built environment on health and well-being

Derek Clements-Croome

Introduction

We live through our senses. What we see, hear, touch, taste and smell affects our human system physiologically and psychologically. At a basic level we need fresh air to live, to nourish our blood with oxygen and then the organs of our body, including our thinking brain. The air has to be warm or cool enough, as well as being clean. We also need light not only to see but also to feel the space in various ways. The aural climate needs to be acceptable. But there are also a host of other factors which subtly influence the human response to the environment, such as aesthetics, greenery, social ambience and the culture of the organisation in which people work (Davis *et al.*, 2011). All these factors contribute to the look and feel of a space. This book aims to lead to more human-centred ways of designing the built environment with deeper meaning and achieve healthier, creative as well as more productive places to work.

Carson, in her (2010) book, *Your Creative Brain*, argues for seven brain sets to maximise imagination, productivity and innovation. These cover:

* Absorb – opening up the mind to new ideas and experiences.
* Envision – using imagination.
* Connect – divergent thinking to generate multiple solutions.
* Reason – the logical ordered mind.
* Evaluate – judging the value of and testing ideas and concepts.
* Transform – creativity that can spring from negativity.
* Stream – thoughts flow in a harmonious and systematic way.

Our knowledge about the brain and mind is increasing rapidly so that our understanding about how we think, how we concentrate and how we get distracted is becoming more evident. Consciousness may be the interaction of the world and the mind and so could remain elusive in spite of brain research but the knowledge from neuroscience is already giving greater insight into what is happening in our minds when we think and act in various ways.

> People work best when all senses are engaged.
>
> (IBI Group Nightingale, 2012)

> Business performance is influenced by the impact of the workplace environment on staff motivation and ability.
>
> (CABE, 2005)

In the Human Spaces Report (2015), *The Global Impact of Biophilic Design in the Workplace*, the research showed that those who work in environments with natural elements, such as greenery, natural materials and sunlight reported:

- 15 per cent higher level of well-being;
- 6 per cent higher level of productivity;
- 15 per cent higher level of creativity

compared to those occupants with no connection with natural elements in the workplace (www.humanspaces.com/2015/ Cooper and Browning). A report by BCO (2012), *Making Art Work in the Workplace*, revealed that 61 per cent of employees believe that art in the workplace increases their creativity besides boosting well-being and productivity.

Antonovski (1979) describes *salutogenic* environments as ones which help to stimulate the mind. The aim is to design to produce ideation or creative environments. But what of the person? Csikszentmihalyi (2014, and TED lecture, February 2004) advocated the concept of *flow* which refers to a person being fully immersed with energised focus on an activity (see Chapter 2). Think of the intense concentration needed by musicians performing in public or writers and composers when creating their stories, poems or music, which requires a state of free flowing thought. However, this is true of any activity requiring concentration either for routine or creative tasks.

How does architecture and the built environment evoke moods and emotions? Pallasmaa (2016) and Desmet (2015) believe buildings go beyond being functional and material servants to our needs because they also house our minds, memories, desires and dreams. People want their environment, whether an office, school or home, to be part of 'the place experience' – a place where they like to be because it allows a rich, diverse range of experiences (Marmot, 2016). Places should let imagination and creativity open up rather than be trampled on by ceaseless information clutter. The smart and thinking city or building is the future as neuroscience helps us to unravel the intangibles that paint the landscape of the brain, the mind interaction with the environment. Brekke (2016) believes this and goes on to say: 'The built environment can become tools for people's wellbeing, and provide safe enclosures combined with opportunities for complex sensorial and social experiences.'

Brains are about 2 per cent of the body weight but consume over 20 per cent of the calorie intake. Brains get tired. For people in jobs where work shift patterns are long, such as doctors and nurses, and where the level of care is vital, one has to realise that towards the end of a 12-hour shift, people become too tired to do their job at the same level of efficiency and effectiveness as when they started the day or night. In practice, this fact tends to be ignored as patients or customers expect a continuous run of efficiency. Heart, head and hands are needed in many jobs. A caring heart and willing spirit never tire but the head and mind do.

Our brains have ultradian rhythms and throughout the day pass though waves of freshness, concentration and tiredness modes (Takenoya, 2006; Arantes, 2015). In the tiredness mode, the brain needs other activities to relax and hence why breakout spaces are so important, whether it is a gym, a social encounter, a sensory garden or a music listening room. Various surveys indicate that many office workers want contemplation spaces whether the brain is in the concentration or tiredness modes. Philips in conjunction with TU Delft (Trevia, 2013) have developed a relaxation space to help employees self-regulate stress by a system of sensors which allow it to be a very adaptive space.

In her (2012) book, *Quiet*, Susan Cain emphasizes the importance of personality traits and discusses in detail the characteristics of extroverts, introverts or a mixture of these called ambiverts and how they react in various situations. She believes management should understand how personality affects communication, working conditions and should support workers' needs much more. The role of personality on the performance of people working is important in assessing what priority should be given to the various aspects of the built environment and the support systems. Marston (1979) describes a profile for personality types he calls Dominant (go-getters), Influential (team players), Steadfast (need structure and routine), and Conscientious (more solitary detailers), and his research shows how their preferences vary.

The Academy of Neuroscience for Architecture (ANFA) was set up in San Diego in 2003 by the American Institute of Architects. The concept of linking these two fields was developed by John Eberhard in his book entitled, *Brain Landscape: The Coexistence of Neuroscience and Architecture* (2009). This part of a neuroscience roundtable discussion was recorded in the *Neuroscience Quarterly* (2003):

GAGE: Why are architects and neuroscientists beginning to work together?

EBERHARD: Architecture has the most impact when the ideas used in building design reflect our understanding of how the brain reacts in different environments. Neuroscientists can help architects understand scientifically what have historically been intuitive observations.

GAGE: Neuroscience has reached a point in its understanding of the brain and how it is influenced by the environment that neuroscientists can work with architects in their designs for environments that enable people to function at their fullest within those environments.

More recent work on the interplay between neuroscience and architecture is described by Michael Arbib in a (2012) paper, 'Brains, machines and buildings', in which he discusses the neuroscience of the architectural experience and examines how brain functions may be incorporated into buildings. A Special Issue of *Intelligent Buildings International Journal* featuring the Academy of Neuroscience for Architecture was published in 2013 (ANFA, 2013).

Architecture and the multi-sensory experience

Our existence is enlivened every waking moment by a symphony of stimuli from people, objects, building spaces, task interest and Nature. This rich array of inputs to the mind and body generates the multi-sensory experience which can colour and enrich the environment for people to live and work in. As in music, the notes of melodies, harmonies and rhythms magically combine in a myriad of ways to inspire the mind, so too in multi-sensory design which weaves a tapestry and diversity of experience for people to flourish.

The idea of taking into account the senses of a building occupant has extended our thinking into how we smell, touch, hear and see things in the built environment, as well as our psychological interactions with the stimuli it provides. Architecture deals not only with materials and form but also with people, their emotions, environment, space and relationships between them. This makes a rich tapestry of stimuli which touch the human body and mind. In order for this human experience to enhance our lives, buildings should provide a multi-sensory experience.

The senses not only mediate information for the judgement of the intellect, they are also channels which ignite the imagination. This aspect of thought and experience through the senses is stimulated not only by the environment and people around us but, when we are inside a building, by the architecture of the space, which sculpts the outline of our reactions. Merleau-Ponty wrote that the task of architecture was to make visible how the world touches us.

Buildings must relate to the language and wisdom of the body. If they do not, they become isolated in the cool and distant realm of vision. However, in assessing the value of a building, how much attention is given to the quality of the environment inside the building and its effects on the occupants? The qualities of the environment together with the people within it affect human physical and mental performance and these qualities should always be given a high priority. This is what might be considered an invisible aesthetic, and together with the visual impact, these make up a total aesthetic.

Buildings can and should provide a multi-sensory experience for people and uplift their spirits. A walk through a forest is invigorating and healing due to the interaction of all the senses. This array of sensory impressions and the interplay between the senses has been referred to as the *polyphony of the senses*. Architecture is an extension of Nature into the person-made realm and provides the ground for perception, a basis from which people can learn to understand and enjoy the world.

The interaction between humans and buildings is more complex than we imagine. In addition to simple reactions that we can measure, there are many sensory and psychological reactions that are difficult to understand and quantify but we must recognise that they happen. The environment we design affects our physical, mental and social well-being. How do we attempt to deal with this in practice?

The World Green Building Council has attempted a more holistic approach to design in their various reports on offices, retail and homes published in 2014 and 2016 (WGBC, 2014; 2016). Realistic metrics are proposed. Health and well-being rating systems are being developed such as the WELL Building Standard and other models like Flourish – described later in this chapter – are being researched.

The British Council for Offices published a report on wearables in the workplace in October 2016 (Taub *et al.*, 2016) that shows how wearable technology is setting a trend for more personalised control of the relationship between the occupant and their workplace. In this report by Arup and Reading University, the following conclusions were drawn:

- *Technology*: Wearables are part of the digital health trend and form a broader goal for technology to be people-centric by enabling increased personalisation. Additionally, they increase people's awareness of a number of health-related issues and can provide fine-grained, real-time data on a greater number of environmental parameters and health indicators than are typically integrated into current building management systems (BMS).
- *Design*: As people are becoming more aware of their health and technology enables mobile working, the fundamental layout and design priorities of workplaces are changing. As the wearables help quantify both sedentariness and stress, office designs will need to creatively support active working and invest more in rest and relaxation spaces, collaborative spaces, inviting dining areas, and strategies that promote a connection to Nature.
- *Metrics*: Combined with data from occupant surveys, environmental monitoring, and business metrics, the added data stream of biometrics from wearables provides an extra dimension to monitoring the impacts of specific interventions to inform design and operations. At the individual level, insights could provide personal guidance on health and individual actions. Aggregated at the company level, insights could help to understand how to make positive adjustments to group behaviour and dynamics.
- *Research*: There will be more research on the relationships between the physical environment, behaviour change, and organisational culture. Such studies that bring together environmental psychology and architecture would have great potential for rich insights into operations and behaviour through a deeper analysis of space utilisation, collaboration, and social interaction.

As to the future, it is reckoned that over the next five years there will be more wearables woven into clothing, more apps to link with wearables, and generally more connected solutions which can aid business as well as indirectly help to improve health in the workplace. Wearable apps will change the way we work and help bring complex business processes to life in a new, simple, visually compelling, action-oriented way while changing wearable devices from gadgets to valuable tools for the business. Futurologists speculate about body digital implants but that raises more questions than answers.

Wearables will enable teams to be more connected to the digital world while being more present in the real world. The key will be to ensure that wearable technology and applications are able to leverage business data to highlight the right information, at the right time, to drive the right business action. Built-in analytic software will make observing trends and patterns derived from the data simpler both for the user and the aggregator.

Wearables for work provide an opportunity to significantly improve productivity, efficiency and even safety, creating tremendous opportunities for those taking advantage of this. However, their introduction needs to be done with sensitivity. As wearable technology becomes more ubiquitous in the workplace, transparency and employee education will go a long way towards resolving these issues.

Finally, technology is not the complete answer. It can enable people to be more aware of their physical and mental states and can support people to work more effectively in their workplaces but IT systems and other technology can be unreliable sometimes, besides being rather rigid in their input requirements. Natural systems such as passive architecture are often simpler, more flexible and durable. A balance between the use of technology and simpler approaches is needed in order to achieve a true multi-sensory experience in the built environment.

Do buildings affect people's health?

Over the past 20 years, it has been empirically assessed that most building environments do have a direct effect on the occupants' physical and psychological health, well-being and performance; however, it is only through more recent studies that a clearer understanding of the occupied environment has been discovered.

This raises the question as to the validity of the codes and standards we have used for years without question concerning air quality, noise, light and temperature. In the UK many head teachers were asked if they felt modern buildings affect learning (Bakó-Biró et al., 2012). Around 78 per cent said they felt there was a clear link between the quality of school design and levels of pupil attainment. Williams (2006) reported a similar conclusion for 12 primary schools, which he assessed using the building quality assessment (BQA) method and compared the BQA scores with examination results. There was a clear correlation between building quality and students' performance.

The report *The Drive Toward Healthier Buildings: The Market Drivers and Impact of Building Design on Occupant Health, Well-Being and Productivity*, published in the USA by McGraw-Hill Construction (2014), in cooperation with the American Institute of Architects, states that 18 per cent of home owners say doctors are their primary source of information about healthy home products and decisions – after friends, family and peers. Yet only 53 per cent of paediatricians, 32 per cent of GPs and 40 per cent of psychiatrists believe buildings affect patient health, presumably because they believe the effects of smoking, alcohol, poverty and a lack of exercise are bigger issues. Similarly a significant number of UK Local Authorities, often those who have financial control, do not believe school buildings have any effect on children's learning (Abdul-Samed and Macmillan, 2005).

The McGraw-Hill Construction Report (2013) is based on the findings of five separate market research studies which included surveys of non-residential architects and contractors and owners; residential builders and architects; US homeowners; human resource executives at US firms; and medical professionals. It showed that in contrast to physicians, 95 per cent of homeowners believe that hospital buildings affect patient/staff health and productivity. Likewise, 90 per cent believe school buildings affect student health and productivity. In addition, 63 per cent of the general public is aware of a link between products and practices they use at home and their health, with 50 per cent indicating an impact on allergies and 32 per cent pointing to an impact on asthma and respiratory illnesses. Human resource executives also recognise the link between buildings and health. In particular, 66 per cent believe that spaces that encourage social interaction are important when making leasing decisions.

Similar results were found in schools. The health of pupils and staff improved and, as a result, learning was enhanced when old or new schools had green credentials in their design (ibid.). This was in addition to the energy reduction benefits.

McGraw-Hill Construction (2014) states that construction industry professionals are paying increasing attention to health in design and construction plans. According to the study, firms focusing on green buildings are more attuned to health issues, and all firms questioned report an increase in addressing occupant health in design and construction. After many years of concentrating on minimising resource demands for energy and water, there has been a shift to balance this need with human values.

This report shows the results of a survey of US non-residential property owners and found significant benefits from healthy buildings:

- 47 per cent believed there was a reduction in the cost of healthcare ranging from 1 per cent to 5 per cent;
- 66 per cent believed there was improved employee satisfaction;
- 56 per cent believed there was lower absenteeism;
- 21 per cent believed there was higher employee productivity.

There is a need to create greater public awareness of the health impacts of buildings; to increase the focus on better tools and methodologies to collect data and measure healthy impacts; and to encourage building codes to place increased emphasis on healthier building practices. This has been realised by the World Green Building Councils and the UK Green Building Council and is reflected in their reports (UK Green Building Council, 2016; World Green Building Council, 2013; 2014; 2016).

Well-being

The World Health Organisation defines health as: 'Health is a state of complete physical, mental and social well-being and not merely the absence of disease or infirmity.' The term 'well-being' reflects one's feelings about oneself in relation to the world and is found in the models proposed by Maslow (1943), Diener and Biswas-Diener (2008), Seligman (2011) and Dolan (2014). There is a growing interest in well-being shown by governments (OECD, 2013) and research (Huppert *et al.*, 2005; Juniper *et al.*, 2009; 2011; Anderson and French, 2010; Burton *et al.*, 2011; Clements-Croome, 2014).

Warr (1998a; 1998b; 2002) proposed a view of well-being defined by two principal dimensions: (1) arousal which may range from low to high levels; and (2) a scale ranging between pleasure and displeasure. Together they represent the 'content of feelings' (Warr, 2002). Warr goes on to propose three axes for the measurement of well-being: (1) pleasure to displeasure; (2) comfort to anxiety; and (3) enthusiasm to depression. Very low arousal typifies boring environments but very high arousal describes more pressurised ones. However, the questionnaires used to elicit responses are finely graduated so that respondents can express a wide range of feelings, whether positive or negative, covering a wide range of arousal levels.

Steemers and Manchanda (2010) have proposed another set of defining attributes that encompass health, comfort and happiness (see Chappells, 2010). These include the job and its environment, involving cultural aspects and outside work factors that characterise one's state of well-being at any point in time, and these can overlap with one another. Bluyssen (2014) writes extensively about how to assess occupants' well-being in buildings.

Well-being is only one aspect of mental health; other factors include personal feelings about motivation, one's competence, aspirations and degree of personal control. Well-being is connected with overall satisfaction, happiness and quality of life, and is thus a much more encompassing word than the neutral, perhaps over-used, word 'comfort'.

We experience life through our senses, and the environment we provide for people to interact with is important. A building and its environment can help people produce more creative work, because they are happier and more satisfied when their minds are concentrated on the central stimulus task, which is the job in hand. Good building design can help, together with other factors, to achieve this. At very low (sluggish) or very high levels (nervousness) of arousal or alertness, the capacity for performing work is low; at the optimum level the individual can concentrate on work while being aware of, but not distracted by peripheral stimuli from the physical environment. Different types of work tasks require different environmental settings for an optimum level of arousal to be achieved. It is necessary to assess if a sharper or leaner indoor environment is required for the occupants' good health and high productivity, and to redefine comfort as one of the defining attributes of well-being.

The *Times Higher Education* reported on a study (Newman, 2010) that reviewed the impact of well-being on staff and research performance. The Higher Education Funding Council for England is encouraging universities to invest in well-being, which can reduce absenteeism and staff turnover. A report commissioned by the Health Work Wellbeing Executive, UK, stated that, for every £1 spent, well-being brings a return of £4.17 (PricewaterhouseCoopers LLP, 2008). The business value of healthy environments is well documented in evidence described by the World Green Building Council (WGBC, 2014) and Browning (2012), for example.

Well-being depends on the management ethos of the organisation, the social ambience and personal factors, but the physical environment also has a major role to play (Clements-Croome, 2004a; 2004b). Anderson and French (2010) have discussed the deeper significance of well-being, and Heschong (1979) has reported that productivity tends to be increased when occupants are satisfied with their environment. The proposal here is that well-being is achieved when all the factors in Maslow's (1943) pyramid of needs are satisfied (Table 1.1).

In his motivation–hygiene theory, Herzberg (1966) distinguished between 'hygiene' factors (e.g. salary, working conditions, fringe benefits) which can prevent dissatisfaction, and motivational factors (e.g. achievement, responsibility, recognition), which actually lead to improved effort and performance. Evans and Stoddart (1990) proposed a socio-ecological model of health (Figure 1.1) wherein the environmental and genetic sources of stimulation lead to individual responses and behaviour and ultimately to our state of well-being.

Morris *et al.* (2006) developed the drivers–pressures–state–exposure–effects–actions (DPSEEA) context model (Table 1.2) which is based on earlier work by the WHO that illustrated how social, economic, environmental and political drivers lead to impacts on health and well-being, and require action to improve them.

Table 1.1 Maslow's hierarchy of needs in the workplace

Need	Achieved through
Physiological	Comfortable working conditions, support systems
Safety	Safe working conditions, job security
Social	Group relationships, informal activities, open communication
Esteem	Regular positive feedback, promotion and reward
Self-actualisation	Challenging job, encouraging creativity, autonomy and responsibility

Source: (Maslow, 1943).

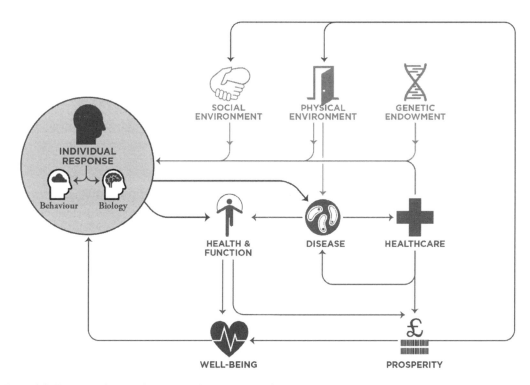

Figure 1.1 Evans and Stoddart's socio-ecological model of health
Source: Evans and Stoddart (1990); Morris *et al.* (2006).

Figure 1.2 shows the pathway from the drivers that act on the environmental systems and result in levels or states of sound, light, heat and air quality, for example, to which human beings are exposed. These states impact on their physiological and psychological systems, and cause positive or negative states of health and well-being. Measurements can be made to help determine which actions should be implemented.

Table 1.2 Elements of the modified DPSEEA context model

Element	Description
Drivers	Society level: social, economic or political influences on the environment
Pressures	Factors resulting from drivers that modify or change the environmental state
State	The resultant environment that has been modified due to the pressure
Exposure	Human interaction with the modified environment
Effects	Human health effects
Actions	Policy and practice designed to address particular factors identified in the chain
Context	Individual level: social, cultural, economic and demographic factors that influence a person's exposure to the modified environment or which lead to a health effect

Source: Morris *et al.* (2006).

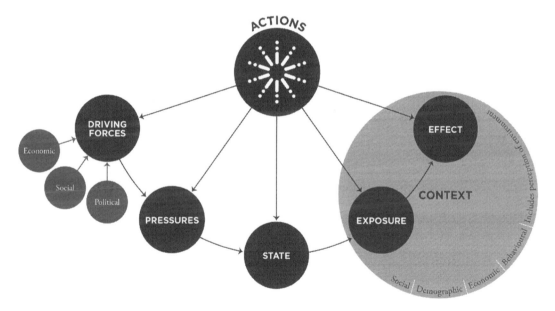

Figure 1.2 The DPSEEA context model
Source: Adapted from Morris *et al.* (2006).

Mental well-being

The author Valerie Martin, when asked when was she happiest, replied that she did not pursue happiness but could not deny it happened when least expected – a view from a hill, a scent from a bit of greenery, a deer pausing in a field, a dog's enthusiastic greeting – happiness floods in (*FT* Weekend, 6/7 February 2016, p. 10). Happiness is elusive but seemingly small unexpected things can change one's mood (Desmet, 2015). However, in his book, *Happiness by Design* (2014), Paul Dolan shows how we can increase the possibilities of designing happier places for people to live and work.

In discussing how built environments influence behaviour and well-being Dolan *et al.* (2016) describe the SALIENT checklist which they have applied in real-world settings. The SALIENT mnemonic identifies seven important elements that can be used to explore the design of built environments to enhance well-being: Sound, Air, Light, Image, Ergonomics, Nature and Tint. Image refers to positive factors like the use of artwork to give interest but not too much to result in clutter. Tint refers to colour. Dolan *et al.* (ibid,) describe and present evidence on how these factors affect well-being.

The mind and body are intimately connected via biochemical systems which themselves are interconnected. Thus stimulation of the physical sense receptors after processing in the brain results in a subjective response. The sense of smell, for example, can spark off memories. A lack of daylight can be depressing. Beauty can delight us. Physical stimuli are received in the cognitive part of the brain and give rise to feelings after interaction with the emotional parts of the brain.

Mental well-being can have two perspectives: (1) a *hedonistic* one defined by the subjective experience of happiness and life satisfaction; and (2) a *eudaimonic* one described by positive psychological functioning through positive social connections and self-realisation and often referred to as human flourishing. Both of these are represented in the Maslow hierarchy of needs. OECD (2013) describes assessing well-being by life evaluation, affect (feelings) and eudaemonia as expressed through life experiences.

Seligman (2011) in his book, *Flourish*, proposes the PERMA model: Positive Emotion; Engagement; Relationships; Meaning; and Achievement to lead a way to a more enriched life and this reflects those ideas discussed by Maslow. The work by Seligman (2011) and Diener and Biswas-Diener (2008) perhaps covers the most comprehensive range of attributes that can contribute to happiness and well-being by including in their research a psychological flourishing scale which adds some aspects on accomplishment, moral character and citizenship, including but going beyond those attributes described by Maslow.

When designing buildings, the aspiration is that people will feel more positive than negative and will not be stressed in a way which is detrimental to their health. Stress can arise from many things such as bureaucratic management, a lack of social ambience, a lack of amenities, unreliable support systems, poverty, social deprivation, personal problems but also the physical environment in which they are placed. Simple things like greenery inside and outside, natural light, views onto Nature, fresh air, fragrance, interesting decor and furnishings and layout can all contribute to uplift a person's mood and well-being. These things have an important role to play in design even though many of them are not measurable and may be considered 'soft' metrics. It requires imagination rather than money to design in this way. There are other factors that can be measured such as temperature, ventilation, light levels, moisture and noise. In addition, personal sensors now common in the form of wearables allow the physiological, mood and stress states to be measured (Taub *et al.*, 2016). Brown *et al.* (2014) describe how sensors (RFID tags) have been used to study how organisational structure and spatial configuration of work environments combine to influence communication between employees. This means we have an interconnected person/building/environment system which can be assessed.

There is also the need to assess if the design has been successful using various post-occupancy evaluations (POE), and here economic performance indicators could include days absent, medical conditions, and self-assessed productivity besides personal fitness data from wearable sensors worn by occupants. They may be willing to share some of this data in order to provide feedback to aid understanding and help to detect weak links between people and their environmental setting which could, if acted upon, lead to improvements in building performance.

The Warwick-Edinburgh Mental Well-Being Scale (WEMWBS) originated in the Warwick University Medical School and is one of the POE methods that has been used in the UK. Others include BUS and the Leesman Index. Currently the WELL Building Standard (2015) from the USA, discussed in Chapter 2, is now beginning to be used in the UK but could undergo modifications, as most POE approaches do. The short form of WEMWBS is a good way to find out about feelings and thoughts in different environmental settings which can act as a background indicator to see if the environment is a contributory factor to negative or positive well-being (Tennant *et al.*, 2007).

A simple example of how the built environment affects the mind is demonstrated in the work relating indoor air quality as assessed by the CO_2 levels to learning in schools (Bakó-Biró *et al.*, 2012) and decision-making in commerce (Satish *et al.*, 2012). This research showed CO_2 levels as low as 600 ppm can affect decision-making in companies and levels in the range 2000–5000 ppm in classrooms detrimentally affect learning, when these were tested using a battery of concentration tasks. Other peer-reviewed research showed similar results. Similarly natural light, smellscapes, soundscapes, greenery and other environmental factors can enhance mood, but if they are lacking, they can disturb, distract or irritate the mind, causing lapses in concentration. These negative effects can be transitory or be more long-lasting and give rise to stress.

Allen and Allen (2015) describe a host of factors that affect mental health in households in various ways. Cold and hot conditions; overcrowding; air and noise pollution; damp conditions; lack of green space; lack of access to public transport, work or culture can all lead to a sense of deprivation.

We spend about a third of our life sleeping and the built environment can affect the quality of sleep. Noise can waken us but even if not awoken, the quality defined by sleep patterns can still be impaired. Sleeping in warm unventilated bedrooms can dry out the respiratory system. Research by Strom-Tjesen *et al.* (2015) shows it is preferable to have a window open while sleeping to ensure a suitable supply of fresh air. In winter, it may be a small opening but it is better than the window being closed, remembering that the insulation provided by duvets and nightwear is substantial. Cross-ventilation will be further improved if it is convenient to have an internal door open. Ventilation can improve sleep quality and the next day's work performance.

Burton (2015) concluded that for human flourishing there should be well-defined open green spaces with plenty of trees and green verges, gardens, green living walls and terraces; walkways; roadways with slow traffic; housing with plenty of fresh air, daylight, effective heat and sound insulation and easy access to cultural activities. All these factors help to prevent loneliness and illness by encouraging walking and play and this adds to the communal value of the neighbourhood.

Another rating tool for homes is the Home Quality Mark (BRE, 2015) which emphasises five factors:

- the overall running costs;
- the impact on health and well-being;
- the environmental footprint;
- resilience to flooding and overheating;
- digital connectivity.

A deficiency in any of these factors, which cover a mixture of economic issues, sustainability, safety, and the health and support system, can lead to stressful conditions for the householder.

But, in addition, residents need easy access to public transport and a rich range of cultural activities so life has meaning and they have homes to treasure and thrive in.

The WELL Building Standard (2015) is a performance-based system for assessing the features of the built environment which affect human health and well-being. It has seven primary factors which cover fresh clean air, water, light, comfort, nourishment, fitness and mind. The standard was based on feedback from the public, medics, building designers and other professionals. There are subtleties here such as recognising the need to pay attention to circadian lighting and not just using functional systems assessed by lighting levels only, and the need to support mental and emotional health in the various ways that have been already described. However good the built environment is, it still requires people to have some responsibility too by eating, drinking, and exercising healthily and not smoking.

Social well-being

In 2013, Affinity Sutton and Catalyst commissioned the Housing Associations Charitable Trust (HACT) and Daniel Fujiwara from Simetrica to undertake a ground-breaking piece of work that culminated in the publication of *Measuring the Social Impact of Community Investment: A Guide to Using the Wellbeing Valuation Approach* (Trotter *et al.*, 2014; Fujiwara and Vine, 2015) and the Social Value Bank, the largest bank of social values to be developed using a consistent methodology. Large national datasets, including the British Household Panel Survey (BHPS) and Understanding Society, were used to identify how people's well-being correlated to other aspects of their life, such as employment status or feelings about their neighbourhood. Changes in well-being associated with these factors were monetised, using econometric approaches now implemented in UK government departments as a measure of impact.

This well-being valuation work has rapidly become the default approach in the housing sector and is gaining traction in other sectors. Since the initial research was released, additional work has been done on the value of outcomes relating to homelessness services and indirect health benefits by Fujiwara *et al.* (2014) and Trotter *et al.* (2015). The next phase of research, looking at the English Housing Survey, has the potential to create at least as much impact for housing providers, by giving them the ability to consider quantitatively, for the first time, the social impact on tenants' lives of a range of outcomes related to core housing activity.

Effects of environmental factors on physiological well-being

> How people feel about their physical surroundings can impact on not just mental health and wellbeing, but also physical disease.
>
> (Scottish Government, 2006)

Well-being at work can be affected by a range of environmental factors, such as sick building syndrome (SBS), the thermal environment, indoor air quality and freshness, olfactory aspects, light, colour, the sound climate, the space layout for active working, biophilic design, and other factors.

Sick building syndrome

Sick building syndrome (SBS) is defined as the case when 20 per cent of a building's occupants complain of a similar medical condition, while in the building, due to an unknown cause over a period of at least two weeks (Abdul-Wahab, 2011). Some research has questioned whether the underlying factors of SBS are perhaps biased towards those who complain more than others, or those who are more sensitive and more susceptible to environmental influences. Nevertheless many surveys have shown that people can feel unwell when they are working in a building but recover when they leave it. The symptoms are usually associated with the respiratory system or they maybe cerebral (including headaches, unusual tiredness, lethargy), tired eyes or dry skin, or musculoskeletal discomfort. Symptoms may manifest as minor irritations or even as pain.

Health is the result of a complex interaction between the physiological, psychological, personal and organisational resources available to individuals and the stress placed upon them by their physical and social environment at work and home. A deficiency in any area increases stress and decreases human performance. Research by Weiss (1997) at Rochester University in New York suggested that the mind can affect the immune system. Stress can decrease the body's defences and increase the likelihood of illness, resulting in a reduction in well-being. Stress arises from a variety of sources: the organisation, the job, the person and the physical environmental conditions. It can affect the mind and body which in turn can weaken the immune system, leaving the body more vulnerable to infection caused by the environmental conditions. Stress in biological terms arises from the hypothalamus reacting to stress by releasing adrenocorticotropic hormone (ACTH), which in turn increases the amount of the hormone cortisol in the blood to a possibly damaging level and affects the brain cells involved in memory. This chain of events interferes with human performance, and productivity falls as a consequence.

People spend about 90 per cent of their lives in buildings, so the internal environment has to be designed to limit the possibilities of infectious disease, allergies and asthma, and building-related health symptoms, referred to as 'SBS symptoms'. Anything in the environment that blocks or disturbs the sensory systems in an undesirable way will affect health and work performance. Thus, lighting, sound, air quality and thermal climate are all conditions around us that can affect our health.

In researching the impacts of the environment on people, it is common to read that environmental factors can act as stressors. Odours, noise, air quality, temperature and light tend to affect humans through four different mechanisms: physiological, affective (moods, feelings, attitudes), stressful (mental and emotional) and psychosomatic (body and mind).

Stressors can cause increased heart rate, vomiting, shallow breathing and muscle tension. They can affect brain rhythms and alter the alpha, beta and theta patterns, which are correlated with mood and affect. Affective states influence judgement, productivity, interpersonal relations, self-image, morale and aggression. Thus, one can see the chain of possible physiological and psychological reactions that may occur when exposed to the environment. There are clues here also as to how physiological measures may aid our understanding of human reaction to the environment.

The survey of 2000 office workers described by BCO (2014) shows the factors which are important and those found irritating. Occupants reported preferences for lots of natural light, access to outdoor spaces, contemplation spaces, support from colleagues, and private as well as collaborative spaces. The main irritants were noise in open plan areas; lack of natural light; lack of colour; lack of greenery; lack of artwork; lack of fresh air; no personal control of temperature; lack of privacy; clutter; and inflexible space.

We experience life through our senses, and intelligent buildings should be a multi-sensory experience. In general, post-occupancy evaluation data show that people are very positive about spaces that are airy, fresh, have natural light, and views out onto, preferably, natural landscapes (Clements-Croome, 2006). If an environment is to be conducive to health and well-being, it should display the following characteristics:

- a fresh thermal environment;
- ventilation rates sufficient to provide clean fresh air with good distribution and acceptable levels of CO_2 and low levels of indoor pollutants (particulates, allergens, VOCs, NO_2);
- plenty of daylighting and this means a shallow plan is preferable to a deep plan;
- no lighting glare;
- views out and onto natural settings if possible;
- acceptable acoustic climate;
- spatial settings to suit various quiet or team working;
- flexible space layouts to allow for active working, human interaction and breakout spaces;
- ergonomic workplaces that have been designed to minimise musculoskeletal disorders;
- the landscaped surroundings should be properly considered as part of the design;
- minimum pollution from external air and noise.

Personal control of these factors, wherever possible, is important. Central control for items such as security is fine, but people prefer to have some degree of control over their immediate physical environment (Ulrich, 1991). The study by Boerstra et al. (2013; 2014), using data from the European HOPE (Health Optimisation Protocol for Energy-Efficient) Buildings project (Roulet et al., 2006; Bluyssen, 2014) shows that occupants with a high degree of personal control over their thermal and indoor air quality environment feel they are more healthy and productive than those with a low amount of control. The increase in productivity between no to full control was concluded to be at least 6 per cent. In addition, occupants were more comfortable and suffered fewer sick building symptoms. It should also be noted that some forms of control were more effective (e.g. external shading) than others (e.g. radiator valves). Often the interface between the person and the controls is poorly designed. The usability characteristic of controls needs to be considered much more by manufacturers.

Normally we say that these environmental factors, if they are at acceptable levels, can make a place comfortable. Later we will see that comfort alone is not enough to achieve a stimulating, creative and productive workplace. There has been an extensive body of research on thermal comfort and this was reviewed by de Dear et al. (2013). Some of the many issues discussed included:

- *Adaptive control* (Nicol et al., 2012) for naturally ventilated and air-conditioned buildings is now transcending the steady state model proposed by Fanger (1970; 2002).
- *Personal control* is important: work is quoted showing that comfort, perceived health and self-assessed productivity are related to occupants' perceived control through simple means, such as knowing that one can open a window (Leaman and Bordass, 1999; 2006).
- *Satisfaction*: users are dissatisfied when a building and its systems are over-complicated with poor usability rendering personal control too complicated and unreliable (ibid.);
- *Pleasant aspects of air movement*: standards and guidelines are too conservative and are more concerned with negative aspects like drafts. Clements-Croome (1996; 2008) showed that temperature and air movement acting together can produce fresh stimulating environments. Tweed et al. (2014), in their research on domestic properties, show that the perceived need to 'air' the property was of prime importance.

The review by de Dear *et al.* (2013) focuses on comfort for the thermal environment only but humans perceive the environment as a whole as stimuli from many sources load the human sensory system and compete for attention. We have to consider Indoor Environmental Quality if occupants' needs are going to be met.

The thermal environment

Markham in his classic book, *Climate and the Energy of Nations* (1944), asks which conditions of temperature and relative humidity lead to feelings of oppressiveness, laziness and lethargy which inhibit productivity. Today the essence of this question remains much debated and yet this, as Markham effectively argues, affects the energy of people and hence ultimately the productivity of a nation.

It is probably true that most research and surveys on environmental conditions and their effects on performance have been concerned with temperature and indoor air quality. The sensors in the skin and the olfactory system receive the stimuli concerned with the thermal experience and generate the signals which pass to the brain. Much of this work is referenced in Clements-Croome (2004a; 2006; 2013).

Cao and Wei (2005) described evidence which suggests that low temperatures tend to cause aggression, and high temperatures tend to cause aggression, hysteria and apathy. The question they investigated in the banking sector was 'Do temperature variations cause investors to alter their investment behaviour?' They hypothesised that lower temperatures lead to higher stock returns due to investors' aggressive risk-taking, and higher temperatures can lead to higher or lower stock returns as aggression and apathy become competing effects on risk-taking. Here we begin to see how the environment may affect decision-making evoking responses coloured by emotion. This is an issue that has been researched more recently by Satish *et al.* (2011; 2012).

Cui *et al.* (2013) carried out chamber room studies, using 36 subjects completing questionnaires and a memory typing task to study the influence of temperature on human thermal comfort, motivation and performance. They concluded that learning was affected by temperature especially when it changed frequently; warm discomfort was more detrimental to performance and motivation than cold discomfort and so they recommended a slightly cool to neutral setting (this would correspond to Fanger's predicted mean vote (PMV) = 0 to -0.5). However, they thought the changes in performance were due to a change in motivation rather than a change in temperature.

The underlying mechanisms explaining how temperature affects performance are beginning to be probed and understood. Lan *et al.* (2011), for example, found that an increase of CO_2 in the blood decreases oxygen saturation in the blood, both of which are likely to affect mental work but many questions on this issue remain.

In addition to this, the work of Bakó-Biró *et al.* (2012) on the effects of CO_2 on learning mentioned above, and other work referenced there and in Wargocki *et al.* (2006) and Wyon and Wargocki (2013) support the contention that the physical environment affects performance. There remain many more questions that need to be researched. Wyon and Wargocki identify some of these but there is enough evidence already to encourage designers to take a more holistic and in-depth view of the conditions they provide for building occupants.

Air, warmth or cold, daylight, noise, space and ergonomics are all important in designing the workplace. However, in the depths of winter or at the height of summer, the temperature tends to be the issue that workers comment about most frequently. The current sustainability agenda features energy as a very important factor, and this is closely related to the temperature at which we maintain our buildings. A UK survey carried out by Office Angels and the Union of Shop, Distributive and Allied Workers (USDAW) (USDAW, 2006) drew the following conclusions.

- Heat exhaustion begins at about 25°C.
- 24°C is the maximum air temperature recommended by the World Health Organisation for workers' comfort (but note that in the UK there is no legislation covering the maximum allowed temperature).
- 16°C is the minimum temperature recommended by the UK Workplace (Health, Safety and Welfare) Regulations 1992 (13°C for strenuous physical work).
- 78 per cent of workers say their working environment reduces their creativity and ability to get the job done.
- 15 per cent of workers have arguments over how hot or how cold the temperature should be.
- 81 per cent of workers find it difficult to concentrate if the office temperature is higher than the norm.
- 62 per cent of workers state that, when they are too hot, they take up to 25 per cent longer than usual to complete a task.

The well-established work on adaptive thermal comfort done by Nicol *et al.* (2012) and Humphreys *et al.* (2016) shows that the internal temperature should be chosen in relation to the monthly mean temperature. Furthermore, the study by Oh (2005), comparing conditions in Malaysian offices with those in the UK, showed that people do adapt to temperature, but not to air quality. Olfactory reactions to pollutants in contrast to temperature are more similar across countries.

Indoor air quality and freshness

Indoor air quality is as important as temperature (Clements-Croome, 2008). Fresh air is, like water, vital to life. A danger with sealing buildings to reduce their energy consumption is that there will be insufficient fresh air, so it is important to build in a controlled air supply such as trickle ventilators or properly located windows that can be opened a little or a lot depending on the seasonal weather. Tweed *et al.* (2014) conclude from their research on energy in homes that many residents feel the need to 'air' their property and this can override other concerns such as heating or costs. Even in cold weather, the perceived need to ventilate is a priority. Hybrid ventilation systems are common which means a fan can be used when needed but windows and doors are the most common ways people like to use when possible to encourage air flow and movement.

'Freshness' is an under-used term in design, yet occupants often talk of the need for a fresh environment (Chappells, 2010). Many factors can contribute, such as colour, spatiality and, more often, air quality. Air quality is a combination of the CO_2 level, temperature, relative humidity and air movement. Chrenko (1974) researched thermal freshness using a seven-point scale, where subjects rated the freshness from 'much too stuffy' to 'much too fresh', and found that freshness was dependent on air velocity and temperature. Clements-Croome's (2008) study, based on UK office surveys, proposed a relationship between fresh air requirements and air temperature for a relative humidity range of 40–60 per cent and average air velocities of 0.2 m/s. For a 'moderately' fresh environment, as judged by a sample of 223 UK office workers, fresh-air rates of 2.2 l/s per person at 20°C, 6.3 l/s at 25°C and 17.9 l/s at 30°C were found to be required. Environments judged by a similar population as 'very fresh' would need higher amounts of fresh air.

Olfactory aspects

The link between odour and scents and work performance is less well understood, but Fisk (1999) concludes that the literature provides substantial evidence that some odours can affect some aspects of cognitive performance. He refers to work by Baron (1990), Dember *et al.* (1995), Knasko (1993), Ludvigson and Rottman (1989), and Rotton (1983). Aroma essences have been used in the air-conditioning systems in the Tokyo office building of the Kajima Corporation (Takenoya, 2006). Tillotson (2008; 2012) describes work on Scentsory Design.

The smell environments of towns and cities are incredibly important and combine with other sensory information to impact directly on people's everyday experiences of different places, streets and neighbourhoods (Henshaw, 2014). The same might be said of soundscapes, as described by Schafer in his book, *The Tuning of the World* (1977). Sensory mapping has now become an important way that planners can begin to understand the real experience of the places they are designing (McLean, 2013). This approach is equally valid for spaces inside buildings too.

Light

Daylight has a primary role in setting the mood tone of the building. Light is reviewed in a report by Veitch and Galasiu (2012), who cover in detail the effects of light on health. Daylight has a strong psychological effect on people, but reactions are linked to sensing the views out of the building, colour, shadow and spaciousness. Human perception is based on the reaction to stimuli from many sources at a particular instant. The Well Building Standard refers to the human circadian rhythms for melatonin, cortisol and alertness levels, which all are influenced by daylight.

Veitch – as reported by Emily Wojcik in 2012 for the American Psychological Association (www.apa.org) – concludes that when people can control their lighting levels and also the colour temperature, their mood is better and they experience improved well-being. One might expect that this would lead to higher productivity but Veitch does not assume this. However, earlier research (Galasiu *et al.*, 2007; Veitch *et al.*, 2008; Veitch *et al.*, 2010) concluded that combinations of automatic and personal control of lighting, daylight harvesting and occupancy sensors save energy and give more occupant satisfaction in open plan offices and this leads to better health and well-being, which, in turn, are likely to raise productivity.

Colour

Wright (1995) demonstrates vividly the importance of colour psychology. Lacy (1996) lists some of the therapeutic effects of colours, as shown in Table 1.3. Whitehead (UK Green Building Council, 2016, p. 22) shows how colour can be used in design to great effect.

Cooper and Browning (2015) describe the impacts of various colours which tend to centre on green, blue, yellow and white for the sample of offices in this survey as:

motivation: blue, green and white
productivity: blue, green, yellow and white
inspiring workers: yellow, green and white
happiness in the workplace: green, blue, brown and white
creativity: yellow, green and white
enthusiasm: green, blue and white
stress: grey only.

Table 1.3 Effects of colours on well-being

Colour	Effect
Red	Energises, activates the emotions, increases the blood pressure and affects the muscular system
Pink	Tranquillising, relaxes the muscles, reduces tension, calms the emotions
Orange	Stimulates the mind, can release blocked emotions, encourages people to be outgoing
Peach	Activates creative impulses, induces better relationships
Yellow	Stimulates the nervous system, changes pessimism to optimism; too much of this colour overcharges the system
Green	Touches deep-seated emotions, can start to release past traumas; induces peace and harmony
Blue	Calms and heals the mind, reduces blood pressure and gives one a greater awareness
Royal blue	Healing for the mind, giving a greater depth to the sense of integrity
Turquoise	Relaxing, cooling, soothing for the nervous system. Helps a person to cope with life
Violet	Releases inadequacies
Magenta	Can help with mental and emotional depression, purges the past to make way for a new beginning

Source: Lacy (1996).

All this work shows that colour should not be ignored in design.

The sound climate

The importance of quiet areas for locating buildings and the effect on people's health has been studied by Shepherd *et al.* (2013). The surfaces of buildings set the boundaries for sound. How a building sounds is just as important as how it looks (Shields, 2003). The shape of interior spaces and the texture of surfaces determine the pattern of sound rays throughout the space. Every building has its own characteristic sound – intimate or monumental, inviting or rejecting, hospitable or hostile. A space is conceived and appreciated through its echo as much as through its visual shape, but the acoustic concept usually remains an unconscious background experience.

Buildings and systems need to be designed so that sound levels do not intrude on the activities undertaken in the space. Façades need to attenuate outside noise from entering the building. However, spaces can be too quiet, so one has to relate the sound level to the type of work being undertaken within the building.

The work of Alvarsson on the advantages of natural sounds will be mentioned in the section on biophilic design.

Space layout for active working

Before the Industrial Revolution people lived actively and sat down much less than today. Today office workers can sit 7 or even as much as 15 hours per day (Levine, 2015). Add to this sedentary home life, then add on 8 hours sleep and it means we walk around only 1–4 hours a day. The human body needs to move around otherwise muscles become slack, blood circulation is sluggish and generally we are less healthy. Our alertness and attention drop and hence productivity is lower. Walking helps us to keep lean by burning off the calories we eat; if we do not, then fat accumulates.

Levine gives the following energy expenditure figures:

10–20 kcal/h – sitting (about 5 per cent above basal energy expenditure);
20–40 kcal/h – standing;
175 kcal/h – standing playing violin (www.caloriecount.com);
100–250 kcal/h – walking 1–2 mph.

Of course, these figures depend on your weight, speed of activity and other factors but they give a comparison between these activities and show that in order to burn off, say, 2000 calories, one needs to do a lot more than sitting. Levine concludes that excessive sitting contributes to many chronic diseases, such as obesity, heart problems, cancer, diabetes and this can be explained by the alterations that occur in physiological and molecular mechanisms (Ekelund *et al.*, 2016).

We need offices to be designed to allow active working and this will have a big impact on the way we arrange and lay out space. In addition, we need to select furniture which is ergonomically designed (Hermans, 2016). Sit–stand desks are now available. Moving about leads to another advantage in that we mingle more and this aids informal or formal face-to-face communication. Marmot and Ucci (2015) edited a series of papers on physical activity, sedentary behaviour and the indoor environment, which discuss the evidence on the effects of sedentary working on health.

De Regules (2016), in discussing complexity science, refers to the Center for Complexity Science building at the National Autonomous University of Mexico, in which maximum adaptability was required by using reconfigurable interactive white walls which also help to encourage occupants to interact and interchange spontaneous ideas. Social buildings encourage informal human communication and from that creativity can be kindled.

Biophilic design

The location of the building with respect to Nature is important. Ulrich (1984) showed how views out from hospital windows onto greenery improved patient recovery rates. Alvarsson *et al.* (2010) showed that the sounds of Nature aid physiological stress recovery. Greenery and still or running water refresh the body and spirit in any climate. There is growing evidence that landscape surrounding buildings can relieve occupants' stress (Beil and Hanes, 2013; Rainham *et al.*, 2013). The UK Houses of Parliament issued POSTnote 538 in October 2016 on *Green Space and Health*, which summarised the evidence for physical and mental health benefits from contact with Nature.

The human race lived and worked in rural settings throughout history until about the last 300 years. We were hunter-gatherers. With the advent of the Industrial Revolution the wrench came and people dashed to towns and cities to work, unaware of the disconnect with Nature that they were experiencing. Biophilia means a love of life or living systems (Wilson, 1984), whether they are flora or fauna. Now we see the advantages that biophilic design can bring to environments in terms of freshness and aesthetics but above all it can help to improve health and well-being (Browning, 2012; Gillis and Gatersleben, 2015). The Japanese recognise the health benefits of forest bathing (*shinrin-yoku*) originating from not only the visual impact but also the fragrances and essential oils that trees emit, making walking in natural settings calming to the mind and this can also lead to decreased glucose levels but increased levels of the hormone serum adiponectin, for example. The fractal patterns in Nature awaken our inner aesthetic senses, responding to the visual richness and diversity. All these factors can affect corti-sol levels, pulse rates, blood pressure, glucose levels, and the serotine-melatonin balance, which, in turn, can affect mood and energy levels. These effects can easily be measured today with all the array of wearable technology available. The research by Roe *et al.* (2013) uses mobile elec-troencephalography (EEG) to measure the emotional experience of walkers in different urban environments and showed that urban green space enhances mood.

> Biophilia offers a healing environment and allows people to draw emotional support from their settings. This psychological vitality of built space depends on the high number and the high quality of visual and intuitive sensory interactions among elements of a space and its users. Such interactions provide a multi-sensory experience. The elements that construct a space together with the openings to the outside world and the air within it govern how people respond to the whole design. Physiology and psychology reactions govern interac-tions between structural elements, the space and human beings.
>
> (Salingaros, 2015)

Urban parks care for the environment – providing storm control, CO_2 conversion, wildlife diversity, softening the raucous quality of noise, offsetting city pollution – and public health in terms of improving mood, mental and physical well-being, says Jane Owen (*FT Weekend*, House and Homes, 6/7 February 2016, p. 1). She went on to report that Natural England reckon that if everyone had access to green space, this would save the healthcare system £2.1 billion a year.

The economic case is vividly demonstrated by Browning (2012) in terms of attendance rates at schools, reduction in crime, increases in worker productivity and quicker recovery rates in hospitals. Property values for homes or commercial buildings in Nature landscape settings are higher than those that are not. Green space lets children play with friends and also encourages people to walk or cycle more. These qualities inspired the Garden City idea of Ebenezer How-ard and Patrick Geddes in the early twentieth century for Letchworth Garden City in the UK. Now we see the garden city concept reborn as a vital ingredient of new or regeneration schemes for cities in Europe, the USA or China, for example. Housing estates in natural settings with trees and greenery have social and healing values. Loneliness, crime, stress and isolation are reduced but walkability, sense of community and sensorial beauty are increased.

Mangone *et al.* (2014) studied the effects on the environment of incorporating a substantial number of plants into office spaces and found that they had a positive, statistically significant effect on thermal comfort. Interior plants can reduce buildings' operating energy consumption rates because the set temperatures for Winter and Summer can be lower or higher respectively, thus decreasing heating or cooling loads. Mangone's experiments showed that the presence of greenery had a psychological influence on people's perceptions of the environment. Other research has shown that plants can lower CO_2 levels and alter humidity enough to give a feeling of freshness. Interior landscaping has to be properly designed to be effective. Knight (Knight and Haslam, 2010) describes how plants and artwork make spaces more interesting to occupants.

Other factors

Due to the now ubiquitous use of mobile phones, computers and other electronic equipment, there is increasing electromagnetic pollution. However, the effects of this on health are still not well known (Clements-Croome, 2000a; 2004b). Computers can cause eye strain, repetitive strain injuries, poor posture and associated aches and pains, so work patterns need to include 'breaks' for users to walk, stand and move around besides having a break from screen time (Hermans, 2016).

The effect of ionisation on human health has always been debated. Nedved (2011) gives an up-to date account of the knowledge in this area.

Feng Shui is the Chinese art and practice of positioning objects, buildings, and furniture, based on a belief in patterns of yin and yang and the flow of chi that have positive and negative effects. Too much clutter, for example, de-energises places. Feng shui is now accepted in the West as many international companies work in China where it is used in assessing designs to ensure the energy flows within the building are optimal (www.fengshuisociety.org.uk).

Watson *et al.* (2016) carried out research on the social value of buildings. Buildings are part of the local community and increasingly companies, schools, churches and universities seek to weave their missions into the fabric of the village, town or city. This gives a deeper meaning and relevance to the daily life of communities nearby.

Beyond environmental comfort

> Perfect truth in short must realise the idea of a systematic whole.
>
> (Bradley, 1914)

The word 'comfort' is perhaps over-used. It has a neutral but long-term durable quality. It is usually seen as a pleasant or relaxed state of a human being in relation to their environment but surely that is only part of what we need for the concentrating mind. Is one highly attentive when comfortable or is there a danger of being bored, losing attention or even falling asleep? Cabanac (2006) writes about pleasure and joy and their role in human life, and indicates how transients are important in providing variety and contrast for the human sensory system to respond to (see Chapter 4 in this volume). During the day we hope for and seek joyful moments, perhaps a tree in blossom, pleasant air movement or changing light patterns. There is an echo of this in Maslow's book, *Religions, Values and Peak Experiences* in 1964, when he writes about peak experiences which can be transitory, momentary or longer-term but trigger happiness and uplift in mood. Cabanac introduced the term *alliesthesia* which means a stimulus may give rise to a pleasant or unpleasant sensation depending on the internal state of the person (de Dear, 2011). Our experience of the environment is the result of an interplay of heat, light, noise and many other factors. Buildings should provide a multi-sensory experience. The senses need stimulation to react to, otherwise boredom sets in.

Malnar and Vodvarka (2004) comment, 'The problem with most of the research on the thermal environment is that it has centred on thermal comfort or thermal neutrality.' They go on to quote other work. Wilson (1984) states: 'As with the auditory area of research, the approaches concentrate on preventing feelings of discomfort, rather than producing positive responses – such as interesting, invigorating – to thermal conditions.'

Langdon (1973) commended a new way of thinking about thermal comfort by replacing a passive model with an active one in which a self-regulatory system has an open-ended interaction with the physical environment in forms governed by social constraints.

Well-being is a more comprehensive term than comfort. Ong (2013) presents a set of essays entitled *Beyond Environmental Comfort*, which stretch the meaning of comfort into new directions. Vink (2012) in his editorial relating to comfort of products like chairs and cars, for example, calls for a new model for comfort based on the work of De Looze *et al.* (2003), which is applicable to the built environment field (Figure 1.3).

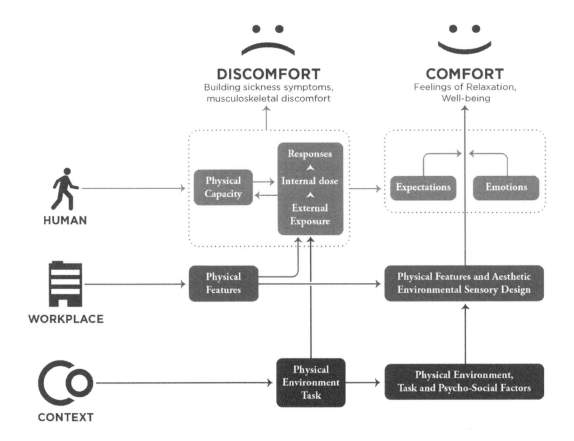

Theoretical Model of Comfort and Discomfort
Adapted from De Looze, M. et al : Ergonomics. 46 (10). 983-007

Figure 1.3 Adapted De Looze model of comfort and discomfort
Source: De Looze *et al.* (2003).

The impact of the environment on people is difficult to predict because the environment has an effect which is more than the sum of its parts (de Dear, 2004; Bluyssen, 2014). Another complication is that sensory modalities interact. Bluyssen (2014) reviews the literature on interactions between noise and heat; noise and lighting; and air quality and thermal comfort.

This interactive characteristic is also evident when we compare our reactions in, say, a black and then a white room. The same-sized room can make one feel 'closed in' or 'more open'. Then do the same comparison with low (feel more closed in) and high (feel more spacious) height rooms. Feelings can be affected by colour or room size in these two simplified examples but then the environment is a complex array of stimuli so measuring the overall reaction of people to it is complex. How does architecture influence our moods, thoughts and health? Lehrer (2011) reviews research that shows some unexpected links between various design factors such as colour and room height, for example, with various aspects of work performance.

Gou *et al.* (2014) carried out research on the gap between comfortable and stimulating illuminance settings. Levels of 400–500 lux were felt to be neutral and comfortable whereas some periods with levels above 900 lux were perceived as more stimulating for the task being undertaken. Perhaps this indicates that comfort is a backdrop which needs to be non-distracting, but human beings also need sensory change from the stimuli around them brought about through the work task, the people and the built environment. It is a complex balance that needs to be achieved.

Barrett *et al.* (Barrett and Barrett, 2010; Barrett and Zhang, 2012; Barrett *et al.*, 2016) believe that there is no real understanding of the holistic impacts of built spaces on people despite the huge amounts of knowledge available on individual aspects such as heat, light and noise. The outcome of his HEAD (Holistic Evidence and Design) project is the SIN Model which has three main dimensions: stimulation level; individualisation; and naturalness:

- *Stimulation* arises from the amount of information in the setting in which triggers such as colour, aromas, greenery, or things that are changing such as formal or informal social contacts or changes in the natural setting give variety, context and interest. An example of a building designed to be enjoyable and uplifting is the atrium in the Kajima office in Tokyo described by Takenoya (2006), in which aroma and bio-music are used intermittently to provide variety and stimulation. Complexity, colour and texture, for example, give contrast and make the environment more interesting. Over-stimulation can give confusing and hectic signals which can increase stress levels whereas too little stimulation can be boring (Bluyssen, 2014).
- *Individualisation* is the occupants' personal environment and includes factors such as personal control, flexibility and one's identity with a space.
- *Naturalness* is the basic environmental setting and this is where the comfort backdrop forms an important foundation.

The holistic experience is the interplay between these three dimensions of stimulation; individualisation and naturalness.

Kano *et al.* (1984) proposed a model of product and service satisfaction in the 1980s which defines three essential attributes:

- *threshold attributes*: customers expect these as a fundamental set of requirements (comfort criteria);
- *performance attributes*: though not absolutely necessary, they increase customers' enjoyment;
- *excitement attributes*: these provide the extra sense of surprise and enjoyment (bonus factors).

These are a dynamic interactive set of attributes (Figure 1.4).

Kim and de Dear (2012) adapted these and described Kano's classification in terms of *basic factors*, *proportional factors* and *bonus factors*. From their survey of 351 different office buildings, they identified basic and proportional factors:

- *Basic factors*: levels of temperature and sound; amount of space; visual privacy; flexible furniture; colours and textures; workplace cleanliness. These are minimal requirements.
- *Proportional factors*: air quality; light; visual comfort; sound privacy; ease of interaction; comfort of furniture; cleanliness; building maintenance. Satisfaction increased linearly as these elements improved.
- *Bonus factors*: colour, social climate, greenery, views, changing daylight, air movement. These factors act like triggers that can impact mood and add pleasure to one's experience. Other factors could be aesthetics and decor.

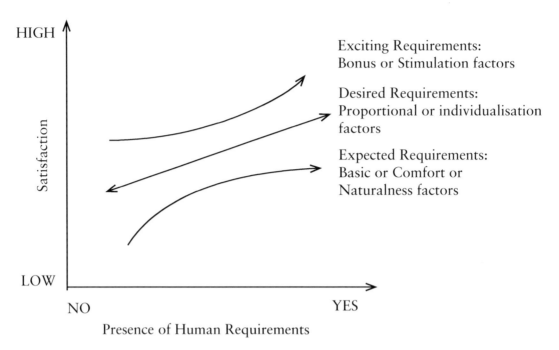

Figure 1.4 Kano's satisfaction model

Source: Adapted from Kim and de Dear (2012) and Bluyssen (2014).

One can see a connection here with the thinking behind the SIN model as the Stimulating element corresponds to the Bonus factor in the Kano model; Naturalness corresponds to the Basic factors; Individualisation corresponds to the Proportional factors and includes personal control.

The aim of the EU PERFECTION project was to help enable the application of new building design and technologies that improve the impact of the indoor built environment on health, comfort and feeling of safety and positive stimulation (Desmyter *et al.*, 2010; Bluyssen, 2014). Desmyter *et al.* (2010) suggested some indicators of positive stimulation which are similar to the response triggers proposed above.

The Flourish model

The aim is to create an environment in which people thrive. The reasoning for this model is based on the work of Barrett *et al.* (2016) and Kim and de Dear (2012), which goes beyond comfort and reaches out towards acquiring the ideal state of well-being, as described by Maslow (1943), Seligman (2011), and Diener and Biswas-Diener (2008). The model is based on three kinds of factors: (1) the *environmental* factors; (2) the *perceptions and feelings* people have in various environmental settings; and (3) the *economic consequences* of the environments created (World Green Building Council, 2014; UK Green Building Council, 2016).

- *Environmental factors* consist of a normal layer featuring standard comfort health and safety guidelines for temperature, sound, light, ventilation (for the waking and sleeping states). Various codes, guides and handbooks prescribe these.
- *Perception and feeling* factors recognise there is a relationship between health and some of the features we are dealing with in a proportional way. For example, as ventilation

increases from 8 l/s person to 25 l/s person, illnesses decrease as the research by Fanger (1970; 2002), Wargocki *et al.* (2006) have shown. So there is not a single number or narrow band to choose for design, such as temperature, for example, but rather an individual or proportional layer from which a choice can be made. In selecting a figure, one has to study the evidence for offices, schools, retail outlets or homes. Often the decision is made on low energy and cost but this has to be offset by the savings accrued by better health and productivity as evidenced by less absenteeism and presenteeism.

• Then there is the *Sparkle* or 'wow' layer which includes things like views on Nature, daylight, colour, decor, layout, aesthetics, or green space around the building. These features are mainly non-quantifiable but are important. These seemingly small factors can suddenly make one feel better in spirit – a bit like getting up in the morning and feeling a little sluggish then opening the curtains on to a beautiful sunny morning and feeling quivers of happiness. Some of the research is beginning to give some design data for biophilic design (Browning *et al.*, 2012) but in general it is things we should do even though these factors are 'soft' metrics and do not generally have numbers. We do know, however, facts such as, for example, that homes with sea or country views fetch premium prices. Buildings in cities are particularly challenging but with careful creative thought they can be lovable, joyful and soulful places for people to live and work.

We need to capture all three layers if we are going to provide buildings where people thrive and flourish for living or work. Figure 1.5 shows the Flourish model (UK Green Building Council, see Clements-Croome, 2016b, p. 14).

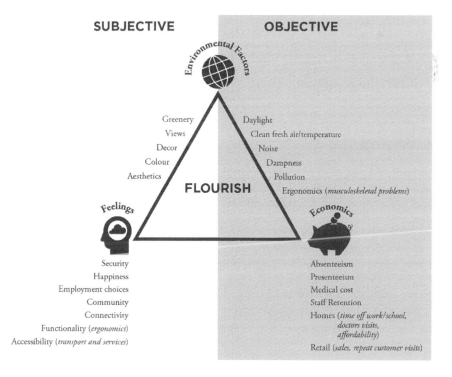

Figure 1.5 The Flourish model
Source: UK Green Building Council (2016).

We can conclude from the work described in this section that comfort is not enough. We need to continue to develop a deeper understanding about the effects of the environment on the health and well-being of people and widen our scope of design to produce more flourishing, stimulating, creative and productive places for people to work in and enjoy.

References

Abdul-Samed, Z. and Macmillan, S. (2005) The valuation of intangibles explored by primary school design. In Emmitt, S. (ed.) *Proceedings of the CIB W096 Conference on Designing Value: New Directions in Architectural Management*, November, Technical University of Denmark, Lyngby.

Abdul-Wahab, S.A. (2011) Sick building syndrome in public buildings and workplaces. In Clements-Croome, D.J. (ed.) *The Interaction between the Physical Environment and People*. Berlin: Springer-Verlag.

Alvarsson, J.J., Weins, S. and Nilsson, M.E. (2010) Stress recovery during exposure to nature sound and environmental noise. *International Journal of Environmental Research and Public Health*, 7(3): 1036–1046.

Anderson, J. and French, M. (2010) Sustainability as promoting well-being: psychological dimensions of thermal comfort. Personal communication, Institute of Well-Being, University of Cambridge, Cambridge, UK.

ANFA (2013) Selected papers from the Academy of Neuroscience for Architecture Conference, September 2012 in San Diego. *Intelligent Buildings International*, 5: S1.

Allen, M. and Allen, J. (2015) Health inequalities and the role of the physical and social environment. In Barton, H. *et al.* (eds) *The Routledge Handbook of Planning for Health and Well-Being*. London: Routledge, pp. 89–107.

Antonovski, A. (1979) *Health, Stress and Coping*. San Francisco: Jossey–Bass.

Arantes, B. (2015) Neuroscience: the next great competitive advantage. *Work & Place*, October: 10–13. Available at: www.steelcase.com

Arbib, M.A. (2012) Brains, machines and buildings: towards a neuromorphic architecture. *Intelligent Buildings International*, 4(3): 147–168.

Bakó-Biró, Z., Clements-Croome, D.J., Kochhar, N., Awbi, H.B. and Williams, M. (2012) Ventilation rates in schools and pupils' performance. *Building and Environment*, 48: 215–223.

Baron, R.A. (1990) Environmentally induced positive affect: its impacts on self-efficacy, task performance, negotiation and conflict. *Journal of Applied Social Sociology*, 20(5): 368–384.

Barrett, P. and Barrett, L. (2010) The potential of positive places: senses, brain and spaces. *Intelligent Buildings International*, 2: 218–228.

Barrett, P., Barrett, L. and Zhang, Y. (2016) Teachers' views of their primary school classrooms. *Intelligent Buildings International Journal*, 8(3): 176–191.

Barrett, P.S., Davies, F., Zhang, Y. and Barrett, L. (2015) The impact of classroom design on pupils' learning: Final results of a holistic, multi-level analysis, *Building and Environment*, 89: 118–133.

Barrett, P. and Zhang, Y. (2012) Teachers' views on the designs of their primary schools. *Intelligent Buildings International*, DOI:10.1080/17508975.2012.672305.BCO (2012) *Making Art Work in the Workplace*, Research Report by International Art Consultants in partnership with the British Council for Offices. Available at: www.bco.org.uk

BCO (2014) *Making the Business Case for Well-being*, The 2014 Well-being at Work Study British Council for Offices; Morgan Lovell and Hatch. Available at: www.bco.org.uk/Research/Publications/Making_the_Business_Case_for_Wellbeing.aspx

Beil, K. and Hanes, D. (2013) The influence of urban natural and built environments on physiological and psychological measures of stress – a pilot study. *International Journal of Environmental Research and Public Health*, 10(4): 1250–1267.

Bluyssen, P.M. (2014) *The Healthy Indoor Environment: How to Assess Occupants' Well-Being in Buildings*. London: Routledge.

Boerstra, A., *et al.* (2013) Impact of available and perceived control on comfort and health in European offices. *Architectural Science Review*, 56(1): 30–41.

Boerstra, A.C., Loomans, M.G.L.C. and Hensen, J.L.M. (2014) Personal control over indoor climate and productivity. In *Proceedings of Indoor Air Conference 2014*, Hong Kong.

Bradley, F.H. (1914) *Essays on Truth and Reality*. Oxford: Clarendon Press.

BRE (2015) *Home Quality Mark: Technical Manual*. SD 232.0.0. Beta England.

Brekke, H. (2016) How does the built environment affect behaviour and cognition? In Fritz, A. (ed.) *Conscious Cities: An Anthology No. 1*. London: The Cube and the Museum of Architecture.

Brown, C., Efstratiou, C., Leontiadis, I., Quercia, D., Mascolo, C., Scott. J. and Key, P. (2014) The architecture of innovation: tracking face-to-face interactions with ubicomp technologies. In *Proceedings of the ACM International Joint Conference on Pervasive and Ubiquitous Computing (Ubicomp 2014)*. Seattle, Washington, USA, September 2014.

Browning, W. (2012) *The Economics of Biophilia*. New York: Terrapin Bright Green.

Burton, E. (2015) Mental well-being and place. In Barton, H. *et al.* (eds) *The Routledge Handbook of Planning for Health and Well-Being*. London: Routledge, pp. 150–161.

Burton, E.J., Bird, W., Maryon-Davis, A., Murphy, M., Stewart-Brown, S., Weare, K. and Wilson, P. (2011) *Thinking Ahead: Why We Need to Improve Children's Mental Health and Wellbeing*. London: Faculty of Public Health of the Royal College of Physicians of the United Kingdom.

Cabanac, M. (2006) Pleasure and joy, and their role in human life. In Clements-Croome, D.J. (ed.) *Creating the Productive Workplace*. London: Routledge, pp. 40–50.

CABE (2005) *The Impact of Office Design on Business Performance*. Design Council CABE. Available at: www.designcouncil.org.uk

Cain, S. (2012) *Quiet*. London: Penguin.

Cao, M. and Wei, J. (2005) Stock market returns: a note on temperature anomaly. *Journal of Banking and Finance*, 29: 1559–1573.

Carson, S. (2010) *Your Creative Brain*. San Francisco: Jossey-Bass.

Chappells, H. (2010) Comfort, well-being and the socio-technical dynamics of everyday life. *Intelligent Buildings International Journal*, 2(4): 286–298.

Chrenko, F.A. (ed.) (1974) *Bedford's Basic Principles of Ventilation and Heating*, 3rd edn. London: H.K. Lewis, pp. 154–180.

Clements-Croome, D.J. (1996) Freshness, ventilation and temperature in offices, *Building Services Engineering Research and Technology*, 17(1): 21–27.

Clements-Croome, D.J. (2000a) Computers and health in the work place. In *Proceedings of Healthy Buildings*, University of Technology, Helsinki, 1: 119–124.

Clements-Croome, D.J. (2000b) *Creating the Productive Workplace*. London: Routledge.

Clements-Croome, D.J. (2004a) *Intelligent Buildings: Design, Management & Operation*. London: Thomas Telford.

Clements-Croome, D.J. (2004b) *Electromagnetic Environments and Health in Buildings*. London: Routledge.

Clements-Croome, D.J. (2006) *Creating the Productive Workplace*, 2nd edn. London: Routledge.

Clements-Croome, D.J. (2008) Work performance, productivity and indoor air. *Scandinavian Journal of Work Environment and Health*, Supplement(4): 69–78.Clements-Croome, D.J. (2013) *Intelligent Buildings: Design, Management & Operation*. London: ICE Publishing.

Clements-Croome, D.J. (2014) *Sustainable Intelligent Buildings for Better Health, Comfort and Well-Being*, EU Report for Denzero Project led by Debrecen University supported by the TAMOP-4.2.2A-11/1/KONV-2012–0041 and co-financed by the European Union and the European Social Fund. Available at: www.derekcroome.com

Clements-Croome, D.J. (2016a) Intelligent liveable buildings: health and well-being perspectives. Lecture at School of Architecture and Civil Engineering, Bath University, 4 March. Available at: www.derekcroome.com

Clements-Croome, D.J. (2016b) *Health and Wellbeing in Homes*. UK Green Building Council. Available at: www.ukgbc.orgCooper, C., Browning, W. (2015) Human spaces: the global impact of biophilic design in the workplace. Available at: http://humanspaces.com; http://humanspaces.com/global-report/key-messages/

Csikszentmihalyi, M. (2014) *Flow and the Foundations of Positive Psychology: The Collected Works of Mihaly Csikszentmihalyi*. Dordrecht: Springer.

Cui, W., *et al.* (2013) Influence of indoor air temperature on human thermal comfort, motivation and performance. *Building and Environment*, 68: 114–122.

Davis, M.C., Leach, D.J. and Clegg, C.W. (2011) The physical environment of the office: contemporary and emerging issues. *International Review of Industrial and Organisational Psychology*, 26: 193–235.

De Dear, R. (2004) Thermal comfort in practice. *Indoor Air*, 14(S7): 32–39.

De Dear, R. (2011) Revisiting an old hypothesis of human perception: alliesthesia. *Building Research and Information*, 39(2): 108–117.

De Dear, R., *et al.* (2013) Progress in thermal comfort research over the last twenty years. *Indoor Air*, 23(6): 442–461.

De Looze, M.P., *et al.* (2003) Sitting comfort and discomfort and the relationships with objective measures. *Ergonomics*, 46: 985–997.

Dember, W.N., Warm, J.S. and Parasuraman, R. (1995) Olfactory stimulation and sustained attention. In Gilber, A.N. (ed.) *Compendium of Olfactory Research. Explorations in Aroma-chology: Investigating the Sense of Smell and Human Response to Odors, 1982–1994*. Dubuque, IA: Kendall Hunt, pp. 39–46.

De Regules, S. (2016) Complex interactions. *Physics World*, 29(4): 27–30.

Desmet, P.M.A. (2015) Design for mood: twenty activity-based opportunities to design for mood regulation. *International Journal of Design*, 9(2): 1–19.

Desmyter, J., *et al.* (2010) A review of safety, security accessibility and positive stimulation indicators, Perfection Workshop at VTT Helsinki, 4 February. Final Report, Performance Indicators for Health Comfort and Safety of the Indoor Environment, 30 August. Available at: www.ca-perfection.eu/media/files/Perfection_D14_final.pdf

Diener, E. and Biswas-Diener, R. (2008) *Happiness: Unlocking the Mysteries of Psychological Wealth*. Malden, MA: Free Press.

Dolan, P. (2014) *Happiness by Design*. London: Allen Lane.

Dolan, P., Foy, C. and Smith S. (2016) The SALIENT Checklist: gathering up the ways in which built environments affect what we do and how we feel. *Buildings*, 6(1); 9. DOI:10.3390/buildings6010009.

Eberhard, J. (2009) *Brain Landscape: The Coexistence of Neuroscience and Architecture*. New York: Oxford University Press.

Ekelund, U., *et al.* (2016) Does physical activity attenuate, or even eliminate, the detrimental association of sitting time with mortality? A harmonised meta-analysis of data from more than 1 million men and women. *Lancet*, July 27, dx.doi.org/10.1016/S0140–6736 916) 30370–1.1.

Evans, R. and Stoddart, G. (1990) Producing health, consuming health care. *Social Science Medicine*, 31: 1347–1363.

Fanger, P.O. (1970) *Thermal Comfort: Analysis and Applications in Environmental Engineering*. Copenhagen: Danish Technical Press.

Fanger, P.O. (2002) Human requirements in future air-conditioned environments. *Advances in Building Technology*, 1: 29–38.Fisk, W.J. (1999) Estimates of potential nationwide productivity and health benefits from better indoor environments: an update. In Spengler, J.D., Samet, J.M. and McCarthy, J.F. (eds) *Indoor Air Quality Handbook*. New York: McGraw-Hill.

Fujiwara, D. and Vine, J. (2015) *The Wellbeing Value of Tackling Homelessness*. London: HACT. Available at: www.hact.org.uk/sites/default/files/uploads/Archives/2015/9/Homelessness%20and%20wellbeing%20analysis.pdf

Galasiu, A.D., *et al.* (2007) Energy lighting control systems for open-plan offices: a field study. *Leukos*, 4(1): 7–29.

Gillis, K. and Gatersleben, B. (2015) A review of psychological literature on the health and wellbeing benefits of biophilic design. *Buildings*, 5(3): 948–963, DOI:10.3390/buildings5030948.

Gou, Z., *et al.* (2014) Visual alliesthesia: the gap between comfortable and stimulating illuminance settings. *Building and Environment*, 82: 42–49.

Henshaw, V. (2014) *Urban Smellscapes*. London: Routledge.

Hermans, V. (2016) Office work innovation: what about wellbeing? *Modern Economy*, 7: 815–821.

Herzberg, F. (1966) *Work and the Nature of Man*. New York: World Publishing Company.

Heschong, L. (1979) *Thermal Delight in Architecture*. Cambridge, MA: MIT Press.

Humphreys, M., Nicol, N. and Roaf, S. (2016) *Adaptive Thermal Comfort*. London: Routledge.

Huppert, F.A., Baylis, N. and Keverne, B. (2005) *The Science of Well-being*. Oxford; Oxford University Press.

IBI Group Nightingale (2012) *Sense Sensitive Design*. Available at: www.ibigroup.com

Juniper, B., *et al.* (2011) Testing the performance of a new approach to measuring employee well-being. *Leadership and Organisation Development Journal*, 25(4): 344–357.

Juniper, B.A., White, N. and Bellamy, P. (2009) Assessing employee well-being – is there another way? *International Journal of Workplace Health Management*, 2(3): 220–230.

Kano, N., *et al.* (1984) Attractive quality and must-be quality. *Journal of the Japanese Society for Quality Control*, 14(2): 39–48 (in Japanese).

Kim, J. and de Dear, R. (2012) Nonlinear relationships between individual IEQ factors and overall workspace satisfaction. *Building and Environment*, 49(1): 33–40.

Knasko, S.C. (1993) Performance mood and health during exposure to odours. *Archives of Environmental Health*, 48(5): 305–308.

Knight, C. and Haslam, S.A. (2010) The relative merits of lean, enriched, and empowered offices: an experimental examination of the impact of workspace management. *Journal of Experimental Psychology: Applied*, 16: 158–172.

Lacy, M.L. (1996) *The Power of Colour to Heal the Environment*. London: Rainbow Bridge.

Lan, L. *et al.* (2011) Effects of thermal discomfort in an office on perceived air quality, SBS symptoms, physiological responses and human performance. *Indoor Air*, 21: 376–390.

Langdon, F.J. (1973) Human sciences and the environment in buildings. *Building International*, 6(January–February): 106.

Leaman, A. and Bordass, B. (1999) Productivity in buildings: the 'killer' variables. *Building Research & Information*, 27: 4–19.

Leaman, A. and Bordass, B. (2006) Productivity in buildings: the 'killer' variables. In Clements-Croome, D.J. (ed.) *Creating the Productive Workplace*. London: Routledge, pp. 153–180.

Lehrer, J. (2011) Building a thinking room. *The Wall Street Journal*, April 30.

Levine, J.A. (2015) Sick of sitting. *Diabetologia*, 58: 1751–1758.

Ludvigson, H.W. and Rottman, T.R. (1989) Effects of odours of lavender and cloves on cognition, memory, affect, and mood. *Chemical Senses*, 14(4): 525–536.

Malnar, J.M. and Vodvarka, F. (2004) *Sensory Design*. Minneapolis, MN: University of Minnesota Press.

Mangone, G., *et al.* (2014) Constructing thermal comfort: investigating the effect of vegetation on indoor thermal comfort through a four season thermal comfort quasi-experiment. *Building and Environment*, 81: 410–426.

Markham, S.F. (1944) *Climate and the Energy of Nations*. New York: Oxford University Press.

Marmot, A. (2016) Space on Demand: Coworkspace and Space Matchmaker Apps., BCO Report. Available at: www.bco.org.uk

Marmot, A. and Ucci, M. (eds) (2015) Special Issue on physical activity, sedentary behaviour and the indoor environment. *Building Research and Information*, 43(5).

Marston, W. (1979) *The Emotions of Normal People*. Minneapolis: Persona Press Inc.

Maslow, A.H. (1943) A theory of human motivation. *Psychology Review*, 50(4): 370–396.

McGraw-Hill Construction (2013) *New and Retrofit Green Schools: The Cost Benefits and Influence of a Green School on Its Occupants*. Smart Market Report. Available at: MHC_Analytics@mcgraw-hill.com

McGraw-Hill Construction (2014) *The Drive Toward Healthier Buildings: The Market Drivers and Impact of Building Design and Construction on Occupant Health, Well-Being and Productivity*. Smart Market Report. Available at: MHC_Analytics@mcgraw-hill.com

McLean, K. (2013) *Sensory Maps of Cities*. Available at: www.sensorymaps.com)

Morris, G.P., Beck, S.A., Hanlon, P. and Robertson, R. (2006) Getting strategic about the environment and health. *Public Health Journal*, 120: 889–907.

Nedved, M. (2011) Ventilation and the air ion effect in the indoor environments: impact on human health and well-being. In Abdul-Wahab, S.A. (ed.) *Sick Building Syndrome in Public Buildings and Workplaces*. Berlin: Springer-Verlag.

Newman, M. (2010) Get happy, and get on with it. *Times Higher Education*, 21 January, pp. 34–36.

Nicol, F., Humphreys, M. and Roaf, S. (2012) *Adaptive Thermal Comfort: Principles and Practice*. London: Routledge.

OECD (2013) *OECD Guidelines on Measuring Subjective Well-being*. Paris: OECD Publishing. Available at; http://dx.doi.org/10.1787/9789264191655-en

Oh, S.Y.J. (2005) Indoor air quality and productivity in offices in Malaysia, BSc dissertation, School of Construction Management and Engineering, University of Reading, Reading, UK.

Ong, B.L. (2013) *Beyond Environmental Comfort*. London: Routledge.

Pallasmaa, J. (2016) Body, mind and imagination: neuroscience and the mental essence of architecture. In Fritz, A (ed.) *Conscious Cities: An Anthology No. 1*. London: The Cube and the Museum of Architecture.

PriceWaterhouseCoopers LLP (2008) *Building the Case for Wellness*. Available at: www.dwp.gov.uk/docs/hwwb-dwp-wellness-report-public.pdf (accessed 26 March 2013).

Rainham, D., Cantwell, R. and Jason, T. (2013) Nature appropriation and associations with population health in Canada's largest cities. *International Journal of Environmental Research and Public Health*, 10(4): 1268–1283.

Roe, J., Aspinall, P.A., Mavros, P. and Coyne, R. (2013) Engaging the brain: the impact of natural versus urban scenes using novel EEG methods in an experimental setting. *Environmental Sciences*, 1(2): 93–104.

Rotton, J. (1983) Affected and cognitive consequences of malodorous pollution. *Basic and Applied Psychology*, 4(2): 171–191.

Roulet, C.A., *et al.* (2006) Perceived health and comfort in relation to energy use and building characteristics. *Building Research and Information*, 34(5): 467–474.

Salingaros, N.A. (2015) *Biophilia and Healing Environments: Healthy Principles For Designing the Built World*. New York: Terrapin Bright Green, LLC.

Satish, U., *et al.* (2011) Impact of CO_2 on human decision making and productivity. Abstract 574, Indoor Air Conference, Austin, TX.

Satish, U., *et al.* (2012*)* Is CO_2 an indoor air pollutant? Direct effects of low-to-moderate CO_2 concentrations on human decision-making performance. *Environmental Health, Perspectives*, 120: 1671–1677.

Schafer, R.M. (1977) *The Tuning of the World*. New York: Knopf.

Scottish Government (2006) *Health in Scotland 2006: Annual Report of the Chief Medical Officer*. Available at: www.scotland.gov.uk/Publications/2007/11/15135302/10 (accessed 26 March 2013).

Seligman, M. (2011) Flourish. New York: Free Press,

Shepherd, D., Welch, D., Dirks, K. and McBride, D. (2013) Do quiet areas afford greater health-related quality of life than noisy areas? *International Journal of Environmental Research and Public Health*, 10(4): 1284–1303.

Shields, B. (2003). Learning's sound barrier. *Newsline*, 26: 10–11.

Steemers, K. and Manchanda, S. (2010). Energy efficient design and occupant well-being: case studies in the UK and India. *Building and Environment*, 45: 270–278.

Strom-Tjesen, P., Zukowska, D., Wargocki, P. and Wyon, D.P. (2015) The effects of bedroom air quality on sleep and next-day performance. *Indoor Air*. DOI:10.1111/ina.12254.

Takenoya, H. (2006) Air conditioning systems of the K I Building, Tokyo. In Clements-Croome, D.J. (ed.) *Creating the Productive Workplace*. London: Routledge.

Taub, M., Clements-Croome, D.J. and Lockhart, V. (2016) *The Impacts of Wearables on Designing Healthy Office Environments: A Review*. BCO Report. Available at: www.bco.org.uk

Tennant, R., Hiller, L., Fishwick, R., Platt, S., Joseph, S., Weich, S. and Stewart-Brown, S. (2007). The Warwick-Edinburgh mental well-being scale (WEMWBS): development and UK validation. *Health and Quality of Life Outcomes*, 5(1) 63.

Tillotson, J. (2008) JENTIL: responsive clothing that promotes an 'holistic approach to fashion as a new vehicle to treat psychological conditions'. In The Body – Connections with Fashion: Conference

Proceedings 2008. Proceedings of the Tenth Annual IFFTI Conference, RMIT School of Fashion and Textiles, Melbourne, Victoria.

Tillotson, J. (2012) Live scent | evil stench. In *This Pervasive Day: The Potential Perils of Pervasive Computing*. London: Imperial College Press, pp. 53–68.

Trevia, F.G. (2013) Take your time: combine nature and technology to relieve work-related stress in the office environment. Master of Science Design for Interaction, TU Delft Faculty of Industrial Design Engineering.

Trotter, L., Vine, J., Leach, M. and Fujiwara, D. (2014) *Measuring the Social Impact of Community Investment: A Guide to Using the Wellbeing Valuation Approach*. HACT. Available at: www.hact.org.uk/measuring-social-impact-community-investment-guide-using-wellbeing-valuation-approach

Tweed, C., *et al.* (2014) Thermal comfort practices in the home and their impact on energy consumption. *Architectural Engineering and Design Management*, 10(1–2): 1–24.

UK Green Building Council (2016) *Health and Wellbeing in Homes*, July. Available at: www.ukgbc.org. www.ukgbc.org/resources/publication/health-wellbeing-and-productivity-offices-next-chapter-green-building; www.ukgbc.org/resources/publication/health-wellbeing-and-productivity-retail-report; www.ukgbc.org/resources/publication/uk-gbc-task-group-report-healthy-homes

Ulrich, R.S. (1984) View through a window may influence recovery from surgery. *Science*, 224: 420–421.

Ulrich, R.S. (1991) Effects of interior design on wellness: theory and recent scientific research. *Journal of Health Care Interior Design*, 1(3): 97–109.USDAW (Union of Shop, Distributive and Allied Workers) (2006) *The Guardian*, Work section, 8 July. Available at: www.guardian.co.uk/theguardian/2006/jul/08/work (accessed 30 Aug. 2012).

Veitch, J.A., *et al.* (2008) Lighting appraisal, well-being and performance in open-plan offices: a linked mechanisms approach. *Lighting Research and Technology*, 40: 13–151.

Veitch, J.A., *et al.* (2010) *Lighting and Office Renovation Effects on Employee and Organisational Well-being*. NRC Report IPC-RR-306.

Veitch, J.A. and Galasiu, A.D. (2012) The physiological and psychological effects of windows, daylight, and view at home. Review and Research Agenda No. IRC-RR-325. NRC Institute for Research in Construction, Ottawa, Canada.

Vink, P. (2012) Editorial: comfort and discomfort studies demonstrate the need for a new model. *Applied Ergonomics*, 43: 271–276.

Wargocki, P., Seppanen, O., Andersson, J., Boerstra, A., Clements-Croome, D., Fitzner, K. and Hanssen, S.O. (2006) *Indoor Climate and Productivity in Offices*. Federation of European Heating and Air-conditioning Associations (REHVA) Guidebook no 6.

Warr, P. (1998a) What is our current understanding of the relationships between well-being and work? *Journal of Occupational Psychology*, 63: 193–210.

Warr, P. (1998b) Well-being and the workplace. In Kahneman, D., El Diener, X. and Schwarz, N. (eds) *Foundations of Hedonic Psychology: Scientific Perspectives on Enjoyment and Suffering*. New York: Russell Sage.

Warr, P. (2002) *Psychology at Work*, 5th edn. Harmondsworth: Penguin Books.

Watson, K.J., Evans, J., Karvonen, A. and Whitley, T. (2016) Capturing the social value of buildings: the promise of social return on investment (SROI). *Building and Environment*. DOI:10.1016/j.buildenv.2016.04.007

Weiss, M.L. (1997) Division of behavior and cognitive science. PhD thesis, Rochester University, New York.

WELL Building Standard (2015) ASC/all/DV/S001/Feb15/V1.0 21, info@wellcertified.com (International Well Building Institute, Washington, DC 20037).

Williams, B. (2006). Building performance: the value management approach. In Clements-Croome, D.J. (ed.) *Creating the Productive Workplace*. London: Routledge.

Wilson, E.O. (1984) *Biophilia*, Cambridge, MA: Harvard University Press.

Wilson, F. (1984) *A Graphic Survey of Perception and Behaviour for the Design Professions*. New York: Van Nostrand Reinhold.

World Green Building Council (WGBC) (2013) *The Business Case for Green Building*. Available at: www.worldgbc.org/files/1513/6608/0674/Business_Case_For_Green_Building_Report_WEB_2013-04-11.pdf

World Green Building Council (WGBC) (2014) *Health, Wellbeing and Productivity in Offices: the Next Chapter for Green Building.* Available at: info@ukgbc.org or office@wgbc.org See Clements-Croome, D.J. *Viewpoint on Beyond Comfort* .pp. 32–33.

World Green Building Council (WGBC) (2016) *Health, Wellbeing and Productivity in Retail: The Impact of Green Buildings on People and Profit.* World Green Building Council. Available at: info@ukgbc.org or office@wgbc.org led by UK Green Building Council.

Wright, A. (1995) *The Beginner's Guide to Colour Psychology.* London: Kyle Cathie.

Wyon, D. and Wargocki P. (2013) How indoor environment affects performance. *ASHRAE Journal,* 55(3): 46–52.

Further reading

Achor, S. (2010) *The Happiness Advantage.* New York: Random House.

Agha-Hossein, M., Birchall, S. and Saryu, V. (2015) *Building Performance Evaluation in Non-Domestic Buildings.* BG 63, BSRIA.

Agha-Hossein, M.M., El-Jouzi, S., Elmualim, A.A., Ellis, J. and Williams, M. (2013) Post-occupancy studies of an office environment: energy performance and occupants' satisfaction. *Building and Environment,* 69: 121–130.

Akhlagi, F. (1996) Ensuring value for money in FM contract services. *Facilities,* 14(1/2): 26–33.

Allen, J.G., MacNaughton, P., Satish, U., Santanam, S., Vallarino, J. and Spengler, J,D. (2015) Associations of cognitive function scores with carbon dioxide, ventilation, and volatile organic compound exposures in office workers: a controlled exposure study of green and conventional office environments. *Environmental Health Perspectives.* DOI: 10.1289/ehp.1510037

AlWaer, H. and Clements-Croome, D.J. (2010) Key performance indicators and priority setting in using the multi-attribute approach for assessing sustainable intelligent buildings. *Building and Environment,* 45(4): 799–807.

Bakó-Biró, Z., Kochhar, N., Clements-Croome, D.J., Awbi, H.B. and Williams, M. (2007) Ventilation rates in schools and learning performance. In *Proceedings of CLIMA 2007, WellBeing Indoors.* The 9th REHVA World Congress, Helsinki, Finland, pp. 1434–1440.

Bakó-Biró, Z., Kochhar, N., Clements-Croome, D.J., Awbi, H.B. and Williams, M. (2008) Ventilation rates in schools and pupils' performance using computerised assessment tests. Indoor Air 2008, Copenhagen, The 11th International Conference on Indoor Air Quality and Climate.Baldry, C. (1999) Space: the final frontier. *Sociology,* 33(3): 1–29.

Barrett P., *et al.* (2013) A holistic, multi-level analysis identifying the impact of classroom design on pupils' learning. *Building and Environment,* 59: 678–689.

Baue, B. (2006) *Opening the Umbrella of Socially Responsible Investing to Include Energy Efficient Mortgages,* SRI World Group, Inc. Brattleboro VT. Available at: www.socialfunds.com/news/article. cgi/1934.html (accessed 8 October 2009)

Bell, J., Mabb, J, Garcia-Hansen, V., Bergman, B. and Morawska, L. (2003) Occupant health and productivity: an Australian perspective. In Yang, J., Brandon, P.S. and Sidwell, A.C. (eds) *Proceedings of the CIB 2003 International Conference on Smart and Sustainable Built Environment* (SASBE 2003), pp. 687–694.

Bellenger, P.E. (2010) Modeling a sustainable world, Presidential Address. *ASHRAE Journal,* 52(8): 18–22.

Berglund, B. and Gunnarsson, A.G. (2000) Relationships between occupant personality and the sick building syndrome explored. *Indoor Air,* 10: 152–169.

Bergs, J. (2002) The effect of healthy workplaces on the well-being and productivity of office workers. Plants for People Symposium, Reducing Health Complaints at Work, Amsterdam.

Bernstein, H. and Russo, M. (2013) *Smart Market Report.* McGraw-Hill Construction. Available at: MHC_Analytics@mcgraw-hill.com

Betthäuser, G. (2013) *Leesman Review,* Issue 10, p. 2.

Black, C. (2008) *Working for a Healthier Tomorrow: Review by Dame Carol Black.* London: HMSO.

Bluyssen, P.M., *et al.* (2010) A top-down system engineering approach as an alternative to the traditional over-the-bench methodology for the design of a building. *Intelligent Buildings International Journal,* 2(2): 98–115.

Booy, D., Liu, K., Qiao, B. and Guy, C.A. (2008) Semiotic model for a self organising multi-agent system. In DEST2008 – International Conference on Digital Ecosystems and Technologies. Phitsanulok, Thailand: IEEE.

Bowen, P. (2005) Integrated approach for information communication technology (ICT) and control system infrastructures within buildings: an independent study. Converged Building Technologies Group. Available at: www.intelligentbuildings.com/PDF/library/smartBuildings/CBTG_ROI_Model. pdf (accessed 8 Feb. 2009).

Boyce, P.B. (1997) *Illumination: Handbook of Human Factors and Ergonomics*, ed. Salvendy, G. New York: Wiley Interscience, pp. 858–890.

Boyden, S. (1971) Biological determinants of optimal health. In Vorster D.J.M. (ed.) *The Human Biology of Environmental Change*. Proceedings of a conference held in Blantyre, Malawi, April 5–12, 1971. London: International Biology Program.

Braungart, M. and McDonough W. (2009) *Cradle to Cradle*. London: Vintage.

BSRIA (2012) *The Value of BREEAM*. Report by J. Parker. BG 42/2012.

BSRIA (2012) *The Soft Landings Core Principles*. BSRIA BG38.

Building Regulations (2000a) *Part L2A: Conservation of Fuel and Power in New Buildings other than Dwelling*. London: HMSO.

Building Regulations (2000b) *Part L2B: Conservation of Fuel and Power in Existing Buildings other than Dwellings*. London: HMSO.

Burr, A. (2008) *CoStar Study Finds Energy Star LEED Buildings Putperform Peers*. Bethesda, MD: CoStar Realty Information Inc. Available at: www.costar.com/News/Article.aspx?id=D968F1E0DCF73712B0 3A099E0E99C679 (accessed 8 October 2009).

CABA Report (2007) *Introduction to Commercial Building Control Strategies and Techniques for Demand Response*. Canada: Continental Automated Buildings Association.

Carbon Trust (2002) *Low Carbon Technology Assessment 2002: Making Our Investment Count*. London: Carbon Trust.

Carder, P. (1997) Benchmarking, performance, measurement and incentivisation, Milwaukee, WI: Johnson Controls [CDROM]. In Clements-Croome, D.J. (2004) *Intelligent Buildings: Design, Management and Operation*. London: Thomas Telford.

Chun, C., Kwok, A., Mitamura, T., Miwa, N. and Tamura, A. (2008) Thermal diary: connecting temperature history to indoor comfort. *Building and Environment*, 43: 877–885.

CIBSE (Chartered Institution of Building Services Engineers) (1999) *Environmental Factors Affecting Office Worker Performance: A Review of the Evidence*. Technical Memorandum 24. London: CIBSE.

CIBSE (2008) *Guide M: Maintenance Engineering and Management*. London: Chartered Institution of Building Services Engineers.Clark, L.A. and Watson, D. (1988) Mood and the mundane: relationships between daily events and self-reported mood. *Journal of Personality and Social Psychology*, 54: 296–308.

Clements-Croome, D.J. (1990) Building services engineering: the invisible architecture. *Building Services Engineering Research and Technology*, 11(1): 27–31.

Clements-Croome. D.J. (2013) Can intelligent buildings provide alternative approaches to heating, ventilating and air conditioning of buildings?, Dreosti Lecture, *RACA Journal*, 29(6): 22–33.

Clements-Croome, D.J., *et al.* (2007) *High Quality Building Services Based on Whole Life Value*. Reading: University of Reading.

Clements-Croome, D.J., *et al.* (2009) Master planning for sustainable liveable cities. Paper presented at 6th International Conference on Green and Efficient Building and New Technologies and Products Expo, Beijing, Ministry of Construction, March 29.

Clements-Croome, D.J., Awbi, H.B., Bakó-Biró, Z., Kochhar, N. and Williams, M. (2008) Ventilation rates in schools. *Building and Environment*, 43(3): 362–367.

Clements-Croome, D.J. and Li, B. (2000) Productivity and indoor environment. In Proceedings of Healthy Buildings Conference, University of Technology, Helsinki, 1: 629–634.

Construction Industry Council (2002) *Design Quality Indicator*. Available at: www.dqi.org.uk (accessed 26 March 2013).

Conti F. (1978) *Architecture as Environment*. New York: Harcourt Colleges Publications.

Cooper, P. (2010) Offsite prefabrication is crucial for sustainable refurbishment. *Modern Building Services*, 7(1): 24.Daly, S. (2010) Ecobuild Conference at Earls Court London and Personal Communication (Heath Avery).

Davidson, R.J. (2003) Report by M. Henderson. *The Times*, 2 September, p. 4.

Davidson, R J. and Begley, S. (2012) *The Emotional Life of your Brain*. Harmondsworth: Penguin.

Deary, I. (2001) *Intelligence: A Very Short Introduction*. Oxford: Oxford University Press.

De Dear, R. and Brager, G.S. (2001) The adaptive model of thermal comfort and energy conservation in the built environment. *International Journal of Biometeorology*; 45: 100–108.

De Dear, R. and Brager, G.S. (2003) Historical and cultural influences on comfort expectations. In Cole, R. and Lorch, R. (eds) *Buildings, Culture and Environment: Informing Local and Global Practices*. Oxford: Blackwell.

De Marco, T. and Lister, T. (1987) *People Ware: Productive Projects and Teams*. New York: Dorset House Publishing.

Duangsuwan, J. and Liu, K. (2008) Multi-agent control of shared zones in intelligent buildings, *International Conference on Computer Science and Software Engineering*, 1: 1238–1241.

Edwards, B. (2002) *Rough Guide to Sustainability*. London: RIBA Publications.

Egan Report (1998) *Rethinking Construction*. London: HMSO.

Eichholtz, P., Kok, N. and Quigley, J. (2009) *Doing Well by Doing Good? An Analysis of the Financial Performance of Green Office Buildings in the USA*. London: RICS. Available at: www.rics.org/site/download_feed.aspx?fileID=20&fileExtension=PDF (accessed 8 October 2009).

Eley Associates (2001) *The Collaborative for High Performance Schools, Best Practices Manual*. San Francisco: Eley Associates.

Elliott, C. (2009) Intelligent buildings: systems engineering for the built environment. *Intelligent Buildings International Journal*, 1(1): 75–81.

Emes, M.R., Smith, A. and Marjanovic-Halbard, L. (2012) Systems for construction: lessons for the construction industry from experiences in spacecraft systems engineering. *Intelligent Buildings International Journal*, 4(2): 67–88.

Evans, R., Haryott, R., Haste, N. and Jones, A. (1998) The long term costs of owning and using buildings. In Macmillan, S. (ed.) *Designing Better Buildings: Quality and Value in the Built Environment*. London: Routledge, pp. 42–50.

Everett, R. (2009) The 'Building colleges for the future' program: delivering a green and intelligent building agenda. New Review of Information Networking, 14(1): 3–20.

Farshchi, M.A. and Fisher, N. (2006) Emotion and the environment: the forgotten dimension. In Clements-Croome, D.J. (ed.) *Creating the Productive Workplace*. 2nd edn. London: Routledge.

Ferguson, G.S. and Weisman, G.D. (1986) Alternative approaches to the assessment of employee satisfaction with the office environment. In Wineman, J.D. (ed.) *Behavioral Issues in Office Design*. New York: Van Nostrand Reinhold, pp. 85–108.

Fisk, W.J. (2000a) Health and productivity gains from better indoor environments and their relationship with building energy efficiency. *Annual Review of Energy Environment*, 25(1): 537–566.

Fisk, W.J. (2000b) Review of health and productivity gains from better IEQ. *Proceedings of Healthy Buildings*, Helsinki, 4: 24–33.

Fisk, W.J., Black, D.R. and Brunner, G. (2012) Changing ventilation rates in US offices: implications for health, work performance, energy, and associated economics. *Building and Environment*, 47: 368–372.

Fogg, B J. (2009) A behaviour model for persuasive design. Persuasive 09, Proceedings of the 4th International Conference on Persuasive Technology, Article 40.

Fontaine, J.R.J., Scherer, K.R., Roesch, E.B. and Ellsworth, P.C. (2007) The world of emotions is not two-dimensional. *Psychological Science*, 18: 1050–1057.

Genslers (2013) Workplace survey. Available at: www.gensler.com/uploads/documents/2013

Goleman, D. (2009) *Ecological Intelligence*. London: Allen Lane.

Gray, C. and Flanagan, R. (1989) *The Changing Role of Specialist and Trade Contractors*. London: Chartered Institute of Building.

Greenfield, S. (2014) *Mind Change: How Digital Technologies Are Leaving Their Mark on Our Brains.* New York: Rider.

Gruneberg, S. (2000) The growth and survival of firms in the heating and ventilating industry. PhD thesis, Faculty of the Built Environment, The Bartlett School of Graduate Studies, University College London.

Guerra-Santin, O. and Itard, L. (2010) Occupants' behaviour: determinants and effects on residential heating consumption. *Building Research and Information*, 38(3): 318–338.

Haghighat, F. and Donnini, G. (2007) Impact of psycho-social factors on perception of the indoor air environment studies in 12 office buildings. *Building and Environment*, 34: 479–503.

Haslam, C., Haslam, S.A., Knight, C., Gleibs, I., Ysseldyk, R., and McCloskey, L.G. (2014) We can work it out: group decision-making builds social identity and enhances the cognitive performance of care home residents. *British Journal of Psychology*, 105: 17–34.

Heerwagen, J.H. (1998) Productivity and well-being: what are the links? American Institute of Architects Conference on Highly Effective Facilities, Cincinnati, OH.

Hidalgo, C.A. (2008) Thinking outside the cube. *Physics World*, 21(12): 34–37.

Himanen, M. (2004) The intelligence of intelligent buildings. In Clements-Croome, D.J, *Intelligent Buildings: Design, Management and Operation*. London: Thomas Telford.

Hirigoyen, J. and Newell, G. (2009) Developing a socially responsible property investment index for UK property companies. *Journal of Property Investment & Finance*, 27(5): 511–521.

Hughes, W., Ancell, D., Gruneberg, S. and Hirst, L. (2004) Exposing the myth of the 1:5:200 ratio relating initial cost, maintenance and staffing costs of office buildings. In Khosrowshahi, F. (ed.) *Proceedings of 20th Annual ARCOM Conference*, 1–3 September 2004, Heriot Watt University, Association of Researchers in Construction Management, vol. 1, 373–381.

Isen, A.M. (1990) The influence of positive and negative effect on cognitive organisation: some implications for development. In Stein, N., Leventhal, B. and Trabasso, B. (eds) *Psychological and Biological Approaches to Emotion*. Hillsdale, NJ: Lawrence Erlbaum.

ISO. BS EN ISO 28802 (2012) *Ergonomics of the Physical Environment*. London: BSI Publications.

Ivanov, P. (1996) Scaling behaviour of heartbeat intervals obtained by wavelet-based time-series analysis. *Nature*, 383(6598): 323–327.

John, G. and Clements-Croome, D.J. (2005) Innovative approach to building systems integration problems: using systems theory, technological forecasting and scenario planning. In *Proceedings of the Third Innovation in Architecture, Engineering and Construction Conference (AEC 2005)*, Amsterdam, Netherlands, 14–18 June, pp 385–394.

John, G., Clements-Croome, D.J., Lo, H. and Fairey, V. (2005) Contextual prerequisites for the application of ILS principles to the building services industry. *Journal of Engineering, Construction and Architectural Management*, 12(4): 307–328.

Johnson, E. (2007). Building IQ: intelligent buildings are becoming part of global real estate market. *Journal of Property Management*, May. Available at: www.highbeam.com/doc/1G1-164222376.html (accessed 8 Feb. 2009).

Jones, P. (2006) *Ove Arup: Master Builder of the Twentieth Century*. New Haven, CT: Yale University Press.

Jowitt, P. (2010) Presidential address at Institution of Civil Engineers, London 3 November 2009. *Civil Engineering*, 163, CE1, 3–8.

Kaku, M. (2011) *Physics of the Future*. London: Allen Lane.

Keeling, T., Clements-Croome, D., Luck, R. and Pointer, P. (2012) How the sensory experience of buildings can contribute to wellbeing and productivity. In Nicol, F. (ed.) *The Changing Context of Comfort in an Unpredictable World*. Windsor, UK: NCEUB.

Keeling, T., Clements-Croome, D., Luck, R. and Pointer, P. (2013) Wireless sensor networks for monitoring people and their close environment. In Clements-Croome, D.J. (ed.). *Intelligent Buildings*. London: Thomas Telford.

Kelly, N. (2008). Smart buildings help NG Bailey to cut carbon. *Business Green*. June. Available at: www.computing.co.uk/computing/news/2219427/smart-buildings-help-ng-bailey (accessed 8 Feb. 2009).

Kok, N., Miller, G.N. and Morris P. (2012) The economics of green retrofits. *JOSRE*, 4(1): 2–22.

Kurzweil. R. (2005) *The Singularity is Near*. New York: Viking Press.

Kwon, S-H., Chun, C. nd Kwak, R-Y. (2001) Relationship between quality of building maintenance management services for indoor environmental quality and occupant satisfaction. *Building and Environment*, 46: 2179–2185.

Latham Report (1994) *Constructing the Team*. London: HMSO.

Le Doux, J. (1996) *The Emotional Brain*. New York: Simon & Schuster.

Lee, S Y. (2006) Expectations of employees towards the workplace and environmental satisfaction. *Facilities*, 24(9/10): 343–353.

Lehmann, M.L. (2011) How sensory design brings value to buildings and their occupants. *Intelligent Buildings International*, 3: 46–54.

Lehman, M.L. (2016) *Adaptive Sensory Design*. London: Routledge.

Lehrer, J. (2012) *Imagine: How Creativity Works*. Edinburgh: Canongate.

Libeskind, D. (2002) The walls are alive. *The Guardian*, 13 July.

Liu, K., Lin, C. and Qiao, B. (2008) A multi-agent system for intelligent pervasive spaces. In Proceedings of IEEE International Conference on Service Operations and Logistics, and Informatics (SOLI), pp. 1005–1010.

Liu, K., Nakata, K. and Harty, C. (2009) Pervasive informatics: theory, practice and future directions. *Journal of Intelligent Buildings International*.

Loftness, V. and Haases, D. (eds) (2013) *Sustainable Built Environments*. Berlin: Springer.

Lu, X., Clements-Croome, D.J. and Viljanen. M. (2010) Integration of chaos theory and mathematical models in building simulation. *Automation in Construction*, 19(4): 447–457.

Lüzkendorf, T. and Lorenz, D. (2011) Capturing sustainability related information for property valuation. *Building Research and Information*, 39(3): 256–273.

Macmillan, S. (2006) Added value of good design. *Building Research and Information*, 34(3): 257–271.

Mahdavi, A. (2006) The technology of sentient buildings, *ITU A|Z*, 3(1/2): 24–36.

Mawson, A. (2002) *The Workplace and Its Impact on Productivity*. London: Advanced Workplace Associates Ltd.

McCarter, R. (2010) *Frank Lloyd Wright*, 6th edn. London: Phaidon.

McDougall, G., Kelly, J., Hinks, J. and Bititci, U. (2002) A review of the leading performance measurement tools for assessing buildings. *Journal of Facilities Management*, 1(2): 142–153.

McMeeken, R. (2014) Building 2050: the cities of the future, *CIBSE Journal*, January, Careers Special Supplement, 22–24.

Mendell, M.J., *et al.* (2013) Association of classroom ventilation with reduced illness absence: a prospective study in California elementary schools, *Indoor Air*, 23: 515–528.

Mendell, M., Fisk, W.J., Kreiss, K., Levin, H., *et al.* (2002) Improving the health of workers in indoor environments: priority research needs for a national occupational research agenda. *American Journal of Public Health*, 92(9): 1430–1440.

Meyer, H. (1999) Fun for everyone, *Journal of Business Strategy*, 20(2): 13–17.

Meyers-Levy, J. and Zhu, R. (2007) The influence of ceiling height, *Journal of Consumer Research*, 34, August, 174–186.

Miller, N.G., *et al.* (2009) Green buildings and productivity. *Journal of Sustainable Real Estate*, 1(1): 65–91.

Nadel, S. (2012) The rebound effect; large or small? An American Council for an Energy Efficient Economy (ACEEE) White Paper. Available at: www.aceee.org

Newell. G. (2009) Developing a socially responsible property investment index for UK property companies. *Journal of Property Investment & Finance*, 27(5): 511–521.

Newsham, G.R., *et al.* (2013) Do green buildings have better indoor environments? New evidence. *Building Research and Information*, 41(4): 415–432.

Nicol, J.F. and Humphreys, M.A. (1973) Thermal comfort as part of a self-regulating system. *Building Research and Practice*, 1: 174–179.

Niemala, R., *et al.* (2001) Assessing the effect of the indoor environment on productivity. Paper presented at the 7th REHVA World Congress, Clima 2000, Naples, 15–18 September.

Niemala, R., *et al.* (2002) The effect of air temperature on labour productivity in call centres. *Energy and Buildings*, 34: 759–764.

Noy, P., Liu, K., Clements-Croome, D.J. and Qiao B. (2007) Design issues in personalising intelligent buildings, in Proceedings of 2nd International Conference on Intelligent Environments, Athens, July 5–6, IET.

Oliver, P. (2008) *The Encyclopaedia of Vernacular Architecture of the World*. 3 vols. Cambridge: Cambridge University Press.

Owen, R. (2009) CIB White Paper on IDDS Integrated Design and Delivery Solutions CIB Publication 328.

Pacheco-Torgal, F., *et al.* (2013) *Nanotechnology in Eco-efficient Construction*. Cambridge: Woodhead Publishing.

Pacheco-Torgal, F. and Labrincha, J.A. (2013) The future of construction materials research and the seventh UN millennium development goal: a few insights. *Construction and Building Materials*, 40: 729–737.

Pelenur, M.L. and Cruickshank, H J. (2013) Investigating the link between well-being and energy use: an explorative case study between passive and active energy management systems. *Building and Environment*, 65: 26–34.

Pelletier, M. and Bose, A. (2010) Article by Ben Coxworth, Student creates cost-effective self healing concrete? Available at: gizmag.com@mcsv81.net

Persily, A. (2010) Using ASHRAE's new IAQ guide. *ASHRAE Journal*, 52(5): 75–82.

Preller, L., Zweers, T., Brunekreef, B. and Boleiji, J.S.M. (1990) Indoor Air Quality '90, Fifth International Conference on Indoor Air Quality and Climate, 1: 227–230.

Qiao, B., Liu, K. and Guy C. (2006) A multi-agent system for building control. In *Proceedings of IEEE/WIC/ACM International Conference on IAT*, December 2006, Hong Kong.

Qiao, B., Liu K. and Guy C. (2007) Multi-agent building control in shared environment. In *Proceedings of the 9th International Conference on Enterprise Information* Systems, 12–16, June 2007, Madeira, Portugal.

Ratcliff, R. (2008) Intelligent building technology can deliver up to 40% energy savings. *Intelligent Building Design*. April, Web. 8 Feb. 2009. Available at: www.energy-online.net/stories/articles//energy_management/building_controls/intelligent_building_desig/

Reed R., *et al.* (2009) International comparison of sustainable rating tools. *JOSRE*, 1(1): 1–22.

Rehm, M. and Ade, R. (2013) Construction costs comparison between green and conventional office buildings. *Building Research and Information*, 41(2): 198–208.

Roelofsen, P. (2001) The design of the workplace as a strategy for productivity enhancement. Paper presented at the7th REHVA World Congress, Clima 2000, Naples, Italy.

Scherer, K.R. (1999) Appraisal theory. In Dalgleish, T. and Power, M.J. (eds) *Handbook of Cognition and Emotion*. Chichester: Wiley.

Shapiro, S. (2009) Valuing green: BRE makes the financial case for building green. Available at: www.greenbuildinglawblog.com/2009/09/articles/valuing-greencbre-makes-the-financial-case-for-building-green/# (accessed 8 October 2009).

Shove, E. (1999) Converging conventions of comfort, cleanliness and convenience. *Journal of Consumer Policy*, 26: 395–418.

Sivunen, M., Kosonen, R. and Kajander, J. (2014) Good indoor environment and energy efficiency increase monetary value of buildings. *REHVA Journal*, 51(4): 6–9.

Sorrell, J. (2005) Royal Society seminar on the promotion of health. Annual Lecture, Scarborough, UK, 7 June.

Spataru, C. and Gauthier S. (2014) How to monitor people 'smartly' to help reducing energy consumption in buildings. *Architectural Engineering and Design Management*, 10(1–2): 60–78.

Stokols, D. (1992) Establishing and maintaining healthy environments: toward a social ecology of health promotion. *American Psychologist*, 47(1): 6–22.

Strelitz, Z. (2006) Briefing for good design. Speech at the Launch of the CIBSE Intelligent Buildings Group at the Royal Society, on 19 October.

Strelitz, Z. (2008) *Buildings that Feel Good*. London: RIBA Publishing.

Sundell, J., *et al.* (2011) Ventilation rates and health: multidisciplinary review of the scientific literature. *Indoor Air*, 21: 191–204.

Swan, M. (2012) Sensor mania! The Internet of Things, wearable computing, objective metrics and the quantified self 2.0. *Journal of Sensor and Actuator Networks*, 1(3): 217–225.

Thomas, K. (2009) *Strategic Overview: Managing Environmentally Sustainable ICT in Further and Higher Education*. Bristol: JISC.

Thompson, B. and Jonas, D. (2008) Workplace design and productivity: are they inextricably interlinked? Property in the Economy Report, *RICS*, 4–41.

Tizard, G. and Mocford, J. (2008) *New Build: Delivering IT*. Available at: http://info.rsc-eastern.ac.uk/files/events/_883_DoncasterCollegeTizardMockford.ppt (accessed 18 March 2009).

Towers Watson (2014) *The Business Value of a Healthy Workforce*, Staying@Work Survey Report, Towers Watson and National Business Group on Health, TW-NA-2012–29407 (United States).

UKGBC (2016) *Health, Wellbeing & Productivity in Retail: The Impact of Green Buildings on People and Profit*. Available at: www.betterplacesforpeople.org

US Green Building Council (2003) *Making the Business Case for High Performance Green Buildings*. Washington, DC: US Green Building Council. Available at: www.usgbc.org/Docs/Member_Resource_Docs/makingthebusinesscase.pdf (accessed 26 March 2013).

van der Voordt, D.J.M. (2003) *Costs and Benefits of Innovative Workplace Design*. Center for People and Buildings, Delft & Centrum Facility Management, Naarden.

Vischer, J.C. (2008) Towards an environmental psychology of workspace: how people are affected by environments for work. *Architecture Science Review*, 51(2): 97–108.

Vorster, D.J.M. (1971) *Human Biology of Environmental Change*. London: International Biological Programme.

Wargocki, P. (2007) Improving indoor air quality improves the performance of office work and schoolwork. Technical University of Denmark, Kgs. Lyngby, Denmark Available at: www.inive.org/members_area/medias/pdf/Inive%5CIAQVEC2007%5CWargocki_2.pdf (accessed 10 Aug. 2009).

Wargocki, P. and Wyon, P. (2007) The effect of moderately raised classroom temperatures and classroom ventilation rate on the performance of schoolwork by children. *HVAC&R Research*, 13(2): 193–220.

Wheeler, G. and Almeida, A. (2006) These four walls: the real British office. In Clements-Croome, D.J. (ed.) *Creating the Productive Workplace*. London: Routledge, pp. 357–377.

Williams, J. (2007) The challenge in further education and skills: e-mentors lead the way. *Becta 2007 Annual Review*, pp. 20–21. Available at: http://publications.becta.org.uk/download.cfm?resID=33625 (accessed 23 December 2008).

Williams, L.E. and Bargh, J.A. (2008) Experiencing physical warmth promotes interpersonal warmth. *Science*, 322: 606–607.

Woods, J. (1989) Cost avoidance and productivity in owning and operating buildings. In Cone, J. and Hodgson, M. (eds) *Occupational Medicine: State of the Art Reviews*, 4(4).

Wu, S. and Clements-Croome, D.J. (2005) Critical reliability issues for building services systems. In *Proceedings of the Fourth International Conference on Quality and Reliability*, Beijing, pp. 559–566.

Wyon, D. (1996) Indoor environmental effects on productivity, keynote address in Indoor Air 1996, Paths to Better Building Environments, Atlanta, GA: ASHRAE, 5–15.

Yang, F. and Bouchlaghem, D. (2010) Genetic algorithm-based multi-objective optimisation for building design. *Architectural Engineering and Design Management*, 6(1): 69–82.

Zeiler, W., *et al.* (2014) Occupants' behavioural impact on energy consumption: 'human-in-the-loop' comfort process control. *Architectural Engineering and Design Management*, 10(1–2): 108–130.

Chapter 2

The business case for sustainable healthy buildings

Health, productivity and economic consequences

Derek Clements-Croome

Employers are recognising that good health is a total business issue, and a lack of it affects work performance.

(Towers Watson, 2014)

For an organisation to be successful and to meet the necessary targets, the performance expressed by the productivity of its employees is of vital importance. Today technology allows people to work while they are travelling or at home or other places, and this goes some way to improving productivity because people feel freer to work best suited to their needs in time or space. There are still, however, many people who have a regular workplace that demarcates space for quiet work alone but which is linked to other collaborative workspaces, as well as social and public spaces. People produce less when they are tired, have personal worries, or are suffering stress due to dissatisfaction with the job or the organisation. The physical environment sets the landscape and this can enhance an individual's work by putting people in a better mood, whereas an unsatisfactory environment can hinder work output.

Mental concentration is vital for good work performance. Absolute alertness and attention are essential if one is to concentrate. There is some personal discipline involved in attaining and maintaining concentration, but again the environment can be conducive to this by affecting one's mood or frame of mind; however, it can also be distracting and can contribute to a loss of concentration. Many surveys of offices (BCO, 2014) show occupants requesting more break-out spaces where they can think, reflect, meditate or contemplate. This reflects the need to shut off from the ever increasing speed and volume of information flow bombarding us every day. Greenfield (2014) shows how digital technology is affecting our brains and everyday lives in terms of thinking patterns and lifestyles. Various studies at Ball State University Centre for Media Design, for example, show that the amount of screen time people spend on mobiles, computers, tablets and television can be as much as 8 hours per day. How we use our brain each day can lubricate our well-being, so a balance of screen time, enjoying a stroll in the fresh air, enjoying music or a myriad of other non-screen activities is generally healthier. This means that the break-out spaces for office workers are particularly important to allow them to use the many parts of the brain, not just a few.

A number of personal factors, which depend on the physical and mental health of an individual, and a number of external factors, which depend on the physical and social environment besides the work-related systems of management, influence the level of productivity. Essentially good health and well-being are the drivers to improving not only productivity but also creativity.

Fisk (1999) has looked at the associations between the transmission of infectious disease, respiratory illnesses, allergies and asthma, sick building syndrome (SBS) symptoms, thermal environment, lighting and odours. He concluded that, in the USA, the total annual cost of respiratory infections was then about $70 billion and that of allergies and asthma was $15 billion. He showed that a 20–50 per cent reduction in SBS symptoms corresponded to an annual productivity increase of $15–38 billion and, for office workers, there is a potential annual productivity gain of $20–200 billion. Fisk (2000a; 2000b) reported that, in the USA, respiratory illnesses alone caused the loss of about 176 million workdays and the equivalent of 121 million days of substantially restricted activity.

Losses in productivity are due not only to absenteeism but occur also by people present at work but not feeling at their best because of environmental factors and this is called presenteeism (Johns, 2010). Prochaska *et al.* (2011) state that the sickness presenteeism costs in the USA are over $150 billion per year and account for 71 per cent of the total cost of lost productivity. There is now a growing number of wellness programmes as companies become more aware of these absenteeism and presenteeism costs. Goetzel *et al.* (2016) conclude that socially responsible companies that invest in health and well-being have greater business success than those that do not.

The UK has a similar problem (Black, 2008) and work absenteeism plus presenteeism waste the nation about £100 billion per year (ONS, 2012; DWP, 2014). *The Times* reported in 'Raconteur on talent management' on 31 January 2017 that in the UK across the public and private sectors, the days off per year average between 4 and 11. Any measures that decrease sick building syndrome, musculoskeletal problems or mental stress save companies and the National Health Service costs. In 2013, there were 131 million working days lost through sickness absence (ONS, 2013; CBI UK Report, 2014) due to the following illnesses (Table 2.1).

These illnesses are due to several causes but the environment is a significant one. Lighting, whether a lack of daylight or poor artificial lighting, can be depressing and also lead to headaches. A lack of fresh air can affect respiratory, nose and throat conditions. Poor furniture design can cause backaches. Further data from the Chartered Institute of Personnel and Development (CIPD) (2016) (shown in *The Times*, 2017) showed that reasons to call in sick included flu, sick bugs, migraine, stress, head colds, all of which are sensitive to the environment, especially factors like fresh air, temperature and lighting.

Comparing the data across countries for different years is difficult but one can conclude that the data does show at least that in the USA and the UK, with working populations of 200 and

Table 2.1 Million of days lost per year due to illness or disorders in the UK in 2013

Illness or disorder	Million days per year lost
Musculoskeletal disorders (neck and back problems)	30.6
Minor illnesses	27.4
Other	21.7
Mental stress	15.2
Stomach problems	8.7
Respiratory conditions	5.3
Eye, ear, nose, throat	5.2
Heart, circulation	5.0
Urinary problems	3.2
Headaches and migraines	1.7
Serious mental health	1.0

30 million people respectively, that a lack of health and well-being are significant problems which impact the productivity of a nation.

The World Green Council Report (WGBC, 2014) states:

> Costs of ill-health vary by sector and country, and are rarely comparable, but the impact is clear:
>
> - The annual absenteeism rate in the US is 3 per cent per employee in the private sector, and 4 per cent in the public sector, costing employers $2,074 and $2,502 per employee per year respectively.
> - The cost of sickness to the employer is estimated at an average £595/employee/year in the UK, while poor mental health specifically costs UK employers £30 billion a year through lost production, recruitment and absence.
> - The aggregate cost to business of ill-health and absenteeism in Australia is estimated at $7 billion per year, while the cost of 'presenteeism' is estimated to be $26 billion·

Fisk (1999) and Clements-Croome (2000a; 2000b) state that, in office buildings, the salaries of workers exceed the building energy and maintenance costs and the annual construction rental costs by a factor of at least 25. Evans et al. (1998) concluded that business costs including salaries exceeded operating costs by 40:1 and capital costs by 200:1. This means that small increases in productivity of 1 per cent or less are sufficient to justify additional capital expenditure to improve the design and construction quality of the building and its services. Ultimately, this will result in a healthier working environment, as well as reduced energy and maintenance costs. Whatever the ratios, it is the salary costs which predominate.

The importance of air quality has been referred to in Chapter 1. Fisk (1999) argues how poor air quality can affect the transmission of infectious disease and the incidence of respiratory illness, allergies and asthma, increase the likelihood of sick building syndrome (SBS) and decrease worker performance. Air quality plays a major role in managing these issues. Air quality is a major issue because it only takes a few seconds for air to be inhaled and its effect to be transmitted to the bloodstream and hence the brain. Clean, fresh air is vital for clear thinking, but it is not the only issue to be considered.

The direct effects of poorly performing environments can be summarised as follows:

- lost work hours due to sickness;
- inability to reach true operational potential;
- reduction in gross domestic product;
- reduced company profits;
- a demoralised workforce;
- increased operational and maintenance costs;
- increased staff turnover.

The issue, therefore, becomes one of health risk and the economic consequences directly at an organisational level and indirectly at a national level. If company performance is a factor associated with the individual, then the building design should concentrate on user-centred design principles for healthy workplaces.

Higher ventilation rates up to about 25 l/s per person tend to lead to reductions in sick building syndrome symptoms, absenteeism due to illness and respiratory ailments (Sundell et al., 2011). Mendell et al. (2013) conclude a 1 l/s per person increase in fresh air ventilation rate over the range 2–20 l/s per person is associated with a 1.0–1.5 per cent decrease in illness absenteeism.

In later work Fisk *et al.* (2012) provided quantitative estimates of benefits and costs of providing different amounts of outdoor air ventilation in US offices and their effect on sick building syndrome (SBS) symptoms, work performance, short-term absence, and building energy consumption. Some of the annual economic benefits were $13 billion by increasing minimum ventilation rates from 8 to 10 l/s per person; $38 billion by increasing them from 8 to 15 l/s per person. The benefits of increasing minimum ventilation rates far exceeded any increased energy costs because the benefits yielded improved health and performance while decreasing absenteeism. This means that perceptions that assume that higher fresh air supply rates are expensive are incorrect, because they fail to take into account the consequences of higher fresh rates and the value they bring of healthier conditions and the consequent effect of them increasing productivity.

Roelofsen (2001) has described a study of 61 offices (7000 respondents) in the Netherlands which showed that people were off work for an average of 2.5 days/year because of unsatisfactory indoor environmental conditions. This represented a quarter of the total average absenteeism. Other work by Preller *et al.* (1990) and Bergs (2002) reveals a close correlation between sick leave and building-related health complaints.

Eley Associates (2001) found that healthy buildings lead to better work performance, and this is supported by other work such as that by Bell *et al.* (2003) Clements-Croome (2006; 2013; 2014) Fanger (2002) and Mendell *et al.* (2002).

The rapid developments in technology can aid productivity in some ways, but they have also brought some negative issues. These are described by van der Voordt (2003) and include getting used to technology, ICT reliability problems and time loss associated with logging onto computer systems and searching for information, besides the need for frequent updating.

Measurement of productivity

Reliable methodologies are evolving that will produce the evidence we need to convince clients to invest in better buildings, which will help to improve staff performance and increase value for money – bearing in mind that about 90 per cent of the costs of running a typical commercial office building is the staff salaries. A lack of productivity shows up in many ways, such as absenteeism, presenteeism, arriving late and leaving early, over-long lunch breaks, careless mistakes, overwork, boredom, and frustration with the management and the physical and social environments.

The Behaviour Model (Fogg, 2009) for persuasive design defines human behaviour in terms of motivation, ability and the trigger or prompt to undertake a certain action:

Behaviour or Performance = Motivation x Ability x Trigger (MAT)

When motivation and ability act together, then at a certain point this prompts or triggers an opportunity for a particular behavioural response (ibid.). Motivation arises from the job interest; the organisation's ethos and culture; the support systems; and the social climate, but the built environment also has a role to play and this has often been not realised or has been ignored. Productivity depends on performance so assessing motivation and opportunities for a sample of subjects with similar abilities and doing the same kind of work would be one way to enable a comparison of performance levels between different environments.

It is often said that productivity cannot be measured and it is not easy to do so, but the following four approaches have had some success. In their work on the effect of environment on productivity, Clements-Croome and Li (2000) have proposed a holistic model that considers the impact of the social ambience, the organisation, the well-being of the individual and the physical environmental factors, and have derived relationships between productivity and job satisfaction, stress, physical environment, SBS and other factors. The data collected from office surveys using nine-point scale questionnaires was analysed using the Analytical Hierarchical Process (AHP).This multifunctional approach resulted in a diagnostic tool that can be used to assess weak and strong factors in any given internal environment.

Another practical approach is given by Wargocki *et al.* (2006) who have proposed a method for integrating productivity into the life-cycle cost analysis of building services (see Chapter 14 in this volume).

Juniper *et al.* (2009; 2010; 2011; 2016a; 2016b) have described another practical route to evaluating well-being and productivity.

Satish *et al.* (2011; 2012) have used a strategic management simulations (SMS) methodology approach to measure the impact of environmental factors on performance. The research by Satish shows that poor air quality can undermine decision-making, hence company productivity (see Chapter 8 in this volume).

Agha-Hossein *et al.* (2013) compared occupants' reactions to the environment in two buildings and used post-occupancy evaluation (POE) techniques to assess employees' perceived productivity, well-being and enjoyment at work. She refers to the work of Meyer (1999), Vischer (2008) and others that show how an enjoyable workplace with a stimulating physical environment can improve occupants' morale, satisfaction, perceived well-being and productivity.

Mention has been made of the survey work by Leaman and Bordass (2006). They have carried out POE over many years referred to as BUS (Building User Studies) and conclude that when occupants are satisfied with their overall comfort, then productivity tends to increase (see ibid., p. 161). The term 'overall comfort' used here seems to be a mixture of factors, including personal health and mood besides functional, convenience and environmental factors.

Lee (2006) concludes from his research on the perception (what one actually feels or senses) and expectation (what one hopes to feel) levels of employees that when the resulting physical environment is below their expectations, the occupants feel dissatisfied but if it exceeds expectation levels, it does not seem to increase satisfaction. Distractions are viewed negatively and privacy positively (Ferguson and Weisman, 1986). Lee found that the control of temperature and ventilation showed the biggest difference between perception and expectation but, most importantly, satisfaction with the physical environment is positively related to job satisfaction.

The WGBC (2014) report in respect of offices suggests how to measure the following features:

- *economic metrics* – covering absenteeism, staff turnover and retention, medical costs, medical and physical complaints, revenue breakdown;
- *perceptual* – feelings assessed by self-reported attitudes via questionnaires, interviews;
- *physical design and operation* – by direct environmental measurements and also measuring people's physiological responses using various forms of wearable sensor technology.

The WGBC (2016) report describes a Retail Metrics Framework which is based on the following features:

- *environment* – lighting, air quality, thermal factors, sound, layout look and feel, inclusive design, biophilia, amenities and community space;
- *experience* of employers and customers as they perceive them;
- *economics* – the costs to the employers such as absenteeism as in WGBC (2014) and value issues like the sales, dwell time, return customers.

Such frameworks let clients and designers check the real issues using authoritative sources and encourage an integrated visionary approach. They also encourage the users to be involved and they collect data using various evolving technologies and environmental mapping approaches, which will help to improve and understand how design needs to move forward to harness a healthy well-being culture in architecture.

Gensler (2013) in a US survey found that:

- US workers struggle to work effectively.
- There is a need to balance focus and collaborative working to afford higher job satisfaction and performance.
- Personal choice drives performance and innovation and improves the workplace experience.
- Thinking holistically about the need for focus, collaboration, learning and social ambience leads to a variety of spaces offering anywhere working policy.
- The drivers of focus are functionality, satisfactory noise levels and design look and feel.
- The drivers of balance are meeting space, circulation and support space, and in-office amenities.
- The drivers of choice are a variety of spaces, tools, policy to let employees match their space to their needs.
- Less space per person is a false economy as work effectiveness decreases.
- Offices provide a 'home' for 'work families'.
- Buildings can give employees a sense of pride.

Gensler use their Workplace Performance Index SM (WPI) derived from a web-based measurement and analysis pre- and post-occupancy evaluation tool for work environments, to help clients understand specifically what comprises space effectiveness so that design solutions can be tailored accordingly. The UK workplace survey for 2016 by Gensler gives WPI scores in various work settings (www.gensler.com/research).

Peer-reviewed research and case studies used in the World Green Building Council (WGBC, 2013) report, *The Business Case for Green Building*, show that:

- Green buildings do not necessarily cost more and they do appeal to tenants because they command higher rents and sale prices. Rehm and Ade (2013) also recognised that integrated team working saves time and costs, which enable green sustainable buildings to be designed and built with no or little extra cost.
- Operating costs are lower because of reduced energy and water use plus reduced maintenance.
- Better environments affect employees and lead to higher staff retention rates.
- Workplace illnesses and hence absenteeism are reduced, while well-being is higher than in conventionally designed offices where high quality environments have not always been a priority.

The McGraw-Hill Construction (2014) report, *The Drive to Toward Healthier Buildings*, states metric and benefits for healthier buildings in ranked order as judged by owners and managing directors of companies as:

- self-assessed productivity;
- lower absenteeism;
- reduced healthcare costs;
- improved employee satisfaction;
- improved employee engagement;
- improved ability to attract new talent.

Self-assessed productivity and satisfaction can be measured using subjective scales like the BUS surveys by Leaman and Bordass (1999; 2006) but the other four factors can show quantitative data. The Leesman Index is another satisfaction survey approach (info@leesmanindex.com). In time, we will advance the metrics and measures, for example, by the increased use of wearables (embedded wireless sensors in clothing or accessories) and more comprehensive feedback will lead to enhanced POE (Spataru and Gauthier, 2014).

Sivunen *et al.* (2014) state that building owners and tenants can financially benefit from sustainability and improved indoor environmental quality via:

- reduced life-cycle costs;
- extended building and equipment life span;
- longer tenant occupancy and lease renewals;
- reduced churn costs;
- reduced insurance costs;
- reduced liability risks;
- added brand value.

The work of Lorenz and Lützkendorf (2011) as well as the previous work referred to above, confirms these conclusions.

McGraw-Hill Construction (2014) states that there is a lot of valid research that supports the hypothesis that the built environment affects human health, and some of this has been referred to already. The environment can ease or increase stress. Physiological or psychological stress can supress the immune system, making people more susceptible to infections.

Too often buildings are seen as costly static containers rather than as investments, which, if they are healthy and sustainable, can add value. Boyden (1971) distinguished between needs for *survival* and those for *well-being*. Human beings have physiological, psychological and social needs. Heerwagen (1998) pinpointed the well-being needs relevant to building design as:

- social milieu;
- freedom for solitary or group working;
- opportunities to develop self-expression;
- an interesting visual scene;
- acceptable acoustic conditions;
- contrast and random changes for the senses to react to;
- opportunities to exercise or switch over from work to other stimulating activities;
- clean fresh air.

Stokols (1992) states that physical, emotional and social conditions together are a requisite for good health.

In practice, investors, developers and clients often agree that sustainable healthy buildings are desirable but they want quantified economic evidence to persuade them to finance such projects. Social awareness is changing about the need for sustainable green buildings. The US Green Building Council published a report in 2003 entitled *Making the Business Case for High Performance Green Buildings* and some of its conclusions included:

- higher capital costs are recoverable in a comparatively short time;
- integrated design lowers operating costs;
- better buildings equate to better employee productivity;

- new appropriate technologies may enhance health and well-being;
- healthier buildings can reduce liability;
- tenants' costs can be significantly reduced;
- property value will increase;
- communities will notice your efforts;
- using best practices yields more predictable results, but remember that occupancy behaviour affects the performance;
- respect the landscape and open space near the building.

Macmillan (2006) discusses the types of value created in the built environment which contribute to the assets of the building owners; the corporate identity; the occupants; the community; the ecology; the culture of the place where buildings are and the history of our civilisation.

Interactive architecture and the environment

Digital and built environments combine to offer personal interaction in the workplace setting. As embedded sensory technology develops and its benefits are realised, personalisation is set to remain and the connectivity of building occupants with their surroundings will intensify. Wearable sensors are likely to be part of a personalisation family together with various Apps and forms of augmented reality (Lehman, 2016). Sensors can be embedded into clothing or accessories, attached in the form of a thin film to the skin. Sensors can be embedded in the body even but more practically in surrounding objects and structures.

For example, Chuck Hoberman at the Harvard Graduate School of Design (*Financial Times*, 2016) is carrying out research on putting various actuators in structures and this dynamic architecture means that façades will become communication channels as well as climatic moderators. James Law in Hong Kong has coined the term cybertecture and features this in the Cybertecture Egg in Mumbai, in which interactive features monitor the health and wellness of occupants who can also customise their views with real-time virtual scenery. Davis *et al.* (2013) have developed the Textile Mirror, which has its textural structure altered by emotional signals from the viewer.

Wearable devices referred to in Chapter 1 are being developed beyond health monitoring into everyday practicalities, such as paying bills. Fitbits can monitor steps and stairs walked as well as having calorie inputs and outputs which can be refined with a sugar App, for example. These applications can encourage attention to improving fitness and nourishment regimes (BCO, 2016). Physiological measures include heart rate, blood pressure, cortisol and glucose levels, brain waves, respiratory rates and muscle tension.

Indications are that there will be sales of 237 m wearables and 38 m virtual reality devices by 2020. The market is slowly but steadily increasing and this will affect the way we become more aware of our personal health, fitness and our surroundings. Office clients and occupants can pre-glimpse and even participate in the office being designed, either new or refurbished.

Advantages of wearables

- Increased awareness of health and fitness.
- Learning how one's body and mind respond in various conditions.
- On-line data connects with doctor so save appointment times.
- Early diagnosis to help prevention better than cure.
- Devices can be integrated into clothing as well as wristbands and other accessories.
- Weak spots in the office environment can be detected.

Disadvantages of wearables

- Privacy, see data sharing section.
- More data and information available so we need Big Data analytic solutions.
- Market is open to gimmicks.
- Like computers and smart phones, devices need regular updating.

Data sharing

When it comes to data sharing there are choices:

- No data sharing.
- Selective data sharing, for example, share one's health data with your doctor.
- Open data sharing, for example, wearable air quality monitors provide valuable data helping to establishing improved air quality, and everyone gains, making this a case of sharing for the common good.

The human body network

Everything in the human body is connected. Network physiology research shows that heart rate fluctuations are random for people who are less healthy but the distribution of fluctuations could be described by a single function for healthy people. Ivanov (1996) concludes that there seems to be an underlying temporal structure to the heart beat fluctuations which can be defined by power laws for the different body systems. Measurements have shown co-ordinated activity between diverse organ systems, so, for example, signal bursts occurred at the similar times for brain EEG, heart rate, respiratory rate and eye movements except when in deep sleep. The strongest coupling was in the fully awake state (Cartwright, 2016). In the future we could see these measurements – some are already on sensor devices – on wearables, which, when synchronised with analytic software, could indicate various levels of health.

Note, perceptions are not always the reality, hence, it is vital we have co-ordinated data collection systems using modern developments, such as wireless sensor networks connecting people to their environment and building, to obtain measured data in real time. Perceptions can be coloured by emotions, and reactions to a multitude of stimuli can be dominated by one perceived negative or positive factor which skews the judgement.

Well-being and productive environments

> People crave social areas that get them bumping into each other and sparking innovation Spaces that are more organic and fluid will always yield better creativity, productivity and at the end of the day, efficiency. Try to move from Mondrian to Miro.
>
> (Parker, 2014)

Warr (2002) has described ten features of jobs that have been found to be associated with well-being. He believes that stable personality characteristics and age and gender are also significant. Environmental determinants of well-being are described by Warr as: the opportunity for personal control; the opportunity to use one's skills; externally generated goals; variety in the job and location; the cultural context and prospects; availability of money; physical security which includes the physical environment; supportive supervision; the opportunity for interpersonal contact; and job status in society. Warr reviews work which indicates that greater well-being is significantly associated with better job performance, lower absenteeism and a lower probability of the employee leaving the organisation. Both the organisation and personal factors play a role.

The work of Fogg (2009) underlies the worker performance model highlighted by Heerwagen (1998) and referred to earlier in the context of occupants' behaviour with regard to energy consumption. Here it is the basis for understanding how the productivity of people in the workplace is influenced by various factors.

Performance = Motivation x Ability x Opportunity

The person has to have the ability to undertake the work; the organisation has to provide the opportunity which includes providing support systems and amenities, such as interesting break-out contemplation spaces. Motivation arises from several sources. The individual must enjoy and want to do the job but the environment can enhance this by providing a stimulating backdrop with variety for them to do their work. The design of the built environment has an influence on motivation and opportunity by providing not only the functional elements but also the 'sparkle' which makes the environment enjoyable to work in (see Chapter 1, the section 'Beyond environmental comfort').

The built environment provides a physical and social ambience that affects motivation; the provision of individual control and a healthy environment can enable ability to flourish; communications systems, restaurants, break-out spaces and other amenities aid workers' motivation even further, by providing opportunities for task implementation. Earlier we referred to BCO (2014); in their report they noted that more office occupants were asking for contemplation spaces now and these require planning, remembering that 'power napping' is more common besides other mindfulness approaches to refresh and aid creativity. Today there is also a debate about the downsides of long sedentary work periods and the need to stand or move around, which helps to avoid musculoskeletal problems developing.

Mindfulness training is about developing a constant sense of awareness and an ability to remain in the present moment, often referred to as ability to focus or concentrate (Dolan, 2014). The difficulty is, in practice, there are a myriad of distractions which disrupt concentration. Dolan (2014) writes that distraction saps attentional energy because energy is wasted switching between different things that attract our attention, and he goes on to say that multitasking can make us feel as if we are more productive but actually the opposite is true because concentration requires a focus on one thing at a time.

Buildings moderate climates, which helps to keep the body healthy and enhance well-being. Some buildings demand closely controlled environments, and various systems can be installed in order to achieve this, but many buildings can take advantage of the body's ability to adapt and interact in a compensatory way with other senses. Mention has been made of wireless sensor networks that link a building directly with the occupant by means of sensors embedded in the building structure and in the clothing people wear, that enable occupants to monitor their personal reactions and responses to the environment.

If we are to understand how we can construct more productive environments, we have to understand more about the nature of work and how the human system deals with work. Quality, and hence productive, work means we need good concentration. When we are about to carry out a particular task, we need to settle down, get in the mood and then concentrate.

The idea of *flow* was introduced in Chapter 1. When an individual is in a state of flow, he or she may be distracted or may become naturally tired, and the process then repeats itself.

Our attention span usually lasts for about 90–120 minutes and then natural fatigue comes into play and our concentration drops, but after a creative break we pick up again, concentrate for another spell of time, and the pattern repeats itself over the waking day. This is the so-called *ultradian rhythm*. Csikszentmihalyi (1990) and De Marco and Lister (1987) have described this as a concept of *flow*. Mawson (2002) describes their work, which claims that individuals take about 15 minutes to ramp up to their concentration level. Mawson believes that there is a significant loss of productivity from distraction, which for a well-managed office has been identified by the *Harvard Business Review* (2012) as being approximately 70 minutes of lost productivity in a typical 8-hour day. This distraction is mainly due to general social buzz and phones ringing with the subsequent conversations.

Davidson (2003; Davidson and Begley, 2012) led a research study at the University of Wisconsin-Madison which showed that positive thinking (good mood, optimism) can promote good health because the body's defences (the immune system) are stronger. This suggests that the balance between the mind and the body is a sensitive one. So how relevant is this in the workplace? Various stressors can arise from conflicts within the physical, social or organisational environment. People adapt to these stressors in various ways, but some will be weakened and, if conditions are very stressful, many will be affected.

There is substantial evidence, as described by Heerwagen (1998) that positive mood is associated with the physical environment and everyday events such as social interactions (Clark and Watson, 1988). Even more telling is research which has shown that a positive mood aids complex cognitive strategies (Isen, 1990) whereas negative mood, due to distractions, discomfort, health risks or irritants arising from the physical or social environments, restricts attention and hence affects work performance. Because positive moods directly affect the brain processes (Le Doux, 1996) it can be concluded that many aspects of building environmental design can enhance task performance. Heerwagen (1998) distinguishes between direct effects, such as overheating, noise or glare, and indirect effects arising from mood and/or motivational factors. Several positive-mood-inducing factors have already been mentioned – aesthetics, freshness, daylight, views out, greenery, colour, personal control, spatial aspects and how the buildings link with nature.

Mood, feelings and emotions affect people's decision-making. Mood can be influenced by several environmental factors, such as the 'Monday effect' or weather conditions. A body of psychological literature shows that temperature and sunlight are the important meteorological variables that affect people's mood, and this in turn influences behaviour. Compare, for example, your mood on a fresh sunny day with that on a dull rainy overcast day. Cao and Wei (2005) stated that the research to date has revealed that stock market returns are associated with nature-related variables such as the amount of sunshine, the daylight-saving time change, the length of the night, and the lunar phases of the moon.

The internal built environment matters in all the ways that have been described in Ong (2013). It is an intrinsic part of our existence. Betthäuser (2013) calls for a new effective and economic workplace model. His argument is that people are beginning to view their workplace in a more emotional way because the office can offset the brutality of the news media and transport stress. The workplace can be a kind of sanctuary offering safety, enjoyment and a place to fulfil creativity. He believes we need to provide a more organic and responsive place to meet occupants' needs. These thoughts are echoed in the earlier editions of *Creating the Productive Workplace* (Clements-Croome, 2000b; 2006) in which a model for productivity which embraces social, personal, organisational and environmental factors together is advocated. Flexible approaches to workplace design are the hallmark of the Workplace Trends Report 2012 (Sodexo, 2012; Gensler, 2013; BCO, 2014).

Good design adds value and if there is any increase in costs. the payback period will be under 3 years. In addition, energy and other resources will be used more efficiently and effectively.

Apple have new offices due to be completed in 2017 located in Cupertino in San Francisco Bay and aspire to design and build the best office building in the world (*The Times*, 2013, pp. 4–5). The universal credit given to Apple products will imbue the minds of many with high expectations. The preview shows a ring structure set in a wooded landscape which will accommodate about 12,000 people. Using renewable energy and other means of being resource-efficient such as 70 per cent use of natural ventilation, the building is expected to reach the highest sustainability rating levels. The interior should give occupants an aesthetic and social experience with lots of natural light and views out of Nature but also one that allows collaboration by having fluid and agile space while allowing the functional aspects to be highly effective. This is a building with a vision.

Step into a cathedral, a restaurant or an office and feel the ambience they offer. This can affect one's mood, well-being and work effort as an individual or as a team. Space can be patterned to encourage formal or informal working so, in a way, can condition human behaviour. There are many subtle factors we need to know more about. For example, do high ceilings encourage abstract thought and creativity as some believe (Meyers–Levy and Zhu, 2007)? Often assumptions about higher occupancy densities or low ceiling heights are made on a cheap cost basis but may in the end have human consequences which make them more expensive. Designing for function and convenience alone is not enough. In the words of Volker Buscher, a Director at Arup (McMeeken, 2014): 'I think we are going to see the Age of the "humane" engineer – engineers who think not just about functions but also about emotions.'

Health and well-being offer economic advantages which more than offset any costs in providing the environments to achieve this. After all the designing is done and the building is operating, there remains the person with all their unique qualities, expectations and personal habits, likes and dislikes. Shawn Achor (2010) is a passionate advocate of positive thinking and he suggests that everyone should try and make room each day for recognising some meaningful event and time for some fun, meditation, generosity, kindness and gratitude. The time spent on these actions can be small but the rewards are vast. The building can provide the setting but we as individuals have to be receptive and proactive too. Architecture provides the setting for health, motivation and creativity.

References

Achor, S. (2010) *The Happiness Advantage*. New York: Random House.

Agha-Hossein, M.M., El-Jouzi, S., Elmualim, A.A., Ellis, J. and Williams, M. (2013) Post-occupancy studies of an office environment: energy performance and occupants' satisfaction. *Building and Environment*, 69: 121–130.

BCO (2014) *Making the Business Case for Well-being*, The 2014 Well-being at Work Study London: British Council for Offices; Morgan Lovell and Hatch. Available at: www.bco.org.uk/Research/Publications/Making_the_Business_Case_for_Wellbeing.

BCO (2016) *The Impact of Wearables on Office Workplaces*. Report by Derek Clements-Croome (Reading University) Mallory Taub (Arup) Vicki Lockhart (Arup) for BCO. Available at: www.bco.org.uk/Research/Publications/Wearables

Bell, J., Mabb, J., Garcia-Hansen, V., Bergman, B. and Morawska, L. (2003) Occupant Health and productivity: an Australian perspective. In Yang, J., Brandon, P.S. and Sidwell, A.C. (eds) *Proceedings of the CIB 2003 International Conference on Smart and Sustainable Built Environment (SASBE 2003)*, pp. 687–694.

Bergs, J. (2002) The effect of healthy workplaces on the well-being and productivity of office workers. Plants for People Symposium, Reducing Health Complaints at Work, Amsterdam.

Betthäuser, G. (2013) *Leesman Review*, Issue 10, p. 2.

Black, C. (2008) *Working for a Healthier Tomorrow*. London: TSO.

Boyden, S. (1971) Biological determinants of optimal health. In Vorster D.J.M. (ed.) *The Human Biology of Environmental Change*. Proceedings of a conference held in Blantyre, Malawi, April 5–12, 1971. London: International Biology Program.

Cao, M., and Wei, J. (2005) Stock market returns: a note on temperature anomaly. *Journal of Banking & Finance*, 29: 1559–1573.

Cartwright, J. (2016) Revealing the network within. *Physics World*, 29(2,): 29–31.

CBI UK Report (2014) *Getting Better, Workplace Health as a Business Issue*. Available at: www.cbi.org. uk/media/2727613/getting-better.pdf

Clark, L.A. and Watson, D. (1988) Mood and the mundane: relationships between daily events and self-reported mood. *Journal of Personality and Social Psychology*, 54: 296–308.

Clements-Croome, D.J. (2000a) Computers and Health in the Work Place. In *Proceedings of Healthy Buildings*, University of Technology, Helsinki, 1: 119–124.

Clements-Croome, D.J. (2000b) *Creating the Productive Workplace*. London: Routledge.

Clements-Croome, D.J. (2006) *Creating the Productive Workplace*, 2nd edn, London: Routledge.

Clements-Croome, D.J. (2013) *Intelligent Buildings: Design, Management & Operation* London: ICE Publishing.

Clements-Croome, D.J. (2014) *Sustainable Intelligent Buildings for Better Health, Comfort and Well-Being*, EU Report for Denzero Project led by Debrecen University supported by the TAMOP-4.2.2A-11/1/ KONV-2012–0041 and co-financed by the European Union and the European Social Fund.

Clements-Croome, D.J. and Li, B. (2000) Productivity and indoor environment. In *Proceedings of Healthy Buildings Conference*, University of Technology, Helsinki, 1: 629–634.

Csikszentmihalyi, M. (1990) *Flow: The Psychology of Optimal Experience*. New York: Harper and Row.

Davidson, R.J. (2003) Report by M. Henderson. *The Times*, 2 September, p. 4.

Davidson. R J. and Begley, S. (2012) *The Emotional Life of Your Brain*. Harmondworth: Penguin.

Davis, F., *et al*. (2013) Actuating mood: design of the textile mirror. Seventh International Conference on Tangible, Embedded and Embodied Interaction, Demo and Paper, February 10–13, 2013. Barcelona, Spain.

De Marco, T. and Lister, T. (1987) *People Ware: Productive Projects and Teams*. New York, Dorset House Publishing,

Dolan, P. (2014) *Happiness by Design*. London: Allen Lane.

DWP (2014) A million workers off sick for more than a month. Department for Work and Pensions, press release, 10 February. Available at: www.gov.uk/government/news/a-million-workers-off-sick-for-more-than-a-month (accessed 15 July 2016).

Eley Associates (2001) *The Collaborative for High Performance Schools: Best Practices Manual*. San Francisco: Eley Associates.

Evans, R., Haryott, R., Haste, N. and Jones, A. (1998) *The Long-Term Costs of Owning and Using Buildings*. London: Royal Academy of Engineering.

Fanger, P.O. (2002) Human requirements in future air-conditioned environments. *Advances in Building Technology*, 1: 29–38.

Ferguson, G. S. and Weisman, G.D. (1986) Alternative approaches to the assessment of employee satisfaction with the office environment. In Wineman, J.D. (ed.) *Behavioural Issues in Office Design*. New York: Van Nostrand Reinhold, pp. 85–108.

Fisk, W.J, (1999) Estimates of potential nationwide productivity and health benefits from better indoor environments: an update. In Spengler, J.D., Samet, J.M. and McCarthy, J.F. (eds) *Indoor Air Quality Handbook*. New York; McGraw-Hill.

Fisk, W.J. (2000a) Health and productivity gains from better indoor environments and their relationship with building energy efficiency. *Annual Review of Energy Environment*, 25(1): 537–566.

Fisk, W.J. (2000b) Review of health and productivity gains from better IEQ. In *Proceedings of Healthy Buildings, Helsinki*, 4: 24–33.

Fisk, W.J., Black D.R, and Brunner, G. (2012) Changing ventilation rates in US offices: implications for health, work performance, energy, and associated economics. *Building and Environment*, 47: 368–372.

Fogg, B.J. (2009) A behaviour model for persuasive design, Persuasive 09. In *Proceedings of the 4th International Conference on Persuasive Technology*, Article 40.

Financial Times (2016) Money, page 5, 16 March.

Gensler (2013) *Workplace Survey*. Available at: www.gensler.com/uploads/documents/2013

Goetzel, R.Z., *et al.* (2016) The stock performance of C. Everett Koop Award Winners compared with the Standard and Poor's 500 Index, *Journal of Occupational and Environmental Medicine*, 58(1): 9–15. DOI:10.1097/JOM.

Greenfield, S. (2014) *Mind Change: How Digital Technologies Are Leaving Their Mark on Our Brains*. New York: Rider.

Harvard Business Review (2012), May 17.

Heerwagen, J.H. (1998) Productivity and well-being: what are the links? Paper presented at American Institute of Architects Conference on Highly Effective Facilities, Cincinnati, OH, USA.

Isen, A.M. (1990) The influence of positive and negative effect on cognitive organisation: some implications for development. In Stein, N., Leventhal, B. and Trabasso, B. (eds) *Psychological and Biological Approaches to Emotion*. Hillsdale, NJ: Lawrence Erlbaum/

Ivanov, P. (1996) Scaling behaviour of heartbeat intervals obtained by wavelet-based time-series analysis, *Nature*, 383(6598): 323–327.

Johns, J. (2010) Presenteeism in the workplace: a review and research agenda, *Journal of Organisational Behaviour*, 31: 519–542.

Juniper, B.A., Bellamy, P. and White, N. (2011) Testing a new approach to evaluating employee well-being. *Leadership and Organization Development Journal*, 32(4): 344–357.

Juniper, B.A., Bellamy, P. and White, N. (2016) Evaluating the well-being of public library workers. *Journal of Librarianship and Information Science* (in press).

Juniper, B.A., Walsh, E., Richardson, A. and Morley, B.M. (2016) A new approach to evaluating the well-being of PhD research students. *Assessment & Evaluation in Higher Education* (in press).

Juniper, B.A., White, N. and Bellamy, P. (2009) Assessing employee well-being – is there another way? *International Journal of Workplace Health Management*, 2(3): 220–230.

Juniper, B.A., White, N. and Bellamy, P. (2010) A new approach to evaluating the well-being of the police. *Occupational Medicine*, 60(7): 560–565.

Leaman, A. and Bordass, B. (1999) Productivity in buildings: the 'killer' variables. *Building Research & Information*, 27: 4–19.

Leaman, A. and Bordass, B. (2006) Productivity in buildings: the 'killer' variables. In Clements-Croome, D.J. (ed.) *Creating the Productive Workplace*. London: Routledge, pp. 153–180.

Le Doux, J. (1996) *The Emotional Brain*. New York: Simon & Schuster.

Lee, S.Y. (2006) Expectations of employees towards the workplace and environmental satisfaction. *Facilities*, 24(9/10): 343–353.

Lehman. M. (2016) *Adaptive Sensory Environments*. London: Routledge.

Lorenz, D. and Lützkendorf, T. (2011) Sustainability and property calculation: systematisation of existing approaches and recommendations for future action. *Journal of Property Investment & Finance*, 29(6): 644–676.

Macmillan, S. (2006) Added value of good design. *Building Research and Information*, 34(3): 257–271.

Mawson, A. (2002) *The Workplace and Its Impact on Productivity*. London: Advanced Workplace Associates Ltd,

McGraw-Hill Construction (2014) *The Drive Toward Healthier Buildings: The Market Drivers and Impact of Building Design and Construction on Occupant Health, Well-Being and Productivity*, Smart Market Report. MHC_Analytics@mcgraw-hill.com

McMeeken, R. (2014) Building 2050: the cities of the future. *CIBSE Journal*, January, Careers Special Supplement, 22–24.

Mendell, M.J., *et al.* (2013) Association of classroom ventilation with reduced illness absence: a prospective study in California elementary schools, *Indoor Air*, 23: 515–528.

Mendell, M., Fisk, W.J., Kreiss, K., Levin, H., *et al.* (2002) Improving the health of workers in indoor environments: priority research needs for a national occupational research agenda. *American Journal of Public Health*, 92(9): 1430–1440.

Meyer, H. (1999) Fun for everyone. *Journal of Business Strategy*, 20(2): 13–17.

Meyers-Levy. J. and Zhu. R. (2007) The influence of ceiling height, *Journal of Consumer Research*, 34(August): 174–186.

Ong, B.L. (2013) *Beyond Environmental Comfort*. London: Routledge.

ONS (2012) *Sickness Absence in the Labour Market, April 2012*. Office for National Statistics. Available at: http://webarchive.nationalarchives. gov.uk/20160105160709/http://www.ons.gov.uk/ons/dcp 171776_265016.pdf (accessed 15 July 2016).

ONS (2013) *Labour Force Survey*. Office of National Statistics. Available at: www/ons.gov.uk/ons/dcp 171776 353899.pdf

Parker, M. (2014) *The Guardian*, 25 June.

Preller, L., Zweers, T., Brunekreef, B. and Boleiji, J.S.M. (1990) Indoor air quality '90. *Fifth International Conference on Indoor Air Quality and Climate*, 1: 227–230.

Prochaska, J.O., *et al.* (2011) The wellbeing assessment for productivity: a wellbeing approach to presenteeism, *Journal of Occupational and Environmental Medicine*, 53(7): 735–742: DOI:10.1097/JOM.

Rehm, M. and Ade, R. (2013) Construction costs comparison between green and conventional office buildings. *Building Research and Information*, 41(2): 198–208.

Roelofsen, P. (2001) The design of the workplace as a strategy for productivity enhancement. Paper presented at the 7th REHVA World Congress, Clima 2000, Naples, Italy.

Satish, U., *et al.* (2011) Impact of CO_2 on human decision making and productivity. Indoor Air Conference, Austin, TX, Abstract 574.

Satish, U., *et al.* (2012) Is CO_2 an indoor air pollutant? Direct effects of low-to-moderate CO_2 concentrations on human decision-making performance. *Environmental Health, Perspectives*, 120: 1671–1677.

Sivunen, M., Kosonen, R. and Kajander, J. (2014) Good indoor environment and energy efficiency increase monetary value of buildings. *REHVA Journal*, 51(4): 6–9.

Sodexo (2012) *Workplace Trends Report*, Ocak 2012, Available at: http://viewer.zmags.com/publication/ 16fdba6d#/16fdba6d/1

Spataru, C. and Gauthier, S. (2014) How to monitor people 'smartly' to help reducing energy consumption in buildings? *Architectural Engineering and Design Management*, 10(1–2); 60–78.

Stokols, D. (1992). Establishing and maintaining healthy environments: toward a social ecology of health promotion. *American Psychologist*, 47(1): 6–22.

Sundell, J., *et al.* (2011) Ventilation rates and health: multidisciplinary review of the scientific literature, *Indoor Air*, 21: 191–204.

The Times (2013) Technology Review, 4 November 2013, pp. 4–5.

The Times (2017) Raconteur on Talent Management, 31 January 2017.

Towers Watson (2014) *The Business Value of a Healthy Workforce*, Staying@Work Survey Report, Towers Watson and National Business Group on Health, TW-NA 2012-29407(United States).

US Green Building Council (2003). *Making the Business Case for High Performance Green Buildings*. Washington, DC: US Green Building Council. Available at: www.usgbc.org/Docs/Member_Resource_ Docs/makingthebusinesscase.pdf (accessed 26/3/2013)

van der Voordt, D.J.M. (2003) *Costs and Benefits of Innovative Workplace Design*, Center for People and Buildings, Delft & Centrum Facility Management, Naarden: Summary & Book Review.

Vischer, J.C. (2008) Towards an environmental psychology of workspace: how people are affected by environments for work, *Architecture Science Review*, 51(2): 97–108.

Wargocki, P., Seppanen, O., Andersson, J., Boerstra, A., Clements-Croome, D., Fitzner, K., and Hanssen, S.O. (2006) *Indoor Climate and Productivity in Offices*. Guidebook no 6. Brussels: Federation of European Heating and Air-conditioning Associations (REHVA).

Warr, P. (2002) *Psychology at Work*, 5th edn. Harmondsworth: Penguin Books.

World Green Building Council (WGBC) (2013) *The Business Case for Green Building.* Available at: www.worldgbc.org/files/1513/6608/0674/Business_Case_For_Green_Building_Report_WEB_2013-04-11.pdf

World Green Building Council (2014) *Health, Wellbeing and Productivity in Offices: The Next Chapter for Green Building.* London: World Green Building Council. Available at: info@ukgbc.org or office@wgbc.org.

World Green Building Council (2016) *Health, Wellbeing and Productivity in Retail: The Impact of Green Buildings on People and Profit,* World Green Building Council. Available at: info@ukgbc.org or office@wgbc.org

Chapter 3

The multi-sensory experience in buildings

Briony Turner, Derek Clements-Croome and Kay Pallaris

The buildings we admire are ultimately those which, in a variety of ways, extol values we think worthwhile – which refer . . . whether through their materials, shapes or colours, to such legendarily positive qualities as friendliness, kindness, subtlety, strength and intelligence.

(de Botton, 2006)

Designing a productive workplace

While Chapter 1 established the links between 'good design', productivity and well-being, in this chapter we draw on research about the senses and office-related studies to demonstrate how buildings can be designed to be conducive to a positive multi-sensory experience. Specifically, we look at the workplace and propose that, in order to design a productive workplace, it is essential to consider how the environment is making us feel, behave and act within it. As the workplace continues to evolve, the case is made for a sensory palette framework to drive a systems approach to building service design, enabling the integration of the multi-modal sensory relationship of people to their environment. Technological advances, in the form of wearables that monitor our physiological response, offer the opportunity to capture empirical data, further enabling the investigation of various environmental settings on our physical and mental well-being.

The evolution of the productive workplace

As our culture of work has evolved and adapted over time, so has the design of the workplace. Its purpose, however, has arguably always been to increase the productivity and efficiency of employees and to maximise the bottom line. Taylorism at the beginning of the twentieth century was illustrated by factory-like rows and rows of desks with a strong demarcation between bosses and workers. Traditionally, productive workplace design has attempted to control the environmental conditions, keeping the focus of individual workers on their assigned task, minimising any distraction. This was achieved by creating a workplace design devoid of sensory stimuli that might detract from the task in hand, including minimising the opportunities for, and distractions of, social interaction.

Over the next 100 years, social attitudes as well as technology changed radically. Hierarchical attitudes faded and technology now affords more personal control. Function is no longer the single factor dominating workplace design; the experience for the occupants, once side-lined, is becoming increasingly important. Cramming people into smaller and smaller areas resulted in stressful working environments and has proved to be a false economy.

As we have moved away from designing workspaces that contain individual booth structures to open plan offices, later to hot-desking and, more recently, to incorporating stylish break-out areas, so the possibilities have emerged for social interaction and increased transparency between hierarchies. Such design promises an environment that is actively conducive to the exchange of ideas for creative collaboration and co-working. However, the notion that group work is the only way to encourage a creative workforce is being challenged (Cain, 2012). There is a need to strike a balance between quiet spaces for personal contemplation and thought, together with spaces for cooperative exchange of ideas and information.

More recently, the design of office fit-outs has become a corporate tool to communicate a powerful brand identity. Studies like the CABE and BCO (2005) report 'The Impact of Office Design on Business Performance' have demonstrated how new office designs can motivate employee and customer attraction and retention. Office design has become a thriving industry in recent years with many online design blogs promoting how a 'branded office' can 'accommodate the creative needs of an artistic workforce' (Palolini, 2012; Ames, 2013; Hughes, 2016).

Another strong turn in office design has focused on preventing ergonomic problems resulting from sedentary working. Furniture product companies, especially those based in Scandinavia and Germany, are creating product lines that both assist with the provision of an inspiring and motivating workplace and also help to address musculo-skeletal problems which feature significantly in the absenteeism statistics. Consideration of sedentary activity has received increasing attention from researchers, given its health consequences. 'Environmental restructuring' of the workplace by providing 'sit-stand' desks in order to limit or restrict sedentary behaviour has been found to be one of the most promising types of reduction interventions. The studies available for review, however, remain limited and are considered to have given insufficient attention to the behavioural motivation of employees through education or information provision (Gardner *et al.*, 2016). A recent trend in fit-out design to encourage less sedentary behaviour in the workplace has included incorporation of areas for physical activity such as ping-pong tables, commonly referred to as the 'Google office'. However, some believe this has taken the workplace too far into the realms of play, away from the purpose of work, where the office is 'treated like a playground' (Myerson, 2016).

The very notions of productivity and what constitutes the workplace are rapidly changing as we head towards what is being dubbed by some as the 'Fourth Industrial Revolution' involving the fusion of multiple technological developments, their interaction across biophysical and digital domains and the advent of smart and connected machines and systems (Schwab, 2016). Mobile internet and cloud services have made redundant our need to be physically located in one place on a daily basis. This is enabling agile, more flexible working practices – people working in cafés, at home or in pop-up offices. Incubator spaces have arisen, providing shared work spaces for the self-employed. Firms are embracing this challenge and starting to devise and embed mobile workplace strategies. This flexibility is welcomed, yet the impact of merging our personal, social and home spaces with work is yet to be fully understood. There is now a dedicated multi-disciplinary domain of research called 'Human-Computer Interaction' to improve understanding and new technologies to aid the relationships between computational systems and human actors and action (EPSRC, 2012).

Looking into the future, the technological turn, particularly with regard to computing power and data mining capacity, suggests that our working culture will need to adapt further. It will also necessitate a re-examination of what is, and what should constitute, the workplace (see Figure 3.1). For instance, many present-day technically dependent occupations such as frontline health professionals will start to require a change in focus from technical knowledge, how to operate equipment, the diagnosis and the personalisation of treatments,

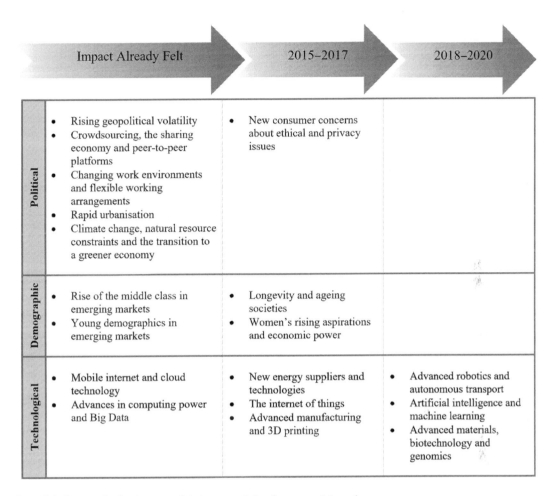

	Impact Already Felt	2015–2017	2018–2020
Political	• Rising geopolitical volatility • Crowdsourcing, the sharing economy and peer-to-peer platforms • Changing work environments and flexible working arrangements • Rapid urbanisation • Climate change, natural resource constraints and the transition to a greener economy	• New consumer concerns about ethical and privacy issues	
Demographic	• Rise of the middle class in emerging markets • Young demographics in emerging markets	• Longevity and ageing societies • Women's rising aspirations and economic power	
Technological	• Mobile internet and cloud technology • Advances in computing power and Big Data	• New energy suppliers and technologies • The internet of things • Advanced manufacturing and 3D printing	• Advanced robotics and autonomous transport • Artificial intelligence and machine learning • Advanced materials, biotechnology and genomics

Figure 3.1 Drivers for business model change and timeframes anticipated

Source: adapted from WEF (2016).

Note: this is based on the responses of Chief Human Resources Officers and other senior talent and strategy executives of 371 companies of today's largest global employers.

towards a focus on effective translation and communication of results produced from data mining (WEF, 2016).

The development of more creative and interpersonal skillsets such as persuasion, cognitive flexibility (in switching between and/or simultaneously considering multiple concepts), emotional intelligence (being aware of, and understanding, others' reactions) and teaching others will rise by 2020, according to a study by the World Economic Forum (WEF) (see Figure 3.2). Consideration of multi-sensory stimuli within workplace design can help create environments conducive to the enhancement and facilitation of these attributes.

Making sense of the multi-sensory experience

To design spaces that benefit our well-being requires knowledge of how the body responds to the multiple stimuli it receives from the environment. The nature of the stimuli that is designed,

Anticipated Top Ten Skills Required in a Workplace	
In 2020	**In 2015**
1. Complex Problem Solving	1. Complex Problem Solving
2. Critical Thinking	2. Coordinating with Others
3. Creativity	3. People Management
4. People Management	4. Critical Thinking
5. Coordinating with Others	5. Negotiation
6. Emotional Intelligence	6. Quality Control
7. Judgement in 2020 and Decision-making	7. Service Orientation
8. Service Orientation	8. Judgement and Decision-making
9. Negotiation	9. Active Listening
10. Cognitive Flexibility	10. Creativity

Figure 3.2 Top ten skills
Source: redrawn from WEF (2016).

Table 3.1 Summary understanding of our sensory modalities

Sensory modalities	Sense
Haptic – Tactioception	Sense of touch
Visual – Ophthalmoception	Sense of vision/sight
Auditory – Audioception	Sense of hearing/Sense of the perception of sound
Gustatory – Gustaoception	Sense of taste
Olfactory – Olfacception	Sense of smell
Thermoreception/Themoception	Sense of temperature
Vestibular – Equilibrioception	Sense of balance
Interoception	Sense of the physiological condition of the entire body
Nociception	Sense of pain
Proprioception	Sense of limb/body position without visual cues: the ability to perceive position, weight, and resistance of objects in relation to the body
Kinesthesia (often incorporated into proprioception)	Sense of movement: the ability to sense the extent, direction, or weight of body movement

Sources: (Craig, 2002; Craig, 2009; Macpherson, 2010; Haverkamp, 2012; Matthen, 2012; Stokes *et al.*, 2014; Schulz, 2015).

be it the design and/or placement of objects (desks, chairs) in a space, the physical form of the building and internal layout, opportunities for social interaction together with the workplace culture, all interact to create a multi-sensory experience. An understanding of how we sense the environment stems from the study of the senses.

It is now commonly believed that we experience more than the five commonly known senses of vision, hearing, touch, taste, and smell (Craig, 2002; 2009; Macpherson, 2010; Haverkamp, 2012; Henshaw, 2012; Matthen, 2012; Stokes *et al.*, 2014; Schulz, 2015). Table 3.1 sets out the additional sensory modalities defined within what represents just a small sample of research from philosophy, bio-physiology and, more recently, from neuroscience data. The brain does not perceive environmental stimuli in isolation. Instead, sensory receptors process the signals and then relay these to the brain, each interacting and converging, resulting in the perceptions, emotions and experiences we feel and respond to. Each sense provides only a partial perspective on a complex whole that is only perceptible through the coordinated processing of multiple senses (O'Callaghan, 2016).

The two senses of proprioception and interoception tell us what the internal body itself is doing and as such, allow an individual to evaluate their personal physical state in response to stimuli. Proprioception refers to the sense of joint position and movement that are essential for maintaining posture and coordinating movement. Simply explained, interoception is the sense of organ function, giving rise to the conscious perceptions of bodily processes such as hunger and heart-beat (Schulz, 2015). Interoception has come to refer to the multi-modal integration of sensory channels resulting in one's complete perception of one's personal physiological condition (Craig, 2002; 2009; Ceunen et al., 2016). In effect, interoception can be thought of being not just the sense of the physiological condition of the body but also as the 'sense of well-being' that is necessary for the generation of both the motivation and attention necessary to influence behavioural decisions regarding survival and quality of life (Craig, 2002). Recent knowledge suggests that interoception is not restricted to mere sensations, but relies upon learned associations, memories and emotions which together give rise to the subjective representation of the body state (Ceunen et al., 2016).

Insights into the functioning of the sensory systems provide vital clues for how we should design the built environment so that it is as responsive to our basic human needs as the natural world it has replaced. The architect, Juhani Pallasmaa, in his publication, *The Eyes of the Skin* (2012), challenges the dominance of the visual sense, asserting that the senses can be regarded as extensions of the sense of touch because the senses as a whole define the interface between the skin and the world. The skin generally reads the texture, weight, density and temperature of our surroundings. The combination of sight, sound and touch allows the person to get a scale of space, distance or solidity. He stipulates that design dominated by the visual sense has given rise to 'a cultural condition and environment that generates alienation, abstraction and distance instead of promoting the positive experiences of belonging, rootedness and intimacy' (Pallasmaa, 2011, p. 51).

Drawing on product optimisation design, a multi-sensory design approach termed 'synesthetic design' offers an alternative to traditional visual sensory bias by providing the systematic incorporation of all five senses. The aim of synesthetic design is 'to coordinate all sensations stimulated by an object in a manner that results in a pleasant, harmonious overall appearance while coinciding with the particular function(s) desired' (Haverkamp, 2012, p. 14). The term itself is derived from Greek, 'syn' indicates together and 'aisthesis' means sensation. Unlike conventional design, it enables cross-sensory correlations and a design strategy that caters for a systematic approach that optimises correlations between the senses.

Designing for multi-sensory well-being

The 2014 British Council for Offices' survey of 2000 UK office workers showed that one in four believed their work environment did not support their physical well-being (BCO, 2014). Dissatisfied respondents were particularly unhappy with a lack of colour (80 per cent), a lack of greenery (64 per cent) and a lack of art (61 per cent) in their workplaces (BCO, 2015). On a global scale, the Human Spaces Survey (Human Spaces, 2015b) found that 58 per cent of 7,600 office workers in 16 countries (of which 85 per cent of offices surveyed were located in an urban environment) did not report having plants in the office and 47 per cent reported

Table 3.2 The sensory appeal of the five elements most wanted in the office

%*	Most desired office element*	Sensory design cues
44	Natural light	• Natural light has a balance of wavelengths compared to fluorescent lighting, that is conducive to the functioning of our photoreceptors in the eye • Contrast of light and shade aiding shape (lines and curves) perception and perception of space condition • Colour hue determined by light wavelength; short wavelengths make people feel cool, calmer. Long wavelengths make people feel warmer and invoke more rapid muscular response.
17	View of the sea	• Natural landscapes provide a harmonic contemplative visual stimulus which allows attention and therefore productivity to be restored
15	Bright colours	• Bright colours (in moderation) associated (especially in Feng Shui practices) with higher energy, motivation and inspiration for the flow of creative ideas
20	Indoor plants	• Related to having access to natural landscapes for restorative contemplation • Plants also help to improve the acoustic soundscape as they absorb, diffract and reflect sound noise, depending on the room's physical properties • Work to improve indoor air quality (depending on plant type), thereby altering the PH and oxygen levels, which impact our chemoreceptors and interoceptors and therefore our bodily function
19	Quiet working space	• Quiet spaces provide an improved acoustic environment by removing distraction and vibration that impact our visual and tactile sensory systems, thus enhancing concentration and attention

Note: *based on the study of 7,600 survey responses by Human Spaces (2015b).

no natural light. Just under half (47 per cent) reported having felt stressed in their workplace within the last three months and 28 per cent of respondents reported that they did not have a quiet space to work in their office. The five elements most desired in the office revealed by the survey (see Table 3.2) were inherently linked to nature and the sensory experience of the workplace.

Designing for quality attention

High productivity requires high and sustained levels of concentration. Many personal health and social factors can affect this, including: low self-esteem, low morale, inefficient work organisation, or poor social relations. External environmental distractions such as excessive heat or noise can further exacerbate one's interoceptive condition, physically manifested as lethargy, headaches and physical ailments, all of which feature in surveys carried out on building sickness syndrome (Abdul-Wahab, 2011). Additionally, with the advent of emails, texts, messaging applications and the increasing prevalence of a networked, online mentality, concentration disruptors are no longer limited to the physical surrounding environment.

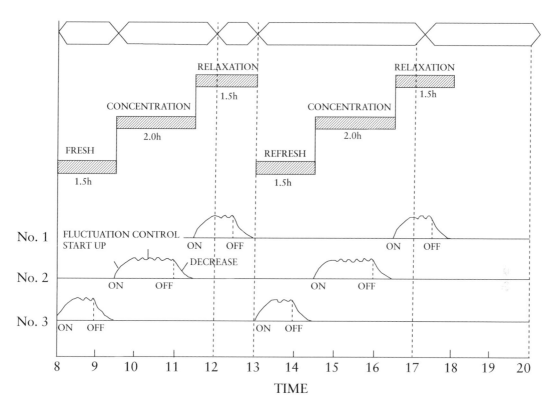

Figure 3.3 Atrium fragrance control scenario for the Kajima building in Tokyo
Source: Takenoya (2006).

It is possible to alter the opportunity for heightened attention through several design factors. Colour is one approach; the Human Spaces (2015b) study identified the colours blue, green, yellow and white as office colours that have a significant impact on workers' productivity. In the Kajima building in Tokyo (see Figure 3.3), aroma fragrances are used to condition the air. This research shows that aromas can help people feel a sense of freshness to offset fatigue, enabling employees to concentrate (Takenoya, 2006).

Designing for acoustic refuge should also be key in a workplace. Quiet can also heighten personal creativity as the space is providing an individual with opportunities to collate ideas and assimilate thoughts.

Designing for social interaction and collaboration

Social interaction and collaboration are vital to an organisation as they help to improve internal knowledge assimilation. In an increasingly networked world, the development and maintenance of professional relationships take place in both physical and digital environments. This affects the opportunity to further or hinder the intimacy necessary for strong social relations (Wilson, 2016). The notion of creating and supporting workplace environments that engender intimacy is particularly important in today's flexible mode of working, especially where projects require multi-disciplinary team working and collaboration. Understanding co-workers' temperaments, personality preferences, communication styles and what drives and motivates each individual, which can only be completely deciphered from face-to-face communication, can result in a more productive team. Building services, particularly those relating to internet and communications provision, should consider not merely servicing spaces, but also spaces that provide valuable conduits for social interaction and productivity.

Spatial experiments by geographers at the University of Sheffield found a strong relationship between ambient sound and the readiness of participants to engage in communication with strangers. Their research showed that before participants could feel secure enough to reveal personal characteristics and be receptive to having their preconceptions 'unsettled', the design of the spaces in which encounters take place have to promote emotional security. Factors such as the size and configuration of space, the relationship between primary and secondary space, the acoustics, issues of ownership, and surveillance all contributed to generating meaningful encounters (Mayblin *et al.*, 2015). Furthermore, bad acoustics reduced the willingness of participants to form smaller groups or paired bonds but increased the likelihood of collaboration with a wider group (as well as shouting across the space). Spaces that echoed less (in their example due to lower ceilings and soft flooring) reduced reverberation which, in turn, resulted in increased one-to-one interaction and an improved sense of security. Through other experiments, they were able to verify Rodaway's hypothesis that auditory perception 'involves the whole body whilst at the same time giving the immediate impression of sensing from a particular point or dedicated organ . . .' (Rodaway, 1994, p. 91). This, while a discrete experiment, suggests questioning of the appropriateness and perhaps indicates that further research is required when applying open plan design in workplaces which are dependent upon strong inter-personal relations for collaborative working.

The ease of wayfinding is also an important consideration. People remember sensory experiences of places and draw on these memories when perceiving a new or familiar environment. If the employee is bombarded with information from many different sensory channels, then 'cue conflict' may result and navigation of the space(s) may be impeded. Taking this into account, a well-designed space will have cues and signs, some or all of which users of the space will infer from past interpretation, enabling a level of wayfinding ease.

Designing to nourish the brain to enhance creativity

Natural elements are often associated with perceived well-being, as indicated by the Human Spaces study (2015a) (see Table 3.3). As we transition to living in increased virtual worlds we have much to learn from Nature's building systems, which possess self-adaptive and

Table 3.3 Natural elements positively linked to well-being at work

Country	Natural elements positively linked to well-being at work
UK	Light, wood and stone materials
France	Views of nature and open water
the Netherlands	Views of trees
Denmark	Natural light and green space
United Arab Emirates	Views of water such as the ocean, lakes or ponds
Sweden	Natural light had a positive impact on levels of happiness at work

Source: Human Spaces (2015a).

self-awareness properties and contain self-repair systems. Embedding natural elements into the design of a workplace has the potential to promote harmonious sensory experiences that will aid our organic growth and nourishment.

'The 14 Patterns of Biophilic Design' (see Table 3.4) has been developed for designers from a review of over 500 publications relating to biophilic responses in order to identify flexible and adaptive design patterns. This offers a powerful tool that can be used by built environment professionals for interiors and exteriors (Browning *et al.*, 2014) to reconnect the human sensory systems to the biophysical reality and the meaning that these natural elements conjure up. For instance, the rustling of leaves, the fragrance of flowers, birdsong, the sound of flowing water, the spaciousness of landscapes (particularly horizons between earth, sky and water), a light breeze and fresh, cool, clean air are all details that are remembered in terms of the emotional response they provoke. A walk outside has the ability to calm and soothe and refocus the mind, by re-stimulating and rebalancing our sensory receptors. A walk outside in a natural environment can therefore promote creativity.

A study looking at London city lawyers revealed that they had become habituated into reacting to the seasons in a stylistic sense, the trigger for the changing season being changes in clothes available in shops rather than awareness of changing environmental conditions (Hitchings, 2013). Reasons given (for not noticing the changing external environment) included convenient access on site to facilities (work cafés, supermarkets, gyms) and the constant controlled indoor conditions all year round (some moving from home to car to office to car to home) with minimal exposure to external conditions. During the summer it took the weather being constantly sunny for 'unusual' forms of practice, e.g. congregating outside, to occur. Furthermore, results for those interviewed indicated that once indoor habits were established of not accessing green space immediately outside the office during breaks, for fear it would disrupt the productive pace built up to meet deadlines and professional performance requirements, they became difficult to unlearn, with green space being viewed as a resource for others to enjoy only.

There are two learning points from this study. As designers, it is worth questioning striving for the creation of a constant thermal environment and considering the role design can play in socialising occupants into indoor behaviours. Second, designers could investigate, perhaps through biophilic cues, facilitating social interaction that encourages outdoor sociability where there are green spaces nearby. This might go beyond the physical design, to the design of working culture incorporating 'walking meetings' within natural spaces to help with refreshing and nourishing the brain (Merchant, 2013).

In the UK, there is growing interest in how green infrastructure can be integrated into buildings and used indoors as a building service, not just as a biophilic service to contribute to improving the health, well-being and productivity of employees but also to simultaneously improve the energy-efficiency of office buildings and enhance the resilience of the internal microclimates of buildings to a changing climate (Dover, 2015; 2016).

Designing for personal and responsive control

It is also important to note that an individual's circadian rhythms, physiologically and psychologically, change during the course of a day. This means there is a large variation in these needs, and also behaviour patterns, between one individual and another. This needs to be catered for by providing a flexible workplace where, for example, the individual can accommodate their different energy levels. Having easy access to an outdoor garden can be a simple yet effective way of rapidly restoring levels of concentration and fatigue.

Table 3.4 The 14 Biophilic Patterns and the ways in which they support cognitive performance (CP)

Sensory qualities of Nature's elements	Sensory patterns in Nature	Sensory perceptions from Nature
1. Visual Connection with Nature A view to elements of Nature, living systems and natural processes CP: Mental engagement/attentiveness	**8. Biomorphic Forms and Patterns** Symbolic references to contoured, patterned, textured or numerical arrangements that persist in Nature	**11. Prospect** An unimpeded view over a distance, for surveillance and planning. CP: Boredom, irritation, fatigue
2. Non-Visual Connection with Nature Auditory, haptic, olfactory, or gustatory stimuli that engender a deliberate and positive reference to nature, living systems or natural processes CP: Positively impacted	**9. Material Connection with Nature** Materials and elements from Nature that, through minimal processing, reflect the local ecology or geology and create a distinct sense of place. CP: Blood pressure and creative performance	**12. Refuge** A place for withdrawal from environmental conditions or the main flow of activity, in which the individual is protected from behind and overhead. CP: Concentration, attention and perception of safety
3. Non-Rhythmic Sensory Stimuli Stochastic and ephemeral connections with Nature that may be analysed statistically but may not be predicted precisely CP: Attention and exploration	**10. Complexity and Order** Rich sensory information that adheres to a spatial hierarchy similar to those encountered in nature	**13. Mystery** The promise of more information, achieved through partially obscured views or other sensory devices that entice the individual to travel deeper into the environment
4. Thermal and Airflow Variability Subtle changes in air temperature, relative humidity, airflow across the skin, and surface temperatures that mimic natural environments CP: Concentration		**14. Risk/Peril** An identifiable threat coupled with a reliable safeguard
5. Presence of Water A condition that enhances the experience of a place through seeing, hearing or touching water CP: Concentration, memory restoration, perception and psychological responsiveness		
6. Dynamic and Diffuse Light Leverages varying intensities of light and shadow that change over time to create conditions that occur in nature		
7. Connection with Natural Systems Awareness of natural processes, especially seasonal and temporal changes characteristic of a healthy ecosystem		

Source: Adapted from Browning et al. (2014). Note: The Patterns of Biophilic Design report also identifies the ways in which the patterns support stress reduction as well as emotion, mood and preference enhancement and provides the evidence basis and an indication of the rigour of support (from anecdotal to peer-reviewed).

As embedded sensory technology improves, the potential to incorporate reactive environments into workplace design will provide opportunities for smarter personal control of the environment. Being able to control thermal and indoor air quality not only renders a perception of feeling healthier but it can also result in higher productivity levels compared with those given less control (Boerstra *et al.*, 2013). Interactive architecture, defined as 'architecture that is programmed to respond to a person or inputs by changing its shape, colour, temperature, humidity, or other quality' (Davis *et al.*, 2013, p. 100), provides exciting potential for enhancement of productivity through responsive design. In its more complex form, it can be programmed to learn from its inputs or a response that a person gives to it, so that it can mediate that environment (ibid., p. 100). Where described as an interactive built environment (IBE), it can suggest a combination of the digital and physical environments that mediate daily workplace interactions, particularly those requiring smarter responsiveness.

Multiple sensory stimuli have been used by researchers from the Netherlands and from Philips in the design of an adaptive relaxation space facility to reduce workplace stress (Philips, 2013; Desmet, 2015). This GRIP project demonstrated how multi-sensory design of an adaptive relaxation space helped employees to self-regulate workplace stress. Its features included:

- the configuration of the space, i.e. partitions slowly enclose/lift to contract or expand triggered by sensors in the floor as an employee enters the space;
- generative sound, generated by the occupants;
- brightness levels of lighting (set to a rhythm of eight breaths a minute);
- trigger design to encourage employees to find the space.

The study also drew on the experience of mindfulness trainers, to help encourage paced breathing and meditation by users of the space. What is particularly interesting about this example is that the employee is provided with the opportunity to have intuitive control over the space. Within the GRIP project, some of the sensors in the space inform and adjust the sensory stimuli based on physiological signals from the user. This reverses the normal experience of the user being stimulated to have a specific sensory response created by the design of the space.

The potential of wearable technology for workplace well-being

We are now in the Conscious Technology Age (Glenn, 2015) of citizen-centric networked data. This offers opportunities to collect further empirical data to understand the links between design and well-being better. Technology-enhanced garments have embedded sensors that enable us to measure our physiological response (such as levels of arousal) or behavioural expressions (such as body movement). Another technique is to carry out sensory journeys with occupants/users of the space within an environment or an existing design similar to the one to be refurbished. Mapping occupants' sensory reactions and feelings, observing their interaction with the space and its contents, their movements and social interactions could reveal hidden work structures, sensory needs and desires within the target occupants (Kolko, 2011).

A method to aid the unobtrusive mapping of occupants' sensory experiences is to make use of rapidly developing wearable technology. The BCO (2016) has recently published a list of wearable devices (see Table 3.5) currently available that provide data relevant to the seven concepts of the WELL Building Standard and are also relevant to other health and well-being-related

Table 3.5 Availability of wearables now and in the future to meet elements of the WELL Building Standard

Concept	Topic	Wearables available	Wearables examples	Design opportunities
Air	Indoor air quality	✓	CleanSpace	Media Filtration Dehumidification UV germicidal irradiation Entryway walk-off systems Low-emitting/non-toxic material selection Ventilation rates
Water	Hydration	✓	WaterMinder	Exemplary drinking water quality. Ready access to potable drinking water
Nourishment	Balanced diet	✓	Healbe	Prominent positioning and clear labelling of healthy food options Adequately sized, equipped and attractive eating spaces
Light	Light properties	✓	SunSprite Netatmo June	Circadian lighting
Fitness	Physical activity	✓	Fitbit Garmin Jawbone Misfit Apple Watch	Attractive stairs with effective wayfinding. Active furnishings (sit–stand, treadmill desks). On-site physical activity spaces. Proximity to walking and cycling paths. Showers and locker rooms
Comfort	Ergonomics	✓	Lumo Lift	Ergonomically adjustable seats and desks
	Distracting sound	✓	Here Active Thermodo	Implementation of more extensive acoustic criteria
	Thermal comfort	✓		Individual control of localised thermal conditions
Mind	Stress	✓	Mindwave EMOTIV	Incorporation of nature Focus on role of artwork and colour in design Rest and relaxation spaces

Source: BCO (2016).

standards, including that of the Institute of Building Biology's certification programme. Such measurements can complement self-reporting of the user's self-perceived mood. These devices and products will necessarily increase awareness in individuals of how their bodies function and respond to different environments and, therefore, how their workplace might be affecting their personal productivity, data that previously has not been easily accessible outside of a research project. This will have ramifications for understanding work style and how not only individuals but also managers arrange workloads, demands and deliverables. While such technology is promising, there is still an apparent dominance of the visual aesthetic and the tactile sense of thermal comfort within the WELL Building Standard and within the wearables available. Additionally, a recent BCO review of commercial buildings, working with facilities management teams, and human resources teams, found very few examples in the UK using such technology compared with the USA, home of the WELL Living Lab, and other countries in Europe (BCO, 2016).

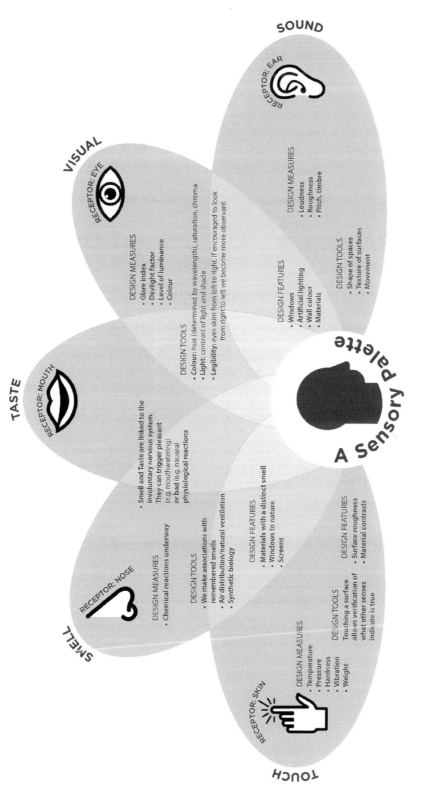

SOUND

RECEPTOR: EAR

DESIGN MEASURES
• Loudness
• Roughness
• Pitch, timbre

DESIGN TOOLS
• Shape of spaces
• Texture of surfaces
• Movement

DESIGN FEATURES
• Windows
• Artificial lighting
• Wall colour
• Materials

VISUAL

RECEPTOR: EYE

DESIGN MEASURES
• Glare index
• Daylight factor
• Level of luminance
• Colour

DESIGN TOOLS
• Colour: hue (determined by wavelength), saturation, chroma
• Light: contrast of light and shade
• Legibility: eyes skim from left to right. If encouraged to look
  from right to left we become more observant

A Sensory palette

TASTE

RECEPTOR: MOUTH

• Smell and Taste are linked to the
  involuntary nervous system.
  They can trigger pleasant
  (e.g. mouthwatering)
  or bad (e.g. nausea)
  physiological reactions

SMELL

RECEPTOR: NOSE

DESIGN MEASURES
• Chemical reactions underway

DESIGN TOOLS
• We make associations with
  remembered smells
• Air distribution/natural ventilation
• Synthetic biology

DESIGN FEATURES
• Materials with a distinct smell
• Windows to nature
• Screens

DESIGN FEATURES
• Surface roughness
• Material contrasts

DESIGN TOOLS
Touching a surface
allows verification of
what other senses
indicate is true

DESIGN MEASURES
• Temperature
• Pressure
• Hardness
• Vibration
• Weight

RECEPTOR: SKIN

TOUCH

Figure 3.4 A sensory palette framework to inform healthy workplace design

Conclusion: towards a sensory palette for a healthy workplace design

Our experience of the workplace is ever-changing and this has implications for how we should design the next generation of workplaces. The responses of the office workers in both the BCO and Human Spaces surveys suggest that even current practice and value sets are not realising the productivity potential that workplace design can yield. We already have a wealth of knowledge about the sensory response of the human body. Wearable technology offers the opportunity to further enhance our knowledge of how design decisions affect employees' physiological and psychological well-being, both at the individual and collective level. Such technology will have implications for the way we design, refurbish and build workplaces, placing an even greater emphasis on the human-centric, experiential perspective, a perspective embedded at the heart of a multi-sensory approach to workplace design (Taub *et al.*, 2016). Employers are realising that greater consideration of their staff within workplace design has multiple rewards, enabling them to provide a healthier working environment while simultaneously improving profitability and staff retention. With less absenteeism, there are potential savings for the health sector too.

Chapter 1 describes the Flourish model, which is an example of a multi-sensory conceptual approach to design. Here we summarise a number of existing design tools and design features that can be used to implement the Flourish model approach to design healthier workplaces. We propose a sensory palette framework to inform workspace fit-out to design an environment that not only improves the productivity of employees but also encourages them to thrive and flourish (see Figure 3.4). If conducting a refurbishment, or designing from scratch, the notion of the sensory palette itself could be used to provoke curiosity, to encourage occupants of the space to engage in the design process and help identify elements within the current workplace inspiring sensory delight or producing sensory overload.

Designing with this sensory approach in mind might at first encounter cost hurdles. This approach can be seen as potentially resulting in higher investment requirements with higher design fees allocated for the additional employee engagement and potentially higher investment required in elements of the office redesign. A traditional workplace valuation approach considers costs in terms of occupancy per square footage. However, productivity is beginning to play an increasingly central role in what is considered economic value for money, thereby shifting the emphasis from employee floorspace ratios to designing productive working environments. Furthermore, given the increased autonomy of employees and their potential instant access to data about their physiological state in the workplace, if the workplace is not delivering the productive, enticing, healthy environment they need to undertake their work, employees will have a well-informed basis upon which to express dissatisfaction and act. The workplace of the future must rapidly transition to incorporate environments conducive to our sense of well-being. This can only be achieved by creating workplaces that enable employees to flourish.

References

Abdul-Wahab, S.A. (2011) *Sick Building Syndrome*. Berlin: Springer.

Ames, P. (2013) The best offices are branded offices: why you should brand your space. Office Genie. Available at: www.officegenie.co.uk/blog/20130612-five-reasons-should-consider-office-branding (accessed 2 July 2016).

BCO (2014) *Making the Business Case for Wellbeing: The 2014 Wellbeing at Work Study*. London: Morgan Lovell and Hatch. Available at: www.bco.org.uk

BCO (2015) *Putting People First: Designing for Health and Wellbeing in the Built Environment*, eds Clements-Croome, D., Aguilar, A.M. and Taub, M. British Council for Offices. Available at: www.bco.org.uk

BCO (2016) *Report on Wearables Technology and Impact on Office Design and Management*, eds Clements-Croome, D., Taub, M. and Lockhart, V. British Council for Offices. Available at: www.bco.org.uk

Boerstra, A., Beuker, T., Loomans, M. and Hensen, J. (2013) Impact of available and perceived control on comfort and health in european offices. *Architectural Science Review*, 56(1): 30–41.

Browning, W.D., Ryan, C.O. and Clancy, J.O. (2014) *14 Patterns of Biophilic Design*. New York: Terrapin Bright Green, LLC. Available at: www.terrapinbrightgreen.com/wp-content/uploads/2014/04/14-Patterns-of-Biophilic-Design-Terrapin-2014e.pdf (accessed 27 March 2016).

CABE and BCO (2005) *Impact of Office Design on Business Performance*. Available at: http://webarchive.nationalarchives.gov.uk/20110118095356/http:/www.cabe.org.uk/files/the-impact-of-office-design-on-business-performance.pdf (accessed 4 August 2016).

Cain, S. (2012) *Quiet: The Power of Introverts in a World that Can't Stop Talking*. Harmondsworth: Penguin.

Ceunen, E., Vlaeyen, J.W.S. and Van Diest, I. (2016) On the origin of interoception. *Frontiers in Psychology* 7(226): 1–15.

Craig, A.D. (2002) How do you feel? Interoception: the sense of the physiological condition of the body. *Nature Review Neuroscience*, 3(8): 655–666.

Craig, A.D. (2009) How do you feel – now? The anterior insula and human awareness. *Nature Review Neuroscience* 10(1): 59–70.

Davis, F., Roseway, A., Carroll, E. and Czerwinski, M. (2013) Actuating mood: design of the textile mirror. In *Proceedings of the 7th International Conference on Tangible, Embedded and Embodied Interaction*, pp. 99–106.

de Botton, A. (2006) *The Architecture of Happiness*. Harmondsworth: Penguin.

Desmet, P.M.A. (2015) Design for mood: twenty activity-based opportunities to design for mood regulation. *International Journal of Design*, 9: 2.

Dover, J.W. (2015) *Green Infrastructure: Incorporating Plans and Enhancing Biodiversity in Buildings and Urban Environments*. London: Earthscan.

Dover, J.W. (2016) *Design Principles Guide*. ARCC network. Oxford: UKCIP. Available at: www.arcc-network.org.uk/wp-content/greensky/summary-challenge-leaflet.pdf (accessed 28 July 2016).

EPSRC (2012) *Report of the EPSRC Review of Human Computer Interaction Research in the UK*. Engineering and Physical Sciences Research Council. Available at: www.epsrc.ac.uk/newsevents/pubs/report-of-the-epsrc-review-of-human-computer-interaction-research-in-the-uk/ (accessed 26 August 2016).

Gardner, B., Smith, L., Lorencatto, F., Hamer, M. and Biddle, S.J.H. (2016) How to reduce sitting time? A review of behaviour change strategies used in sedentary behaviour reduction interventions among adults. *Health Psychology Review*, 10(1): 89–112.

Glenn, J. (2015) *The Age of Conscious-Technology*. Geneva: World Economic Forum Available at: http://reports.weforum.org/global-strategic-foresight/jerome-glenn-the-millennium-project-the-age-of-conscious-technology/ (accessed 29 November 2015).

Haverkamp, M. (2012) *Synesthetic Design: Handbook for a Multi-Sensory Approach*. Berlin: Birkhäuser.

Henshaw, J.M. (2012) *A Tour of the Senses: How Your Brain Interprets the World*. Baltimore, MD: The Johns Hopkins University Press.

Hitchings, R. (2013) Studying the preoccupations that prevent people from going into green space. *Landscape and Urban Planning*, 118: 98–102.

Hughes, K. (2016) 16 Stimulating design offices to stir the senses. Creative Blog, Feb 19 2016. Available at: www.creativebloq.com/design/design-offices-912828 (accessed 15 July 2016).

Human Spaces (2015a) Biophilic design in the workplace. Available at: http://humanspaces.com/report/ (accessed 31 March 2016).

Human Spaces (2015b) The global impact of biophilic design in the workplace. Available at: file:///D:/Downloads/Global-Human-Spaces-report-2015-US-FINAL.pdf (accessed 31 March 2016).

Kolko, J. (2011) *Thoughts on Interaction Design*. 2nd edn. Burlington, VA: Elsevier.

Macpherson, F. (2010) *The Senses: Classical and Contemporary Perspectives*. Oxford: Oxford University Press.

Matthen, M. (2012) *The Oxford Handbook of Philosophy of Perception*. Oxford: Oxford University Press.

Mayblin, L., Valentine, G., Kossak, F. and Schneider, T. (2015) Experimenting with spaces of encounter: creative interventions to develop meaningful contact. *Geoforum*, 63: 67–80.

Merchant, N. (2013) Kill your meeting room, the future's in walking and talking. *Wired*, 3 August 2013. Available at: www.wired.com/2013/03/how-technology-can-make-us-stand-up/ (accessed 15 July 2016).

Myerson, J. (2016) Google has had a negative effect on office design. *Dezeen*. Available at: www.dezeen.com/2016/03/22/google-office-design-negative-effect-interiors-jeremy-myerson/ (accessed 26 August 2016).

O'Callaghan, C. (2016) Objects for multisensory perception, *Philosophical Studies*, 173(5): 1269–1289.

Pallasmaa, J. (2011) Selfhood and the world lived space, vision and hapticity. In Diaconu, M., Heuberger, E., Mateus-Berr, R. and Vosicky, L.M. (eds) *Senses and the City: An Interdisciplinary Approach to Urban Sensescapes*. Reihe, Austria: Forschung und Wissenschaft – Interdisziplinär Bd.

Pallasmaa, J. (2012) *The Eyes of the Skin: Architecture and the Senses*, 3rd edn. Chichester: John Wiley & Sons Ltd.

Palolini, K. (2012) How one branding firm branded its own space: exploring ideas that shape the places we work. *Work Design Magazine*, June 1, 2012. Available at: http://workdesign.com/2012/06/how-one-branding-firm-branded-its-own-space/ (accessed 2 July 2016).

Philips (2013) Adaptive relaxation space: an ambient experience concept. Koninklijke Philips Electronics N.V. Available at: www.newscenter.philips.com/pwc_nc/main/design/resources/pdf/Inside-Innovation-Backgrounder-Adaptive-Relaxation-Space.pdf (accessed 30 March 2016).

Rodaway, P. (1994) *Sensuous Geographies: Body, Sense and Place*. Reprint edn (4 Nov. 2011) .London: Routledge.

Schulz, A. (2015) Interoception. In J.D. Wright (ed.) *International Encyclopedia of the Social and Behavioral Sciences*. Oxford: Elsevier, pp. 614–620.

Schwab, K. (2016) *The Fourth Industrial Revolution*. Geneva: World Economic Forum.

Stokes, D., Matthen, M. and Biggs, S. (eds) (2014) *Perception and Its Modalities*. Oxford: Oxford University Press.

Takenoya, H. (2006) Airconditioning systems of the K I Building, Tokyo. In Clements-Croome, D. (ed.) *Creating the Productive Workplace*. London: Routledge, pp. 334–347.

Taub, M., Clements-Croome, D.J. and Lockhart, V. (2016) *BCO Report: The Impacts of Wearables on Designing Healthy Office Environments*. Available at: www.bco.org.uk

WEF (2016) *The Future of Jobs: Employment, Skills and Workforce Strategy for the Fourth Industrial Revolution*. Geneva: World Economic Forum.

Wilson, A. (2016) The infrastructure of intimacy. *Signs: Journal of Women in Culture and Society*, 41(2): 247–280.

Chapter 4

Pleasure and joy, and their role in human life

Michel Cabanac

Experiments on human subjects showed that the perception of sensory pleasure can serve as a common currency to allow the trade-off among various motivations for access to behaviour. The trade-offs between various motivations would thus be accomplished by the simple maximisation of pleasure. A common currency for motivations as different from one another as physiological, ludic, social, aesthetic, moral, and religious is necessary to permit competition for access to behaviour. Therefore, all motivations can be compared to one another from the amount of pleasure and displeasure they arouse. It follows that the main properties of sensory pleasure should belong also to joy. Indeed, joy and sensory pleasure share identical properties; they are contingent, transient, and they index useful behaviours.

The behavioural final common path

One basic postulate of ethology is that behaviour tends to satisfy the most urgent need of the behaving subject (Tinbergen 1950; Baerends, 1956). One shortcoming of the theories of the optimisation of behaviour proposed by ethologists and behavioural ecologists is that the mechanism, by which behaviour is optimised, is never mentioned. In other words, they do not explain *how* the subject 'decides'. The notion of the *behavioural final common path* is a first step on the way leading to an answer to that question. Paraphrasing Sherrington's image of the motoneuron final common path of all motor responses, McFarland and Sibly (1975) pointed out that behaviour is also a final common path on which all motivations converge. This image incorporates all motivations into a unique category since behaviour must satisfy not only physiological needs but also social, moral, aesthetic, playful motivations. Indeed, it is often the case that behaviours are mutually exclusive; one cannot work and sleep at the same time. Therefore, the brain, responsible for the behavioural response, must rank priorities and determine trade-offs in the decisions concerned with allocating time among competing behaviours. It can be expected that the brain operates this ranking by using a *common currency* (ibid.; McNamara and Houson, 1986). In the following pages pleasure and joy will be proposed as this common currency.

Sensory pleasure

Sensory pleasure possesses several characteristics: Pleasure is contingent, pleasure is the sign of a useful stimulus, pleasure is transient, pleasure motivates behaviour. In the commerce of a subject with stimuli, it has been shown experimentally that the wisdom of the body leads the organism to seek pleasure and avoid displeasure, and thus achieve behaviours which are beneficial to the subject's physiology (Cabanac, 1971). Relations exist between pleasure and usefulness and between displeasure and harm or danger. For example, when subjects are invited to report verbally, the pleasure aroused by a skin thermal stimulus can be predicted knowing deep body temperature (Cabanac *et al.*, 1972; Attia, 1984) (Figure 4.1).

A hypothermic subject will report pleasure when stimulated with moderate heat, and displeasure with cold. The opposite takes place in a hyperthermic subject. Pleasure is actually observable only in transient states, when the stimulus helps the subject to return to normothermia. As soon as the subject returns to normothermia, all stimuli lose their strong pleasure component and tend to become indifferent. Sensory pleasure and displeasure thus appear especially suited to being a good guide for thermoregulatory behaviour (Figure 4.2).

The case of pleasure aroused by eating shows an identical pattern (Figure 4.3). A given alimentary flavour is described as pleasant during hunger and becomes unpleasant or indifferent during satiety. Measurement of human ingestive behaviour confirms the above relationship of behaviour with pleasure; it has been repeatedly demonstrated in the case of food intake (Fantino, 1984: 1995), that human subjects tend to consume foods that they report to be pleasant and to avoid those foods that they report to be unpleasant. Pleasure also shows a quantitative influence: the amount of pleasurable food eaten is a function of alimentary restrictions and increases after dieting. The result is that pleasure scales can be used to judge the acceptability of food.

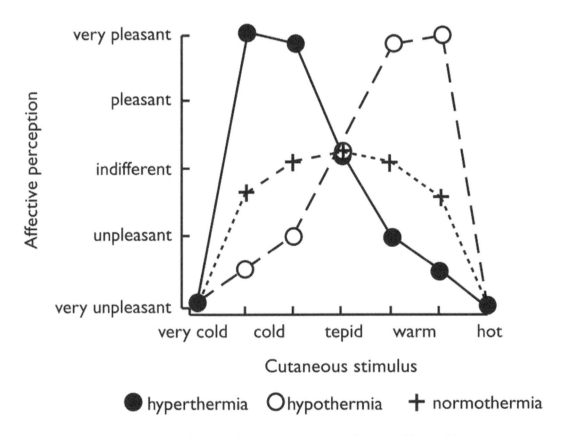

Figure 4.1 Pleasure (positive ratings) and displeasure (negative ratings) reported by a subject in response to thermal stimuli presented for 30 s on his left hand

Source: Cabanac (1986).

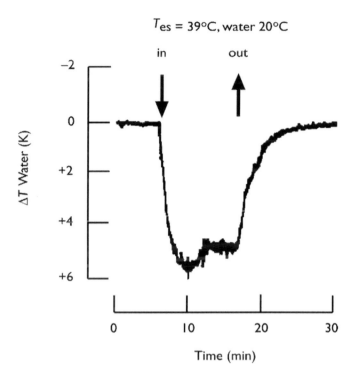

$T_{es} = 39°C$, water 20°C

Figure 4.2 Direct calorimetry of the heat loss by the hand of a hyperthermic subject when his hand was dipped
into highly pleasant cold water at 20°C. The plateau occurring ca. min 12 is a steady state, after initial
deflexion, when heat flow taken from the hand by the cold water is equal to heat flow brought to the
hand by arterial blood. Knowing the flow of water running around the hand it is easy to calculate that
the heat lost by the hand corresponds to ca. 73 W.

Source: Cabanac *et al.* (1972).

Thus, in the cases of temperature and taste, the affective dimension of sensation depends
directly on the biological usefulness of the stimulus to the subject. This was already noticed
by Aristotle (quoted in Pfaffmann, 1960). The word 'alliesthesia' was coined to describe the
fact that the affective dimension of sensation is contingent, and to underline the importance of
this contingency in relation to behaviour (Cabanac, 1971): a given stimulus will arouse either
pleasure or displeasure according to the internal state of the stimulated subject. The seeking of pleasure and the avoidance of displeasure lead to behaviours with useful homeostatic
consequences. Garcia has shown how past history, such as illness, induced in association with
the taste of an ingested substance, can 'stamp in' a change in the affective quality of that taste
(Garcia *et al.*, 1985). The behaviour of subjects instructed to seek their most pleasurable skin
temperature could be described and predicted from their body temperatures and the equations
describing their behaviour were practically the same as those describing autonomic responses
such as shivering and sweating (Cabanac *et al,.* 1972; Bleichert *et al.*, 1973; Marks and
Gonzalez, 1974; Attia and Engel, 1981).

It is possible therefore from verbal reports to dissociate pleasure from behaviour and to
show thus that the seeking of sensory pleasure and the avoidance of sensory displeasure lead to

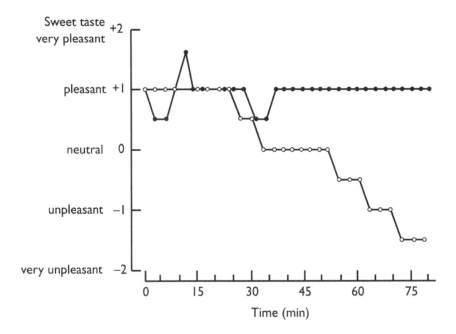

Figure 4.3 Pleasure (positive ratings) and displeasure (negative ratings) reported by a fasted subject in response to the same gustatory stimulus, a sample of sweet water presented repeatedly every third minute. Solid dots, the subject expectorated the samples after tasting; open symbols, the subject swallowed the samples and thus accumulated a heavy sucrose load in his stomach. In the latter case, it can be seen that the same sweet taste that aroused pleasure in the fasted subject aroused displeasure in the satiated subject.

Source: Cabanac (1971).

behaviours with beneficial homeostatic consequences. Pleasure thus indicates a useful stimulus and simultaneously motivates the subject to approach the stimulus. Pleasure serves both to reward behaviour and to provide the motivation for eliciting behaviour that optimises physiological processes. One great advantage of this mechanism is that it does not take rationality nor a high level of cognition to produce a behaviour adapted to biological goals. (Rational is understood, here, in its philosophical acceptation (i.e. reason), and not in its narrower economical sense.) Indeed, conditioned food aversion can be induced during sleep and under anaesthesia (Garcia, 1990). As soon as a stimulus is discriminated, the affective dimension of the sensation aroused tells the subject, animal or human alike, that the stimulus should be sought or avoided.

Pleasure and comfort

Let us keep the examples taken from temperature to understand the difference between comfort and pleasure. Comfort is different from sensory pleasure in that it is a general feeling whereas pleasure applies to the sensation aroused by a precise stimulus. Thermal comfort used to be defined as the 'subjective satisfaction with the thermal environment' (Bligh and Johnson, 1973). However, Figure 4.4 shows that this definition is inadequate. Figure 4.4 simplifies the experimental results presented in Figure 4.1. It can be seen that the cases of 'subjective satisfaction with the thermal environment', boxes P+I, represent a heterogeneous category including

Stimulus

	cold	neutral	warm
hypothermia	U	I	P
normothermia	U	I	U
hyperthermia	P	I	U

Internal state

Figure 4.4 Figure 4.1 simplified into a 3 × 3 matrix. The affective dimension of thermal sensation depends on the subject's internal state. A thermal stimulus feels unpleasant (U), indifferent (I) or pleasant (P) depending on body core temperature. Pleasure occurs only in dynamic situations when a stimulus tends to correct an internal trouble.

Source: Cabanac (1986).

pleasure and indifference. Pleasure, P boxes, occurs when there is an internal trouble, hypo- or hyperthermia. In these cases a pleasant stimulus, e.g. warm skin in a hypothermic subject, tends to correct the trouble, i.e. results in normothermia, and then turns unpleasant, i.e. to follow up with our example, warm skin in a normothermic subject. Pleasure provides 'subjective satisfaction with the thermal environment', but the situation is highly unstable. This led to the new definition of thermal comfort as the 'subjective indifference to the thermal environment' (I.U.P.S. Commission for Thermal Biology, 1987). Defined this way, comfort is stable and can last and is clearly different from pleasure whose characteristic is to be transient.

A feeling of pleasure indicates therefore that everything is right, but this is not a very exciting feeling, whereas pleasure indicates, in a troubled situation, a useful stimulus that should be consumed but will not last once the trouble is corrected.

Conflicts of motivations

If pleasure indicates usefulness, it would be of interest to explore situations with simultaneous and possibly conflicting multiple motivations. Several experiments were conducted where one motivation was pitted against another (e.g. sweet *vs.* sour, temperature *vs.* fatigue, and

	Resulting affective experience		Action
Behaviour 1	a $\longrightarrow$ A		yes
Behaviour 2	B $\longrightarrow$ b		no
Behaviour 1 + Behaviour 2	a + B $\longrightarrow$ A + b		yes

with a < A, and B > b, and with a + B < A + b

Figure 4.5 Mechanism by which a behaviour (behaviour 2) that produces displeasure can be chosen by a subject if another behaviour (behaviour 1) that produces pleasure is simultaneously chosen. The necessary and sufficient condition for the behaviour 2 to occur (action) is that the algebraic sum of affective experience (pleasure) of the yoked behaviours is positive (a + B < A + b). Capital letters B and A indicate larger pleasure than respective small letters a and b.

Source: Cabanac (1992).

chest *vs.* legs). In all these experiments the subjects' behaviours were repeatedly coherent. In the bi-dimensional sensory situations imposed by the experimenters, the subjects described maps of bi-dimensional pleasure in sessions where their pleasure was explored. They tended to move to the areas of maximal pleasure in these maps, in sessions where their behaviour was explored.

Thus, subjects in conflict situations tend to maximise their sensory pleasure as perceived simultaneously in both dimensions explored. In these experiments the subjects tended to maximise the algebraic sum of their sensory pleasure, or to minimise their displeasure. As a corollary of this observation, it can be stated that, in a situation of conflict of motivations, one can predict the future choice of the subject from the algebraic sum of affective ratings of pleasure and displeasure, given by the subject, to the conflicting motivations. This theoretic situation is presented in Figure 4.5.

Such a prediction is not surprising if one considers that, at each instant, all motivations are ranked to satisfy only the most urgent and that there must exist a common currency to actuate the behavioural final common path (McFarland and Sibly, 1975; McNamara and Houston, 1986; Cabanac, 1992). The results of the above experiments show that sensory pleasure fulfilled the conditions required of a common motivational currency, at least in the case of the behaviours selected which have clear physiological implications.

From pleasure and comfort to joy and happiness

Let us now see another implication of the behavioural final common path and the common currency. In everyday life, physiological motivations must compete with other motivations, social, ludic, religious, etc. Since pleasure was the common currency allowing trade-offs

Table 4.1 Joy is to happiness what pleasure is to comfort

	Sensation	*Consciousness*
pleasant	pleasure	joy
indifferent	comfort	happiness

among various physiological motivations, the same currency must also allow comparison of all motivations in order to rank them by order of urgency. In turn, the transience of pleasure can be found also in other aspects of consciousness than sensation. Happiness is considered generally as the aim of life. Yet, the pursuit of happiness is fallacious if one does not know what happiness is. In the same way as there are two different elements in sensation: sensory pleasure (highly positive but transient), and comfort (indifferent but stable), it is possible to recognise two elements in the affectivity of global consciousness: positive and transient joy, and indifferent but stable happiness (Cabanac, 1986; 1995). Happiness is to joy what comfort is to pleasure (Table 4.1). This duality explains the disappointment expressed by many a writer and some philosophers when they deal with happiness. They use the word happiness to describe a pleasant experience which they expect to last and, when they see that it is only transient, erroneously conclude that happiness does not exist. They should have used the unambiguous word joy (for additional discussion on the nature of happiness, see Cabanac (1986; 1995)).

Thus the transience of pleasure can be found also with joy.

Optimisation of behaviour

The word optimality applied to behaviour can be ambiguous because it bears somewhat different meanings when used by ethologists, economists, or physiologists (Lea *et al.*, 1987, p. 627). Ethologists differentiate between goal and cost. Economists differentiate between utility and cost. The goal of a subject, as well as utility, is some entity that an optimal behaviour will tend to maximise, which may appear tautological to the physiologist. The cost is a characteristic of the environment that the optimal behaviour will tend to minimise. All would agree that an optimal behaviour gives the maximal net benefit (or fitness) to the behaving individual. Specialists diverge in their definition of benefit (or fitness). The benefit can be defined in terms of reproductive efficacity (Krebs and Davies, 1981, p.292) as well as financial profit and physiological function (McFarland, 1985, p. 576). We are concerned here with this last aspect: physiological benefit.

To the physiologist, a behaviour is optimal when it leads to homeostasis. Optimal behaviour could be recognised easily when subjects instructed to seek their most pleasurable skin temperature selected stimuli which, after data analysis, could be described by mathematical models identical to the models describing the autonomic responses (Cabanac *et al.*, 1972; Bleichert *et al.*, 1973; Marks and Gonzalez, 1974), or when the best performance coincides with minimal discomfort (Figure 4.6) One may wonder whether optimisation, as seen from the physiological point of view, was also achieved in the experiments quoted above where subjects maximised the algebraic sum of two modalities of sensory pleasure. Physiological criteria of optimisation showed that maximisation of pleasure was the key to optimal behaviour in the experimental conflicts of motivations studied.

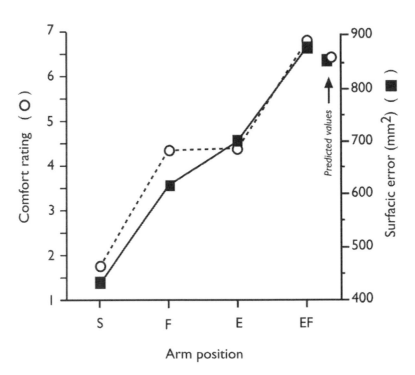

Figure 4.6 Increase in discomfort rate and of the error of performance observed over arm positions. In S, the subject adopted the most comfortable natural position; in F, the wrist was maximally flexed; in E, the arm was maximally extended vertically; and in EF the subject adopted both F and E.

Source: Rossetti et al. (1994).

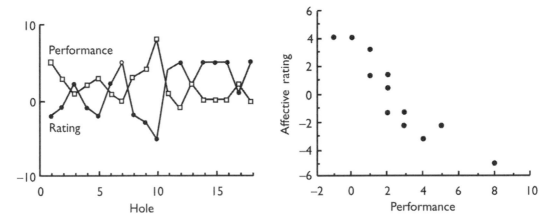

Figure 4.7 Results obtained in the golf video-game on the subject with the highest correlation between performance and affective experience. Left: performance and rating of affective experience plotted over the successive holes of the golf game. The amplitude of the rating scale was open and left to the subject's estimation; positive rating for pleasure and negative rating for displeasure. Right: rating of affective experience (dependent variable) plotted against performance (independent variable). It can be seen that when performance improved (lower scores) pleasure increased. This correlation was significant in 9 subjects out of 10. P = 0.1 in the last subject.

Source: Cabanac et al. (1997).

The hypothesis according to which pleasure would signal optimal mental activity as well was tested empirically (Figure 4.7). Ten subjects played video-golf on a Macintosh computer. After each hole they were invited to rate their pleasure or displeasure on a magnitude estimation scale. Their ratings of pleasure correlated negatively with the difference: par, minus their performance; i.e., the better the performance, the more pleasure reported. This result would indicate that pleasure is aroused by the same mechanisms, and follows the same laws in physiological and cognitive mental tasks and leads to the optimisation of performance.

Conclusion

Knowing that pleasure was an index of the physiological usefulness of a stimulus and of optimal function in a mental activity, the law of the common currency renders inevitable that joy is the index of a useful conscious event. The relationship of joy with usefulness may become non-univocal with the increased complexity of the mind process. It is obvious that among those events or behaviours that arouse joy, there are some for which we cannot foresee how useful they could be. The case of drug addiction comes immediately to mind. The answer to this argument is twofold. First, from a Darwinian point of view, it is not necessary that joy be useful on each mental event. To be passed on to future generations, it is sufficient that joy gives some advantage to the subjects who possess it. From this point of view, we can compare pleasure and joy to curiosity. On some occasions the outcome of curiosity may be noxious. Yet, everybody will agree that curiosity gives an evolutionary advantage to the subjects who possess it. Second, usefulness of sensory pleasure is mostly proximate, usefulness being judged from its immediate survival value. However, sensory pleasure can also be associated with long-term usefulness. Sexual pleasure is a powerful reward of reproductive behaviour. Its usefulness may be assigned to the species, rather than the individual. Similarly, joy can be the sign of an integrative behaviour, useful in the short term for the subject or in the long term for the species. The joy of love may have no immediate survival usefulness (arguably the opposite), but finds its usefulness in the resulting reproductive behaviour. Pleasure as an index of useful sensation can be innate or acquired. Similarly, one may easily accept that homologous joy can be acquired. The hormic joy associated with effort has to be taught and learnt.

Since no behaviour can escape the law of pleasure maximisation, one may question what remains of liberty in such a situation. Human liberty is often ill understood as the freedom to do anything. Actually it is to be understood as the freedom to choose one's own way to maximise pleasure and joy. Among the motivations sorted by Sulzer (1751) as sensory, intellectual, and moral, the last has always been considered by the philosophers as the most rewarding.

References

Attia, M. (1984) Thermal pleasantness and temperature regulation in man. *Neuroscience Biobehavioral Review*, 8: 335–343.

Attia, M. and Engel, P. (1981) Thermal alliesthesial response in man is independent of skin location stimulated. *Physiology and Behavior*. 27: 439–444.

Baerends G.P. (1956) Aufbau des tierischen Verhalten. In Kükenthal, W. and Krumbach, T. (eds) *Handbuch der Zoologie*. Berlin: De Gruyter & Co., Teil 10 (Lfg 7).

Bleichert, A., Behling, K., Scarperi, M. and Scarperi, S. (1973) Thermoregulatory behavior of man during rest and exercise. *Pflügers Archive*, 338: 303–312.

Bligh, J. and Johnson, K.G. (1973) Glossary of terms for thermal physiology. *Journal of Applied Physiology*, 35: 941–961.

Cabanac, M, (1971) Physiological role of pleasure. *Science*; 173: 1103–1107.

Cabanac, M. (1986) Du confort au bonheur. *Psychiatrie française*, 17: 9–15.

Cabanac, M. (1992) Pleasure: the common currency. *Journal of Theoretical Biology*, 155: 173–200.

Cabanac, M. (1995). *La quête du plaisir*. Montréal: Liber.

Cabanac, M., Massonnet, B. and Belaiche, R. (1972) Preferred hand temperature as a function of internal and mean skin temperatures. *Journal of Applied Physiology*, 33: 699–703.

Cabanac, M., Pouliot, C. and Everett, J. (1997) Pleasure as a sign of efficacy of mental activity. *European Psychologist*; 2: 226–234.

Fantino, M. (1984) Role of sensory input in the control of food intake. *Journal of the Autonomic Nervous System*, 10: 326–CC347.

Fantino, M. (1995) Nutriments et alliesthésie alimentaire. *Cahiers de Nutrition et de Diététique*, 30: 14–18.

Garcia, J. (1990) Learning without memory. *Journal of Cognitive Neuroscience*, 2: 287–305.

Garcia, J., Lasiter, P.S., Bermudez-Rattoni, F. and Deems, D.A. (1985) A general theory of aversion learning. *Annals of the New York Academy of Science*, 443: 8–21.

I.U.P.S. Commission for Thermal Biology (1987) Glossary of terms for thermal physiology. *Pflügers Archive*, 410: 567–587.

Krebs, J.R. and Davies, N.B. (1981) *An Introduction to Behavioural Ecology*. Sunderland, MA: Sinauer Associates.

Lea, S.E.G., Tarpy, R.M. and Webley, P. (1987) *The Individual in the Economy*. Cambridge: Cambridge University Press.

Marks, L.E. and Gonzalez, R.R. (1974) Skin temperature modifies the pleasantness of thermal stimuli. *Nature*; 247: 473–475.

McFarland, D.J. (1985) *Animal Behaviour*. London: Pitman.

McFarland, D.J. and Sibly, R.M. (1975) The behavioural final common path. *Philosophical Transactions of the Royal Society, London*; 270: 265–293.

McNamara, J.M. and Houston, A.I. (1986) The common currency for behavioural decisions. *American Naturalist*, 127: 358–378.

Pfaffmann, C. (1960) The pleasures of sensation. *Psychological Review*, 67: 253–268.

Rossetti, Y., Meckler, C. and Prablanc, C. (1994) Is there an optimal arm posture? Deterioration of finger localization precision and comfort sensation in extreme arm-joint postures. *Experimental Brain Research*, 99: 131–136.

Sulzer, M. (1751) Recherches sur l'origine des sentiments agréables et désagréables. *Mémoires de l'Académie de Royale Science belles Lettres Berlin*; 7: 57–100.

Tinbergen, N. (1950) The hierarchical organization of mechanisms underlying instinctive behaviour. *Symposium of the Society of Experimental Biology*, 4: 305–312.

Chapter 5

User-centred workspace design

Applications of environmental psychology to space for work

Jacqueline C. Vischer

As the complexity of work increases, the importance of the psychological and behavioural effects of environmental features in places designed for work has grown. This field, known as the environmental psychology of workspace or workspace psychology, has expanded rapidly since the 1980s and now forms a substantial body of knowledge, not only for researchers but also for organisations in terms of the design, operation and management of space for work. This chapter provides an overview of approaches to studying, understanding and applying workspace psychology to planning for worker comfort and productivity, cost effectiveness of accommodation, technology-supported mobile work, and rapid organisational change.

Space for work – or workspace – is increasingly diverse. Office planning was once based on simple division of workspace into large rooms containing rows of desks and a few private offices for managers and executives. Contemporary workspace includes a range of individual and shared spaces, communal areas and amenities, and access to sophisticated electronic tools (Gillen, 2006). Advances in tele-communications mean that people no longer need to be fixed in space and time to work together. Mobile work, work in public spaces such as airports and hotels, and non-territorial and 'drop-in' or convenience workspace are all increasing. Barriers between work and personal life are breaking down as people seek career opportunities rather than jobs, work different hours, make a social life at work, and sleep, eat and exercise in their employers' buildings. The meaning of workspace in all lines of work is changing and we are finding out more about the psychological impact of physical environments on work.

Companies are increasingly applying quality as well as cost criteria to workspace design (Becker and Kelley, 2004; Preiser and Vischer, 2015; Vischer and Malkoski, 2015). Workspace is no longer a backdrop – that is, a passive setting – for work. Environments are planned and designed to actively support workers' tasks (Nicolaou, 2006; Vischer 1996). Consequently, knowledge of how building occupants behave as a function of their physical environment is increasingly being applied to the creation of supportive, efficient and adaptable workspace. Research indicates that workspace design and management affect not only how people feel about their job, but also affect work performance, employee loyalty and engagement, and the value of human capital to the organisation.

The focus of this chapter, then, is on the behaviour of building occupants – meaning not only workers' actions and responses, but also their attitudes, feelings, expectations, values and beliefs towards their workspace. It is useful to think of the user-environment relation as dynamic and interactive: that is to say, the user's environmental experience includes the consequences of his or her behaviour in that environment. The user/occupant is not a passive receptacle experiencing the built environment statically, as input; her experience of the environment is itself transformed by the activities she is performing. The relationship is better characterised as transactional or negotiated (Gray and Daish, 1996; Moore, 1980; Vischer, 2008a).

Satisfaction and productivity

Studies aimed at analysing and understanding the relationship of users to their workspace have largely focused on two outcomes: user satisfaction and worker productivity. While acknowledging that both outcomes are difficult to measure, the implicit logic that features of workspace design can be evaluated in terms either of how much workers like them or of how much more work is produced because of them has been hard to displace. Typically, user satisfaction is measured through survey responses in the form of ratings of various environmental features, and effects on productivity are assessed either in the form of self-report ('are you more or less productive as a function of workspace features?') or pre- and post-measures of task performance.

The extent to which environmental characteristics affect users' satisfaction has guided research on the environmental psychology of office environments since the 1980s and often still does (Marans and Spreckelmeyer, 1981; Ornstein, 1999; Veitch *et al.*, 2007). Post-occupancy evaluation relies on survey questionnaires that ask building users to identify what they 'like' and 'dislike' about their work environment, on the assumption that users' self-reported satisfaction with individual features is a *de facto* measure of building quality. If users feel positive (satisfied), the workspace is successful, whereas if they are dissatisfied, the building (its design, management, work environment) is not performing or has somehow failed. Substantial knowledge of users' preferences has emerged from workspace satisfaction research. For example, user surveys consistently find that office workers are dissatisfied with 'open plan' workspace, whether this is due to noise levels, distractions, lack of privacy, or the sameness of 'cubicles' (Borzykowski, 2015; Churchman *et al.*, 1990; Hedge, 1986; Konnikova, 2014; Maher and von Hippel, 2005). However, the prevalence of this finding has not prevented employers from favouring some form of open plan – in part, because it is cheaper to construct and more flexible to reconfigure than a traditional partitioned office layout, and in part because more desks and more equipment can be fitted into open plan layouts. A more useful research question is the degree to which workers are supported in the performance of their tasks by different open plan layouts – in other words, to what degree is their ability to work affected? Studies show that, on the positive side, open workstations facilitate communication by enabling workers to exchange information rapidly and informally and support flexible work-group participation. On the negative side, the open environment can generate noise and distractions that prevent workers from concentrating on their tasks (Davis *et al.*, 2011). Moreover, the trend towards densification of workspace contributes towards distracting noise levels that many experience as a loss of privacy (Vischer, 2012).

Whether workers like or dislike workspace features pertains more closely to happiness research than to understanding how effectively the physical environment supports work (Kolbert, 2010; Stone and Mackie, 2013). More complex models of user-environment interaction – such as how well people can perform tasks, access needed tools, engage in appropriate communication, and identify territory – are needed to guide research into workplace performance, that is, the effectiveness of workspace whose explicit objective is to support the performance of work. A performing workplace is designed to optimise worker productivity (Clements-Croome, 2006). The concept of productivity is used for a wide range of desired behavioural outcomes (Haynes, 2007; Ouye, 2008). Many studies use respondents' self-reports of 'improved' or 'reduced' productivity because research measuring quantifiable output per worker or team is more complex to execute (Bordass and Leaman, 2004; Oseland, 2009).

Part of the difficulty of measuring the effects of workspace on worker productivity is confusion about definitions. There are at least three types of productivity that are influenced by environmental design, each of them in different ways. Each of the three categories – individual, group, and organisational productivity – denotes a variation in scale of environmental influence (Vischer, 2006). Individual productivity is typically evaluated at the scale of the individual workpoint, examining how the micro-environment – specifically the environmental conditions, such as lighting and visual conditions, variations in temperature and humidity, furniture ergonomics, and noise privacy – influences individual task performance in terms of effects on speed and error rates as well as on incidence of illness and absenteeism. The productivity of groups sharing workspace, such as a teamwork environment, is typically evaluated in terms of the quality and quantity of group processes, such as rate of innovations, number of creative ideas, and speed of decision-making. Teamwork is affected by the design and layout of the team workspace, including access and circulation, as well as by ambient conditions, such as noise. Group processes are affected by workgroup size and the relative proximity of team members. Other environmental determinants of workgroup effectiveness include the positioning of work areas and shared space, and access to shared tools and equipment (Heerwagen et al., 2004; Oseland et al., 2011).

A third level of productivity is assessed in terms of an organisation's accommodation, that is, its overall work environment, including appearance and location, workspace and amenities, communications tools and technology, and the ways these are used. Accommodation supports business objectives and increases competitive advantage to varying degrees. The organisation-accommodation (O-A) relationship evolves and changes over time as a function of cultural and business changes inside the organisation (Vischer, 1996). The quality of support that the organisation obtains from its accommodation can range from highly positive – actively supporting work – through neutral and poor, to highly negative. In a positive O-A relationship workers' tasks are supported, and in a negative O-A relationship workers' time and attention are lost dealing with adverse environmental conditions. The O-A relationship is dynamic and evolving as firms become attuned to the benefits of adjusting and updating workspace in response to changing business tools and processes. Locational advantages and ease of access, balancing consolidation under one roof (centralisation) with dispersion of different groups in different facilities over manageable distances, and amenities such as fast elevators, convenient bathrooms, adequate parking, and attractive eating areas all affect organisational effectiveness (van der Voordt, 2004; Vischer, 2006). Studies have shown that both worker performance and organisational success are compromised 'when the physical environment interferes with actions taken towards achievement [of objectives]' (McCoy and Evans, 2005).

Individual task performance is measured using tools for ergonomic analysis as well as questionnaire surveys that focus on the effects on workers of ambient conditions, such as lighting, noise levels, furniture comfort, temperature, and indoor air quality. Team effectiveness studies tend to be more dependent on indirect measures, such as social network analysis, gaming, and comparing outcomes among comparable workgroups in different environments (Horgen et al., 1999; Springer, 2011). Reviewing methods for evaluating organisational (O-A) effectiveness has led to the conclusion that none is entirely satisfactory, as this is an elusive concept to define and measure, although tools are available.

While evidence accumulates that workspace design influences workers' effectiveness, accounts of workspace change suggest that employees resist 'social engineering' solutions where employers envision a work environment aimed at eliciting maximum work performance (Vischer, 2011). Such an approach violates the socio-spatial contract, the implicit social contract between worker and employer that promises to provide a certain level of workspace quality in return for the worker's energy, effort and knowledge (Vischer, 2005a). Contract violations cause workers to feel devalued and increase resistance to workspace change. In many organisations, moving workers out of enclosed offices and into open workspace is a socio-spatial contract violation: the status, confidence and responsibility that the employer communicates through private enclosed workspace are called into question by allocating workspace that is the same as everyone else's.

Managers who consider supportive workspace to be an investment in their workforce need to use research evidence to guide their environmental design decisions. Evidence-based design causes workspace planning and design alternatives to be tested empirically, or evaluated in terms of published research results before a decision is made (Hamilton and Watkins, 2008; Vischer and Zeisel, 2008). Like information technology, workspace can and should be a tool for performing work. In order to design workspace as a tool for work, reliable information is needed on what workers do, how they perform tasks, and ways in which they are or are not helped by workspace elements. Such an approach applies to all three categories of productivity: individual task performance, teamwork effectiveness, and organisational accommodation.

Concept of workspace comfort

The connection between workspace satisfaction and productivity is functional comfort. The term comfort is frequently applied to interior conditions, especially to temperature and ventilation in commercial buildings. For example, temperature, air speed and relative humidity measure thermal comfort; air speed, circulation and freshness measure ventilation comfort; and brightness, contrast conditions and luminance measure lighting comfort. The results of comfort studies form the basis for comfort standards in buildings. The term adaptive comfort refers to the interactive nature of human comfort in terms of user control over environmental conditions (Nicol and Stevenson, 2013). Others point out that comfort is socially and culturally defined and the users' experience of workspace is in part a function of the organisational culture (Chappells, 2010; Cooper, 2009).

Functional comfort assesses the degree of support for their tasks that workers obtain from their physical environment. Measuring functional comfort offers more than feedback on worker satisfaction by capturing the impact of workspace features on work performance at the three productivity levels of individual tasks, team or collaborative work, and organisational effectiveness. In expanding functional to workspace comfort, the model recognises that, while assessing the degree to which the environment supports work provides useful diagnostic data on building performance, occupants' experiences are more complex and have multi-level effects (Vischer, 2008b). As shown in Figure 5.1, functional comfort is one of three constituents of workspace comfort. Physical comfort, defined in terms of meeting building codes and comfort standards, ensures that people feel healthy and safe in the buildings they occupy. Without physical comfort there can be neither functional nor psychological comfort. Both physical and functional comfort are affected by psychological comfort: people's sense of belonging, territory and environmental control, often expressed through the need for privacy.

The functional comfort approach has been applied to diagnosing workplace performance in numerous office buildings (Rioux et al., 2013; Vischer, 2005b; Vischer and Malkoski, 2015). Levels of functional comfort are diagnosed using reliable feedback from building occupants. A standardised survey questionnaire measures occupants' experience, thereby avoiding the temporal and calibration limitations of instrument-based data collection. However, instrumentation is often useful to help interpret users' responses. Occupants' ratings on a series of five-point

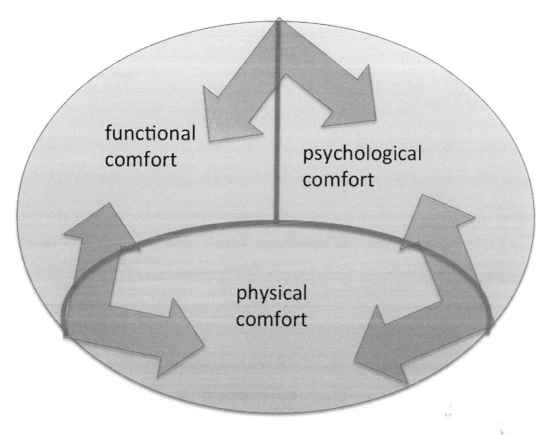

Figure 5.1 Tri-partite model of workspace comfort

scales assess how much or how little specific environmental features (for example, temperature, air quality, lighting, human and equipment noise levels, space for meetings, access to equipment) support their work. Data are analysed to provide a profile of functional comfort for a given work environment, the results providing a diagnostic yardstick for designers, planners and managers. A functionally comfortable workspace is a performing workplace, signifying to employers that they are receiving a return on their workspace investment. Sometimes relatively small changes can lead to important improvements in workers' functional comfort and therefore overall productivity; there is also evidence that functional comfort and psychological comfort have interactive effects.

Workspace diagnosed as functionally uncomfortable slows down work and increases worker fatigue, leading to workspace stress. In unsupportive environmental conditions, workers are employing their energy to solve environmental problems. Consequently, their effectiveness is compromised, energy for creative thinking and innovation is reduced, and the value of its human capital is not realised by the organisation (Vischer, 2007). The notion of environmental support for work means not just receiving support from, but also being able to act on, the environment to achieve a desired, supportive result. Stress occurs when elements of the physical environment interfere with the attainment of work objectives. Potential physical stressors that interfere with task performance, motivation and social relationships 'can influence physiological processes, produce negative affect, limit motivation and performance, and impede social interaction' (Evans and Cohen, 1987).

While workers' satisfaction ratings provide information on attitudes, measuring functional comfort yields a more useful diagnosis of workplace performance (Francescato *et al.*, 2017). Balancing environmental demands with the skills and abilities of users to act on their environment is a way of defining optimal workspace for creativity and flow (Csikszentmihalyi, 2003). The concepts of positive stress and of environmental competence recognise that some environmental challenge is necessary to ensure active engagement (Pedersen, 1999; Selye, 1979). Moreover, workspace cannot be designed to be a one-time, final, and permanent ergonomic support for all office tasks, but rather needs to be adaptable and negotiable to be most supportive to users. Users need the skills and opportunities to engage with and adjust their environment successfully, over time and with changing task requirements, in order to optimise comfort and manage workspace stress successfully.

Measuring levels of functional comfort in a building provides an indicator of both more stressful/least comfortable and of less stressful/more supportive environmental elements. Reliable occupant feedback shows that all workspace environments fall somewhere on the continuum ranging from functionally comfortable and supportive of work to dysfunctional and stressful.

Psychological comfort

Psychological comfort links psychosocial aspects of work with the environmental design and management of workspace through territoriality, privacy and environmental control (Augustin, 2009; Vischer, 2005a). Psychological comfort is a function of a sense of belonging (territorial appropriation), along with loyalty and commitment to the organisation, and environmental control, all of which are mediated by the socio-spatial contract and the behavioural expectations it implies.

The primary component of psychological comfort is sense of territory – both individual and group territory. Territory has psychological value, both as space for one's work and as symbolic of one's place in the organisation. Underlying these is a behavioural schema expressed in terms of the personalisation and appropriation of space: marking territory and constructing boundaries of social and environmental control. Workspace personalisation and space appropriation behaviours are more noticeable in offices where denser and more open office configurations have been installed (Wells and Thelen, 2002). The introduction and use of new technology and better communications tools also affect workers' perceptions of and attitude towards their physical environment and territory (Cascio, 2000; Lai *et al.*, 2002). Territorial boundaries are not simply physical elements that enclose space: territoriality signifies sense of privacy, social status and control. When people move out of private enclosed offices into open workstations, studies show they judge their environment more negatively, citing lack of privacy, acoustic conditions, and confidentiality problems (Brennan *et al.*, 2002; Rishi *et al.*, 2000). These reasons are given irrespective of whether or not their work is confidential, or of whether or not they need to be alone to perform tasks effectively. Complaints about lack of privacy abound in studies of workspace change, independent of physical characteristics such as furniture configuration and partition height (Haans, 2007; McElroy and Morrow, 2010). On the other hand, data collected from professionals in open workstations who were not faced with a territorial threat, such as an imminent move, indicated that the demands of the job are more important than individual privacy (Kupritz, 1998).

Environmental control affects workers on at least two levels: mechanical or instrumental control, and control over process, or empowerment. Experimental efforts to increase users' control over their environment provide evidence of beneficial psychological effects (Niemala *et al.*, 2002). Environmental control can be mechanical, such as chairs and worktables that are raised and lowered, shelving and tables on wheels, operable windows, switchable lights, and a door to open and close. Evidence indicates a positive psychological impact from mechanical control in situations where employees are informed and even trained to make use of the controls available (McCoy and Evans, 2005; Tu and Loftness, 1998). An important form of environmental control is the opportunity for personalisation (Chalmers, 2015). Behaviours such as placing symbolic objects, family photographs, plants and posters in individual and team workspace increase sense of belonging, loyalty and morale.

Opportunities for employees to participate in workspace decision-making increase empowerment and sense of environmental control, both directly linked to psychological comfort. Studies have shown that worker participation in the design process has a positive effect on people's response to and feelings about their workspace (Lee and Brand, 2005). People who are informed about workspace-related decisions and who participate in decisions about their own space are more likely to feel territorial about their workspace and to have feelings of belonging and ownership. This enables positive coping with environmental demands and encourages workers to find their own ways of solving environmental problems (Vischer, 2007).

Finally, research suggests a connection between workers' psychological traits and their reactions to the built environment at work. In focusing on cognitive processes, this line of inquiry addresses the effects of users' individual differences and how workers' evaluation of their workspace affects their perception of themselves at work (Elsbach, 2003). Not only do employees' cognitive and affective processes affect their perception of their work environment, but their perception and assessment of their workspace influence how they see themselves as workers and their professional effectiveness (Fischer *et al.*, 2004). Studies comparing open with enclosed office users indicate that extraverts respond more positively to more possibilities for communication, and therefore do better in open office settings than workers with more introvert personalities (McCusker, 2002).

Conclusion and directions for future research

While considerable knowledge has accrued from studying the environmental psychology of workspace, important gaps remain. Findings to date have given rise to new and important questions that are fruitful directions for future research. The future of this field of study aims to strengthen theoretical frameworks and lend greater coherence to existing knowledge.

The results of environmental satisfaction research offer a broad and comprehensive database of people's workspace preferences. However, satisfaction is not a practical outcome for measuring workplace performance. While occupants' ratings provide data on their likes and dislikes, satisfaction studies generate little information about environmental support for task performance, about adding value to business processes, or reasons why owners and managers should invest in workspace improvement. Measuring functional comfort provides diagnostic data on workspace support to individuals and teams. Results are applied to prioritising decisions about how and when to intervene to solve environmental problems and effect improvement through removing, replacing or changing workspace features. User feedback on ambient conditions can be used to diagnose building systems problems that are amenable to intervention and correction. Functionally comfortable workspace leads to better individual task performance and increased teamwork effectiveness, both of which improve organisational productivity.

Measuring productivity in terms of occupants' self-reports is prone to social influence and lack of clarity about what exactly is being measured. However, more objective productivity indicators such as reduced illness rates, increased speed and accuracy of task completion, and improved customer relations, are also used as measures of environmental effects on productivity. Moreover, characteristics of the work environment affect the creation and transmission of knowledge in organisations (Vischer, 2010; Von Krogh et al., 2000). Companies are interested in understanding how knowledge accrues in their organisations and how to distribute and share new knowledge. Workspace plays an important role in these processes. Worker productivity in the knowledge economy is less a matter of improving speed and accuracy of routine tasks and increasingly a function of generating new ideas, being creative, working effectively in teams, and generating knowledge that adds value to the organisation (Holman et al., 2003). The concept of 'ba' – conditions that support and encourage knowledge creation, not only through the design of space but also through the nature and operations of the social and cultural environment – offers researchers a new and promising direction for analysing how features of the work environment add value to an organisation's human capital (Nenonen, 2004).

Finally, psychological comfort – the feeling of belonging – is an important predictor of employee retention and reducing costly staff turnover. More extensive measurement of territorial behaviour and appropriation at work will yield more information about how and why environmental features affect employees' sense of privacy and support constructive appropriation behaviours. A better understanding of territoriality, privacy and environmental control will help organisations determine how and to what degree investment in environmental quality will affect both recruitment and retention of high-quality employees.

All three types of workspace comfort interact with the sustainability or the 'green' qualities of commercial buildings (Baird, 2010; Brown et al,. 2009; Leaman and Bordass, 2007). Workspace psychology looks, first, at the effects of sustainable building features, such as natural ventilation, water recycling and passive cooling technology on occupants and their work; and, second, at the behavioural changes anticipated from users as a result of sustainable design features in buildings where they work. Such behaviours might include turning off lights when leaving, dropping blinds on sunny windows to reduce heat gain, and using public transport to get to and from work. Some studies indicate a positive effect on psychological comfort where occupants are proud of working in sustainable buildings and feel empowered to make these kinds of decisions, while others show little evidence of more supportive workspace in sustainable buildings. Anecdotal evidence exists of buildings supplied with innovative sustainable design features that occupants have either not wanted or not been able to use. There is also evidence that giving occupants a more active role and responsibility for changing their behaviour in environmentally sustainable buildings is a necessary condition for their success.

The environmental psychology of workspace is a rich and diverse field of study that is growing fast. As human beings in all parts of the world spend increasing amounts of time at work, the effects of the physical environment on occupants' performance, health and morale urgently need to be understood. The knowledge yielded by workspace psychology research will inform employers' decisions as well as corporate investments in the work settings they create, and will assist and improve the building industry as designers, facilities managers, leasing agents and construction professionals draw on it. Business managers also need to understand more about how workspace affects their personnel as companies become more agile by making on-going changes to workspace and even dispersing co-workers to more than one geographic locale (Beard, 2012; Harrison et al., 2004). Finally, all indications are that a better understanding of occupant comfort is a prerequisite for successful sustainability and an effective impact on climate change.

References

Augustin, S. (2009) *Place Advantage: Applied Psychology for Interior Architecture*. New York: John Wiley & Sons, Inc.
Baird, G. (2010) *Sustainable Buildings in Practice: What the Users Think*. London: Routledge.
Beard, C. (2012) Spatial ecology learning and working environments that change people and organizations. In Alexander, K. and Price, I. (eds) *Managing Organizational Ecologies: Space, Management and Organization*. London: Routledge.
Becker, F. and Kelley, T. (2004) *Offices at Work: Uncommon Workspace Strategies that Add Value and Improve Performance*. San Francisco: Jossey-Bass.
Bordass, B. and Leaman, A. (2004) Post-occupancy evaluation. In Preiser, W.F.E. and Vischer, J.C. (eds) *Assessing Building Performance*. London: Routledge, pp. 72–78.
Borzykowski, B. (2015) Available at: www.bbc.com/capital/story/20150804-cant-focus-blame-your-desk (accessed 17 October 2015).
Brennan, A., Chugh, J.S. and Kline, T. (2002) Traditional versus open office design: a longitudinal study. *Environment and Behavior*, 34(3): 279–299.
Brown, Z., Dowlatabadi, H. and Cole, R. (2009) Feedback and adaptive behavior in green buildings. *Intelligent Buildings International*, 1: 296–315.
Cascio, W. (2000) Virtual workplaces: implications for organizational behavior. In Cooper, C. and Rousseau, D. (eds) *Trends in Organizational Behavior*, vol. 6. *The Virtual Organization*. New York: Wiley.
Chalmers, L. (2015) Women's spatial practices in the routine office, Winnipeg 1960–1990. PhD dissertation. Ryerson and York Universities, Toronto.
Chappells, H. (2010) Comfort, well-being and the socio-technical dynamics of everyday life. *Intelligent Buildings International*, 2: 286–298.
Churchman, A., Stokols, D., Scharf, A., Nishimoto, K. and Wright, R. (1990) Effects of physical environmental conditions in offices on employee stress and well being. Paper presented at 22nd International Congress of Applied Psychology, Kyoto, Japan.
Clements-Croome, D. (ed.) (2006) *Creating the Productive Workplace*, 2nd edn. London: Routledge.
Cooper, I. (2009) Comfort in a brave new world. *Building Research & Information*, 37(1): 95–100.
Csikszentmihalyi, M. (2003) *Good Business: Leadership, Flow, and the Making of Meaning*. New York: Viking.
Davis, M., Leach, D. and Clegg, C. (2011) The physical environment of the office: contemporary and emerging issues. In Hodgkinson, G.P. and Ford, J.K. (eds) *International Review of Industrial and Organizational Psychology*, vol. 24. Chichester: John Wiley & Sons, Ltd.
Elsbach, K.D. (2003) Relating physical environment to self-categorizations: identity threat and affirmation in a non-territorial office space. *Administrative Science Quarterly*, 48(4): 622–654.
Evans, G.W. and Cohen, S. (1987). Environmental stress. In Stokols, D. and Altman, I. (eds) *Handbook of Environmental Psychology*, vol. 1. New York: John Wiley & Sons, Inc., pp. 571–610.
Fischer, G-N., Tarquinio, C., and Vischer, J.C. (2004) Effects of the self schema on perception of space at work. *Journal of Environmental Psychology*, 24(1): 131–140.
Francescato, G., Weidemann, S. and Anderson, J.R. (2017) Evaluating the built environment from the users' perspective: implications of attitudinal models of satisfaction. In Preiser, W., Hardy, A. and Schramm, U. (eds) *Building Performance Evaluation: From Delivery Process to Life Cycle Phases*. New York: Springer.
Gillen, N.M. (2006) The future workplace, opportunities, realities and myths: A practical approach to creating meaningful environments. In Worthington, J. (ed.) *Reinventing the Workplace*, 2nd edn. Oxford: Architectural Press, pp. 61–78.
Gray, J. and Daish, J. (1996) *User Participation in Building Design and Management: A Generic Approach to Building Evaluation*. London: Architectural Press.

Haans, A., Kaiser, F.G. and de Kort, Y.A.W. (2007) Privacy needs in office environments: development of two behavior-based scales. *European Psychologist*, 12: 93–102.

Hamilton, D. and Watkins, D. (2008) *Evidence-based Design for Multiple Building Types* New York: John Wiley and Sons, Inc.

Harrison, A., Wheeler, P. and Whitehead, C. (2004) *The Distributed Workplace*. London: Spon Press.

Haynes, B. (2007) An evaluation of office productivity measurement. *Journal of Corporate Real Estate*, 9(3): 144–155.

Hedge, A. (1986) Open versus enclosed workspace: the impact of design on employee reactions to their offices. In Wineman, J.D. (ed.) *Behavioural Issues in Office Design*. New York: Van Nostrand Reinhold.

Heerwagen, J., Kampschroer, K., Powell, K. and Loftness, V. (2004) Collaborative knowledge work environments. *Building Research and Information*, 32(6): 510–528.

Holman, D., Wall, T.D., Clegg, C.W., Sparrow, P. and Howard, A. (eds) (2003) *The New Workplace: A Guide to the Human Impact of Modern Working Practices*. New York: John Wiley & Sons, Inc.

Horgen, T., Joroff, M., Porter, W. and Schon, D. (1999) *Excellence by Design*. New York: John Wiley & Sons, Inc.

Kolbert, E. (2010) Everybody have fun: What can policymakers learn from happiness research? *New Yorker*, March 22, pp. 72–74.

Konnikova, M. (2014) The open office trap. *New Yorker* blog, 7 January.

Kupritz, V.W. (1998) Privacy in the workplace: the impact of building design. *Journal of Environmental Psychology*, 18: 341–356.

Lai, J., Levas, A., Chou, P., Pinhanez, C. and Viveros, M. (2002) Bluespace: personalizing workspace through awareness and adaptability. *International Journal of Human-Computer Studies*, 57(5): 415–428.

Leaman, A. and Bordass, B. (2007) Are users more tolerant of green buildings? *Building Research and Information*, 35(6): 662–673.

Lee, S.Y. and Brand, J. (2005) Effects of control over office workspace on perceptions of the work environment and work outcomes. *Journal of Environmental Psychology*, 25(3): 323–333.

Maher, A. and Von Hippel, C. (2005). Individual differences in employee reactions to open-plan offices. *Journal of Environmental Psychology*, 25(2): 219–229.

Marans, R. and Spreckelmeyer, K. (1981) *Evaluating Built Environments: A Behavioral Approach*. Ann Arbor, MI: University of Michigan, Institute for Social Research and Architectural Research Laboratory.

McCoy, J.M. and Evans, G.W. (2005) Physical work environment. In Barling, J., Kelloway, E.K. and Frone, M.R. (eds) *Handbook of Work Stress*. Thousand Oaks, CA: Sage, pp. 219–245.

McCusker, J.A. (2002) Individuals and open space office design: The relationship between personality and satisfaction in an open space work environment. Dissertation Abstracts International: Section B Sciences and Engineering, 63(2-B), August.

McElroy, J.C. and Morrow, P.C. (2010) Employee reactions to office redesign: a naturally occurring quasi-field experiment in multi-generational setting. *Human Relations*, 63(5): 169–191.

Moore, G.T. (1980) Holism, environmentalism and the systems approach. *Man-Environment Systems*, 10(1): 11–21.

Nenonen, S. (2004) Analysing the intangible benefits of work space. *Facilities*, 22(9–10): 233–239.

Nicol, F. and Stevenson, F. (2013) Adaptive comfort in an unpredictable world. *Building Research and Information*, 41(3): 255–258.

Nicolaou, L. (2006) Emerging building forms and accommodation solutions: new building typologies for distinctive place-making. In Worthington, J. (ed.) *Reinventing the Workplace*, 2nd edn. Oxford: Architectural Press, pp. 205–219.

Niemala, R., Rautio, S., Hannula, M. and Reijula, K. (2002) Work environment effects on labor productivity: an intervention study in a storage building. *American Journal of Industrial Medicine*, 42(4): 328–335.

Nonaka, I. and Toyama, R. (2007) Why do firms differ? The theory of the knowledge creating firm. In Ichijo, K.I. and Nonaka, I. (eds) *Knowledge Creation and Management*. Oxford: Oxford University Press, pp. 13–31.

Ornstein, S.W. (1999) A post-occupancy evaluation of workplaces in São Paolo, Brazil. *Environment and Behavior*, 31(4): 435–462.

Oseland, N. (2009) Enhancing interaction. *Facilities Management*, November: 22–23.

Oseland, N., Marmot, A., Swaffer, F. and Ceneda, S. (2011) Environments for successful interaction. *Facilities*, 29(1–2): 50–62.

Ouye, J.A. (2008) In search of measuring workplace productivity. Paper presented at the ProWork Seminar, May 2008, Helsinki, Finland. New Ways of Working Network.

Pedersen, D. (1999) Dimensions of environmental competence. *Journal of Environmental Psychology*, 19(3): 303–308.

Preiser, W.F.E. and Vischer, J.C. (eds) (2015) *Assessing Building Performance*, 2nd edn. New York: Routledge.

Rioux, L., Rubens, L., Le Roy, J. and Le Comte, J. (eds) (2013) *Le confort au travail*. Quebec: Presses de l'Université Laval.

Rishi, P., Sinha, S.P. and Dubey, R. (2000) A correlational study of workplace characteristics and work satisfaction among Indian bank employees. *Psychologia*, 43(3): 155–164.

Selye, H. (1979) The stress concept and some of its implications. In Hamilton, V. and Warburton, D.M. (eds) *Human Stress and Cognition: An Information-Processing Approach*. London: Wiley, pp. 11–32.

Springer, T. (2011) Measuring work and work performance. New Ways of Working White Paper. February.

Stegmeier, D. (2008) *Innovations in Office Design: The Critical Influence Approach to Effective Work Environments*. New York: John Wiley & Sons, Inc.

Stone, A. and Mackie, C. (2013) *Subjective Self-Being: Measuring Happiness, Suffering, and Other Dimensions of Experience*. New York: National Academies Press.

Sundstrom, E., McIntyre, M., Halfhill, T. and Richards, H. (2000) Work groups: From the Hawthorne studies to work teams of the 1990s and beyond. *Group Dynamics: Theory, Research, and Practice*, 4(1): 44–67.

Tu, K.J. and Loftness, V. (1998). The effects of organizational workplace dynamics and building infrastructure flexibility on environmental and technical quality in offices. *Journal of Corporate Real Estate*, 1(1): 46–63.

Van der Voordt, T. (2004) Productivity and employee satisfaction in flexible workplaces. *Journal of Corporate Real Estate*, 6(2): 133–148.

Veitch, J., Charles, K., Farley, K. and Newsham, G. (2007) A model of satisfaction with open-plan office conditions: COPE field findings. *Journal of Environmental Psychology*, 27(3): 177–189.

Vischer, J.C. (1989) *Environmental Psychology in Offices*. New York: Van Nostrand Reinhold.

Vischer, J.C. (1996) *Workspace Strategies: Environment as a Tool for Work*. New York: Chapman and Hall.

Vischer, J.C. (2005a) *Space Meets Status: Designing Performing Workspace*. London: Routledge.

Vischer, J.C. (2005b) Measuring the impact of moving on building users: can new workspace change organisational culture? *Ecolibrium*, September: 22–27.

Vischer, J.C. (2006) The concept of workplace performance and its value to managers. *California Management Review*, 49(2): 62–79.

Vischer, J.C. (2007). The effects of the physical environmental on work performance: towards a model of workspace stress. *Stress and Health*, 23(3): 175–184.

Vischer, J.C. (2008a) Towards a psychology of the work environment: comfort, satisfaction and performance. In Grech, C. and Walters, D. (eds) *Future Office*. London: Routledge, pp. 25–32.

Vischer, J.C. (2008b) Towards an environmental psychology of workspace: how people are affected by environments for work. *Architectural Science Review*, 51(2): 97–108.

Vischer, J.C. (2009) Applying knowledge on building performance: from evidence to intelligence. *Intelligent Buildings International*, 1: 239–248.

Vischer, J.C. (2010) Human capital and the organisational environment. In Burton-Jones, A. and Spender, J.C. (eds) *Oxford Handbook of Human Capital*. Oxford: Oxford University Press, pp. 477–498.

Vischer, J.C. (2011) User empowerment in workspace change. In Finch, E. (ed.) *Facilities Change Management*. London: Wiley-Blackwell.

Vischer, J.C. (2012) The changing meaning of workspace: planning space and technology in the work environment. In Mallory-Hill, S., Preiser, W. and Watson, C. (eds) *Enhancing Building Performance*. London: Wiley-Blackwell, pp. 89–98.

Vischer, J.C. and Fischer, G.-N. (2005) Issues in user evaluation of the work environment: recent research, *Le Travail Humain*, 68(1): 73–96.

Vischer, J.C. and Malkoski, K. (2015) *The Power of Workspace for People and Business*. Melbourne, Australia: Schiavello.

Vischer, J.C. and Zeisel, J. (2008) Bridging the gap between research and design. *World Health Design*, July: 57–61.

Von Krogh, G., Nonaka, I. and Nishiguchi, T. (eds) (2000) *Knowledge Creation: A Source of Value*. New York: St. Martins Press.

Wells, M. and Thelen, L. (2002) What does your workspace say about you? The influence of personality, status and workspace on personalization. *Environment and Behavior*, 34(3): 300–321.

Chapter 6

Change makers
Rethinking the productive workplace through an art and design lens

Jeremy Myerson

Introduction

Making the workplace more productive is most commonly addressed from a technical perspective. We typically place our faith in science, technology, engineering and mathematics to create the offices in which we think we can work most effectively. And we do it for a reason – a logical, rational approach yields the metrics and data on which design decisions can be justified to others. Nobody would deny that reasonable air quality, proper illumination or efficient spatial organisation – all factors which impact on productivity – depend to a considerable extent on competent scientific calculation. But this rigid technocratic approach often misses a vital point: the human beings who work in offices aren't nearly as rational and logical as the data on which their workplaces are constructed. In fact, they often behave in ways that defy the logic of technical systems altogether.

In the rush to develop standards and metrics around every aspect of the workplace, we tend to overlook those factors which cannot be so easily quantified in a neat table of data. Often denigrated as 'soft' factors (as opposed to the hard stuff that the real workplace scientists and engineers grapple with daily), these nevertheless play right to the core of the human condition in their exploration of such things as behaviour, experience or well-being. And they impact significantly on productivity despite the ambiguity or fuzziness that surrounds them. Take lighting as an example: most building codes specify a quantity of light but fail to note *quality* of light, its aesthetic effect, its impact on mood and ultimately on how people work.

Designers and artists operate in this more ambiguous terrain more comfortably than engineers or scientists; they are trained to handle ambiguity better and their expertise lends itself more easily to experimental and experiential thinking around the workplace. Furthermore, the practical emphasis in design on ethnographic research, sketching, making and prototyping is a bonus when it comes to fitting people to workspace. At least that was the belief when I set up a research lab for workplace futures in the Helen Hamlyn Centre of Design at the Royal College of Art in 1999. This chapter is an experiment in itself – an attempt to rethink key aspects of the productive workplace through an art and design lens, by retracing my steps through a series of the projects that revealed new ideas and insights about how people really want to work.

Over more than 15 years, under my direction, the Helen Hamlyn Centre of Design conducted more than 40 collaborative projects with industry partners in the workplace field, as well as leading major research studies funded by the UK Research Councils. What I discovered from analysis of this body of practice-based research were both the strengths and weaknesses of our approach. From an art and design perspective, we certainly reached those parts that other disciplines couldn't reach in terms of understanding and measuring human interaction and experience at work; however, the qualitative outputs that resulted from our creative enquiry sometimes struggled to convince decision-makers in business, for whom the small datasets and specific contexts (a by-product of the design-led approach) were less than compelling.

Four areas emerged from my analysis of the Helen Hamlyn Centre of Design portfolio as essential contributions of design research to the productive workplace. The ability to influence behaviour, enhance experience, explore sensation and affect well-being are not exclusive to an art and design approach, but these are core themes on which design researchers can hang their hat, and for which their skills and aptitudes are especially well suited.

Influencing behaviour

When we started the Helen Hamlyn Centre of Design in 1999, two big themes were on the millennial horizon. The first was the rise of home working, which briefly threatened a rethink of office property strategy; the second was the rise of open plan working, as the walls came tumbling down in offices. Both trends involved significant behavioural change. Could a design-led research approach identify and influence behaviours? Our first public event as a research centre in 1999 was called Work At Home, a symposium on home working preceded by an ethnographic study of home workers (Myerson, 1999). This study identified four models based on the 'borders' that people construct to protect and enable work within the home. Two were successful models of working at home; two were unsuccessful.

The first we called the Contained Work model, where the borders constructed around work are solid, allowing little that doesn't belong to pass in or out, and clearly defining the parameters of work within the home. Spatial borders are marked; temporal borders are defined; time plans and schedules are adhered to. Psychologically, the distinction between home and work is clear in the worker's mind. Sitting at the opposite end of an axis in terms of the degree of separation of work from home was the Permeable Work model. Here the borders are constructed to allow a planned integration of work and home activities and easy two-directional access. Work is often not confined to the workspace; domestic and work activities are intertwined or run in parallel.

The other two models demonstrated conditions where borders were not successfully constructed or maintained. In the Overflowing Work model, work has burst its banks and flooded the home. The work is not contained by spatial or temporal borders, it cannot be shut or folded away, the worker is constantly investing more and more time in the work and neglecting other basic functions of home life. Its counterpart is the Imploding Work model where resources are drained or channelled away from work, and less and less work is achieved. Workspace shrinks – psychologically and practically; plans disintegrate; motivation and discipline weaken in the face of competing demands and constant interruptions and diversions (visitors, babies, builders, depression).

These four models were fleshed out with scenarios, sketch designs and prototypes to show how borders might be erected and maintained between work and home. A follow-on study by Yuko Tsurumaru (2000) collaborated with the National Group on Homeworking and the Design Council to observe six households around the UK and prototype low-tech products – from workstools to tabletop organisers – that would aid certain types of industrial homeworking, such as electronic assembly or sewing. By working backwards from behavioural insights derived from interviews, observations and design interventions, we developed a whole new way to look at the subject of home working. The idea of 'borders' became a governing design principle that influenced behaviours in the home.

Open plan working challenged design research in different ways. The chief problem identi-fied here was a lack of privacy perceived by office workers whose walls were removed. A study called Head Space by Tim Parsons (Parson, 2001) looked at ways to create greater psychologi-cal privacy for people in large open plan offices, using a range of artefacts on and around the desk as research tools to encourage new social rituals at work. A research rationale was devel-oped that directed the project towards the provision of greater psychological privacy over the erecting of purely physical boundaries (booths, cabins, caves, screened-off areas, and so on).

Through a series of observations in bustling media offices, Parsons discovered that ter-ritorial and physical elements to aid concentration and privacy tend to be ineffective and irrelevant if the mind is unsettled and unfocused on the job in hand. He created a series of cultural experiments to give people greater psychological privacy without the need to create private enclaves or even give workers any more personal space. Prototypes were placed in a range of offices for testing. One object was an 'Umbrella Chair', which featured an umbrella in the backrest that could be opened to provide an acoustic shield and act as a sign saying 'do not disturb me' (Figure 6.1). Another positioned a 'desk post box' on the edge of a worker's personal domain to avoid mail and document deliveries from colleagues interrupting the flow of concentration.

Figure 6.1 The Umbrella Chair designed by Tim Parsons as a cultural probe to test psychological privacy in open plan space (2001)

Some interventions were more successful than others, but the use of creative probes and artefacts to map and guide user behaviour in the workplace represented a novel addition to the research landscape. As the knowledge economy gathered pace, subsequent Helen Hamlyn Centre for Design projects extended the design research repertoire in the behavioural arena. In Space for Thought (Greene and Myerson, 2009), researcher Catherine Greene used a novel drawing exercise as part of a series of interviews with 20 knowledge workers in order to understand their different workspace needs. In each interview a simple graphic research tool was introduced to engage participants in thinking about how they used the office building. Each participant was presented with a grey box on a piece of paper, the box representing the office building, and they were invited to describe their mobility in relation to the office by drawing their movements in and around the box. This drawing technique proved effective in encouraging participants to describe their working patterns and habits in ways that would be hard to capture in words.

The study identified four key typologies of knowledge worker (Figure 6.2). Each of these typologies interacts with the office in a different way: the 'Anchor' is desk-based, almost always in one spot; the 'Connector' moves around within the building; the 'Gatherer' makes journeys away from the office but always returns; and the 'Navigator' is rarely in the office at all, working for the organisation at arm's length. What we learnt was that for the Anchor, comfort remains the most important issue; for the Connector, more adaptable types of furniture are needed; the Gatherer wants more choice and control of his or her environment; and the Navigator requires a more welcoming alternative to the standard hot-desk provided on the occasions they visit the building.

Similar design methods were used when the research team was commissioned by Johnson Controls to find new ways for companies to better support employees in making more sustainable choices at work. The Sustainable Cultures study (2012) held interviews and workshops in three multinational companies from three different industry sectors (consumer goods, financial services and real estate) (Crumbleholme et al., 2014). From the outset, it was clear that people

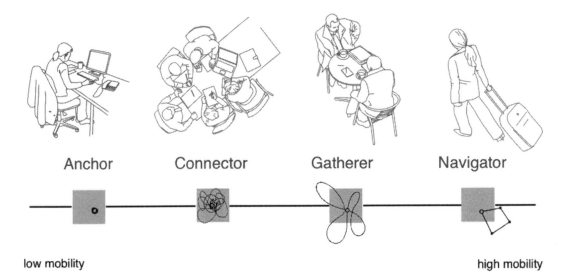

low mobility   high mobility

Figure 6.2 Four typologies of knowledge worker created by Catherine Greene, Space for Thought
Source: Greene and Myerson (2009).

had a wide variety of views on what sustainability in the workplace should mean. These were based on people's perceptions of the various costs and benefits to both company and employee of being sustainable.

The research team identified four different workplace behaviours towards sustainability. The Housekeeper culture puts the responsibility of sustainability on the employee without the company bearing any costs itself – its attitude is 'waste not, want not' to cut down on the use of resources. The Pragmatist believes that sustainability should not entail any cost to the employee or the company – its motto is 'it has to work for everyone'. The Libertarian believes sustainability is the responsibility of the company and not employees – its message is 'free will should prevail'. The fourth cultural model, the Campaigner, advocates that both the company and employees should shoulder the burden – 'we all need to take urgent action'.

This framework of four cultures was developed into an online toolkit for company managers responsible for sustainability, facilities and communications. The toolkit presents examples of how different initiatives – for example, saving energy – might be tailored to Pragmatist, Housekeeper, Libertarian and Campaigner cultures, providing practical guidelines on how to roll out a campaign to change behaviour at work.

Enhancing experience

As well as mapping behaviours at work, our exploration of the productive workplace from an art and design angle looked closely at experience. In recent times, it has become more apparent that the single-minded pursuit of management efficiency in modern office design has tended to overlook the importance of individual psychological comfort at work. As a result, many workplace environments are designed as psychologically impoverished 'lean' spaces, which do nothing to enhance the company culture. When more psychologically enriched settings are attempted, these are often highly customised and expensive one-offs that are difficult to build and replicate.

In a project called Living Stages (Privett and Jarvis, 2013), architect and researcher Imogen Privett looked at how theatre design could provide an inexpensive blueprint to create more expressive and effective office environments for people, using a simple 'kit of parts' approach. Drawing on the idea of 'maximum effect through minimal means', the project began with archival research into the pioneers of Modernist stage design, among them Edward Gordon Craig and Adolphe Appia. A set of six scenographic techniques used to create mood and atmosphere was identified, based on the application of light and shadow, projection, screens, levels, colour and vista. These fundamental techniques were then developed into a 'vocabulary' of effects that could be adapted to the office environment to investigate how we might be able to create emotional landscapes at work to respond to people's psychological needs (Figure 6.3).

The project described a modular set of stage componentry akin to systems furniture, designed to enhance certain cultures of performance at work by changing mood, ambience and layout in any given setting. Through the study we came to a key way of thinking about the workplace as a combination of *process* and *experience* – what we do and how we feel. Much workplace design tends to focus on one at the expense of the other. Some offices, for example, support working processes and practices efficiently but fail to create a positive, welcoming experience; others generate a great ambience or look visually arresting but are incoherent in terms of enabling work process.

We were interested in having the best of both worlds, and Privett followed up her workspace project on learning from theatre design with a study looking at how the design of certain types of urban public space might have lessons for designing better group experiences at work. Living

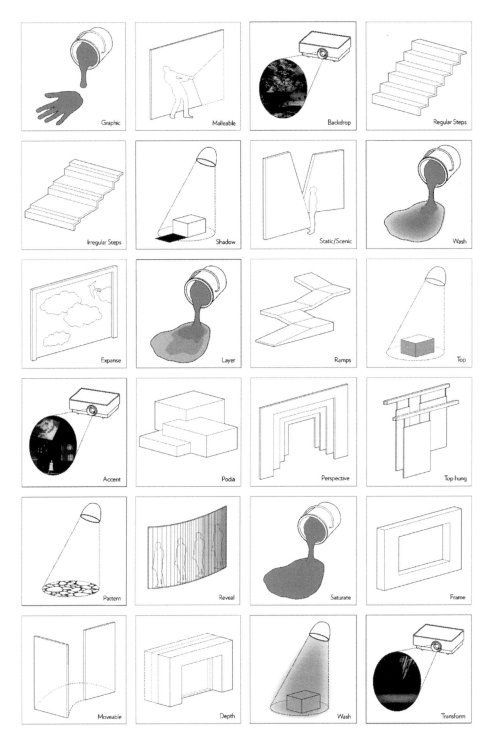

Figure 6.3 Vocabulary of stage techniques adapted for use in office design by Imogen Privett, Living Stages
Source: Privett and Jarvis (2013).

Cities (Privett, 2013) investigated how adaptable and imaginative temporary urban events, such as markets, festivals or pop-ups might inform the development of a more agile and flexible office landscape. The study articulated a series of key design elements to enhance social interaction and communication at work. Its formula for improving collective experiences became part of a book (Myerson and Privett, 2014) that analysed the whole issue of balance between experience and process in the workplace.

Living Cities was not our only foray into the city realm to look for ways to improve the human experience of the workplace. In Workscapes (Koslowski, 2012), architectural researcher Benjamin Koslowski created a design framework based on four urban planning principles to show how workspace could be reprogrammed to be more socially dynamic and interactive by addressing programmable surfaces, circulation, large objects and points of interaction. Koslowski's work drew heavily on two schemes for Parc de la Villette in Paris in the 1980s and on the theories of American urban planner Kevin Lynch, author of *Images of the City* (1960). The focus was especially on making the experience of work environments more understandable and legible, encouraging greater movement and interaction (Figure 6.4). Workscapes was subsequently developed into a planning toolkit in partnership with Herman Miller.

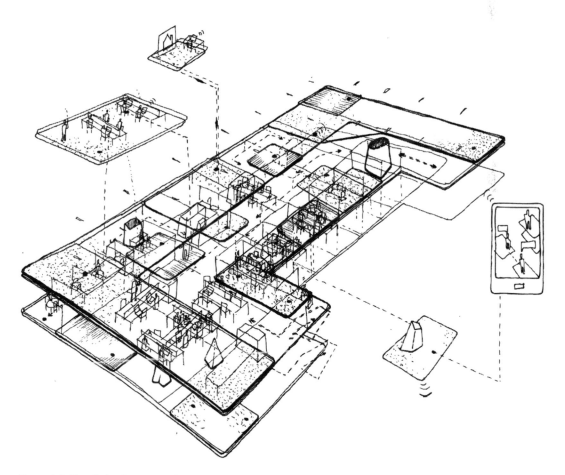

Figure 6.4 Sketch by Benjamin Koslowski explores urban planning principles of programmable surfaces and wayfinding objects in office space (Workscapes 2012)

Exploring sensation

Many work experiences are of a sensory nature and a natural extension of our research in this area explored the creation or evaluation of different sensations at work. In *Light Volumes, Dark Matters* (2010), Claudia Dutson questioned why levels of artificial light in commercial interiors such as offices and showrooms are increasing, and examined the impact of high levels of light on the people who have to work under them. In challenging a mechanical interpretation of productivity that is directly linked to the brightness of light in a space, she used a series of design research tools to build an alternative, more sustainable case for how workspaces should be lit. These included a linguistics exercise (Figure 6.5) to show the self-defeating nature of providing excessive levels of artificial light, which have a damaging effect on the health and well-being of employees as well as on the environment through greater energy consumption. Through use of such novel research tools, Dutson opened a widespread debate on the applicability and usefulness of current lighting codes.

In another lighting study, industrial designer Tom Jarvis (Privett and Jarvis, 2013) built on Imogen Privett's work in Living Stages, which had defined a vocabulary of low-cost stage techniques to create mood and atmosphere in the workplace. Jarvis designed one practical application of the research – a top-hung, illuminated screen system to support private concentration and informal collaboration in the open plan office by creating an enclosure of illuminated surfaces. Jarvis tested a lightweight system capable of hanging from a suspended ceiling in three UK offices to investigate the psychological requirements of office workers in situations where they are required to concentrate or collaborate (Figure 6.6). Data was collected from more than 60 office workers in relation to screen variables such as translucency (low to high), colour (calm to vivid), illumination (soft to intense) and arrangement (open to closed), in order

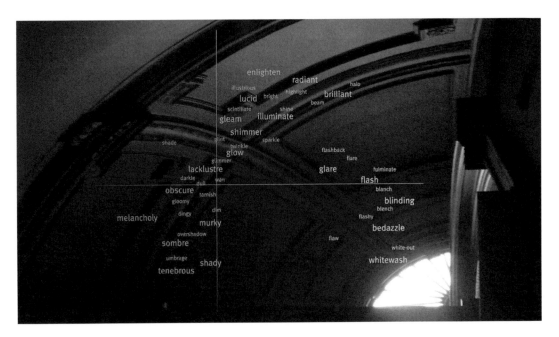

Figure 6.5 Linguistics exercise by Claudia Dutson explores the meanings of light across a spectrum of intensity
Source: Dutson (2010).

Figure 6.6 Designer Tom Jarvis (left) supervises a user research session in his prototype illuminated enclosure, Haworth, London (2013)

to define the precise specifications of the new system. Full-size prototyping of this type – a characteristic of design research – is useful for understanding sensory preferences in the workplace.

Sensory experience was also central to work by Harriet Harriss and Suzi Winstanley in *Capture It* (2005), a study that looked at the future workplace for the multi-generational knowledge worker. In carrying out design-based ethnographic research with individuals and organisations in the UK and Japan, the researchers devised a series of sensory probes to gather data – these included a Japanese-inspired 'Knowledge Blossom' installation that gave workers an opportunity to tie their thoughts to a physical 'tree' in the office. Their study identified a need among older workers for more reflective and contemplative spaces that feel closer to nature, with softer, more tactile surfaces in natural materials replacing harsh grey, steel and glass – the brusque masculinity of the corporate environment. *Capture It* also provided insights more generally into the well-being needs of a multi-generational workforce and prefigured later research on workplace demographics and well-being at the RCA.

Affecting well-being

The fourth major theme of our design research for the workplace relates to affecting well-being. Our first venture into this area was with The Heart-Friendly Office (2002), a project led by Mike Bond and Martin Coyne, which looked at ways in which workplace designers could help reduce levels of heart disease in the UK. Linked to the British Heart Foundation's workplace health programme, this project provided a bridge between medical factors (high cholesterol, high blood pressure, obesity, and so on) and design factors (such as local environmental controls, catering provision, and spatial adjacencies). It resulted in a communication campaign to encourage architects and developers to do more to create a healthier workplace.

Given the Helen Hamlyn Centre for Design's general focus on design for ageing populations, we swiftly developed the well-being theme to apply to older people facing extended working lives. Against a background of a shortfall in pension funds, newly introduced age discrimination legislation and growing management interest in retaining experience and knowledge in the workforce, Jeremy Gay's Work Well project (Gay, 2005) developed a series of inclusive design principles and furniture proposals to support older people at work. Concepts ranged from health-monitoring chairs and seating that encourages exercise to modular micro-stations for work on the move (Figure 6.7). Each proposal was designed to affect well-being.

Figure 6.7 Seating design to encourage exercise at work, Jeremy Gay, Work Well (2005)

Work Well's body of research was followed up by Welcoming Workplace (Myerson and Bichard, 2009), which was funded by two UK Research Councils as part of the Designing for the 21st Century initiative. This much larger study looked at ways to rethink office design so that growing numbers of older people could participate in the knowledge economy, and it became our largest research engagement with the productive workplace. We studied around 80 office workers aged over 50 in three knowledge-intensive industries: pharmaceuticals, technology and financial services. Working with academic partners in Japan (the University of Kyushu) and Australia (the University of Melbourne), we engaged a group of senior knowledge workers who rarely draw attention to themselves – typically, mature research chemists, process engineers and financial analysts who comprise the 'corporate memory' of their employers and whose departure from the organisation would leave a hole in the knowledge base.

We interviewed these people in their organisations in London, Yokohama and Melbourne, and also quizzed the discipline managers responsible for their welfare and productivity in such areas as facilities, estates, human resources, occupational health and diversity. Based on what we learnt, we then built experimental work settings for them to experience changes to the environment in terms of lighting, acoustics, furniture, technology and ambience over a period of up to two weeks. These interventions were designed to gather additional information on needs and aspirations. The project generated its own intellectual property and registered designs, including a Rain Curtain (Figures 6.8 and 6.9), Office Garden and Dynamic Lighting system – innovations that could be licensed by industry.

What we discovered about the well-being needs of older knowledge workers cast a dark shadow over the much-hyped move to open plan working. Our research found that key aspects of knowledge work, such as individual concentration on complex tasks, were poorly catered for by the general design of the open plan office. An overriding emphasis on collaboration and teamwork neglected the fact that knowledge work requires intense periods of deep, uninterrupted concentration and thinking, often undertaken alone. To achieve this, people often had no option but to take work home. For older knowledge workers, the need for dedicated spaces to concentrate on work was mirrored by the need for suitable spaces to contemplate – to think, relax and physically recuperate during the working day, shielded from the daily social grind of being constantly on show. Well-planned contemplation space was identified as a missing dimension in office design.

It was not simply a case that this group chose to arbitrarily dismiss the importance of social interaction at work; nobody wanted to go back to the bad old days of long corridors, private rooms and communication by formal memo. But even the act of collaboration itself was seen as poorly served by bland open plan areas in which physical proximity is no substitute for project settings which really support group working through enhanced display media, lighting, layout and protocols of use.

The Welcoming Workplace study produced design guidance for architects and developers of office buildings, in association with the British Council for Offices. It gave pause for thought on one-size-fits-all open plan, by advocating a range of dedicated settings for concentration, collaboration and contemplation, each with special features to address the particular demands of knowledge work and the physical consequences of the ageing process. Ultimately, what emerged from the study was a call for an inclusive, commonsense approach towards workspace that works for everyone engaged in the knowledge economy. The study was described in detail in *New Demographics, New Workspace* (Myerson et al., 2010). It focused strongly on the well-being of older people at work, but in prototyping and testing experiential settings, it also explored behaviour, experience and sensory input.

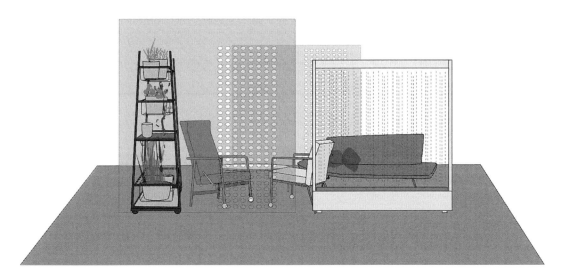

Figures 6.8 and 6.9 Rain Curtain designed by Catherine Greene as part of prototype zone for contemplation, Welcoming Workplace (2009)

Conclusion

Discussion of workplace projects undertaken by the Helen Hamlyn Centre for Design at the RCA since 1999 has revealed the use of a number of different qualitative research tools and methods that derive specifically from art and design-based enquiry. In creating user scenarios and frameworks (*Work At Home, Sustainable Cultures*), in adopting drawing or wordplay techniques to gather data (*Space for Thought, Light Volumes, Dark Matters*), in transposing practical elements from other fields such as urban planning (*Workscapes, Living Cities*), in designing cultural probes to be placed in the environment (*Head Space, Capture It*), and in prototyping experiential settings with different levels of sensory input (*Living Stages, Welcoming Workplace*), our research has opened up new perspectives on the human condition.

Thinking about what it is to be human in any environment goes right to the core of art and design education and practice; and this is the angle that we have brought to the debate about creating the optimum workplace for productivity. We would not claim that such studies are a substitute for more scientific forms of research – however, they do provide an added layer or perspective on how people perform in space. The overall approach is relational and experiential, providing insights into how people really behave and feel in relation to certain conditions and certain stimuli. We believe this has value to the property industry as it contemplates constructing the next generation of productive workplaces, but more work still needs to be done to really get the message across that creative design indicators should count as much as technical or statistical evidence.

References

Bond, M. and Coyne, M. (2002) *The Heart-Friendly Office: A Communication Tool for Architects and Designers*. London: Helen Hamlyn Centre for Design with British Heart Foundation, Royal College of Art.

Crumbleholme, L., Greene, C. and Myerson, J. (2014) Sustainable cultures: engaging employees in creating more sustainable workplaces and workstyles. *Facilities*, 32(7/8): 438–454.

Dutson, C. (2010) *Light Volumes, Dark Matters*. London: Helen Hamlyn Centre for Design with Megaman, Royal College of Art.

Gay, J. (2005) *Work Well: Inclusive Furniture for Older Office Workers*. London: Helen Hamlyn Centre for Design with Kinnarps, Royal College of Art.

Greene, C. and Myerson, J. (2011) Space for thought: designing for knowledge workers. *Facilities*, 29(1/2): 19–30.

Greene, C., Myerson, J. and Puybaraud, M. (2012) Sustainable for All: Pragmatists, Libertarians, Housekeepers and Campaigners are making the workplace greener. In Junghans, A. and Jensen, P.A. (eds) *Proceedings of the 11th EuroFM Research Symposium*. Copenhagen, Denmark.

Harriss, H. and Winstanley, S. (2005) *Capture It: A Future Workplace for the Multi-Generational Knowledge Worker*. London: Helen Hamlyn Centre for Design with DEGW, IDEO and Megaman, Royal College of Art.

Koslowski, B. (2012) *Workscapes: Exploring New Directions in Office Design*. London: Helen Hamlyn Centre for Design with Herman Miller, Royal College of Art.

Lynch, K. (1960) *The Image of the City*. Cambridge, MA: MIT Press.

Myerson, J. (ed.) (1999) *Work At Home: Proceedings of a Thinktank on Homeworking*. London: Leonard Cheshire/Royal College of Art.

Myerson, J. and Bichard, J. (2009) Welcoming workplace: rapid design intervention to determine the office environment needs of older knowledge workers. In Inns, T. (ed.) *Design for the 21st Century*, vol. 2: *Interdisciplinary Methods and Findings*. London: Gower.

Myerson, J., Bichard, J. and Erlich, A. (2010) *New Demographics, New Workspace: Office Design for the Changing Workforce*. London: Gower.

Myerson, J. and Privett, I. (2014) *Life of Work: What Office Design Can Learn from the World Around Us*. London: Black Dog Publishing.

Parsons, T. (2001) *Head Space: Privacy in Open Plan Offices*. London: Helen Hamlyn Centre for Design with IDEO and Steelcase, Royal College of Art.

Privett, I. (2013) *Living Cities: Temporary Urban Events and the Workplace*. London: Helen Hamlyn Centre for Design, Royal College of Art.

Privett, I. and Jarvis, T. (2013) *Living Stages: What Can Workplaces Learn from Theatre Design?* London: Helen Hamlyn Centre for Design with Haworth and Philips Lighting, Royal College of Art.

Tsurumaru, Y. (2000) *Home Industry: New Tools for Manual Pieceworkers*. London: Helen Hamlyn Centre for Design, Royal College of Art.

Part II

Research evidence

Chapter 7

Lessons from schools for productive office environments
The SIN model

Peter Barrett

Challenges and value of establishing real-world impacts of work environments

Measuring the impact of physical spaces on the health, well-being and performance of occupants is the facilities management 'holy grail'. But it is tremendously difficult to do. This difficulty derives from the complexity of the situation and comes in two parts. First, there is the issue of what to measure in relation to human performance. Second, there is the web of design factors that might impact and how they are related. Both are knotty problems in offices, and together they really are a substantial challenge.

But does this matter? The answer has to be an emphatic 'yes'. Large amounts of money are invested in the creation and running of the built environment. It has been estimated that in the UK this amounts to around 20 per cent of GDP (Barrett, 2007; 2008). It can also be estimated, from a line-by-line examination of the SIC categories used to structure economic activities, that around 13 million of the UK working population, that is around 46 per cent, work in office situations (Office for National Statistics, 2011). It is not really surprising that for most organisations, their accommodation costs are probably the second biggest budget item after staffing. Not only are huge amounts of money being expended on office accommodation, but, as will be seen below, the value derived from this expenditure is not at all clearly understood. Of course, shelter is provided and company images are created, but what impact does this investment have on the productive factor within office-based work – the staff? Given this situation, it is easy to see how expenditure on space could be seen as a cost to be minimised. Given the size of the budgets involved, how much better it would be if the decisions could take into account their impact on staff productivity.

The dangers of *not* clearly understanding these productivity impacts can be highlighted through the issue of Green buildings and energy conservation. This is confronted head-on with the argument that energy costs are only around 2 per cent of total building budgets over a 30-year life-cycle, once staff salaries are factored in, so even if they can be measured and controlled, they will never overshadow the massive issue of worker productivity, which, it is known, can be in tension with energy-saving initiatives (Tom, 2008). It is not that one should dominate the other, and it is conceivable that clever design could achieve both (Kershaw and Lash, 2013), however, it is the case that 'what gets measured gets done' and this can significantly skew calculations when rather intangible staff considerations are put up against clearly measurable energy costs. The analogous argument can be seen to operate around the issue of open plan offices. These have become very widespread on the back of clear cost savings, weighed against unclear impacts on workers. Recent work has started to challenge this asymmetry, finding that the 'benefits of enhanced "ease of interaction" were smaller than the penalties of increased noise level and decreased privacy resulting from open-plan office configuration' (Kim and de Dear, 2013). That said, these findings are based on user perceptions/satisfaction.

The performance metrics problem

This brings the focus to the first area of complexity, namely, human performance metrics. Light is thrown on this by a fairly recent benchmark, a multi-author book on building performance evaluation (BPE) (Mallory-Hill *et al.*, 2012; Barrett, 2013). This sets out the steady evolution of BPE over the last 40 years. It is probably old news that it can be beneficial to listen to users, but BPE, it seems, demands much more. It is stated that: 'For BPE to be objective, actual performance of buildings is measured against established performance criteria . . . objective, quantifiable and measurable "hard" data, as opposed to soft criteria . . . qualitative . . . subjective' (Mallory-Hill *et al.*, 2012, pp. 27–28). However, hardly anywhere is evidence of the type aspired to actually reported. Through a survey of the literature it is concluded in the book that: 'productivity is difficult to define' (ibid., p. 169), with the consequence that the most common approach uses perceptions gleaned from occupant surveys with occasional interviews. The World Green Building Council has a solution in principle (World Green Building Council, 2015), that is, to link organisational outcomes with worker perceptions of their office spaces, and assessments of the physical conditions and amenities. It is, however, acknowledged that although sickness and absence and complaints data may be accessible, meaningful measures of revenue/productivity are less easy to access.

So, although there is a considerable body of work focused on office accommodation, a web-based forum of over 450 corporate real estate (CRE) and facilities management (FM) professionals came to a dramatic, collective view that 'CRE&FM currently has no objective way of evidencing the value it brings to business' (Varcoe, 2012).

Complexity in the design factors

Turning to the second area of complexity, the design factors that might be influential, the field of internal environment quality (IEQ) takes a 'scientific' approach that should be consonant with the desire for hard metrics mentioned above. IEQ research has primarily focused on the 'big four' readily measurable aspects of: heat, light, sound and air quality, and although impressive individual sense impacts have been identified, it has been a struggle to explain variations in overall human performance with these variables. The following perspectives illustrate the difficulty of addressing a comprehensive, interactive, multi-sensory view of the impact of built environments on humans. Bluyssen *et al.* (2011) highlight the importance of complex interactions in understanding IEQ. They suggest the individual factors 'can cause their effects additively or through complex interactions (synergistic or antagonistic)' (ibid., p. 2632). Huang *et al.* reinforce the interactive nature of IEQ, stating, 'Physical environmental parameters are all interrelated and the feeling of comfort is a composite state involving an occupant's sensations of all these factors' (2012, p. 305). Cao *et al.* (2012) state that researchers have realised that people's discomfort is usually not determined by a single factor but instead reflects the integration of physiological and psychological influences caused by many factors.

Kim and de Dear (2012) are a recent exception to the tight focus on the 'big four', primarily because their study was based on an existing POE database that included 15 dimensions of satisfaction in offices. Interestingly 'amount of space' and other layout/privacy issues came out with some of the strongest satisfaction scores. However, even these authors argue powerfully that there is currently no consensus as to the relative importance of IEQ factors on overall satisfaction. Away from the laboratory some exceptions have gained traction, for example, Ulrich's (1984) classic evidence of the positive healing effects of views of nature. But progress from this promising start still falls a long way short of comprehensively addressing the design challenge. The difficulty of studying multiple dimensions in the field is illustrated by the problems encountered when the impressive Heschong Mahone (Heschong Mahone Group, 1999; 2003) day-lighting studies were extended to include other issues. It is also evident in Tanner's (2000; 2009) struggle to coherently analyse the multiple aspects impacting on learning rates in schools. In workspaces, the WGBC (2015) lists a wide range of possible physical measures of workspaces, but notes it is an area 'complicated by the range of components'.

So there exists an important research challenge regarding the issue of better understanding, and evidencing, the holistic, interactive impacts of the characteristics of office spaces on the workers in them.

A new perspective: SIN

Leaving the issue of measuring productivity to one side for the moment, this section focuses on progress made on the second challenge, that of addressing the complexity in the elements of the physical spaces to be considered.

The SIN concept

To address the challenge of taking an holistic view, an over-arching conceptual perspective is needed to synthesise the alternative design factors into a coherent framework. One way forward is to use the simple notion that the effect of the built environment on users is experienced via multiple sensory inputs in particular spaces (Derval, 2010; Lehman, 2011), which are resolved in the user's brain. These latter mental mechanisms can provide a basis for understanding the combined effects of sensory inputs on users of buildings at a level of resolution where 'emergent properties' (Checkland, 1993), such as impacts on productivity, may be evident. This resonates with the field of study undertaken by the Academy of Neuroscience for Architecture (ANFA), based in San Diego. The suggestion is that the structuring of the brain's functioning can be used to drive the selection and organisation of the environmental factors to be considered, not just their inherent measurability. This has been termed neuro-informed thinking (Barrett et al., 2013) and has drawn especially on Rolls' (2007) detailed description of the brain's implicit system.

In real-world situations, individuals experience spaces holistically and interactively. The resultant complexity exceeds the cognitive limits of humans, so that perception becomes an 'ill-posed question', in which the brain endeavours to represent reality probabilistically, as best it can using Gestalt grouping rules (Wolfe et al., 2006) collecting the stimuli into usable experiences, called 'percepts' (Eberhard, 2007). These perceptions are intricately linked to memory, which relies on a type of matching and recognition of sensory information circuits (ibid., p. 106).

The sequential process from sense input to response clarifies how these competing influences interact and how the human brain seeks to make optimal judgements between alternatives. Rolls (2007) argues that human behaviour is ultimately motivated by 'primary reinforcers', drawn from our external experience, that are related to survival needs, such as: for clean non-putrified air, bounded temperature, the absence of natural dangers, light, shelter, reasonable stimulation and food hoards. This sensory information about the world is collected as raw data that then enters the orbitofrontal cortex of our brain where the value of the environmental stimulus is assessed. This appears to happen by a pattern-matching process against alternative strings of neuronal associations that are built up and progressively updated. This individual learning process links the elements of situations observed to the built-in primary reinforcers, so giving previously neutral inputs reward value as 'secondary reinforcers', for example, the sight of food rather than its taste. This reward calculation then feeds forward to the amygdala where individuals hold a sense of the correlation between the prospective actions and the potential rewards.

Thus, when experiencing spaces, we will receive a range of sensory inputs that will create an implicit or unconscious response. It seems that the implicit response alone does not automatically create behaviour in humans, but is represented in a range of relatively few emotional states or moods, that do have an important impact by providing quite weak 'back projections', so influencing the cognitive evaluation of what is being experienced. The above discussion gives some indication of the research evidence on human sense perception, impacts and the underlying cognitive calculations involved. Building on this at a level of broad principles, it has been proposed that three *design* principles can be seen to emerge (Barrett and Barrett, 2010):

- the role of naturalness;
- the opportunity for individualisation;
- appropriate levels of stimulation.

The rationale for the choice of these principles is summarised below.

First, as our emotional systems have evolved over the millennia in response to our natural environment, it does not seem unreasonable to suggest that our comfort is likely to be rooted in key dimensions of 'naturalness' that should, therefore, infuse the design process. The stress here is, of course, on the positive aspects of naturalness, such as clean air.

Second, the brain functioning described in the section above highlights the personal way in which individuals build connections between primary reinforcers and complex representations of secondary reinforcers. Taken together with the situated nature of memory, these personal value profiles lead to highly individual responses to spaces. This provides a sound basis to raise the potential importance of 'individualisation' as an additional, key, underlying design principle. This appears to play out in two ways: particularisation and personalisation. Particularisation concerns accommodating the functional needs of very specific types of users, for example, younger or older people. Personalisation concerns an individual's preferences resulting from their personal life experiences of spaces. These, of course, will vary greatly from person to person, but the desire is evident in the way people seek to individualise spaces.

Third, lying behind the detail of design elements for general and particular needs, there is also a recurrent theme regarding the general level of stimulation that is appropriate for particular activities. In broad terms, this may vary from buildings designed for relaxation, such as homes, to those designed to stimulate, such as theatres, but also variation will be appropriate within buildings. In the context of judging design competitions, Nasar (1999) reinforces the central importance of the level of stimulation produced. Drawing on an extensive literature review, he suggests that combinations of pleasantness (or unpleasantness) and different levels of arousal yield either excitement (or boredom) or relaxation (or distress).

These three design principles have been typified more memorably, in reverse order, as the SIN factors, and are shown in Figure 7.1.

Within this novel organising framework it is possible to structure the full range of relevant factors (e.g. light, layout, etc.). Although this perspective was published as a *speculation* in 2010 (Barrett and Barrett, 2010), the next section summarises the findings from applying these

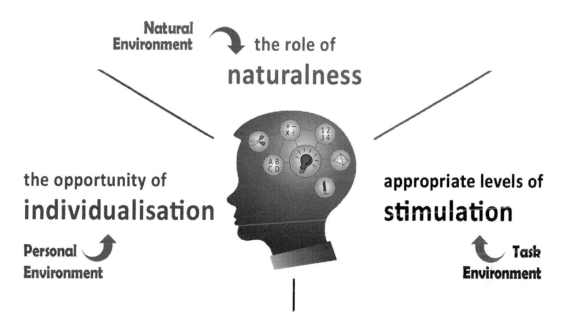

Figure 7.1 SIN design principles

ideas in a relatively simple educational situation where, crucially, a clear connection to measured learning rates provides an opportunity to make an explicit link to impacts on human performance. This supports the utility of framing the physical factors to be considered using the SIN model and provides a basis for considering implications for offices later.

SIN applied to schools and learning

A focus on primary school classrooms carries huge benefits as an ideal 'natural' research design for this knotty problem. The children are in one space for the great majority of their time and there are metrics of their academic progress over a year. If spaces have an impact on human performance, it should show up in this situation! Based on an extensive literature review of putative physical design features linked to evidenced impacts on learning in schools (Barrett and Zhang, 2009), the three SIN principles were operationalised to structure ten design parameters as follows:

- *Stimulation* design parameters: visual complexity and colour.
- *Individualisation* design parameters: ownership (personalisation and distinctiveness), the flexibility of the layout and connection (or way-finding).
- *Naturalness* design parameters: light, temperature, air quality, sound and links to nature.

This approach addressed taking a comprehensive view of possible factors. Then, in combination with measures of these factors and measures about individual pupils and of their academic progress, plus a knowledge of which classroom each pupil was in, multilevel statistical modelling could be used. This allowed the complex interactions of the various elements to be addressed so that the effects of, for example, pupil characteristics such as special educational needs, could be isolated in the analysis and controlled for. In this way, it was possible to isolate the effects on learning attaching specifically to the classroom design level of the analysis.

After three years the EPSRC-funded HEAD (Holistic Evidence and Design) study reached a successful conclusion (Barrett *et al.*, 2015; 2015b). Based on a detailed study of 153 classrooms in 27 English schools in Blackpool, Hampshire and Ealing, involving 3766 pupils, it has been possible to establish the evidence for how important classroom design is for learning and which of the factors involved are particularly important. Based on this large sample, by fixing the variables to their averages apart from the classroom design parameters, it has been modelled that variations in the physical characteristics of the classrooms explain 16 per cent of the variation in the learning progress of the pupils who spent a year in these spaces. This is a much bigger impact than anyone expected.

The impact is driven by seven of the ten factors. Sound, links to nature and connection, despite showing a statistically significant relationship to learning when considered on their own, drop out of the multi-level analysis where pupil effects are controlled for and the design parameters compete with each other. This is a measure of the danger of single factor analyses. To give a flavour of the results, the 'top ten tips' to make the classroom as effective a learning space as possible are set out in Box 7.1.

Box 7.1　Top ten tips for effective primary school learning spaces

The first two tips focus on the level of background *stimulation* provided by the visual appearance of the classroom. Until now it has been argued by some that de-cluttering is best and by others that exciting spaces are best. The clear evidence of the HEAD research is that somewhere in the middle is actually optimal.

Tip 1 Manage the Visual Complexity

A mid-level of visual complexity is to be sought. The basic complexity of the floor plan and ceiling structure is the starting point. Teachers can then build on this with the displays, aiming for a lively feel, without it becoming chaotic!

Tip 2 Use Colour Carefully

Young children do seem to like bright colours, but for effective learning a combination of quite a calm background colour for the walls with some brighter highlights, say, the teaching wall or a feature area, seems best. Then the effect of the furniture and displays, etc. has to be factored in. Try to avoid an overall colour scheme that is 'shouting at you' or feels really boring and go for something somewhere in the middle.

The next two tips are to do with how well the classroom supports the pupils as *individuals*. How well can they relate to it as 'their' space.

Tip 3 Choose the Right Level of Flexibility

A classroom that has defined learning zones, that are suited to the pupils' stage of development, assists learning. Given the usual blended learning approach to teaching seen, this means more complex floor plans and a range of zones for the more play-based learning of KS1 children and bigger, simpler spaces for KS2 pupils, as the learning becomes more formal.

Tip 4 Engender Ownership

Having aspects of the classroom that reflect the individual pupils is important. A space that is not just a soulless box. This can be in the design of the basic space augmented by something that the pupils have all created together that makes the classroom instantly recognisable. At a more detailed level, pupils' work on the wall, names/pictures on drawers and pegs, etc. all help. This is all supported by good quality, child-centred furniture and equipment.

The last group of tips are to do with the *naturalness*, or healthiness, of the classroom. This is obvious in many ways, as to function well as learners we need to be well nourished.

Tip 5 Maximise Daylight

Daylight is good for us. Where possible, it should be maximised, but subject of course to avoiding problems with glare. Obstructing the windows with large items of furniture or covering them with pupils' work is not usually a good idea. Depending on the orientation and size of the windows, blinds may need to be used, but only as much as necessary. Of course there will be times when artificial light is needed and good quality lighting is important to keep up attention levels.

Tip 6 Ensure Adequate Ventilation

Again a very basic human requirement – oxygen! An average classroom with 30 children in it will develop poor air quality within 30 minutes if no fresh air is introduced. This is important as poor air makes pupils drowsy, not a good basis for learning. So the provision and active use of opening windows are recommended as poor air quality was very commonly encountered.

Tip 7 Control the Temperature

Provision of local control via a thermostat in the classroom is ideal so the space can be controlled to be cool but comfortable. Problems of overheating from the sun should be avoided by careful selection of the orientation of windows, but if unavoidable, then external shading will be needed.

After all this detail, the last three tips are more general:

Tip 8 Attack on All Fronts!

The impact on learning of the above actions is spread pretty evenly across all seven areas. So, don't focus on one or two only, but try to assess and address all of them together.

A large part of this is increased awareness as to what matters – easier now the evidence has been established.

Tip 9 Remember to See the Classroom as Another Teaching Tool

The above are the specific aspects that have been shown to have positive (and, if ignored, potentially negative) impacts on learning. The physical features of the classroom should be seen as a set of levers that can be actively used to positive effect.

Tip 10 Don't Assume a 'Good' School Means a 'Good' Classroom

From the HEAD study we know that there are typically more and less effective classrooms in the same school. Sometimes it is to do with the different orientations of classrooms and other times it comes from the different things individual teachers do with their spaces. So it is essential to design/assess every classroom as an individual case. This argues for 'inside-out' design.

It can be seen that the actions involved are often quite simple. However, the fact that there was wide variation in each of these factors across our sample indicates that they are not so obvious in practice, although many of the issues are cheap to do and easy to implement – now we have the evidence! It is also notable that a wide spread of factors is in play, as summarised in Figure 7.2. There is no such thing as a 'silver bullet' factor.

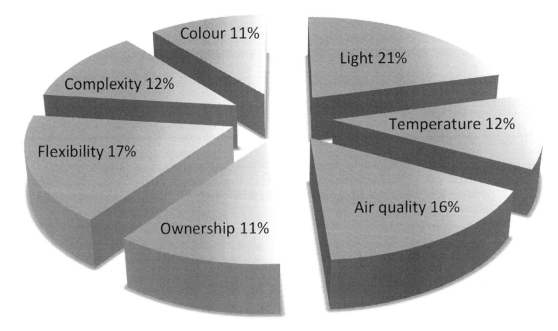

Figure 7.2 Balance of impacts of factors involved

It should be stressed that the last point given in Tip 10 was quite unexpected. It seemed obvious that school-level things like the playgrounds and play-sets, the specialist teaching rooms, such as for cookery, would be relevant. However, at least in relation to learning, they simply did not compare with the force of the variation in the local spaces that pupils occupied for most of their time.

For schools, these findings are important as they relate to the primary business of education – learning – and they are actionable both at the design stage and through users' choices. Beyond this, the approach taken and the results discovered raise interesting opportunities for other types of space, like offices, where brain-work is also taking place.

Implications for offices

Performance in offices

Unlike for schools, in offices there is not a relatively simple, individual measure of occupant performance. There are in fact many possible performance measures with a focus mainly on individual and collective productivity, sometimes on creativity and to a reasonable extent on well-being. These are summarised by Clements-Croome (2006), who goes on to say: 'There are measures that can be quite easy to employ for repetitive office work, however, apart from basic qualities like speed and accuracy, it is much more elusive to assess quality.' Further, given the importance of innovation to business success, it is essential, but much more difficult, to measure impacts on innovative behaviour. From extensive experience, Hodulak (2012) suggests that spaces for innovation should provide for: communication, concentration, collaboration, flexibility, diversity and comfort. This complex of requirements reflects the almost contradictory nature of the innovation process, which normally has to pass cyclically through expansive, creative stages and narrowing, implementation stages (Van de Ven *et al.*, 1999).

So performance in office situations could be studied where repetitive, measurable work is carried out, such as, for example, processing insurance claims or proof-reading. However, this carries dangers of over-emphasising this more measurable work over creative work that may be crucial, but less easy to quantify. In this context the lessons of the HEAD schools' project gain valency as they focus on a fundamental human function – learning – that is commonly proposed to be a key organisational capacity for survival and growth (Garvin *et al.*, 2008).

A SIN-ful view of offices

Taking the ten top tips summary in Box 7.1, the last three would seem to translate well to offices. It is important to take an holistic perspective and to try to consider all aspects together, rather than fixating about one or two, maybe more measurable, factors. It is the space 'as experienced' in its entirety by an occupier that should be considered. Even more, this needs to be addressed at the level of individual spaces, expecting significant variations within buildings, and then the design options should be actively employed as tools to create the optimal conditions to support workers' performance. If the impact is anything like 16 per cent variation in, let's say, productivity, then the value of this to the business is enormous. The space design consideration is not simply a cost to minimised, but rather an investment, the benefit of which is to be maximised. So how can this be done? The following are *suggestions* derived by analogous translation from schools to offices.

First, in the area of the appropriate level of *stimulation*, it would seem highly likely that a mid-level is optimal in offices for a broad range of activities, especially where the focus is on acquiring and applying knowledge. Thus, attention should be paid to colour schemes and the overall visual complexity of the spaces created, including wall displays. Sterile spaces should be avoided, but so too should cluttered, chaotic spaces. However, this principle does link to the 'task' being undertaken and if this is of a creative sort, then it could be expected that there could be some different emphases at play. Williams *et al.* (2014) have carried out extensive research on the desirable features of creative spaces, drawing on the experiences of a wide range of contributors. Of 62 'recipes', 32 specifically mention the physical environment. These recipes have been analysed using the SIN framework (Williams and Barrett, 2014) and in the area of stimulation there is a call for 'affordances' in the enriched appearance of the spaces so that they connect people, ideas and information. This can involve displays and access to whiteboards to share/stimulate ideas. However, a more subtle issue is also proposed alongside this, which is the provision of triggers to help people switch cognitive gears (Louis and Sutton, 1991) between the creative, divergent, phase of the innovation cycle and the reflective, convergent phase (Van de Ven *et al.*, 1999). This could involve the dynamic use of colour and other visual features to signal hoped-for changes in thinking styles.

This leads into the second area of *individualisation* where the analysis of the conditions for creative recipes is very fully represented, especially around the availability of flexibility. But first, for 'normal' work the proposition would be that staff will work better in conditions where they feel some ownership of the space they are in, where they do not feel it is an anonymous box. Given that workers spend many hours in their offices, this does not seem a crazy suggestion. So within reason, surely staff should be given the opportunity to put their mark, individually or collectively, on the spaces they occupy. This may be especially so where the task being carried out is difficult and the confidence of the worker needs to be bolstered. The reason for saying this is that a subject-based analysis of the HEAD data finds that for mathematics, specifically, 'ownership' is extremely influential, and this is a subject where confidence is known to be a huge factor/problem. Where the task confronted also demands creativity, then Williams and Barrett summarise McCoy as stating that

> [the] creative achievement is enhanced by the degree to which people are empowered . . . to adapt their physical environment to their unique needs, enabled to communicate and collaborate freely, and permitted to demonstrate their shared professional focus through the display of team artefacts.
>
> (2014, p. 83)

The second element of this resonates with the HEAD project's findings on the provision of diverse learning zones for play-based learning. The provision of flexible options can be designed in, achieved through 'official' adaptations, or achieved by 'users' unofficial hacking'. This last point indicates that there can be a tension between efficiency-orientated business drivers and the optimal provision of spaces that support innovative work. This need not be a problem, but if it is, it may need more active consideration at times. If this does not happen, then maybe a tolerant attitude to local hacks is at least a possibility!

The third area is the achievement of *naturalness*, or good comfort conditions. These are a prerequisite to functioning as natural organisms. The impact of these factors on children's learning is a strong indication that similar impacts on productivity in offices can be expected. Interestingly, recent research, specifically on offices and the impact of poor air quality on worker functioning (Allen *et al.*, 2015) has found dramatic detriments to a range of cognitive functions, with the negative impacts rising in a fairly linear fashion from very low levels (500 ppm of CO_2 – well below 'acceptable' levels) in normal office conditions. This aspect simply cannot be ignored. We won't repeat the argument already given about the preferencing of easily quantifiable aspects such as energy, but the scale of the price paid in productivity from poor environmental conditions has to be taken more seriously. In situations where there are creative imperatives at work, then the analysis of the HEAD project data by subject provides an interesting insight. Specifically for writing, 'links to nature' are of particular salience among school children and it would seem from the educational literature this could be driven by the creativity especially needed in this subject. This is reinforced in Williams *et al.*'s (2014) assembly of creative recipes where 'hacks' are noted to address lighting, unwanted sound and bringing in nature to the office via plants. That said, it would seem that, for users, these comfort factors are to a great extent invisible, out of control, taken-for-granted hygiene factors. In their contribution Robertson and Jones go further and ironically set out a 'recipe for mediocrity'. This highlights many sub-optimal naturalness factors and suggests that in order to achieve facilities that will *stifle* creativity: 'Appoint buildings managers and administrators who love the building more than people . . . Impress on them that their job is to protect the building from the infestation of people' (ibid., p. 82). Well they make their point (!) and this will resonate with many office workers' first-hand experience.

In summary, it can be seen that, by drawing on the HEAD project results via their evidenced insights for impacts of the holistic physical environment on the cognitive performance of pupils, indications can be derived for office workers, although the nature of their task demands (repetitive vs creative) requires some finessing of the ideas. So, it is proposed that the SIN framework provides a route map of major areas to be considered and allows more detailed findings about offices to be levered in within a balanced overall consideration. That said, the problem of measuring productivity itself remains as a challenge.

Future opportunities

Mallory-Hill *et al.* rightly stated that the range of internal environment quality dimensions studied is broadening in response to an increasing appreciation of the 'subtle psychological, cognitive and social influences [that provide] a rich frontier for future . . . building research' (2012, p. 176). It is suggested here that the SIN framework has demonstrated its top-down utility in framing a holistic representation of the physical environment. The HEAD project on schools also indicates the scale and nature of the cognitive impacts of the holistic physical environment. Put simply, with double digit impacts involved, this is a business-critical issue. The contribution of office design to worker productivity should be optimised.

The clarity of this argument is still somewhat obscured by the absence of clear productivity metrics for most types of office work. One strategy to help resolve this obstacle is to triangulate workers' perceptions of their environment to measured performance in the laboratory, for example: 'perceived thermal satisfaction of occupants is reflected in objective measurement of office work performance [with] practical implications . . . boost[ing] workplace productivity' (Tanabe *et al.*, 2015). The HEAD project also provides a clue as to how to expand our understanding of the holistic office environment through analogies. Just as the schools' work points to impacts on learning, so studies in other situations with clearer performance metrics than offices allow insights to be derived and applied to various aspects of office performance. For example, it has been suggested (Mallory-Hill *et al.*, 2012) that exceptions to the problem of measurement may be found in the literature about manufacturing facilities and about activities, such as libraries, with clear usage metrics. Impacts on prisoners could also provide insights about effects, such as re-offending, that may have implications for longer-term career patterns, albeit a recent study only focused on the 'big four' and subjective views (Dogbeh *et al.*, 2015).

Studies of hospitals and of dementia care may also throw a light on health and, in the latter case, provide insights where occupants have a reduced mental capacity to handle complexity (Zeisel *et al.*, 2003). Further, work in the retail environment can link directly to metrics on buying behaviour and inform notions around the impacts of environmental factors on motivations for alternative choices. Interestingly in the retail area there is the classification of utilitarian vs hedonic shoppers (Kaltcheva and Weitz, 2006), which in some loose sense may parallel standardised and creative work. Drawing on these various areas and their insights into different cognitive functions, it may be that progressively productivity can be better understood.

Overall, it is proposed that for a better understanding of the impacts and value of the physical design of offices a broad holistic approach is needed that reflects spaces *as experienced*. In this it seems likely that multi-level modelling has tremendous potential to facilitate the untangling of competing effects. This top-down journey should not preference measurable factors over important factors. Over time the measurability of the wide range of factors involved will improve. In terms of performance metrics, it may be that a combination of user satisfaction/laboratory work, together with analogous studies of holistic situations, with a range of relevant performance measures available, may allow some traction to be gained on the knotty issue of office productivity.

If this can be achieved, then the 'soft' factors, when compared against more easily measurable features can be actively managed. As the relevant design factors and their impacts become clearer, organisations will be in a position to make balanced investment decisions, based on evidence. This will enable them to deliver spaces to workers that optimally support them in their endeavours for the organisation. Ideally, this will extend to dynamic options that actively and intelligently support different types of office task, as they arise.

References

Allen, J.G., Macnaughton, P., Satish, U., Santanam, S., Vallarino, J. and Spengler, J.D. (2015) Associations of cognitive function scores with carbon dioxide, ventilation, and volatile organic compound exposures in office workers: a controlled exposure study of green and conventional office environments. *Environmental Health Perspectives*, 124(6): 805–812.

Barrett, P. (2007) Revaluing construction: an holistic model. *Building Research and Information*, 35: 268–286.

Barrett, P. (2008) *Revaluing Construction*. Oxford: Blackwell.

Barrett, P. (2013) Enhancing building performance. *Construction Management and Economics*, 31: 780–781.

Barrett, P. and Barrett, L. (2010) The potential of positive places: senses, brain and spaces. *Intelligent Buildings International*, 2: 218–228.

Barrett, P., Barrett, L. and Davies, F. (2013) Achieving a step change in the optimal sensory design of buildings for users at all life-stages. *Building and Environment*, 67: 97–104.

Barrett, P.S., Davies, F., Zhang, Y. and Barrett, L. (2015a) The impact of classroom design on pupils' learning: final results of a holistic, multi-level analysis. *Building and Environment*, 89: 118–133.

Barrett, P.S. and Zhang, Y. (2009) *Optimal Learning Spaces: Design Implications for Primary Schools*. SCRI Report, 2. Salford: University of Salford.

Barrett, P.S., Zhang, Y., Davies, F. and Barrett, L. (2015b) *Clever Classrooms: Summary Report of the HEAD Project*. Salford: University of Salford.

Bluyssen, P.M., Janssen, S., Van Den Brink, L.H. and De Kluizenaar, Y. (2011) Assessment of wellbeing in an indoor office environment. *Building and Environment*, 46: 2632–2640.

Cao, B., Ouyang, Q., Zhu, Y., Huang, L., Hu, H. and Deng, G. (2012) Development of a multivariate regression model for overall satisfaction in public buildings based on field studies in Beijing and Shanghai. *Building and Environment*, 47: 394–399.

Checkland, P. (1993) *Systems Thinking, Systems Practice*. Chichester: John Wiley & Sons Ltd.

Clements-Croome, D. (ed.) (2006) *Creating the Productive Workplace*. London: Routledge.

Derval, D. (2010) *The Right Sensory Mix*. Heidelberg: Springer.

Dogbeh, A., Jomaas, G., Bjarløv, S.P. and Toftum, J. (2015) Field study of the indoor environment in a Danish prison. *Building and Environment*, 88: 20–26.

Eberhard, J.P. (2007) *Architecture and the Brain: A New Knowledge Base from Neuroscience*. Atlanta, GA: Ostberg.

Garvin, D., Edmondson, A. and Gino, F. (2008) Is yours a learning organization? *Harvard Business Review*, March: 109–116.

Heschong Mahone Group (1999) *Daylighting in Schools*. Fair Oaks, CA: Pacific Gas and Electric Company.

Heschong Mahone Group (2003) *Windows and Classrooms: A Study of Student Performance and the Indoor Environment*. Fair Oaks, CA: Californian Energy Commission.

Hodulak, M. (2012) Programming spaces for innovation. In Mallory-Hill, S., Preiser, W. and Watson, C. (eds) *Enhancing Building Performance*. Oxford: Blackwell.

Huang, L., Zhu, Y., Ouyang, Q. and Cao, B. (2012) A study on the effects of thermal, luminous and acoustic environments on indoor environmental comfort in offices. *Building and Environment*, 49: 304–309.

Kaltcheva, V. and Weitz, B. (2006) When should a retailer create an exciting store environment? *Journal of Marketing*, 70(1): 107–118.

Kershaw, T. and Lash, D. (2013) Investigating the productivity of office workers to quantify the effectiveness of climate change adaptation measures. *Building and Environment*, 69: 35–43.

Kim, J. and De Dear, R. (2012) Nonlinear relationships between individual IEQ factors and overall workspace satisfaction. *Building and Environment*, 49: 33–44.

Kim, J. and De Dear, R. (2013) Workspace satisfaction: the privacy-communication trade-off in open-plan offices. *Journal of Environmental Psychology*, 36: 18–26.

Lehman, M.L. (2011) How sensory design brings value to buildings and their occupants. *Intelligent Buildings International*, 3: 46–54.

Louis, M.R. and Sutton, R.I. (1991) Switching cognitive gears: from habits of mind to active thinking. *Human Relations*, 44: 55–76.

Mallory-Hill, S., Preiser, W. and Watson, C. (eds) (2012) *Enhancing Building Perfomance*. Chichester: Wiley-Blackwell.

Nasar, J. (1999) *Design by Competition: Making Design Competition Work*. Cambridge: Cambridge University Press.

Office for National Statistics (2011) Labour Force Survey Employment status by occupation, April–June 2011. Newport: Office for National Statistics.

Rolls, E.T. (2007) *Emotion Explained*. Oxford: Oxford University Press.

Tanabe, S.-I., Haneda, M. and Nishihara, N. (2015) Workplace productivity and individual thermal satisfaction. *Building and Environment*, 91: 42–50.

Tanner, C. (2000) The influence of school architecture on academic achievement. *Journal of Educational Administration*, 38: 309–330.

Tanner, C.K. (2009) Effects of school design on student outcomes. *Journal of Educational Administration*, 47: 381–399.

Tom, S. (2008) Managing energy and comfort: don't sacrifice comfort when managing energy *ASHRAE Journal*, June: 18–26.

Ulrich, R. (1984) View through a window may influence recovery from surgery. *Science*, 224: 420–421.

Van De Ven, A., Polley, D., Garud, R. and Venkataraman, S. (1999) *The Innovation Journey*. Oxford: Oxford University Press.

Varcoe, B. (2012) *CRE&FM Futures Forum: Final Report*. Zurich.

Williams, A. and Barrett, P. (2014) Creating sensory-sensitive spaces. In Williams, A., Jones, D. and Robertson, J. (eds) *BITE: Recipes for Remarkable Research*. Rotterdam: Sense.

Williams, A., Jones, D. and Robertson, J (eds) (2014) *BITE: Recipes for Remarkable Research*. Rotterdam: Sense.

Wolfe, J. *et al.* (2006) *Sensation and Perception.* Sunderland MA: Sinauer Associates.

World Green Building Council (2015) *Health, Wellbeing and Productivity in Offices: The Next Chapter for Green Building.* Toronto: World Green Buiding Council.

Zeisel, J., Silverstein, N.M., Hyde, J., Levkoff, S., Lawton, P.M. and Holmes, W. (2003) Environmental correlates to behavioral health outcomes in Alzheimer's special care units. *The Gerontologist*, 43: 697–711.

Chapter 8

Effects of indoor air quality on decision-making

Usha Satish, Piers MacNaughton and Joseph Allen

Productivity

Human productivity has been defined as the level of worker or workforce efficiency. Typically, this is measured as work output in a given time frame or specific work output compared to average output. Research on human decision-making and productivity has shown that cognitive variables are an important determinant of efficiency levels. While there has been a lot of focus on fundamental cognitive parameters such as memory, perception, speed and basic judgement, only recently have we started looking at metacognitive variables that are central to our day-to-day functioning and integral to overall productivity. Some of these metacognitive variables include staying focused on the task at hand, processing incoming information and using it appropriately, managing crises, and strategizing optimally to achieve goals. When thinking about productivity in the workplace, it is critical to understand how the environment affects these metacognitive abilities as they are the most closely aligned with employees' actual work functions.

Indoor air quality (IAQ)

Indoor air quality (IAQ) is a broad umbrella term that covers a wide range of exposures that may be experienced in the office. IAQ is affected by buildings' materials and furnishings breaking down or off-gassing in the space. Over time, materials wear down and can be inhaled as particles, ingested as dust, or even enter the bloodstream dermally. In the case of off-gassing, volatile and semi-volatile organic compounds (VOCs and SVOCs), a term for compounds that are applied in the solid or liquid form but enter the gas phase, are released into the air. These compounds range from benzene, a component of gasoline, to formaldehyde, which is often used in resins and adhesives. An often unconsidered set of VOCs are those created by the occupants themselves. People not only bring in food, cleaning agents, and office supplies to the office but also generate bioeffluents. While the odors associated with bioeffluents are easily perceived by occupants (and often reported), a more concerning aspect is infectious agents. Similar to components of dust, viruses and bacteria can be directly inhaled or contacted as they settle on to surfaces. In order to exhaust all these contaminants, buildings are ventilated with outdoor air. Depending on the location of the building, outdoor air pollution may pose another significant source of indoor contaminants. As we spend 90 percent of our time indoors, most of our exposure to pollution of outdoor origin occurs indoors (Klepeis *et al.*, 2001) (Figure 8.1). Of particular concern are particulate matter and combustion byproducts from vehicles and power plants.

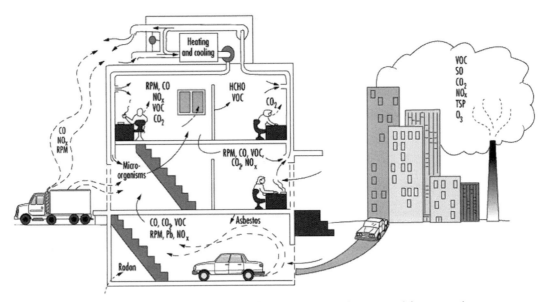

CO = carbon monoxide; CO₂ = carbon dioxide; HCHO = formaldehyde; NO ₓ = nitrogen oxides; Pb = lead; RPM = respirable particulate matter; VOC = volatile organic compounds.

Figure 8.1 Exposure sources and pathways in a typical office environment
Source: Adapted from Sola (2012).

The literature

The mix of chemicals that we may be exposed to in any one indoor environment opens the door for several pathways to negatively affect our health and performance. The impact of IAQ on worker performance can be broken down into three distinct categories: (1) exposure to toxins in the air can cause illness, which leads to employees missing work; (2) exposures that do not result in increased sick leave may still be causing some morbidity and reduced in-office productivity; and (3) certain contaminants can directly impact cognitive function.

The relationship between the built environment and employee illness became abundantly clear in the early 1980s following a new design paradigm to construct increasingly tight buildings to reduce energy costs in the face of rising oil prices. The prevalence of a diverse set of symptoms increased in many of these buildings without a clear mechanism at the time. Lower air exchange rates magnified the potency of indoor sources, leading to exposures higher than previously observed in buildings. The observation of problem buildings with clusters of sick occupants propelled a new line of inquiry into what was called sick building syndrome (SBS).

Mendell *et al.* (2002) and Wargocki *et al.* (2002) summarized the results of decades of research on the subject. Of the 32 studies investigated by Mendell, carpeting, occupant density, and low ventilation rates consistently surfaced as issues in buildings. More importantly, the physiological effects of these exposures aligned with the types of symptoms reported. Wargocki's review supported these findings and added that increased ventilation rates reduced short-term sick leave and increased productivity.

Until recently, sick leave was the predominant pathway to demonstrate productivity losses attributable to IAQ. As an outcome, sick leave and illness are easy to measure and objective

Table 8.1 Health impacts of ventilation rate in medium office prototype building

Reference	Outcome	Ventilation rate (l/s/person)		Relative risk
		Low	High	
Milton et al., 2000	Short-term sick leave	11.8	23.6	1.5
Brundage et al., 1988	Illness all years	2.1	14.2	1.5
Brundage et al., 1988	Illness 1983 data	2.1	14.2	1.9
Drinka et al., 1996	Illness	22.7	56.7	2.2
Drinka et al., 1996	Influenza	22.7	56.7	4.7
Knibbs et al., 2011	Influenza	7.1	21.2	3.1
Knibbs et al., 2011	Rhinovirus	7.1	21.2	2.1
Knibbs et al., 2011	TB	7.1	21.2	3.3
Hoge et al., 1994	Pneumonia	9.6	14.2	2.0
Stenberg et al., 1994	SBS symptoms	4.0	20.0	5.0

Source: adapted from Fisk et al. (2003).

indicators of health. Table 8.1 highlights several of the studies that have linked ventilation in offices with illness.

Milton et al. (2000) found that employees were 1.5 times as likely to miss work at 11.8 l/s/person (25 cfm/person), which exceeds the ASHRAE 62.1 guidelines, compared to doubling that rate to 23.6 l/s/person (50 cfm/person). This is equivalent to 5 days of sick leave per employee per year attributable to lower ventilation, or a cost to the employer of approximately $400 per employee per year.

More difficult to assess is the impact these illnesses and symptoms have on workers in the office. Often referred to as presenteeism, this concept represents workers who are in the office but are not able to perform at their best because of their symptoms. Workers with depression report 5.6 hours per week of lost productive time compared to 1.5 hours a week for workers without depression (Stewart et al., 2003). In fact, the lost productive time at work exceeded the lost productive time due to absenteeism. Seasonal allergies, which affect approximately 13 percent of the workforce, can also affect productivity. A study in a call center found that 7 percent fewer of the employees with allergies met the productivity standard (e.g. number of calls, call time, etc.) than those without allergies (Burton et al., 2001). Some extent of this disengagement by illness is attributable to the indoor environment. For example, ventilation impacts not only objective symptoms like throat dryness and respiratory symptoms, but also subjective reports of having difficulty thinking clearly and feeling bad (Wargocki et al., 2000). In addition, SBS symptoms are correlated with stress, and stress affects both performance and engagement (Mendelson et al., 2000). Productivity in the office is closely tied to the well-being of the workforce, which is mediated by environmental conditions.

There is no doubt that absenteeism and presenteeism play a large part in the overall productivity of the workforce, but there is a hidden cost, which even the individual employee may not be aware of, that may be just as significant. Employees are aware of their time away from work and their engagement, but they may not know how their performance is being affected when they are working diligently at their desk. IAQ can have direct impacts on cognitive function; the challenge is finding a tool to measure cognitive function that is objective and sensitive.

Common cognitive test batteries, developed to identify clinical manifestations of mental disease, may not be sensitive enough to quantify the performance of a highly-functional office worker. For example, Wargocki et al. (2000) found slight improvements in speed of addition and the Tsai-Partington test, which entails tracing a line through 2-digit numbers sequentially, at lower indoor CO_2 concentrations; however, these results were mostly non-significant. It is frequently found that these building blocks (e.g. memory, speed, perception) can be intact in normal functioning individuals and yet overall productivity may be impacted. This is because productivity is more than the sum of these building blocks and requires metacognitive abilities (e.g. task orientation, information management, crisis responses, and strategy). A tool used in more recent research to address this need is the Strategic Management Simulations (SMS). This tool with its long history of evaluation of human productivity might potentially offer a deeper understanding of the impact of IAQ on human productivity.

Strategic Management Simulations (SMS)

The SMS product has a long history in assessing human decision-making and its impact on job performance and human productivity. Further, it has been demonstrated to be sufficiently robust in assessing and training across a number of professions. Writers concerned with instructional technology view the complexity approach as one of the more significant bases for skill acquisition in today's requirements of learning. The SMS measures complex human behaviors required for effectiveness in many workplace settings. The system assesses both basic cognitive and behavioral responses to task demands, as well as cognitive and behavioral components commonly considered as executive functions. Participants are exposed to diverse computer-generated situations that are proven to match real-world, day-to-day challenges.

The SMS (Strategic Management Simulation Systems) is comprised of a set of evaluation techniques that have their roots in complexity theory. High levels of predictive validity,

Table 8.2 Nine of the cognitive domains assessed by the SMS test and their definitions

Cognitive domain	Definition
Basic activity level	Overall ability to make multiple decisions. Completes designated tasks; follows through with appointments and tasks as needed. Designs activity toward goals.
Focused Activity Level	Capacity to pay attention to situations at hand. Completes tasks with precision and in a timely manner.
Applied Activity Level	Capacity to make decisions that are geared toward overall goals. Ability to take a task to completion with the overall job goal in focus.
Task Orientation	Capacity to make specific decisions that are geared toward completion of tasks at hand. Ability to stick to a time line and finish tasks.
Crisis Response	Ability to plan, stay prepared and strategize under emergency conditions. Reflects the ability to handle unexpected changes with efficiency.
Information Management	Ability to gather and use information in order to accomplish tasks and overall goals. This reflects the ability to actively seek out available resources and opportunities that could lead to task accomplishment and use the information in a productive and creative manner.
Breadth of Approach	Ability to make decisions along multiple dimensions and use a variety of options and opportunities to attain goals. Reflects the capacity to shift thinking styles when and as needed toward productive functioning.
Strategy	Ability to reflect and bring forth well-integrated solutions with the help of optimal use of information and planning. Capacity to remain productive both in the short and long term.

reliability, and applicability of the SMS simulations to real-world settings have been repeatedly demonstrated across multiple professions, cultures, and continents (predicting an individual's achievement and future success level on indicators such as "job level at age," "income at age," "promotions," "number of persons supervised," and so forth) (Streufert et al., 1988). Table 8.2 lists the primary learning skill dimensions that are the focus of the SMS training program.

IAQ research with an SMS tool

Prior research with the SMS simulation demonstrates that this technique is able to discriminate differences in human functioning under a variety of conditions in normal individuals (papers on leadership, etc.), individuals using different medications (effects of beta-blockers, caffeine, antihistamines, alcohol, marijuana, and tranquilizers) and under conditions of illness (allergy, brain injury) (Breuer and Satish, 2003; Satish et al., 2004; Satish et al., 2006; Satish et al., 2008; Swezey et al., 1998). Recently, the SMS simulation has been used to test the impacts of IAQ on decision-making performance.

The CogFx study conducted by Harvard T.H. Chan School of Public Health, Syracuse University, and SUNY Upstate Medical Center tested the impacts of VOCs, CO_2, and ventilation on cognitive function. Some 24 participants spent six full workdays over two weeks in the Syracuse Center of Excellence Total Indoor Environmental Quality (TIEQ) lab. On each day, the environmental conditions were altered, unbeknown to the participants (Table 8.3).

The conditions were designed to represent real office conditions. The ventilation targets were 9.4 l/s/person (20 cfm/person), which is the ASHRAE 62.1–2010 standard ventilation rate, and 18.9 l/s/person (40 cfm/person) (ASHRAE, 2016). The CO_2 and VOC targets were derived from the EPA Building Assessment and Survey Evaluation (BASE) study of 100 non-problem office buildings in the USA (EPA, 1998). The average VOC concentration in those buildings was 453 $\mu g/m^3$ and the highest average CO_2 concentration was 1405 ppm. At the ASHRAE 62.1 standard, occupant-generated CO_2 will reach a steady-state concentration of approximately 950 ppm, the day 2 target CO_2 concentration. CO_2 levels were increased on day 2 and 3 by injecting pure CO_2 into the space, and VOC target concentrations were reached by adding

Table 8.3 CO_2, VOC and ventilation rate targets during each testing condition in the TIEQ lab at the Syracuse Center of Excellence

DAY	1	2	3	4	5	1&6
CO_2 (ppm)	550	950	1400	950	950	550
Ventilation (cfm/person)	40	40	40	20	20	40
VOCs (ppb)	50	50	50	50	550	50
CONDITION	GREEN+	MEDIUM CO_2	HIGH CO_2	GREEN	CONVENTIONAL	GREEN+

in materials commonly found in conventional office environments, such as building materials, office supplies, adhesives, and cleaning agents (Allen *et al.*, 2015).

Participants scored 61 percent higher during the green building condition than the same participants scored during the conventional environment. Cognitive function scores more than doubled on the two green+ days compared to the conventional day. Participants' cognitive function scores decreased by 16 percent and 51 percent when CO_2 concentration increased from 550 ppm to 950 ppm and 1400 ppm respectively. Participants performed nearly the same on the SMS test on the two green+ days, despite being 9 days apart, which shows the internal validity of the conditions and the SMS test. When modeling the effect of the test conditions on cognitive function scores, 81 percent of the variability in average scores was explained by the test condition and the participants' baseline ability on the SMS test. Based on this evidence, it can be concluded that VOCs, CO_2 and ventilation all had significant, independent effects on SMS scores (Allen *et al.*, 2015).

The impact of each of these IAQ parameters on cognitive function scores has been reevaluated in separate studies using the SMS test. Satish *et al.* (2012) tested cognitive performance at 600 ppm, 1000 ppm and 2500 ppm. When plotted against the results from the CogFx study, a clear dose-response emerges, with cognitive test scores decreasing at each higher exposure to CO_2, despite differences in the length of exposure (half day vs. full day) and the population of participants (graduate students vs. knowledge workers) (ibid.). In another study, Satish *et al.* tested the impact of VOCs from paints on the cognitive function of painters. While the VOC mix differed from the CogFx study due to the different sources, in both cases the majority of cognitive domains were impacted (Satish *et al.*, 2013). Lastly, Maddalena *et al.* (2015) tested ventilation rates at and above ASHRAE standards and found significant improvements in cognitive performance on the SMS test at higher ventilation rates.

Implications

Given the body of literature that now supports the association between indoor air quality and productivity, why is the commercial industry hesitant to optimize the indoor environment? There are several key frameworks in place that promote the status quo and inhibit changes to the design and operation of buildings.

First, the regulatory framework around indoor air quality is focused on managing the risk of indoor exposures. The American Society of Heating, Refrigerating, and Air Conditioning Engineers (ASHRAE) defines its ventilation standard 62.1 around acceptable minimums, and in practice these minimums are seen as sufficient for occupants, despite benefits seen at higher ventilation rates (ASHRAE, 2016). The same strategy is used for chemicals that may be introduced into the environment. In the United States, the Toxic Substances Control Act (TSCA) does not require companies to test the safety of new chemical compounds, which can cause a significant gap between when people are first exposed to a chemical, when the health impacts are discovered, and when the chemical is regulated. In Europe, Registration, Evaluation, Authorization, and Restriction of Chemicals (REACH) requires baseline testing by manufacturers based on the amount being produced, but testing will not be detailed enough to detect more nuanced health impact pathways. As a result, we regularly detect a plethora of VOCs and SVOCs in indoor environments originating from the chemicals used in the production of building materials, furnishings, and office supplies without a clear picture as to the impact these chemicals may have on our cognitive function.

Second, the owner/manager/tenant relationship causes a split incentive system in the commercial sector. The tenant receives the benefits of improved air quality, which far outweigh the costs of improving IAQ. While the energy costs may be trivial compared to the increase in employee productivity, they fall on the building management and constitute a significant portion of their budget. Their budget is set by the owner, who will only increase their budget if they believe there is demand for improved IAQ in the building. Only 34 percent of owners claim to market IAQ in spaces, and only 21 percent of tenants say they have observed this despite 74 percent of tenants reporting that they consider IAQ either directly or indirectly when buying or leasing a space. Of the 21 percent of tenants who saw owners marketing IAQ, only 54 percent were confident that the claims were valid (Hamilton *et al.*, 2016). Clearly owners' perceptions of tenant expectations are misaligned with reality, and tenants are lacking trust in owners' decision-making around IAQ. Furthermore, this ignores the 26 percent of tenants who do not consider IAQ when leasing, which indicates that the benefits of improved IAQ are not universally accepted.

Lastly, the costs of improving IAQ are often perceived to be greater than they are in practice. Owners, managers and tenants all overestimate the costs of improving IAQ when asked what would be the cost to double ventilation rates from 9.4 to 18.9 l/s of outdoor air per person and improve filtration from a minimum efficiency reporting value (MERV) 6 to MERV 11. Despite costs being less than $30 per occupant per year, owners predicted costs at $80, property and facility managers at $100, and tenants at $115. The perceived benefit of improved IAQ needs to exceed these perceptions, rather than the actual costs, in order for a decision about ventilation changes to be made. The perceived benefits are similarly underestimated: only 41 percent of these stakeholders were willing to pay $15 per occupant per year for the same improvement in IAQ (Hamilton *et al.*, 2016).

In actuality, the benefits of improved IAQ are several orders of magnitude larger than stakeholders realize. A follow-up paper on the CogFx study compared the benefits of increased ventilation in terms of increased productivity against the associated energy costs and environmental impacts. In agreement with Hamilton *et al.* (2016), energy costs were less than $40 per person per year to double ventilation rates from 9.4 l/s/person to 18.9 l/s/person in all the climate zones investigated. When the increased ventilation rate was coupled with an energy recovery ventilator (ERV), which captures some of the latent heat exhausted from the building, the costs were reduced to less than $18 per person per year and the environmental impacts were essentially neutralized; in many climate zones and system types, a system running at 18.9 l/s/person with an ERV uses less energy and results in fewer greenhouse gas emissions than a system running at 9.4 l/s/person without an ERV. Using the cognitive data from the CogFx study, the same change in ventilation resulted in an 8 percent improvement in cognitive function compared to the distribution of knowledge workers (i.e. administrative, technical, professional and managerial employees) who have taken the SMS test in the past (Figure 8.2) (MacNaughton *et al.*, 2015).

This is equivalent to a $6,500 difference in salary for an equivalent shift in the distribution of compensation for knowledge workers. This figure does not include the impacts of ventilation on absenteeism, which has been estimated to be on the order of $400 per person per year, or presenteeism, which has not yet been quantified (Milton *et al.*, 2000). It also does not include the impact of chemical exposures on cognitive function; in the CogFx study, the cognitive deficits were even greater when VOC-emitting materials were added to the space (the conventional condition) than when ventilation rates were reduced (the green condition).

The solutions to IAQ problems are evident from the previous discussion: absenteeism, presenteeism, and cognitive function can be optimized by removing sources of chemicals from the office and increasing ventilation rates and filtration. The onus is on property owners, building managers, and tenants to advocate for these changes as regulation, codes, and even green

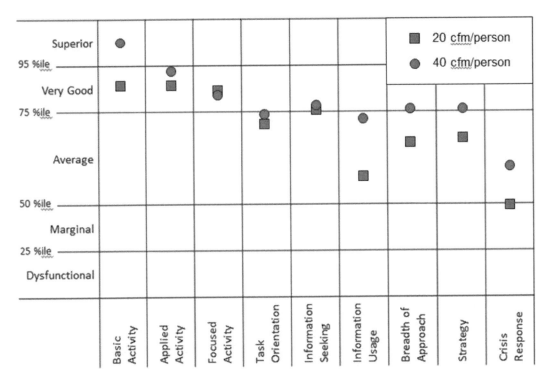

Figure 8.2 Average cognitive scores on the SMS tool of 24 participants in a green building at 9.4 l/s/person (20 cfm/person) and 18.9 l/s/person (40 cfm/person) of outdoor air relative to normative data from ~70,000 people

Source: Adapted from MacNaughton *et al.* (2015).

building standards are designed to mitigate risks and ensure a minimally acceptable level of comfort, and will lag behind scientific evidence. In the design phase, high-performing HVAC systems can be installed with sufficient tonnage to accommodate higher outdoor air ventilation rates, and low chemical content building materials can be preferentially selected. In the operations phase, building managers and tenants can choose health-conscious suppliers and operate HVAC systems at or above design levels. Importantly, building managers can establish a rigorous IAQ testing and commissioning program, which will identify or prevent many IAQ problems before they have a significant effect on the occupants.

These solutions which can bolster employee productivity are usually overlooked or disregarded by company presidents, CEOs, and business owners. The success of a business is typically tracked through the use of key performance indicators (KPIs). Factors that influence the performance of the workforce will have a significant effect on the company's triple bottom line (people, profit, planet), and therefore should be assessed with the same, or greater, rigor as KPIs, which only target financial outcomes. An analogous term, Health Performance Indicators (HPIs), can be used to track these upstream impacts on the workforce and company as a whole, as well as drawing attention to the importance of employee health and productivity in the success of a company. The HPIs in the built environment are encapsulated by the nine foundations of a healthy building: ventilation, air quality, thermal health, moisture, dust and pests, safety and security, water quality, lighting and views, and noise (ForHealth.org, 2016). Allen *et al.* (2015) have summarized the evidence on how these factors affect employee health and productivity to make this information accessible to practitioners outside the realm of public health, to cross-pollinate academic fields that are currently siloed, and to translate 40 years of public health research into practice.

References

Allen, J.G., MacNaughton, P., Santanam, S., Satish, U., and Spengler, J. (2015) Associations of cognitive function scores with carbon dioxide, ventilation, and volatile organic compound exposures in office workers: a controlled exposure study of green and conventional office environments. *Environmental Health Perspectives*, 123(10). DOI: 10.1289/ehp.1510037.

ASHRAE (2016) *Standard 62.1–2016 Ventilation for Acceptable Indoor Air Quality*. Atlanta, GA: American Society for Heating, Refrigeration, and Air-Conditioning Engineers, Inc.

Breuer, K. and Satish, U. (2003) Emergency management simulations: an approach to the assessment of decision-making processes in complex dynamic crisis environments. In González, J.J. (ed.) *From Modeling to Managing Security: A Systems Dynamics Approach*. Kristiansand: Norwegian Academic Press, pp. 145–156.

Brundage, J.F., Scott, R.M., Lednar, W.M., Smith, D.W. and Miller, R.N. (1988) Building-associated risk of febrile acute respiratory diseases in army trainees. *JAMA*, 259(14): 2108–2112. DOI: 10.1001/jama. 1988.03720140028029.

Burton, W., Conti, D., Chen, C., Schultz, A. and Edington, D. (2001) The impact of allergies and allergy treatment on worker productivity. *Journal of Occupational and Environmental Medicine*, 43(1): 64–71.

Drinka, P.J., Krause, P., Schilling, M., Miller, B.A., Shult, P. and Gravenstein, S. (1996) Report of an outbreak: nursing home architecture and influenza A attack rates. *Journal of the American Geriatrics Society*, 44(8): 910–913. DOI: 10.1111/j.1532-5415.1996.tb01859.x.

EPA (1998) *Building Assessment Survey and Evaluation*. Available at: www.epa.gov/iaq/base/study_over view.html (accessed 22 Jan. 2015).

Fisk, W.J., Seppänen, O., Faulkner, D. and Huang, J. (2003) Economizer system cost effectiveness: Accounting for the influence of ventilation rate on sick leave. In *Proceedings of Healthy Buildings Conference*, Singapore.

ForHealth.org. (2016). Nine foundations of a healthy building. Available at: www.forhealth.org

Hamilton, M., Rackes, A., Gurian, P.L. and Waring, M.S. (2016) Perceptions in the U.S. building industry of the benefits and costs of improving indoor air quality. *Indoor Air*, 26(2): 318–330. DOI: 10.1111/ ina.12192.

Hoge, C.W., Reichler, M.R., Dominguez, E.A., Bremer, J.C., Mastro, T.D., Hendricks, K.A., *et al.* (1994) An Epidemic of pneumococcal disease in an overcrowded, inadequately ventilated jail. *The New England Journal of Medicine*, 331(10): 643–648. DOI: 10.1056/NEJM199409083311004.

Klepeis, N.E., Nelson, W.C., Ott, W.R., Robinson, J.P., Tsang, A.M., Switzer, P., *et al.* (2001) The National Human Activity Pattern Survey (NHAPS): A resource for assessing exposure to environmental pollutants. *Journal of Exposure Analysis and Environmental Epidemiology*, 11: 231–252. DOI: 10.10.8/sj. jea.7500165.

Knibbs, L.D., Morawska, L., Bell, S.C. and Grzybowski, P. (2011) Room ventilation and the risk of airborne infection transmission in 3 health care settings within a large teaching hospital. *AJIC: American Journal of Infection Control*, 39(10): 866–872. DOI: 10.1016/j.ajic.2011.02.014.

MacNaughton, P., Pegues, J., Satish, U., Santanam, S., Spengler, J.D. and Allen, J. (2015) Economic, environmental and health implications of enhanced ventilation in office buildings. *International Journal of Environmental Research and Public Health*, 12. DOI: 10.3390/ijerph120x0000x.

Maddalena, R., Mendell, M.J., Eliseeva, K., Chan, W.R., Sullivan, D.P., Russell, M., *et al.* (2015) Effects of ventilation rate per person and per floor area on perceived air quality, sick building syndrome symptoms, and decision-making. *Indoor Air*, 25(4): 362–370. DOI: 10.1111/ina.12149.

Mendell, M.J., Fisk, W.J., Kreiss, K., Levin, H., Alexander, D., Cain, W.S., *et al.* (2002) Improving the health of workers in indoor environments: priority research needs for a national occupational research agenda. *American Journal of Public Health*, 92(9): 1430–1440.

Mendelson, M., Catano, V. and Kelloway, K. (2000) The role of stress and social support in Sick Building Syndrome. *Work & Stress*, 14(2): 137–155. DOI: 10.1080/026783700750051658.

Milton, D.K., Glencross, P.M. and Walters, M.D. (2000) Risk of sick leave associated with outdoor air supply rate, humidification, and occupant complaints. *Indoor Air*, 10(4): 212–221. DOI: 10.1034/j.1600-0668.2000.010004212.x.

Satish, U., Cleckner, L. and Vasselli, J. (2006) Pilot study of using strategic management simulation to assess human productivity. Paper presented at the AWMA/EPA Conference: Indoor Air Quality – Problems, Research, and Solutions, Durham, NC, USA, 17–17 July.

Satish, U., Cleckner, L. and Vasselli, J. (2013) Impact of VOCs on decision making and productivity. *Intelligent Buildings International*, 5(4), 213–220. DOI: 10.1080/17508975.2013.812956.

Satish, U., Mendell, M.J., Shekhar, K., Hotchi, T., Sullivan, D.P., Streufert, S. and Fisk, W.J. (2012) Is CO_2 an indoor pollutant? Direct effects of low-to-moderate CO_2 concentrations on human decision-making performance. *Environmental Health Perspectives*, 120(12): 1671.

Satish, U., Streufert, S., Dewan, M. and Voort, S. (2004) Improvements in simulated real-world relevant performance for patients with seasonal allergic rhinitis: impact of desloratadine. *Allergy*, 59(4): 415–420.

Satish, U., Streufert, S. and Eslinger, P.J. (2008) Simulation-based executive cognitive assessment and rehabilitation after traumatic frontal lobe injury: case report. *Disability & Rehabilitation*, 30(6), 468–478.

Sola, X.G. (2012) Indoor air quality. In *Encyclopaedia of Occupational Health and Safety* (4th ed., Vol. VI). Geneva: International Labour Office.

Stenberg, B., Eriksson, N., Höög, J., Sundell, J. and Wall, S. (1994) The Sick Building Syndrome (SBS) in office workers: a case-referent study of personal, psychosocial and building-related risk indicators. *International Journal of Epidemiology*, 23(6): 1190.

Stewart, W.F., Ricci, J.A., Chee, E., and Morganstein, D. (2003) Cost of lost productive work time among US workers with depression (1538–3598). *Journal of American Medical Association*, 289(23): 3135–3144.

Streufert, S., Pogash, R. and Piasecki, M. (1988) Simulation-based assessment of managerial competence: reliability and validity. *Personnel Psychology*, 41(3): 537–557. DOI: 10.1111/j.1744-6570.1988.tb00643.x.

Swezey, R.W., Streufert, S., Satish, U. and Siem, F.M. (1998) Preliminary development of a computer-based team performance assessment simulation. *International Journal of Cognitive Ergonomics*, 2(3): 163–179.

Wargocki, P., Sundell, J., Bischof, W., Brundrett, G., Fanger, P.O., Gyntelberg, F., *et al.* (2002) Ventilation and health in non industrial indoor environments: report from a European Multidisciplinary Scientific Consensus Meeting (EUROVEN). *Indoor Air*, 12(2): 113–128. DOI: 10.1034/j.1600-0668.2002.01145.x.

Wargocki, P., Wyon, D., Sundell, J., Clausen, G. and Fanger, P.O. (2000) The effects of outdoor air supply rate in an office on perceived air quality, Sick Building Syndrome (SBS) symptoms and productivity. *Indoor Air*, 10(4): 222–236.

Chapter 9

Workplace productivity
Fatigue and satisfaction

Shin-ichi Tanabe and Naoe Nishihara

Introduction

Building-related carbon dioxide emissions, or the sum of the commercial and residential sectors, account for nearly one-third of the total emissions in Japan and worldwide, and have shown most increase.

The COOL BIZ campaign has been promoted by the Japanese government since the summer of 2005 in order to reduce the amount of emissions from the commercial sector. This campaign involves raising the preset temperature for cooling and modifying the business dress code in offices during summer (Doi, 2006). The Energy Conservation Center, Japan (ECCJ, 2005) reported that 1.2 percent of the annual energy consumption of a heating, ventilation, and air conditioning system can be saved by raising the temperature set point during summer from 26°C to 28°C. There has been a wide movement for mitigating the preset temperature in offices and public facilities in Japan.

Although the conservation of energy is an important issue, the indoor environmental quality has to be maintained concurrently to maintain the comfort and performance levels of the workers in an office. The salary costs of workers in a typical commercial building are about two orders of magnitude more expensive than the operational energy and maintenance costs of the buildings (CIBSE, 1999; Nishihara and Tanabe, 2010).

Seppänen *et al.* (2006) proposed an equation that demonstrates the association between indoor air temperature and relative performance of office workers: the performance decreases with increasing the indoor temperature >22°C. On the other hand, Pilcher *et al.* (2002) conducted a meta-analysis of thermal effects on task performance. Their analysis indicated that performance peaked across a broad range of temperatures from 21°C to 27°C. De Dear *et al.* (2013) concluded, from an extensive literature review, that the effects of thermal comfort on task performance and productivity remain ambiguous owing to the diverse definitions of productivity.

The relationship between thermal environment and workers' productivity should be evaluated in light of the underlying mechanism. In this chapter, we focus on fatigue and individual thermal satisfaction to explain the relationship between thermal environment and worker performance.

Conceptual diagram for the effect of thermal environment on productivity

A conceptual diagram for the evaluation of the effect of thermal environment on productivity is proposed as shown in Figure 9.1. Human responses are considered to be important intermediate

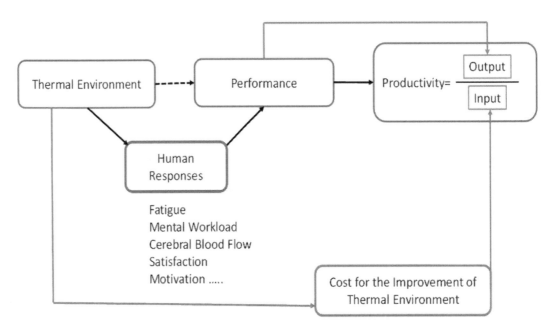

Figure 9.1 Conceptual diagram for the effect of thermal environment and productivity

factors, affecting the performance of the workers via the indoor environment. In our studies, we have focused on fatigue and individual thermal satisfaction. Evidence from subjective experiments and field surveys are described to explain Figure 9.1 in the following sections.

The call center study

Tanabe *et al.* (2009) performed a field survey at a call center in Japan to investigate the effect of indoor air temperature on call response rate. The field survey was conducted in a call center, with a floor area of 458 m², located on the fourth floor of a building. The main business contents of the call center were guidance, consultation, and technical support for their customers.

The surveyed data were collected between February 18, 2004 and February 1, 2005. Throughout the survey, a cumulative total of 13,169 persons' call data were collected. The call control system installed in this call center estimates the incoming call load each day based on the records from the previous year and assigns an appropriate number of operators, because the numbers of incoming call varied by season and time of day. During the survey, there were usually 70–120 operators per day working in the call center. They all wore their own ordinary clothes and could adjust their clothes accordingly. The office hours of the call center were 8:45 to 19:00, Monday through Saturday. The analyses were based on the data gathered on the weekdays; data for Saturday were excluded.

The call center was conditioned normally during the survey period, that is, without any intervention from observers. The air-conditioning system was equipped with a central controlling system and additional package-type air-conditioning systems with its operation and preset

Figure 9.2 A call center

temperature deferred to the occupants. The air-conditioning system operated from 8:00 to 20:00 on business days, and had shifted from heating to cooling on April 20 and cooling to heating on November 2. The preset temperature for heating was 23.0°C and for cooling was 25.0°C. The air temperature and relative humidity were measured every 10 minutes by a small data logger (1.1 m above floor level) in the center of the office. Measurements used for analyses were conducted from 8:50 to 19:00, corresponding to the office hours.

Call data were collected automatically for each operator daily. The permissible rate of abandonment was set to be less than 5 percent by the supervisor throughout the survey period. The call response rate was calculated by taking the average of number of calls handled per hour by each operator. The call response rate represents the processing speed of the call center, based on the assumption that the favorable conditions of correspondence are maintained as less than 5 percent of the rate of abandonment, in which an appropriate balance of incoming calls and call responses is achieved. Since the efficiency of call center services is defined as sufficient correspondence without delay in responding to the incoming calls, the call response rate was used as the index of performance in this study.

The relationship between indoor air temperature and call response rate over one year is shown in Figure 9.3. A linear regression model weighted by the number of relevant operators was obtained with a correlation coefficient of -0.69. Based on the regression model, the increase in air temperature by 1.0°C is associated with a decrease in call response rate by 0.15 calls/h. Thus, increasing the indoor air temperature by 1.0°C from 25.0°C to 26.0°C would

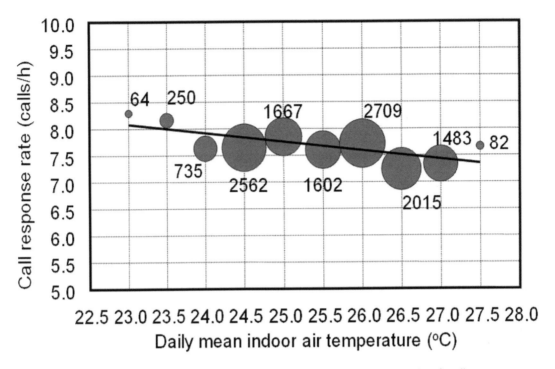

Figure 9.3 Relationship between indoor air temperature and call response rate using data for all seasons

decrease the call response rate from 7.79 to 7.64 calls/h, which is a 1.9 percent loss in call response performance.

Does performance decrease upon short-term exposure to a moderately hot environment?

The answer is no. Task performance does not decrease with short-term exposure in a moderately hot environment; however, workers feel more fatigued.

Tanabe and Nishihara (2004) reported the effects of a moderately warm environment on work performance corresponding to a COOL BIZ office. They tested the effect of exposure to temperatures of 25.5°C, 28.0°C, and 33.0°C on office work performance via a subjective experiment in a climate chamber. The effect differed inconsistently between task types, while there was a clear trend of greater mental fatigue with higher temperature.

College-aged subjects, 20 male and 20 female, participated in the experiment (ibid.). The chamber was conditioned at operative temperatures of 25.5°C, 28.0°C, and 33.0°C with still air. Before exposure to these three conditions, a practice session at an operative temperature of 25.5°C was conducted. Relative humidity was controlled at around 50 percent. Subjects wore a uniform with an insulation value of 0.76 clo. The task performance tests were conducted on computers for 1.5 hours.

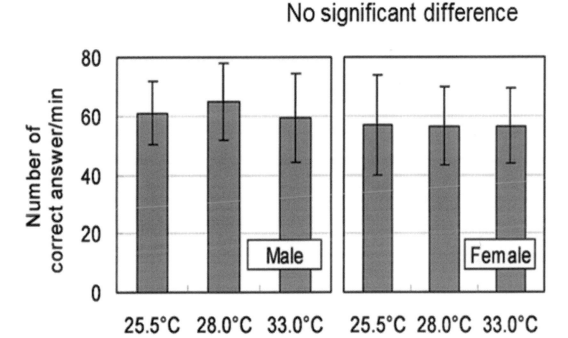

Figure 9.4 Performance of the addition task

The performance of an addition task is shown in Figure 9.4. For both male and female subjects, there was no significant difference in the performance of the addition test under the environmental conditions. However, it is difficult to evaluate the effect of thermal environment on productivity by measuring task performance alone.

We used the Evaluation of Subjective Symptoms of Fatigue questionnaire (Yoshitake, 1973) to evaluate the feeling of fatigue. This questionnaire consists of three categories: group I consists of 10 terms regarding drowsiness and dullness; group II consists of 10 terms regarding difficulty in concentration; and group III consists of 10 terms regarding projection of physical disintegration. Mental fatigue (group II) appeared to be most severe in subjects who were in the room with an operative temperature of 33.0°C.

Effect of high temperature on cerebral blood flow

Near infrared spectroscopy

In near infrared spectroscopy, near infrared light is produced by laser diodes and carried to the tissue via optical fibers (Figure 9.5). The light emerging from the tissue is returned to the instrument through another optical fiber by a detector, and incident and integrated values of transmitted light intensities are recorded every second. The sampling rate in our study was 2,000 times per second. Changes in the concentration of the chromophores oxygenated hemoglobin "ΔO_2Hb" and deoxyhemoglobin "ΔHHb" were calculated using the modified

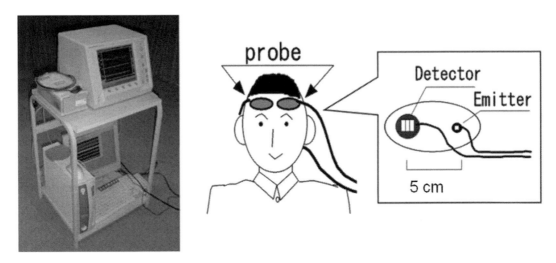

Figure 9.5 Near infrared spectrometer (NIRO-300)

Beer-Lambert equation in µM = 10^{-6} mol units. The changes in concentration of total hemoglobin were calculated:

$$\Delta\text{total Hb} = \Delta O_2 Hb + \Delta HHb$$

The probes were placed on the subject's forehead.

Previous studies reported that an increase in $\Delta O_2 Hb$ and Δtotal Hb and decrease in ΔHHb are the typical near infrared spectroscopy findings during brain activation and mental work. The mechanism was explained as follows: blood is necessary for brain activity, but the brain has small glucose and O_2 reserves. Therefore, blood flow supply to this region is important. The $\Delta O_2 Hb$ and Δtotal Hb increase with brain activity. However, the consumption of O_2 during brain activity is much lower than the increase in cerebral blood flow. Therefore, ΔHHb decreases with brain activity.

According to the results of split-brain studies, the left brain dominates linguistic abilities, calculations, math, and logical abilities whereas the right brain dominates spatial ability. Moreover, in right-handed people, the language center is located in the left side of the brain.

Cerebral blood flow and the difficulty level of tasks

The relationship between the changes in cerebral blood oxygenation and the difficulty level of a task was evaluated in subjective experiments (Tanabe and Nishihara, 2004). Four tasks were conducted: single-digit addition, double-digit multiplication, triple-digit addition, and triple-digit multiplication. The more difficult the type of task, the more oxygenated hemoglobin and total hemoglobin concentration were required for their performance. There was a significant correlation between the subjective value of mental demand for tasks and the left-side Δtotal Hb. The correlation between the rate of change in mental demand and left-side Δtotal Hb, based on the single-digit addition task, is shown in Figure 9.6. Monitoring cerebral blood oxygenation

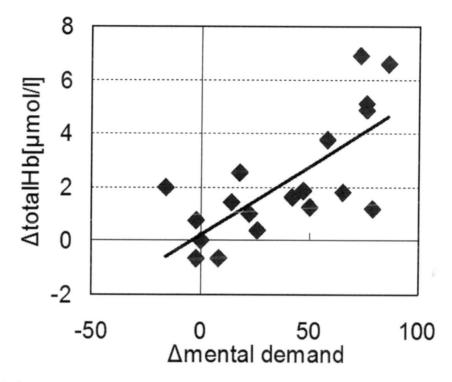

Figure 9.6 Correlation between the rate of change in mental demand and left-side Δtotal Hb during the single-digit addition task

changes could be applied to the evaluation of the input-side parameter of productivity to indicate the degree of mental effort required to perform the task.

Does short-term exposure to a moderately hot environment affect cerebral blood flow?

A subjective experiment was conducted to study the effect of a moderately hot environment on cerebral blood flow (Tanabe *et al.*, 2007). Twelve right-handed male subjects were exposed, in a climatic chamber, to two operative temperature levels of 26.0°C and 33.5°C in a balanced order. Before exposure to these two conditions, they participated in a practice session under an operative temperature of 26.0°C the first time. In this study, in order to increase their motivation to the same level, they were informed that the top 6 performers of the computer tasks could earn one hour's worth of bonus. Therefore, it could be assumed that subjects were highly motivated. After adaptation to the thermal environment for 50 minutes, three types of calculation tasks (single-digit addition, triple-digit addition, and triple-digit multiplication) were assigned to subjects.

Subjects felt that the 33.5°C environment was hotter and stuffier compared to that at 26.0°C. There were no significant differences in task performances between the 26.0°C and 33.5°C conditions. Moreover, the subjects complained of mental fatigue more frequently in the 33.5°C environment than in the 26.0°C environment.

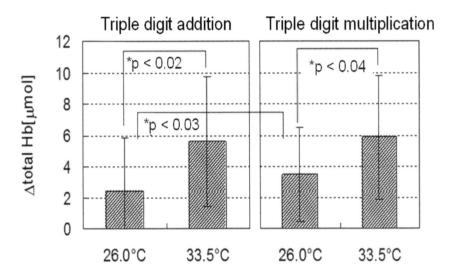

Figure 9.7 Δtotal Hb and task performance

The results showed that there was no significant difference in task performances between the 26.0°C and 33.5°C conditions, but the increase in Δtotal Hb was higher at 33.5°C than that at 26.0°C. Hotter environments required more cerebral blood flow to maintain the same level of task performance (Figure 9.7).

Does improving thermal satisfaction have a positive effect on performance?

Thermal satisfaction is important for achieving optimal performance in offices with moderately high temperatures. A subjective experiment was conducted in a climate chamber to objectively evaluate the effect of improving the thermal environment (Tanabe *et al.*, 2015). Reduction of clothing insulation and control of air movement around the occupants are examples of ways to improve satisfaction with thermal environment. To reduce clothing insulation, both reducing clothing items and changing the type of office chair can be considered.

Three cooling items were used in this study: a desk fan, a type of work shirt with integrated fans, and an office chair with mesh fabric. The desk fan (Figure 9.8 (a)) can be turned off, or adjusted to three levels of air volume, and allows for oscillation of the direction of air movement. The shirt with integrated fans (Figure 9.8 (b)) can be switched off or operated at two air supply rates. For the office chair (Figure 9.8 (c)), the back and seat areas comprise mesh material that allows air movement and the removal of heat and moisture.

The experiment was conducted in a climate chamber on Tuesdays to Fridays from September 18 to November 4, 2007. The experiment lasted from 12:00 to 18:00. The chamber was air-conditioned during the experiment. The layout of the chamber and a picture taken during the experiment are shown in Figure 9.9. Desk fans were placed on the left corner on the workstation.

(a) Desk fan   (b) Air-conditioned   (c) Mesh office chair
                                    shirt

Figure 9.8 Cooling items used in the study

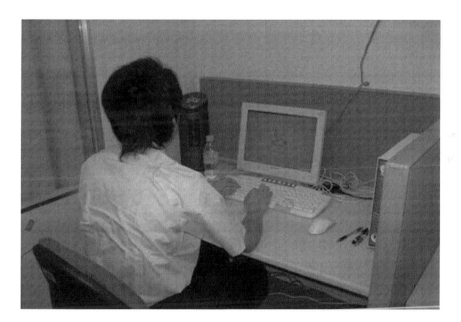

Figure 9.9 A subject during the experiment

Eleven Japanese male students (age: 22.4 ± 1.6 years; height: 171.9 ± 4.7 cm; weight: 60.6 ± 4.8 kg) were recruited and divided into four groups, each containing two or three subjects. Each group participated in the experiment once a week, repeated at the same time and day. To keep the subjects motivated, they were told that they would receive a bonus depending on their performance. Experimental conditions were set according to a combination of operative temperature, clothing insulation, and use of cooling items (Table 9.1).

Table 9.1 Experimental conditions

Conditions	25.5°C-Suit	28.5°C-Suit	28.5°C-CB	28.5°C-DF	28.5°C-ALL
Clothes	Suit 0.96 clo	Suit 0.96 clo	Short-sleeved shirt without a tie 0.57 clo	Short-sleeved shirt without a tie 0.57 clo	Short-sleeved shirt without a tie 0.57 clo
Cooling Items	None	None	None	Desk fan (Adjustable)	Desk fan, air-conditioned shirt, mesh office chair (Adjustable)

In the "25.5°C-Suit" scenario, the operative temperature was set at 25.5°C with a clothing ensemble of a suit jacket, tie, long-sleeved business shirt, short-sleeved T-shirt, thin trousers, underwear, socks, and leather shoes (0.96 clo). The "28.5°C-Suit" scenario repeated the same clothing ensemble with an operative temperature of 28.5°C, simulating an increased temperature set point while not modifying the dress code. In the "28.5°C-CB" scenario, the operative temperature was 28.5°C, with a lightweight business ensemble of a short-sleeved business shirt, short-sleeved T-shirt, thin trousers, underwear, socks, and leather shoes (0.57 clo). In the "28.5°C-DF" scenario, the desk fan was used with an operative temperature of 28.5°C and a lightweight clothing ensemble. In the "28.5°C-ALL" scenario, the desk fan was used, and the air-conditioned shirt was worn instead of a standard short-sleeved business shirt, while the other clothing items matched those in scenario 28.5°C-CB.

The mesh office chair was used only in 28.5°C-ALL; all other scenarios used a chair with normal cushions. In scenarios 28.5°C-DF and 28.5°C-ALL, the subjects were allowed to adjust the speed of the desk fan and the direction of air movement, and could select whether the fan should operate in the oscillating mode; moreover, the speed of the fan incorporated into the shirt could be adjusted. Relative humidity was set at 50 percent. Fluorescent lights on the ceiling were controlled to provide an illumination of 750 lx at the desk level. The main noise sources during the experiment consisted of the fan of the air-conditioning system, the desk fans, and the air-conditioned shirts; noise from the operation of personal computers; and any noise made by the subjects.

Eating was not allowed during the experiment. Subjects were provided with bottles of plain mineral water and were allowed to drink whenever necessary. Prior to exposure, the subjects practiced the experimental procedures. The condition during this session was the same as in the "28.5°C-Suit" scenario. The experimental conditions were balanced for order of presentation.

The physical parameters measured in the chamber were air temperature, mean radiant temperature, relative humidity, carbon dioxide concentration, and desktop illumination. The experimental procedure is shown in Figure 9.10. They performed three sessions consisting of the multiplication task for 30 minutes, proofreading for 25 minutes, and a creative thinking task for 20 minutes. Exposure to the experimental conditions lasted 338 minutes, of which 225 minutes involved simulated office tasks.

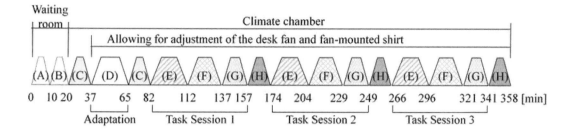

(A) Change clothes and instruction

(B) Rest in waiting room

(C) Votes on indoor environment, subjective vote on fatigue, vote on sleepiness, finger pulse wave measurement, and P-Tool

(D) Rest in the climate chamber

(E) Multiplication task

(F) Proofreading task

(G) Creative thinking task

(H) NASA-TLX and vote on concentration + (C)

Figure 9.10 The experimental procedure

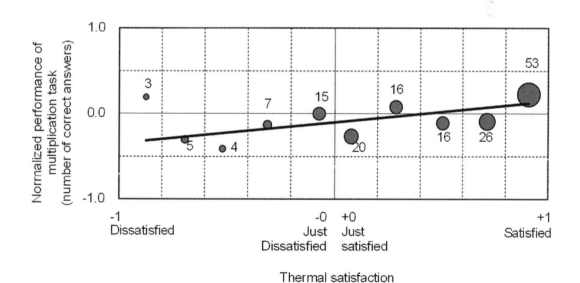

Figure 9.11 Thermal satisfaction and standard score of multiplication task (y = 0.245x − 0.103, R^2 = 0.403, p < 0.001, n = 165)

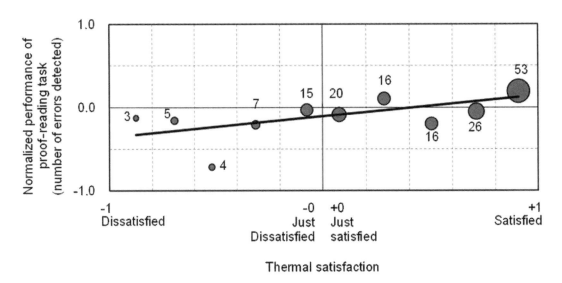

Figure 9.12 Thermal satisfaction and standard score on the proofreading task ($y = 0.254x - 0.107$, $R^2 = 0.464$, $p < 0.001$, n = 165)

To determine the effect of thermal satisfaction on the performance of simulated office work, the thermal satisfaction votes after each task session were correlated with performance in the multiplication (number of correct answers) and proof-reading (number of errors detected) tasks.

The data set for the thermal satisfaction votes (intervals of 0.2) was averaged and compared with the corresponding normalized performance. The relationship between thermal satisfaction and normalized performance in the multiplication task is shown in Figure 9.11 and that between thermal satisfaction and normalized performance in the proofreading task is shown in Figure 9.12. The size of the plots in the figures represents the number of votes used for calculating the averages. The coefficients of determination (R2 value) of linear regression, as weighted by the number of corresponding votes, were 0.403 for the multiplication task and 0.464 for proofreading. From the results, performance in the multiplication and proofreading tasks was higher when subjects were thermally satisfied.

Conclusion

In this chapter, the experiments regarding the effect of moderately high temperature on productivity were reviewed.

1   The call center study conducted over one year showed that increasing the indoor air temperature by 1.0°C from 25.0°C to 26.0°C would result in decreased call response rate, which is a 1.9 percent loss in call response performance.
2   The effect of short-term exposure to a moderately hot environment on task performance showed inconsistent results among the task types. The subjects complained of mental fatigue.
3   The effect of short-term exposure to a moderately hot environment on cerebral blood flow was estimated using near infrared spectroscopy. The results showed that increased

cerebral blood flow was required to maintain the same level of task performance under hot conditions than that at thermal neutral conditions. To evaluate the task performance, cost of maintaining the performance, namely, fatigue and mental effort, is important when evaluating and predicting productivity.

4   The experimental findings demonstrate that the performance of simulated office work, i.e. multiplication and proof-reading tasks, improved when individual thermal satisfaction was higher. Based on the evidence that subjective thermal satisfaction among employees influences objective measurements of workplace performance, the evaluation of thermal satisfaction in real offices has clear practical benefits for improving workplace productivity.

References

CIBSE (1999) Environmental factors affecting office worker performance: a review of evidence. CIBSE Technical Memoranda TM24. Windsor: Reedprint Limited.

de Dear, R., Akimoto, T., Arens, E., Brager, G., Candido, C., Cheong, K.W., *et al.* (2013) Progress in thermal comfort research over the last twenty years. *Indoor Air*, 23(6): 442–461.

Delpy, D.T., Cope, M., van der Zee, P., Arrige, S., Wray, S. and Wyatt, J. (1988) Estimation of optical pathlength through tissue from direct time of flight measurement. *Physics in Medicine and Biology*, 33: 1433–1442.

Doi, K. (2006) COOL BIZ, *Japanese SHASE J*, 80(7), 5–7 (in Japanese).

Nishihara, N. and Tanabe, S. (2010) Management of indoor climate (Productivity). *Handbook of Heating, Air-Conditioning and Sanitary Engineers*, 5, p. 562 (in Japanese).

Pilcher, J.J., Nadler, E. and Busch, C. (2002) Effects of hot and cold temperature exposure on performance: a meta-analytic review, *Ergonomics*, 45(10): 682–698.

Seppänen, O., Fisk, W.J. and Lei, Q.H. (2006) Effect of temperature on task performance in office environment. Proceedings of the 5th International Conference on Cold Climate HVAC (CD-ROM)

Tanabe, S., Haneda, M. and Nishihara, N. (2015) Workplace productivity and individual thermal satisfaction. *Building and Environment*, 91: 42–50.

Tanabe, S., Kobayashi, K., Kiyota, O., Nishihara, N. and Haneda, M. (2009) The effect of indoor thermal environment on productivity by a year-long survey of a call centre. *Intelligent Buildings International*, 1(3): 184–194.

Tanabe, S. and Nishihara, N. (2004) Productivity and fatigue. *Indoor Air*, 14(s7): 126–133.

Tanabe, S., Nishihara, N. and Haneda, M. (2007) Indoor temperature, productivity, and fatigue in office tasks. *HVAC&R Research*, 13(4): 623–633.

The Energy Conservation Center, Japan (2005) *Guidebook for Energy Conservation in Building of FY2005*. Available at: www.eccj.or.jp/office_bldg/index.html (accessed 19 April 2016) (in Japanese).

Yoshitake, H. 1973. *Occupational Fatigue: Approach from Subjective Symptom*. Tokyo, Japan: The Institute for Science of Labor (in Japanese).

Chapter 10

Proving the productivity benefits of well-designed offices

Nigel Oseland

Defining productivity

It seems that whenever a group of workplace professionals come together (regardless of whether managers, designers, or researchers), the discussion will soon turn to the relationship between the built environment and productivity. A lively debate on how to measure productivity usually ensues, eventually reaching the conclusion that measuring productivity in the modern office is virtually impossible. For over thirty years, the pursuit of measuring office worker productivity has been referred to as 'the search for the holy grail' (Conrath, 1984). There is a view that the relationship between office design, or environmental conditions, and productivity is elusive and intangible – a myth even. That in itself is not a problem, but one consequence of believing that the impact of office design on productivity cannot be readily demonstrated, is that it is often completely ignored.

From a business perspective, ignoring the effect of the office design on worker performance is not only naïve but also irresponsible. Furthermore, because of (wrongly) perceived measurement difficulty and lack of evidence, the potential impact of office design on business performance is generally excluded from the business case for workplace projects. Thus, the business case is simply weighted in terms of reducing property costs, e.g. by saving space. This perpetuates the notion that property is a cost burden rather than a potentially lucrative return on investment for the business. Furthermore, in completed projects, the effect of the office design on productivity is not thoroughly tested. Therefore, we may never fully understand whether the design had a beneficial or negative impact on business performance. Hence, as long as the new office design reduces property costs, it is deemed as successful, regardless of the consequences for the business.

Clearly a balance of cost savings and performance benefits is required. Saving property costs while reducing business performance is a short-sighted, rather than a sustainable, solution. Reducing costs without adversely affecting performance is better and saving costs while improving performance is the best solution. All approaches require monitoring the impact of the office design on performance.

The terms productivity and performance are used interchangeably, there are many definitions of productivity but it is often simply defined as the 'ratio of output to input'. The output usually refers to achieving a goal or completing a task or another form of performance. Input usually refers to the time and effort applied to achieve the output, but it could also refer to other required resources, such as money, space and equipment. In terms of achieving a balanced design, productivity could actually be considered in terms of the ratio of business performance to property costs. So, reducing costs while maintaining performance would be considered productive, whereas saving costs and reducing performance would not be productive. This approach to productivity was illustrated by Oseland and Bartlett (1999) in their productivity matrix, see Figure 10.1.

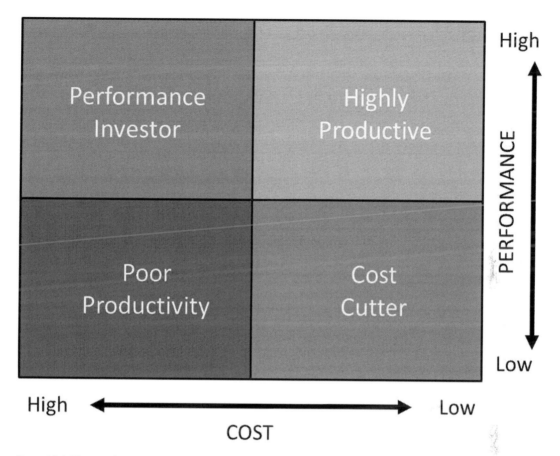

Figure 10.1 The productivity matrix

The productivity equation is also affected by the proportion of property to employee costs in a business. For some time researchers have illustrated that employee costs are a much higher proportion of a business's overall cost base than property. For example, as far back as 1965, the National Bureau of Standards estimated employee costs to be approximately 85 per cent (Wargocki, 2012), with property costs at 15 per cent. More recently property costs are reported to be closer to 10 per cent (Alker, 2014), see Figure 10.2. Therefore, large savings in property costs could easily be offset by small changes in employee performance. Several researchers have proposed that an increase in performance of approximately 15 per cent would cover the cost of the property by offsetting the equivalent in employee costs, see Oseland (1999) for a review.

The 15 per cent performance calculation explained above is actually an under-estimation as in some organisations the employees are expected to generate revenue for the business in the order of three times their income. In such organisations, just a 5 per cent increase in performance, reflected in pure revenue, could offset the property costs. A more recent report by the British Council for Offices (Harris and Hawkeswood, 2016) suggests that while property costs are around 15 per cent of business costs, the employee costs are closer to 55 per cent with

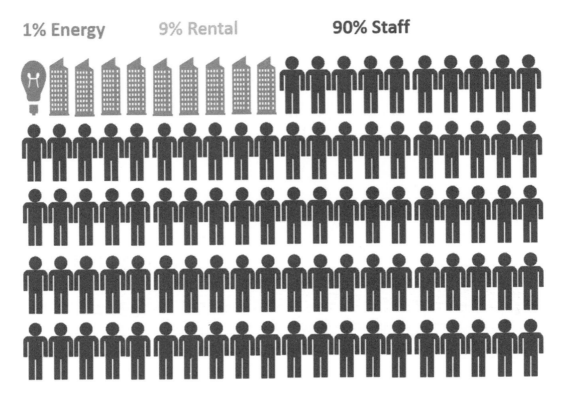

1% Energy   9% Rental   **90% Staff**

Figure 10.2 Business life-cycle operating costs

the remaining 30 per cent made up of other business costs. While these figures require further verification, they indicate that the increase in performance to cover the property costs may be considerably higher than previously thought. Nevertheless, based on revenue, an increase in performance of approximately 25 per cent could cover the property costs of business.

Measuring productivity

Despite the current lack of confidence, measuring the productivity of the workforce dates back at least 7,000 years. The Sumerians kept individual records of each worker's daily performance and compared it with the cost of feeding and accommodating them. Of course, the performance of the Sumerian worker would have been relatively easy to calculate, for example, by measuring the output of their construction work or farming. While output is an appropriate performance metric for some office work, for most twenty-first-century businesses, it is not so straightforward.

In the modern office, work may include elements of creativity, management, collaboration, client entertainment and sharing knowledge, etc. Some work tasks will require much effort but not have any immediate deliverables, or revenue generation, associated with them. For example, a day spent networking or entertaining clients (at dinner or on a golf course) may not be considered productive by colleagues, especially if it did not result in an immediate sale or contract. While their view would likely change if the day out resulted in a sale, would it still be considered a productive day if no deal was made on the day but nevertheless it resulted in revenue generation several months later?

The length of time spent working is, on its own, not a reliable performance metric. Failing to complete a task due to inefficiency or spending the day delivering an output which is then not accepted by the client are considered unproductive time. Nevertheless, the office design should allow employees to conduct their work duties with minimal distraction or downtime. Similarly, absenteeism is a useful proxy for productivity simply because if people are not working, then they cannot be productive, but when at work we also want to increase their performance, or at least ensure it does not drop due to poor office design or facilities.

The reality is that modern office work is varied for the individual, the business and the sector. That does not mean that productivity cannot be measured, it just means it is difficult, multivariable and not generic. Back in the early 1990s, organisations such as ASHRAE (Levin, 1992) hosted a series of seminars and workshops, resulting in proposed measures of office worker productivity, see Table 10.1. While there are practical difficulties associated with most of these measures, the list nevertheless highlights the wide range of methods of monitoring productivity.

Most organisations will have performance metrics that they understand are relevant to them and that they report regularly. Generic business metrics such as revenue, margin and profitability, etc. are likely to be more reported in the boardroom than, say, creativity, meeting deadlines or accuracy. Organisations may also have other more pertinent metrics they report, such as fee-earning hours for lawyers, papers published for researchers, the number of claims processed in insurance companies, calls converted to sales in contact centres, drawings issued on time for designers, staff utilisation for consultancies, etc. The World Green Building Council (WGBC) recently published a framework for assessing the impact of the design and operation of the office on health, well-being and productivity, see Figure 10.3 (Alker, 2014).

The *Physical* refers to gathering information about the physical office environment itself, either through direct measurement or user evaluation. *Perceptual* refers to underlying attitudes

Table 10.1 ASHRAE's proposed productivity metrics

Item	Metric
1	Absence from work, or workstation; unavailability on telephone
2	Health costs including sick leave, accidents and injuries
3	Observed downtime and interruptions to work
4	Controlled independent judgements of work quality, mood, etc.
5	Self-assessments of productivity
6	Component skills, task measures, such as speed, slips and accuracy
7	Output from pre-existing work groups
8	Total unit cost per product or service
9	Output change in response to graded reward
10	Voluntary overtime or extra work
11	Cycle time from initiation to completion of a discrete process
12	Multiple measures at all organisational levels
13	Individual measures of performance, health and well-being at work
14	Time course of measures and rates of change

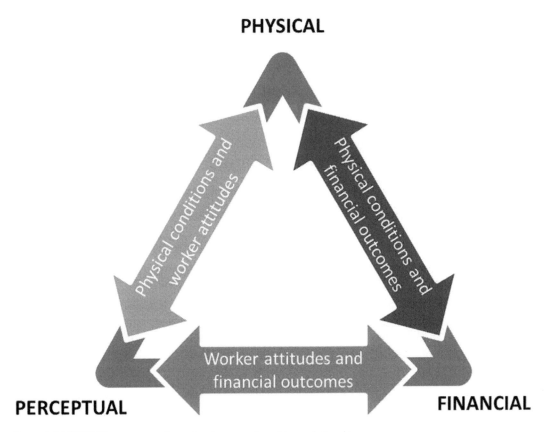

Figure 10.3 WGBC's summary of metrics framework and key relationships

about the workplace and self-reported productivity in the workplace. Under *Financial*, the WGBC include:

1 Absenteeism
2 Staff turnover/retention
3 Revenue breakdown
4 Medical costs
5 Medical complaints
6 Physical complaints.

While the more business-related performance metrics, in particular, points 1–3 above, are more familiar to the board, their relationship to office design is confounded by other variables. Business performance is dependent not only upon the office design but also is affected by the workforce's capability, market demand, brand, advertising, legacy, investment and organisational factors, etc. The difficulty in measuring productivity is therefore not the metric *per se* but untangling the direct impact of the office design from other relevant factors. To achieve this requires a baseline and/or control group so that interventions, such as office design, can be identified and isolated. For example, many retail organisations monitor the sales in their outlets across the country on a weekly basis, and some even report the sales per floor area (£ per m²); this allows them to more easily observe the impact of any initiatives such as regional advertising, new management or a recent shop fit-out. However, such comprehensive monitoring is not currently practised by office-based businesses. Thus, when the effect of the office design on performance is evaluated, it tends to be a one-off measurement without context.

Evidence for productivity

Despite the continuous ignoring of the impact of office design on productivity, there is abundant evidence to suggest a clear relationship. Empirical research on the impact of environmental conditions on worker performance has been conducted since the early twentieth century. Over the last 20 years there have been many literature reviews cataloguing productivity research including the following four notable publications from large institutions:

1   The Chartered Institution of Building Service Engineers (CIBSE) report, *Technical Memoranda 24 Environmental Factors Affecting Office Worker Performance: Review of Evidence* (Oseland, 1999) covered the definition of productivity, reviewed 149 papers showing the impact of environmental conditions on performance and showed how previous authors had monetised the benefits.
2   The Commission for Architecture and the Built Environment (CABE) and British Council for Offices (BCO) joint report, *The Impact of Office Design on Business Performance* (Morrell, 2005) reviewed 111 papers on productivity. The authors explored the types of metrics commonly used and proposed a model for capturing data and reporting case studies.
3   The Royal Institution of Chartered Surveyors (RICS) report, *Workplace Design and Productivity: Are They Inextricably Linked?* (Thompson, 2008) reviewed 57 papers on productivity, stressed the need to understand the link to productivity and detailed how to monetise productivity benefits.
4   Carnegie Mellon University's database for *Health, Productivity and the Triple Bottom Line* (Loftness, 2007) includes 297 case studies which highlight the impact of environmental conditions on performance and health in offices, hospitals and schools.

Several of the previous reviews acknowledge that organisational and motivational factors are likely to have the biggest impact on productivity, but nevertheless conclude that environmental factors may account for only a 5–15 per cent increase in productivity (Oseland, 1999). At first sight, this percentage seems low, but as illustrated earlier, the proportion of employee costs is much higher than property costs for most organisations, so that a 15 per cent increase in performance has a dramatic impact on a business's revenue.

Subjective measures, such as self-assessed performance, are better than no measure at all. However, the most convincing research studies are those where the effect on performance is quantified using more objective (possibly built-in business) measures, rather than subjective ones, carried out in the real world, rather than a laboratory. Such studies are rare, but there are a handful often referred to in the productivity literature as described below.

For example, Kroner, Stark-Martin and Willemain (1994) examined the performance of staff in the West Bends Mutual insurance company during a move to new premises. The new office offered an improved space layout, better designed windows, a more efficient ventilation system and new workstations which provided individual control over task lighting, heating and cooling. They recorded the number of insurance claims processed over a period of 51 weeks covering before and after the move. Kroner and colleagues calculated a 15.7 per cent overall increase in performance (claims processed) after the move to the improved working environment, see Figure 10.4. In addition, they found that disabling the new workstations, i.e. removing individual control, reduced the performance gain to 12.7 per cent. Kroner and colleagues concluded that individual control results in a 2.8 per cent increase in performance; the vice-president of the insurance company estimated the increase in performance from the new workstations to be more like 5 per cent.

Call centres have many objective performance measures in place, such as call waiting time, length of call and closed enquiries, etc. Tham *et al.* (2003) controlled the temperature and fresh air supply rate in a tropical call centre over a nine-week period. They found that operator performance, i.e. reduced 'talk time', improved by 4.9 per cent when the air temperature was decreased from 24.5°C to 22.5°C at a low fresh air supply rate (9.8 l/s/person). They then found an 8.8 per cent improvement in operator performance when the fresh air supply rate was increased (22.7 l/s/person).

While not an office *per se*, post offices provide another environment with objective performance measures, i.e. the quantity of mail sorted. Kourigin and Mikheyen (1965) found that increasing the level of noise, via loudspeakers, resulted in a decrease in the numbers of sorted letters. Windheim and McLean ([1986] 1994) studied the retrofit of a Reno post office.

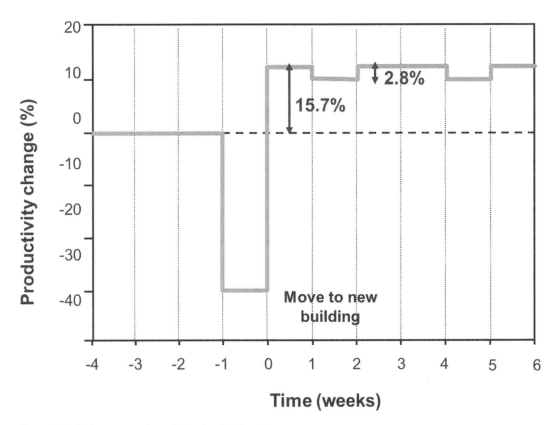

Figure 10.4 Performance gains at West Bends Mutual

Improved lighting was installed along with a sloping ceiling aimed at improving acoustics and temperature control. The output of two sorting sections was monitored before and after the retro-fit over a period of one year. The number of pieces of mail sorted per hour initially increased by 8 per cent and later settled at a 6 per cent increase compared to the pre-project average.

The impact of daylight, view and ventilation on worker performance at the Sacramento Municipal Utility District was studied by Heschong (2003) and colleagues. Initially they continuously monitored the call handling time of 100 workers in the incoming call centre. They found that the call centre staff with the best views out of a window, calculated by the size of the window and vegetation content, processed calls 6–12 per cent faster than those with no view. Both daylight and greenery are considered basic biophilic needs, important for optimal performance (Browning *et al.*, 2012).

The previous highlighted studies illustrate that, as expected, research in real offices using more objective measures tend to be in workplaces where the performance is based on timed output and is more easily quantified. However, more recent research is focusing on using cognitive assessment tasks, as a proxy for performance, in real offices.

For example, Heschong (2003) went on to study the performance of a further 200 office workers at Sacramento Municipal Utility District, using a series of cognitive assessment tests, taken at the worker's own desktop computer. Office workers were found to perform 10–25 per cent better on mental function and memory recall tests when they had the best possible views outside versus those with no view. They also found that in both studies (call centre and offices), the glare from the windows decreased performance by 15–21 per cent.

A more recent example is that of Carter and Jeffery (2015) who carried out a range of cognitive performance tests to estimate productivity benefits before and after a redesign of the National Grid's offices in Warwick. Three cognitive performance tests were administered in the office, each analysing attributes considered vital to the National Grid, such as creativity and lateral thinking. After the office fit-out there was an 8 per cent improvement in performance on the cognitive tests, which the National Grid believes equates to a potential £20M per year of increased productivity. The authors also report an additional two hours or more collaborative activity per week per person, equating to 5 per cent increase in collaborative activity and cross-team working. Employees also 'gained back 5% in productive time due to improved access to meeting spaces'.

The challenge with using in-situ cognitive tests as proxy measures of performance is translating the results into ones which represent all work activities and all employees. While the National Grid pro-rated the 8 per cent gain across all staff, they do recognise that the £20M relates more to potential productivity gains rather than actual ones.

A classic study that used performance tasks in a real-world situation is DeMarco and Lister's (1987) Coding War Games. They studied 600 software developers at 92 different companies and asked them to complete a series of benchmark coding and testing tasks. Each participant worked alone at their workstation and logged the amount of time they spent completing the coding task. Prior to the coding they asked the participants whether they considered their workplace to be quiet, private and free from interruptions, etc. DeMarco and Lister found that the participants who performed in the top quartile, i.e. the quickest time with least errors, rated their workspace much more positively than those who performed in the bottom quartile. Interestingly, DeMarco and Lister comment that the data does not exactly prove that a better workplace will help people perform better, it may only indicate that people who perform better tend to gravitate toward organisations that provide better workplaces.

Quantifying productivity benefits

With so much evidence published, it is a wonder that the relationship between office design and productivity is so often ignored and the business case for new projects is based on space and costs savings alone. As indicated above, possible reasons for doubt are:

- The research has been carried out in a range of environments (laboratory, simulations) which may or may not have a direct relationship with the office worker productivity.
- Different performance metrics are used which may not reflect core office work activity.
- Beneficial results reported by such studies vary dramatically, with productivity gains covering a very large range.
- A wide range of environmental factors are studied (temperature, light and noise, etc.) either individually or combined.

In response to issues with research credibility, Oseland and Burton (2012) carried out a literature review of productivity research and conducted a meta-analysis which accounted for the above factors. They reviewed over 200 productivity research papers, and analysed 75 credible studies with 135 quantified performance benefits. Their raw data indicated productivity gains of 0–160 per cent.

The unique aspect of Oseland and Burton's literature review is that they weighted the reported percentage changes in performance according to the relevance of the research study to real offices and office workers. They weighted the raw data results by:

- *Research environment* – Referring to the place where the productivity research was carried out. For example, a real office was more highly weighted than a laboratory study.
- *Performance metric* – Referring to the measurement made to evaluate the change in productivity. For example, in-house business metrics were weighted more highly than self-reports.
- *Activity time* – Referring to the amount of time that the measurement might be observed in a real office building. For example, computing tasks were weighted more highly than mental arithmetic or paper-based tasks, as more time is usually spent computing in the office.

The weighted results were then averaged for each of the various environmental design factors; the average predicted percentage change increase in performance is highlighted in Table 10.2. The authors provided a range of effects and proposed that the actual figure used would depend upon the confidence with how likely the upper increase in performance is

Table 10.2 Weighted effect of design factors on performance (%)

Design factor	Un-weighted Average	Weighted predicted increase in performance		
		Average	Lower	Upper
Lighting	9.5	1.1	0.1	2.0
Noise	27.8	1.4	0.2	1.7
Temperature	17.0	1.2	0.0	1.9
Ventilation	9.0	1.4	0.2	1.7
Control	8.0	1.2	0.3	2.1
Furniture	15.7	2.1	1.0	2.1
General/mixed	15.9	2.7	1.2	3.2

to be achieved, for example, based on the project budget. They used an existing tool called the *Design Excellence Evaluation Process* (DEEP), see Whitehead (2001). DEEP was used to help identify the potential impact on comfort of the improvements made to the building under various planning scenarios. Alternatively, a percentage of the ideal/highest budget could be used to weight the upper predicted increase in performance.

The authors believe that their revised figures are ones that are more likely to be accepted by financial directors when used in building a business case for office design projects. They tested their model on an office refurbishment pilot for the UK MoD. Again, while some of the figures are low, it must be remembered that just a 5 per cent gain in performance could offset the property costs.

The 'general/mixed' data refers to studies where multiple factors were applied, such as an overall office refurbishment. However, Oseland and Burton also proposed a 'rule of thumb' for determining the effect of a number of the individual factors. Their proposal is based on the law of diminishing returns backed up by three multifactor studies:

$$P_O = P_1 + \tfrac{2}{3} P_2 + \tfrac{1}{3} P_3 \ldots$$

Where:

P_O = the overall percentage performance change
P_1 = percentage performance change due to 1st environmental factor
P_2 = percentage performance change due to 2nd environmental factor
P_3 = percentage performance change due to 3rd environmental factor

The ranges in the Table 10.2 and the rule of thumb above clearly require further testing. Nevertheless the authors conducted a substantial review of productivity research and have offered a more realistic framework for understanding and using the results from those studies, than using the raw data alone.

Designing for productivity

In motivation theory, Maslow (1943) argued that people cannot reach their maximum potential unless a hierarchy of needs are met. The lowest order needs relate to health and safety plus security and basic comfort, such as temperature, noise and daylight. In Herzberg's (1959) *Two Factor Theory*, he proposed that not providing for these basic working conditions, or 'hygiene factors', could have a negative effect on performance. However, he also proposed that resolving the hygiene factors may not necessarily increase performance; that requires motivators, including organisational factors such as challenging work, recognition, responsibility and opportunity, etc. Providing a good working environment is therefore critical both to removing barriers to performance and motivation.

Many researchers and workplace consultants have presented guidance on how to create the productive workplace. In their book *Improving Office Productivity: A Guide for Business and Facilities Managers*, Oseland and Bartlett (1999) go one step further and provide a spreadsheet tool to evaluate whether an office adheres to a set of design principles that will enhance the occupants' performance. Their 100-item checklist is broken down into five broad categories:

- *Location & Access* – Transport nodes, journey time, signage and ease of access, etc.
- *Design & Layout* – Clear circulation routes, team co-location/zones, occupational density, storage and ergonomics, etc.

- *Facilities & Amenities* – Provision of meeting spaces, booking systems, tea-points and restaurant, quiet spaces, personal lockers and showers, etc.
- *Environmental Conditions* – Temperature control, daylight and glare, air quality and acoustic barriers, etc.
- *Infrastructure & Support* – Connectivity between locations, follow-me phones, facilities Service Level Agreements (SLAs), helpdesks and regular occupant feedback, etc.

As mentioned earlier, it is generally recognised that office design may account for an overall improvement in performance of up to 5–15 per cent, with organisational factors accounting for higher performance gains. Due to the ratio of staff to property costs, it is very worthwhile pursuing the 5–15 per cent gain. The most important point is that property savings are not considered out of the context of performance gains, as small savings could potentially have a hugely negative impact on performance. Monitoring the impact of design on performance is therefore critical.

Measuring the impact of office and environmental design factors on individual and business performance is difficult but not impossible. The relationship between good design and performance is well documented in the research literature. However, the difficulty is in: (1) separating out extraneous non-design factors from the performance change; and (2) developing (or expecting) a generic productivity measure that applies to all sectors. Despite these difficulties, the impact of office design on performance should not be simply ignored. Proxy measures such as satisfaction and self-assessed performance can be recorded and case studies compiled to further demonstrate the impact of design on productivity.

References

Alker, J. (2014) *Health, Wellbeing & Productivity in Offices: The Next Chapter for Green Building.* London: World Green Building Council.

Browning, B. *et al.* (2012) *The Economics of Biophilia: Why Designing with Nature in Mind Makes Financial Sense.* New York: Terrapin Bright Green.

Carter, S. and Jeffery, H. (2015) National Grid: How workplace design has boosted productivity. *Personnel Today*, September. Available at: www.personneltoday.com/hr/national-grid-workplace-design-boosted-productivity/ (accessed August 2016).

Conrath, D.W. (1984) White collar productivity: the search for the holy grail. *Journal of Business Ethics*, 3(1): 29–33.

DeMarco, T. and Lister, T. (1987) *Peopleware: Productive Projects and Teams.* New York: Dorset House Publishing Company.

Harris, R. and Hawkeswood, A. (2016) *The Proportion of Underlying Business Costs Accounted for by Real Estate.* London: British Council for Offices.

Herzberg, F. (1959) *The Motivation to Work.* New York: John Wiley & Sons, Inc.

Heschong, L. (2003) *Windows and Offices: A Study of Office Workers' Performance and the Indoor Environment.* Fair Oaks, CA: Heschong Mahone Group, prepared for California Energy Commission.

Kourigin, S.D. and Mikheyen, A.P. (1965) *The Effect of Noise Level on Working Efficiency.* Joint Publications Research Service.

Kroner, W.M., Stark-Martin, J.A. and Willemain T. (1994) Environmentally responsive workstations and office-worker productivity. *ASHRAE Transactions*, 100(2): 750–755.

Levin, H. (1992) Workshop on productivity and the indoor environment: Preface to workshop proceedings. Baltimore, MD: ASHRAE.

Loftness, V. (2007) *Health, Productivity and the Triple Bottom Line.* Carnegie Mellon University: Center for Building Performance and Diagnostics. Available at www.cmu.edu/iwess/workshops/absic_dec_2007/BIDS%20ABSIC_FINAL%202007.pdf (accessed August 2016).

Maslow, A.H. (1943) A theory of human motivation. *Psychological Review* 50: 370–96.

Morrell, P. (2005) *The Impact of Office Design on Business Performance*. London: Commission for Architecture and the Built Environment (CABE) and British Council for Offices (BCO).

Oseland N.A. (1999) *Environmental Factors Affecting Office Worker Performance: A Review of Evidence, TM24*. London: Chartered Institution of Building Service Engineers.

Oseland, N.A. and Bartlett, P. (1999) *Improving Office Productivity: A Guide for Business and Facilities Managers*. Harlow: Pearson Education Limited.

Oseland, N.A. and Burton, A. (2012) Quantifying the impact of environmental conditions on worker performance for inputting to a business case. *Journal of Building Survey, Appraisal and Valuation*, 1(2): 151–164.

Tham, K.W. *et al.* (2003) Temperature and ventilation effects on the work performance of office workers: study of a call-center in the Tropics. *Proceedings of Healthy Buildings* 3: 280–286.

Thompson, B. (2008) *Workplace Design and Productivity: Are They Inextricably Linked?* London: Royal Institution of Chartered Surveyors.

Wargocki, P. (2012) Satisfaction and self-estimated performance in relation to indoor environmental parameters and building features. Paper presented at Workplace Trends: Wellbeing and Performance. London: Merlin Events & Marketing. Available at: www.slideshare.net/maggieprocopi/workplace-trends-2012-thermal-and-air-quality-effects-on-performance-pawel-wargocki (accessed August 1016).

Whitehead, T. (2001) *Design Excellence Evaluation Process*. London: Defence Estates.

Windheim, L. and McLean, R. (1994) Personal communications with the Reno Post Office, 1986. Cited in Romm, J., and Browning, W. (eds) (1994) *Greening the Building and the Bottom Line*. Colorado: Rocky Mountain Institute.

Chapter 11

Optimising well-being and productivity through an ergonomics-based approach

Stephen Bowden

This chapter is about health, well-being, productivity and the science of ergonomics. The immediate question in people's minds may be, 'What has ergonomics to do with well-being?' This question may well have been preceded or immediately followed by 'What is ergonomics?' Perhaps the most important question that should be asked, however, is 'What has ergonomics to do with optimising productivity?' This latter question is an important one to be addressed by anyone who is interested in the design, management and use of workplaces. The level of productivity is the single most important determinant not only of a country's standard of living (Economic Policy Institute, 2000) but also in terms of individual employee productivity as a core component of a company's ability to generate revenue (Prochaska *et al.*, 2011).

At the time of writing, the UK Economy is growing at its fastest rate for nine years — faster than any of the other G7 nations yet . . . the UK is 30 per cent less productive than the USA, Germany, France and 10 per cent less productive than Italy (Bloom, 2015). Clearly, UK workers are struggling to work productively in their workplaces. It is in this context that the relationship between ergonomics, well-being and productivity is explored.

Ergonomics

Ergonomics, otherwise known as human factors (HF), is concerned with designing systems and working environments to best meet the requirements of people using them, based on their physical, psychological and social attributes. The history of ergonomics can be traced back over hundreds of years. For example, Bernardino Ramazinni (1633–1714) was a medical practitioner who wrote about the work-related complaints of his patients.

It was during World War II, however, that the formal history of ergonomics was established through its application in the improvement of the effectiveness of military equipment and control systems. Nowadays the goal of ergonomics is considered to be the well-being of individuals, organisations and national economies (Wilson and Sharples, 2015). The goal of well-being is clearly enshrined in the ISO's (International Standards Organisation) definition of ergonomics which is:

> Ergonomics produces an integrated knowledge from the human sciences to match jobs, systems, products and environments to the physical and mental abilities and limitations of people. In doing so it seeks to safeguard safety, health and wellbeing whilst optimising efficiency and performance.

In essence, ergonomics/HF fits the task to the human as eloquently described by Kroemer and Grandjean (1997) in their classic textbook of occupational ergonomics, *Fitting the Task to the Human*.

The following specialisms within ergonomics as described by Wilson and Sharples (2015) may be used in fitting the task to the human:

- *Physical ergonomics*: Fit, clearance, reach, access, tolerance, workload, manual handling, health and safety, workplace layout, displays and controls, product and equipment design, environment, tools.
- *Cognitive (psychological) ergonomics*: Information processing, sensing, perception, decision-making, problem-solving, reaction, mental workload, fatigue, stress, interface design, reliability, communication and fault diagnosis.
- *Organisational (social) ergonomics*: Attitudes, motivation, satisfaction, job and team design, hours and patterns of work, pacing, implementation of change.
- *Systems ergonomics*: taking a holistic approach to design and evaluation that integrates the physical, cognitive and organisational/social.

In summary, ergonomics/HF is concerned with designing systems and working environments to best meet the well-being of people addressing their physical, psychological (cognitive) and social attributes.

Ergonomics focuses on people or the human factor within the system.

The human factor within socio technical systems

The importance of the person/human factor within the system has been highlighted in highly complex socio-technical safety critical system disasters which have led to loss of life and great financial loss.

Gordon (1998) illustrates how, within the context of the Piper Alpha disaster in 1988, the performance of a highly complex socio-technical system is dependent upon the interaction of technical, human, social, organisational, managerial and environmental factors. Piper Alpha was the world's worst offshore oil disaster in which 167 men died and losses of £3.4 billion were incurred. This example may seem extreme and somehow removed from everyday work carried out within our places of work in buildings and offices. The risk of such serious consequences as death and serious injury remain from fire, for example, but there are hidden costs that are substantial, which stem from not placing the human factor at the centre of design of our buildings and offices which are complex socio-technical systems, as will be mentioned later in the chapter.

Hidden costs and the human factor

The cost of sickness absence to employers in the UK in 2013 was £28.8 billion, equivalent to just under 7 per cent of GDP (PwC Research, 2013). The cost of sickness absence is, however, dwarfed by the hidden cost of presenteeism which has been quoted by Main *et al.* (2005) as being as high as seven times the cost of absenteeism, and as such should attract the attention of anyone interested in the financial performance of an organisation.

The nature of presenteeism will be discussed later in this chapter but its source and associated substantive cost lie within the human issues that occur in an organisation's workforce. McClelland and Suri (2005) have pointed out that if human issues are not articulated in a clear and manageable form, they are likely to be very easily pushed aside when the pressure of costs, schedules and technical issues comes to bear.

An example of human issues being pushed to one side has manifested itself in recent times wherein the purely open plan office concept has given way to open plan collaborative forms as the predominant choice for office design. Both forms of office design have common features which include fewer interior walls, enabling larger floor areas that allow greater numbers of employees to be accommodated.

Increasing the density of workers housed within an office space has been the principal driver for change as employers have seen this as an important part of reducing overheads, with savings to be made in either rental, land, or build costs and lower servicing charges, i.e. total cost per square foot. The trend of designing open plan collaborative offices has taken place without the full consideration of the capabilities of individual office workers, who are at the centre of the socio-technical system (STS). As described later, leaving out either the social or technical elements of a system will lead to suboptimal system performance. This is reflected in the UK where office density has increased from 11.8m^2 per person in 2009 to 10.9m^2 per workstation in 2013 (Bedford et al., 2013).

The current focus on collaborative forms of open plan offices has taken hold despite long-standing evidence from the scientific literature that open plan office design can be counterproductive in terms of impact on employee well-being and productivity.

A brief synopsis of the relevant literature is provided in Table 11.1.

Table 11.1 A brief synopsis of the impact of open plan office design on office workers

Author(s)	Subject matter, source	Main findings
Aoife Brennan et al. 2002	Traditional versus open office design: a longitudinal field study Environment and Behaviour 34(3): 279–299	Lack of privacy and confidentiality and increased noise
Kaarlela-Tuomaala et al. 2009	Effects of acoustic environment on work in private office rooms and open-plan offices – longitudinal study during relocation Ergonomics 52(11): 1423–44	Negative effects of acoustic environment increased significantly, including increased distraction, reduced privacy, increased concentration difficulties
Kim and de Dear 2013	Workspace satisfaction: The privacy-communication trade-off in open plan offices Journal of Environmental Psychology 36: 18–26	The open plan proponents' argument that open plan improves morale and productivity appears to have no basis in the research literature
A. Seddigh et al. 2014	Concentration requirements modify the effect of office type on indicators of health and performance Journal of Environmental Psychology 38: 167–174	In order to prevent poor health and loss of performance, organisations with open-plan office environments should have action plans in order to lower the amount of distraction and cognitive stress
Bergström et al. 2015	Work environment perceptions following relocation to open-plan offices: A 12-month longitudinal study Work 50(2): 221–228	The results of the study indicate that employees' perception of health, work environment and performance decreased during a 12-month period following relocation from individual offices to open-plan offices.

Human-centred design and ergonomics

Designs that are in any way counterproductive to employee well-being should be avoided as they will either cause or exacerbate business inefficiencies within employment cost. Interestingly, Harris (2016) documented that 55 per cent of business costs relate to staff salaries with the remaining 45 per cent comprising of business costs (30 per cent) and property (15 per cent).

Some of the reasons that human issues may be pushed aside in favour of office construction and operating costs include but are not limited to the following reasons:

- the benefits of an ergonomics approach are not clearly understood by organisations;
- human performance is seen as difficult to quantify in comparison to office construction and operating costs;
- ergonomic and health and safety professionals tend to shy away from economic arguments.

Furthermore, the following fallacies are commonly used to push aside ergonomics. Pheasant (1996) described the Five Fundamental Fallacies as:

1   The design is satisfactory for me – it will, therefore, be satisfactory for everyone else.
2   The design is satisfactory for the average person – it will, therefore, be satisfactory for everyone else.
3   The variability of human beings is so great that it cannot possibly be catered for in any design, but since people are wonderfully adaptable, it doesn't matter anyway.
4   Ergonomics is expensive, and since products are purchased on appearance and styling, ergonomic considerations may conveniently be ignored.
5   Ergonomics is an excellent idea. I always design things with ergonomics in mind – but I do it intuitively and rely on my common sense so I don't need tables of data or empirical studies.

As 55 per cent of business costs to an organisation are related to the employment of staff, a systems ergonomics approach should be adopted to address any business inefficiencies in this major business cost, recognising that the human factor is central to an organisations performance. To quote Oxenburgh *et al.* (2004):

> Eventually all work comes down to people, even those whose work is seemingly remote from people, for example, accountants will find that they need to look more closely at the people side of the business – people are an asset, not just a cost.

Oxenburgh's assertion of work eventually coming down people first is based on Human Centred Design (HCD). The person/human factor within the system is central to an ergonomics/HF approach as shown in Figure 11.1. Systems ergonomics is used to implement an HCD approach to the design of organisations. HCD can be seen as the way for organisations to enhance the well-being and productivity of their employees. McClelland and Suri (2005) state: 'The goal of HCD is to focus attention on the critical human issues throughout the design and development process so that the inevitable trade-offs between commercial and technical issues can be made in a balanced way.'

The British Council of Offices' (BCO) recent publication, *Putting People First* (British Council of Offices, 2015) highlights the movement towards including the individual's health and well-being in the design of the built environment:

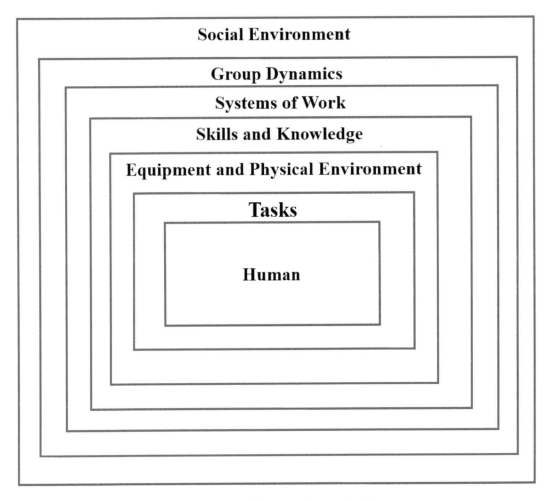

Figure 11.1 Factors which apply to an ergonomics/HF approach to work design

Successful implementation of health and wellness strategies will require both a better understanding of related medical science research and a deeper collaboration between owners, architects, engineers, contractors and facility management to identify design criteria that go beyond comfort and the building and additionally incorporate personalisation and user experience.

Kirk *et al.* (2015) describe the benefits of HCD:

- Inspires new ideas and design directions.
- Creates new paradigms and value for existing product or service offerings.
- Increases real and perceived value of a design.
- Provides better experiences for people using a design.
- Avoids wasting development effort on a bad design idea.

- Makes a weak idea much better and turns a good idea into a great one.
- Reduces exposure to product liability issues.
- Reduces customer complaints and product recalls.
- Creates a more efficient design process in relation to:

  - faster, more precise definition of functionality;
  - faster choice of appropriate interaction technologies;
  - earlier determination of design performance targets;
  - more cost-effective way of assigning design team effort.

Figure 11.1 illustrates that the human is at the centre of the work design. An ergonomics/HF approach places the human, their well-being and individual productivity at the centre of their organisation.

A variety of methods are used to measure both the abilities of the person and the demands of the work so as to determine the match or mismatch between the two. Methods include HCD, socio-technical systems (STS), task analysis, systems analysis, job content definition, investigating work roles, and measures of the physical workplace and how they relate to the range of variability inherent in the working population. Many of the issues in an ergonomics analysis have direct implications for performance, quality and have an indirect impact on the attitudes people have about various aspects of their work.

The application of HCD involves an ergonomics/HF approach called the socio-technical system (STS). When considering the technical side of the system, a STS approach to the design of workplaces is recommended to reduce the chance of system failure. Given that office environments are complex STS systems, designers should ensure that both the human factor and technical systems are considered without bias to either side.

Waterson (2015) illustrates the proponents that affect performance, which is defined in terms of production output, quality, employee well-being and job satisfaction, and is a function of the degree to which the design of the social and technical systems are considered to be complementary, as well as indicating the relative effort placed upon the parallel design of both systems. If more effort is placed on the design of one system compared to another, then suboptimal performance of the overall system is predicted to be the net outcome.

Clegg (2000) provides a set of 19 principles for STS design that can be used to design balanced productive work systems. Clegg expanded upon earlier work by Albert Cherns in 1976 and 1986. Three of the 19 principles are:

1 *Design is systemic.* All aspects of system design are interconnected. Leaving out one part (e.g. the human aspects) will inevitably lead to the suboptimal performance of the whole system.
2 *Values and mind-sets are central to design.* Attitudes and values on the part of designers, managers, users, etc. will shape the outcomes of design. It may be helpful at the outset of design to state clearly any possible biases and leanings towards possible design options.
3 *Design is socially shaped.* Design is subject to social movements and trends, these may sometimes manifest themselves as fads and fashions.

As described earlier, the aim of ergonomics is considered to be the well-being of individuals, organisations and national economies (Wilson and Sharples, 2015). At this point it is worth discussing the terms 'health' and 'well-being' as there is confusion and misunderstanding around their meaning and use.

Health and well-being defined

The terms 'health' and 'well-being' are not synonymous, yet they are terms that are often used together as if they are one and the same thing. The situation is probably compounded by the lack of understanding and clear definition of what the term 'well-being' means. The terms, however, are associated and so it may be of value to describe what each term means:

- Health refers simply to a mental and physical state being absent from disease.
- Well-being is a dynamic holistic concept describing an individual's positive emotional, mental, physical and social state. It provides a sense of individual resilience to assist in managing their daily life – in essence, how happy an individual is with his or her lot in life.

Examples of distinguishing the terms include a person suffering from a physical health condition that does not impact on their state of well-being. For example, a para-Olympian or a person with asthma, diabetes or rheumatoid arthritis can have a state of good well-being but may not enjoy good health. Important concepts of health are active life expectancy and disability-free years of life.

As mentioned earlier, ergonomics/HF is concerned with designing systems and working environments to best meet the well-being of people by addressing their physical, psychological (cognitive) and social attributes.

At this point it is worth exploring the construct of well-being, particularly as the G7 (the world's largest economies) is currently focussing on human well-being as an economic measure as a means to assess national productivity, in addition to the traditional means used. Well-being is defined as: 'The balance point between an individual's resource pool and the challenges faced' (Dodge *et al.*, 2012), as illustrated in Figure 11.2.

Well-being emerges from physical, psychological, social and environmental factors that influence our view of ourselves in the context of the world around us. These factors form the basis of each individual's perception of their well-being.

First of all, it is worth noting that the physical, psychological and social attributes that form the basis of each individual's perception of their well-being are the basis of the specialisms within ergonomics/HF as described above. The see-saw concept described by Dodge *et al.* (2012) illustrates the need for individuals to return to a set-point for their well-being in equilibrium. In

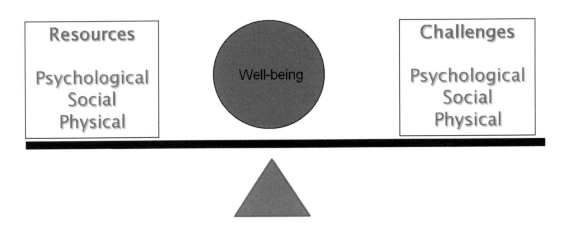

Figure 11.2 Well-being

essence, an individual is in a state of stable well-being when they have the psychological, social and physical resources they need to meet a particular psychological, social and/or physical challenge. (The maintenance/restoration of stable well-being is achieved through an ergonomics approach which will be described later in the chapter.) It should be noted that, as Pheasant (1996) described, people vary in terms of shape, size, strength, dexterity, mentality and taste. Likewise an individual's sense of well-being is diverse. When individuals have more challenges than resources, the see-saw dips, along with their well-being, and vice versa. Each time an individual meets a challenge, the system of challenges and resources moves into a state of imbalance, as the individual is forced to adapt his or her resources to meet this particular challenge.

Well-being and presenteeism

If an individual's perception of their own well-being remains out of balance, a decline in their productivity can result, potentially leading to ill health, presenteeism and absenteeism. Absenteeism is well recognised as a cost to organisations. The sibling of absenteeism, presenteeism, is less well known. Typically, presenteeism is defined as the act of employees attending work when ill. It is better described, however, as 'the sub-optimal performance of those still at work'.

Definitions of presenteeism have evolved over time, as described by Johns (2010) in an excellent review of the literature on presenteeism in the workplace. These definitions are:

- Attending work, as opposed to being absent (Smith, 1970).
- Exhibiting excellent attendance (Canfield and Soash, 1955; Stolz, 1993).
- Working elevated hours, thus putting in 'face time', even when unfit (Simpson, 1998; Worrall et al., 2000).
- Being reluctant to work part-time rather than full-time (Sheridan, 2004).
- Being unhealthy but exhibiting no sickness absenteeism (Kivimäki et al., 2005).
- Going to work despite feeling unwell (Aronsson et al., 2000; Dew et al., 2005).
- Going to work despite feeling unhealthy or experiencing other events that might normally compel absence (e.g., child care problems) (Evans, 2004; Johansson and Lundberg, 2004).
- Reduced productivity at work due to health problems (Turpin et al., 2004).
- Reduced productivity at work due to health problems or other events that distract one from full productivity (Hummer et al., 2002; Whitehouse, 2005).

The final definition above will be used to describe the concept of presenteeism as it is able to incorporate all potential causes of presenteeism, including those that are not primarily caused by the onset of disease and are under the direct control of architects, directors, senior managers and facilities.

The UK government states that presenteeism has generally been found to be costlier than absenteeism and suggests that organisations may wish to assume that the cost of presenteeism is at least the same as that for absenteeism. This is a conservative estimate. The cost of presenteeism in Australia's workforce has been estimated as being nearly four times more than absenteeism (Medibank Private, 2005), with Main et al. (2005) indicating that presenteeism costs an organisation up to a staggering seven times the cost of absenteeism.

Merrill et al. (2013) have stated that the use of a multipronged integrated approach to well-being improvement can enhance employee job performance. Furthermore, Gandy et al. (2014) point out that the construct of well-being as a broader framework for understanding and improving employee productivity in both healthy and unhealthy employees can provide explanatory power for productivity above and beyond what can be attributed to health status. The point that Gandy et al. (2014) raise is an important one as many of the assessment methods used are based on the assumption that the cost of presenteeism is confined to those who are attending work while ill.

Clearly the variance in the published data concerning the cost of presenteeism to organisations will raise doubts as to its validity. Nevertheless, the data published so far and the improving understanding indicate that the cost of absenteeism is the tip of the iceberg compared to the cost of presenteeism to an organisation.

Furthermore, Goetzel *et al.* (2016) describe how the stock performance of companies who invest in the health and well-being of their employees outperforms the stock performance of those companies who do not invest in the health and well-being of their employees by a ratio of three to one.

Presenteeism

There are two forms of presenteeism that are not primarily caused by the onset of disease: physical presenteeism and psychological presenteeism. Both these forms of presenteeism have precursor events that distract the individual from full productivity. Figure 11.3 represents the

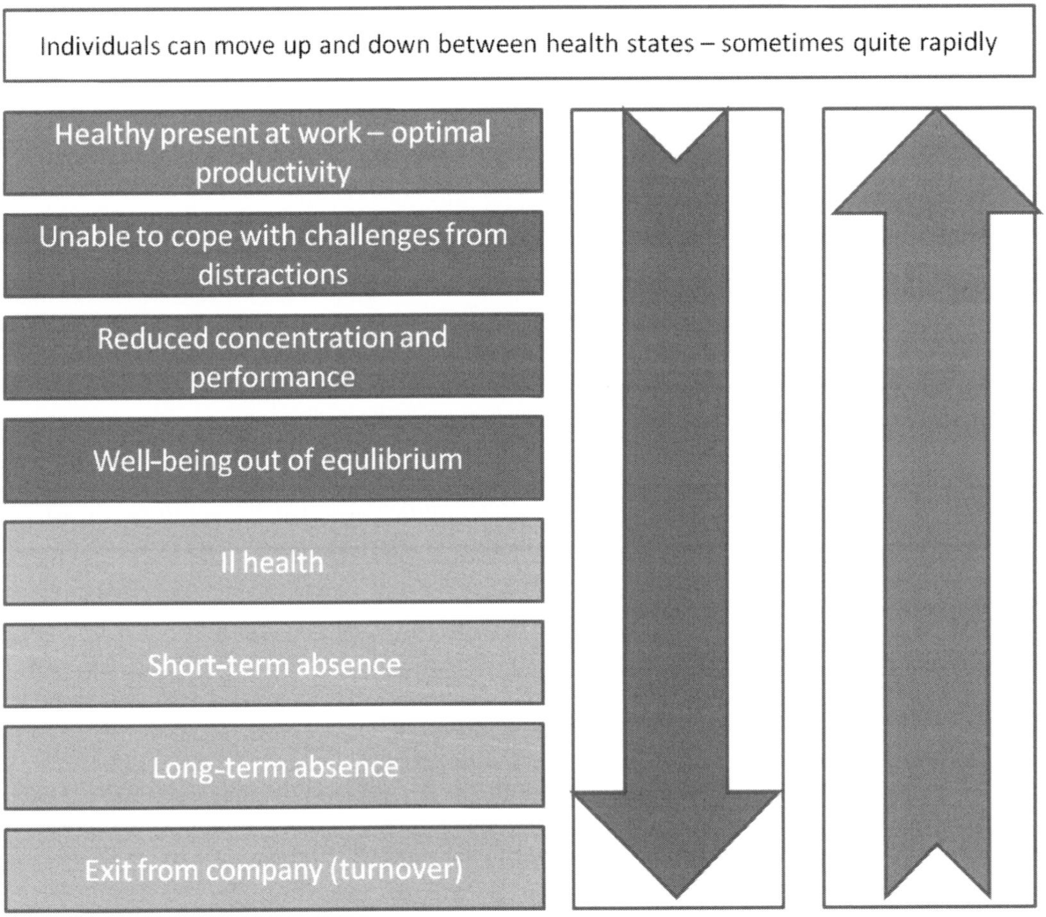

Figure 11.3 Potential travel through health states

Source: Reproduced with permission from COPE Occupational Health and Ergonomics Ltd.

health states that an individual will pass through if the exposures that have caused them to move out of the first health state of 'Healthy present at work – optimal productivity' are not checked. Unfortunately, individuals are usually already at the stage of ill health with associated loss of productivity by the time they decide to consult their General Practitioner or attend a consultation with an occupational health professional. An ergonomics/HF approach to understanding the resources and challenges faced by the user at the earliest stages of any design will mitigate the risk of the user moving away from optimal productivity and moving into a state of presenteeism.

It should be understood that presenteeism has both positive and negative connotations regarding a person's health state and productivity in relation to their work. A person may be on a rehabilitation programme under the care of a health professional, moving from absence to being present at work but performing suboptimally (presenteeism) until fully rehabilitated (the upward arrow in Figure 11.3). On the other hand, a person may be moving from a state of presenteeism to absence and potential exit from an organisation due to either ill health or other non-health-related factors (the downward arrow in Figure 11.3). Despite the direction of travel, this group of individuals are performing suboptimally while still being at work and as such can be considered to be performing the act of presenteeism.

Distractions, well-being, presenteeism and ill health

The nature of the process that causes presenteeism is in the form of a distraction that is either physical, psychological or social in nature and prevents an individual from fully concentrating on the task that they are responsible for completing. The lack of sufficient concentrated time on the individual task causes deadlines to be missed and performance to suffer. The loss in performance causes an individual's perception of their well-being to move out of equilibrium and, if they cannot control the situation, well-being will suffer, leading to presenteeism and potentially ill health. Distraction is the keyword here, as distraction in its various forms prevents individuals from concentrating on the tasks that they are responsible for which may lead to ill health.

Writing in the *Wall Street Journal*, Helen Shellenbarger (Shellenbarger 2013) draws together the results of a number of research papers setting out the impact of interruptions causing disturbances in concentration:

- an interruption of even 2 seconds is long enough for people to lose the thread of a difficult or complex task;
- the average time spent on a task before being interrupted: 12 min. 40 secs;
- the average time elapsed before returning to work on the same task: 25 min. 26 secs;
- the average time required, after resuming a difficult task, to get back to the same level of intense concentration: 15 min.;
- the percentage of tasks that are interrupted when people work in open plan offices: 63 per cent;
- the percentage of tasks interrupted when people work in private offices: 49 per cent.

From Shellenbarger's article, it can readily be seen how the inability of an individual to maintain concentration on the task at hand can impact negatively on performance, leading to the slippery slope down the health states as set out in Figure 11.3.

Individuals can move up and down between health states. In some cases of mental health problems, the passage from a perceived one of being in a healthy state with optimal productivity to ill health and long-term absence can be very rapid – somewhat like walking off a cliff.

In some of these cases, the rehabilitation process can be protracted with the prospect of full rehabilitation an unlikely one. A group of Swedish researchers have reinforced earlier research outcomes that sickness presenteeism is a risk factor for deterioration in health and sickness absence, particularly as a result of mental health problems (Tayloyan *et al.*, 2012).

Distractions can be caused but not necessarily limited to any one or a combination of the following sources:

- culture/management style;
- salary;
- work load;
- noise;
- physical discomfort (MSDs);
- interruptions;
- lack of privacy;
- poor thermal and air quality environments.

Economic analysis

There are three main types of economic models that can be used to analyse the costs and benefits of ergonomic designs (Oxenburgh *et al.*, 2004):

- financial appraisal – return on investment analysis;
- cost-effectiveness analysis;
- cost-benefit analysis.

Cost-benefit analysis is the most complete model as it attempts to include the social and cultural aspects of any proposal. Cost-benefit analysis is a tool to convince otherwise sceptical management that the value of people must not be underestimated and that workers are the key to profit (ibid.).

It should be understood, however, that, as stated in a seminal paper (Corlett 1998):

> To leave cost benefit analysis to accountants, economists, even to ergonomists, is to build in a cause for failure. The utility of professionals, particularly in combination is undoubted but the understanding of what has to be measured can come only with the aid of those involved.

Many accounting approaches used by organisations to measure expense only focus on cost reduction. They address questions such as, Can taxation be reduced? Can a function of the business be outsourced? These are important questions but in essence do not address the key question of productivity but only focus on a narrow window of the organisation's true operating costs.

The aim of the ergonomics/HF approach is to enable management to understand clearly that good working conditions lead to improved productivity and profit through a better understanding of how the physical, social and psychological challenges placed upon the individual affect the businesses performance. Good ergonomics is good economics and in order to demonstrate this, Oxenburgh *et al.* (2004) provide seven cases studies showing how a cost-benefit analysis can be used to demonstrate the financial benefits derived from an ergonomics-/HF-based approach.

In one case study of a large scale experiment where retail workers were at the centre of an intervention involving an ergonomics and physiotherapy service, payback was achieved within nine months. This period of time to achieve payback of less than one year is not unusual in well-designed ergonomics interventions.

In each of these studies a productivity assessment tool in the form of a computer programme is used to measure cost-benefit/productivity in order to allow management to assess the value of an ergonomic intervention.

Conclusion

The chapter discusses how well-being and productivity can be optimised through an ergonomics approach to the design of places of work. Focus is placed on the importance of the human factor in design and how a human-centred design can yield positive effects on not only well-being and productivity but also on the financial performance of business.

This chapter provides a better understanding of how poor perceptions of well-being can lead to presenteeism, ill health and loss of productivity. Health and well-being are terms that are currently in regular use without a proper understanding of their meaning and application in today's workplace. The definition of presenteeism as 'Reduced productivity at work due to health problems or other events that distract one from full productivity' is used to illustrate that presenteeism is caused not only by ill health conditions but also by the design of the environment which exposes workers to unnecessary distractions. Attention is drawn to the underestimation of the cost of presenteeism to organisations and how human-centred design can optimise workers' well-being and productivity.

References

Bedford, D., Harris, R., King, A., Hawkeswood, A. (2013) *Occupier Density Study September 2013*, London: BCO.

Bloom, J. (2015) Why the productivity gap? BBC News, May.

British Council of Offices (2015) *Putting People First: Designing For The Health And Wellbeing In The Built Environment*. London: British Council of Offices.

Clegg, C.W. (2000) Sociotechnical principles for system design. *Applied Ergonomics*, 31: 463–477.

Corlett, E.N. (1998) Cost-benefit analysis of ergonomic and work design changes. In Obourne, D. (ed.) *International Review of Ergonomics*. London: Routledge, pp. 85–104.

Dodge, R., Daly, A., Huyton, J., and Sanders, L. (2012) The challenge of defining wellbeing. *International Journal of Wellbeing*, 2(3): 222–235. DOI:10.5502/ijw.v2i.

Economic Policy Institute (2000) The link between productivity growth and living standards. Available at: www.epi.org/publication/webfeatures_snapshots_archive_03222000/ (accessed December 2015).

Gandy W, *et al.* (2014) Comparing the contributions of well-being and disease status to employee productivity. *Journal of Occupational and Environmental Medicine*, 56(3): 252–257.

Goetzel, R.Z. *et al.* (2016) The stock performance of C. Everett Koop Award Winners compared with the Standard & Poor's 500 Index. *Journal of Occupational & Environmental Medicine*, 58(1): 9–15.

Gordon, R.P.E. (1998) The contribution of human factors to accidents in the offshore oil industry. *Reliability Engineering and System Safety*, 61: 95–108.

Harris, R. (2016) *The Proportion of Underlying Business Costs Accounted for by Real Estate*. London: BCO.

Johns, G. (2010) Presenteeism in the work place: a review and research agenda, *Journal of Organizational Behaviour*, 31: 519–542.

Kirk, D. *et al.* (2015) Involving people in design research. In Wilson, J.R. and Sharples, S. (eds) *Evaluation of Human Work*, 4th edn. London: CRC Press.

Kroemer, K.H.E. and Grandjean, E. (1997) *Fitting the Task to the Human: A Textbook Of Occupational Ergonomics*, 5th edn. London: Routledge.

Main, C. *et al.* (2005) Validity of the HSE stress tool: an investigation within four organizations by the Corporate Health and Performance Group; *Occupational Medicine*, 55(3): 208–214.

McClelland, I. and Suri, J.F. (2005) *Evaluation of Human Work*, 3rd edn. London: Routledge.

Medibank Private (2007) *Econtech Economic Modelling of the Cost of Presenteeism in Australia*. Available at: www.medibank.co.au

Merrill, R.M., Aldana, S.G., Pope, J.E., *et al.* (2013) Self-rated job performance and absenteeism according to employee engagement, health behaviours, and physical health. *Journal of Occupational and Environmental Medicine*, 55(1): 10–18.

Oxenburgh, M., Marlo, P.S.P. and Oxenburgh, A. (2004) *Increasing Productivity and Profit Through Health and Safety. The Financial Returns from a Safe Working Environment*. 2nd edn. London: CRC Press.

Pheasant, S. (1996) *Bodyspace: Anthropometry, Ergonomics and the Design of Work*, 2nd edn. London: CRC Press.

Prochaska, J.O. *et al.* (2011_ The wellbeing assessment for productivity. *Journal of Occupational and Environmental Medicine*, 53(7): 735–742.

PwC Research (2013) Rising sickness bill is costing UK business £29bn a year – July. Available at: http://pwc.blogs.com/press_room/2013/07/rising-sick-bill-is-costing-uk-business-29bn-a-year-pwc-research.html

Shellenbarger, H. (2013) The biggest office interruptions are . . . *Wall Street Journal*, Sept. 10.

Tayloyan, M., Aronsson, G., Leineweber, C. and Westerlund, H. (2012) Sickness presenteeism predicts suboptimal self-rated health and sickness absence: a nationally representative study of the Swedish working population. *PLoS One*, 7(9): e44721. DOI: 10.1371/journal.pone.0044721.

Waterson, P. (2015) Sociotechnical design of work systems. In Wilson, J.R. and Sharples, S. (eds) *Evaluation of Human Work*, 4th edn. London: CRC Press.

Wilson, J.R. and Sharples, S. (2015) *Evaluation of Human Work*, 4th edn. London: CRC Press.

Chapter 12

Lighting for productive workplaces

Jennifer A. Veitch

Introduction

'Productivity' means 'the effectiveness of productive effort, especially in industry, as measured in terms of the rate of output per unit of input' (*Oxford English Dictionary*, 2016). Organisational productivity is more than merely the production rate of a factory, or the output speed of an individual worker. It is better understood as the result of the balance between the inputs (costs) and outputs (values) averaged over all the contributions across the organisation. This is the *efficiency* definition of organisational productivity (Pritchard, 1992). Organisations are productive when their costs are lower than the value of the outputs produced. It is useful to apply this to studying the effects of the work environment because the effects may occur on both sides of the equation, as will be seen. Changes to the work environment have direct effects on input costs because of their technical performance (e.g. changing energy bills by implementing a new lighting system), and indirect effects on both input costs and output values through their effects on employees.

In the early days of electric lighting, in the late nineteenth and early twentieth centuries, the focus was largely on the quantity of light and the possibility of using electric light to supplement daylight was comparatively new. Today, our understanding of good lighting is more nuanced. The model of integrated lighting quality (Veitch, 1998) shown in Figure 12.1 has widespread support. Good lighting, in any setting, is achieved by simultaneously considering the effects of the lighting on the people using the space – bearing in mind that these may include a variety of individual needs and characteristics at one time – together with contextual factors relating to the architectural setting and to the economic and environmental circumstances. This model is consistent with the efficiency definition of organisational productivity in that good lighting uses as little energy as possible, addresses any limitations on purchase, installation, and maintenance costs, and fully considers the needs of those who will use it. (Although it was created with interior lighting for people in mind, this definition can easily be extended to consider outdoor lighting, or applications, such as greenhouses, in which the primary 'users' are not humans.)

This model underpins the structure of this chapter, which has as its primary focus the lighting conditions that meet individual needs for people at work, because these are the conditions that will both reduce input costs and lead to increased output value. The chapter ends with integrated recommendations for lighting that will support organisational productivity. The sections that lead up to this integration provide the necessary background understanding of the internal processes through which these needs might be met: sensation, perception, cognition, emotion, etc. These processes occur in parallel, and of course are not limited to responses to light. Veitch (2012) discussed these processes in relation to other work environment conditions.

Box 12.1 discusses the early experiment with lighting and productivity.

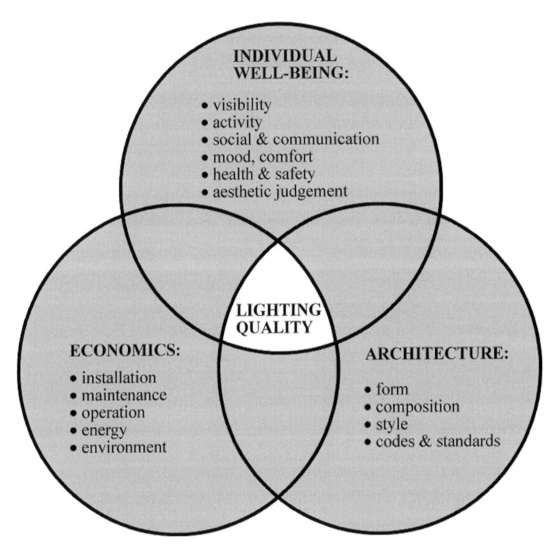

Figure 12.1 Lighting quality lies at the intersection of meeting user needs, respecting the economic and environmental context of the project, and integrating with the architectural character of the setting

Source: Veitch (1998).

Box 12.1   The Hawthorne experiments and productivity

One often hears about the set of experiments conducted at the Western Electric factory at Hawthorne, Illinois, in the 1920s (Roethlisberger and Dickson, 1939). These industrial production experiments apparently demonstrated that electrical assembly work is unaffected by light level: Work performance was said to have continued to improve when light levels increased, decreased, and stayed the same (Snow, 1927).

The "Hawthorne effect" is often cited as an example of participant expectancy biases (in which participants behave in a manner that fulfills what they believe to be expected of them) because the workers were aware that they had been selected to take part in the tests. The results arguably set back environmental psychology research for decades because they seemed to show that the working conditions were not important (Gifford, 2002). We now know that the apparent failure of the illumination experiments at the Hawthorne plant occurred for many reasons, including poor experimental design and limitations imposed by the industrial hosts (Izawa *et al.*, 2011, Levitt and List, 2011). At the time, however, the illumination experiments' results led the research team to focus on the relationships between management and employees and the social relations in employee groups, which they believed were the most profound influences on productivity. Interest in lighting and the physical work environment became somewhat of a fringe activity within psychology, where it has remained until recently (de Kort and Veitch, 2014). In that time organizational psychology has provided a more nuanced view of what constitutes a productive workplace than was considered at Hawthorne, and the fields of environmental psychology, human factors and ergonomics, architecture, interior design and environment-behaviour research have developed the knowledge base that this book presents.

In the decade since the publication of the second edition of *Creating the Productive Workplace* (Veitch, 2006), revolutionary changes have occurred in both lighting technology and in our understanding of how light influences behaviour and physiology. We have much to learn before we can comprehensively apply light and lighting to influence health and well-being (Commission Internationale de l'Eclairage, 2016),[1] but we have a stronger basis than ever before for many recommendations related to circadian regulation (the timing of physiological processes on a 24-hour cycle). Meanwhile, both light source technologies (particularly light-emitting diodes, LEDs) and lighting controls have advanced exponentially in sophistication and performance, bringing with them the promise of dramatic energy savings for lighting in all buildings, including workplaces. The urgency of the need to reduce electricity consumption and associated greenhouse gas emissions makes the rapid adoption of these new technologies critical. The chapter reflects these developments in both technology and knowledge, but also retains its grounding in the fundamentals expressed in the model of integrated lighting quality.

Eye and brain: sensation

Light is defined as 'radiation that is considered from the point of view of its ability to excite the human visual system' (CIE, 2011). This radiation is generally considered to be within the range 380–780 nm. It was formerly thought that electromagnetic radiation received at the eye stimulated two cell types, the rods and cones, which were responsible for sending information to the brain, where the visual cortex processed the information and decoded images. This understanding was thought to be so fundamental that the fundamental unit for light, the *candela*, is defined in relation to the human spectral luminous efficiency curve for photopic vision (Conférence Générale des Poids et Mesures, 1979). This spectral luminous efficiency curve (known as V_λ) was derived based on brightness perception experiments (CIE, 1978), which showed a peak at 555 nm. Light is the only unit of physical measurement to be defined in terms of an effect on humans.

We now know, however, that when radiation between ~380 and ~780 nm reaches the retina, many photoreceptor types convert the physical energy to signals sent to many brain structures and it has many effects beyond stimulating a visual response. In 2001 we learned that intrinsically photoreceptive retinal ganglion cells (ipRGCs) respond to light by sending signals through the retino-hypothalamic tract, and that these signals regulate melatonin production by the pineal gland (Berson *et al.*, 2001; Berson *et al.*, 2002; Hattar *et al.*, 2002). These findings triggered a tremendous expansion of research efforts that have since shown that the results of 380–780 nm radiation detected at the eye are more complex than we could have imagined. There are at least five types of ipRGCs (Ecker *et al.*, 2010). There are cross-connections between ipRGCs and the rods and cones; among these, ipRGCs influence vision indirectly by contributing to pupil size (Gooley *et al.*, 2011). The various subtypes of ipRGC have different spectral sensitivities and project to a wide variety of brain structures, with a variety of effects on behaviour and physiology. This chapter will consider effects on cognition, emotion, alertness, and circadian regulation.

Thus, the official definition of light is too restrictive and may need official attention and revision. For convenience, this chapter will use the word 'light' without restricting its meaning to only those processes related to vision: 'Light is electromagnetic radiation between 380 and 780 nm detected by the human eye, weighted according to the appropriate spectral sensitivity function for the process under consideration' (CIE, 1978).

Much attention has focused on identifying the spectral sensitivity function of the ipRCGs. Indeed, the demonstration that these cells respond differently than rods and cones was part of the evidence base that led to their identification (Brainard *et al.*, 2001). It has been clear since the work began that ipRGCs generally are most sensitive in the short wavelengths (Brainard and Provencio, 2006), and the first consensus report on this important issue emerged in 2014 (CIE, 2015; Lucas *et al.*, 2014). Figure 12.2 illustrates the current view on the integrated spectral sensitivity of ipRGCs (notwithstanding the differences that may exist between subtypes).

This is important because of its implications both for measurement of the dose and for the design of suitable light sources. When we measure light exposure conventionally, we use units of *luminance* to describe the quantity of light coming from a surface (in candelas per square metre) and *illuminance* to describe the quantity of light falling on a surface (lumens per square metre, or lux), but these are weighted according to the visual spectral efficiency function. To understand effects of light that do not require vision, such as circadian regulation, we need to know the dose in terms of spectral luminous flux (radiance or irradiance, units of energy) correctly weighted by a spectral sensitivity function. These new units would be used to make specific recommendations about, for example, the necessary light exposure for circadian regulation. A future edition of this chapter might be able to make such recommendations, but the knowledge of today leaves us with only general statements.

Responses to light exposure are now known to depend on at least six parameters: the spectrum, intensity, and duration of exposure, its spatial distribution, its timing in relation to the circadian system, and the history of prior light exposures (Figueiro, 2013). Responses that rely on visual perception also involve interpretation, and are further modified by expectations and experiences (CIE, 2014). This complexity makes the job of understanding how light can contribute to a productive workplace challenging and interesting.

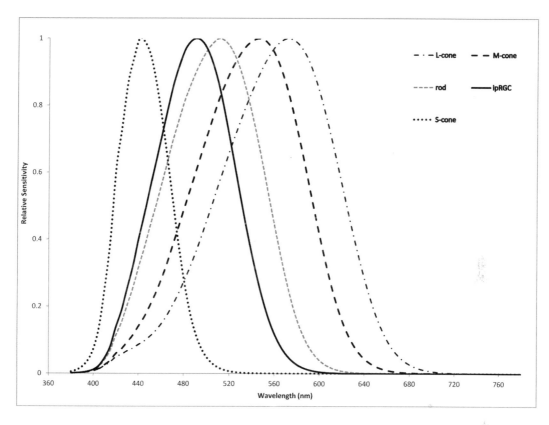

Figure 12.2 There are five known photoreceptive cells in the human retina, each with a different action spectrum, shown here as relative sensitivity normalized to their peaks. Data used to prepare this figure are from CIE (2015).

Seeing and interpreting: perception, cognition, and emotion

Seeing the task

The fundamental understanding of visual performance has not changed. Our ability to see fine details is a function of the size of the details, their contrast, the quantity of light, the speed with which they are moving (if any), and our visual capabilities (Boyce, 2014). With respect to the quantity of light, there is a very broad range across which visual performance does not change (the plateau), but for a given task there is a point at which the quantity becomes insufficient, and performance drops rapidly for lower quantities (the escarpment) (Boyce and Rea, 1987). This relationship is captured in existing recommendations and guidance for light levels (illuminance) in workplaces, such as the Illuminating Engineering Society's *Lighting Handbook* (DiLaura *et al.*, 2011) and the Society of Light and Lighting's *SLL Code for Lighting* (Raynham, 2013). For most common tasks, 300 lx is the recommended desktop illuminance; however, this value will be higher for workers with poor vision (including older workers), and for very small tasks or those that involve motion (e.g. objects moving on a conveyor belt).

Our models of visual performance demonstrate the importance of the task size and contrast for visibility. These variables exert more powerful influences on visual performance than does light level, at least across the range of light levels one might encounter in an interior (Rea and Ouellette, 1991). If there is a visual performance problem, changing the task by increasing its size or contrast will more quickly solve the problem than will increasing the light level. Even when increasing the light on the task is the solution, the energy-efficient choice is to use a task light rather than to light the whole space. In addition, poorly positioned light sources, whether for ambient or task lighting, can reduce task contrast by casting a veil of light across the target one wishes to see; think of the difficulty of reading a computer screen when direct sun falls on it. In this case the solution is to change the geometry of the light source and the task.

Many light sources deliver light with cyclical variations in light output, known as temporal luminous modulation. For older technologies, such as incandescent and fluorescent lighting systems, this was a property of the generic technology. Low-frequency temporal variations in light output, such as the 100 or 120 Hz operation (depending on the mains supply) of a fluorescent lighting system on a magnetic ballast, have long been known to affect visual performance (Wilkins, 1986). The problem was thought to be solved with the advent of electronic ballasts operating at 40 kHz (Veitch and McColl, 1995). Energy-efficiency regulations in many countries resulted in the widespread adoption of electronic ballasts, which had the desirable side effect of removing conditions that could disrupt eye movements, reduce visual performance, and contribute to headaches in susceptible individuals (Wilkins et al., 2010).

However, the advent of LEDs has brought the potential for temporal luminous modulation back to workplaces. The design of the electronics to run LEDs varies between devices, with the result that there is a wide variety of performance seen in currently available products (Poplawski and Miller, 2011). Furthermore, many dimmable LEDs reduce their output using pulse-width modulation at a moderately high frequency (e.g. 400–600 Hz), which means that the 'off' portion of each cycle varies in length, depending on the dimming level (e.g. at 30 per cent dimming, the light source will be on 30 per cent of the time and off 70 per cent of the time – the duration will depend on the cycle frequency). The IEEE published a recommendation to limit temporal luminous modulation from LED products in 2015 (IEEE Power Electronics Society, 2015), which provides guidance on how to limit risks to viewers based on the modulation frequency and the modulation depth. According to this recommendation, the 100 per cent modulation of a pulse-width-modulation dimming system would be acceptable only for frequencies greater than 1100 Hz. There is not yet a requirement for manufacturers to report the temporal luminous modulation properties of their products, so that it is difficult to determine whether or not a given system might pose a risk, although it is clear that if modulation depth is very low and modulation frequency is very high, the risk of adverse consequences is reduced.

Colour rendering describes the effect of a light source on the colour appearance of objects. Good colour rendering adds to workplace lighting in several ways. Tasks that have a colour component are performed better when colour rendering is high (O'Donell et al., 2011). For some occupations (e.g. dentistry and visual arts), colour matching accuracy (also known as colour fidelity) is critical. The existing metric is the CIE General Colour Rendering Index (R_a, known in North America as CRI) (CIE, 1995). The current recommendation (in some places, a requirement) for R_a is that it be at least 80. For settings where colour fidelity is critical, 90 would be recommended. There is an argument to be made that we could lower illuminance recommendations somewhat by using high colour rendering light sources (higher than typically used today), making use of the colour information to maintain visual performance while giving the best possible colour appearance to the environment (Papamichael et al., 2016). Given that there is an inherent trade-off between the luminous efficacy of a light source and its colour rendering, reducing illuminance would ensure that energy-efficiency goals are achieved while colour rendering is improved.

The advent of LEDs has brought renewed attention to colour rendering by re-exposing known limitations to R_a (CIE, 2007). LED products can be disadvantaged by the R_a calculation, and may deliver a better colour appearance to objects than their R_a, values would suggest. A new system for calculating a colour fidelity metric was proposed in North America in 2015 (Illuminating Engineering Society of North America, 2015), and international groups are now evaluating it as a possible replacement for R_a. The new system provides more detailed information about light source colour, including a colour fidelity metric known as R_f, and a colour gamut metric known as R_g. (Colour gamut is the range of all colours that the light source can create.) There is evidence to suggest that the gamut size relates to colour preferences, with a larger gamut being preferred over a smaller one (e.g. Dangol *et al.*, 2015). Some manufacturers report the new metrics. If colour rendering is important to the circumstances, look for R_f values > 90. In any case, consider a trial installation or a mock-up of a proposed LED lighting system to verify that the colour properties are well suited to the needs of that workplace.

The colour appearance of a light source is described by its correlated colour temperature (internationally, the symbol is T_{cp}; in North America it is known as CCT). Correlated colour temperature is a function of the spectrum of the white light source; in general, when a white light source has relatively more short-wavelength radiation in the spectrum, the CCT will be higher and the colour will be described as cooler. Typical workplace lighting in North America and Europe is in the range of 3000–4000 K, and occasionally as high as 5000 K, although light sources with much higher T_{cp} are on the market (8000–17000 K) because of an assumption that more stimulation to the ipRGCs will be a good thing.

For decades there have been attempts to demonstrate that light sources with higher T_{cp} are beneficial, particularly to visual performance. There is good experimental evidence that light sources with more short wavelength content can decrease pupil size and thereby increase depth of field (Berman *et al.*, 1991), which in turn can improve performance in a visually demanding task (Berman *et al.*, 1993). This led to suggestions that illuminance could be reduced if high T_{cp} light sources are used, thereby reducing energy use while maintaining visual performance (Berman, 1992). However, the evidence for the visual performance benefit of high T_{cp} light sources has been difficult to obtain for tasks and light levels typical of offices (Boyce *et al.*, 2003), and field investigations have found that these installations are not well received by occupants (Wei *et al.*, 2014); in particular, very high T_{cp} (6500 K and higher) at a low illuminance can be perceived as unpleasantly cold (Akashi and Boyce, 2006). Box 12.2 discusses LEDs, eye health, and the 'blue light hazard'.

Box 12.2   LEDs, eye health, and the 'blue light hazard'

White LEDS operate by converting short-wavelength (usually blue, sometimes violet) light to white by passing the light through a phosphor coating. This is conceptually similar to a fluorescent lamp, except that the fluorescent lamp uses ultraviolet radiation that is not emitted from the lamp because of the glass tube. The spectral power distribution of a white LED, regardless of its correlated colour temperature, generally shows a peak in the blue range of the spectrum, around 450 nm. This peak is relatively higher for LEDs with higher correlated colour temperatures. However, the total radiation in this spectral range is typical of other common light sources – there is not more 'blue light' from an LED than other sources we use in homes, shops, and offices.

The 'blue light hazard' is a form of retinal damage that can occur when one is exposed to very high levels of short-wavelength radiation, as would be the case if one stared at the sun or at a welder's arc. Guidance for protection from this and other photobiological hazards is found in international standards such as IEC 62471:2006/CIE S009:2002. The standard classifies light sources into risk groups using the spectral output of the light sources, the spectral weighting function for the hazard, and (where appropriate) the time course for the effect. The exposure calculation is based on a fixed geometry typical of the way the light source is intended to be used. For light sources intended for interior applications, this is the distance that produces an illuminance of 500 lx (roughly, the distance from the ceiling to the top of a desk).

White light LEDs used for general illumination – like all other white light sources for general illumination – are shown to be in risk group 0; they pose no risk for blue light hazard or other common photobiological problems. The U.S. Department of Energy has written a fact sheet on this topic that provides greater detail (http://apps1.eere.energy.gov/buildings/publications/pdfs/ssl/opticalsafety_fact-sheet.pdf).

Perceiving and experiencing the space

The whole environment – the lighting equipment (luminaires), windows or skylights, and interior design including surface finishes – makes up the lighting system. Repaint white walls in a deep purple colour, and one changes the light levels, colours, and distribution of light dramatically.

People generally judge more spacious rooms as being more pleasant (Inui and Miyata, 1973; 1977). Among the design features that contribute to judged spaciousness is the presence of a window (Stamps, 2010). Employees consistently express strong and consistent preferences for access to windows over windowless spaces (Farley and Veitch, 2001; Veitch et al., 2003), although being next to the window can bring with it undesirable temperature variations that reduce overall environmental satisfaction (Veitch et al., 2005).

Spaces with light surfaces appear more spacious (Stamps, 2010), which probably contributes to the consistent results favouring lighting schemes that deliver wall luminances that are at least 30 cd/m² (Loe et al., 1994; Newsham et al., 2004; Newsham et al., 2005; Veitch and Newsham, 2000). People also prefer lighting schemes that provide visual interest in the form of variations in light and dark across the space, rather than a uniform light distribution (Loe et al., 1994; Newsham et al., 2005; Veitch and Newsham, 2000).

Newsham et al. (2005) cautioned that although some variability in light level across the space is desirable and contributes to its attractiveness, there can be too much variability, at which point attractiveness drops. This will be particularly true if the variability is patterned, either spatially or with excessive colour contrast (Wilkins, 2016). Studies that have analysed images using a statistical method called Fourier analysis have found that when the visual characteristics of what we view differ statistically from what is found in nature, it causes discomfort. This discomfort is correlated with brain activity that indicates more effortful processing. Some individuals are more susceptible than others, particularly those who suffer from migraine headaches (Wilkins, 2016). Thus, pronounced stripe patterns – as might be found in a large space with rows of luminaires that direct light down in a dark ceiling – are to be avoided, as are strong colour contrasts.

Another source of discomfort is glare, or light that is more intense than the background level to which one is adapted, when it shines directly in the eyes. Outdoors, it is easy to shield the eyes by looking away, using a shade, or wearing sunglasses; indoors these options might not be available. The geometric arrangement of light sources and work surfaces, whether vertical or horizontal, needs careful attention to prevent this problem. Discomfort is less when the light source is daylight (Osterhaus, 2001), and when it occurs together with an interesting or attractive view (Ariës et al., 2010; Tuaycharoen and Tregenza, 2005). Illuminating engineers have developed mathematical models to predict discomfort arising from glare (e.g. the Unified Glare Rating (CIE, 1995) and the Daylight Glare Probability (Wienold and Christoffersen, 2006)), which may be used at the design stage to assist with glare prevention.

Providing adequately light room surfaces with a moderate degree of variability leads to the judgement that the space is attractive, but the exact preferences differ from one person to another (Newsham and Veitch, 2001). After many years of investigation, it is now clear that providing individual control over the light level in the workstation provides results that are good for the individual, the organisation, and the environment. The preference differences between individuals mean that at best, half of the employees will experience their personal preference with any fixed light level (Newsham and Veitch, 2001). By providing individual control, each individual can work under conditions that they personally prefer. This leads to the judgement that the lighting is of higher quality (Boyce et al., 2006a; Newsham and Veitch, 2001). One study also found that individual control enabled individuals to maintain their motivation throughout the workday, whereas it declined among those without control (Boyce et al., 2006a).

Several independent replications, in both laboratory and field conditions, have shown that when employees work in lighting conditions that they judge to be of higher quality, the benefits are threefold. These conditions include a mixture of direct and indirect light (usually about 40 per cent uplight and 60 per cent downlight) (Veitch and Newsham, 2000), with individual control over light level at the workstation level. The environment benefits because, on average, the individual controls lead to ~10 per cent lower energy use than would be the case at any likely fixed light level (Boyce et al., 2006b; Galasiu et al., 2007). The individual benefits because they experience better mood, higher environmental and job satisfaction, and fewer problems with visual and physical discomfort (Veitch et al., 2008; Veitch et al., 2010; Veitch et al., 2013). Finally, the employing organisation benefits from individuals who are more engaged in work tasks (Veitch et al., 2013), report less time away from work, and are more committed to their organisations and have less intent of leaving (Veitch et al., 2010).

LED technologies exist that can allow individuals to choose the light source spectrum as well as light level. There are few studies with this very new technology, making it difficult to determine whether or not it will be a cost-effective way to add to the degree of personalisation allowed to individuals. Moreover, there are design questions about the feasibility of having different light source spectra side-by-side in a large space; it might be the case that it is only practical to offer individual colour-tuning in an enclosed space. One study to date has examined the effects of providing individual control over light source spectrum. There was weak evidence that providing individual control had a small beneficial effect on the mood of people with this control, which is one link in the evidentiary chain above; however, the authors noted that the participants were unfamiliar with the concept of colour tuning, and questioned whether people had been able to express a stable preference, as they were able to do with light level dimming (Veitch et al., 2012). This technology will need further development and study before it will be clear what its benefits and costs might be.

Activation and alertness

General principles

Our understanding of these processes has greatly expanded since the previous versions of this chapter (Veitch, 2000; 2006). Light received at the eye by the ipRGCs results in signals to many brain structures, not all of which have yet received the same degree of research attention. Because of this, knowledge in this domain is at a preliminary level, and specific recommendations are few. Enough is known to support general principles of healthful lighting, as were expressed by the CIE in 2004 (CIE, 2004/2009). These are shown in Table 12.1.

As we learn more about how light influences physiological and psychological processes through the ipRGCs, our understanding will become more refined and will support more detailed recommendations (CIE, 2016). At present, two broad categories of influence are recognised: accumulative effects of patterns of light and dark exposure that influence circadian regulation (circadian processes are those that occur in daily patterns on an approximately 24-hr cycle), and acute effects on mental processes, including alertness and mood (Cajochen, 2007).

Circadian regulation: waking and sleeping

Circadian regulation is principally controlled by the secretion of the hormone melatonin. In all vertebrate species studied, darkness prompts melatonin secretion, and light exposure suppresses melatonin (Brainard and Provencio, 2006; CIE, 2004/2009). Thus, melatonin levels increase in the evening hours and overnight. Melatonin secretion drops quickly in the morning, during light exposure; for most of the active hours of the day there is no circulating melatonin. In humans, melatonin causes sleepiness and reduced alertness (Arendt and Skene, 2005).

Light detection by the ipRGCs does not include image information; these cells respond to the total light exposure and integrate this exposure over time. For organisms in the natural world, this system ensures that biological processes are synchronised to the day–night cycle of dawn and dusk. Humans, however, have the ability to change light exposures at will using electric light, which leads to the use of light and dark exposure to influence circadian rhythms. Note that it is the overall pattern of exposure over the 24-hour day that will determine an individual's circadian response, meaning that for most people the workplace lighting is not the only, nor always the principal, contributor. Obtaining the proper daily light exposure may be understood as partly a matter of developing good personal health habits, similar to nutrition or exercise.

That being said, people who are exposed to a higher light level over the day show higher levels of circulating melatonin at night, meaning a larger amplitude of the melatonin rhythm

Table 12.1 Principles of healthy lighting as articulated by the International Commission on Illumination (CIE, 2004/2009)

- The daily light dose received by people in Western (industrialized) countries might be too low.
- Healthy light is inextricably linked to healthy darkness.
- Light for biological action should be rich in the regions of the spectrum to which the non-visual system is most sensitive.
- The important consideration in determining light dose is the light received at the eye, both directly from the light source and reflected off surrounding surfaces.
- The timing of light exposure influences the effects of the dose.

(Harb *et al.*, 2015; Noguchi *et al.*, 2004). The greater daytime light exposure, whether provided by windows in the workplace or with elevated levels of electric light, results in a stronger circadian signal that supports better sleep quality (Boubekri *et al.*, 2014; Harb *et al.*, 2015; Münch *et al.*, 2012).

Given that circadian regulation is controlled by light detected through the ipRGCs, which are more sensitive to short-wavelength light (see Figure 12.2), this might explain the results of two field studies that have tested the effects of fluorescent lamps that were designed to increase short-wavelength light exposure and therefore to provide greater ipRGC stimulation. Viola, James, Schlangen and Dijk (2008) found that employees who worked under 17,000 K (short-wavelength-enhanced) lamps reported better sleep quality at night and better alertness and ability to concentrate by day than those who worked under standard 4000 K lamps. Similarly, Mills, Tomkins, and Schlangen (2007) had found that over three months employees working under 17,000 K lamps reported less fatigue and less daytime sleepiness than those under 2900 K lamps. In both cases the light levels (in lux) remained the same for the experimental conditions.

A third investigation focused specifically on female industrial assembly workers with a permanent morning shift starting at 06:00, comparing the standard fixed lighting for this task (1000 lx at 4000 K) with a system using a 6500 K light source slowly increasing in intensity from 1000 lx to 2000 lx (Canazei *et al.*, 2014) between 08:00 and 10:00, then staying at that level until the shift end at 14:00. This dynamic lighting system increased the light exposure considerably, particularly in the short wavelengths, but the study design does not permit differentiation between the effects of the increase in intensity and those from the change in light source spectrum. The dynamic system was associated with small to medium-sized physiological and self-report effects consistent with the hypothesis of an influence on circadian regulation, such as shorter sleep latency and increased heart rate variability.

Circadian regulation depends on the pattern of light and dark exposure – one needs a period of time each day in darkness, during which melatonin is produced, as well as an adequate light exposure. There is good evidence that evening light exposures, including light from display screens, disrupts circadian rhythms by delaying melatonin production (Chang *et al.*, 2015; Figueiro *et al.*, 2011; Gooley *et al.*, 2011). Employers cannot control light exposure outside of working hours, of course, but they can encourage good light exposure habits at home by discouraging the practice of responding to emails after working hours and by limiting overtime that results in high light exposures during the evening hours.

The importance of maintaining a suitable rhythm of light and dark exposure to preserve a regular circadian rhythm of melatonin production that supports many physiological processes cannot be over-emphasised. Several serious health consequences are associated with circadian rhythm disruptions (Stevens and Zhu, 2015), including cancer, obesity, and depression. Indeed, in 2007 the International Agency for Research on Cancer classified shiftwork as *probably carcinogenic to humans* (group 2A) on the basis of research on the effects of night-time light exposure and circadian rhythm and sleep disruption in humans together with the experimental evidence from animals (IARC Monographs Working Group on the Evaluation of Carcinogenic Risks to Humans, 2010). In some countries, the cancer risk from shift work is a recognised occupational health issue and individuals with cancer who can demonstrate long-term exposure to shift work may receive compensation from workplace safety insurance programmes.

Recommendations for night-time lighting in shift work settings are intended to address two problems: aiding staff to regulate circadian rhythms, and providing adequate stimulation to maintain alertness during the shift (the latter is discussed below). The timing of light and dark patterns must be in relation to the shift schedule, and success in the effort depends on the co-operation of the employee because it is the 24-hour pattern that determines the result. Light exposure before the nadir of core body temperature (which occurs 2–3 hours before the end of sleep when the rhythms are entrained) will delay the clock (shifting the temperature nadir to a later time); light exposure just after the temperature nadir will advance the clock (so that the next temperature nadir will happen earlier). If one knows the starting point for the individual, a pattern of light exposure and darkness can be developed to enable an adjustment to a suitable new circadian rhythm given the shift work schedule, provided the shift is not too rapid and this new pattern is practised consistently. Smith and Eastman (2012) have presented a practical approach to this, which includes adjustments for days off. Similar considerations arise in using light and dark exposure to aid in adjustment to new time zones when travelling (Revell and Eastman, 2005), for employees who need to be alert while on business travel.

Alertness, vitality, and emotion

Independent of circadian rhythm regulation, light exposure has acute (i.e., immediate) effects on physiology and behaviour. These processes are only beginning to be understood, but there are interesting hints about how to influence overall well-being.

Immediate effects of light on alertness, both by day and night (e.g. for night-shift workers) appear to follow a separate pathway from circadian regulation (Cajochen, 2007). One of the ways in which we know this is that the effects occur during the day, when melatonin is already suppressed (Smolders et al., 2012), as well as at night in the presence of melatonin. This pathway appears to be more sensitive to longer wavelengths (i.e. red light) than the ipRGCs, another indication of a separate process (Kayumov et al., 2005; Sahin and Figueiro, 2013; Sahin et al., 2014). However, there is no precise information as yet about the spectral sensitivity of this system.

There is mounting evidence that increased light exposure during the day has beneficial effects on immediate well-being. Early studies of the effects of light exposure on mood and well-being showed that people who are exposed to higher levels over a period of weeks tend to report fewer depressive symptoms (Espiritu et al., 1994) and stronger feelings of vitality (Partonen and Lönnqvist, 2000). Contemporary studies have used momentary experience sampling to obtain respondents' feelings on a frequent basis over the day, together with light exposure monitoring. Using this method, we now see that feelings of vitality are stronger immediately following periods of bright light exposure (> 1000 lx white light) (aan het Rot et al., 2008; Smolders et al., 2013; Smolders and de Kort, 2014). Moreover, aan het Rot et al. (2008) also found that social interactions were less quarrelsome and more agreeable immediately following bright light exposure. One possibility is that bright light exposure alters the availability of serotonin in the brain, a neurotransmitter that is key to positive emotional experiences (aan het Rot et al., 2007). These results support the first principle of healthy lighting (CIE, 2004/2009) (see Table 12.1), but do not yet provide sufficient clarity to specify what the best light level might be.

As noted above, advances in lighting and controls technologies have made it feasible to offer the opportunity to change both the light source spectrum (generally expressed as correlated colour temperature) and level. This has increased interest in possible applications of the growing body of knowledge about photobiology and photochemistry, either to increase light exposure to adjust for presumed limitations in light exposure (Canazei et al., 2014), or by tuning the lighting system to settings connected to particular tasks.

Several published papers have reported tests of a variable lighting system in classrooms, each paper reporting investigations in a different geographic locale: Germany (Barkmann et al., 2012), Mississippi, USA (Mott et al., 2012), and the Netherlands (Sleegers et al., 2013). The variable lighting system had between four and seven pre-set conditions that the classroom teachers were instructed to use to aid the students in becoming active; calm; focused; or a standard setting for instruction. The variable lighting system was compared to a standard, fixed system used in other classrooms. In each investigation, concentration tests were the principal dependent measure (there were others in some but not all of the investigations); for the variable lighting system these tests were performed under the 'focus' lighting (1000 lx at 6500 K). There were mixed results, with some grades showing increased concentration in the variable lighting condition, but others not. Some authors have interpreted these results as evidence of a cognitive effect of the increased short-wavelength exposure related to ipRGC stimulation. However, a competing hypothesis cannot be ruled out: That the use of the 'focus' setting to administer other tests during the school year had created a stimulus-response association between concentrating and the bright, cold light. Only a study that paired different special lighting settings with focused concentration can determine whether the effect is a psychological association of stimulus and response, or has a physiological basis in the light exposure. Regardless of what underlying process explains them, these findings suggest that it is possible to cue tasks and improve their performance with specific lighting settings, which may in some circumstances be sufficient to warrant use of these advanced systems.

Integrated lighting recommendations

Having reviewed the various physiological and psychological processes through which light can affect individuals and contribute to their well-being, we now turn to integrating this information into a single set of recommendations for workplace lighting. This chapter cannot provide the level of detail required for every possible workplace, nor is it a replacement for applicable regional or international standards and recommendations. Resources providing more detail include the *IES Lighting Handbook* (DiLaura *et al.*, 2011), the *SLL Code for Lighting* (Raynham, 2013), and the European standard EN 12464–1 (Comité Européen de Normalisation, 2011).

Table 12.2 shows integrated lighting recommendations that balance the needs of individuals to see the task, to be comfortable, to work in a pleasant environment, and to receive suitable stimulation for circadian regulation and immediate alertness. Achieving the right lighting for the workplace will also depend on local building energy regulations, and on considerations of total system costs including installation and maintenance.

There can be apparent conflict between some of these requirements, particularly the suggestion that light exposures need increasing as compared to energy-efficiency regulations. One means to resolve such conflicts is to focus on good design principles, putting light only where it is needed, and only when it is needed, by using controls for detecting occupancy and dimming when daylight is available. An investigation comparing a typical grid lighting system of parabolic-louvred luminaires with an advanced, workstation-specific system combined with occupancy, daylight-linked dimming, and individual controls found that the design change alone reduced the lighting energy use by 42 per cent; when all of the controls were enabled, the new system consumed 69 per cent less energy than the original (Galasiu *et al.*, 2007) while providing the same target light level for each employee's working area.

Readers who compare this chapter with previous versions will find that many recommendations are unchanged (Veitch, 2000; 2006). This may come as a surprise, given the dramatic change in lighting technologies and controls in recent years. However, human fundamental needs themselves have not changed, although our understanding of them has expanded along with the tools for providing for them. As always, to light a productive workplace requires

Table 12.2 Lighting guidelines for productive workplaces, based on office research

Mediating process	Guidelines
Seeing the task	• Deliver the appropriate horizontal and vertical illuminances for tasks and viewers
	• Control unwanted light (glare), both direct and reflected
	• Maximise colour fidelity (colour rendering)
	• Check the flicker properties of LED light sources – seek those with low-amplitude modulation, at modulation frequency rates > 3 kHz if possible
Perceiving and experiencing the space	• Keep vertical surfaces bright, above 30 cd/m² (200 lx vertical on a light-coloured wall)
	• Overall luminance ratios in the direction of view should have a ratio of maximum:minimum of ~1.5:1
	• Use lighting designs with both direct (~60%) and indirect (40%) components
	• To prevent discomfort, avoid creating striped patterns and high colour contrasts
	• Design to allow users' preferred range of illuminances (in offices, average between 300–500 horizontal illuminance)
	• Provide individual controls over light level (the best way to facilitate individuals' receiving preferred conditions); consider providing spectrally-tunable light to also give individual control over light source spectrum
	• Keep controls simple and responsive; always provide manual over-ride options
	• Create interest by integrating luminance variability with architecture
	• Maximise access to daylighting and windows, but protect against thermal and glare problems
Circadian regulation	• Investigate the specific light exposure schedules needed to aid night-shift workers
	• Use daylight as much as possible to facilitate higher light exposures and suitable spectral distributions
	• Inform all staff about good light hygiene habits (avoiding light at night, screens before bed); consider workplace policies to limit display screen use after working hours
Alertness	• Consider providing for increased light levels during daytime, within energy limits – but only if glare can be avoided
	• Use daylight as much as possible to facilitate higher light exposures that can contribute to immediate well-being and more co-operative social behaviour
	• For night shift workers, use light sources that do not have high short-wavelength content (i.e., low correlated colour temperature), as these may facilitate alertness at work with less circadian rhythm disruption

solving several problems at once, taking into consideration the parallel processes that are at play. The job is more demanding than the original Hawthorne researchers could have imagined; we also know now that it is more rewarding. Achieving high-quality lighting in workplaces means that employers, employees, and the environment all benefit.

Note

1 Known by the acronym of its French name, CIE, the Commission Internationale de l'Eclairage (International Commission on Illumination) is a technical, scientific and cultural, non-profit autonomous organisation devoted to international cooperation and exchange of information among its member countries on all matters relating to the science and art of lighting. It is recognised by the International Standards Organisation as an international standardisation body. Further information is available at www.cie. co.at/cie.

References

aan het Rot, M., Benkelfat, C., Boivin, D.B. and Young, S.N. (2007) Bright light exposure during acute tryptophan depletion prevents a lowering of mood in mildly seasonal women. *European Neuropsychopharmacology*, 18(1): 14–23.

aan het Rot, M., Moskowitz, D.S. and Young, S.N. (2008) Exposure to bright light is associated with positive social interaction and good mood over short time periods: a naturalistic study in mildly seasonal people. *Journal of Psychiatric Research*, 42(4): 311–319.

Akashi, Y. and Boyce, P.R. (2006) A field study of illuminance reduction. *Energy and Buildings*, 38(6): 588–599.

Arendt, J. and Skene, D.J. (2005) Melatonin as a chronobiotic. *Sleep Medicine Reviews*, 9(1): 25–39.

Ariës, M.B.C., Veitch, J.A. and Newsham, G.R. (2010) Windows, view, and office characteristics predict physical and psychological discomfort. *Journal of Environmental Psychology*, 30(4): 533–541.

Barkmann, C., Wessolowski, N. and Schulte-Markwort, M.J. (2012) Applicability and efficacy of variable light in schools. *Physiology and Behavior*, 105(3): 621–627.

Berman, S.M. (1992) Energy efficiency consequences of scotopic sensitivity. *Journal of the Illuminating Engineering Society*, 21(1): 3–14.

Berman, S.M., Fein, G., Jewett, D.L. and Ashford, F. (1993) Luminance-controlled pupil size affects Landolt C task performance. *Journal of the Illuminating Engineering Society*, 22(2): 150–165.

Berman, S.M., Greenhouse, D.S., Bailey, I.L., Clear, R.D. and Raasch, T.W. (1991) Human electroretinogram responses to video displays, fluorescent lighting, and other high frequency sources. *Optometry and Vision Science*, 68(8): 645–662.

Berson, D.M., Dunn, F.A. and Takao, M. (2001) Phototransduction by ganglion cells innervating the circadian pacemaker [ARVO abstract]. *Investigative Ophthalmology & Visual Science*, 42(4): S113 Abstract nr 613.

Berson, D.M., Dunn, F.A. and Takao, M. (2002) Phototransduction by retinal ganglion cells that set the circadian clock. *Science*, 295(5557): 1070–1073.

Boubekri, M., Cheung, I.N., Reid, K.J., Wang, C.H. and Zee, P.C. (2014) Impact of windows and daylight exposure on overall health and sleep quality of office workers: a case-control pilot study. *Journal of Clinical Sleep Medicine*, 10(6): 603–611.

Boyce, P.R. (2014) *Human Factors in Lighting*. 3rd edn. London: CRC Press.

Boyce, P.R., Akashi, Y., Hunter, C.M. and Bullough, J.D. (2003) The impact of spectral power distribution on the performance of an achromatic visual task. *Lighting Research and Technology*, 35(2): 141–161.

Boyce, P.R. and Rea, M.S. (1987) Plateau and escarpment: the shape of visual performance. in *Proceedings of the 21st Session of the CIE, Venice, Italy, June 17–25, 1987*. Vienna, Austria: Commission Internationale de l'Eclairage.

Boyce, P.R., Veitch, J.A., Newsham, G.R., Jones, C.C., *et al.* (2006a) Lighting quality and office work: Two field simulation experiments. *Lighting Research and Technology*, 38(3): 191–223.

Boyce, P.R., Veitch, J.A., Newsham, G.R., Jones, C.C., *et al.* (2006b) Occupant use of switching and dimming controls in offices. *Lighting Research and Technology*, 38(4): 358–378.

Brainard, G.C., Hanifin, J.P., Rollag, M.D., Greeson, J., *et al.* (2001) Human melatonin regulation is not mediated by the three cone photopic visual system. *The Journal of Clinical Endocrinology and Metabolism*, 86(1): 433–436.

Brainard, G.C. and Provencio, I. (2006) Photoreception for the neurobehavioral effects of light in humans. In *Proceedings of the 2nd CIE Expert Symposium on Lighting and Health, Ottawa, Canada*. Vienna, Austria: CIE, pp. 6–21.

Cajochen, C. (2007) Alerting effects of light. *Sleep Medicine Reviews*, 11(6): 453–464.

Canazei, M., Dehoff, P., Staggl, S. and Pohl, W. (2014) Effects of dynamic ambient lighting on female permanent morning shift workers. *Lighting Research and Technology*, 46(2): 140–156.

Chang, A.M., Aeschbach, D., Duffy, J.F. and Czeisler, C.A. (2015) Evening use of light-emitting eReaders negatively affects sleep, circadian timing, and next-morning alertness. *Proceedings of the National Academy of Sciences of the United States of America*, 112(4): 1232–1237.

Comité Européen de Normalisation (CEN) (2011) *Light and Lighting – Lighting of Work Places – Part 1: Indoor Work Places* (EN 12464–1). Brussels, Belgium.

Commission Internationale de l'Eclairage (CIE) (1978) *Light as a True Visual Quantity: Principles of Measurement* (CIE 41–1978 (TC-1.4)). Paris, France.

Commission Internationale de l'Eclairage (CIE) (1995a) *Method of Measuring and Specifying Colour Rendering Properties of Light Sources* (CIE 013.3–1995). Vienna, Austria.

Commission Internationale de l'Eclairage (CIE) (1995b) *Discomfort Glare in Interior Lighting* (CIE 117–1995). Vienna, Austria.

Commission Internationale de l'Eclairage (CIE) (2004/2009) *Ocular Lighting Effects on Human Physiology and Behaviour* (CIE 158:2009). Vienna, Austria.

Commission Internationale de l'Eclairage (CIE) (2007) *Colour Rendering of White LED Light Sources* (CIE 177:2007). Vienna, Austria.

Commission Internationale de l'Eclairage (CIE) (2011) *ILV: International Lighting Vocabulary* (CIE S 017/E:2011). Vienna, Austria.

Commission Internationale de l'Eclairage (CIE) (2014) *Guide to Protocols for Describing Lighting* (CIE 213:2014). Vienna, Austria: CIE.

Commission Internationale de l'Eclairage (CIE) (2015) *Report on the First International Workshop on Circadian and Neurophysiological Photometry, 2013* (CIE TN 003:2015). Vienna, Austria. Available at: www.cie.co.at/index.php?i_ca_id=978.

Commission Internationale de l'Eclairage (CIE) (2016) *Research Roadmap for Healthful Interior Lighting Applications* (CIE 218:2016). Vienna, Austria.

Conférence Générale des Poids et Mesures (CGPM) (1979) *Comptes Rendus des séances de la 16e Conférence Générale des Poids et Mesures*. Paris. Available at: www.bipm.org/utils/common/pdf/CGPM/CGPM16.pdf.

Dangol, R., Islam, M.S.Z., Hyvärinen, M., Bhushal, P., Puolakka, M. and Halonen, L. (2015) User acceptance studies for LED office lighting: preference, naturalness and colourfulness. *Lighting Research and Technology*, 47(1): 36–53.

de Kort, Y.A.W. and Veitch, J.A. (2014) From blind spot into the spotlight: Introduction to the special issue 'Light, lighting and human behaviour'. *Journal of Environmental Psychology*, 39(1): 1–4.

DiLaura, D.L., Houser, K.W., Mistrick, R.G. and Steffy, G.R. (2011) *The Lighting Handbook*. 10th edn. New York: Illuminating Engineering Society of North America.

Ecker, J.L., Dumitrescu, O.N., Wong, K.Y., Alam, N.M., *et al.* (2010) Melanopsin-expressing retinal ganglion-cell photoreceptors: cellular diversity and role in pattern vision. *Neuron*, 67(1): 49–60.

Espiritu, R.C., Kripke, D.F., Ancoli-Israel, S., Mowen, M.A., *et al.* (1994) Low illumination experienced by San Diego adults: association with atypical depressive symptoms. *Biological Psychiatry*, 35(6): 403–407.

Farley, K.M.J. and Veitch, J.A. (2001) *A Room with a View: A Review of the Effects of Windows on Work and Well-Being*. Ottawa, ON: NRC Institute for Research in Construction. Available at: http://doi.org/10.4224/20378971.

Figueiro, M.G. (2013) An overview of the effects of light on human circadian rhythms: Implications for new light sources and lighting systems design. *Journal of Light and Visual Environment*, 37(2–3): 51–61.

Figueiro, M.G., Wood, B., Plitnick, B. and Rea, M.S. (2011) The impact of light from computer monitors on melatonin levels in college students. *Neuroendocrinology Letters*, 32(2): 158–163.

Galasiu, A.D., Newsham, G.R., Suvagau, C. and Sander, D.M. (2007) Energy saving lighting control systems for open-plan offices: a field study. *Leukos*, 4(1): 7–29.

Gifford, R. (2002) *Environmental Psychology: Principles and Practice*. 3rd edn. Victoria, BC: Optimal Books.

Gooley, J.J., Chamberlain, K., Smith, K.A., Khalsa, S.B.S., *et al.* (2011) Exposure to room light before bedtime suppresses melatonin onset and shortens melatonin duration in humans. *Journal of Clinical Endocrinology and Metabolism*, 96(3): E463–E472.

Harb, F., Hidalgo, M.P.L. and Martau, B. (2015) Lack of exposure to natural light in the workspace is associated with physiological, sleep and depressive symptoms. *Chronobiology International*, 32(3): 368–375.

Hattar, S., Liao, H.W., Takao, M., Berson, D.M. and Yau, K. (2002) Melanopsin-containing retinal ganglion cells: architecture, projections, and intrinsic photosensitivity. *Science*, 295(5557): 1065–1070.

IARC Monographs Working Group on the Evaluation of Carcinogenic Risks to Humans (2010) *IARC Monographs on the Evaluation of Carcinogenic Risks to Humans: Volume 98 – Painting, Firefighting, and Shiftwork*. Lyon, France. Available at: http://monographs.iarc.fr/ENG/Monographs/vol98/mono98.pdf.

IEEE Power Electronics Society (2015) *IEEE Recommended Practices for Modulating Current in High-Brightness LEDs for Mitigating Health Risks to Viewers* (S1789–2015). New York: Institute for Electrical and Electronics Engineers, Inc. (IEEE).

Illuminating Engineering Society of North America (IESNA) (2015) *IES Method for Evaluating Light Source Color Rendition* (IES TM-30-15). New York: IESNA.

Inui, M. and Miyata, T. (1973) Spaciousness in interiors. *Lighting Research and Technology*, 5(2): 103–111.

Inui, M. and Miyata, T. (1977) Spaciousness, behaviour, and the visual environment. *Journal of Light and Visual Environment*, 1(1): 59–63.

Izawa, M.R., French, M.D. and Hedge, A. (2011) Shining new light on the Hawthorne illumination experiments. *Human Factors*, 53(5): 528–547.

Kayumov, L., Casper, R.F., Hawa, R.J., Perelman, B., *et al.* (2005) Blocking low-wavelength light prevents nocturnal melatonin suppression with no adverse effect on performance during simulated shift work. *Journal of Clinical Endocrinology and Metabolism*, 90(5): 2755–2761.

Levitt, S.D. and List, J.A. (2011) Was there really a Hawthorne effect at the Hawthorne plant? An analysis of the original illumination experiments. *American Economic Journal: Applied Economics*, 3(1): 224–238.

Loe, D.L., Mansfield, K.P. and Rowlands, E. (1994) Appearance of lit environment and its relevance in lighting design: experimental study. *Lighting Research and Technology*, 26: 119–133.

Lucas, R.J., Peirson, S. N., Berson, D.M., Brown, T., Cooper, H. M. *et al.* (2014) Measuring and using light in the melanopsin age. *Trends in Neurosciences*, 37(1) 1–9.

Mills, P.R., Tomkins, S.C. and Schlangen, L.J.M. (2007) The effect of high correlated colour temperature office lighting on employee wellbeing and work performance. *Journal of Circadian Rhythms*, 5: 2.

Mott, M.S., Robinson, D.H., Walden, A., Burnette, J. and Rutherford, A. S. (2012) Illuminating the effects of dynamic lighting on student learning. *SAGE Open*, 2(2): 1–9.

Münch, M., Linhart, F., Borisuit, A., Jaeggi, S.M. and Scartezzini, J.-L. (2012) Effects of prior light exposure on early evening performance, subjective sleepiness, and hormonal secretion. *Behavioral Neuroscience*, 126(1): 196–203.

Newsham, G.R., Marchand, R.G. and Veitch, J.A. (2004) Preferred surface luminances in offices, by evolution. *Journal of the Illuminating Engineering Society*, 33(1): 14–29.

Newsham, G.R., Richardson, C., Blanchet, C. and Veitch, J.A. (2005) Lighting quality research using rendered images of offices. *Lighting Research and Technology*, 37(2): 93–115.

Newsham, G.R. and Veitch, J.A. (2001) Lighting quality recommendations for VDT offices: A new method of derivation. *Lighting Research and Technology*, 33: 97–116.

Noguchi, H., Ito, T., Katayama, S., Koyama, E., Morita, T. and Sato, M. (2004) Effects of bright light exposure in the office. In *Proceedings of the CIE Expert Symposium on Light and Health*. Vienna, Austria: Commission Internationale de l'Eclairage, pp. 153–156.

O'Donell, B.M., Colombo, E.M. and Boyce, P.R. (2011) Colour information improves relative visual performance. *Lighting Research and Technology*, 43(4): 423–438.

Osterhaus, W.K.E. (2001) Discomfort glare from daylight in computer offices: what do we really know?. In *Proceedings of Lux Europa 2001*. Reykjavik, Iceland: Organizing Committee of Lux Europa 2001, pp. 448–456.

Oxford English Dictionary (2016) Productivity, n.2. In *Oxford English Dictionary Online*. Oxford, UK: Oxford University Press. www.oed.com/view/Entry/152001?redirectedFrom=productivity#eid

Papamichael, K., Siminovitch, M., Veitch, J.A. and Whitehead, L. (2016) High color rendering can enable better vision without requiring more power. *Leukos*, 12(1–2): 27–38.

Partonen, T. and Lönnqvist, J. (2000) Bright light improves vitality and alleviates distress in healthy people. *Journal of Affective Disorders*, 57(1–3): 55–61.

Poplawski, M. and Miller, N.J. (2011) Exploring flicker in solid-state lighting: What you might find, and how to deal with it. Paper presented at Illuminating Engineering Society of North America Annual Conference. Austin, TX, Oct. Available at: http://e3tnw.org/Documents/2011 per cent20IES per cent-20flicker per cent20paper per cent20poplawski-miller-FINAL.pdf.

Pritchard, R.D. (1992) Organizational productivity. In Dunnette, M.D. and Hough, L.M. (eds) *Handbook of Industrial and Organizational Psychology*. 2nd edn. Palo Alto, CA: Consulting Psychologists Press, pp. 443–471.

Raynham, P. (ed.) (2013) *SLL Code for Lighting*. London: Chartered Institution of Building Services Engineers.

Rea, M.S. and Ouellette, M.J. (1991) Relative visual performance: a basis for application. *Lighting Research and Technology*, 23(3): 135–144.

Revell, V.L. and Eastman, C.I. (2005) How to trick mother nature into letting you fly around or stay up all night. *Journal of Biological Rhythms*, 20(4): 353–365.

Roethlisberger, F.J. and Dickson, W.J. (1939) *Management and the Worker*. Cambridge, MA: Harvard University Press.

Sahin, L. and Figueiro, M. G. (2013) Alerting effects of short-wavelength (blue) and long-wavelength (red) lights in the afternoon. *Physiology & Behavior*, 116–117: 1–7.

Sahin, L., Wood, B.M., Plitnick, B.A. and Figueiro, M.G. (2014) Daytime light exposure: Effects on biomarkers, measures of alertness, and performance. *Behavioural Brain Research*, 274: 176–185.

Sleegers, P.J.C., Moolenaar, N.M., Galetzka, M., Pruyn, A.T.H., *et al.* (2013) Lighting affects students' concentration positively: findings from three Dutch studies. *Lighting Research and Technology*, 45(2): 159–175.

Smith, M.R. and Eastman, C.I. (2012) Shift work: health, performance and safety problems, traditional countermeasures, and innovative management strategies to reduce circadian misalignment. *Nature and Science of Sleep*, 4: 111–132.

Smolders, K.C.H.J. and de Kort, Y.A.W. (2014) Bright light and mental fatigue: effects on alertness, vitality, performance and physiological arousal. *Journal of Environmental Psychology*, 39: 77–91.

Smolders, K.C.H.J., de Kort, Y.A.W. and Cluitmans, P.J.M. (2012) A higher illuminance induces alertness even during office hours: findings on subjective measures, task performance and heart rate measures. *Physiology and Behavior*, 107(1): 7–16.

Smolders, K.C.H.J., de Kort, Y.A.W. and van den Berg, S.M. (2013) Daytime light exposure and feelings of vitality: results of a field study during regular weekdays. *Journal of Environmental Psychology*, 36: 270–279.

Snow, C.E. (1927) Research on industrial illumination. *The Tech Engineering News*, 8(6): 257, 272–274, 282.

Stamps, A.E., III (2010) Effects of permeability on perceived enclosure and spaciousness. *Environment and Behavior*, 42(6): 864–886.

Stevens, R.G. and Zhu, Y. (2015) Electric light, particularly at night, disrupts human circadian rhythmicity: is that a problem? *Philosophical Transactions of the Royal Society of London B: Biological Sciences*, 370(1667): 2014–2120.

Tuaycharoen, N. and Tregenza, P.R. (2005) Discomfort glare from interesting images. *Lighting Research and Technology*, 37(4): 329–341.

U.S. Department of Energy. Safety fact sheet. Available at: http://apps1.eere.energy.gov/buildings/publications/pdfs/ssl/opticalsafety_fact-sheet.pdf

Veitch, J.A. (1998) Commentary: On unanswered questions. In Veitch, J.A. (ed.) *Proceedings of the First CIE Symposium on Lighting Quality*. Vienna, Austria: CIE, pp. 88–91.

Veitch, J.A. (2000) Creating high-quality workplaces using lighting. In Clements-Croome, D.J. (ed.) *Creating the Productive Workplace*. London: E & FN Spon, pp. 207–223.

Veitch, J.A. (2006) Lighting for high-quality workplaces. In Clements-Croome, D.J. (ed.) *Creating the Productive Workplace*. 2nd edn. London: Routledge.

Veitch, J.A. (2012) Work environments. In Clayton, S.D. (ed.) *The Oxford Handbook of Environmental and Conservation Psychology*. Oxford: Oxford University Press, pp. 248–275.

Veitch, J.A., Charles, K.E., Newsham, G.R., Marquardt, C.J.G. and Geerts, J. (2003) *Environmental Satisfaction in Open-Plan Environments: 5. Workstation and Physical Condition Effects*. Ottawa, ON: NRC Institute for Research in Construction. [Online]. Available at: www.nrc-cnrc.gc.ca/obj/irc/doc/pubs/rr/rr154/rr154.pdf.

Veitch, J.A., Dikel, E.E., Burns, G.J. and Mancini, S. (2012) *Office Light Source Spectrum: Effects of Individual Control on Perception, Cognition, and Comfort* (NRCC-RR-386). Ottawa, ON.

Veitch, J.A., Geerts, J., Charles, K.E., Newsham, G.R. and Marquardt, C.J.G. (2005) Satisfaction with lighting in open-plan offices: COPE field findings. In *Proceedings of Lux Europa 2005*. Berlin, Germany: Deutsche Lichttechnische Gesellschaft e. V. (LiTG), pp. 414–417.

Veitch, J.A. and McColl, S.L. (1995) Modulation of fluorescent light: flicker rate and light source effects on visual performance and visual comfort. *Lighting Research and Technology*, 27(4): 243–256.

Veitch, J.A. and Newsham, G.R. (2000) Preferred luminous conditions in open-plan offices: Research and practice recommendations. *Lighting Research and Technology*, 32: 199–212.

Veitch, J.A., Newsham, G R., Boyce, P.R. and Jones, C.C. (2008) Lighting appraisal, well-being, and performance in open-plan offices: alinked mechanisms approach. *Lighting Research and Technology*, 40(2): 133–151.

Veitch, J.A., Newsham, G.R., Mancini, S. and Arsenault, C.D. (2010) *Lighting and Office Renovation Effects on Employee and Organizational Well-Being* (NRC-IRC RR-306). Ottawa, ON. Available at: http://nparc.cisti-icist.nrc-cnrc.gc.ca/npsi/ctrl?action=shwart&index=an&req=20374532&lang=en.

Veitch, J.A., Stokkermans, M.G.M. and Newsham, G.R. (2013) Linking lighting appraisals to work behaviors. *Environment and Behavior*, 45(2): 198–214.

Viola, A.U., James, L.M., Schlangen, L.J.M. and Dijk, D.-J. (2008) Blue-enriched white light in the workplace improves self-reported alertness, performance and sleep quality. *Scandinavian Journal of Work, Environment and Health*, 34(4): 297–306.

Wei, M., Houser, K.W., Orland, B., Lang, D.H. *et al.* (2014) Field study of office worker responses to fluorescent lighting of different CCT and lumen output. *Journal of Environmental Psychology*, 39: 62–76.

Wienold, J. and Christoffersen, J. (2006) Evaluation methods and development of a new glare prediction model for daylight environments with the use of CCD cameras. *Energy and Buildings*, 38(7): 743–757.

Wilkins, A.J. (1986) Intermittent illumination from visual display units and fluorescent lighting affects movement of the eyes across text. *Human Factors*, 28(1): 75–81.

Wilkins, A.J. (2016) A physiological basis for visual discomfort: Application in lighting design. *Lighting Research and Technology*, 48(1): 44–54.

Wilkins, A.J., Veitch, J.A. and Lehman, B. (2010) LED lighting flicker and potential health concerns: IEEE Standard PAR1789 update. In *Proceedings of the Energy Conversion Congress and Exposition (ECCE) 2010 IEEE, 12–16 Sept., 2010*. New York: Institute of Electrical and Electronics Engineers, pp. 171–178.

Chapter 13

The Robert L. Preger Intelligent Workplace™

The Living Laboratory at Carnegie Mellon University

Volker Hartkopf, Vivian Loftness, Azizan Aziz, Khee Poh Lam, Steve Lee, Erica Cochran and Bertrand Lasternas

Introduction

This chapter presents a vision for sustainable, flexible, and user-based workplaces for the future as demonstrated in the Robert L. Preger Intelligent Workplace at Carnegie Mellon University, and introduces the building science research this 'living laboratory' has supported toward linking high performance workplaces to gains in environmental and human outcomes.

KEY QUESTION: The integrated systems that form the built environment represent no single company's core business, nor does it fall under the purview of a single governmental agency's core mission. It is instead the result of many decisions, influenced by numerous actors working in succession or at times in concert, that often fall short in delivering environmental quality, organizational and technological flexibility, or resource sustainability. Should universities assume leadership to address these weaknesses?

Challenges

- Worldwide growth of nonrenewable resource consumption and resource waste.
- Finite land, material and energy resources (2009 world-wide peak of oil production).
- Poor indoor and outdoor environmental quality.
- 50 percent of world population living on less than $2/day.
- The United States of America's leadership in fashion and short-term investments.

The built environment in the USA:

- creates 40 percent of land-fill waste by weight, and 30 percent by volume;
- consumes almost 40 percent of the US primary energy for operation and an additional 10–20 percent for building materials production;
- contributes over 500 million tons of CO_2 into the atmosphere per year from the generation of the electricity used for building operations (67 percent of total electricity use);
- produces 18 percent of the US total annual CO_2 emissions in cement production;
- offers potential for health and productivity savings in the range of $20–200 billion annually through improved practices and systems integration.

The Robert L. Preger Intelligent Workplace: The Living and Lived-In Laboratory

Every Architecture, Building Science, and Building Engineering program should have an Intelligent Workplace – a living laboratory of component and subsystem innovations and a testing ground for the next generation of building systems integrated for indoor environmental quality and resource sustainability.

The Robert L. Preger Intelligent Workplace™ (IW) (Figure 13.1) is a 7000 sq ft living laboratory of component and subsystem innovations in an occupied, lived-in laboratory of integrated passive-active systems for sustainability. Developed with leading practitioners and manufacturers

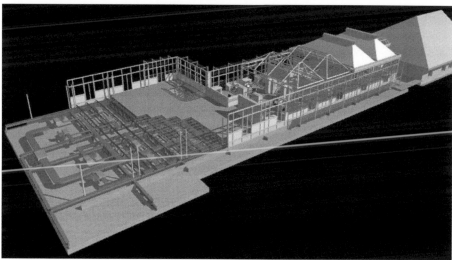

Figure 13.1 The Intelligent Workplace™, a 700m² rooftop extension at Carnegie Mellon University, has flexible, floor-based infrastructures to support research and organizational dynamics

of high performance building systems, the Intelligent Workplace is an ongoing test bed for advances in building enclosure, mechanical, lighting, telecommunications and interior systems as well as the next generation of building controls to support human health and productivity as well as the highest level of environmental sustainability (Hartkopf and Loftness, 2004).

This IW living lab is the result of an unprecedented collaboration between the Center for Building Performance and Diagnostics, the first National Science Foundation Industry/University Cooperative Research Center in the building industry, and the Advanced Building Systems Integration Consortium (ABSIC), a collaborative body of industry and government leaders in the built environment. Occupied in 1997 and continuously being adapted, the IW is a rooftop extension of Margaret Morrison Carnegie Hall on the Carnegie Mellon campus. The Intelligent Workplace has the highest level of thermal, air, light, and plug load sensors and controllers of any university laboratory, supporting ongoing research on the impacts of grid-enabled climate and occupancy-based sensor and control networks for energy conservation and environmental quality.

For more than 15 years, the Intelligent Workplace has provided a forum for education, demonstration and research with a global constituency focused on:

- innovations in enclosure, lighting, HVAC, power and data networking, as well as interior systems to achieve the highest level of thermal, air, visual, acoustic, and spatial quality;
- innovations in spatial flexibility and collaborative work environments to meet the changing nature of work and organizations;
- innovative product assemblies for ensuring performance in an integrated setting;
- "state of the art" IT systems as well as sensing, actuating, and controls technologies to enable effective performance of systems to achieve sustainability in building operations;
- training on material, component, and systems choices and their integration for performance;
- hands-on training with instrumentation and metrics for evaluating performance and occupancy comfort;
- field-validated development of computational tools for design, simulation and management.

The IW enables the interchangeability and side-by-side demonstrations of innovations in HVAC, enclosure, lighting, interior, networking and control components and assemblies. Most importantly, as a "lived-in" office, research, and educational environment, the IW provides a testing ground to assess the performance of new products in an integrated, occupied setting.

Tested, transferable goals of the Intelligent Workplace™

1   *Individual productivity and comfort.* High performance workplaces must ensure individual comfort, health and productivity with quality enclosure, HVAC, lighting and interior systems that deliver thermal, acoustic, visual and air quality, as well as spatial and ergonomic support.
2   *Organizational flexibility.* High performance workplaces must ensure sustained individual productivity and collaborative creativity in the face of ongoing organizational and technological change through user-centric, customizable plug-and-play infrastructures.
3   *Technological adaptability.* High performance workplaces must support advances in technology and connectivity for individual and collaborative work, through accessible and open interior systems and engineering infrastructures that support changing technological demands.
4   *Environmental sustainability.* High performance workplaces must demonstrate the highest level of environmental sustainability in energy, water, material use and assembly design, for health, resource efficacy, just-in-time delivery, flexibility, and maintainability, with a focus on life-cycle design and natural conditioning.

Systems integration for performance

The Intelligent Workplace was not envisioned as a one-time "show-and-tell" demonstration project, but rather as a dynamic environment for teaching and researching the effects of building components, assemblies and systems – in an integrated and occupied setting – on indoor environmental quality and human health and task performance (Loftness, 2001). The IW also provides the platform to explore broad environmental and ecological issues such as recyclability of building products and assemblies, design for disassembly and long-term resource management.

The IW is conceived as a modular system, the units of which can be continuously reconfigured to adapt to the needs of changing office environments, to changes in the location and density of individual and collaborative space and technologies, including changes in the level of workspace enclosure for physical, visual and acoustic privacy without compromising indoor environmental quality.

Design approaches to absorb change and avoid obsolescence: Flexible Grid – Flexible Density – Flexible Closure systems

To avoid frequent environmental quality failures, or median and long-term obsolescence of building infrastructures, it is critical to invest in user-based infrastructures that are modular, reconfigurable, and expandable for all key services – ventilation air, thermal conditioning, lighting, data/voice and power networks. The dynamic reconfigurations of space and technology typical in buildings today cannot be accommodated through the existing service infrastructures – either the "blanket systems" for uniform open plan configurations or the idiosyncratic systems for unique configurations. Instead, what are needed are flexible infrastructures capable of changing both location and density of services:

> Flexible Grid – Flexible Density – Flexible Closure Systems are a constellation of building subsystems that permit each individual to set the location and density of HVAC, lighting, telecommunications, and furniture, as well as the level of workspace enclosure.

These services can be provided by separate ambient and task systems where users set task requirement and the central system responds with the appropriate ambient conditions, or they can be fully relocatable, expandable task/ambient systems (Loftness and Aziz, 2009) (Figure 13.2).

Advanced buildings today demonstrate that modular, floor-based infrastructures may more effectively support the dynamic workplace. Since networking, ventilation and thermal conditioning need to be delivered to each workstation and team space, services from the floor or at desktop offer a greater ease of reconfiguration than ceiling-based systems. In addition, floor-based systems such as HVAC diffusers or cabling and outlet terminal units can be continuously relocated, added or subtracted, to meet changing organizational or individual needs. With modular floor-based services, the ceiling can become more playful and elegant — as a light and acoustic diffuser – defining working groups and working neighborhoods as well as re-exposing the beautiful ceilings of landmark buildings (Hartkopf et al., 1999). Today, a number of industry partnerships are forming to offer collaborative solutions to flexible infrastructures through both floors or ceilings – data/voice, power, lighting, thermal conditioning and ventilation.

EXISTING SERVICE/UTILITY

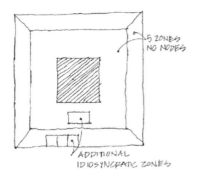

CONCEPT OF GRID & NODES

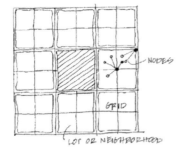

Figure 13.2 The future of high performance offices are flexible infrastructures with micro-zoning and user reconfigurability of heat, light, air, networks and spatial settings for individual and collaborative work

Flexible work environments are more critical than ever. Interactive multimedia and web-based technologies create the possibility of working within ever-changing teams, both locally and globally. This requires that work environments must be responsive to ever-changing organizational and rapidly evolving technological circumstances (Loftness, 2008).

Eliminate or reduce waste in design, construction and operation

The Intelligent Workplace exemplifies how building design and engineering can result in a 70–90 percent reduction of emissions and waste during the production of materials, components and assemblies for the structure, façade, roof and floor plenum when compared to a conventional building. This includes the reduction of NOx by 90 percent, SO_2 by 70 percent, and CO_2 by 80 percent. Selecting recycled aluminum and steel rather than virgin materials, benign low energy finishes, manufacturing assemblies in factories with no waste, and material transportation by water, where possible, were critical to environmental performance in the design phases.

In addition to ensuring complete recycling of all by-products in manufacturing, the IW's modular design and its off-site fabrication led to no on-site waste during the construction phase, from the steel structure to the façade erection to interior fit-out. This also resulted in a reduced potential for injury and significant time savings during construction, which ultimately led to capital savings through shortened delivery time.

In the operation of the IW, the greatest reduction in waste is through natural conditioning by passive and active solar heating and cooling, natural ventilation for six or more months, and daylighting 100 percent of the work places during daylight hours. Also in the operational phase, material waste is reduced through reconfigurable and relocatable interior systems, with modular interfaces to the HVAC, lighting, and networking systems. The just-in-time support of organizational and technological change ensures that the building is meeting flexibility and adaptability requirements without redundancy or waste. Accessible plenums, bolted and pinned assemblies (rather than welded and caulked) and plug-and-play technologies allow for component-by-component, or system-by-system change-out of technology without destruction or waste. Flexible, plug-and-play infrastructures also ensure that the building is a renewable asset for its investors and will not become a "straitjacket" that eventually has to be discarded in whole or in part.

The integrated, modular and demountable systems in the IW reflect the fact that buildings are made from components with different life cycles. While the structural system should have a life of 100 years, plug-and-play design ensures the potential for additions and relocations with columns and trusses that can be redeployed. While the envelope as a system should have a life of 50–100 years, the potential to exchange glazing materials, photovoltaics and other components is supported as soon as superior performance becomes economically feasible. While lighting and HVAC components have a life of 25–50 years, modular, accessible, plug-and-play infrastructures will support easy relocation and densification changes without waste of the high quality light fixtures and thermal and air quality "terminal units." While interior systems have considerably less "life expectancy" from 10–25 years, and computing technologies might have a useful life of 2–5 years, even these systems can be designed for reconfiguration, upgrading, and eventual disassembly for recycling.

In summary, the waste management and environmental benefits of the IW include the following:

1   The materials, components and systems require a fraction of the energies during their production and assembly and produce a fraction of the emissions of comparable systems.
2   During the construction phase, waste is eliminated through prefabrication and modular design.
3   During the operational phase, the management of obsolescence supports organizational and technological changes on-demand. This is enabled through relocatable infrastructures: HVAC, lighting, power, communication and interior systems. The fact that major building components and systems have different life cycles is accounted for through the use of the modular, plug-and-play systems that allow for easy change-out and advancement of technology as the need or opportunity arises.
4   The design for disassembly anticipates a complete decommissioning of the building and its constituent parts. The "long-life systems" such as structure and enclosure can be redeployed elsewhere. Or, as in all other cases, the materials of non-unified components in subsystems can be completely recycled.

Design ascending then cascading energy systems

The Intelligent Workplace is designed to maximize energy conservation and passive energies before using energy cascades that maximize mechanical energies. The "ascending strategy" uses insulated and airtight enclosure assemblies, high performance glazing, shading, natural ventilation and building mass to maximize the number of hours for which no electric lighting is needed and the number of months for which no cooling, heating or ventilation is needed. Passive strategies such as cross-ventilation, stack ventilation, fan-assisted ventilation and night ventilation are an ongoing area of research, alongside passive solar heating and daylighting through time of day and seasonal window management.

Mechanical systems are engineered to maximize passive conditioning. When wind or thermally induced ventilation is no longer viable naturally, economizer ventilation with 70 percent heat recovery is provided by an enthalpy recovery air handler. When outdoor humidity levels exceed the effective comfort zone for economizers, desiccant cooling is the next level of mechanical assist. Only when all else fails, during the hottest days, does refrigerant cooling provide comfort. Research on active system controls to support passive conditioning is an ongoing area of research in the "living lab," from HVAC central system controls to micro-zoning terminal unit controls to night ventilation linked to increasing thermal mass through phase change materials.

Electric lighting is also engineered to maximize passive conditioning. Daylighting is pervasive in the IW, providing 100 percent of the workspaces' light for 80 percent of the work hours throughout the year. Daylight redirection through dynamic external louvres and manual and automated interior blinds support effective daylighting even on low light days in spaces that measure as much as 20 meters window wall to window wall. Every light fixture is an IP addressable point of control, enabling occupancy, daylight levels, and user preferences to support highly individualized lighting control for visual quality and energy efficiency. Research on façade assemblies for effective daylighting distribution and electric lighting control innovations is a long-term focus of the Center.

Complementing these passive energy strategies with responsive mechanical systems, the Intelligent Workplace is a test-bed for "cascading" energy systems designed to make maximum use of limited natural resources. In an area of research affectionately called IWESS, for Intelligent Workplace Energy Supply Systems, our present cascading system – a bio-diesel generator, concentrating solar collectors and photovoltaic panels – can be bundled to provide the building's power generation with high temperature reject heat used to drive desiccant and absorption systems, and low temperature reject heat used for space heating and hot water (Figure 13.3). The availability of the campus grid to absorb excess electricity and steam is invaluable to achieve cascading energy performance in these combined heating, cooling and power generation approaches, with 70 percent efficiencies rather than the 30 percent typical in the USA.

Over 15 years of testing and updates, the energy performance of the Intelligent Workplace living lab is 20 percent of a standard US office building (Figure 13.4). Yet there are still areas for innovation, including:

- reducing infiltration and heat loss/heat gain through the roof ridge vents and in the under-floor plenum;
- seasonally reducing glass area by shading, insulation or modulating solar heat gain coefficients;
- introducing additional thermal mass through phase change materials to maximize night cooling potential;
- updating the desiccant and enthalpy recovery air handling unit, possibly introducing two systems to separate the north and south zones;

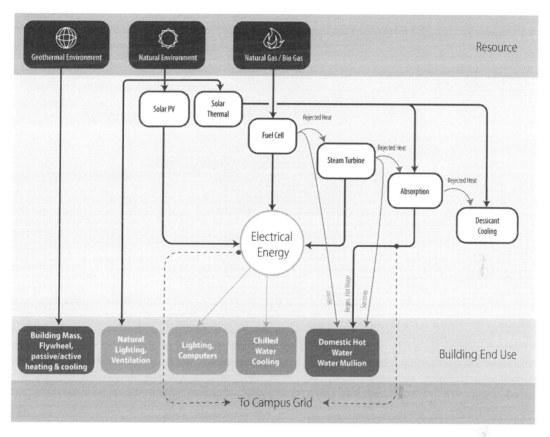

Figure 13.3 Cascading energy systems combining power, cooling and heating make maximum use of limited resources

- microzoning thermal controls so each workstation can use occupancy, passive conditioning and user preference for control, with expert feedback for energy savings;
- updating the electric lighting from T-5 lamp sources to LED, maintaining the focus on individually addressable and continuous dimming controls with daylight harvesting;
- testing future generations of Intelligent Workplace Energy Supply Systems that cascade power to power to cooling to heating to hot water.

Some of the research, development and demonstration innovations might best be directed at a new, larger living laboratory at Carnegie Mellon University. A new 'Invention Works' building proposal is designed to be a Building-as-Power-Plant (BAPP) integrating advanced enclosure, heating, ventilation, air-conditioning and lighting technologies with innovative distributed energy generation systems, so that all of the building's energy needs for heating, cooling, ventilating and lighting are met on-site, and excess energy is exported (Figure 13.5).

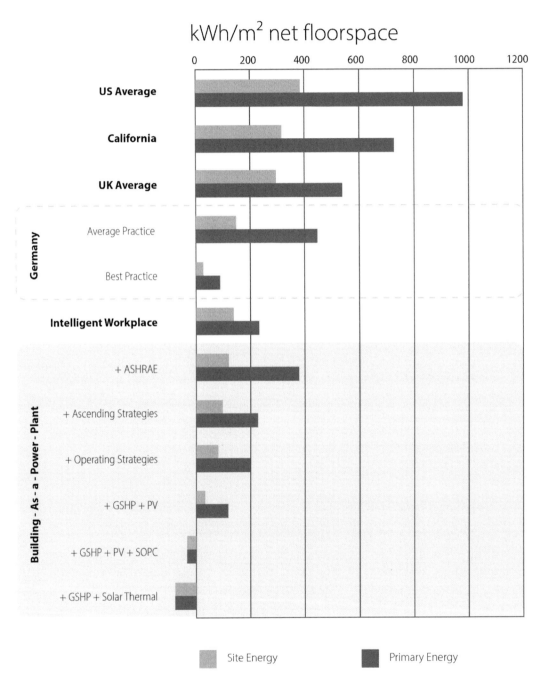

kWh/m² net floorspace

Figure 13.4 Comparisons of site and primary energy performance of the Intelligent Workplace, at 20 percent of standard US office buildings, and future living labs that demonstrate buildings as power plants (BAPP)

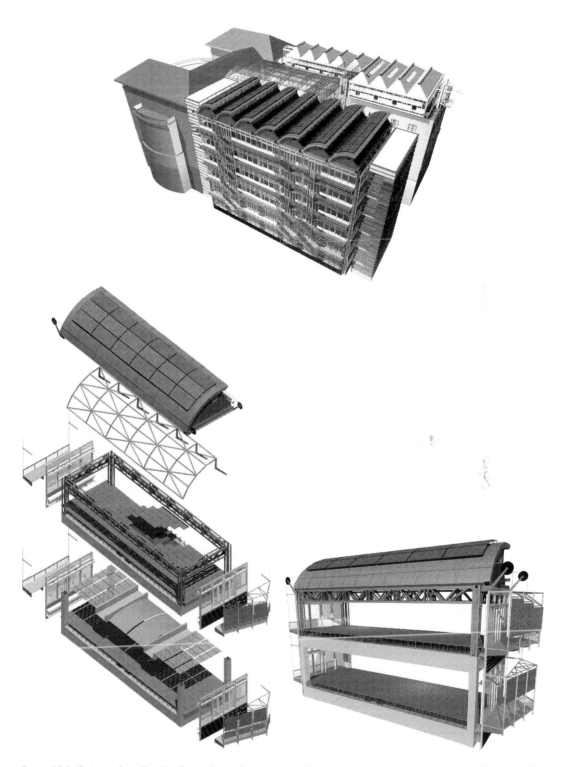

Figure 13.5 Column-free, flexible floor plans, plug-and-play infrastructures, modular interiors, combined cooling, heating and power with solar PV and thermal collectors would make the new Invention Works living laboratory a Building as Power Plant

A living laboratory for building science research and education

Carnegie Mellon University's Intelligent Workplace has supported almost 20 years of graduate and undergraduate thesis projects, with groundbreaking results in each of the following research areas:

- Advanced building systems research – developing and testing innovations in integrated mechanical, lighting, enclosure and interior systems.
- Indoor environmental quality (IEQ) research – testing systems integrations that improve thermal comfort, acoustic quality, visual quality and air quality.
- Environmental monitoring research – expanding the post-occupancy evaluation toolkits to include quantitative measurements of integrated environmental conditions (POE+M).
- Environmental controls research – demonstrating the potential for building occupants to act as sensors and controllers through innovations in IP addressable building systems for IEQ and energy savings.
- Lab and field-tested advanced software research – developing innovative algorithms and software tools for designing and operating buildings for the highest level of energy conservation and environmental quality, from BIM to BEM.

Advanced building systems research — developing and testing innovations in integrated mechanical, lighting, enclosure and interior systems

In advanced building systems research, the faculty and students in the CBPD are actively researching innovative components and integrated mechanical, lighting, enclosure and interior systems in the IW living lab, towards achieving the highest level of thermal, air, acoustic, and visual quality as well as deep energy and material conservation.

Ming Qu, now Associate Professor of Architectural Engineering in the School of Civil Engineering at Purdue University, completed a dissertation in 2008 that proved the viability of high temperature solar concentrators for solar absorption cooling and heating in the Intelligent Workplace (Figure 13.6). Supported by DOE and the Advanced Building Systems Integration Consortium, this research combined experimental and model-based performance analysis in the IW:

> This solar cooling and heating system incorporates 52 m^2 of linear parabolic trough solar collectors; a 16 kW double effect, water–lithium bromide (LiBr) absorption chiller, and a heat recovery heat exchanger with their circulation pumps and control valves. It generates chilled and heated water, dependent on the season, for space cooling and heating. This system is the smallest high temperature solar cooling system in the world. Performance of the system has been tested and the measured data were used to verify system performance models developed in the TRaNsient SYstem Simulation program (TRNSYS). On the basis of the installed solar system, base case performance models were programmed; and then they were modified and extended to investigate measures for improving the system performance. The measures included changes in the area and orientation of the solar collectors, the inclusion of thermal storage in the system, changes in the pipe diameter and length, and various system operational control strategies. It was found that this two bay solar thermal system could supply 39 percent of cooling and 20 percent of heating energy for this building space in Pittsburgh, PA, if it included a properly sized storage tank and short, low diameter connecting pipes. Guidelines for the design and operation of an efficient and effective solar cooling and heating system for a given building space were developed.
>
> (Qu *et al.*, 2010a; Qu *et al.*, 2010b)

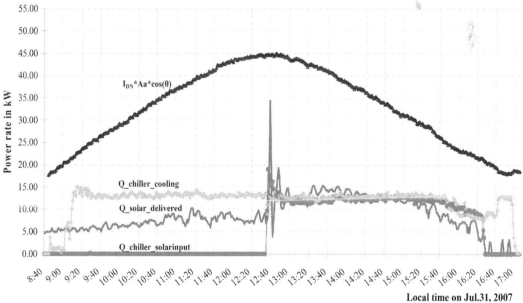

Figure 13.6 Solar concentrators and LiBr absorption chiller system could generate 39 per cent of the cooling and 20 per cent of the heating in the IW

Source: Qu *et al.* (2010).

Mode One Results: Thermal Load Follow		
Annual Net Energy Import	104,613	MJ
Annual Net Thermal Energy Export	31,827	MJ
Annual Net Electrical Energy Import	136,440	MJ
Hours of Operation	5,158.5	Hours
Heating Hours Not Met	2,773	Hours
Cooling Hours Not Met	2,986	Hours
Regeneration Hours Not Met	3,184	Hours
Total Energy Used	834,821	MJ
Total Fuel Consumption	9,025	Gallons
Total Fuel Energy Consumption	1,228,845	MJ
Average Annual Efficiency	68%	

Table 13: IWESS Thermal Load Follow Simulation Results

Figure 13.7 Combined Cooling, Heating, Power, and Ventilation systems (CCHP/V) with biodiesel fuels yield an average annual efficiency of about 68 per cent and a peak of 78 per cent for the IW

Source: Betz (2009).

Fred Betz, now Senior Sustainable Design Consultant at Affiliated Engineers in Madison Wisconsin completed a dissertation in 2009 that proved the viability of Combined Cooling, Heating, Power, and Ventilation systems (CCHP/V) with biodiesel fuels, through an on-site installation at CMU integrated with the HVAC in the IW (Figure 13.7).

> Carnegie Mellon University's Departments of Architecture and Mechanical Engineering have designed and installed a biodiesel fueled engine-generator with heat recovery equipment to supply electric and thermal power to an office building on campus, the Intelligent Workplace (IW). The installation was completed in early September 2007, and was commissioned through April of 2008 with standard off-road low sulfur Diesel (LSD) fuel. Additional baseline testing was conducted with LSD until October 2008, when the transition was made to a 100 percent soybean oil-based biodiesel. The turbocharged Diesel engine-generator set is operated in parallel with the local electric utility and the campus steam grid. The system is capable of generating 25 kW of electric power while providing 18 kW of thermal power in the form of steam from an exhaust gas boiler and 19 kW in the form of heated water from the engine coolant. The steam is delivered to a double-effect Lithium-Bromide (Li-Br) absorption chiller, which supplies chilled water to the IW for space cooling in the summer or hot water for space heating in the winter. Furthermore, the steam can be delivered to the campus steam grid during the fall and spring when neither heating nor cooling is required in the IW. The thermal energy recovered from the coolant provides hot water for space heating in the winter, and for regenerating a solid desiccant dehumidification ventilation system in summer . . . The results show that for efficient and effective performance of a CHP system in a high performance building it is essential to have electrical and thermal grids available to export and/or import CHP energy. The grids allow the CHP system to operate continuously at the design load. The grids also provide back-up in case of system outage. The results of operating the biodiesel fueled CHP system in the IW yields an average annual efficiency of about 68 percent and a peak of 78 percent.
> (Betz *et al.*, 2008; Betz, 2009; Betz and Archer, 2009)

Indoor environmental quality (IEQ) research – testing systems integrations that improve thermal comfort, acoustic quality, visual quality and air quality

In the research area of IEQ, the faculty and students in the CBPD are actively researching in the IW living lab the integrated parameters of thermal, acoustic, visual and air quality that contribute to physiological, psychological and social health, comfort and well-being.

Yun Gu, now Research Scientist at Phillips Lighting completed a dissertation in 2011 that demonstrated the impact of personalized lighting and daylighting control accompanied by real-time knowledge and expert feedback to improve office users' satisfaction, task performance, and energy savings (Figure 13.8).

> This dissertation provides field laboratory data demonstrating that individual control helps achieve lighting energy reduction and improve office worker satisfaction without task performance decrement. The study also provides laboratory evidence that real-time knowledge and feedback help to achieve further energy reduction while sustaining high user satisfaction and task performance.
> *Office occupants need personal environment control to achieve the 80 percent satisfaction.* In a test environment with fixed 500 lux ceiling light delivery (typical in US offices),

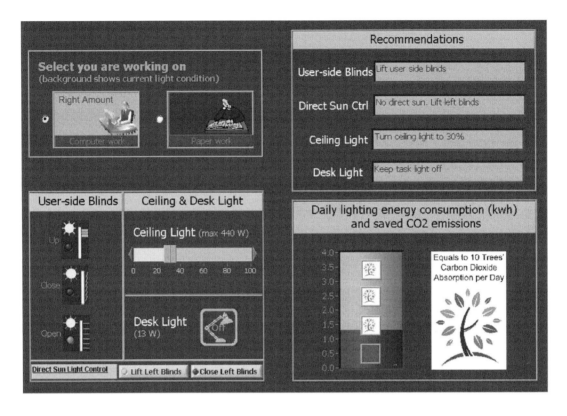

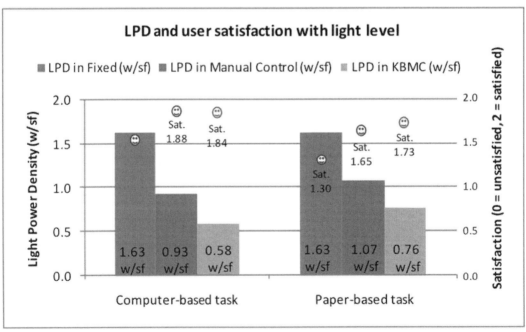

Figure 13.8 Individual control of ambient, task and daylight yields **40** per cent energy savings and high satisfaction, rising to **60** per cent savings with dashboards offering real-time, knowledge-based individual control

only 53 percent of occupants were satisfied with the light level on the work surface for either computer-based task or paper-based task. When occupants manually operated blinds, dimmed ceiling luminaires and turned task light on or off in the test space, over 80 percent user satisfaction could be achieved.

Manual controls for ambient light, task light and blinds can save as much as 40 percent of the energy, while increasing satisfaction from 50 percent to 80 percent. Separated ambient and task light, with personal glare-free daylight control and dimmable ambient light and task lights, are keys to user satisfaction and energy savings. The flexibility of occupants to manipulate blinds and light settings based on personal preference and task requirements offers 40 percent energy savings compared to a fixed office lighting design in a daylit office.

Real-time feedback and expert knowledge for understanding the lighting and daylighting choices further reduce energy by 20 percent, for a total of 60 percent over fixed level ceiling luminaire output, while maintaining the high level of satisfaction. Real-time feedback on environmental conditions, energy consumption, and emission consequences, alongside expert recommendations helps office occupants understand their options for setting blinds and lights. Office users equally ranked the value of the four categories of information as useful in helping them make decisions. Total energy consumption is now reduced by 60 percent compared to fixed ceiling luminaire settings in a daylit office, with user satisfaction rates rising from 53 to over 80 percent.

(Gu, 2011)

Joonho Choi, now Assistant Professor in the School of Architecture at the University of Southern California, completed a dissertation in 2010 that demonstrated the potential of human bio-signals such as heart rate and skin temperatures to act as thermal comfort controllers yielding 93 percent satisfaction rates with thermal conditions (as compared to < 60 percent in thermostat-controlled offices), no change in task performance, and 5.9 percent in cooling energy savings (Figure 13.9).

By necessity, existing automatic control systems disregard individual characteristics such as health status, age, gender, lifestyle, ethnic or cultural origin, body fat percentage, etc., which may affect physiological responses. As a consequence, these systems have serious limitations in ensuring individual thermal satisfaction. While there have been many efforts to overcome the limitations of current technology and to improve individualized control, they are still based on pre-set programmable parameters and require physical access to controllers. In addition, most of the attempts to make smart controllers for buildings have dealt primarily with optimizing mechanical building components to deliver uniform conditions, largely ignoring whether a generated thermal environment by building systems meet actual users' comfort and satisfaction. Over-cooling and over-heating are common, unnecessary results.

Thermal control innovations for building mechanical systems are critically needed to demonstrate that meeting the physiological needs of occupants can actually save energy and improve environmental quality while enhancing user satisfaction. The thermo-regulation of the human body has a biological mechanism, homeostasis, which enables it to maintain a stable and constant body temperature by changing physiological signals including skin temperatures and heart rate. These signal patterns have the potential to provide information about each individual's current thermal perception.

This project established an adaptive thermal comfort controller driven by ongoing human physiological responses in bio-signals, and resulted in significant increases in thermal comfort and

Skin temperature and generated air temperature pattern by different clo-values

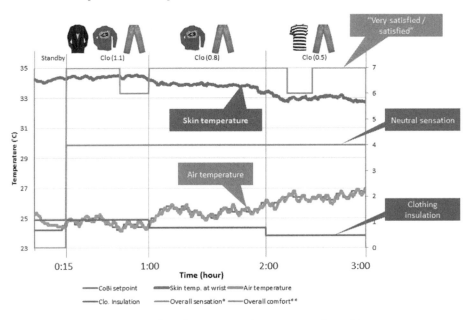

Figure 13.9 Skin temperature is an excellent thermostat, reflecting personal variables over time
Source: Choi (2010).

measured energy savings without compromising task performance. After confirming the optimum driver of skin temperature, and the body locations for a sensor, the sensor-controller was ergonomically and economically refined, and data mining algorithms incorporated in a wireless configuration to support the optimum control of HVAC terminal units. Since the system uses a data-driven approach, the controller predicts thermal sensation based on the dataset of individual bio-signals and indoor/outdoor climate conditions collected in real-time in the IW test room (Figure 13.9). This prediction principle can also be used for multi-occupancy space controls by adopting a negotiation strategy for a consensus to maximize the thermal comfort of all the space occupants while minimizing energy use for heating or cooling. A bio-sensing adaptive HVAC system controller could substantially improve occupant comfort, health, and well-being while advancing environmental sustainability with energy savings, at a small first cost for existing or new buildings (Choi, 2010; Choi and Loftness, 2012; Choi *et al.*, 2012).

Environmental monitoring research – expanding the post-occupancy evaluation toolkits to include the technical attributes of building systems and the quantitative measurements of integrated environmental conditions (POE+M)

User satisfaction assessment, IEQ monitoring and up-to-date records of the technical attributes of building systems are equally critical components of post-occupancy evaluations. Over 40 years with ongoing support from GSA, the CBPD faculty and students have refined toolkits in the IW for the side by side and before and after evaluation of office, school, lab and assembly facilities worldwide. This National Environmental Assessment Toolkit (NEAT) combines on-site physical measurements of thermal, air, lighting and acoustic conditions, both on-line and on-site user satisfaction questionnaires, and records of the technical attributes of building enclosure, lighting, interior and HVAC systems, to generate statistically significant guidelines for sustaining or improving the quality of the indoor environment. (Loftness *et al.*, 2003; Aziz *et al.*, 2012).

Ying Hua, now Associate Professor in the College of Human Ecology at Cornell, completed a dissertation in 2007 that contributed significantly to the development of the NEAT toolkit and its potential to uncover critical linkages between the attributes of buildings, indoor environmental quality and worker effectiveness.

The dissertation focused attention on

> the collaborative spaces in workplaces, to identify layout scenarios of these spaces on the basis of extensive literature review and a large-scale field study of twenty-seven federal workplace settings. Six new layout-scale spatial variables were proposed for workplace studies to amend the workstation characteristics studied in the existing literature. They are: distance from individual workstation to nearest meeting space; distance from individual workstation to nearest shared copy/print area; distance from individual workstation to nearest shared kitchen or coffee area; percent of floor space dedicated to meeting spaces; percent of floor space dedicated to shared service and amenity spaces; and openness . . . The results in this study present a coherent view of how particular layouts can support or inhibit collaborative work. They also suggest a particular type of spatial organization to support collaborative work, namely, a uniformly distributed clustered organization of shared spaces (M6, M7, and C4) as preferable to centralized space solutions or randomly distributed spaces (Figure 13.10).

> (Hua *et al.*, 2010; 2011)

Types of shared print spaces in US offices

	Diagram	Description	% of sites	MEAN distance workstation to shared service (ft)	Standard Deviation distance (ft)
C1	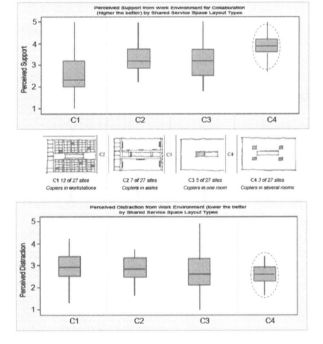	Copiers randomly located in vacant workstations	44%	65.08	52.12
C2		Copiers on main circulation aisles	26%	36.09	18.85
C3		Copiers in dedicated space, centralized (usually in the core)	18%	87.15	48.52
C4		Copiers in dedicated spaces, distributed	12%	41.18	24.28

Dedicated copy / print rooms are associated with higher levels of perceived support for collaboration...

and with lower levels of perceived distraction from the work environment.

(n=308, Ying 2007)

Figure 13.10 Studies of meeting, kitchen and print spaces in federal office buildings revealed that distributed yet centrally accessible enclosed spaces improve collaboration and reduce distraction

Source: Hua *et al.* (2011).

Jihyun Park, now a Research Associate in the Center for Building Performance and Diagnostics, completed a dissertation in 2015 gathering over 1600 workstation data sets, across more than 65 office buildings, to identify linkages between the attributes of buildings, indoor environmental quality and worker effectiveness, with a focus on whether humans are good sensors. This thesis demonstrated:

> an integrated approach to POE+M by leveraging occupants as sensors to quickly capture IEQ conditions in a work environment, and identify critical factors in the physical environment that impact building occupant comfort, satisfaction, health, and performance. This approach provides practical IEQ assessment methods and procedures centered on the occupants' perspective, and addresses the significant discrepancy between major IEQ standards and actual human perception (Park *et al.*, 2013). Through multivariate regression, multiple correlation coefficients, and Pearson correlation statistical analysis of the database of 1,600 workstations, the thesis demonstrated that humans are effective direct and indirect sensors for certain IEQ metrics, but not for others, with findings comparable to complex instrumentation. Moreover, the thesis identified that present environmental thresholds are not adequate for capturing acceptable thermal, acoustic, visual and air quality conditions for occupant satisfaction, due to omitted human factors and physical workspace characteristics (Figure 13.11).
>
> (Park *et al.*, 2013; Park, 2015)

Environmental controls research — demonstrating the potential for building occupants to act as sensors and controllers through innovations in IP-addressable building systems for IEQ and energy savings

The Intelligent Workplace is one of the most sensored and controllable workplaces worldwide, shifting from traditional settings with one control for every 20 occupants to 20 controls for every occupant. With the emergence of wireless sensors and controllers and the Internet of Things (IoT), the IW is a testbed for the engagement of occupants as both sensors and controllers for the improvement of environmental quality and energy conservation. In 2010, the CBPD faculty began a long term collaboration with the students of Dr. Bernd Bruegge in the Institut for Informatik at the Technical University of Munich (TUM). Through this collaboration, the IW has been the laboratory for Bachelor, Masters and PhD thesis projects related to using the capabilities of smartphones to provide communication, expert feedback and consulting, and intuitive control.

With the support of the TUM team led by Professor Bruegge and PhD graduate *Sebastian Peters*, every occupant in the Intelligent Workplace has smartphone access to every sensor and controller in their personal and shared workspaces.

We can control each ceiling light and task light individually, as well as radiant panels, cooling chilled beams, motorized windows, fans and more. We can also see local temperatures, humidity, particulate and CO_2 readings, daylight and electric light levels, and the energy use of all of our desktop technologies (Figure 13.12). Smartphone-based switches and text reminders help us to turn off office technologies remotely in case we forget. If enabled, "Geofencing" controls allow our phone's localization (GPS, Bluetooth, and other location finders) to automatically turn off selected technologies when we leave the office, so even reminders are unnecessary. This is the "Internet of Things" for offices in action.

The true power of the Internet of Things in buildings, however, is the ability to customize our environment to individual needs at the lowest energy demand. For those who prefer lower lighting for computer work, the smart phones let you dim the light with a gesture,

Cooling season user satisfaction with air temperature at 0.6m

CBPD, CMU, Cooling Season (n=446)

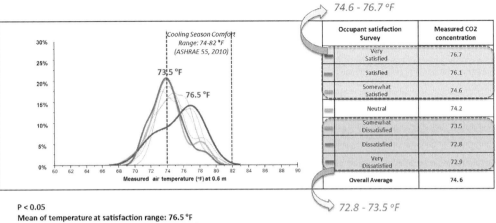

74.6 - 76.7 °F

Occupant satisfaction Survey	Measured CO2 concentration
Very Satisfied	76.7
Satisfied	76.1
Somewhat Satisfied	74.6
Neutral	74.2
Somewhat Dissatisfied	73.5
Dissatisfied	72.8
Very Dissatisfied	72.9
Overall Average	74.6

72.8 - 73.5 °F

P < 0.05
Mean of temperature at satisfaction range: 76.5 °F
Mean of temperature at dissatisfaction range: 73.5 °F

Temperature Satisfaction by "Size of Zone"

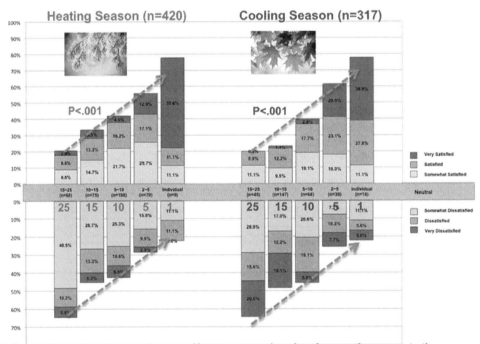

The smaller the thermal zone (fewer people sharing a thermostat), the greater the satisfaction with air temperature in the workstation.

Figure 13.11 US office occupants are much more comfortable at 74.6–76.7°F in summer (above), and only achieve ASHRAE's mandate for 80 per cent satisfied in individually controlled zones (44 buildings, n = 737) (below)

Source: Park (2015).

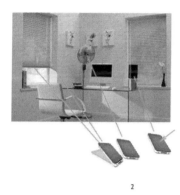

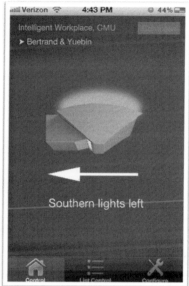

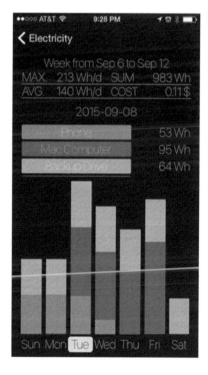

Figure 13.12 Smart phones will support intuitive gesture control of every fixture (top), provide energy use information (bottom right) and readings of individual sensors and set points (bottom left)

Source: Peters (2016).

using the phone's compass and gyroscope (Peters, 2011). For those who want less air conditioning, a smart phone controller could allow us to lower the fan speed or partially close the diffuser. The mutually supportive opportunity for saving energy and increasing indoor environmental quality is long overdue (Peters, 2016).

The power of user interfaces and the Internet of Things form the subject of a 2014 IW dissertation focused on the development of Intelligent Dashboards for Occupants (ID-O). *Ray Yun*, now an Assistant Professor at Hongik University, developed innovative energy dashboards for office workers focused on communication/feedback, expert consulting, and multiple levels of control (C³; Figure 13.13). The impact of nine critical interventions for behavioral change were studied in his dissertation, structured in three sets: (1) Instructional interventions – education, advice and self-monitoring; (2) Motivational interventions – goal setting, comparison and engagement; and (3) Supportive interventions – communication, control and reward. With a focus on controlling plug loads, the fastest growing energy end use in commercial buildings, the nine-month controlled field experiment with 80 office workers revealed that occupant dashboards for controlling desktop technology, with ongoing energy communication and expert consulting generated by the occupants' own data set, can generate up to 40 percent energy savings in plug loads (Yun, 2014).

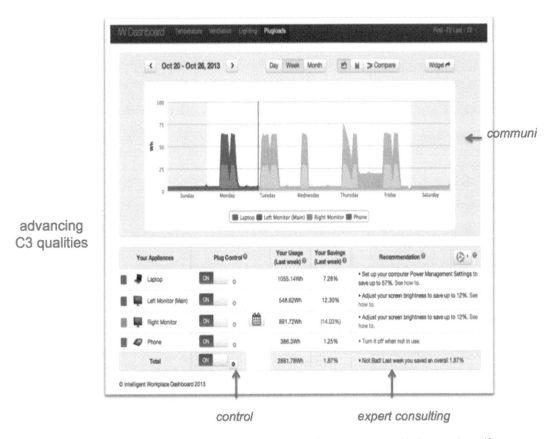

Figure 13.13 Desktop energy feedback and control dashboards for occupants yielded as much as **40** per cent sustained savings from an already efficient workstation

Source: Yun (2014).

Lab and field-tested advanced software research – developing innovative algorithms and software tools for designing and operating buildings for the highest level of energy conservation and environmental quality, from BIM to BEM

The CBPD has been developing dynamic life-cycle building information models (DLC-BIM) focused on Total Building Performance to ensure best practices in sustainable and green architecture. The DLC-BIM supports multi-disciplinary and concurrent multi-domain building-related design and operational decision-making, developed and refined through the power of test-beds such as the IW. The model structure is primarily based on the Industry Foundation Class (IFC) schema that captures the "static" building information generated during the design and construction process to support building performance predictions using various building simulation tools (energy, CFD, lighting, acoustics, etc.) and benchmark evaluations (e.g. LEED) with advanced design optimization. DLC-BIM then captures "dynamic" (operational) building information generated from large-scale occupancy detection and environmental sensing network for ongoing commissioning, whole building performance monitoring and advanced adaptive controls based on occupant behavioral studies. Specific applications include Occupancy Behavior-based Predicted HVAC Control; Passive, Active and Hybrid HVAC and Controls; Dynamic 3-D Architectural Model and Sensor Information Visualization; Representing and Evaluating Performance Metrics including Embodied Energy and Carbon Content in Primary Building Materials.

Omer Karaguzel, now an Assistant Professor at Carnegie Mellon University, completed a dissertation in 2013 that developed computational methods and procedures to extend the current boundaries of simulation-based performance quantification of multi-functional solar PV systems for building enclosures, by introducing a building systems integrative photovoltaic (BSiPV) modeling and analysis approach through a multi-domain parametric framework (Figure 13.14). This research used the Intelligent Workplace's dynamic PV louvers for empirical testing of computational code development, with transformative findings:

- The empirical studies revealed that the proposed model with the use of device-under-test data, can accurately predict the solar power generation of an existing building integrated PV system in the form of an external louvre with mean bias error indices as low as 2.95 percent and 2.60 percent for operating PV current and power, respectively.
- Sensitivity analyses conducted on the PV performance model indicate the global solar radiation intensity on the plane of the PV module as the most influential factor for the solar power generation with peak deviations of 116 percent and 117 percent from the mean values of PV power and current, respectively.
- Results of simulation-based sensitivity analyses reveal that the length of the overhang integrated PV systems can be the most dominant factor affecting both energy consumption and generation characteristics in addition to daylight utilization effectiveness of south-facing perimeter office spaces under heating- and cooling-dominated climates.
- The area of PV integrated glazing systems with respect to opaque and clear glazing area is found to be the most influential design factor for all climate types.
- Solar and visible transmittance of semitransparent PV systems can be influential to net energy balance if such systems are deployed on glazing assemblies under high solar radiation conditions (i.e. under cooling-dominated climates and in an unshaded urban context).

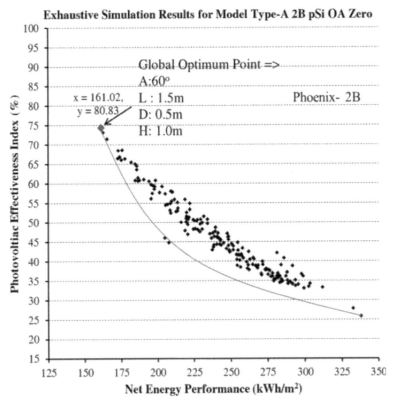

Figure 13.14 Pyranometers on the PV surface for solar radiation measurements (above) and parametric simulation results of the optimum alternatives for a PV system integrated in external shading devices

Source: Karaguzel (2013).

- Solar cell material type of two different PV modules (e.g. mono-crystalline versus poly-crystalline silicon materials) with the same peak power ratings may not be significant in terms of affecting variations in net energy balance and PV power generation with relative importance percentages of 0.4 percent and 1.4 percent, respectively.
- Simulation-based results also show that geometrically and electrically optimized BSiPV systems on south-facing façades of typical medium-sized office buildings in the US context can offset around 14.7 percent and 16.8 percent of annual total source energy consumption under heating- and cooling-dominated climates, respectively.
- Results also indicate that significant energy savings (25.4 percent for heating and 26.1 percent for cooling-dominated climates) can be achieved in whole building energy balance with respect to national benchmark models, given the contribution of the optimized BSiPV systems' energy yield when combined with pertinent high-performance enclosure measures.

(Karaguzel, 2013)

The computational models and parametric search procedures developed in this dissertation support energy-efficient and optimal design of high-performance buildings equipped with multi-functional solar PV systems so as to achieve reduced heating, cooling, and electric lighting energy consumption and maximize the generation of renewable solar power while maintaining acceptable levels of thermal and visual comfort conditions for the occupants.

Jie Zhao, now a Research Scientist at Lutron, completed a dissertation in 2015 demonstrating "Design-Build-Operate Energy Information Modeling for Occupant-Oriented Predictive Building Control," moving from controlled experimentation in the IW to a partnership with a newly awarded Living Building – the Phipps Center for Sustainable Landscapes.

This dissertation has developed and demonstrated the concept of design-build-operate Energy Information Modeling infrastructure (DBO-EIM), which can be used at different stages of the entire building life-cycle to improve energy and thermal comfort performance (Figure 13.15). The whole process is tested using a median-size office building in Pittsburgh, PA. At the design stage, for the purpose of design decision-making, the author demonstrates a parametric BEM process in the test-bed building. The case study results show that the proposed design case building has better energy performance than the baseline, selected design alternatives, and various benchmark buildings. At the commissioning and early operation stages, the author introduces an EnergyPlus model calibration method using empirical data that are collected from the test-bed building. The final calibrated model has a mean biased error of 1.27 percent and a coefficient of variation of the root mean squared error of 6.01 percent. This calibration method provides a scientific and systematic framework to conduct high accuracy EnergyPlus model calibration. At the operation stage, on the basis of the calibrated EnergyPlus model, the author develops an occupant-oriented mixed-mode EnergyPlus predictive control (OME+ PC) system. Given the Pittsburgh weather context and current operation assumptions, the simulation results suggest a 29.37 percent reduction in annual HVAC energy consumption. In addition, OME+ PC enables building occupants to control their thermal environment through an internet-based dashboard. In summary, this dissertation has demonstrated that the original design stage EnergyPlus model can be updated and utilized through the entire building life cycle.

(Zhao, 2015)

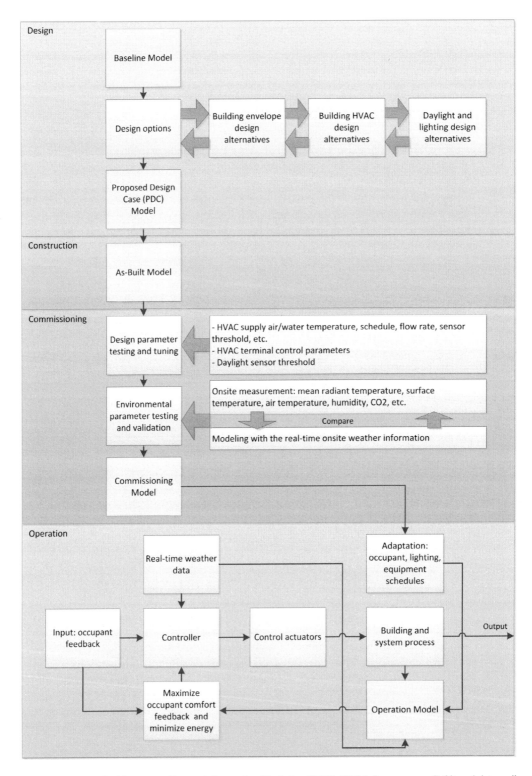

Figure 13.15 Design-build-operate Energy Information Modeling (DBO-EIM) infrastructure (left), and data collection and system integration architecture (right)

Source: Zhao (2015).

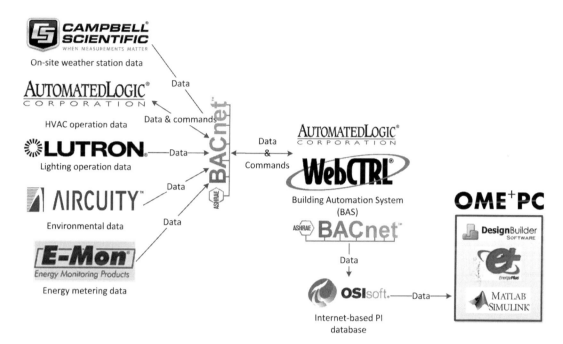

Figure 13.15 Continued

Conclusion

What more can be said? Every Architecture, Building Science, and Building Engineering program should have an Intelligent Workplace, a living laboratory of component and subsystem innovations and the testing ground for the next generation of building systems integration for indoor environmental quality and resource sustainability. These "living laboratories" should be seen as scientific instruments to rival engineering and science labs, with ongoing collaboration with the building industry for research and education of a new generation of building scientists and practitioners. In truth, universities should not only have living laboratory buildings, the campuses themselves should be considered energy, water, materials and environmental labs to ensure that the next generation of graduates lead in practice and innovation for our shared future.

References

Aziz, A., Park, J., Loftness, V., and Cochran, E. (2012) Field measurement protocols for evaluating indoor environmental quality and user satisfaction in relation to energy efficiency. U.S. DOE The Energy Efficient Buildings Hub, Department of Energy.

Betz, F. (2009) Combined cooling, heating, power, and ventilation. PhD dissertation, Carnegie Mellon University, Pittsburgh, PA.

Betz, F. and Archer, D. (2009) Biodiesel fueled engine generator with heat recovery: comparing biodiesel to diesel performance. Paper presented at ASME 2009 3rd International Conference on Energy Sustainability, Vol. 2, San Francisco, California, USA, July 19–23.

Betz, F., Archer, D., Damm, C. and Goodwin, B. (2007) Biodiesel fueled engine generator with heat recovery. In *Proceedings of ES2008 Energy Sustainability*, August 10–14, 2008, Jacksonville, FL.

Choi, J. (2010) CoBi: bio-sensing building mechanical system controls for sustainably enhancing individual thermal comfort. PhD thesis, Carnegie Mellon University, Pittsburgh, PA.

Choi, J., and Loftness, V. (2012) Investigation of human body skin temperatures as a bio-signal to indicate overall thermal sensations. *Building and Environment*, 58: 258–269.

Choi, J., Loftness, V., and Lee, D.W. (2012) Investigation of the possibility of the use of heart rate as a human factor for thermal sensation models. *Building and Environment*, 50: 165–175.

Gu, Y. (2011) The impacts of real-time knowledge based personal lighting control on energy consumption, user satisfaction and task performance in offices. PhD dissertation, Carnegie Mellon University, Pittsburgh, PA.

Hartkopf, V. and Loftness, V. (2004) Architecture, the workplace, and environmental policy. In Resnick, D.P. and Scott, D.S. (eds) *The Innovative University*. Pittsburgh, PA: Carnegie Mellon University Press, pp. 181–194.

Hartkopf, V., Loftness, V. and Mill, P. (1985) Building performance criteria. In Rush, R. (ed.) *The Building Systems Integration Handbook*. New York: John Wiley & Sons, Inc.

Hartkopf, V., *et al.* (1999) The GSA Adaptable Workplace Laboratory: 'Cooperative Buildings: Integrated Information' .In Streitz, N.A., Siegel, J. Hartkopf, V. and Konomi, S. (eds) *Organizations and Architecture*. Berlin, Germany: Springer.

Hua, Y., Loftness, V., Kraut, R., and Powell, K.M. (2010) Workplace collaborative space layout typology and occupant perception of collaboration environment. *Environment and Planning B: Planning and Design*, 37(3): 429–448.

Hua, Y., Loftness, V., Heerwagen, J., and Powell, K.M. (2011) Relationship between workplace spatial settings and occupant-perceived support for collaboration. *Environment and Behavior*, 43(6): 807–826.

Karaguzel, O. (2013) Simulation-based parametric analysis of building systems integrative solar photovoltaics. PhD dissertation, Carnegie Mellon University, Pittsburgh, PA.

Loftness, V. (2008) Innovation in office design. In Solomon, N. (ed.) *Architecture: Celebrating the Past, Designing the Future*. Chichester: John Wiley & Sons, Inc.

Loftness V., *et al.* (2001) 'Smart buildings', facility, supporting sustainable organizational and technological change though appropriate spatial, environmental and technical infrastructures. In Teicholz, E. (ed.) *Facility Design and Management Handbook*. New York: McGraw-Hill.

Loftness, V and Aziz, A. (2009) Towards a global concept of collaborative space. In Lahlou, S. (ed.) *Designing User Friendly Augmented Work Environments*. New York: Springer.

Loftness, V., Aziz, A., Srivastava, V., and Hua, Y. (2003) 'Creating a national environmental assessment toolkit (NEAT!),' Productivity protocols for the field evaluation of baseline environmental quality. In Proceedings of the US Green Building Council (USGBC) International Green Building Conference, November 12–14, 2003, Pittsburgh, PA.

Qu, M., Yin, H., and Archer, D. (2010a) A solar thermal cooling and heating system for a building: experimental and model based performance analysis and design. *Solar Energy*, 84(2): 166–182.

Qu, M, Yin, H., and Archer, D. (2010b) Experimental and model based performance analysis of a linear parabolic trough solar collector in a high temperature solar cooling and heating system. *Journal of Solar Energy Engineering*, 132.

Park, J. (2015) Are humans good sensors? Using occupants as sensors for indoor environmental quality assessment and for developing thresholds that matter. PhD thesis, Carnegie Mellon University, Pittsburgh, PA.

Park, J., Aziz, A., and Loftness, V. (2013a) Indoor environmental quality assessment for energy savings and increased user comfort. In Proceedings of the US Green Building Council (USGBC) GREENBUILD International Conference and Expo, Philadelphia, PA.

Park J., Aziz A., and Loftness, V. (2013b) Post occupancy evaluation for energy conservation, superior IEQ, and increased occupant satisfaction. Paper presented at IFMA's World Workplace Conference and Expo 2013, Philadelphia, PA.

Peters, S. (2011) A framework for the intuitive control of smart home and office environments. Masters thesis in Informatics. TUM.

Peters, S. (2016) MIBO: a framework for the integration of multimodal intuitive controls in smart buildings. PhD thesis in Informatics, TUM.

Yun, R. (2014) Persistent workplace plug-load energy savings and awareness through energy dashboards: feedback, control, and automation. In CHI'14 Extended Abstracts on Human Factors in Computing Systems, ACM.

Yun, R., Aziz, A., Lasternas, B., Zhang, C. *et al.* (2014) The design and evaluation of intelligent energy dashboard for sustainability in the workplace. In Proceedings, HCI International 2014, Creta Maris, Heraklion, Crete, Greece, June 22–27, 2014, Springer Verlag.

Yun, R., Lasternas, B., Aziz, A., Loftness, V., *et al.* (2014) Toward the design of a dashboard to promote environmentally sustainable behavior among office workers. In *Persuasive Technology*. Berlin: Springer, pp. 253–265.

Zhao, J. (2015) Design-build-operate energy information modeling for occupant-oriented predictive building control. PhD dissertation, Carnegie Mellon University, Pittsburgh, PA.

Chapter 14

Thermal and IAQ effects on school and office work

Pawel Wargocki and David P. Wyon

Thermal effects

Office work

Thermal conditions can affect the performance of office work through at least six different mechanisms (Wyon, 1996c): (1) thermal discomfort distracts attention; (2) warmth lowers arousal (the state of activation of an individual) (e.g. Provins, 1966; Willem, 2006), exacerbates building-related symptoms and has a negative effect on cognition (e.g. Wyon, 1974; Lan *et al.*, 2011a); (3) cold conditions decrease finger temperatures and thus have a negative effect on manual dexterity (e.g. Meese *et al.*, 1982); (4) rapid temperature swings have the same effects on office work as slightly raised room temperatures, while slow temperature swings merely cause discomfort (e.g., Wyon, 1979); (5) vertical thermal gradients reduce perceived air quality or lead to a reduction in room temperature that then causes complaints of cold at floor level (e.g. Wyon and Sandberg, 1996); and (6) raised temperatures can result in increased carbon dioxide (CO_2) concentration in the blood, which may cause headaches (e.g. Lan *et al.*, 2011a).

Effects on arousal

Provins (1966) was one of the first to formulate the principle that moderate heat stress lowers arousal, while higher levels of heat stress, i.e. at and above the sweating threshold, raise arousal. Easterbrook (1959) had already summarised a great deal of evidence for the effects of arousal on mental performance, showing that raised arousal leads to reduced cue-utilisation, or breadth of attention, whatever the external or internal driving factor may be. These conclusions are well supported by the research summarised below, but as yet there is no corresponding evidence that arousal is raised by moderately cool conditions, below thermal neutrality.

Under moderately warm conditions, above neutrality, it is possible to avoid sweating by reducing metabolic heat production. This leads to a lowering of arousal, as people relax and generally try less hard to work fast. This is often a completely unconscious response to warmth. Aspects of mental performance with a low optimal level of arousal, such as memory (Wyon *et al.*, 1979) and creative thinking (Wyon, 1996a), are improved by exposure to a few degrees above thermal neutrality. Similar effects are to be expected for unprepared vigilance, which requires the greatest possible breadth of attention.

Temperature swings

Mental performance has been studied as a function of dynamic temperature swings, with periods up to 60 minutes and amplitudes up to 8 degrees about individually preferred temperatures, by Wyon *et al.* (1971; 1973; 1979). These three experiments were summarised by Wyon (1979). Subjective tolerance of temperature swings was greater while working than while resting. The performance of routine work requiring concentration was reduced by small and relatively rapid temperature swings (peak-to-peak amplitudes up to 4 degrees and periods up to 16 minutes). Physiological response to cold appeared to take place faster than response to warmth under these conditions, so their net effect was equivalent to a slight increase in room temperature in terms of its effect on the rate of loss of heat from the body. Large temperature swings (peak-to-peak amplitudes approaching 8 degrees and periods approaching 32 minutes) had a stimulating effect that actually increased rates of working, but were subjectively unacceptable. It would seem that there is no advantage in imposing temperature swings in indoor environments designed for mental work.

Drifting temperatures

Kolarik *et al.* (2009) studied whether moderately drifting operative temperatures can affect performance. No consistent effects were observed. The effects of changing temperature on cognitive performance were also examined by Valančius and Jurelionis (2013). The only significant result was that decreasing the temperature had a positive effect on an arithmetic task and increased accuracy in a Tsai-Partington test. Tham and Willem (2010) showed that increased accuracy in a Tsai-Partington test indicates raised arousal, which improves concentration and would thus be expected to benefit arithmetic calculations.

Individual control

Individual control of the thermal environment may be necessary if optimal performance is to be achieved. Wyon (1996b) showed that individual control equivalent to ±3 degrees would be expected to improve the performance of mental tasks requiring concentration by 2.7 per cent. A decrease of this magnitude (2.8 per cent) in the rate of claims-processing in an insurance office had been demonstrated by Kroner *et al.* (1992) when individual microclimate control devices in an insurance office were temporarily disabled. Wyon showed that this degree of individual control (±3 degrees) would be expected to improve the group mean performance of routine office tasks by 7 per cent, and the performance of manual tasks for which rapid finger movements and a sensitive touch are critical by 3 per cent and 8 per cent respectively. Thermal conditions above the group mean for thermal neutrality will still reduce the group mean performance of mental work, but the expected benefits of individual control for group performance were shown to be greater under warm conditions than they are at the group optimum. This was true up to 5 degrees above the group optimum.

Thermal gradients

In rooms where the airflow must remove a high heat load, and particularly if this is to be done by displacement rather than by complete or partial mixing, air temperature at head height will usually be 2–3 degrees higher than at floor height. Cold feet and warm air to breathe is the exact opposite of human requirements, and an individual who wishes to avoid building-related symptoms or sensations of dryness at head height will often be forced to lower the room temperature to such an extent that it will be too cold for whole body heat balance. Over 40 per cent of subjects in a study were found to experience local thermal discomfort even when displacement ventilation had been adjusted to provide preferred whole-body heat loss, when 72 subjects were exposed for one hour to two typical winter and two typical summer conditions in an office module by Wyon and Sandberg (1990). In a later experiment by Wyon and Sandberg (1996), in which over 200 subjects were exposed for one hour to vertical temperature differences of 0, 2 and 4 degrees K per metre, with room temperatures resulting in the same three states of whole body heat balance at each vertical temperature difference, local thermal discomfort was found to be unaffected by vertical temperature difference, but highly sensitive to whole body heat balance. Similar results had been reported by Ilmarinen *et al.* (1992) and Palonen *et al.* (1992), but with only six subjects. These experiments indicate that thermal gradients are only a problem because they lead to an increase in air temperature in the breathing zone. Even if the individual has a choice in the matter, it is an uncomfortable one, between feelings of dryness at head height and a room temperature that is too low for comfort. Whichever is chosen, the end result is likely to be that the performance of office work is reduced by vertical temperature differences.

Performance in cold conditions

In a study by Meese *et al.* (1982), 600 South African factory workers were randomly assigned to work for 6.5 hours at 24°C, 18°C, 12°C or 6°C in the same clothing ensemble. Performance of a wide range of simulated industrial tasks involving finger strength and speed, manual dexterity, hand steadiness and a number of well-practised manipulative skills was found to decline monotonically with room temperature below thermal neutrality. The critical room temperature for unimpaired performance was either 18°C or 12°C, depending on the task. Finger speed and fingertip sensitivity were measurably impaired at the air temperature preferred for thermal comfort (18°C), in comparison with the air temperature (24°C) at which finger temperatures were at their maximum value. Finger strength was maintained at 18°C and 12°C but was measurably reduced at 6°C. A realistic laboratory simulation of one of the heaviest tasks still performed manually in industry was also part of the series: the proportion of poor welds made with a heavy but counterbalanced spot-welding apparatus was three times greater at 6°C than it was at 18°C.

Physiological effects

Lan *et al.* (2011a; 2014) investigated cognitive performance when subjects felt thermally neutral (at 22°C) and thermally warm (at 30°C). They showed that cognitive tests and tasks measuring the ability to perform office work were negatively affected at the higher temperature. They attributed these effects to the physiological responses to raised temperature that occurred: increased heart rate, respiration rate, blood gas levels of carbon dioxide and reduced visual acuity. Whether the effects were due to elevated temperature, the distraction of thermal discomfort or some combination of the two mechanisms could not be determined. In another study, Lan *et al.* (2010) attributed the negative effects on cognitive performance to physiological reactions when ambient temperature was reduced from 21°C to 17°C or increased to 28°C, but with data from only three subjects, the effects on heart rate variability (HRV) and EEG, although they were as would be expected if arousal had decreased as temperatures increased, did not reach significance. Subjectively reported motivation was lower at 17°C and still lower at 28°C. EEG was shown to be affected by temperature by Lee *et al.* (2012), who compared responses at 20.5°C and 24°C and concluded that a slightly cool thermal environment would be more beneficial than a neutral environment for tasks that require attention.

Studies reporting no effects on performance

Some experiments have found no effect of increased temperature on cognitive performance (e.g., Tanabe *et al.*, 2007; Maula *et al.*, 2015). Absent results are often due to the insufficient power of the experimental design, and absent or anomalous results can be due to the unintended confounding of two environmental factors. Hedge and Gaygen (2010) reported that increasing temperature seemed to improve performance in an office building. If true, this would be good news for energy conservation in air-conditioned buildings. However, a simpler explanation of their anomalous finding is that the ventilation system in the building was a Variable Air Volume (VAV) system, so that when the temperature increased, the outdoor air supply rate will have increased as well; this interpretation is strongly supported by the negative correlation between temperature and the carbon dioxide concentration, and between temperature and the concentration of volatile organic compounds that was found in this observational study. The apparently positive effect of increased temperature seems likely to have been due to improved indoor air quality, as changes in these two factors were confounded.

Relationship between temperature, thermal sensation and performance

Based on the results from 24 studies investigating the effects of temperature on the performance of office work, Seppänen *et al.* (2006a) derived a relationship between temperature and work performance, suggesting that performance is reduced by about 1 per cent for every 1°C change. Studies in existing buildings support this prediction. A small cross-sectional study in a telecommunication call centre indicated that in the area where temperatures remained below 25°C, operator performance was better: average talk-time was 5–7 per cent lower than it was on the sunny side of the call centre (Niemelä *et al.*, 2002). Temperatures above 25.4°C caused qualified nurses providing medical advice in a call centre to work 16 per cent more slowly when writing up their reports after the call was over (i.e. wrap-up time increased) (Federspiel *et al.*, 2002). A third field experiment was performed in an office building in the Tropics by Tham (2004). Call centre operator performance, as indicated by average talk-time, improved by 4.9 per cent when the air temperature was decreased by 2°C from 24.5°C at the normal outdoor air supply rate of 10 L/s/p. A subsequent analysis of total call-handling time (Tham, pers. comm.) confirmed the reality of these effects. Thermal discomfort increased at the lower temperature but no other subjective symptoms were affected. The productivity of call centre operators in the Tropics could thus be improved by maintaining conditions on the cool side of thermal neutrality.

An attempt to relate thermal discomfort to performance was made by Roelofsen (2001), who correlated Fanger's PMV model (Fanger, 1970) with Gagge's two-layer model (Gagge *et al.*, 1986). His analysis indicated quite large effects on performance. A quantitative relationship between thermal sensation and performance was established by Lan *et al.* (2011b), who showed that a slightly cool environment would be optimal for cognitive performance. They also compared their model with those of Seppänen *et al.* (2006a) and Roelofsen (2001) and showed that thermal discomfort has smaller effects on performance than they predict, probably because people can partially compensate for thermal stress by exerting more effort, as suggested by Hancock and Vasmatzidis (1998). They therefore suggested that PMV limits in workplaces should be set in the range between –0.5 and 0 instead of between –0.5 and +0.5 as stipulated in the present standards.

School work

A comprehensive set of experiments on the effects of classroom temperatures on the performance of schoolwork was carried out in Sweden (Wyon, 1970). In these experiments, three parallel classes of 9–10-year-old children were exposed for two hours to each of three classroom temperatures: 20°C, 27°C and 30°C, encountered in balanced order, and four classes of 11–12-year-old children were similarly exposed to 20°C and 30°C in the morning and the afternoon in a 2x2 design, again in balanced order of presentation of conditions (Holmberg and Wyon, 1969). The temperatures were artificially raised in these experiments. The children performed a number of school exercises, including numerical tasks (addition, multiplication, number checking) and language-based tasks (reading and comprehension, supplying synonyms and antonyms) so that their rate of working and the number of errors they made could be quantified. The children's performance of both types of task was significantly lower at 27°C and 30°C in comparison with 20°C. In the numerical tasks, the effect was on rate of working, but reading comprehension as well as reading speed was reduced by raised temperatures. The negative effects of raised classroom temperatures were significant in the afternoon, when the children were fatigued, but not in the morning. The magnitude of the negative effect of temperature on performance was for some tasks as high as 30 per cent. The appearance and behaviour of the children were systematically observed in these studies from behind one-way glass and both were significantly affected by raised classroom temperature (Holmberg and Wyon, 1972): the children became visibly hot but were very slow to adjust their clothing; girls became restless but continued to work, while boys began to behave in an undisciplined way and could be seen to concentrate less well. In another experiment in which groups of four 12-year-old boys were exposed to 20°C (the reference condition), 23.5°C and 27°C in balanced order, no effects of the intermediate temperature could be shown (Wyon, 1969), while the highest temperature caused children to perform schoolwork more slowly and to complete a diagnostic test of cue-utilisation (the Tsai-Partington test) more rapidly, indicating that raised temperatures have their effect on children in school by reducing arousal or alertness.

Schoer and Shaffran (1973) reported three experiments, in which 10–12-year-old pupils in matched pairs were assigned either to a classroom without cooling (where the temperature was about 26°C), or to an adjacent air-conditioned classroom (where the temperature was about 22.5°C). Each group then worked in the same classroom every school day for 6–8 weeks and their performance was significantly better in the classroom that was always cool, on average by 5.7 per cent. However, the subjects knew they were taking part in an experiment (because they were taken by bus each day to the specially constructed classrooms and instructed by experimenters who were not their normal class teachers), knew when they were being tested (because each test was performed under maximum effort conditions and timed with a stopwatch), and by talking to each other over 6–8 weeks must have known that there was a difference in temperature between the two classrooms. The observed difference in performance could thus have been due to a gradual process of discouragement and growing resentment between two groups of pupils. This interpretation is supported by the original authors' own analysis, showing that the difference in performance between the groups increased over time, while the parallel processes of acclimatisation, familiarisation and learning would all be expected to reduce over time the negative effects of temperature on performance.

In field intervention experiments in Scandinavian school classrooms (Wargocki and Wyon, 2007a; 2007b), the temperature was manipulated by either operating or idling split cooling units. In the first experiment, the average air temperature in the classrooms was about 20°C when cooling was provided, or 23.6°C in the warmer reference condition. In the second experiment, which was run in the same two classrooms the following summer, the corresponding air temperatures were 21.6°C and 24.9°C. The classrooms were mechanically ventilated with 100 per cent outdoor air. The interventions used a repeated-measures crossover design that was balanced for order of presentation: each experiment was carried out in two parallel classrooms at a time and each condition lasted for a week. Both teachers and pupils were blind to interventions. During the experiments, the teachers and pupils were allowed to open the windows and doors as usual, and the teaching environment and daily routines remained as normal as possible. During each week the children performed tasks resembling typical schoolwork: addition, multiplication, subtraction, number comparison, logical thinking (i.e. grammatical reasoning), proof-reading from dictation and reading and comprehension. The duration of the tasks was short enough to ensure that children could not normally complete them in the time available. Up to 10 minutes was allocated for each task. When the temperature was reduced from 25°C to 20°C, the performance of two arithmetical and two language-based tests improved significantly, as had been reported by Holmberg and Wyon (1969) nearly 40 years earlier. The improvement was in terms of speed, except in the case of the proof-reading exercise where the speed was fixed by the rate of dictation. In this task, reducing the air temperature reduced the percentage of errors missed in one experiment and led to an increase in false-positive identifications in another, indicating that subjects were trying harder.

An empirical dose-response relationship between the performance of schoolwork and classroom temperature was developed. It shows that reducing classroom air temperature by 1°C improved the speed of performance by about 2 per cent. If only data from those tasks in which performance was significantly affected by the interventions were used to establish the relationship, reducing classroom air temperature by 1°C would improve performance speed by about 4 per cent. Reducing classroom temperature would not have a measurable effect on errors. These effects are comparable with those observed for adults (Seppänen *et al.*, 2006a) and higher than the effects found by Haverinen-Shaughnessy and Shaughnessy (2015), who performed a cross-sectional study in 70 elementary school and 140 fifth-grade classrooms. They measured the air temperature in each classroom for a week-long period between January and April and correlated it with a state-wide assessment of learning that included students' individual test scores in mathematics, reading and science. Average indoor temperature was 23°C and it varied between about 20°C and 25°C. Modelling showed that there was a 12–13-point increase in mathematics score for each 1 degree decrease of temperature (as the average score was 2,286 points, this was 0.5 per cent/degree).

Sarbu and Pacurar (2015) examined the performance of 18 university students in a classroom over a period of 36 days. The temperatures were manipulated in the classroom by operating or idling the air cooling and changing the air cooling set-point, and they remained between 22°C and 29°C. The students repeatedly performed two attention tests: the concentrated attention test (the Kraepelin test) and the distributive attention test (the Prague test). The results showed that the performance of students on both tests followed an inverted-U curve, similar to what was observed for the effects of temperature on the performance of office work by adults (Seppänen *et al.*, 2006a; Lan *et al.*, 2011b). The temperatures for optimal performance were higher (about 27–28°C) for the Prague test and lower (about 25–26°C) for the Kraepelin test, as would be expected if the change in performance followed the psychological theory of arousal – moderately higher temperatures reduce the arousal/stress level and are thus beneficial for tests requiring high cue-utilisation, as is the case for the Prague test.

Bakó-Biró *et al.* (2012) also observed thermal effects on simple psychological tasks that support the arousal interpretation. They performed an intervention study in eight primary schools in 16 classrooms, in which they improved air quality by retrofitting classrooms with an external ventilation system installed in a window. In one school, due to system failure, the ventilation rate was high throughout but classroom temperature was reduced from 25.3°C to 23.1°C. At the higher temperature, simple reaction time and choice reaction time were 6 per cent longer and the performance of a colour-word vigilance task was 8 per cent worse, as would have been expected had arousal been lower at the higher temperature.

The Adaptive Thermal Comfort (ATC) model and performance

The Adaptive Thermal Comfort theory assumes that thermal comfort can be obtained at higher temperatures by two mechanisms (de Dear and Brager, 2001): (1) by adaptive behaviours such as adjusting clothing, opening windows or reducing activity level; and (2) by becoming habituated to higher temperatures, so that the physiological responses that take place become acceptable. It is assumed that if higher temperatures are found acceptable, they will have no negative effects on performance (de Dear et al., 2013; Leyten and Kurvers, 2013).

Hancock and Vasmatzidis (1998) suggested that a zone of psychological and physiological adaptability exists, in which people can tolerate thermal stress and within which there will be no effects on cognitive performance. However, as indicated by the study of Lan et al. (2011a), increasing temperatures and the physiological responses that occur result in symptoms such as headaches or difficulty in concentrating and thinking clearly that can reasonably be expected to have direct negative effects on cognitive performance unless more effort is exerted to counteract them. Tanabe et al. (2007) showed that this is only possible for a limited time.

Pepler and Warner (1968) showed in a climate chamber experiment that thermal conditions providing optimum comfort may not give rise to maximum efficiency. In these experiments young American subjects, dressed in standard clothing that they were not allowed to adjust, performed mental work at different temperatures. The original report measured performance in terms of errors made per hour, but percentage errors were constant across temperature conditions, so work rate is a better predictor of productivity. These subjects were most thermally comfortable at 27°C, but that was the temperature at which they exerted least effort and worked the most slowly. They worked fastest at 20°C even though most of them felt uncomfortably cold at this temperature, as in the call centre experiment by Tham (2004) discussed above, indicating that physiological effects can outweigh the effects of thermal discomfort.

Future experiments must examine the underlying mechanisms more closely, but it is already clear that some adaptive behavioural adjustments will reduce productivity, as when more breaks from work are taken or when work rate is deliberately or unconsciously reduced to avoid thermal discomfort.

Indoor air quality (IAQ) effects

Office work

The mechanisms by which indoor air quality affects performance are not well understood, but it seems reasonable to assume that people who do not feel very well and experience building-related symptoms, such as headaches and difficulty in concentrating and thinking clearly when the air quality is poor, will not work very well. Other possible mechanisms for an effect of poor air quality on performance include distraction by odour, sensory irritation, allergic reactions, or direct toxicological effects. Studies of adult subjects performing simulated office work (Bakó-Biró et al., 2005) showed that increased air pollution caused by gaseous emissions from typical building materials, furnishings and office equipment caused subjects to exhale less carbon dioxide. This must either be a consequence of reduced metabolic rate due to reduced motivation to perform work in polluted air, or a consequence of physiological changes leading to inefficient gas exchange in the lungs when polluted air is inhaled, resulting in a higher concentration of carbon dioxide in the blood. The latter mechanism is known to cause head-aches and difficulty in thinking clearly. A raised concentration of carbon dioxide in the blood of subjects performing mental work was observed by Zhang *et al.* (2016a; 2016c), and it was significantly higher when either bioeffluent or CO_2 levels in the room had been increased. In the early studies performed by the New York State Commission on Ventilation (1923) in the 1910s, the performance of simulated office work (including addition and typing) could not be shown to be significantly reduced by low ventilation rates that resulted in CO_2 concentrations as high as 3000–4000 ppm.

Laboratory experiments altering pollution loads

An important turning point in understanding the effects of indoor air quality on the performance of mental work and on the cognitive skills that are essential for office work were the studies by Wargocki *et al.* (1999; 2000b; 2002), summarised by Wyon (2004). In an intervention experiment, Wargocki *et al.* (1999) altered the indoor air quality in a normal office while the health, comfort and performance of the occupants were measured. Indoor air quality was altered by decreasing the pollution load, i.e. by physically removing a pollution source without informing the subjects, while maintaining an outdoor air supply rate of 10 L/s per person. The major pollution source was a carpet that had been used for 20 years in an office and was present behind a partition in a quantity corresponding to the floor area of the office in which the exposures took place. Thirty subjects performed different cognitive tests and typing and addition tasks to simulate typical office work during 4.5-hour exposures. The indoor air quality caused 70 per cent to be dissatisfied with the air quality when the used carpet was present and 25 per cent when it was absent. The presence of the used carpet caused subjects to type 6.5 per cent more slowly, to make 18 per cent more typing errors, and to experience more headaches. Lagercrantz *et al.* (2000) replicated the study of Wargocki *et al.* (1999) in a similarly standard daylit office with a different group of subjects and the same carpet. Meta-analysis of the two studies by Wargocki *et al.* (2002) confirmed that their results are compatible. The original study of Wargocki *et al.* (1999) was repeated in the same office by Bakó-Biró *et al.* (2004) with six cathode ray tube visual display units (CRT/VDU) that had been in operation for about 500 h, corresponding to approximately three months of normal office use, as the pollution source. Some 40 per cent of the subjects reported that they were dissatisfied with the air quality when the VDUs were present behind the screen, while only 10 per cent were dissatisfied when they were absent. Combining the observed effects on the speed and accuracy of typing and the decrease in speed of proof-reading, it could be shown that overall text-processing would be performed 9 per cent more slowly if the VDUs were present.

Wargocki *et al.* (2000a) combined the results from different studies and showed that the performance of office tasks improves linearly as a function of the proportion finding the air quality acceptable (upon entering a space): a 10 per cent reduction in the percentage dissatisfied with the air quality corresponds to about a 1 per cent increase in the performance of office work.

Laboratory experiments altering outdoor air supply rate

In the studies described above, indoor air quality was modified by installing or removing the pollution source, keeping the subjects blind to conditions. Indoor air quality can also be modified by changing the ventilation rate. Wargocki *et al.* (2000a) increased the outdoor air supply rate from 3 to 10 or to 30 L/s per person with the original pollution source, a used carpet, always present behind the partition. Some 60 per cent were dissatisfied with the resulting indoor air quality at the lowest ventilation rate and 30 per cent were dissatisfied at the highest rate. It was possible to show that the performance of the text-typing task improved by about 1 per cent for every two-fold increase in the outdoor air supply rate. The performance of the addition and proof-reading tasks followed the same trend, but the effects did not reach significance. In an open-ended test of creative thinking, subjects provided 10 per cent more answers and more original answers at 10 L/s per person than at 3 L/s per person.

Park and Yoon (2011) showed that the performance of typing, addition and memorisation improved by on average 2.5–5 per cent when ventilation rates were increased from 5 to 10 to 20 L/s per person. In their experiments, the main pollutants were volatile organic compounds emitted from the new finishing materials that were present in the chamber where the experiments were carried out.

Maddalena et al. (2015) examined the effects of changing ventilation rates when the main sources of pollution were typical building materials (outdoor air supply rates 0.8–5.5 L/s/m²) and human bioeffluents (2.5–8.5 L/s per person – the resulting CO_2 levels were 1800 ppm and 900 ppm, respectively). Subjects were exposed for 4 hours and performed a battery of tests measuring the skills and abilities needed for decision-making (SMS: Strategic Management Simulation, Streufert et al., 1988) in different scenarios in which this was critical. They showed that if diluting pollutants emitted from building materials, then humans significantly improved decision-making performance, although the effect was quite small. Koskela et al. (2014) increased the outdoor air supply rate from 2 to 28 L/s per person in a climate chamber where the main pollution sources were the subjects themselves. The resulting CO_2 levels were 2200 ppm and 600 ppm, respectively. They were not able to demonstrate any effects on the performance of typing tasks (psychomotor performance) or on working memory although 36 subjects were exposed for 3.5 hours to the two levels of air quality created in the chamber. Zhang et al. (2016a; 2016b) exposed subjects to three levels of bioeffluents by modifying the outdoor air supply rate: the resulting CO_2 levels were 500 ppm, 1000 ppm and 3000 ppm. Only at the highest level was the performance of an addition task significantly reduced: other performance tests and tasks such as text typing were not affected. These results suggest that the pollutant concentrations in the study by Koskela et al. (2014) were too low for any effects on performance to appear. These results also suggest that the effects of indoor air quality on cognitive performance can depend on the type of pollutants present, so that the outdoor air supply rate may not always be an adequate indicator of potential effects on performance – the level of exposure would be a more pertinent indicator, as postulated by Carrer et al. (2015).

For most workplaces, Seppänen et al. (2006b) suggested a quantitative relationship between office work and the outdoor air supply rate that predicts that work performance will on average increase by approximately 1.5 per cent for each doubling of the outdoor air supply rate.

Possible effects of CO_2 on performance

Three independent experiments showed that CO_2 itself at the levels typically occurring indoors can have negative effects on cognitive performance. Kajtár and Herczeg (2012) reported a decrease in the performance of a proof-reading task during exposure to added CO_2 at 3000 ppm. This effect was, however, observed in only one of several exposures. Experiments by Satish et al. (2012) exposing subjects for 2.5 hours to CO_2 levels that had been raised by releasing pure CO_2 and of Allen et al. (2015) exposing them similarly for an entire working day demonstrated conclusively that exposures to CO_2 at levels as low as 1000 ppm systematically reduced the performance of the SMS test battery. Subsequent experiments by Zhang et al. (2016a; 2016b; 2016c) could not confirm that adding CO_2 had any effect on performance.

They exposed subjects to different levels of CO_2 as high as 4900 ppm, which is close to the 8-hour occupational exposure limit. Zhang *et al.* did not use the SMS test battery but used different psychological tests and tasks such as text typing and arithmetical calculations. This suggests that increasing the level of pure CO_2 may increase arousal/stress, but to an extent that does not decrease the performance of normal office work. Adding this stress to an already stressful task, such as the SMS test battery, has negative effects on the performance of that task. Levels of task difficulty must be considered an important additional variable when the effects of the indoor environment on cognitive performance are examined.

Field studies

No field measurements have been carried out in which the performance of office work was quantified and air quality was measured by quantifying the proportion dissatisfied. In one study performed in the field by Wargocki *et al.* (2004), replacing the used bag ventilation filter with a new one improved the performance of call centre operators by 10 per cent because the pollution load in the occupied volume was reduced, as in the interventions made in the laboratory studies described above, so that the air quality was improved. Unfortunately, the percentage dissatisfied with the air quality was not obtained.

There have been few field studies in which the outdoor air supply rate was modified and the performance of office work was measured. Wargocki *et al.* (2004) showed that the performance of call centre operators improved by 6 per cent when the outdoor air supply rate was increased from 2.5 to 25 L/s per person, but only when new bag filters had been installed in the ventilation system; with used bag filters, an increase in the ventilation rate reduced measured performance by 8 per cent. In a study by Federspiel *et al.* (2004), the performance of call centre operators improved by 2 per cent when the outdoor air supply rate was increased from 8 to 94 L/s per person, while an increase from 8 to 20 or 53 L/s per person reduced their performance, probably because used bag filters were in place, as in the field intervention experiment by Wargocki *et al.* (2004). Tham *et al.* (2003) showed that the performance of call centre operators in an office building improved by 9 per cent when the outdoor air supply rate was increased from 10 to 23 L/s per person with no bag filters (electrostatic filters were being used instead).

These field studies validate the laboratory experiments described above and show that indoor air quality had a greater effect on the performance of real office work in the field than would be predicted from the laboratory experiments that examined simulated office work. Call centres were selected for field experiments because the work performed by operators is a good paradigm for many other kinds of multitasking, and because unlike almost all other types of office work, it is routinely timed with great accuracy. Call centre operators perform high-level office work, dealing directly with customers and thus having to solve unexpected problems under pressure. Their work requires concentration, verbal communication, logical thinking under time pressure, visual attention and very often the use of sophisticated computer software. These skills are common to most office tasks, so if call centre performance is affected by changes in the indoor environment, other office tasks are likely to be similarly affected. Talk-time can be considered a conservative indicator of performance, as customers dissatisfied with the quality of service would be likely to prolong the call in order to achieve their goal.

The effects on sickness absence

Sickness absence rates may be considered to be a 'field' indicator of environmental effects on performance. Milton *et al.* (2000) showed that the risk of short-term sick leave associated with respiratory diseases caused by infection was significantly higher in offices with 12 L/s per person compared to offices ventilated with 24 L/s per person. Using the results of Milton *et al.* (2000) and the theoretical model of Riley (1979), Fisk *et al.* (2003) derived a relationship between sick-leave and ventilation rate. The relationship was derived from studies using sick-leave or short-term illness as outcomes and predicts a 10 per cent reduction in illness or sick leave when the outdoor air change rate is doubled.

School work

Effects on cognitive tests

Myhrvold *et al.* (1996), Coley *et al.* (2007), Ribic (2008), Bakó-Biró *et al.* (2012) and Sarbu and Pacurar (2015) used psychological and neurobehavioural tests to examine the effects of indoor air quality and outdoor air supply rate on the performance of schoolwork and learning. Myhrvold *et al.* (1996) found a weak association between CO_2 levels and simple reaction time that suggested a positive effect of increased ventilation on performance: CO_2 was reduced from 1500 to 4000 ppm to <1000 ppm. In this experiment and in the experiments described below, CO_2 was not considered to be a pollutant but an indicator of the efficiency of ventilation and outdoor air supply rate when the main sources of pollution were humans (CO_2 is a major human bioeffluent). Ribic (2008) observed improved performance on the d2 test, a standard test for measuring concentration and attention, when CO_2 concentration was reduced from around 3800 ppm to 870 ppm (absolute level). Sarbu and Pacurar (2015) found that the performance of students on two psychological tests requiring concentration and cue-utilisation (the Kraepelin test and the Prague test) improved linearly when CO_2 levels were reduced from about 2000 ppm to 500 ppm. Coley *et al.* (2007) and Bakó-Biró *et al.* (2012) improved the air quality in classrooms by either allowing students to open the windows or retrofitting the classrooms with an external ventilation system especially designed for the purpose of the experiments, installed in the window and making it possible to either deliver outdoor air or to recirculate the air already in the classroom. In the former study, the levels of CO_2 were reduced from about 2900 ppm to 690 ppm and this had a significant and positive effect on tests measuring reaction time; the authors concluded that the power of attention was improved. In the latter study, the ventilation rate was increased from about 1 L/s per person to 8 L/s per person (the corresponding CO_2 levels were about 1500–5000 ppm and <1000 ppm). This intervention significantly improved the performance of tests examining reaction time, concentration and attention, recognition and memory. The effects were from about 3 per cent to 15 per cent.

Effects on actual schoolwork

Wargocki and Wyon (2007a; 2007b) carried out three experiments in late summer and in winter, in which the outdoor air supply rate per person was increased from about 3 to 9.5 L/s per person, using the existing mechanical ventilation system, after increasing the fan capacity and rebalancing the system to direct more outdoor air to first one and then the other of the two classrooms in which performance was being measured. The children's usual teachers administered parallel versions of language-based and numerical performance tasks representing different aspects of schoolwork, from reading to mathematics. When the outdoor air supply rate increased, the speed at which the children performed four numerical and two language-based tasks improved significantly, and in the case of one numerical task, the percentage of errors was significantly reduced. An empirical dose-response relationship between the performance of schoolwork and classroom ventilation was developed based on these results and it indicates that doubling the outdoor air supply rate would improve the performance of schoolwork in terms of speed by about 8 per cent. If data only from those tasks in which performance was significantly affected by the interventions is used to establish the relationship, doubling the outdoor air supply rate would improve the performance of schoolwork in terms of speed by about 14 per cent. Increasing the outdoor air supply rate would not have a measurable effect on the performance of schoolwork in terms of errors. These studies were repeated by Petersen *et al.* (2016) with very similar results. In the study by Bakó-Biró *et al.* described above, the time needed to solve simple mathematics tests was reduced when ventilation rate was increased from about 0.3–0.5 to 13–16 L/s per person (Bakó-Biró *et al.*, 2007).

Effects on standardised tests and learning

Haverinen-Shaughnessy *et al.* (2011) measured CO_2 levels in 100 fifth grade classrooms in 100 schools and showed that poor ventilation reduced the number of pupils managing to pass language and mathematics tests. A linear relationship was found, suggesting 3 per cent more pupils passed the tests for every 1 L/s per person increase in ventilation up to 7 L/s per person. In another study in 140 fifth grade classrooms in 70 schools, Haverinen-Shaughnessy and Shaughnessy (2015) showed that mathematics scores improved by about 0.5 per cent for every 1 L/s per person increase in ventilation rate in the range from 0.9 to 7 L/s per person. Mendell *et al.* (2015) performed two-year-long measurements in 150 classrooms in 28 schools and showed that increasing ventilation rates had positive effects on mathematics and English scores, although only in the latter case did the effects reach statistical significance: a 10 per cent increase in ventilation resulted in a 0.6 point increase in the score obtained in the English test. This was a very small effect, as the average scores for this test were about 350–380 points. Toftum *et al.* (2015) evaluated academic achievement by using the scores from a standardised Danish test battery, adjusted for a socioeconomic reference score, that includes mainly language-based and mathematics tests. The lowest national test scores were generally found for pupils in classes with CO_2 concentrations above 2000 ppm, although the association was not significant. Pupils in schools with some means of mechanical ventilation scored on average higher in the national tests than pupils in schools with natural ventilation, probably because the efficacy of ventilation was higher. Murakami *et al.* (2006) examined whether changing air quality affects learning by college students. A recorded lecture on DVD was played, so that each class received the same amount and type of education and the same information from the same teacher. The students answered questions to examine how much they had learnt during the class. Indoor air quality was modified by changing the outdoor air supply rate between 0.4 h^{-1} and 3.5 h^{-1}. Unfortunately, air temperatures also changed between conditions, from about 24–25°C at the higher ventilation rate to 27–28°C at the lower rate, so the change in air quality was confounded with a change in temperature. Increasing ventilation rate (and reducing the temperature) improved the average score obtained by about 6–8 per cent. In addition to the objective measurements of performance, the students were asked to make their own estimate of their performance. The magnitude of the change in self-estimated performance was smaller than was measured objectively.

  Ito *et al.* (2006) replicated the studies by Murakami *et al.* (2006). They obtained very similar results, except that the magnitude of the change in self-estimated performance was greater than was measured objectively, not smaller.

The studies described in this sub-section validate the use of simple tests to predict progress in learning.

Effects on sickness absence

Several studies have examined whether increasing classroom ventilation rate decreases sickness absence, although there is no clear evidence that short-term absence affects the academic performance of students (Mendell and Heath, 2005). Simons et al. (2010) found high student absenteeism to be associated with poor ventilation in 2751 New York schools. Shendell et al. (2004) found student yearly absence to decrease by 0.5–0.9 per cent when the CO_2 concentration decreased by 1000 ppm in 434 American classrooms, while Gaihre et al. (2014) observed a much larger effect (0.2 per cent increase in sick absence for each 100 ppm increase in CO_2) in 60 Scottish classrooms. In another very comprehensive study in 162 Californian classrooms, Mendell et al. (2013) observed that sickness absence decreased by as much as 1.6 per cent for each additional 1 L/s per person of ventilation rate.

Effects of particles and SVOCs on performance of schoolwork

Very few studies have examined whether specific pollutants in the classroom affect performance. Two experiments examined whether removing airborne particles in classrooms would improve the performance of schoolwork. Mattsson and Hygge (2005) installed electrostatic air cleaners that were operated or disabled in two pairs of classrooms. Five tests similar to schoolwork were applied. When the air cleaners were operated, children 'stating themselves to be sensitive to airborne particulate contaminants' experienced a significantly greater reduction in eye and airway irritation, and these pupils scored about 25 per cent higher on one of the five performance tests (finding synonyms), but the authors themselves cite 'multiple testing' (i.e. chance) as a possible reason for this isolated result.

Wargocki et al. (2008) installed electrostatic air cleaners in six classrooms in three schools, all mechanically ventilated with 100 per cent outdoor air. The interventions were implemented in a cross-over design in parallel classrooms. Airborne particle concentrations were lower in all size ranges the more outdoor air a given school provided to its classrooms (as would be expected if there were significant indoor sources of particles), and were reduced by operating the air cleaners, more markedly in the smaller size ranges. Operating the electrostatic air cleaners also reduced settled dust on horizontal surfaces. There were, however, no effects on the performance of a wide range of tasks selected to be characteristic of schoolwork, including the language-based and mathematics tasks used by Wargocki and Wyon (2007a). As increasing the outdoor air supply rate had improved the performance of these tasks, it was inferred that the observed negative effects should be attributed to gaseous pollutants and not to the particles that were present.

Hutter et al. (2013) showed that the cognitive performance of about 600 pupils in the first and second grade in nine elementary schools improved with reduced levels of tris(2-chlorethyl)-phosphate (TCEP) in PM10, PM2.5 and dust. They also found an association between a polycyclic aromatic hydrocarbon and cognitive performance. In parallel to these observations, Hutter et al. (2013) observed that lower carbon dioxide levels (indicating a higher ventilation rate) were associated with improved performance. Cognitive performance was measured using the Standard Progressive Matrices test, which is a non-verbal assessment tool for measuring the reasoning component of general intelligence. It was performed by the pupils for a period of about 45 minutes. TCEP is a phosphororganic compound used widely in plasticizers, flame retardants and floor sealing and is currently a substance of very high concern because of its possible long-term health effects.

Sleep quality and next day performance

Two relatively small experiments provide some support for an effect of indoor air quality on sleep quality. In one of them, students in identical corridor rooms slept with windows open or closed, and the resulting peak CO_2 concentrations and ventilation rates were as follows: between 1000 ppm and 2500 ppm (corresponding to 0.4 h^{-1} to 1 h^{-1}) or between 3000 ppm and 4500 ppm (corresponding to 0.2 h^{-1} to 0.3 h^{-1}). Objective sleep measures showed no differences, while students reported more awakenings during the night and that they better remembered dreams in the windows-open condition (Laverge and Janssens, 2011). In another experiment, also performed in identical corridor rooms, students slept with high and low rates of ventilation with outdoor air achieved by covertly operating or idling a small fan mounted in the air-intake aperture. The resulting average CO_2 levels were about 850 ppm and 2400 ppm, respectively. This time, students reported that the air in their room was perceived to be more fresh, that they felt more refreshed and that their mental state was better in the condition in which the fan was operated. The objectively measured sleep efficiency (time in bed spent asleep) was higher and their performance on the concentration test taken in the morning was better when the fan was operated (Strøm-Tejsen et al., 2016). Yet another study showed that elderly subjects sleeping with an air outlet device directed towards the head of the sleeping person had a shorter sleep onset latency (measured objectively) and that their heart rate variability was reduced (Zhou et al., 2014).

Self-estimated performance

Many studies show that self-estimated performance will improve with improved indoor environmental quality, both in the case of laboratory and field experiments (e.g., Akimoto et al., 2010; Hedge and Dorsey, 2013; Tanabe et al., 2013; 2015; Thatcher and Milner, 2014). They also show that the self-recalled sickness absence would be improved (Pejtersen et al., 2011). None of the above studies simultaneously obtained self-estimated performance and objectively measured performance. An increase in self-estimated performance may simply indicate high satisfaction and improved well-being (e.g. Wargocki et al., 2012), or an expectation that performance has improved. When Kroner et al. (1992) monitored the self-estimated performance of insurance claim assessors during a move to new office premises, it was unchanged even during the period immediately after the move had taken place, during which the time taken to resolve an insurance claim increased by 30 per cent on average. In the studies of Murakami et al. (2006) and Ito et al. (2006) mentioned above, self-estimated performance did not predict the magnitude of objectively measured performance. Self-estimated performance should therefore be used with extreme caution when documenting the effects of the indoor environment on cognitive performance.

References

Akimoto, T., Tanabe, S., Yanai, T. and Sasaki, M. (2010) Thermal comfort and productivity: evaluation of workplace environment in a task conditioned office. *Building and Environment*, 451: 45–50.

Allen, J., Macnaughton, P., Satish, U., Santanam, S., Vallarino, J. and Spengler, J. (2015) Associations of cognitive function scores with carbon dioxide, ventilation, and volatile organic compound exposures in office workers: a controlled exposure study of green and conventional office environments. *Environmental Health Perspectives*, 124(6): 805–812.

Bakó-Biró, Z., Clements-Croome, D., Kochhar, N., Awbi, H. and Williams, M. (2012) Ventilation rates in schools and pupils' performance. *Building and Environment*, 48: 215–223.

Bakó-Biró, Z., Kochhar, N., Clements-Croome, D., Awbi, H. and Williams, M. (2007) Ventilation rates in schools and learning performance. In Proceedings of CLIMA 2007, Helsinki, Finland: FINVAC, pp. 1434–1440.

Bakó-Biró, Z., Wargocki, P. Weschler, C. and Fanger, P. (2004) Effects of pollution from personal computers on perceived air quality, SBS symptoms and productivity in offices. *Indoor Air*, 14: 178–187.

Bakó-Biró, Z., Wargocki, P., Wyon, D. and Fanger, P. (2005) Indoor air quality effects on CO_2 levels in exhaled air during office work. In Proceedings of Indoor Air 2005, Beijing, China, 1(1): 76–80.

Carrer, P., Wargocki, P., Fanetti, A., Bischof, W., Fernandes, E., *et al.* (2015) What does the scientific literature tell us about the ventilation–health relationship in public and residential buildings? *Building and Environment*, 94: 273–286.

Coley, D., Greeves, R. and Saxby, B. (2007) The effect of low ventilation rates on the cognitive function of a primary school class. *International Journal of Ventilation*, 62: 107–112.

de Dear, R., Akimoto, T., Arens, E., Brager, G., *et al.* (2013) Progress in thermal comfort research over the last twenty years. *Indoor Air*, 23(6): 442–461.

de Dear, R. and Brager, G. (2001) The adaptive model of thermal comfort and energy conservation in the built environment. *International Journal of Biometeorology*, 45: 100–108.

Easterbrook, J. (1959) The effect of emotion on cue-utilisation and the organisation of behaviour. *Psychological Review*, 66: 183–201.

Fanger, P. (1970) *Thermal Comfort. Analysis and Applications in Environmental Engineering*, New York: McGraw-Hill.

Federspiel, C., Fisk, W., Price, P., Liu, G., *et al.* (2004) Worker performance and ventilation in a call-center: analyses of work performance data for registered nurses. *Indoor Air*, 14(s8): 41–50.

Federspiel, C., Liu, G., Lahiff, M., Faulkner, D., *et al.* (2002) Worker performance and ventilation: analyses of individual data for call-center workers. In Proceedings of Indoor Air 2002, Monterey, CA, ISIAQ, 1, pp. 796–801.

Fisk, W., Seppänen, O., Faulkner, D. and Huang, J. (2003) Cost benefit analysis of ventilation control strategies in an office building, In Proceedings of Healthy Buildings 2003, Singapore: NUS, 3, pp. 361–366.

Gagge, A., Fobelets, A. and Berglund, L. (1986) A standard predictive index of human response to the thermal environment. *ASHRAE Transactions*, 92(2): 709–731.

Gaihre, S., Semple, S., Miller, J., Fielding, S. and Turner, S. (2014) Classroom carbon dioxide concentration, school attendance, and educational attainment. *Journal of School Health*, 849: 569–574.

Hancock, P. and Vasmatzidis, I. (1998) Human occupational and performance limits under stress: the thermal environment as a prototypical example. *Ergonomics*, 41(8): 1169–1191.

Haverinen-Shaughnessy, U., Moschandreas, D. and Shaughnessy, R. (2011) Association between substandard classroom ventilation rates and students' academic achievement. *Indoor Air*, 212: 121–131.

Haverinen-Shaughnessy, U. and Shaughnessy, R. (2015) Effects of classroom ventilation rate and temperature on students' test scores. *PloS One*, 10(8): e0136165.

Hedge, A. and Dorsey, J. (2013) Green buildings need good ergonomics. *Ergonomics*, 563: 492–506.

Hedge, A. and Gaygen, D. (2010) Indoor environment conditions and computer work in an office. *HVAC&R Research*, 162: 123–138.

Holmberg, I. and Wyon, D. (1969) The dependence of performance in school on classroom temperature. *Educational & Psychological Interactions*, 31, 20pp. Malmö, Sweden: School of Education.

Holmberg, I. and Wyon, D. (1972) Systematic observation of classroom behaviour during moderate heat stress. *Educational and Psychological Interactions*, 37, 18pp. Malmö, Sweden: School of Education.

Hutter, H., Haluza, D., Piegler, K., Hohenblum, P., *et al.* (2013) Semivolatile compounds in schools and their influence on cognitive performance of children. *International Journal of Occupational Medicine and Environmental Health*, 264: 628–635.

Ilmarinen, R., Palonen, J. and Seppänen, O. (1992) Effects of non-uniform thermal conditions on body temperature responses in women. In Proceedings of the 41st Nordiska Arbetsmiljömötet, Reykjavik, Iceland: Arbetsmiljöstyrelsen, 1, pp. 181–182.

Ito, K., Murakami, D, Kaneko, T. and Fukao, H. (2006) Study on the productivity in classroom Part 2. Realistic simulation experiment on effects of air quality /thermal environment on learning performance. In Proceedings of Healthy Buildings 2006, Lisbon, Portugal: ISIAQ, pp. 207–212.

Kajtár, L. and Herczeg, L. (2012) Influence of carbon-dioxide concentration on human well-being and intensity of mental work. *Quarterly Journal of Hungarian Meteorological Services* 116; 145–169.

Kolarik, J., Toftum, J., Olesen, B. and Shitzer, A. (2009) Occupant responses and office work performance in environments with moderately drifting operative temperatures RP-1269. *HVAC&R Research*, 155: 931–960.

Koskela, H., Maula, H., Haapakangas, A., Moberg, V. and Hongisto, V. (2014) Effect of low ventilation rate on office work performance and perception of air quality: a laboratory study. In Proceedings of *Indoor Air 2014*, Hong Kong, PRC: ISIAQ, 8, pp. 23–24.

Kroner, W., Stark-Martin, J. and Willemain, T. (1992) Using advanced office technology to increase productivity: the impact of environmentally responsive workstations ERWs on productivity and worker attitude. Troy, NY, USA: Rensselaer Polytechnic Institute, Center for Architectural Research.

Lagercrantz, L., Wistrand, M., Willén, U., Wargocki, P., Witterseh, T. and Sundell, J. (2000) Negative impact of air pollution on productivity: previous Danish findings repeated in new Swedish test room. In Proceedings of Healthy Buildings 2000, Espoo, Finland: ISIAQ, 1, pp. 653–658.

Lan, L., Lian, Z. and Pan, L. (2010) The effects of air temperature on office workers' well-being, workload and productivity-evaluated with subjective ratings. *Applied Ergonomics*, 421: 29–36.

Lan., L., Wargocki, P. and Lian, Z. (2011b) Quantitative measurement of productivity loss due to thermal discomfort. *Energy and Buildings*, 435: 1057–1062.

Lan., L., Wargocki, P. and Lian, Z. (2014) Thermal effects on human performance in office environment measured by integrating task speed and accuracy. *Applied Ergonomics*, 45: 490–495.

Lan, L., Wargocki, P., Wyon, D. and Lian, Z. (2011a) Effects of thermal discomfort in an office on perceived air quality, SBS symptoms, physiological responses, and human performance. *Indoor Air*, 21(5): 376–390.

Laverge J. and Janssens A. (2011) IAQ exposure of sleeping occupants under different residential ventilation configurations. In Proceedings of Roomvent 2011, Trondheim, Norway: SINTEF, Paper 125.

Lee, H, Choi, Y. and Chun, C. (2012) The effect of indoor air temperature on occupants' attention ability based on the electroencephalogram analysis. In Proceedings of Healthy Buildings 2012, Brisbane, QLD, Australia: ISIAQ.

Leyten, J. and Kurvers, S. (2013) Letter to the Editor. *Indoor Air*, 23: 439–440.

Maddalena, R., Mendell, M., Eliseeva, K., Chan, W., *et al.* (2015) Effects of ventilation rate per person and per floor area on perceived air quality, sick building syndrome symptoms, and decision-making. *Indoor Air*, 25(4): 362–370.

Mattsson, M. and Hygge, S. (2005) Effect of particulate air cleaning on perceived health and cognitive performance in school children during pollen season, In Proceedings of Indoor Air 2005, Beijing, China: Tsinghua University Press, pp. 1111–1115.

Maula, H., Hongisto, V., Östman, L., Haapakangas, A., Koskela, H. and Hyönä, J. (2015) The effect of slightly warm temperature on work performance and comfort in open-plan offices: a laboratory study. *Indoor Air*, 26(2): 286–297.

Meese, G., Kok, R., Lewis, M. and Wyon, D. (1982) Effects of moderate cold and heat stress on factory workers in Southern Africa, 2: skill and performance in the cold. *South African Journal of Science*, 78: 189–197.

Mendell, M., Eliseeva, E., Davies, M. and Lobscheid, A. (2015) Do classroom ventilation rates in California elementary schools influence standardized test scores? Results from a prospective study. *Indoor Air*, 26(4): 546–557.

Mendell, M., Eliseeva, E., Davies, M., Spears, M., Lobscheid, A., Fisk, W. and Apte, M. (2013) Association of classroom ventilation with reduced illness absence: a prospective study in California elementary schools. *Indoor Air*, 236: 515–528.

Mendell, M. and Heath, G. (2005) Do indoor pollutants and thermal conditions in schools influence student performance? A critical review of the literature. *Indoor Air*, 15: 27–52.

Milton, D., Glencross, P. and Walters, M. (2000) Risk of sick-leave associated with outdoor air supply rate, humidification and occupants complaints. *Indoor Air*, 10: 212–221.

Murakami, S., Kaneko, T, Ito, K. and Fukao, H. (2006) Study on the productivity in classroom Part 1. field survey on effects of air quality/thermal environment on learning performance. In Proceedings of Healthy Buildings 2006, Lisbon, Portugal: ISIAQ, pp. 271–276.

Myhrvold, A., Olsen, E. and Lauridsen, Ø. (1996) Indoor environment in schools: pupils' health and performance in regard to CO_2 concentrations. In Proceedings of Indoor Air 1996, Nagoya, Japan: ISIAQ, 4, pp. 369–374.

New York State Commission on Ventilation (1923) Report of the New York State Commission on Ventilation. New York: Dutton.

Niemelä, R., Hannula, M., Rautio, S., Reijula, K. and Railio, J. (2002) The effect of air temperature on labour productivity in call centres: a case study. *Energy and Buildings*, 34: 759–764.

Palonen, J., Ilmarinen, R., Seppänen, O. and Wenzel, C. (1992) Thermal comfort in sedentary conditions with vertical temperature and velocity gradient. In Proceedings of the 41st Nordiska Arbetsmiljömötet, Reykjavik, Iceland: Arbetsmiljöstyrelse, pp. 190–191.

Park, J. and Yoon, C. (2011) The effects of outdoor air supply rate on work performance during 8-h work period. *Indoor Air*, 21(4): 284–290.

Pejtersen, J., Feveile, H., Christensen, K. and Burr, H. (2011) Sickness absence associated with shared and open-plan offices; a national cross sectional questionnaire survey. *Scandinavian Journal of Work, Environment & Health*, 37(5): 376–382.

Pepler, R. and Warner, R. (1968) Temperature and learning: an experimental study. *ASHRAE Transactions*, 74: 211–219.

Petersen, S., Jensen, K., Pedersen, A. and Rasmussen, H. (2016) The effect of increased classroom ventilation rate indicated by reduced CO_2 concentration on the performance of schoolwork by children. *Indoor Air*, 26(3): 366–379.

Provins, K. (1966) Environmental heat, body temperature and behavior: an hypothesis. *Australian Journal of Psychology*, 18: 118–129.

Ribic, W. (2008) Nachweis des Zusammenhangs zwischen Leistungsfähigkeit und Luftqualität, *HLH Lüftung/Klima – Heizung/Sanitär* – Gebäudetechnik, 59: 43–46 (in German).

Riley, R. (1979) Indoor spread of respiratory infection by recirculation of air. *Bulletin Europeen Physiopathologie Respiratoire*, 15: 699–705.

Roelofsen, P. (2001) The design of the workplace as a strategy for productivity enhancement. In Proceedings of CLIMA 2001, Napoli, Italy.

Sarbu, I. and Pacurar, C. (2015) Experimental and numerical research to assess indoor environment quality and schoolwork performance in university classrooms. *Building and Environment* 93: 141–154.

Satish, U., Mendell, M., Shekhar, K., Hotchi, T., Sullivan, D., Streufert, S. and Fisk, W. (2012) Is CO_2 an indoor pollutant? Direct effects of low-to-moderate CO_2 concentrations on human decision-making performance. *Environmental Health Perspectives*, 120(12): 1671.

Schoer, L. and Shaffran, J. (1973) A combined evaluation of three separate research projects on the effects of thermal environment on learning and performance. *ASHRAE Transactions*, 79, pp.97–108.

Seppänen, O., Fisk, W. and Lei, Q. (2006a) Effect of temperature on task performance in office environment. In Proceedings of Cold Climate HVAC Conference, Moscow.

Seppänen, O. Fisk, W. and Lei, Q. (2006b) Ventilation and performance in office work. *Indoor Air*, 16: 28–35.

Shendell, D., Prill, R., Fisk, W., Apte, M., Blake, D. and Faulkner, D. (2004) Associations between classroom CO_2 concentrations and student attendance in Washington and Idaho. *Indoor Air*, 145: 333–341.

Simons, E., Hwang, S., Fitzgerald, E., Kielb, C. and Lin, S. (2010) The impact of school building conditions on student absenteeism in upstate New York. *American Journal of Public Health*, 1009: 1679–1686.

Streufert, S., Pogash, R. and Piasecki, M. (1988) Simulation-based assessment of managerial competence: reliability and validity. *Personnel Psychology*, 41(3): 537–557.

Strøm-Tejsen, P., Zukowska, D., Wargocki, P. and Wyon, D. (2016) The effects of bedroom air quality on sleep and next-day performance. *Indoor Air*, 26: 679–686.

Tanabe, S., Haneda, M. and Nishihara, N. (2015) Workplace productivity and individual thermal satisfaction. *Building and Environment*, 91: 42–50.

Tanabe, S., Iwahashi, Y., Tsushima, S. and Nishihara, N. (2013) Thermal comfort and productivity in offices under mandatory electricity savings after the Great East Japan earthquake. *Architectural Science Review*, 561: 4–13.

Tanabe, S., Nishihara, N. and Haneda, M. (2007) Indoor temperature, productivity, and fatigue in office tasks. *HVAC&R Research*, 134: 623–633.

Tham, K. (2004) Effects of temperature and outdoor air supply rate on the performance of call center operators in the Tropics. *Indoor Air*, 14(s7): 119–125.

Tham, K. and Willem, H. (2010) Room air temperature affects occupants' physiology, perceptions and mental alertness. *Building and Environment*, 451: 40–44.

Tham, K., Willem, H., Sekhar, S., Wyon, D., Wargocki, P. and Fanger, P. (2003) Temperature and ventilation effects on the work performance of office workers (study of a call center in the tropics), In Proceedings of Healthy Buildings 2003, 3: 280–286.

Thatcher, A. and Milner, K. (2014) Changes in productivity, psychological wellbeing and physical wellbeing from working in a 'green' building. *Work*, 493: 381–393.

Toftum, J., Kjeldsen, B., Wargocki, P., Menå, H., Hansen, E. and Clausen, G. (2015) Association between classroom ventilation mode and learning outcome in Danish schools. *Building and Environment*, 92: 494–503.

Valančius, R. and Jurelionis, A. (2013) Influence of indoor air temperature variation on office work performance. *Journal of Environmental Engineering and Landscape Management*, 211: 19–25.

Wargocki, P., Frontczak, M., Schiavon, S., Goins, J., Arens, E. and Zhang, H. (2012) Satisfaction and self-estimated performance in relation to indoor environmental parameters and building features. In Proceedings of Healthy Buildings 2012, Brisbane, QLD, Australia: ISIAQ. Available at: http://escholarship.org/uc/item/451326fk).

Wargocki, P., Lagercrantz, L., Witterseh, T., Sundell, J., Wyon, D. and Fanger, P. (2002) Subjective perceptions, symptom intensity and performance: a comparison of two independent studies, both changing similarly the pollution load in an office. *Indoor Air*, 12: 74–80.

Wargocki, P. and Wyon, D. (2007a) The effects of outdoor air supply rate and supply air filter condition in classrooms on the performance of schoolwork by children: ASHRAE 1257-RP. *HVAC&R Research*, 132: 165–191.

Wargocki P. and Wyon, D. (2007b) The effects of moderately raised classroom temperatures and classroom ventilation rate on the performance of schoolwork by children: ASHRAE 1257-RP. *HVAC&R Research*, 132, pp. 193–220.

Wargocki, P., Wyon, D., Baik, Y., Clausen, G. and Fanger, P. (1999) Perceived air quality, Sick Building Syndrome SBS: symptoms and productivity in an office with two different pollution loads. *Indoor Air*, 9: 165–179.

Wargocki, P., Wyon, D. and Fanger, P. (2000a) Productivity is affected by the air quality in offices. In Proceedings of Healthy Buildings 2000, Espoo, Finland: ISIAQ, 1, pp. 635–640.

Wargocki, P., Wyon, D. and Fanger, P. (2004) The performance and subjective responses of call-centre operators with new and used supply air filters at two outdoor air supply rates. *Indoor Air*, 14(s8): 7–16.

Wargocki P., Wyon, D., Lynge-Jensen, K. and Bornehag, C. (2008) The effects of electrostatic filtration and supply air filter condition in classrooms on the performance of schoolwork by children: ASHRAE 1257-RP. *HVAC&R Research*, 14(3): 327–344.

Wargocki, P., Wyon, D., Sundell, J., Clausen, G. and Fanger, P. (2000b) The effects of outdoor air supply rate in an office on perceived air quality, Sick Building Syndrome SBS symptoms and productivity. *Indoor Air*, 10: 222–236.

Willem, H. (2006) Thermal and indoor air quality on physiological responses, perception and performance of tropically acclimatized people. PhD thesis, National University of Singapore.

Wyon, D. (1970) Studies of children under imposed noise and heat stress. *Ergonomics*, 13(5): 598–612.

Wyon, D. (1974) The effects of moderate heat stress on typewriting performance. *Ergonomics*, 17: 309–318.

Wyon, D. (1979) Human responses to cyclic changes in the thermal environment. Editions INSERM, 75: 153–161.

Wyon, D. (1996a) Creative thinking as the dependent variable in six environmental experiments: a review. In Proceedings of Indoor Air 1996, Nagoya, Tokyo: ISIAQ, 1, pp. 419–422.

Wyon, D. (1996b) Individual microclimate control: required range, probable benefits and current feasibility In Proceedings of Indoor Air 1996, Nagoya. Tokyo, Japan: ISIAQ, 1, pp. 1067–1072.

Wyon, D. (1996c) Indoor environmental effects on productivity. In Proceedings of IAQ´96 Paths to Better Building Environments, Atlanta, USA: ASHRAE, pp. 5–15.

Wyon, D. (2004) The effects of indoor air quality of performance and productivity. *Indoor Air*, 14(s7): 92–101.

Wyon, D., Andersen, I. and Lundqvist, G. (1979) The effects of moderate heat stress on mental performance. *Scandinavian Journal of Work, Environment & Health*, 5: 352–361.

Wyon, D., Asgeirsdottir, T., Kjerulf-Jensen, P. and Fanger, P. (1973) The effects of ambient temperature swings on comfort, performance and behaviour. *Archives des Sciences Physiologiques*, 27: 441–458.

Wyon, D., Bruun, N., Olesen, S., Kjerulf-Jensen, P. and Fanger, P. (1971) Factors affecting the subjective tolerance of ambient temperature swings. In Proceedings of the 5th International Congress for Heating and Ventilating, Copenhagen, Denmark: Danish Technical Press, 1, pp. 87–107.

Wyon, D. and Sandberg, M. (1990) Thermal manikin prediction of discomfort due to displacement ventilation. *ASHRAE Transactions*, 96(1), Paper 3307.

Wyon, D. and Sandberg, M. (1996) Discomfort due to vertical thermal gradients. Indoor Air, 6: 48–54.

Zhang, X., Wargocki, P. and Lian, Z. (2016a) Physiological responses during exposure to carbon dioxide and bioeffluents at levels typically occurring indoors. *Indoor Air*, DOI: 10.1111/ina.12286.

Zhang, X., Wargocki, P. and Lian, Z., (2016c) Human responses to carbon dioxide, a follow-up study at recommended exposure limits in non-industrial environments. *Building and Environment*, 100: 162–171.

Zhang, X., Wargocki, P., Lian, Z. and Thyregod, C. (2016b) Effects of exposure to carbon dioxide and bioeffluents on perceived air quality, self-assessed acute health symptoms and cognitive performance, *Indoor Air*, DOI: 10.1111/ina.12284.

Zhou, X., Lian, Z. and Lan, L. (2014) Experimental study on a bedside personalized ventilation system for improving sleep comfort and quality. *Indoor and Built Environment*, 23(2): 313–323.

Chapter 15

Measuring the IEQ contribution to productivity and well-being

The importance of the built environment indoor environment quality on economic productivity and the contributing factors which lead to improved performance

Vyt Garnys, Travis Hale and Adam Garnys

Introduction

In many developed countries, global competitiveness is slipping, compared to other developing countries, particularly for labour productivity. As countries transition from manufacturing to service-related industries, their global competitiveness and productivity become increasingly important. Labour productivity, which is the ratio of fiscal output to inputs, is a key measure of how efficiently inputs (e.g. wages) are being used to generate outputs in economies.

Given that labour represents around 90 per cent of the input costs within service-related industries (compared to energy at 1–5 per cent of input costs), improving the labour output (as a result of targeted IEQ improvements) has the potential to lead to significant economic benefits locally, regionally and nationally. In a city, such as Melbourne, in the central City of Melbourne alone a 5 per cent increase in labour productivity would equate to an annual benefit of approximately A$2.1 billion to the local economy.

An improvement of 5 per cent in productivity is achievable through targeted and benchmarked retrofits of the indoor environment. The contribution to worker productivity from the indoor environment is in the order of 1–10 per cent. At a business level, the implementation of targeted retrofits can result in significant financial benefit and even offset the cost of a retrofit in a short period of time.

Targeted improvements to indoor environment quality (IEQ), be they lighting, acoustics, thermal comfort or contaminants, have significant benefits beyond just productivity, including increasing staff retention, improving occupant satisfaction and even reducing absenteeism. For owners, demonstrable productivity improvements can lead to better building rental yields. More work needs to be done, but the importance of productivity cannot be overstated for future growth as countries transition to a service-driven economy that can benefit from increased productivity as a result of improvements to the IEQ of the built environment.

A universal and comparable methodology for assessing productivity from IEQ measurements is needed before benchmark assessments of improvements can be made.

Potential

What is productivity

The Organisation for Economic Co-operation and Development's (OECD) Compendium of Productivity Indicators (OECD, 2015) states:

> Productivity is commonly defined as a ratio between the fiscal volume of output and the volume of inputs. In other words, it measures how efficiently production inputs, such as labour and capital, are being used in an economy to produce a given level of output. Productivity is considered a key source of economic growth and competitiveness and, as such, internationally comparable indicators of productivity are central for assessing economic performance.

Many measures of productivity exist. For example, at a national level, productivity is typically measured as multi-factorial productivity, which measures the residual growth that cannot be explained by the rate of change in the services of labour, capital and intermediate outputs as used for many years by the OECD (2008). Additionally, other productivity measures exist which typically relate to specific industries (e.g. capital productivity) and for the service-related industry, the measure is typically labour productivity.

Labour productivity measures the value of goods and services produced, divided by the hours (or value) of labour used to produce them. In the service-related industries the relative costs of organisations are approximately divided into 0.9 per cent energy, 9 per cent rent and operation, and 90 per cent employee costs (Skopek, 2014; World Green Building Council, 2014). Therefore, the use of labour productivity as a measure of service-related productivity is justified. There is a difference between productivity (fiscal) and efficiency (non-fiscal).

The difficulty arises when assessing the effects from IEQ, as there is no consensus in the literature on how to measure productivity in the built environment, despite more than 20 years of IEQ research and the generally agreed position that both occupant and organisational efficiency (misnamed as productivity in publications) can benefit from an increase of 1–15 per cent attributable to improved indoor environment quality. This problem is discussed, but without quantitative resolution, by Sullivan *et al.* (2013) in their report, *Measuring Productivity in the Office Workplace*.

To address the challenge of quantitative and even financial measurement of office productivity, Garnys and Wargocki conducted workshops on 'Agreeing on a Productivity Index for IEQ', at the International Healthy Buildings Conferences HB2015 Europe, Eindhoven, the Netherlands, and HB2015 America, Boulder, Colorado, at the Facility Management Association of Australia conference, Ideaction 2016, Melbourne, Australia and at HB2017, Lublin, Poland.

The aim of arriving at a comparative productivity index has been agreed in most countries for the purposes of identifying global, country and sector productivity differences and areas for improvement by using a cascade of productivity indices, as shown in the triangular representations in Figure 15.1. Figure 15.2 shows the criteria that the OECD has considered for productivity assessment.

The criteria as shown in Figure 15.2 are generally applicable to IEQ assessments. These assessments must be comparable in their methodologies and frameworks while still being universally achievable within reasonable costs. This is rarely the case for the published studies to date.

Annual assessments are presented as comparative and specific publications by the OECD to governments, who then mine research and survey data to identify areas for attention and improvement, as shown in Figure 15.3.

Cascade of Productivity Measurement

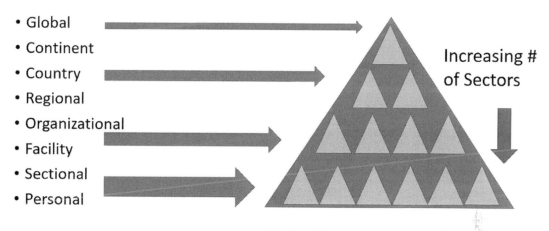

- Global
- Continent
- Country
- Regional
- Organizational
- Facility
- Sectional
- Personal

Increasing #
of Sectors

Productivity Index = Output/Input

Figure 15.1 Schematic pyramidal cascade of Productivity Indices used to analyse and compare variations in productivity

Measurement of Aggregate and Industry-Level Productivity Growth – OECD Criteria

- An accessible guide to productivity measurement
- Improves international harmonisation
- Identify desirable characteristics of productivity measures by reference to a coherent framework
- Assessed against reality of data availability or costs
- Broad trends .. with simpler tools but be aware of significance of simplifications

Figure 15.2 OECD criteria for establishing universal productivity measures
Source: OECD (2001).

With changing knowledge and criteria with respect to IEQ and its effects on occupants, it is important to have regular comparisons between studies that have been conducted using similar protocols, to benchmark assessments from improvements to IEQ and emerging knowledge. Comparison of IEQ-related productivity studies, when used as key performance

OECD Compendium of Productivity Indicators 2015

Figure 15.3 Regular OECD publication of comparative studies between and within countries. The indices allow for immediate high level management.

indices (KPIs), also allows rapid correction of poorly performing assets and assists with design criteria.

While both capital and labour productivity are considered by the OECD, the effect of indoor environment only affects the occupants, so we can prioritise our focus on labour productivity. Care must be taken to remove capital distortions of labour productivity assessments.

Figure 15.4 shows the simplified OECD approach to measuring labour productivity – namely as fiscal output per cost or time of labour. For buildings, we can consider this to be budgeted or actual revenues per labour cost. For service or knowledge industries, the actual final economic output by department is not always quantified. Departmental budgets are a useful surrogate for expected outputs and staff costs and times as inputs to calculate productivity indices. Agreed profit or loss margins can be added to departmental budgets for aggregate reconciliations.

The annual *OECD Compendium of Productivity Indicators* reports provide indices that give a basis for comparison between economies, as shown in Figure 15.5.

OECD – Types of Productivity Measures

- Labour productivity
  - **Quantity index of gross output / Quantity index of labour input**
- Labour remains the single most important input to many production processes
- Labour input is measured as the total number of hours worked
  Quality and degree of international comparability are not always clear
- Hours paid and full-time equivalent persons can provide reasonable alternatives

Figure 15.4 OECD measures of labour productivity as costs or hours

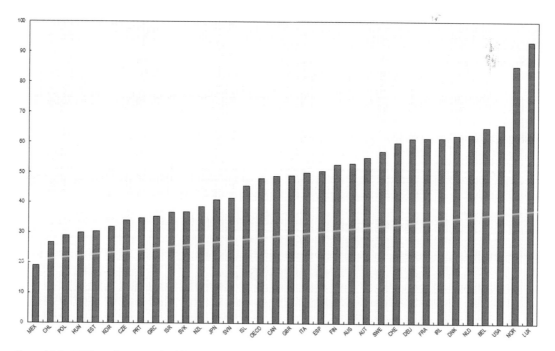

Figure 15.5 GDP per hour worked, labour productivity
Source: OECD (2015) (Figure 1.7).

Furthermore, the indices gives a basis for an analysis of change in the growth of labour, productivity, shown in Figure 15.6, and the relative performance of overall business sectors, but excluding real estate, as shown in Figure 15.7.

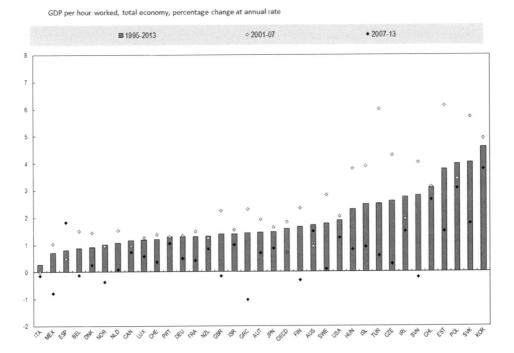

Figure 15.6 Growth in labour productivity
Source: OECD (2015) (Figure 1.8).

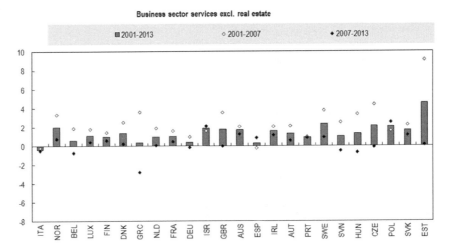

Figure 15.7 Business sector services growth of productivity, excluding real estate. Real value added per hour worked, percentage change at annual rate.
Source: OECD (2015) (Figure 2.1).

The challenge for the sector analysis, particularly for real estate, is that there are capital productivity distortions. Additionally, there are no statistics available for the contribution that buildings make towards the productivity of service-related businesses. In the case of real estate, there are generally only construction and property sales statistics. However, there are examples of data from productivity assessments (Figures 15.5–15.7) and these highlight the ability to make comparisons between countries and sectors – if there is a uniform methodology for calculating productivity.

The pressing need is to assess how buildings contribute to national labour productivity based on their indoor environment characteristics, not just because interior fit-out constitutes about 40 per cent of constructed property costs. This impact is likely to be much larger than the capital productivity of buildings based on construction and property sales. This is particularly important since most business services are conducted from offices and the impact of office design efficiency is currently not being financially quantified. Construction and interior fit-out costs are very high and are known accurately, but the effect of these on occupant productivity, of about an 80 per cent greater quantity over the property operational life, is essentially unknown.

Energy consumption continues to be the key focus of regulators, owners and rating systems despite the long-standing assumption that the relative fiscal magnitude of energy : operations : occupant productivity was of the order of 5 : 15 : 80 per cent respectively and now, 1 : 9 : 14 per cent for new buildings due to energy saving technologies and rising wages.

The World Green Building Council's (2014) *Health, Wellbeing and Productivity in Offices* series of reports have recognised this imbalance of priorities and raised awareness of this important topic by setting out a framework for organisations to measure how their building impacts on their most valuable asset, i.e. their employees.

The built environment's contribution to labour productivity

Most developed economies in the world have been undergoing a structural change over the past few decades, with an ever-decreasing proportion of the employment economy being driven by traditional mainstays, for example, in Australia, by mining and manufacturing (Reserve Bank of Australia, 2010).

As an example of a moderately sized (1–5 million population) global city, we can examine Melbourne, Australia – voted the world's most liveable city 2010–2016 (Economist Intelligence Unit, 2016). For the Melbourne economy, since the 1994–1995 financial year; manufacturing has fallen from 17.7 per cent to 7.2 per cent while 'Professional, Financial and Insurance Services' grew from 6.7 per cent to 21.6 per cent (SGS Economics – Australian Cities Accounts, 2014–2015). This highlights the structural reform underway, and the greater emphasis that needs to be placed on the productivity of service-related industries.

The greatest annual operational cost for the growing service-related industry is labour. Australia's $600 billion property industry houses this labour and allows them to deliver their respective outputs. Consequently, the property industry makes a significant contribution to Australia's service-related labour productivity. Based on information from the City of Melbourne, Property Market Digest (City of Melbourne, 2013), the current value of buildings in Melbourne's Central Business District is approximately A$23 billion. From the City of Melbourne economic profile, the value-added Gross Local Product (GLP) from the office-related industries was approximately A$42.5 billion per annum. Without discount cash flow adjustment, the 20-year value (average lifetime of building prior to major refurbishment) (Adelaide City Council, 2007) of value-added GLP is approximately A$840 billion from the current A$23 billion stock of buildings – a raw capital productivity ratio of 36.5.

The specific drivers for productivity improvement are discussed further in the section on drivers of productivity; however, improvements to the built environment are linked to improvements in occupant satisfaction and productivity. While numerous factors affect an employee's productivity, the contribution of the indoor environment to their performance is of the order of 1–10 per cent (REHVA, Indoor Climate and Productivity in Offices, 2006) in normal office environments and hence are of significant value at a local, state and national level.

How productivity uplift can improve economic development

As an example of Victoria, Australia, a state of 6 million inhabitants, a 5 per cent improvement in total output would be worth A$17 billion to Victoria's Gross State Product (GSP) of $344 billion (in 2012) or a saving of A$6.2 billion in wages of $124.8 billion (in 2012). The overall population of Victoria's capital city, Melbourne is 4 million with a population density of about 3,000 inhabitants per square kilometre and an average salary of A$75,000.

In this chapter, the City of Melbourne is used for the majority of projections, as detailed statistics are kept for the service-related industries in that municipality, however, it is expected that similar benefits would also apply to service-related industries across other comparable cities. In the City of Melbourne (CoM) alone where there is an A$42.5 billion of GLP output for office-related businesses, a 5 per cent improvement would equate to a $2.1 billion benefit annually to the local economy. While increases to productivity translate into wider economic benefit, they can also represent financial benefits to local businesses and public authorities.

For the City of Melbourne Council, the new Council House 2 building (CH2) has reported a 10 per cent "productivity" improvement based on occupant self-assessment compared to Council House 1 (Paevere and Brown, 2008) and 500 Collins Street showed specific tenant performance improvements in its Green Building Council of Australia's 5-Star Rating (Green Building Council of Australia, 2006).

There are few case studies (including a number of older papers) that demonstrate how investment in the built environment can drive improvements in labour efficiency. More recent academic studies have endeavoured to develop methodologies to assess the relationship between IEQ, costs and efficiency and net cost as illustrated by the work of Valancius et al., 2013, Jurelionis (2015) Wargocki et al. (2006), and Fisk et al. (Fisk, 2000; Fisk et al. 2011; Fisk et al., 2003).

How can we achieve this potential?

Drivers of productivity improvements

Labour productivity in the service industry is driven by a number of factors which are highlighted in Figure 15.8; these factors include the indoor climate, the infrastructure, management and facilities. Clearly not all of these factors are under the control of the building owner or facility manager and therefore they are not considered in this chapter, other than to suggest that improvements to each of these factors is likely to elicit a potential improvement to occupant satisfaction and therefore efficiency and productivity gains.

The delivery of indoor climate and indoor environment quality (IEQ) is directly under the control of the building owner or facility manager. Therefore, positive targeted improvements to this area are likely to drive productivity increases more widely.

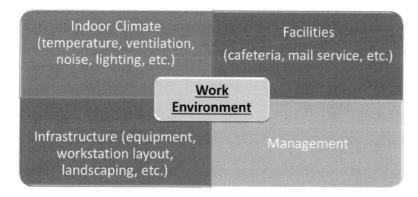

Figure 15.8 The factors that make up the work environment and therefore occupant productivity

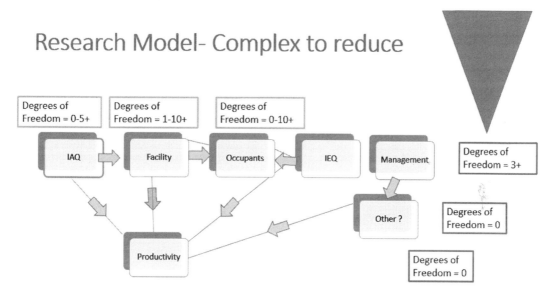

Figure 15.9 Published research methodology for the assessment of human performance efficiency but not financial productivity

The Factors for Developing a Productivity Index must have the following characteristics:

• be practical to obtain the data;
• be affordable for cost/benefit;
• be relevant to the organisation;
• be universally adopted;
• be comparable to other studies.

Attempts to collate disparate research findings into a socially or financially convertible productivity index have failed due to the inherent complexity and lack of relationship between studies, even though each study is valuable in clarifying a particular variable. Figure 15.9 shows the inverted triangle or 'knowledge tree' problem.

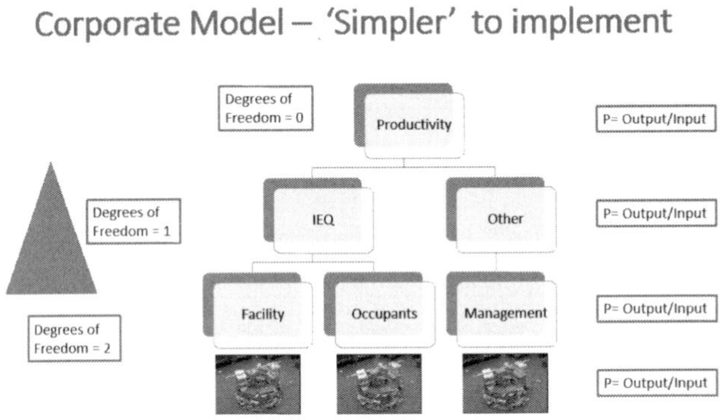

Figure 15.10 Suggested OECD-based model for assessment of labour productivity

Taking the lead from the OECD model, Figure 15.10 shows a more intuitive and simple model to arrive at segregating sectors of varying productivity, which can then be reduced to critical factors able to be analysed from research or organisational practice.

Can we use rating systems to quantify IEQ?

Rating systems provide the basis for organising data and have the following advantages and disadvantages:

- readily available;
- well structured and proven technically;
- accepted by owners and occupiers;
- internally comparable;
- design based ratings, e.g. BREEAM, LEED – weak on post-occupancy evaluation and IEQ, no occupant satisfaction surveys;
- performance based ratings, e.g. NABERS – strong on IEQ and occupant satisfaction – rate as post-occupancy evaluation (POE).

Relative contribution of indoor environment quality

Similar to much of the developed world, most Australian workers now spend 70–90 per cent of their working lives indoors and as a result, building design, its use, and management influence occupant comfort, well-being and productivity (Skopek, 2014; WGBC, 2014). While a detailed analysis of the influence of each of these factors is outside the scope of this chapter, some of the impacts are listed in Table 15.1 with their relative contribution.

Opportunities to capture this potential

Internationally, organisations are examining the relationship between the indoor environment and productivity, with the World Green Building Council releasing a report entitled

Table 15.1 Typical productivity improvements broken down per category

	Higher productivity (%)	Less absenteeism (%)
Good overall indoor environment	10–15	2.5
No air pollution source	3–7	1.5
Adequate ventilation	1–2	0.5
Adjustable temperature	2–3	0.5
Temperature not too high, not too low	7	
Cellular office (max. 4 people)	2–4	Decrease
Good lighting	2–3	
Daylight		0.5
Less noise nuisance	3.9	

As adapted from Leijten (2002).

'Health, Wellbeing and Productivity' in 2014. Furthermore, numerous building rating schemes currently exist which focus on benchmarking of indoor environment quality performance, including the UK BREEAM In-Use, The Green Building Council of Australia's Green Star Performance tool, and the National Australian Built Environment Rating Scheme (NABERS) Indoor Environment (IE) rating tool. The NABERS IE tool is the most-established and refined performance tool worldwide and provides a significant database for benchmark comparisons and emerging productivity estimates. The NABERS IE Protocol requires post-occupancy measurement of the indoor environment and an occupant satisfaction survey to strict protocols based on international standards. The measurements are at prescribed locations, periods and measure temperature, relative humidity, air flow, carbon dioxide levels, carbon monoxide levels, total volatile organic compounds, formaldehyde and PM10 particulates. The NABERS IE Version 2 rating benchmarks against the average rating for the past 12 months.

Conducting benchmarking of IEQ performance through a rating tool prior to refurbishment allows targeted improvements to be made to the building where performance is poor and identification of potential labour productivity opportunities exist.

Following retrofits, surveys and measurements can be conducted to confirm that improvements have been made to the areas of poor performance. Finally, an assessment of occupant satisfaction and financial modelling can be applied to determine the magnitude of labour productivity increases as a result of the retrofit. As an example, CETEC applied this approach to an engineering consulting firm in Melbourne, by conducting occupant satisfaction surveys and physical measurement prior to relocation into new retrofitted offices. Following the targeted retrofit, improvements were seen in each of these measures and internal furbishing of the new premises gave a project payback within 9 months.

An important outcome of this study was that the productivity gains were not uniform throughout the organisation, as shown in Figure 15.11. The gains, measured financially as fiscal output to labour cost ratios, were most marked for the pre-moved areas that had the worst IEQ in the old premises. The arrows show the predicted 13 per cent improvement in productivity with the actual of 12.5 per cent when measured six months after the move to avoid settling in and initial excitement factors.

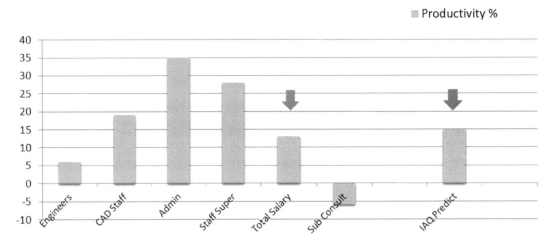

Figure 15.11 Labour productivity gains (vertical axis) six months after relocation

Capturing the potential productivity improvements is important as it maximises the output value relative to the cost of retrofits.

Another recent example is a superannuation trust which contracted CETEC to conduct a pre-occupancy study of IEQ and occupant satisfaction prior to commissioning plant upgrades in four of their operating buildings. There were no upgrades to the interiors other than lighting to the building and the outdoor air-handling systems and the tenants remained the same for this mix of newer and older buildings. The plant upgrades included installation of a dedicated outdoor air-handling system to improve air comfort and better manage temperature and humidity, as well as installing E1 lighting to improve eye comfort and light spread while reducing glare. Following plant upgrades and a 'settling-in' period, a post-occupancy assessment was conducted to determine IEQ performance and occupant satisfaction. Measurements were conducted in accordance with the NABERS IE protocol. Figure 15.12 identifies the average pre- and post-occupancy satisfaction before and after conducting the plant upgrades. It is evident that changes in IEQ have resulted in improvements in general building satisfaction. In the case of this organisation, changes to thermal comfort, air quality and cleanliness and maintenance have made significant improvements in general building satisfaction which had a projected nett impact on labour productivity of 1 to 5 per cent.

Figure 15.13 shows predicted productivity gains for a selection of 10 buildings in Australian cities that have undergone NABERS IE assessment. In the case of the last four, the labour productivity, as calculated pre- and post-occupancy (after refurbishment) is shown. The significantly larger gains of A$100 to A$200 per square metre from labour productivity are compared with the energy gains of A$15 to A$20 per square metre.

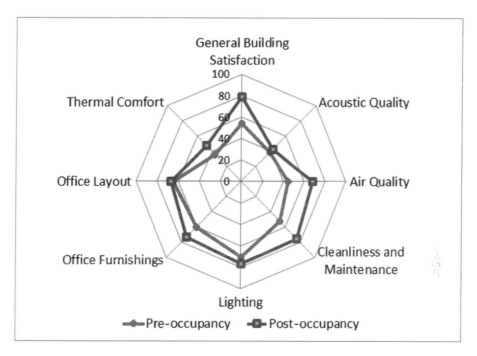

Figure 15.12 Average occupant response before and after HVAC plant and lighting upgrades

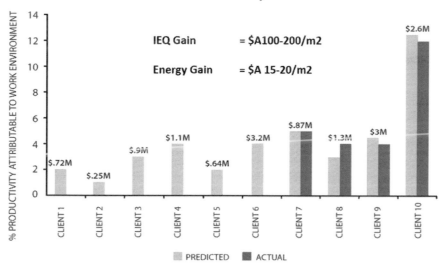

Figure 15.13 Predicted pre- and post-productivity gains from a selection of 10 major Australian buildings surveyed by CETEC

Benefits of investment in the improvement of the built environment

Boosting economies

As developed nations continue to transition from manufacturing to service-related industries, evaluating and increasing labour productivity are becoming increasingly important. Statistics are also kept for labour productivity by main activity, including building sector services, excluding real estate. For example, despite the fact that Australia's national labour productivity has increased from 0.93 per cent (2001–2007) to 1.48 per cent (2007–2013), Australia's labour productivity (real value added per hour worked, percentage changed at annual rate) in business services excluding real estate has decreased from 2.06 per cent in the 2001–2007 period, to 1.24 percent in the 2007–2013 period (OECD, 2015). The contribution of indoor environments, where most people work, is unknown.

Improving occupant satisfaction

Given that building-based workers spend around 70 per cent of their working life indoors, the importance of the indoor environment on occupant satisfaction cannot be overstated. The REHVA Indoor Climate and Productivity in Offices – Guidebook No 6 (REHVA, 2006) highlights that in the European Audit project carried out in 56 European office buildings in 9 countries, it was found that the proportion of persons dissatisfied with air quality varied between 25 and 60 per cent dissatisfied (Bluyssen *et al.*, 1996). Thus improving air quality in the buildings with the highest proportion of dissatisfied persons to the levels observed with the lowest proportion of dissatisfied can be expected to improve the performance of office work by 3–4 per cent.

This gain is significant, and identifies that improving occupant satisfaction (in addition to air quality) can lead to dramatic labour efficiency and productivity increases. Additionally, as shown in Table 15.1, the increases in occupant satisfaction across various factors are linked to decreases in absenteeism and other performance indices.

Increasing staff retention

Occupant satisfaction is not the only potential gain. The training of new labour (especially in service-related industries) can be considered to be cost-intensive. Therefore, increasing staff retention is of great financial value to an organisation.

The Colliers International Office Tenant Survey (2010) identified that excellent indoor air quality and thermal comfort rated second to proximity to public transport in the top office characteristics for staff attraction and retention.

Matt Reeder from Reuters reports that:

> The one-time cost of replacing just one employee can be as much as 150 percent or more of their annual salary. Recruiting, hiring and tracing replacements for lost people add up and companies can also suffer from lost productivity and intellectual capital.
>
> (Reeders, 2011)

Improving building stock and increasing rental yield

Improvements to the IEQ of office buildings offer many benefits to both the occupier and the building owners. The increases in the economic benefits and subsequent higher user satisfaction can also lead to a higher market value of the building, and extend the building life.

In a market where service industries are looking for competitive advantages, and to increase their profitability, any increase to output (e.g. labour productivity increases) is of significant value. This demand for optimal built environments allows building owners to command greater rental prices.

As presented by CETEC at the International Healthy Buildings HB 2015 America Conference, for a Melbourne-based property trust with national building stock of 820,000 square meters in 25 buildings, targeted improvements led to a quality increase of the national portfolio's average NABERS IE star rating (across a three-year programme) from 3.8 to 4.75 as shown in Figure 15.14. This illustrates that responding to baseline ratings can generate improved indoor environments to the base building which would contribute to improved occupied building IEQ and hence labour based efficiency and productivity gains.

Increases to the portfolio NABERS IE Rating average across a three-year period from refreshed buildings commanded greater rental yields which offset the cost of retrofit in a shorter period of time than energy upgrades.

Next steps

The property industry has always been considered to be an important part of national economies based on construction and real estate valuation factors. What has not been factored into

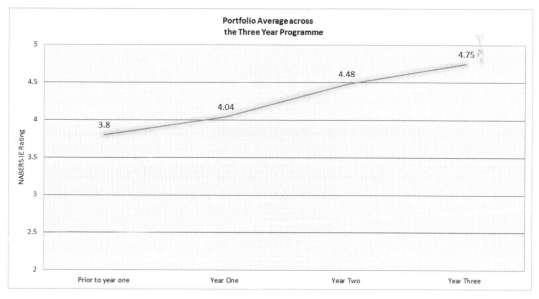

Figure 15.14 Building stock average NABERS IE (Base Building) star rating over a three year period for 820,000 m^2 in 25 Grade 1 office buildings

Source: Callinan *et al.* (2015).

economic modelling is how buildings can leverage GSP by 10 to 100 times. This is important as economies transition from manufacturing to a service industry base, while at the same time buildings and infrastructure ages.

For example, the City of Melbourne's 1200 Building Refurbishment initiative has recognised the benefits of refurbishment for energy and resources savings, but has not made the case for improved labour productivity improvements which far exceed resources savings (City of Melbourne, 2016). Improved labour productivity, rather than being seen as a cost-cutting opportunity, is the advantage for 'growing the economic pie' from increased capacity to deliver efficient goods and services. Therefore, greater assistance and recognition should be given to the property industry as not only a high basis of city, national and international assets, but as a key driver of city, national and international growth and competitiveness. Indoor environment quality improvement through better design in new and refurbished buildings will provide an important mechanism for growth, while maintenance of the indoor environment quality by good facility and human resource management will deliver a significant component of the growth engine for improved labour productivity.

Actions possible by property associations, governments and the general property and construction community are:

- Assess the relative impacts of potential productivity improvements with respect to the grades of building (e.g. P, A, B, C or D). This will allow for a greater focus of retrofit targeting.
- As the definition and understanding of productivity can vary greatly, a standardised system needs to be developed for the classes of office buildings and organisations to benchmark building IEQ and potential productivity.
- Educational and advocacy programmes are required for property professionals and organisations on the issues of IEQ and productivity.
- Information is the key in determining the potential for improvements, and while a standardised programme exists, the quality of the decision-making is tied directly to the quality of data collection. Therefore, accreditation of professionals able to efficiently and accurately interpret and deliver the required information is needed.
- Surveys are required to explore the perceptions within organisations and their opinions on productivity and benchmarking efforts to inform further discussions.

The quality of the indoor environment can play a significant part in national economic positions, provided the importance of productivity is recognised and more data is developed for quantitative assessment.

The proposed steps to assess productivity in commercial buildings are:

1   From financial data, calculate the Productivity Index: Overall Fiscal Turnover/Labour Cost.
2   Measure comprehensive IEQ and occupant satisfaction, e.g. using the NABERS Protocol/
3   Assess each IEQ parameter for productivity contribution.
4   Optimise IEQ productivity index: overall turnover/labour cost
5   Reassess steps 1–4.

The question of adoption rests with each jurisdiction with respect to:

- policy
- practice
- research

- communication
- education.

This method has been successfully adopted in Australia by CETEC Pty Ltd, in a number of case studies, and further discussion is encouraged for global methodology unification to allow comparative translation from building design to post-occupancy assessment to better organisational performance.

References

Adelaide City Council (2007) *Building Refurbishment*. Available at: http://www.adelaidecitycouncil.com/planning-development/building-renovating/building-refurbishment/ (accessed 31 August 2016).

Bluyssen, P.M. and Oliveira-Fernandes, E. *et al*. (1994). European indoor air quality audit project in 56 office buildings. *Indoor Air* 6(4): 221–238.

Callinan, T.M., Noonan, J., and Garnys, V. (2015) A 2014 case study for a commercial office building portfolio of 25 Australian buildings. In *Proceedings of Healthy Buildings 2015 America*, pp. 448–451.

City of Melbourne (2013) *Property Market Report*, September. Available at: http://nla.gov.au/nla.arc-151194 (accessed 31 August 2016).

City of Melbourne (2016) *1200 Buildings*. Available at: www.melbourne.vic.gov.au/business/sustainable-business/1200-buildings/Pages/1200-buildings.aspx (accessed 31 August 2016).

Colliers International Australia/New Zealand Office Tenant Survey Report (2010). Available at: www.colliers.co.nz

Economist Intelligence Unit (2016) *The World's Most Liveable Cities*. Available at: www.economist.com/blogs/graphicdetail/2016/08/daily-chart-14 (accessed 31 August 2016).

Fisk, W.J. (2000) Health and productivity gains from better indoor environments and their relationship with building energy efficiency. *Annual Review of Energy and the Environment*, 25(1):537–566.

Fisk, W.J., Black, D. and Brunner, G. (2011) Benefits and costs of improved IEQ in US offices. *Indoor Air*, 21(5): 357–367.

Fisk, W.J., Brunner, G. and Doug, B. (2011) Benefits and cost of increasing ventilation rates in U.S. offices. Proceedings of the 12th International Conference on Indoor Air Quality and Climate—Indoor Air, Austin, TX, USA, 5–10 June 2011; Paper ID: 219.

Fisk, W.J., Seppänen, O., Faulkner, D. and Huang, J. (2003) Cost benefit analysis of ventilation control strategies in an office building. In *Proceedings of the Healthy Buildings 2003 Conference*, Singapore, Volume 3, pp. 361–366.

Green Building Council of Australia (2006) *500 Collins Street*. Available at: http://www.gbca.org.au/uploads/73/1609/500_Collins_St.pdf (accessed 31 August 2016).

Jurelionis, A. (2015) EP-OP Method for cost-benefit analysis of improved indoor climate and reduced energy consumption in office buildings: case studies. Proceedings of Healthy Building Europe 2015 Paper_ID406.

Leijten, J. (2002) Binnenmilieu, productiviteit en ziekteverzuim [The inside environment, productivity and sick leave]. *Facilities Management*, 15(103): 17–21.

OECD (Organisation for Economic Co-operation and Development) (2001) *Measuring Productivity: OECD Manual: Measurement of Aggregate and Industry-level Productivity Growth*. Paris: OECD.

OECD (Organisation for Economic Cooperation and Development) (2008) *OECD Factbook 2008: Economic, Environmental and Social Statistics*. Paris: OECD.

OECD (Organisation for Economic Cooperation and Development) (2015) *OECD Compendium of Productivity Indicators 2015*, Paris: OECD Publishing, http://dx.doi.org/10.1787/pdtvy-2015-en

Paevere, P. and Brown, S. (2008) *Indoor Environment Quality and Occupant Productivity in the CH2 Building: Post-Occupancy Summary*. March, CSIRO, Report No. USP2007/23, 2008.

Reeder, M. (2011) Want to keep your employees? Try better benefits. Available at: http://blogs.reuters.com/small-business/2011/01/14/want-to-keep-your-employees-try-better-benefits/ (accessed 1 September 2016).

REHVA (2006) *Indoor Climate and Productivity in Offices.* Brussels: REHVA.

Reserve Bank of Australia (2010) *Structural Change in the Australian Economy.* September. Available at: www.rba.gov.au/publications/bulletin/2010/sep/1.html. (accessed 31 August 2016).

SGS Economics and Planning (2015) *GDP by Major Capital City — Australian Cities Accounts 2014–15.* Available at: www.sgsep.com.au/publications/gdp-major-capital-city-2014–2015 (accessed 31 August 2016).

Skopek, S. (2014) *Green + Productive Workplace: The Office of the Future . . . Today.* London: JLL.

Sullivan, J.T., Baird, G. and Donn, M.R. (2013) *Measuring Productivity in the Office Workplace: Final Report.* Wellington, New Zealand: Centre for Building Performance Research, Victoria University.

Valancius, R., Jurelionis, A. and Dorosevas, V. (2013) Method for cost-benefit analysis of improved indoor climate conditions and reduced energy consumption in office buildings. *Energies,* 6(9): 4591–4606.

Wargocki, P., Seppänen, O., Andersson, J., Boestra, A,. Clements-Croome, D., Fitzner, K. and Hanssen, S.O. (2006) *Indoor climate and Productivity in Offices: How to Integrate Productivity in Life Cycle Costs Analysis of Building* Services. Brussels: REHVA.

World Green Building Council (2014) *Health, Wellbeing & Productivity in Offices.* London: WGBC.

Part III

Experiential evidence from surveys and building case studies

Chapter 16

A visual language of the workplace
New planning principles for modularized work

Peter A. Bacevice, Hannah Beveridge and Liz Burow

Introduction

Contemporary popular, professional, and academic discourse is actively engaging with new ways to understand the nature of work and the workplace. Work is a complex economic, social, and vocational pursuit that is fundamental to human nature. Seen from our professional perspective through the interdisciplinary practice of design, architecture, research, and scholarship, work and the workplace are topics to be understood in order to shape a more positive and fulfilling experience of both – and to tell compelling stories of these experiences and change within them.

As organizations come to terms with "new ways of working" driven by all matters of economic and societal change, we engage with leaders in discussions around how to leverage the workplace and its design as strategic business tools. A well-designed workplace serves people. It delights them in unexpected ways. It can symbolize an organization's investment in people and work process efficiency. The workplace is a latent part of the daily rhythms and routines of people, sometimes going unnoticed unless it poses barriers to productivity or engagement. People can often point to elements of the workplace that don't work, but we often find that they require additional tools and language to see the connection between workplace design and work patterns, and to understand how space can have a positive influence on the output and experience of work.

The aim of this chapter is to introduce the reader to what we see as fundamental changes in the nature of work and how the built environment is being used in new ways to shape a more positive work experience for people. We aim to give readers a sense of how we, as strategists, build language and tools that help visualize a strategic link between workplace design and the changing work patterns that define the reality of today's economic landscape.

We argue that the nature of professional work practices is increasingly defined by a more modular and autonomous approach to the organization of work flow. Consequently, workplace design is evolving to accommodate these changes through the utilization of more modular planning principles and the introduction of innovative space types that support more flexible and fluid ways of working. The chapter is structured as follows:

1   We introduce the concept of modularization and summarize what we see as fundamental changes to the nature of work. More precisely, the nature of work implies the organization of work, its institutional patterning, and its relationship to the market economy where it happens.
2   We discuss the implications of these changes on people and their everyday work patterns. Because people are the root of organizational life, we extend our analysis to the implications on organizations and collective work patterns.

3   We introduce our Collaboration and Quiet Index – a framework that enables users to align common spatial characteristics with common aspects of work patterns. We provide two short case studies that illustrate the strategic alignment of work patterns and space.

4   We conclude this chapter with implications for the future and other changes to the language of the workplace.

In recognizing what we set out to accomplish in this chapter, it is necessary for us to establish some key definitions and limits to our effort. While we do not seek to exclude anyone from gaining insight on what we write throughout this chapter, we direct our efforts to the ways that work is experienced by individuals in traditionally corporate, creative, or other institutionalized professions (Meyer and Rowan 1977). When we speak of the workplace, we primarily focus on what would be commonly perceived to be office work, as opposed to a factory or other highly specialized work settings, such as hospitals, retail stores, or other service-based settings.

As authors, each of us is a member of the strategy team within a global architectural practice. In practicing our mission – "our work tells your story" – we aim to discover the unique attributes of our client organizations and their users, to elicit the work patterns and practices that shape their daily experiences, and to develop strategies and guidelines to help our clients use space as a tool to support users and their business. Each one of us is also independently engaged within broader academic discourse through teaching and research. Our perspectives shared here stem from our work with clients, students, colleagues, and other researchers. This work reflects our shared passion for understanding the drivers that motivate people to pursue their professional goals and ambitions. We use participatory and empathic design research methods (Laurel, 2003; Leonard and Rayport, 1997) in our engagements. We believe in disseminating what we learn as a way to engage with the broader community and to invite feedback that challenges and refines our own thinking. This chapter is part of our ongoing efforts to do just that. While this chapter draws from an interdisciplinary landscape and engages with a broad base of theoretical scholarship, we use our limited space here to arrive at practical summaries that we hope will enrich the reader's appreciation with the possibilities of workplace design.

The modularization of work

We summarily describe the current state of the workplace in terms of the accelerating pace by which companies abandon the most hierarchical forms of organization and adopt looser and more decentralized structures and platforms (Davis, 2016; Vallas, 1999). In doing so, the link between space and organizational status is diminishing. Historically, the spatial division of labor (Walker, 1985) would be visible through the size and accessibility of offices, which would indicate the status of the occupants and suggest some aspect of their roles and power. Interior plans correlated with social categories and roles (Hillier and Hanson, 1984). Contemporary spatial division of labor is marked by a more modular and work-pattern-based approach to planning. Instead of planning for roles and social structure, space is planned for projects and work patterns – where people have the autonomy and agency to self-organize and define how space should work for them – either inside or outside of the office; online, or offline.

Two notable outcomes of this change are reshaping the experience of professional work. The first outcome is the emergence of alternative economic models that reorganize work on a peer-to-peer and project-to-project basis (Bauer and Gegenhuber, 2015; Davis, 2016; Sundararajan, 2016). While some of these changes are observable in the evolution of sharing economy and platform capitalism (Davis, 2016) business models at the individual consumer level, these changes are also affecting the nature of work in larger organizations. What it describes is a modularization of knowledge work into discrete tasks that can be accomplished by individuals working as freelancers or independent contractors or working as members of short-term project teams within a more structured organization or network setting. This modularization of knowledge work enables greater levels of individual or team-level autonomy about how to structure work tasks in order to maximize the efficient execution of those tasks.

The second outcome is a growing trend of capturing new forms of value from under-utilized real estate (Duffy, 2008; Lacy and Rutqvist, 2015; Laing, 2013). Several new business models have emerged in recent years that monetize under-utilized real estate and market those spaces as work environments to individual users and larger organizations. One notable example is the emergence of coworking spaces (Garrett, Spreitzer and Bacevice, 2014; Spinuzzi, 2012) that provide shared workspace and a community-focused atmosphere to autonomous workers – including freelancers, entrepreneurs, and people working remotely for other companies. Coworking offers corporate real estate leaders options for providing space to individuals or small groups of people in a very flexible way without the need to sign leases or maintain infrastructure. Coworking also offers building owners a new option for monetizing space without needing to attract a traditional organization.

Office buildings are not the only example of real estate modularization. For example, one application operates a platform that lets users find space in restaurants during off-peak hours, effectively creating part-time coworking spaces when those restaurants would otherwise be sitting empty. Hotels are also evolving as providers of workspace. While hotels have traditionally offered meeting and conference facilities to out-of-town groups and conference organizers, many chains are increasingly re-configuring their meeting and public spaces for short-term use by local groups or users seeking an alternative to a coffee shop.

Even amidst the rise of coworking and the otherwise on-demand availability of space beyond a traditional office setting, the office has not disappeared. Instead, the evolution of office design, the emergence of coworking space, and the proliferation of other wi-fi-equipped publicly available spaces collectively contribute to a spatial infrastructure that supports ubiquitous working and even a blurring of work and other social activities. Consequently, the archetype of a technologically equipped flexible space that offers configuration choice to meet the needs of whatever work or social activity is unfolding in the moment supports the realities of networked professional and social life. Archetypes of space and work modes can be deconstructed to a more modular level and reassembled in a way such that space can be planned to support the micro work patterns that happen within them, while work patterns are sufficiently fluid that they can attach themselves to any one of a range of available spaces and settings inside or outside of any given location.

Changing work patterns

The changes described here affect people and their everyday work patterns in a significant way (Sweet and Meiksins, 2016). In working with users in a range of sectors and professions, we witness how these changes result in greater levels of autonomy in the form of greater control over one's job role as well as more flexibility around where and when work happens (Kelly, Moen and Tranby, 2011). For people working full-time, this means a greater prevalence of working in places outside of an office. This is evidenced by an increase in the number of people working from home, from coworking spaces, or generally on-the-go from a range of spaces (Kelliher and Anderson, 2010; Spreitzer, Garrett and Bacevice, 2015). This autonomy is also evidenced in the growing numbers of people who freelance by choice.

These work patterns are the product of an evolution of several technological and managerial innovations that have unfolded over the last several decades. The changing trajectory of autonomous work roughly parallels the evolution of more sophisticated, cheaper, and user-controlled information and communication technologies that reduce the temporal and location constraints of work while enabling greater levels of asynchrony in work (Lerman and Schmidt, 1999; RAND Corporation, 2004). On the managerial side, responses to global market competition and the pressures to reduce costs have altered the career paths for much of the professional workforce. These changes have meant fewer people staying with one company for their entire career (Farber, 2008) and, instead, frequently changing roles and companies. The worker who once resembled William Whyte's (1956) "organization man" persona is far more likely to work as part of a globally distributed project team or crowdsourced task (Shirky, 2008).

Even as more professional workers establish their careers as freelancers or project workers, the organization is not disappearing. What is changing is the way in which work is organized. In industries where growth depends on continuous innovation of new consumer products and services, the discipline and the department become much less important than the project team. The design thinking approach (Martin, 2009) popularized in business books and contemporary discourse emphasizes the importance of reshuffling teams and involving people in tasks who can bring an outsider's point of view. While common perception might associate design thinking with so-called "creative sectors," such as tech or product design, companies in sectors like finance and insurance are adopting this methodology and realizing the benefits associated with their looser and less hierarchical ways of working.

The "agile" approach to project management and work flow (Highsmith, 2009) is one that fits with a modularized organization of work processes. The agile approach organizes people from different disciplines to work together on the same project team. It also redefines the role of the customer as a stakeholder whose input can refine the final outcome of the project. People working in agile teams experience a balance of both highly focused and highly collaborative work patterns, which change as the project stages evolve. In an agile setting, users have the requisite autonomy to work in the most productive way possible, but they are held accountable in an equitable way for their part of the project and the performance of other team members.

While the use of the agile methodology is well established in the technology sector, we are witnessing a greater adoption of it in a wider range of industries. For example, many financial service companies with which we work have in-house developer and design teams who create new ways to engage with customers through online, mobile, and face-to-face interaction points. We also work with large insurance companies whose growth strategies center on identifying and serving new niche markets, which often involves the reshuffling of teams and expertise in order to cross-pollinate ideas (Brown and Anthony, 2011; Hargadon and Sutton, 2000).

Another example of changing work patterns is witnessed through the growth of employee mobility. A growing number of organizations are breaking the standard practice of assigning one desk seat to each user and introducing programs that support people who work from a range of spaces and locations. Several decades of space utilization study data collected from organizations across a range of sectors indicate that it's not unusual for individually assigned workspace to be occupied less than 50 percent of the time (Worthington, 2009). In some cases, these empty seats are explained by the fact that people are working in the building but may be away from their desk in a meeting or talking elsewhere with a colleague. But for certain groups of users who travel to offsite meetings or who are otherwise on the go, their assigned desks at an office remain unutilized for long stretches of time.

Many organizations are codifying more autonomous ways of working through workplace mobility programs. Mobility programs establish guidelines on the assigning of individual space within an office, the sharing of unassigned space, and the use of technology and online resources for those working outside of the office. Guidelines also define high level workstyle profiles based on the extent of people's internal mobility (within the office) and external mobility (outside of the office). These programs are typically drafted with the support of information technology, human resource, and real estate professionals within the organization. Symbolically, mobility programs are organizational artifacts that legitimize a range of company work patterns within and outside the office environment (see Bechky, 2003). They also reflect an evolution of what previously existed as "telework" or "work from home" programs (Gajendran and Harrison, 2007) that defined a more rigidly defined form of telework. Mobility programs often codify an organization's support for a range of work styles regardless of the time and place of work.

In summary, the changes we describe here are examples of how the organization of work patterns is approached in a modular way. While the fluidity of day-to-day work is nothing new, the affiliation of people and the teams and other structures through which professional work is organized has become increasingly fluid and transient. As work activities and organizational structures are strung together and reshuffled to meet the ebb and flow of business and market fluctuations, architects and designers are, consequently, approaching workplace design in new ways to accommodate this shift. Furthermore, leaders regularly ask us to help them define what it means to create a workplace that attracts people to it, given the choices they have to work from so many other settings beyond a traditional office. When technology enables people to work from anywhere, one key task that strategists and designers face is to help organizations define what it means to create a sense of place of face-to-face interaction in the workplace. Our next section turns to the spatial side of change and describes how the built environment is adapting along these lines.

Adapting the workplace

In describing the evolution of the workplace, we can imagine several traditional spatial archetypes whose configurations suggest specific uses. A large array of cubicles on a floor might suggest a traditional corporate setting of knowledge workers. Large open tables with game rooms nearby and people working from laptops might suggest a tech start-up. A quiet corridor with large offices and plush carpeting might suggest an executive work area. And tall tables with counter stools and a bar might suggest a coffee shop or café. The reality of today's environments is much more complex and ambiguous than these casual descriptions suggest. New designs are rewriting conventional archetypes. CEOs now sit in open plan desks next to the rest of their colleagues. The designs of Wall Street company workspaces and tech company workspaces are beginning to resemble one another because of common work modes. The café or coffee shop is now part of many office settings in urban office towers and in suburban office parks. The actual neighborhood coffee shop is a de facto office for many mobile workers. Hotel lobbies in the hippest of city neighborhoods rival any tech company office for buzz and networking opportunities. The designs of coworking spaces mirror that of some of the most progressive workplace designs in just about any other sector. Even university learning spaces are being designed to mimic the best work environments, while corporate workplaces are incorporating maker-spaces that once were limited to learning environments.

In space planning and design, a key task of a designer is to help clients imagine new possibilities for their space. The process involves engagements that elicit an understanding of how people work and use space – whether that space is in the office or on the go. As organizational life becomes more fluid and as work becomes more modularized, our task as designers and design strategists has evolved in the way we educate and facilitate discussions about space. Just as a typical work day could be seen as modularized – being broken into different activities such as meetings, checking emails, stand-ups, 1-to-1 check-ins, quiet reading – so too can the spaces which support these activities be seen as modular. To help people visualize a connection between work patterns and space, we offer a simple question-based framework for placing activities.

In using this framework, which we define as the *Collaboration and Quiet Index*, we begin by asking users to select a few typical work activities they routinely experience. For example, we might ask people to imagine a weekly team meeting, or an intense period of concentrative work, or a confidential conversation. We then ask them to consider the following variable attributes of a space and place their work activity on the various scales. The outcome of this exercise is an attribute-based description of a space that best supports a given activity.

- *Where does your work happen?* Some activities are best suited when they happen closer to where the team is located, while others are more suitable for happening away from the team. Away from the team could mean located in a centralized work area where other groups mix, or it could mean located offsite where there is value to being in the presence of outsiders. Location can be situated on a scale ranging from *core location* to *peripheral location*, where core and periphery are determined relative to the team in which the work is embedded.

- *Are your work activities best suited to physical boundaries?* One of the most fundamental attributes of space is whether or not it is enclosed by a wall, a door, and/or a ceiling. Likewise, some work activities are suitable for occurring in the open with exposure to other people and activities or in enclosed spaces with a greater degree of physical separation. Boundaries can be situated on a scale ranging from *open* to *enclosed*, where variability is based on elements that bound a space.

- *What level of exposure is suitable for your work?* While boundaries such as walls, doors, and ceilings can enclose a space, each one of those boundaries can be either *transparent* or *solid*. The use of glass can increase the transparency of a space and provide a line of sight into it. Glass or other materials can create a semi-transparent or opaque space that allows light to penetrate while blocking sightlines. Some work activities benefit from the maximum privacy that an enclosed space can offer, while other activities benefit from being seen or overheard by others.

- *How many people are involved in your work?* Work activities are undertaken by individuals and groups. When supporting multiple people, a space can be described based on the number of people it accommodates (capacity) and the amount of space per person it provides (density). Capacity and density can be situated on a scale from *low* to *high*.

- *What kind of technology do you need to do your work?* Some activities such as virtual meetings require sophisticated audio/video technologies to make them happen. Alternatively, some activities require nothing more than a simple whiteboard with markers. Technology varies on a scale from *high-tech* to *low-tech*, where the range is determined relative to the tools needed for the most productive work session. Spaces can greatly vary in the amount of technology with which they are equipped.

- *What is the duration of your work?* Work activities vary greatly in length. While some spaces are more suitable for quick meetings, others are more suitable for lingering. The temporal characteristics of a space can be situated on a scale ranging from *short-term* to *long-term* levels of use or occupancy.

- *What is the mood of your work?* A formal meeting with a client differs from an all-hands meeting of a team. Work moods extensively vary, and spaces can vary to the extent that they *create calm* or *generate buzz*. Similarly, they can draw your attention inward, or they can focus it outward.

We often use these questions in workshops to help users map their work day through a series of spaces (Figure 16.1). As part of our approach, we use a series of image cards that feature the attributes of the scales described above (Figure 16.2). The visuals are a sensemaking tool that enable the user to mentally situate their work along a spectrum of possible spaces and to generate discussions about the assumptions behind their choices. The answers to these questions help us calibrate the right mixture of spaces types within a spectrum of collaborative and quiet settings that support users' current and desired ways of working. It provides us with a visual vocabulary that anchors subsequent discussions in the design process.

To understand the saliency of these questions to the planning and design of workplaces for today's modular ways of working, we will share a few brief examples of how we applied this approach with specific organizations.

Our first example is a large technology company relocating to a new flagship workplace in a major urban location. The company needed a space that would bring disparate teams from around the city into a consolidated office. We engaged in a 4-month-long discovery process

Figure 16.1 Example workshop engagement

Figure 16.2 Collaboration and Quiet Index engagement cards

where we interviewed major groups, facilitated a series of hands-on workshops, and convened multiple staff town hall meetings. The goal was to understand the business drivers and priorities for the groups as well as to determine any unique requirements for specific groups. One of the major requirements of the project was to create zones for employees, customers, and other visitors that often included students and others from the community. The way the teams used space necessitated an activity-based workplace that provided a range of shared collaborative settings to be used for project work. Although everyone was provided with an assigned seat, the number of collaborative seats per person was considerably higher than in their existing space and consumed a greater percentage of the total square footage compared to their existing offices. The discovery engagement revealed the importance of buzz and transparency within these spaces, but with clearly defined boundaries for user groups beyond the employee population. And despite this being a technology company, discussions revealed that users wanted some key spaces to be decidedly low-tech to support certain types of hands-on design thinking activities.

As the discovery process unfolded, one unexpected learning outcome we uncovered was that the company actually had more space than they initially required. This created a planning challenge. On the one hand, the company intended for the space to be one they would "grow into" over time. On the other hand, there was a concern that too much space would make the workplace feel dead of activity. Once this finding was validated, our team engaged in a number of exercises to imagine alternate ways of using the extra space. This challenge created new opportunities. The exercises revealed that the additional space could be consolidated to an entire floor and would actually allow the company to expand its community outreach and innovation programs by providing them with a coworking-like setting on that floor. The company recognized that it would eventually need that floor for employee workspace. Yet they also realized that configuring the space in the near term for academic groups engaged in design thinking activities would actually give them flexibility in the long term in providing space for project teams. The questions we asked revealed that the academic users of the space required a setting that offered more buzz than formality, smaller spaces rather than large ones, and spaces that were more open than enclosed. In the solution, part of the floor would be configured as a large hands-on workshop space that could be used by both employees and students. These requirements were similar to the employee requirements, thus revealing the compatibility between the near-term and long-term planning scenarios. Boundaries were an important variable that the company considered when planning this part of the space. They wanted to provide some element of transparency between students and employees while still controlling the level of student access to the employee workspace and the separate customer space.

Ultimately, the engagement illustrated that the company's needs went beyond the simple statement of "we need more collaborative space." Instead, the design successfully supported the fluidity of headcount requirements between day 1 and day 2 occupancy, the fluidity of project team configurations, and the needs of external users whose presence contributed to the company's sense of place and destination in the work environment.

Our second example is also a large technology company. This company is rapidly growing through the acquisition of smaller companies. The company's workflow is characterized by the agile methodology described earlier in this chapter. Designing to support agile is a major organizational priority. However, many of the companies they acquire vary with respect to their place on the agile learning curve. The company wanted to create a process for rolling out new agile work environments that would provide teams with a framework for creating a suitable agile-supported work environment that could also be reconfigured as project teams evolve. For organizations that embrace agile methodology – where collaboration and communication are the core premises of their work flow – the ability to switch between tasks, acoustic levels, and team configurations is of paramount necessity.

The questions we asked in this engagement focused more on identifying the basic spatial elements of how to support the workflows of agile project teams. We also asked questions to quantify how much space teams required. We employed a hands-on "sandbox" activity that provided teams with a fixed amount of space on a floor plan that they could fill with components that would support agile work flow. We also ran a series of look and feel workshops to gauge their preferences for aesthetic and layout elements. After concluding this process, we developed a "kit of parts" that the company could provide to teams. The kit of parts included a mix of furniture and layout options that teams could configure in any way they desired within the constraints of defined boundaries. As a consequence, the spaces would be sufficiently modular to support the workflows of teams and then could be reconfigured to meet the needs of new groups as project teams were reshuffled. The outcome also provided a roadmap for more efficiently integrating newly acquired teams into this company's broader workflow process. Teams were given sufficient autonomy to self-organize their own space while staying within the parameters defined by the corporate real estate team.

Rather than assigning the same mix of space types to every organization, engaging with users to understand the link between behavior, business processes, and space leads to a more informed design outcome. The establishment of an organization's business goals and the understanding of its culture and aspirations can allow the workplace to support users in their day-to-day endeavors and ensure the organization continues to support desired behaviors. Good work-place design sees an alignment of the activities processes and cultural life of the end users of the space, ultimately leading to maximized utility and efficiency of real estate assets.

Implications

In this chapter, we have outlined a new language for understanding and visualizing the work-place in the context of the broader economic shifts affecting the organization of work. We have illustrated our narrative with examples of how organizations have realigned their work environments to these new ways of working. In our conclusion, we outline some additional language for how to conceptualize the workplace.

First, our chapter has underscored the importance of approaching the workplace through the lens of the project team. The modularization of work into smaller units and more discrete tasks (and the platforms and processes that enable its coordination) shifts the unit of organization away from the department and discipline. Project teams can be understood through analyzing the nodes of a network, which map informal relationships. In contrast, departments and disciplines are mapped through formal organizational charts. As companies increasingly differentiate through solutions for customers and clients, they increasingly organize as project-based organizations. Bauer offers a way to understand the structuring of such organizations: "They succeed in creating a continuous flow of knowledge and people across projects, thereby lowering employee uncertainty and enhancing utilization of capacity. In short, these firms are integrated through rhythm rather than through structure" (2007, p. 45).

A team that is coupled to a particular project may be ephemeral, which necessitates a level of flexibility in the spaces where this work happens. Using a more cogent metaphor, March (1995) refers to disposable organizations that emerge with an efficient means of addressing a particular challenge and subsequently disappear when they are either no longer able to efficiently address the challenge or when the challenge is solved. Political campaigns are a good example of this. Political campaigns or other such team structures use temporary space and move fluidly from place to place. Today's real estate market offers these kinds of organizations an array of on-demand options, including various coworking platforms, for situating their teams in space in an ad-hoc way. While not every team mirrors the transience of a political campaign, the way they use space bears similarity to other project teams.

Second, we have referred to *users* rather than *employees*. This choice is more than semantic. When approaching the planning and design of any space, referencing users offers the designer a more encompassing term for the people occupying space and their relationship to the entity for whom the space is being designed. Any given workplace may house people who are actively employed by the organization or merely associated with the organization as a customer, part-ner, student, or visitor. Likewise, people work from spaces that are not solely designed as work environments and may mix with others who use the space for different purposes.

Third, we propose that the term workplace could yield to a more descriptive term, which we label *work-enabled place*. The semantic difference is rooted in the changing real estate land-scape where building and space use typologies blur and increasingly accommodate a variety of users in a work capacity. When restaurants and hotel lobbies double as workplaces during different times of day or in different zones of the space, the term "work-enabled place" applies. The question-based framework we outlined earlier in this chapter is applicable when planning and designing such spaces because it offers a way to understand the limits of the nature of work activities that could be reasonably supported. For example, a hotel lobby is not likely to support very private work activities because the enclosed space that such work might require would conflict with the more social affordances of the setting. Work-enabled places inherently exhibit functional trade-offs that balance the needs of various user groups.

Finally, we propose that the new language of the workplace necessitates a new way of looking at planning metrics. The planning and design process is moving away from the assumption that each user requires one assigned desk seat. While assigned workspace is not disappearing from the layouts of traditional offices, designers and planners are using metrics such as collaborative seats per person, shared vs. owned seats, and open vs. enclosed meeting room spaces to create more flexible layouts that offer choices to users and options depending on their work mode at any given time. And while standard metrics such as 120 square feet might define the standard size for an enclosed private office, a truly modular floor plan would easily accommodate a transition of that space from an office to any one of a number of meeting room designs as needs evolve. In other words, quantifiable metrics offer a starting point for defining the optimal size of a spatial footprint, but within any given footprint are a growing range of archetypal configurations that support a range of work patterns.

To conclude, the modularization of work necessitates a new language for the planning and design of workplaces. Innovations in the business of real estate further extend the applicability of this new language to a wider range of environments and settings. As these changes evolve, the importance of end user engagement grows because of the coinciding variability of work practices.

References

Bauer, R.M. (2007) Organizations as orientation systems: some remarks on the aesthetic dimension of organizational design. In Shamiyeh, M. and DOM Research Laboratory, (eds), *Organizing for Change – Profession: Integrating Architectural Thinking in Other Fields*. Boston: Birkhaüser, pp. 35–49.

Bauer, R.M. and Gegenhuber, T. (2015) Crowdsourcing: global search and the twisted roles of consumers and producers. *Organization*, 22(5): 661–681.

Bechky, B.A. (2003) Object lessons: workplace artifacts as representations of occupational jurisdiction. *American Journal of Sociology*, 109(3): 720–752.

Brown, B. and Anthony, S.D. (2011) How P&G tripled its innovation success rate. *Harvard Business Review*, 89(6): 64–72.

Davis, G.F. (2016) *The Vanishing American Corporation: Navigating the Hazards of a New Economy*. Oakland, CA: Berrett-Koehler.

Duffy, F. (2008) *Work and the City*. London: Black Dog Publishing,

Farber, H.S. (2008) *Employment Insecurity: The Decline in Worker-Firm Attachment in the United States*. Princeton, NJ: Princeton University, USA Center for Economic Policy Studies.

Gajendran, R.S. and Harrison, D.A. (2007) The good, the bad, and the unknown about telecommuting: meta-analysis of psychological mediators and individual consequences. *Journal of Applied Psychology*, 92(6): 1524–1541.

Garrett, L., Spreitzer, G. and Bacevice, P. (2014) Co-constructing a sense of community at work: the emergence of community in coworking spaces. *Academy of Management Proceedings*, Academy of Management, Philadelphia, 14004.

Hargadon, A. and Sutton, R.I. (2000) Building an innovation factory. *Harvard Business Review*, 78(3): 157–166.

Highsmith, J. (2009) *Agile Project Management: Creating Innovative Products*. Harlow: Pearson Education.

Hillier, B. and Hanson, J. (1984) *The Social Logic of Space*. New York: Cambridge University Press.

Kelliher, C. and Anderson, D. (2010) Doing more with less? Flexible working practices and the intensification of work. *Human Relations*, 63(1): 83–106.

Kelly, E.L., Moen, P. and Tranby, E. (2011) Changing workplaces to reduce work-family conflict schedule control in a white-collar organization. *American Sociological Review*, 76(2): 265–290.

Lacy, P. and Rutqvist, J. (2015) The sharing platform business model: sweating idle assets. In *Waste to Wealth:* New York: Palgrave Macmillan, pp. 84–98.

Laing, A. (2013) *Work and Workplaces in the Digital City.* New York: Center for Urban Real Estate, Columbia University, USA.

Laurel, B. (ed.) (2003) *Design Research: Methods and Perspectives.* Cambridge, MA; MIT Press.

Leonard, D. and Rayport, J.F. (1997) Spark innovation through empathic design. *Harvard Business Review,* 75(6): 102–115.

Lerman, R.I. and Schmidt, S.R. (1999) *An Overview of Economic, Social, and Demographic Trends Affecting the U.S. Labor Market.* Washington, DC: The Urban Institute.

March, J.G. (1995) The future, disposable organizations, and the rigidities of imagination. *Organization,* 2(3–4): 427–440.

Martin, R. (2009) *The Design of Business: Why Design Thinking Is the Next Competitive Advantage.* Boston: Harvard Business Press.

Meyer, J.W. and Rowan, B. (1977) Institutionalized organizations: formal structure as myth and ceremony. *American Journal of Sociology,* 83(2): 340–363.

Shirky, C. (2008) *Here Comes Everybody: The Power of Organizing Without Organizations,* New York: Penguin Press.

Spinuzzi, C. (2012) Working alone together: coworking as emergent collaborative activity. *Journal of Business and Technical Communication,* 26(4): 399–441.

Spreitzer, G., Garrett, L. and Bacevice, P. (2015) Should your company embrace coworking? *MIT Sloan Management Review,* 57(1): 27–29.

Sundararajan, A. (2016) *The Sharing Economy: The End of Employment and the Rise of Crowd-Based Capitalism.* Cambridge, MA: MIT Press.

Sweet, S. and Meiksins, P. (2016) *Changing Contours of Work: Jobs and Opportunities in the New Economy,* 3rd edn. Los Angeles: Sage.

The RAND Corporation (2004) *Research Brief: The Future at Work: Trends and Implications.* Santa Monica, CA. Available at: www.rand.org/content/dam/rand/pubs/research_briefs/2005/RB5070.pdf.

Vallas, S.P. (1999) Rethinking post-Fordism: the meaning of workplace flexibility. *Sociological Theory,* 17(1): 68–101.

Walker, R.A. (1985) Class, division of labour and employment in space. In Gregory, D. and Urry, J. (eds) *Social Relations and Spatial Structures.* New York: St. Martin's Press, pp. 164–189.

Whyte, W. (1956) *The Organization Man.* New York: Simon & Schuster.

Worthington, J. (2009) Urban form for a sustainable future: how sustainable is distributed working in the networked city. *Journal of Green Building,* 4(4): 148–157.

Chapter 17

The people-building interface

It's a two-way street

Judith Heerwagen, Kevin Kampschroer, Bryan C. Steverson and Brian Gilligan

We shape our buildings and thereafter they shape us.

(Winston Churchill)

Those of us in the building business often quote Winston Churchill's observation about buildings. We, too, believe that the design and operation of our buildings shape what we do, how we feel, and how productive we are. But this is only half the truth. People also shape their buildings. They influence building performance and the use of space. They alter conditions to fit their needs and abandon spaces that don't work.

This chapter focuses on this two-way interaction between building inhabitants and the spaces they occupy. We provide an overview of key findings from research on occupant experience in office buildings, drawing largely on research conducted by the US General Services Administration (GSA), supplemented by other relevant findings. The chapter is not intended to be a comprehensive review of the research literature. Much of that is covered in other chapters in this book. Rather, we provide some insights into the people-building interface and explore how this knowledge can shape the design and operations of buildings to achieve both sustainability goals and optimal supports for human health, performance, and well-being.

The key findings from this body of research, identified below, are discussed in more detail in this chapter:

1 Buildings are not inert. They can have medicinal effects that influence our physiological, psychological, and cognitive functioning.
2 Building inhabitants are not passive recipients of design. They often take matters into their own hands, changing the environment to fit their personal needs.
3 Open workplace design has consistent benefits but may require organizational interventions for benefits to be realized.
4 Workplace acoustics consistently receive low ratings across comfort studies. But human-generated noise may be an important factor in productive work. It's complicated.

This chapter will present findings on these four topic areas and then discuss the larger issue of designing more effectively for the people-building interface.

Buildings can have medicinal effects

We know from decades of research that poor building conditions are associated with a range of illnesses, with the most attention on respiratory and neurological problems associated with poor air quality and indoor contaminants (Ten Brinke *et al.*, 1998; Apte *et al.*, 2000;

Institute of Medicine, 2004). There is also evidence from numerous studies that poor indoor environmental quality is also associated with negative psychological, cognitive, and social outcomes (Evans, 2003). A review by Klitzman and Stillman (1989) shows that noise, ergonomic conditions, poor air quality, and lack of privacy are associated with reduced mental health and overall satisfaction in work environments. A more recent review of both offices and hospitals by Rashid and Zimring (2008) also identified the negative effect of numerous individual ambient and spatial factors on cognitive performance, emotional functioning, social support, and stress.

In recent years, attention has begun to shift from studying the negative impacts of the indoor environments to focus on whether – and how – the indoor environment can be designed and operated to improve health and well-being, and not just reduce risks (Sternberg, 2009). In other words, can buildings be more like medicine?

Can a workplace re-design reduce stress?

A GSA research project, conducted by researchers from the National Institutes of Health (NIH), addressed this question in a study of two workspaces in the Denver Federal Center. One was a typical workspace in the building and the other was renovated with the goal of reducing employee stress and creating a better place to work (Thayer *et al.*, 2010). Prior to the NIH research, a GSA post-occupancy evaluation of the building showed that newly renovated workspaces had more positive employee ratings than the un-renovated spaces. However, the study did not incorporate health outcomes so it was not possible to determine if the re-design had benefits beyond improved satisfaction.

The old workspace had mixed types of furnishings, poor overall lighting, and high panel cubicles that blocked access to daylight and views to the outdoor landscape. Some spaces had low frequency noise from the HVAC system. The design changes in the new space included reduced HVAC noise, workstation panels with glazing to enhance access to indoor daylight and views, a sound masking system, and new furnishings. The building also had a centralized break area and a basement space with a pool table, couches, and other amenities paid for by funds raised by the employees. These amenities were available to employees in both of the spaces studied by the NIH team.

The NIH research focused on physiological and subjective measures of stress. Study participants wore heart rate monitors for five days at work and at home to assess heart rate variability, a widely used measure of stress. Study participants also provided salivary cortisol samples five times a day, and responded to a brief electronic survey hourly during work hours to assess psychological functioning.

The physiological results showed that study participants located in the new space had a healthier higher heart rate pattern (lower stress) and lower cortisol levels both at work and at home than those who were located in the un-renovated space (Thayer *et al.*, 2010). The experience sampling, however, did not find differences in subjective measures of stress across the two spaces, suggesting that people were not consciously aware of experiencing physiological stress.

The Denver research was not able to identify the specific environmental factors that contributed to the differences in stress outcomes between the two spaces. A current GSA project is designed to address this gap. The project focuses on identifying the environmental factors (both ambient and spatial) that influence the stress response and other health outcomes. A research team at the University of Arizona Institute on Place and Well-Being is heading up the project. The study is linking, in real time, measures of the ambient environment (thermal, light, acoustics, and air quality) to measures of heart rate variability and movement patterns. In addition to the environmental sensing and HRV, the research methods also include experience sampling and spatial characterization. The spatial analysis identifies key differences in the physical environment, enabling the team to assess how this variation is linked to variation in health outcomes. The study sites are federal government offices that vary in overall design approaches, from cubicles to open plan benching and private offices. Research findings are expected in 2017.

Can indoor daylight be a health benefit?

We have known for a long time that people prefer to be in daylit spaces and value the changes in light quality over the day and season (Heerwagen, *et al.*, 1991a; Galasiu and Veitch, 2006; Heerwagen, 2010). Research has also begun to explore the non-visual health effects of light. For instance, in a study of daylight in hospitals, Benedetti *et al* (2001) found that bi-polar patients in bright rooms stayed in the hospital 3.67 fewer days on average than those who were in rooms with less daylight. Similar results were found by Beauchemin and Hayes (1996) for psychiatric in-patients. Those in the brightest rooms stayed in the hospital 2.6 fewer days on average. However, neither of these studies provides data on the actual light levels in the patient rooms, so it is difficult to draw conclusions about actual daylight exposure levels.

More recent research in a Pittsburgh hospital measured room brightness levels linked to health outcomes. Walch *et al.* (2005) studied 89 patients who had elective cervical and spinal surgery. Half of the patients were located on the bright side of the hospital while the other half were in a hospital wing with an adjacent building that blocked sunlight from entering the rooms. The study team conducted extensive photometric measures of light in each room, including light levels at the windows, on the wall opposite the patient's bed, and at the head of the bed, which would have been at or near the patient's eye level. They also gathered data on patients' use of medication and their psychological functioning the day after surgery and at discharge. Results showed that patients in the brightest rooms took 22 percent less analgesic medicine and experienced less stress. This resulted in a 21 percent decrease in the costs of medicine for those in the brightest rooms.

A study by Boubekri *et al.* (2014) focused on the health impacts of being in windowed vs windowless office spaces. They found that workers in windowless spaces scored poorer on psychological well-being and sleep quality than those in windowed spaces. The authors attributed the differences to greater light exposure in windowed environments. However, they did not provide data on actual light exposures of the study participants.

A research project underway by GSA is addressing the light and health connection in office buildings where interior conditions are variable and where occupants move around much more during the day than hospital patients. Together with the Rensselaer Polytechnic Institute's Lighting Research Center (LRC), GSA is assessing the impact of indoor light (both daylight and electric light) on circadian functioning and affective outcomes. The study includes extensive photometric analysis of the building spaces as well as individual light exposures over a seven-day period in both summer and winter.

The project began with a simple fact: people in industrial societies spend, on average, 86.7 percent of their time indoors, including time at home and at work, 5.5 percent in vehicles and only 7.6 percent outdoors (Klepeis *et al.*, 1996). During the winter months with short days, this means that people will experience daylight primarily indoors.

The GSA project initially focused on the health impacts of daylight, testing the hypothesis that people who work in spaces with more daylight should have better sleep quality at night as well as more positive moods and alertness during the day. The research was conducted in five federal buildings, all designed with daylight as a key factor. A total of 128 study participants wore a device created by RPI (called a "daysimeter") that calculates the amount of circadian stimulus participants received both at work and elsewhere over a seven-day period. The circadian stimulus calculation takes into account the intensity, duration, spectral characteristics, and timing of light entering the eye.

The research team also conducted extensive photometric analysis of each of the buildings to identify the "circadian stimulus potential" of the overall space by measuring a variety of interior locations as well as daylight entering the windows. Outcome measures included sleep quality, mood, and other psychological factors assessed with standardized questionnaires (Figueiro and Rae, 2016). The participants were studied in both the summer and winter months to assess seasonal impacts in five federal buildings, two in the Pacific Northwest, one in western Colorado, and two in Washington, DC.

The results partially supported the hypothesis, but there were numerous surprises:

- Participants received more light at work than anywhere else.
- Participants who had the most circadian stimulus during the day scored better on measures of sleep quality and mood, compared to those who received the lowest circadian stimulus.
- When we took a closer look at the data, participants who had high levels of circadian stimulus in the morning fell asleep faster (as much as 30 minutes faster) than those with lower circadian stimulus levels. Those with lower levels of circadian stimulus also scored lower on sleep quality and mood. This suggests there are health benefits for people when they receive sufficient circadian stimulus at work.
- While the participants who were closest to the windows received the most circadian light, the majority experienced low circadian stimulus at work and many were in biological darkness for much of the day.
- Interior design matters to circadian stimulation. High workstation panels and other furnishings block the penetration of light into the space with the result that only those nearest the windows get sufficient daylight for health.
- Occupant behavior can enhance or impede circadian stimulation. Shade use and the strong tendency to sit perpendicular to the windows to reduce glare also reduce the amount of light entering the eye.

Because the "daylight hypothesis" was only partially supported, the GSA research is currently testing electric light solutions to increase circadian stimulation and alertness in deep or windowless spaces in several federal buildings. The study is testing both portable desktop and ceiling-based light solutions using energy-efficient LEDs that can be programmed for spectrum and intensity to optimize health impacts. This phase of the research focuses on windowless spaces and deep interior spaces far from the windows. Overall project results and best practices derived from the findings are expected in 2017.

Building inhabitants are not passive recipients of design

Numerous studies show high levels of discomfort in many office buildings, especially for thermal and acoustical conditions (Heerwagen et al., 1991a; Kim and de Dear, 2013; Newsham et al., 2013). How do people cope with these problems? Do they passively accept conditions or actively modify their environments? Their choices can have significant effects on their comfort and well-being at work, as well as on building performance.

Coping with discomfort

In a study of seven energy-efficient office buildings in Oregon and Washington, Heerwagen *et al.* (1991a) investigated the comfort coping behaviors of 268 occupants who participated in the study. The coping process is an important component of the relationship between people and buildings and is likely to have an impact on stress, performance, and overall experience (Lazarus, 1966; Lazarus and Folkman, 1984). According to Lazarus and Folkman, people have two basic coping options. They can: (1) alter the situation by changing the environment or their behavior or (2) they can alter their emotional and cognitive responses, such as trying to ignore the problem. It is generally considered healthier and more effective to change the situation or one's behavior than to try to alter emotional or cognitive responses that are more resistant to change.

Using the Lazarus and Folkman framework, the researchers found that study participants used different approaches depending upon the comfort problem (Heerwagen *et al.*, 1991b). The different coping behaviors also had different degrees of success, as measured by whether the behavior resolved the discomfort (Table 17.1). The easiest problem to resolve was sunlight discomfort: 84 percent of the study participants said they closed the window blinds. In contrast, fewer than half said they were able to successful resolve thermal or acoustic discomfort.

The Energy Edge study also showed that people actively altered their personal workspaces to enhance their comfort and psychological experience. Of the 268 study participants, 20–30 percent added lamps and heaters or rearranged furniture, while more than 50 percent added plants, posters, or personal artifacts. Numerous other coping behaviors were evident from walkthrough observations in each building, such as disabling light sensors to keep lights on, de-lamping fixtures when ceiling lights produced glare on the computer screen, covering up air vents to reduce overhead drafts, or putting strips of paper on the vents to see whether air was coming out.

Coping with windowless conditions

Extensive research shows that people prefer windowed environments compared to windowless conditions and value the opportunity for views of the outdoor environment as well as the presence of daylight, sunlight and fresh air from operable windows (Heerwagen and Orians, 1986). Numerous studies also show that windowless spaces, compared to windowed spaces, generate

Table 17.1 Occupants' coping behaviors for different comfort problems

Comfort category	Predominant coping approach to discomfort	Percentage saying coping was successful
Sunlight discomfort	*Environmental* – close shades to reduce glare and heat gain	84
Thermal discomfort	*Behavioral* – drink something hot/cold, change clothing, contact a staff person, go for a walk	57
Ventilation discomfort	*Environmental* – open door or window	49
Acoustic discomfort	*Emotional* – try to ignore the problem and concentrate harder, Just put up with it, "there is nothing I can do"	42

Table 17.2 Comparison of décor items used in windowed and windowless office spaces

Décor type	Windowless offices	Windowed offices
Landscape scenes	83	21
Pictures of natural elements (animals, flowers, plants)	51	24
Cityscapes	13	11
Other (memorabilia, wall hangings)	48	26
TOTALS	193	82

more negative health and well-being outcomes (Chang and Chen, 2005; Aires *et al.*, 2010; Raanas *et al.*, 2011) and poor recovery in hospital intensive care units (Wilson, 1972; Keep *et al.*, 1980). Others have found that the window view itself makes a difference to health and well-being (R. Kaplan, 1983; Ulrich, 1984). Views of nature, especially large trees, were associated with reduced stress in Kaplan's study of work environments and more positive recovery from surgery in Ulrich's hospital study. In a laboratory study, Chang and Chen (2005) tested participants in an office-type setting with simulated views and living plants either present or absent. They found that the condition with both a nature view and live plants had the most positive psychological outcomes.

Given the positive benefits of windows and views, how do people in windowless work environments respond to the less than optimal conditions? In a field study that addressed this question, Heerwagen and Orians (1986) hypothesized that people would create surrogate views to compensate for the lack of connection to the outdoors and the natural environment. The study compared the use of visual décor in windowed and windowless offices that were comparable in size and amount of wall space for décor.

The results showed that people in the windowless offices used significantly more visual décor overall, more surrogate views (especially landscapes), and more nature décor (flowers, animals) than those in windowed spaces (Table 17.2). The results suggest that the opportunity for employees to create pleasant visual environments at work may be an unrecognized well-being benefit.

The findings by Heerwagen and Orians were replicated in a study of 286 office workers in Norway (Bringslimark *et al.*, 2011). The Norwegian study found a five times greater odds of having plants and a three times greater odds of having pictures of nature for workers in windowless spaces as compared to windowed spaces.

Open workspace design has consistent benefits, but may require organizational intervention for benefits to be realized

The movement toward more open work environments coincided with and was stimulated by fundamental changes in the nature of work itself. A study on the skill content of jobs related to technological changes, beginning in 1959, found that demand for routine manual and cognitive work steadily declined while the demand for non-routine and interactive cognitive tasks increased (Autor *et al.*, 2003).

Recognizing these changes, designers responded to the challenge with workplace designs that promote many forms of collaboration and interaction (Heerwagen *et al.*, 2004). The result is an office form that is more visually open with better visual access throughout the space, a greater variety of meeting spaces, quiet rooms, shared filing and storage, and circulation systems that enable views into contiguous spaces to support ongoing awareness of work. These features characterize many workplace projects in US federal buildings that were designed to intentionally support collaboration and improve overall employee experience (US General Services Administration, 2009).

Results from pre- and post-occupancy evaluations of six of these federal projects show that more than 50 percent of the survey respondents rated the new workplaces as better for a number of communication and well-being behaviors (Table 17.3). Fewer than 10 percent rated the workplace as worse for these factors (the remaining percentages said there was "no change"). As can be seen, the majority of survey respondents rated both well-being and communication as better in the new spaces. The highest agreement (82 percent) was for "feeling proud to show the office to visitors."

In addition to the survey research, a research team from the Pacific Northwest National Laboratory (PNNL) conducted social network analysis in one workplace project for the US Coast Guard where improved inter-group collaboration was a key goal. The new design focused on co-location of the targeted groups, enhanced internal visibility, and more spaces for interaction and group work. The social network analysis mapped the frequency and type of interaction within and across groups to identify changes in interaction and information flows. In the old space, the four groups worked in different areas in the building and in one case, on different floors. In the new space, the groups were intentionally co-located on the same floor to encourage more frequent and direct interaction. The overall goal was to move work forward more quickly by sharing information and resolving problems in real time.

The social network analysis showed that two of the target groups interacted significantly more in the new workspace, while the other targeted groups did not (PNNL, unpublished presentation). Further investigation found differences in the culture and behaviors of the four groups. The two groups that interacted more in the new space realized the value of increased communication and quickly revised their work patterns to further improve cross-group collaboration.

For the other two groups, differences in culture and work practices made collaboration difficult. The social network analysis showed no changes in frequency or type of interaction after

Table 17.3 Percentage of respondents rating communication and well-being as higher in the new space

Communication benefits	Percentage rating new workspace as better
Ability to share information quickly	66
Ability to locate others when needed	64
Within group communication	62
Overall group productivity	58
Communicating with other groups	57
Awareness of what people are working on	56
Ability to get timely answers to questions	51
Well-being benefits	
Feeling proud to show the office to visitors	82
Feeling proud of the organization	70
Feeling better about my personal well-being	69
Getting to know people better	58

the groups were collocated. In this case, it was clear that workplace design was insufficient to change behavior, and that an organizational intervention was necessary.

Workplace acoustics and human-generated noise

Acoustic conditions are a consistent problem across workplace studies, mostly associated with open plan or cubicle work environments. The challenges faced by the open plan environment, in particular, arise largely from its fundamental goal: to enhance complex collaborative and cognitive work. Collaboration does not occur only in meeting rooms. Studies of where and how people interact consistently show that much interaction is serendipitous and takes place when people come into contact as they move through space or when they see each other due to increased visibility throughout the space (Heerwagen et al., 2004).

A pre- and post-analysis of six GSA workplace projects, comparing a baseline workspace with high partition cubicles to more open workstations with low panels, found that acoustic satisfaction was low in both environments (US General Services Administration, 2009). Only 21 percent of the survey respondents were satisfied with speech privacy in both old and new workspaces.

Despite this low level of satisfaction, when asked about their own acoustic-related behaviors people reported the following:

- 59 percent said they stop and talk to others in the corridors and workspaces.
- 56 percent said they learn a lot by overhearing others' conversations.
- 53 percent said they often have meetings in their personal workstations.

These survey findings are consistent with behavioral observations of employee interactions in a federal building in Philadelphia (Rashid et al., 2006). The workplace was redesigned to enhance collaborative work practices. The study by researchers from the Georgia Institute of Technology found twice as many face-to-face interactions in the newly renovated space compared to the old space. In both the new and old spaces, 80 percent of the interactions took place in or near individual workstations, and not in corridors or informal social spaces intended for such interaction. This is consistent with other research showing that people have many brief, unplanned, standing conversations across the day (Heerwagen et al., 2004).

It is these common, spontaneous interactions that create the majority of acoustic problems in the workplace. Why are these interactions such a problem? The main issues are distraction and interruption to ongoing thought processes. Acoustic distractions also strain attentional capacity, contribute to "cognitive overload syndrome," lead to mental fatigue, and reduce the time for thinking and reflection.

Given the value of everyday behaviors such as getting quick feedback, checking facts, and moving work forward, it may be difficult to eliminate, or even dramatically reduce, the noise irritations that result for others who are trying to do work requiring focused attention. An example from a software engineering firm that tried to implement quiet hours is informative (Perlow, 1999). The engineers found it difficult to get their individual work done due to continuous interruptions from others. As a result, the group's overall productivity suffered. The firm implemented a policy of quiet time that worked well for a while, resulting in better integration of group work and lowered interruptions to individuals. However, people gradually began to ignore quiet time when they needed to talk to someone and the group reverted to their normal behavioral pattern of continuous interruptions. Many organizations have behavioral protocols and rules for working in open plan environments, but survey findings suggest that these rules may not work as well as intended.

To add more complexity to this situation, research by Mehta *et al.* (2013) suggests that ambient noise (at levels that create some discomfort) may enhance creativity. In a series of laboratory experiments that tested the impact of different levels of human-generated noise, the researchers found that moderate levels of ambient noise (70 dB) compared to lower levels (50 dB) enhanced performance on creativity tasks. High noise (80 dB) had a detrimental effect. Their explanation was related to how the people coped cognitively with noise because it is distracting: "we reason that such a moderate distraction, which induces processing difficulty, enhances creativity by prompting abstract thinking" (2013, p. 786).

How can we optimize the interface between people and buildings?

In this chapter, we have looked at how the characteristics and behaviors of people influence their response to work environments and how these human factors may also influence the operational performance of buildings. Despite findings from numerous studies, we lack standards, structures or even approaches to effectively incorporate human factors into building design and operation. Different organizations have different ways of assessing "user needs," but there is no overall framework that is linked to theory, research, or even a big, central idea.

We propose a framework based on Stephen Boyden's theory of "basic human needs" (Boyden, 1971; Heerwagen *et al.*, 1995; Heerwagen, 2006). Although Boyden identifies the cognitive, social, and physical needs that must be supported to enable optimal human health and well-being, he does not identify environmental features and attributes that are likely to support those needs. Using existing research and theory, we propose a set of features associated with each of the basic needs that are relevant to building design, especially office settings.

To illustrate the basic needs approach, we would like to start, not with buildings, but with zoos. Early zoos focused on keeping animals alive in their exhibition cages so human visitors could look at them. After decades of this approach, zookeepers began to realize that many animals survived, but they did not flourish. They failed to reproduce. They often showed signs of boredom and behaved aggressively toward their fellow animals. They languished physically from lack of exercise. What was missing from their zoo habitats? What did the animals need to flourish?

To answer this question, zoos turned to field biologists who studied animals in their natural habitats and social groupings. This partnership produced a major innovation in zoo design – the ecological zoo that incorporates critical features of natural habitats linked to behavioral needs. The new zoo encourages animals to explore, forage, play, build nests, and maintain social relationships that are closer to those they would experience in the wild, including relationships with other species. Construction materials, vegetation, spatial relationships, light, water features, and behavior settings are selected to provide supports and amenities for the animals' physical, psychological and social well-being. Investments in the new design approach paid off. Zoo attendance and memberships have increased across the country. Animals are flourishing, and zoos are now playing a major role in animal conservation efforts around the world.

What if we used the zoo approach to design sustainable, healthy building habitats for people? This would mean starting with fundamental human needs, rather than with the building form and image. It would require understanding what creates a healthy environment in the broad sense, including psychological and social factors as well as physical health.

What makes a good building habitat for people?

Research in behavioral ecology (Boyden, 1971 Heerwagen and Orians, 1993) addresses the evolved links between the specific needs of organisms, the environments they inhabit, and their survival and well-being associated with living in a good vs a poor habitat. Boyden specifically addresses the needs of humans and the links to survival and well-being. Boyden argues that failure to satisfy survival needs may lead to serious illness and death and that failure to satisfy the well-being leads to psychosocial maladjustment and stress-related illnesses.

Well-being needs proposed by Boyden and others (S. Kaplan, 1983; Stokols, 1992; Ulrich, 1993) include several that are relevant to the work environment:

- behavioral choice and control;
- support for a variety of social experiences;
- privacy, retreat, and social separation when desired;
- a pleasing and meaningful sensory environment;
- connection to nature and natural processes;
- cultural and collective meaning and identity.

Table 17.4 (derived from Heerwagen, 2006) identifies features and attributes of buildings that are likely to support these needs and experiences. Many of these features are key elements of sustainable design, an imperative in many organizations, including the US General Services Administration.

Table 17.4 Features and attributes of building habitats linked to well-being

Experience/Need	Supportive environmental features and attributes
Behavioral choice and control	Personal control of ambient conditions (light, ventilation, temperature, noise); ability to modify and adapt environments to suit personal needs and preferences; multiple behavior settings to support different activities; technology to support mobility; ability to move easily between spaces to achieve comfort and desired behavioral supports
Support for a variety of social experiences	Multiplicity of meeting space types that support different kinds of social behaviors (collaboration, informal conversation, friendship development, confidentiality, general awareness); gathering "magnets" such as food; centrally located meeting and greeting spaces
Privacy, sensory retreat, and social separation when desired	Enclosure; screening materials; ability to maintain desired distances from others; public spaces for anonymity; support for confidentiality of information
A pleasing and meaningful sensory environment	Visual interest; materials selected with sensory experience in mind (touch, visual change, color, pleasant sounds and odors); spatial variability; thermal variability; moderate levels of visual complexity
Connection to nature and natural processes	Daylight; views of outdoor natural spaces; views of the sky and weather; water features; gardens; indoor plantings; outdoor plazas or interior atria with daylight and vegetation; natural materials and décor
Cultural and collective meaning and identity	Incorporation of artifacts and symbols of culture and group identity; sense of uniqueness; places of celebration

A growing body of research in diverse fields is beginning to identify positive outcomes associated with basic needs and the building features and attributes that support these needs (Table 17.4). Many of these benefits are cited in this chapter, including:

- stress reduction associated with improved indoor environmental quality (IEQ), including daylight, electric light, air quality, and views;
- improved overall comfort and satisfaction with improved IEQ and comfort controls;
- improved circadian functioning from better access to indoor daylight;
- social benefits from interior designs that connect people more effectively;
- improved psychological functioning associated with sensory variability, especially daylight.

The research cited in this chapter also indicates some needs are not adequately supported. For instance, workplaces do not provide sufficient privacy or support for behavioral control. Many people are still tethered to their workstations, with insufficient spaces for sensory retreat and privacy and little or no control over ambient conditions. Numerous studies show that lack of control, especially over noise and the social environment, is stressful and is associated with negative affect and subjective experience of stress (Heerwagen et al., 1995).

Numerous studies also show that conflicts can arise between the needs identified in Table 17.4. For instance, enhanced social experience (especially spontaneous and informal conversation) can have negative effects on the need for sensory retreat and focused attention – especially when these behaviors occur in the same space and have few supports for transition between social phases (Perlow, 1999; US General Services Administration, 2009).

We also know from various studies cited in this chapter that people change the environment to make it more compatible with these needs, such as adding visual décor, plants, and comfort devices. People also alter conditions to enhance their comfort, sometimes to the detriment of building operations and energy efficiency (adding lights, fans, covering ventilation vents).

The value of the basic needs approach

At the present time there is no overarching framework for the design and operation of buildings to intentionally support human health, well-being and performance. Much design proceeds with little evidence to support design goals or the expected results. Furthermore, the disciplines that provide the evidence for decision-making work in isolation from one another, which only encourages the proliferation of design approaches based on fad rather than fact.

The overall goal of the basic needs approach is to optimize the interface between people and buildings by ensuring that a wide range of needs and behaviors are addressed. The basic needs in Table 17.4 could be expanded to include supports that are unique to a particular situation, such as extreme security, night work, or underground environments.

The basic needs approach is especially relevant for two critical design phases: (1) initial design thinking; and (2) assessing the potential success of alternatives before a decision is made. The approach can also provide a basis for identifying and alleviating potential conflicts early in the design process as well as identifying potential ways to compensate for a need that may be difficult to achieve, such as providing sensory variability or connection to the outdoors in a windowless space.

In addition to design factors, the approach could also be used to create and implement organizational policy and cultural supports that reinforce the workplace goals. For instance, if the environment provides a wide range of spatial supports for different work needs, but limits mobility supports or expects people to be on view and available to leadership, then this would act against its success.

A project currently underway at GSA is using a similar and compatible approach to identify the links between workspace and health for a variety of needs, from individual and collaborative work to psychological restoration and connection to nature. The aim is to identify the features and attributes of space that, in combination, have the greatest potential to enhance physical and psychological well-being in work environments. The project integrates the expertise and tools of medicine, psychology, building science, sustainability, data analytics, and organizational effectiveness. It's not an easy undertaking, but it is a step toward optimizing the people-building interface for human health and well-being.

References

Aires, M.B.C., Veitch, J.A. and Newsham, G.R. (2010) Windows, view and office characteristics predict physical and psychological discomfort. *Journal of Environmental Psychology*, 30: 533–541.

Apte, M.G., Fisk, W.J. and Daisey, J.M. (2000) Association between indoor CO_2 concentrations and sick building symptoms in US office buildings: an analysis of BASE study data. *Indoor Air*, 14: 178–187.

Autor, D.H., Levy, F. and Murone, R.J. (2003) The skill content of recent technological change: an empirical exploration. *Quarterly Journal of Economics*, 118(4): 1279–1333.

Beauchemin, K.M. and Hayes, P. (1996) Sunny hospital rooms expedite recovery from severe and refractory depressions. *Journal of Affective Disorders*, 40(1): 49–51.

Benedetti, F., Colombo, C., Barbini, B., Campori, E. and Smeraldi, E. (2001) Morning sunlight reduces length of hospitalization in bipolar depression. *Journal of Affective Disorders*, 62(3): 221–223.

Boubekri, M., Cheung, I.N., Reid, K.J., Kuo, N-W., Wang, C-H. and Zee, P.C. (2014) Impact of windows and daylight on overall health and sleep quality of office workers: a case-control pilot study. *Journal of Clinical Sleep Medicine*. 10(6): 603–611.

Boyden, S. (1971) Biological determinants of optimum health. In D.J.M. Vorster (ed.) *The human biology of environmental change: Proceedings of a conference*, Blantyre, Malawi, April 5–12, 1971. London: International Biology Program.

Bringslimark, T., Hartig, T. and Patil, G.G. (2011) Adaptation to windowlessness: do office workers compensate for a lack of visual access to the outdoors? *Environment and Behavior*, 43(4): 469–487.

Chang, C-Y. and Chen, P-K. (2005) Human response to window views and indoor plants in the workplace. *Horticulture Science*, 40(5): 1354–1359.

Evans, G. (2003) The built environment and mental health. *Journal of Urban Health: Bulletin of the New York Academy of Medicine*, 88(4): 536–555.

Figueiro, M. and Rae, M. (2016) Office lighting: a personal light exposure in two seasons: impact on sleep and mood. *Lighting Research and Technology*, 48(3): 352–364.

Galasiu, A.D. and Veitch, J.A. (2006) Occupant preferences and satisfaction with the luminous environment and control systems in daylit offices: a literature review. *Energy and Buildings*, 38(7): 728–742.

Heerwagen, J.H. (2006) Investing in people: the social benefits of sustainable design. In *Proceedings of Rethinking Sustainable Construction*, Sarasota, FL, September 19–22.

Heerwagen, J.H. (2010) The experience of daylight. *D/A Magazine*, issue 15. Paper prepared for the Velux Daylight Symposium, Lausanne, Switzerland.

Heerwagen, J.H., Diamond, R. and Loveland, J.L. (1991a) Energy Edge post-occupancy evaluation project (Report No. DE-AC06–86RLL11659). Washington, DC: US Department of Energy.

Heerwagen, J.H., Diamond, R. and Loveland, J.L. (1991b) Environmental satisfaction, coping, and health outcomes in the office habitat. In *Proceedings of the 1991 International Solar Energy Society Conference*, Denver, CO.

Heerwagen, J.H., Heubach, J.G., Montgomery, J. and Weimer, W.C. (1995) Environmental design, work and well-being. *American Association of Occupational Health Nurses Journal*, 43(9): 458–468.

Heerwagen, J.H., Kampschroer, K., Powell, K. and Loftness, V. (2004) Collaborative knowledge work environments. *Building Research and Information*, 32(6): 510–528.

Heerwagen, J.H. and Orians, G.H. (1986) Adaptations to windowlessness: a study of the use of visual décor in windowed and windowless offices. *Environment and Behavior*, 18(5): 623–630.

Heerwagen, J.H. and Orians, G.H. (1993) Humans, habitats, and aesthetics. In Kellert, S.R. and Wilson, E.O. (eds) *The Biophilia Hypothesis*. Washington, DC: Island Press.

Institute of Medicine (2004) *Damp Indoor Spaces and Health*. Washington, DC: National Academy of Science, Institute of Medicine, Board on Health Promotion and Disease Prevention.

Kaplan, R. (1983) The role of nature in the urban context. In Altman, I. and Wohlwill, J.F. (eds) *Behavior and the Natural Environment*. New York: Plenum Press.

Kaplan, S. (1983) A model of person-environment compatibility. *Environment and Behavior*, 15(3): 314–332.

Keep, P., James, J. and Inman, M. (1980) Windows in the intensive therapy unit. *Anaesthesia*, 35: 257–262.

Kim, J. and de Dear, R. (2013) Workspace satisfaction: the privacy and communication tradeoff in open plan offices. *Journal of Environmental Psychology*, 36: 18–26.

Klepeis, N.E., Nelson, W.C., Ott, W.R., Robinson, J.P., *et al.* (1996) *The National Human Activity Pattern Survey: A Resource for Assessing Exposure to Environmental Pollutants*. Berkeley, CA: Lawrence Berkeley National Laboratory.

Klitzman, S. and Stillman, J.M. (1989) The impact of the physical environment on the psychological well-being of office workers. *Social Science and Medicine*, 29(6): 733–742.

Lazarus, R.S. (1966) *Psychological Stress and the Coping Process*. New York: McGraw-Hill.

Lazarus, R.S. and Folkman, S. (1984) *Stress, Appraisal and Coping*. New York: Springer.

Mehta, R., Zhu, R. and Cheems, A. (2013) Is noise always bad? Exploring the effects of ambient noise on creative cognition. *Journal of Consumer Research*, 39(4): 784–799.

Newsham, G.R., Birt, B.J., Arsenault, C., Thompson, A.J.L., *et al.* (2013) Do "green" buildings have better environments? New evidence. *Building Research and Information*, 41(4): 415–434.

Perlow, L.A. (1999) The time famine: toward a sociology of work time. *Administrative Science Quarterly*, 44: 57–81.

Raanas, R.K., Evensen, K.H., Rich, D., Sjostrom, G. and Patel, G. (2011) Benefits of indoor plants on attention capacity in an office setting. *Journal of Environmental Psychology*, 31: 99–105.

Rashid, M., Kampschroer, K., Wineman, J. and Zimring, C. (2006) Spatial layout and face to face interactions in offices: a study of the mechanisms of spatial effects in face to face interaction in offices. *Environment and Planning B: Planning and Design*, 33(6): 825–864.

Rashid, M. and Zimring, C. (2008) A review of the empirical literature on the relationship between indoor environment and stress in healthcare and office settings: problems and prospects of sharing evidence. *Environment and Behavior*, 40(2): 151–190.

Sternberg, E.M. (2009) *Healing Spaces: The Science of Place and Well-Being*. Cambridge, MA: Harvard University Press.

Stokols, D. (1992) Establishing and maintaining healthy environments: toward a social ecology of health promotion. *American Psychologist*, 47(1): 6–22.

Ten Brinke, J.T., Selvin, S., Hodgson, A.T., Fisk, W.J., Mendell, W.J., Koshland, C.P. and Daisey, I.M. (1998) Development of new volatile organic compound (VOC) exposure metrics and their relationship to "Sick Building Syndrome." *Indoor Air*, 8: 140–152.

Thayer, J.F., Verkuil, B., Brosschot, J.F., Kampschroer, K., *et al.* (2010) The effects of the physical work environment on physiological measures of stress. *European Journal of Preventative Cardiology*, 17(4): 431–439.

Ulrich, R.S. (1984) View through a window may influence recovery from surgery. *Science*, 224: 420–421.

Ulrich, R.S. (1993) Biophilia, biophobia and natural landscapes. In Kellert, S.R. and Wilson, E.O. (eds) *The Biophilia Hypothesis*. Washington, DC: Island Press.

US General Services Administration (2009) *The New Federal Workplace*. Washington, DC: GSA Public Buildings Service.

Walch, J.M., Rabin, B.S., Day, R., Williams, J.N., Choi, K. and Kang, J.D. (2005) The effect of sunlight on postoperative analgesic medication use: a prospective study of patients undergoing spinal surgery. *Psychosomatic Medicine*, 67: 156–183.

Wilson, L.M. (1972) The effects of outside deprivation on a windowless intensive care unit. *Archives of Internal Medicine*, 30: 225–226.

Chapter 18

Workplace
A tool for investment

Kevin Reader

Introduction

In a dynamic global business environment where access to information and services is taking place anytime and anywhere by staff and customers, where the location of workspace is becoming more difficult to define, those companies that are most likely to succeed are using mobile technologies to liberate their employees' workspace from space and time constraints, taking into account employee input and ideas in the design and delivery of their future workplaces.

The link between an organisation's real estate, its impact on its people's performance and the delivery of a series of tangible outcomes remains an untapped source of measurable benefits. What is required is a planning rationale that systematically takes user needs and links them to key business metrics as the basis for decision-making on the future size, location and design of workplaces. What is needed is increased awareness and responsibility within senior management that the workplace does influence and impact business performance and productivity.

The office/workplace needs its relative value and performance assessed in terms of how well it performs for the people who use it. Taking steps to turn the workplace into a machine for work will improve its performance and bring the office of yesterday and today into the twenty-first century.

Simple cost cutting and squeezing people into less space is not a long-term guideline for valid space decisions. Neither is the removal of all formal built workspaces, as we move to a distributed workforce working from home, clients' offices or in transit, as a way of achieving improved business outcomes.

In the following pages we set out our belief that workplace design is far more than simple space planning and the layout of desks. Instead, it is a far more fundamental aspect of a company's business planning which can make a real difference to a company's profitability and its employees' morale, productivity, health and well-being.

Why is the workplace changing?

When effectively linked to a company's business priorities, buildings can contribute to its corporate image, serving both customers and employees, providing spaces that enable improved collaboration, innovation and accelerating the development of new products and services.

We live in an era of transformation – of technology, social values, environments and the way we work. In order to meet an increasingly global and competitive market, organisations are undergoing re-engineering, and work process redesign. Such a transformation means analysing and redesigning core processes around new operating principles and linking these to the design of its workplaces.

The eventual effect of these changes may be networked organisations, in which the traditional boundaries between functions, producers, suppliers and even between competitors are broken down. The goal is to make the work of the organisation more efficient and productive, with fewer resources and at a lower cost base. One of the key aspects of this approach is workplace transformation and the role of the relationship between the employee, their physical and virtual space in their work. Workspace strategies, design and evaluation should be linked to business planning and objectives and thus strengthen core organisational objectives and values.

There is an emerging trend in the relationship between organisations and their buildings, the keystones of which are as follows:

- An organisation's workplaces should deliver an affordable quality environment that supports its business objectives, location and size requirements.
- A building's interior environment should be designed to serve a measurable purpose that advances the organisation towards its performance and business goals.
- The work environment needs to be considered another business tool, like digital and other office technologies, that can be used to improve an employee's ability to deliver their work more effectively.
- The building should provide a safe, secure, humane and functional work environment for its users.
- The building must be environmentally responsible for the organisation and the wider community.

It is increasingly becoming accepted by those involved in the delivery and running of office buildings that it is no longer necessary to accept a compromise between an organisation and its accommodation but seek a mutually beneficial relationship.

Economic and social pressures on the workplace

Trends in workplace design demonstrate that organisations are responding to the increasing cost of office accommodation by looking to derive more measurable benefits from investment in their real estate. Organisations are finding the cost of their accommodation increasingly burdensome. Whether they lease or own their office space, they are faced with the cost of furnishing and equipping the workplace with steadily increasing amounts of office technology, furniture and workers who are demanding higher levels of building-related comfort and services. Organisations are also looking for greater flexibility in lease periods, with the average length in the UK typically now less than five years with a business planning cycle of three years. Typically we are seeing some of the following issues impacting workplaces:

- The increasing sophistication of modern buildings makes them a more costly capital investment as well as more expensive to operate.
- Most office employees now have at least one or two computers per desk with associated equipment. Consequently it costs more to equip them to do their work and requires more power, cooling and ventilation.

- Employees expect and sometimes require an increasing number of other amenities including cafeterias, fitness rooms and multi-faith spaces.
- Increasingly sophisticated building operations and systems require a more highly skilled, trained and paid Facilities Management team.
- Office workers are increasingly aware of the impact of the working environment on their comfort and health and are demanding higher levels and standards of building system performance, ergonomic furniture and environmental testing.
- Knowledge workers will be able to multi-task, process information faster and interact with colleagues and peers and will require workplaces that enable them to operate and collaborate across the globe.
- Increased use of smart-phones, tablets and mobile technologies means the physical boundaries and time restraints of the typical working day are being stretched and manipulated by an increasingly sophisticated workforce.

Organisations are responding to higher operational costs by exploring alternatives to reduce occupancy costs, especially for employees who do not need to be in the buildings on a full-time basis. Implementing such alternatives, however, can be slow and painful, because of the force of habit and also because of the emotional meaning of space in people's work lives.

Given the entrenched nature of many people's attitudes towards their workspace, especially in the context of a corporate system that has in the past often used space as a reward and a symbol of advancement, efforts to reduce occupancy costs by simply accommodating people in less space are likely to be ineffective unless the emotional and interpersonal components of space planning are considered.

The workplace as a tool for investment

A decade ago the world of work was awash with phrases such as 'new ways of working' and 'hot desks'. The office was on its way to becoming paper-free and file-free. For most office employees these ideas have never come to fruition. Few people are required to book a desk every morning, most still deal with reams of paperwork and the filing cabinet is still a feature of many offices. Many companies pay lip service to mobile working by installing Wi-Fi in their public facing areas and enabling a trusted few to work from home on an as-and-when basis. Flat screen technology has seen the L-shaped desk replaced by rows of serried benching, hardly the promised workplace revolution. Instead of making cultural and work behavioural changes, too many companies fall into the trap of tacking on gimmicks and creating workplaces that are supposed to be fun, but bear little resemblance to what people really are looking for in their workplaces.

The emerging workplace model suggests that the boundaries between public and private, work and leisure and domestic environments have been eroded. While good design is a useful tool in attracting and retaining the best staff, it never works in isolation. It is the people not the buildings that produce creative environments, supported by a work culture and management style that encourage agility, collaboration and knowledge sharing.

The success of this approach depends on the concept of a workspace environment with feedback and consultation as a key element of its operation. Systematic feedback from the buildings occupants can both inform and improve decisions on the organisational goals and consumption of resources. The growth of post-occupancy studies are a testimonial to the fact that organisations are seeking to get feedback on the impact their workspace is having on its people and how they compare to their peers.

But despite all these innovations in data gathering, most organisations still see their workspace as an overhead and most employees see their workspace as demarcating personal territory. However, in accepting that people's comfort and a return on the money invested in their workspace are a legitimate and realisable goal, organisations may come to see its accommodation as no more than a tool for getting its employees to get their work done more efficiently.

In adopting the concept of the office as a tool, questions on how much to spend on accommodation are answered by measurement of its performance: investment in building improvements have to show measurable increases in the productivity of the users and a positive impact on the performance of the organisation.

More than just a property project

The strategic business advantage of a planning process designed around feedback from building occupants is that it provides a road map of the design and investment of its future workplaces. If a company wants to select the right combination of workspace alternatives to best meet its corporate goals of increasing its workforce productivity, innovation and collaboration, while lowering operational costs, it needs a sophisticated accommodation strategy, combining human resources planning, technology development, culture change (training & development) and business planning.

Any change to an organisation cannot succeed if imposed on employees by management, facilities staff or building planners. Any integrated planning of space alternatives such as expansion, refurbishment or downsizing has to demonstrate a link between the built environment and the key business outcomes of the organisation. An integrated workplace strategy should contain the following elements:

- careful financial analysis of the costs and benefits to be realised by an accurate definition of the organisations space requirements;
- feedback and mobilisation of the occupants on their functional comfort requirements and genuine work needs;
- analysis of information on the link between a workplace and its impact on the desired business outcomes;
- training of supervisors (champions) in integrated workplace change strategies and techniques, particularly how to manage and motivate a remote workforce;
- preparation of the principles, values and training needed at all levels in the organisation to conform to a new form of workstyle;
- redefinition of output and productivity indicators to conform to any geographically dispersed workgroup configurations;
- redefinition of the meaning of work and the meaning of having a job. 'Work is an activity not a place.'

If companies want alternative working environments that produce results in terms of increased productivity, lower accommodation costs and long-term sustainability, then feedback from users applied to the design process is essential, using pre- and post-occupancy evaluation (POE) and annual health check surveys. To be effective in designing work environments for their staff, managers must address and co-ordinate complex human resources issues, the business strategy, the impact of information technology, as well as building and asset management issues.

Workplace design, construction and operation require reasoned analysis and careful planning to ensure that the right amount of space is provided, which will provide optimal workspaces for employees, to enable them to deliver quality solutions for their employer and customers.

Case studies

The following three case studies are drawn from projects where the author has been involved in workplace strategy, design and delivery. They represent a range of clients who were seeking to achieve more than just a new physical workplace, rather in many cases these clients wanted to achieve a fundamental shift in their approach to how their new workplace would impact the organisation, its people, clients and wider community. Each organisation, therefore, had individual targets and benefits which it was looking to achieve, at the outset with its new workplace. In some cases other objectives were identified along the way or after the projects were completed.

Case study 18.1 Arcadis House London (previously EC Harris)

Context

During periods of expansion EC Harris (Arcadis UK) had previously moved from various offices in order to accommodate its growing number of staff. The primary focus for these relocations was the need to provide more room for more staff.

The success of the organisation had been built on a strong competitive spirit fostered in a close-knit organisational structure. Prior to moving to a new building, the highly cellular office spaces occupied by the organisation had failed to harness and motivate the highly skilled workforce. Divisions between different departments in the company grew and as a result some teams/departments adopted silo working cultures. As a result of this, the driving strategy for a new building was to create an environment that fostered a strong collaborative working culture.

Part of this involved re-establishing the organisation's core values through the creation of a workspace 'Blueprint' that covered more than just the physical aspects, but social and economic drivers. The goal was to use the HQ relocation as a visible catalyst for change at the heart of a much wider business transformation programme as the organisation moved from its traditional business roots into a wider range of building-related consultancy and advisory skills.

This cultural transformation involved establishing a central hub work environment where interaction and collaboration were allowed to become the DNA of the organisation. This concept was to enable meritocratic working practices, as all staff members where given a platform from which they could explore and share new ideas with their colleagues. Knowledge and good practice were placed at the heart of the business for all workers to use in their daily working life. It was important to the CEO that the organisation grew out of the ideas of every staff member.

Outcomes and approach

In addition to property cost reduction, targeted operational benefits were identified relating to the following areas:

- people performance
- operational efficiency
- service quality
- brand perception.

Arcadis relocated its headquarters from Tavistock Square London to a site next to Kings Cross Station, London (Figure 18.1). From identification of the target site, to fit-out of 69,000 sq ft and practical completion, it took the project team a mere six months, the entire HQ staff being relocated over one weekend. Extensive pre-move engagement with business leaders and the staff

Figure 18.1 Arcadis House entrance (landside space)

on the new location and working behaviours enabled the organisation to carry out a seamless migration with zero downtime. The project went on to win the PFM Awards 2007 for Partners in Business Change.

Benefits

Pre- and post-occupancy studies with the organisation and its people have enabled Arcadis to demonstrate Return on Investment through a variety of tangible metrics:

- £3m targeted benefits were realised in under 6 months (against a 12-month target) (Figure 18.2).
- The capital project was delivered 5 per cent below budget and on time.
- Net Profit Margin increased by 13 per cent from pre-move levels.
- Fee turnover per head increased by 7.5 per cent.
- Staff attrition dropped from 24 per cent to 15 per cent, attraction/attrition ratio improved 1:1 to 2.5:1. The use of workspaces increased from 62 per cent to 85 per cent, with desks per head down to 0.7 (Figure 18.3).

- Total Occupancy Cost per head reduced by 36 per cent.
- Overhead costs as a percentage of staff costs reduced by 14 per cent.
- Carbon footprint improved 251 per cent.
- 99 per cent of all waste is now recycled, and paper consumption is down 44 per cent per head.

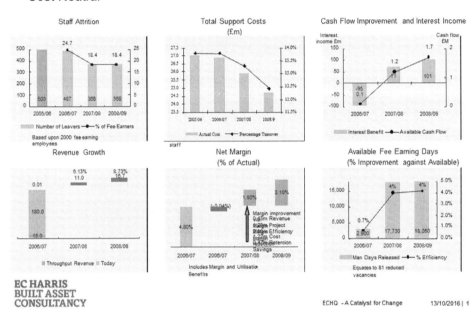

Figure 18.2 Arcadis House benefit graphs

Figure 18.3 Arcadis House work area (airside space)

Business impact

The benefits are still being delivered on a continuous basis and were used to underpin the impact of transforming the business across a further 11 sites within the United Kingdom and across the globe. It had a positive impact on how Arcadis staff and clients viewed the organisation; its culture was fundamentally changed and it became a more attractive employer.

New working practices increased integration, flexibility and transfer of knowledge. Its greatest benefits included increased visibility of leadership and access to the most experienced staff.

Case Study 18.2 Adur District Council and Worthing Borough Council

Context

In 2007, Adur District Council and Worthing Borough Council took the decision to work in partnership. The original aim was to create a single, senior officer structure and shared services across the two Councils and to deliver savings and efficiencies for both Councils. A single senior officer team was created in April 2008 and since then all services have become joint teams, providing joint services to the people of Adur and Worthing.

In 2008, the two Councils commissioned an accommodation study of its principal shared estate buildings which demonstrated that space efficiencies and further cost savings could be achieved by the disposal of at least one of their buildings and consolidating into a smaller portfolio. The accommodation consolidation strategy rested upon the introduction of New Ways of Working (NWoW). This involved investment in its buildings, technology and people, to enable a significant increase in mobile, remote and home working. The introduction of NWoW was essential if the financial benefits were to be achieved, and underpinned the key objectives of the transformation programme. In addition, wider benefits and challenges of a workplace change programme were considered by the Councils, if their ambitious programme was to achieve its goals.

Ultimately the aims were to reduce their combined operating costs, increase overall productivity, making more effective the delivery of the Councils' services to their communities, improving communications and providing the right conditions to thrive and create a more enjoyable workplace for their staff.

Outcomes and approach

Adur and Worthing Councils (AWC) Transformation Programme had seven key objectives and these formed the basis for the development of the final business case, with tangible measurable benefits linked to them. These benefits were based on baseline data gathered in the work that was done previously in 2008 and 2012. The potential sale of the Adur Civic Centre had provided impetus and a deadline for its disposal for redevelopment but a number of key issues became apparent that had to be overcome, not least huge staff resistance to any imposed changes to how and where they worked. Some of the others were as follows:

- existing data centre with insufficient capacity to handle increased traffic and information storage;
- poor alignment of new mobile technologies with programme's timetable and deliverables;

- perception from most teams that the Electronic Data Records Management System would be in place by the end of the programme, when in fact it was only focused initially on one team's filing;
- staff perception that the IT systems had never worked properly before and would certainly not in the future;
- staff viewed any relocation or move between buildings as a recipe for disaster, as in the past they had not been delivered as well as they could have been;
- staff resistance to the NWoW programme and change due to levels of misinformation and lack of understanding of how it could benefit them.

Benefits

From the outset it was apparent that substantial work had to be done with all the staff, managers and elected members to mobilise them and communicate the benefits and why this project was being undertaken. At an internal Managers Conference they committed to continue working together in partnership to deliver cost-effective services while retaining separate identities, and moving towards smaller and smarter local government.

The Councils' priorities were summarised as protecting front line services, while ensuring value for money and lower Council Tax through the following:

- reduction of in operational costs by circa £500,000 per annum;
- sale of Adur Civic Centre for substantial capital sum (£6–£8 million);
- reduction in core estate by 50 per cent and resulting lower carbon footprint;
- reduction in business mileage between Council buildings;
- improved Customer Services in combined new walk-in centre in Worthing (Figure 18.4);
- consolidation of other community services into the remaining two buildings and the creation of a 'Civic Hub' with voluntary sector partners accommodated into the Council buildings;
- sale of community building for circa £350,000 and returned to local housing stock;
- delivery of more flexible and responsive technologies, enabling staff to log on in half the time, enabling 200 hours per day to be returned to delivering more effective local services;
- unified IT platform and technologies enabling staff to work from any location using wired or wireless solutions, including working from home;
- follow me printing and paper-light approach which saved 30–40 per cent in annual printing costs;
- improving communications across services and teams by co-location;
- improved customer experience of dealing with the Councils and an overall improvement in positive customer feedback.

Business impact

One of the key aspects to the whole consolidation programme was the design and delivery of a new single walk-in centre. The age demographics of the two Councils mean they have a higher percentage of older persons than the average for England and moving them to cheaper forms of access, while still a key aim, has to be tempered with the reality of what was needed by their communities.

This programme represented an exemplar of two local Councils, combining their services, making substantial savings, retaining the identity of both Councils and improving its workplaces for its people whilst still protecting key services for its citizens.

Figure 18.4 Customer walk-in space in Worthing

Case Study 18.3 Walsall Council

Context

The public sector of the twenty-first century will be significantly different to that of the twentieth century. To be successful will require new thinking and new ways of working, with measurable and tangible benefits for the organisation, its people and communities.

In September 2006, Walsall's Cabinet adopted its first Corporate Property Strategy with a key objective to introduce new ways of working with a view to reducing the amount of accommodation held by the Council. This strategy was one of a number of drivers that would assist Walsall to transform the way it delivers its services to its communities.

Arising from a reorganisation within the Human Resource and Development (HRD) service, Walsall wanted to put in place new office layouts and working arrangements to optimise floor space and staff efficiency. It was intended that this 'Model Office' was to be used as an exemplar project to promote new ways of working to the rest of the Council, with the following drivers for change:

- support and inform the corporate property strategy by piloting new ways of working;
- embrace, demonstrate and encourage transformation – lead by example;
- reduce HRD's cost base and invest back into the organisation;

- relocate all the HRD teams from seven locations to one location and increase joint working;
- improve the working environment for staff – resolve significant H&S and DDA issues;
- provide a flexible office environment – teams share resources (printers, knowledge, software, etc.);
- provide the platform to radically improve customer service;
- equip HRD staff with a real change management experience.

Outcomes and approach

A Time Utilisation Study (TUS) was carried out of the teams in their seven locations which demonstrated peak occupancy between 50–60 per cent (Figure 18.5). In addition, a staff perception and environmental symptom pattern survey was undertaken, which indicated significant sick building symptom issues with the Civic Centre, resulting in higher than average staff absenteeism levels (Figure 18.6).

Once this work was completed, in-depth user workshops were set up, exploring staff concerns on moving to a more shared workplace environment. These were followed by extensive education and training on new way of working protocols which resulted in a 75 per cent negative view of the change pre-start to a 25 per cent position before the works started to a 4 per cent position post completion.

On completion of the analysis, engagement and studies, a business case based on a set of targeted measurable benefits was signed off by the Council. This was followed by a design, performance specification and tender package which was delivered in a two-stage programme over three months. Finally the project was rounded off with a Post Occupancy Analysis (POA) to establish if the benefits had been delivered and used to inform next steps in the Council's wider property rationalisation plans.

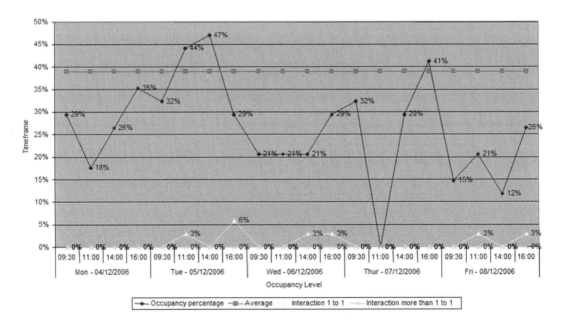

Figure 18.5 Walsall occupancy study graph

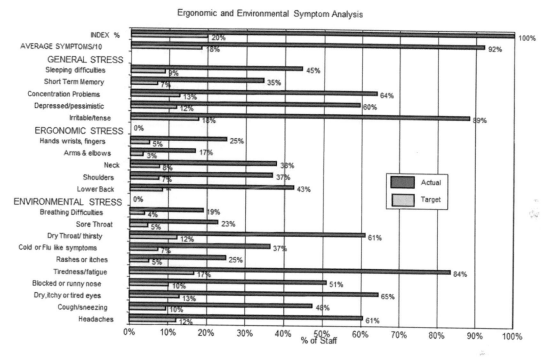

Figure 18.6 Walsall symptom study graph

Benefits

At the outset of the project key potential benefits were established, which were base-lined, tracked and delivered. Some of the key ones are as follows:

- 135 per cent desk occupancy achieved and 150 per cent targeted;
- 50 per cent reduction in staff sickness absenteeism;
- 35–50 per cent reduction in printing costs;
- across all areas £350,000 savings in first year and ROI of 18 months;
- customer satisfaction levels rose from 45 per cent to over 90 per cent.

The Council also base-lined and targeted a number of key outcomes as measures of project success. One of these was staff absenteeism. Figure 18.7 demonstrates this before the project and after. During May 2007 there were over 260 sick days for the 130 staff. The dotted lines are where the refurbishment of the space was completed in two phases and new working practices adopted. By November 2007 the level of days off sick had dropped to 65 out of the 130 staff, resulting in productivity improvements, measured against the delivery of targets.

Business impact

The Council will be using this Model Office as an exemplar project on the benefits of adaptive working across the whole estate. This is seen as the first key part of a change management

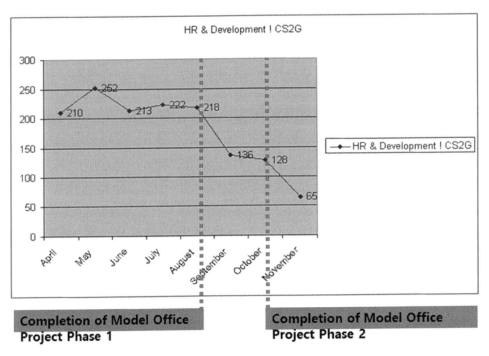

HR & Development ! CS2G

210
252
213
222
218
136
128
65

—◆— HR & Development ! CS2G

April May June July August September October November

Completion of Model Office Project Phase 1

Completion of Model Office Project Phase 2

Figure 18.7 Walsall Absenteeism Reduction Graph

Figure 18.8 Walsall before the transformation

Figure 18.9 Walsall after the transformation

programme which will eventually deal with every aspect of the Council's delivery of services to its customers. The aim is delivering significant operational cost savings and capital receipts from the disposal of buildings and improvements in the delivery of key front line services to the people and communities of Walsall. The final quote from Sharon Carter summarised the success of the 'Model Office Programme' 'The new office space is excellent; our staff have really embraced the change. People are even saying that they don't want to go home.' Figures 18.8 and 18.9 show the before and after states.

Conclusion

We set out a hypothesis that workplaces could be viewed in a business context as a tool to enable people to deliver improved outcomes for their organisation and clients, while supporting the delivery of improved health and well-being for themselves.

Workplaces should no longer be a burden to an organisation but can become a direct contributor to its success in the attraction and retention of talent, improving productivity and delivering positive business outcomes, but it cannot be done in isolation from the needs of its people, their work behaviours and management culture.

The link between an organisation's real estate, its impact on its people's performance and the delivery of a series of tangible outcomes remains an untapped source of measurable benefits. This latent potential within the organisation will only be released if the people are fully engaged in the change process, with enabling technologies and environments, all with the sole objective of delivering a high performing workplace. The methodology required to achieve this requires a radical rethink on how property professionals measure their real estate's performance, combined with a detailed understanding of its impact on their people's performance and outputs, across a range of tangible metrics. Once you can establish the full range of financial and non-financial benefits, you can move from the operational cost per sq ft/m model typically used to a total impact investment model. Only then will the workplace become the tool for investment that senior business leaders are seeking, supporting and delivering the desired business outcomes, while providing its people with the environment they need to do their job more effectively.

Acknowledgements

Arcadis, Information and photographs provided by Arcadis.
Antony Faughnan, Director of Operations Regional Management Team, Arcadis UK.
John Jukes, Workplace Productivity & Well Being Specialist, WESTRA Consulting.
Steve Spinner, Head of Business & Technical Services, Adur & Worthing Councils.
Konrad Thomasson, Workplace Change Consultant, Konvergence Consulting.

Chapter 19

Productivity in buildings

The killer variables: twenty years on

Adrian Leaman and Bill Bordass

Introduction

'Productivity in buildings: the killer variables' first appeared as a presentation at the Workplace Comfort Forum in 1997,[1] and has subsequently been updated in three versions, including earlier editions of this book. The older versions contain additional material: these and many other references can be found at www.usablebuildings.co.uk.

Twenty years on, what have we learned? Has anything substantially changed? The second question is easier to answer than the first. Our conclusions remain basically similar, with many of the same mistakes being made as twenty years ago. Despite a new batch of UK studies into building performance in use (Lorch, 2016), and much wider appreciation of the importance of feedback to help get the best out of people in their workplaces, recent longitudinal studies, e.g. Bunn (2016a), continue to show that workplace productivity is being unnecessarily compromised.

Buildings are complex, interconnected systems; so outcome indicators such as perceived productivity are usually associated with others, like perceived health. The cat's cradle of causality and association differs from one building to the next, making it dangerous to be over-assertive about causation without careful appreciation of contexts. For example, two technically similar buildings may have very different performance outcomes, depending on their occupation and management. In a badly performing office, people with window seats may report much better levels of comfort, health and productivity than those in the middle, while in a better-designed and managed building the 'window effect' may disappear. Similarly, people who only use a building once or twice a week will usually respond more positively than those who are there five days a week.

Here we cover the lessons learned – from our investigators' perspective – then reflect on what we saw to be the killer variables in the past and how we see them now. By 'killer variable', we mean those aspects of buildings which most directly affect perceptions of workplace productivity by building users. By 'perceived productivity', we mean how people think their activities at work are enhanced or reduced by the conditions in the building. Our main standpoint is building performance – how well buildings work to meet the needs of occupants and how successful buildings are technically and environmentally. This necessarily involves understanding the needs of individuals, their host organisations, and the building's fabric, form and technology. Twenty years ago we were also interested in how buildings work from an economic perspective. But we have never studied this in any detail because of the extraordinary difficulty and expense of obtaining robust data (Bordass, 2000).

What have we learned?

Our approach to building performance concentrates on aspects over which clients, designers and, to a lesser extent, facilities managers have some influence and are potentially able to intervene to affect outcomes, hopefully for the better. We draw a clear boundary around things we can examine with confidence and those we cannot. For example, we might ask occupants if their working environment is too noisy, but not about the 'morale' of their colleagues. Occupants will normally be able to tell you accurately whether it is too noisy, but a topic like morale may not mean much to them. So the recent preoccupation with the well-being of building occupants – a diffuse, if not impossibly abstract concept – is outside our terms of reference.

When building occupants know the answers and therefore do not have to speculate, results are more useful. This is like an exit poll after an election. The respondent, having just voted, is likely to give a more accurate response because they actually know the answer. Opinion polls in advance of election day will be less accurate because respondents will tell you how they might vote, not how they actually do. If you ask a building user, 'How do you think your productivity at work is affected by conditions in the building?' and ask them to rate a percentage increase or decrease on an interval scale, most can attempt this with a degree of honesty, if not accuracy – though a few may say: 'With respect to what? I have no yardstick to judge this by.'[2] Perceived productivity measurement like this is close to the limits of what can be achieved effectively with questionnaires. So, as a general rule, only include questions that respondents are likely to know the answers to.

There is also the question of subjectivity. 'The answers are only subjective so cannot be trusted', say some. But how is it possible to measure productivity at work practically and objectively across all kinds of buildings and their occupants? It's fruitless, because each separate type of activity (e.g. software development, marketing, etc.) will require a subtle change to the metric and to the method of measurement, all within changing situations, the vast majority of which will be inaccessible to the researcher.

Although perceived productivity might well be the first variable a researcher might seek to remove from a questionnaire on methodological grounds, from a manager's point of view workplace productivity is one of the most important criteria of success. It is one of the twelve key variables (out of 48 altogether) used to create a Summary Index of occupant satisfaction in the BUS survey.[3] Despite debate about its pitfalls, e.g. Oseland (1999), no-one, to our knowledge, has successfully found a practical alternative.

So also with absenteeism. If you ask about absences, responses may be misleading in various ways. Respondents need to be confident that their honest responses will not be used against them: if they feel they might be identified, they may be nervous about managers seeing what they say. Data of absences from staff or medical records will not pick up people going absent for a few hours because it will only refer to longer periods of time, e.g. when covered by a doctor's sick note. Data culled from, say, Human Resource Department records may also be hard to associate with a particular building. Organisations will say that such data are available, but when examined more closely, interpretation becomes difficult. 'Workplace absenteeism' may be the headline, but the support data may just be based on sick leave, which is not the same (Economist Intelligence Unit, 2014).

We ask respondents how their behaviour changes as a result of being in the building. This is an indirect way of getting at absences. It also picks up comments on more subtle aspects like wearing headphones to mask unwanted noise, or escaping from the building briefly for respite from poor conditions. Figure 19.1 shows the distribution of percentages of respondents who say, 'Yes, they change their behaviour as a result of conditions in the building'. The mean and median are just over 40 per cent across 174 buildings.[4] Almost invariably the reported behaviour will be a coping strategy to help mitigate perceived problems. A typical comment might be: 'I take my lunch breaks outside the building wherever possible, and go home exactly on time every day.' Only a few comments will be positive like: 'I dress more smartly' and 'I try to sit next to the atrium because the quality of light is good there.'

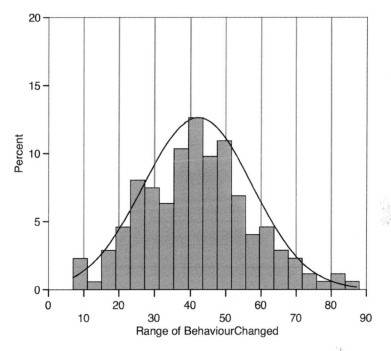

Figure 19.1 The distribution of percentages of respondents who say that they change their behaviour as a result of conditions in the building. Data are drawn from a sub-set of UK buildings in the BUS Methodology dataset.

Note: Mean of distribution = 42.1%; median = 42%; SD = 15.3; Count = 174.

We contextualise statistical ratings with users' comments. For example, if you want to examine how the quality of daylight relates to perceived productivity, you should not choose the study buildings solely on the basis of ratings on lighting quality. Over the past twenty years, most buildings score better on daylight and artificial lighting, largely owing to improvements in lighting and computer screen technology. However, in some buildings, lighting may be the *only* variable that scores well, and may mask other things that are rated poorly. This is one reason why studies that set out to examine educational performance and lighting quality, for example, never seem to reach publication: the method may not properly describe or control for context; and the analysis may be swamped by 'noisy' data that makes results difficult or impossible to interpret.

Analysis by Baird and Dykes (2012) suggests that comments boxes in the BUS questionnaire are usually filled in by about one-third of the respondents. They found that negative comments outweighed positive or neutral and suggested that a ratio of 5 to 1 should prompt an alert, while anything approaching 10 to 1 should warrant immediate investigation. Comments – positive and negative – are significantly associated with the numerical ratings for the corresponding variable. Ratings and comments are usefully associated, so where occupants comment negatively on a topic, they are likely to rate it negatively too. For perceived productivity, the significant correlations are r = 0.67 for positive comments and r = -0.82 for negative comments.

Giving respondents plenty of opportunity to comment is a good way to keep down the length of a questionnaire and get bellwethers of things to come. There is no need to ask about everything: a well-designed questionnaire will extract the answers anyway. For example, the BUS questionnaire does not ask specifically about problems in reception areas, but elicits responses

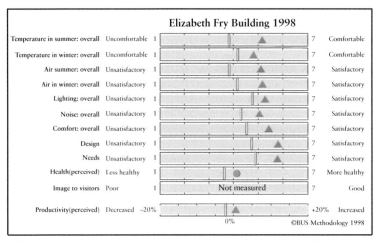

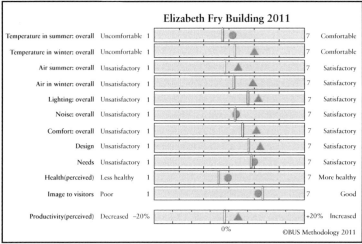

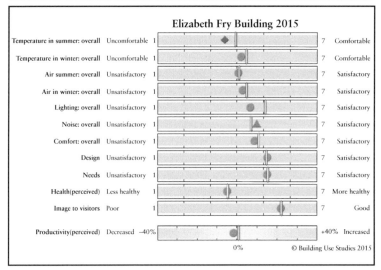

Figure 19.2 'Fingerprints' of BUS Occupant Survey Summary scores for the Elizabeth Fry building

Note:

Figure 19.2 is a simplified representation of BUS ratings (Bunn (2016b)), intended to show the overall pattern or "fingerprint" rather than greater detail, an example of which can be found in Figure 19.3.

where such problems occur. In schools, clashes between daylight strategies and the now omni-present electronic whiteboards were first detected in a teacher's remark in 1995, well ahead of their widespread use.

When studies are repeated at intervals over time, the 'fingerprints' – the general shapes of the average rating scores – tend to be similar, a good indicator of 'robustness' of the method. Figure 19.2 (Bunn, 2016b) shows three fingerprints for the Elizabeth Fry Building[5] from surveys in 1998, 2011 and 2015. The respondents in the buildings may change over time, but the overall pattern of average responses is discernible over time.

Figure 19.3 overlays data for the Rivergreen Centre for studies in 2007 and 2015 (Bunn, 2016b). Mean scores for 2007 are denoted by double-ended vertical arrows and those for 2015

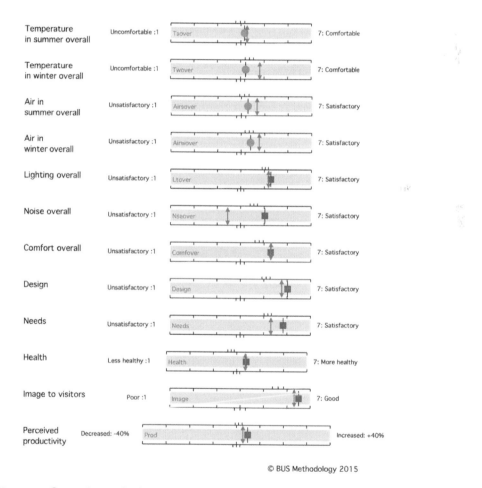

© BUS Methodology 2015

Figure 19.3 Rivergreen Centre: longitudinal survey scores for 12 principal survey variables, 2007 and 2015

Notes:

Squares are mean scores for 2015 significantly better than the British benchmark for 2015: circles are 2015 scores no different from the British benchmark; diamonds are significantly worse than the British benchmark (there are none here).

Double-ended arrows are mean scores for 2007.

The outer facing tick marks for each variable are the upper and lower limits for the test which decides significance. For example, the square for perceived productivity lies outside the extremes of the tick marks, so the score for 2015 is better than the benchmark. The double-ended arrow – the score for 2007 – is also outside these limits, but slightly lower than 2015, meaning that perceived productivity has declined slightly, but is still significantly better than the 2015 benchmark.

Table 19.1 Rivergreen Centre, 2007 and 2015 companies and outcomes

Variable	Mean2007	SD	SE	SE x 1.96	Lower	Upper	Mean 2015	Outcome
Temperature in summer (overall)	4.24	1.69	0.19	0	4	4	4.15	Same
Temperature in winter (overall)	4.89	1.63	0.16	0	5	5	4.21	Worse
Air in summer (overall)	4.54	1.53	0.17	0	5	5	4.28	Same
Air in winter (overall)	4.81	1.74	0.17	0	5	5	4.4	Worse
Lighting (overall)	5.19	1.7	0.16	0	5	5	5.28	Same
Noise (overall)	3.44	1.86	0.18	0	3	3	5.03	Much better
Comfort (overall)	5.35	1.44	0.14	0	5	5	5.29	Same
Design	5.78	1.16	0.11	0	6	6	6.02	Better
Needs	5.23	1.6	0.16	0	5	5	5.83	Better
Health	4.29	1.51	0.15	0	4	4	4.4	Same
Image	6.32	1.08	0.10	0.20	6	7	6.5	Same
Perceived productivity	2.16	15.07	1.49	3	−1	5	4.78	Same

by shapes.[6] For perceived productivity, the score changed from plus 2 per cent in 2007 to plus 4.8 per cent in 2015. Although the value is 2.8 per cent higher, this is still within measurement limits, so not significantly better in the statistical sense. Outcomes for all twelve summary variables including perceived productivity are shown in Figure 19.3 and Table 19.1.

Rivergreen is written up in more detail in Bunn (2007). As far as occupants are concerned, the BUS survey shows it is a good building overall, in the top quartile of the British dataset. In 2007, only one indicator – noise – scored significantly worse than the British benchmark. By 2015, noise scores had improved, as a result of changes to the internal layout and treatment of noise-reflecting surfaces. Most of the other scores were maintained over the 8-year period, apart from wintertime conditions, which deteriorated. The scores for *Image* are an order higher than the others: where a building is distinctive, respondents tend to give this higher ratings. Conversely, in common with many recent British buildings, the rating and benchmark for *Health* tend to be lower. The comments on perceived productivity reflect the ratings: 'This is a relatively comfortable place to work and I don't have a need to fiddle with the controls to try and find a comfortable temperature.' However, 'Productivity drops in summer because of the higher temperatures.'

Rivergreen is a naturally ventilated office. Like many other UK office buildings today, occupant densities have been increasing. It is also relatively rare: most recent UK offices are deeper in plan form, requiring greater management intervention to keep on top of the heating, cooling and ventilation, with all the increased complexity of the technologies required. We might speculate: 'Is the performance of simpler, shallow-plan buildings like Rivergreen less likely to deteriorate over time?', but there are not yet enough longitudinal studies to test this hypothesis. What we do know from case studies is that performance of complicated, highly-serviced buildings can collapse suddenly if economies are made on maintenance and facilities management.

A rare longitudinal study of a naturally-ventilated office is the Woodland Trust's headquarters (Bordass *et al.*, 2014) . Here feedback from detailed studies of an earlier building by the same design team, the National Trust's Heelis building, was used to inform design and management practices (Nevill, 2007). Its design philosophy was similar to the Rivergreen's – 'Keep it simple, and do it well' – an approach that post-occupancy studies have consistently shown to work but many projects sadly lack. The Woodland Trust had better energy performance than Heelis, especially for heating and lighting; good quality at a normal cost (£1,800/m²) and occupant satisfaction levels above British benchmarks on 10 out of 12 indicators. The exceptions were *Noise*, and *Perceived Health*.

One comment from the Woodland Trust 2012 survey is worth quoting fully:

> As I am home-based and (only) come into the building for specific meetings, my productivity suffers little, if at all. I must be absolutely focused and productive during the time I am in the building. Long periods in the building could decrease productivity from past experience of working there full-time, or it's more likely that it's more difficult to be as productive as there's a need to concentrate harder, and if I stay longer than a few hours, although my productivity doesn't decline, as I don't allow it to, I do not feel comfortable and actually begin to feel unwell again.

This observation has many of the features of interest here: a preference to work from home to permit complete concentration and escape noisy distractions; a tendency for people who use the building less to give higher ratings; and deteriorating perceptions of health from those who spend longer times in a building.

The perceived productivity score for Woodland Trust in 2012 was +4 per cent, a good result. It tempts some to take such a figure, multiply it by the number of staff and their average salary, monetise the total 'gain' and promote this with an eye-catching headline. Search online by 'office productivity dollars saved' and you will see a list of studies with claims of this kind. As with most modern research, you must ask first: 'Who is paying?'. Often this will be organisations with vested interests peddling their wares. We think that monetising value like this is a step too far. By all means find out the relative levels of perceived productivity and how the findings compare – better or worse than others; increasing, stable or declining – but do not gild the estimates with spurious authenticity. It is enough to know that the likely gain is 4 per cent (not 4.09 per cent, there is no need to take everything to two places of decimals). Perceived productivity is a relative indicator – it works as a nominal or ordinal statistic (i.e. this is better than that, this is placed here on the scale compared with others), but when used as an absolute real or ratio figure (4.09 per cent, 95 per cent), it loses traction.

The Heelis, Woodland Trust, and Rivergreen are all examples of buildings that work relatively or very well, and are future-proofed to some extent.[7] Their performance may well decline over time, but any fall-off is likely to be slowed because they possess many of the features listed in the following sections.

What of buildings that work less well? We can often learn more from these than the better ones (it is easier to improve building performance by getting rid of the poor features than by adding good ones to a flawed chassis), but these are much less likely to reach publication. For example, recent occupant survey results from an Australian building with a 'five-star' Green-Star[8] rating (which suggests it is energy-efficient and has many features lauded as 'sustainable') revealed that its occupants think less well of it, with perceived productivity scores of close to –10 per cent. We may privately know why such buildings are failing by users' criteria, but the findings are unlikely to reach publication, because they will reflect badly on the developers, owners, designers and management, and the fear is that they will damage professional reputations.

So it cannot be assumed that just because a building rates highly in a tick-box, feature-rating system such as BREEAM, LEED or GreenStar, or is given plaudits and awards for its architectural design, that it will work well for its occupants or for the environment. In fact, awards often give the impression that buildings work well, but rarely take advantage of an assessment to check whether this conclusion is justifiable. Users often know better and can be very insightful about things going wrong. For example, comments from the poorly performing but glamorous building mentioned in the previous paragraph: 'Too much focus on aesthetics and not enough consideration of functionality . . . Wasted space for strange-shaped rooms . . . Privacy is entirely lacking . . . Goldfish have more privacy.' A UK award-winning school was rated very poorly by the staff, while a student said: 'The architecture showed next to no sense. It leaked in the rain and was intolerably hot in sunlight. Pretty perhaps, sustainable maybe, but practical it is not.'

User perceptions can be paradoxical. For example, questionnaire responses may reveal that a building is too hot in summer and too cold in winter but occupants regard overall thermal comfort as OK. This contrariness might baffle survey methodologists who want consistent answers, but it is quite normal. Occupants may nit-pick with their criticisms of the details of humidity, glare and noise, for example, but then say: 'We quite like the way it looks, we feel better for being there, and it's much nicer than where we were before.' We calculate the difference and call it 'forgiveness': users may tolerate some drawbacks as long as they are compensated in some way. For example, occupants will be happier if they have personal control with some elements of choice (e.g., too hot with the window shut or too noisy with it open, but not both together) – what is known as adaptive opportunity. In the Australian building described earlier, the 'forgiveness' score was at the 25th percentile in comparison with the rest of the dataset (that is, in the bottom quarter in comparison with the rest of the dataset), so despite the sparkling aesthetics, the occupants did not think good looks compensated them for the building's failings.

The killer variables – twenty years ago

A 'killer' variable is one that has a critical influence on the overall behaviour of a system. The original version of this paper – Leaman and Bordass (1997) – related to workplaces, particularly offices, and identified four clusters of variables, outlined below.

1   *Personal control.* Research in the 1970s revealed that the range of conditions occupants found 'comfortable' was wider in field studies than in the laboratory. Avoiding discomfort appeared more important than providing comfort, with people more tolerant of conditions where they had more opportunities for control – windows, blinds, switches, thermostats, and so on. This later became known as adaptive comfort theory, which also includes control over personal situations, e.g. where people are not tied to a specific workstation or bound by a dress code. Perversely, the trend in buildings was towards automatic systems that took control away from occupants. In the late 1980s, we discovered that, if not well-designed, built, maintained, managed, and cleaned, buildings of this kind could easily end up as 'sick', particularly the deep plan ones.

2   *Responsiveness.* If personal controls work well, one attribute is system responsiveness: you make an adjustment and conditions rapidly begin to change for the better. In the early 1990s, we began to find the occasional building where occupants reported relatively high degrees of control, even though few control devices were available to them. The reason turned out to be proactive facilities managers who responded rapidly to occupant needs (e.g. if telephoned), and sometimes even learnt to make adjustments in anticipation. Responsiveness is not restricted to environmental controls, but anything that may need adapting to meet changing needs, e.g. reconfiguring furniture and spaces. Sometimes this

is physically difficult (with triangular rooms, for example), or where organisations adopt a completely uniform workstation standard, although space requirements may differ substantially with task, e.g. for surveyors needing to look at large drawings and marketing people working with samples. Sometimes problems are administrative, for example, in some Private Finance Initiative (PFI) buildings, even simple changes have to be made by the contractor not the occupier; and delay, misunderstanding and high cost often stop people requesting them.

3 *Building depth.* In deeper-plan buildings, scores for occupant satisfaction and productivity tended to go down. Greater depth correlated with more complication, presence of air conditioning, less personal control, and more dependence on facilities management, which was often slow to respond to occupants, particularly in public sector buildings. Naturally-ventilated buildings tended to perform better, with shallower plans, more window seats, more personal control and less dependence on management. However, we warned that the 'green' trend to introduce natural ventilation into deeper-plan buildings might not necessarily carry the perceived benefits of natural ventilation with it, because the occupant satisfaction problems associated with air-conditioned buildings were more to do with depth, complexity and management than the air conditioning itself.

4 *Workgroups.* In offices, perceptions of productivity were higher for smaller and more integrated workgroups, either in their own rooms, or in clusters within an open-plan space. An important reason for this was seen to be the 'mapping' between the workgroup's activities, and the available environmental controls. Where the relationship is one-to-one (i.e. everything coincides, as it often does in a single room), the sole occupant will have full control over lighting, blinds, ventilation, heating, cooling, privacy and noise, and can fine-tune these to suit their needs. While this is no longer possible for a workgroup, its members are more likely to come to an agreement: indeed, sometimes we found workgroups using environmental controls – particularly lighting – to reinforce group identity. Overheard conversations of other members of a workgroup may also convey useful information, while noise from unrelated groups may well be regarded as intrusive and distracting.

As is apparent in the discussion above, the four variables are inter-related, and can combine in vicious and virtuous circles. In well-designed and well-managed buildings, we found positive associations between comfort, perceived productivity and energy efficiency (Bordass *et al.*, 1995). Conversely, the 'sick' buildings common in the 1980s and 1990s[9] exemplified vicious circles of associations and causes: an extreme example being the infamous Inland Revenue building in Bootle, Lancashire (BBC News, 2001), which was eventually demolished after all attempts to rectify endemic problems failed. Initially researchers, using large-sample statistical studies, blamed air conditioning as the 'cause', but this turned out to be wrong. There was no single design or management problem, but a system of interactions that spun out of control – including deeper-plan spaces with air conditioning, little or no occupant control of comfort conditions; lack of natural light and outside awareness; complex and poorly maintained building services technology that often did not work properly; and facility managers who lacked both the diagnostic skills to put things right and adequate resources to do so.

The lack of a single cause was the reason why so many of these buildings never improved: it was a question of systemic failure. Many of us will have experienced something similar. In an empty room, conditions may not be exactly to our liking – it might be too cold – but may well be tolerable. As more people come in, the room gets warmer and noisier, and perhaps more convivial. At some point the room's carrying capacity – its ability to support the needs of those in it (like face-to-face conversation) – reaches a threshold, which will vary for different people. Things become uncomfortable, too hot, too noisy for reasonable conversations, and too crowded, at which point people may try to leave or at least move to a cooler or quieter spot.

A version of this is played out in many office buildings around the world. Physical and organisational constraints often mean that flexibility and adaptability are poor. Increasing or reducing densities is one of the few variables that may be manipulated in the short term – but increased density may take the building over its carrying-capacity threshold. Meeting rooms may be converted into desk zones, touch-down workstations introduced (perhaps breaking up working group propinquity), storage areas reduced (or taken offsite), and primary circulation compromised with the original design intent ignored. Users' objections will be over-ridden. A well-regarded building may deteriorate quickly.

The killer variables – ten years ago

In the second edition of this book, we expanded item 3 into 'Ventilation type and building depth' and added a fifth variable:

5   *Design intent*, and how it is communicated to occupants. By design intent, we mean how designers expect particular features to work, how they should be used or operated; and how users interpret this.

In practice:

- Some features might work well if they were actually used. However, occupants do not always appreciate what they are for, perhaps because the item cannot be seen (e.g. with natural ventilation through grilles); its purpose is not clear (e.g. trickle ventilators in office and hospital windows, often present but rarely used); nobody explained the intent (e.g. staff in open-plan offices may not know they are free to use the cellular offices as quiet rooms); or there may be cultural problems (e.g. staff reluctant to use quiet rooms for fear that managers will think they are not at work).
- Some features may need insight to use, which in turn may require explanation and training. This applies not just to electronic controls (lighting controls are too often incomprehensible) but to much simpler things like windows. For example, in a thermally massive building, the design intent might be to close windows during the day and open them at night in hot weather: however, occupants may not understand this, or security and cleaning staff may close them anyway.
- Some may be unusable, for example, where insurers do not allow windows intended for night ventilation to be left open. In one case – a university library – automatic ventilation primarily for night cooling was switched off by management because of fears that students would steal books by throwing them out of open windows to their co-conspirators below!

Donald Norman, writing about everyday artefacts generally (Norman, 2013) identifies the 'design model', the 'user's model' and the 'system image'. Designers tend to know why things are how they are, and may assume that users will see things the same way. But users' mental models are often very different: even when conversing with other designers, they may not share the same system image. Design intent should be made crystal clear: Norman argues that if this is not possible intuitively, then ideally people should only need to be told once. Clarity of design intent is also associated with other effects that improve building performance and the productivity of occupants, including:

- People are more forgiving of sub-optimal conditions when they understand the design intent. We first became aware of this when studying recently completed office buildings designed for and occupied by research organisations and design practices. The clients for these studies expected the occupants – being designers themselves and thinking that they could have done better and sometimes having said so – might be particularly critical of items that did not work quite as well as anticipated. In fact, the opposite was true, possibly because the occupants understood the design intent better and were more tolerant as a result.
- Virtuous circles, where understanding of design intent helps buildings to become better in multiple ways, e.g. with both low energy use and high perceived productivity. Here we have identified two main influences: (1) Design intent tends to be easier to understand in buildings that are intrinsically simpler (e.g. shallow-plan with openable windows), have more components that users can adjust themselves, and where users can clearly perceive the outcomes of their actions. (2) Design intent is more likely to be carried through to operational reality where special care has been taken in briefing, design, construction, commissioning and subsequent management and monitoring. We therefore helped to develop the Soft Landings process (Way *et al.*, 2009) to make these outcomes more likely.

Buildings that work well

Our five killer variables still appear valid. In rather different words, buildings, especially offices, appear to work best for occupants when the following are present:

- *Comfort and control.* An environment that is comfortable for the most of the time, with plenty of opportunities for changing things should conditions deteriorate.
- *Usability.* Clear communication of design intent, so users of all types (not just permanent occupants) understand how things are supposed to work, can intervene to make changes if necessary and get rapid feedback on whether or not the change required has occurred.
- *Rapid response* in meeting immediately perceived needs, not necessarily by having good local control devices. Other strategies include the ability to move about and the responsiveness of management to requests for changes.
- *Shallow plan forms*, preferably demanding less technically complex and less management-intensive systems (with the added benefit of better energy performance).
- *Natural ventilation* of some sort. Some of the best buildings we have reviewed incorporate mixed-mode schemes in which properly integrated and managed mechanical systems are able to supplement or replace the natural ones when necessary. However, to create a good mixed-mode system needs care in design, construction, commissioning and operation which are often lacking.
- *Zoning and density.* Activities that properly fit the spaces and services that support them, not only in spatial capacity (e.g. enough room for everyone, well-integrated workgroups), but for zoning and control of heating, cooling, lighting, ventilation, noise and privacy.
- *Proven low energy use.* Apart from the obvious benefits of lower emissions, this tends to be associated with better briefing, procurement, management and monitoring, which is also likely to lead to better human performance in the workplace.

If you want accurate and believable feedback to help designers and managers improve the next generation of buildings, we think the above list would be a good starting point. However, this is not enough for some. They want proof. Unfortunately, this may lure researchers into the territory of large-sample surveys, physical measurement, statistical modelling and simulation, the scope of which may be hobbled by onerous methodological and inferential requirements. Too often, uncertainty generated by too much emphasis on theory and method creates interpretational barriers which designers, in search of practical advice, find hard to negotiate.

We prefer to start with case studies of real buildings in use, apply tried-and-tested methods to extract indicative and diagnostic information, and only rarely go deeper into further investigation and measurement. This 'drill-down' strategy takes you only to the level of detail you need. You do not collect too much information unnecessarily, or create a muddle with too many results. Flyvbjerg (2006) is an excellent justification for the misunderstood virtues of case studies.

For example, an occupant survey may tell you that perceived productivity is low, as in Figure 19.4, where the average score for the study building is six percentage points below that typical for others in the dataset. From the comments boxes in the questionnaire, it is clear that traders are dissatisfied with a new market hall, in particular, the high ambient temperature and

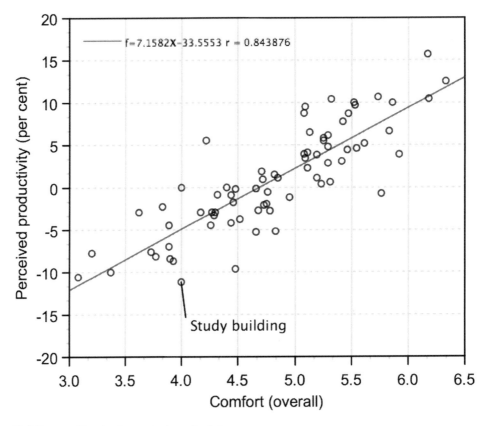

Figure 19.4 Expected levels of perceived productivity

Notes:

Perceived comfort overall score means by building (horizontal axis) plotted against mean perceived productivity scores (vertical axis) for UK buildings from BUS 2014 dataset. The study building highlighted is scoring six percentage points lower than might be expected from the distribution overall.

a low footfall of customers: the two may even be related. The levels of proof required depend on circumstances of the investigation and what you are trying to do. For design and management diagnostics, the information already collected on the market hall may be enough, particularly as it is an unusual building type, for which there may be little comparative information. The next steps would probably be to investigate the reasons for overheating and to carry out a survey of the shoppers who do visit and perhaps do not visit the hall to discern the reasons for the low footfall.

For more detailed academic studies, stricter criteria may apply. (e.g. Robson, 2011). Whatever prevails, we think the most fruitful approach is a case-study building visit coupled with straightforward data-gathering, preferably based on direct contact, interview and measurement. Working remotely with, for example, internet-based occupant surveys or 'smart' metering databases may miss gross anomalies, especially if data cannot be double-checked and resolved.

The increasing emphasis on finding proof may be leading researchers up blind alleys. Take, for example, two growing productivity killers in office buildings – noise and increasing occupant densities. These are related: a trend to more intense use leads to higher occupant densities in open plan offices, so noise and unwanted interruptions increase too. In the worst cases, high density may also be associated with higher temperatures, poorer air quality, less cleanliness, perceptions of unhealthiness and other knock-on effects. A vicious circle of deterioration has started, which may become increasingly difficult to reverse. A solely statistical approach will miss such dynamics, unless backed by on-the-ground case study investigation.

What has changed since the 1980s?

In the past quarter century we have identified the following trends.

- *Control.* Occupants tend to have less control because more and more systems are automated, despite evidence that occupants are happier when they can intervene for themselves. With smartphone interfaces, this might now be changing – but there is a danger that systems might then become too complicated and difficult to manage.
- *Facilities management and maintenance.* In the 1980s, many of the 'sick' buildings we surveyed were poorly managed, maintained and cleaned. The 1990s saw considerable improvements, but since then things seem to have stalled. Reasons include cost-cutting and a trend to outsourcing – so often facilities management contractors do not fully understand the buildings they are managing (particularly if they have unusual design and engineering features) and the occupants they are serving. After a few years some teams eventually do, but this experience can easily be dispersed when contracts are re-tendered, increasingly across whole organisations at 3–5-year intervals. A terrible forgetting curve.
- *Response times* also tended to improve and then get worse, as a result of this outsourcing, to companies who also turn to specialist contractors to correct faults, often adding time-lags, increasing costs, and frequently leading to the treatment of the symptoms of a problem (e.g. replacing a component), but a neglect of the underlying causes (why did it fail?). One aspect of responsiveness has, however, improved: in modern workspaces, occupants (or at least some of them) have more opportunity to move around and so escape from an uncomfortable environment to somewhere different.

- *Deeper plan forms* are widespread, which is leading to more complaints of noise, unwanted interruptions and a lack of perceived control, and makes natural ventilation more difficult to engineer, at least at an economic cost.
- *Natural ventilation* is not achieving its potential, even in shallower buildings. Where present, there are often shortcomings in window design, control and excessive heat gains. If well executed, mixed-mode buildings may offer the best of both worlds, but they are still rare. There seems to be a lack of design and management expertise, and perceptions that natural ventilation and mixed-mode systems are riskier, too expensive or too much trouble. This applies particularly in the (growing) rented sector, which needs to accommodate a wide range of tenants, and in spite of arguments for the greater flexibility of mixed-mode.
- *Zoning and workgroup integrity* are breaking down under intensification of use.
- *Energy and environmental rating schemes* are commonly treated as tick-box compliance at the design stage, rather than underpinning root-and-branch reform of management attitudes and practices to achieve better performance in use based on proven outcomes.

One thing that has definitely improved is user satisfaction with natural and artificial lighting. We first started noticing this in about 2000. The main reason was not the lighting itself but the arrival of flat computer screens. The older cathode-ray (CRT) screens were curved, so could pick up reflections from anything, particularly windows and light fittings, while LCD and LED screens could often easily be angled away from the sources of glare.

The change in screen technology also had a big impact on the layout of open-plan offices. CRT screens tended to be tucked into the inner corners of cruciform or triangular workstation clusters, so some screens almost inevitably picked up glare from the windows. With LCDs, workstation clusters could become long benches perpendicular to window walls – reducing glare but allowing occupation density to be increased.

Why aren't we doing better?

We have defined some circumstances under which people respond well in buildings and the environmental gains that can result. So why is the market going largely in the opposite direction? The answers may lie somewhere in the following:

- Myth-making about workplace performance, especially the supposed efficacy of open plan offices and the generic assumption that they increase productivity. Do people really communicate better in open plan spaces, if we factor in their real work tasks? Some will, some won't. What about the increasing numbers who wear earphones and headsets to keep out the unwanted noise (while probably listening to something distracting)? Corporate management and designers seem to be more at ease with the concept of open plan than the many who have to work in it.
- Increasing complication of requirements, process and products, with deliberate over-complication often cynically treated as a business opportunity.
- Excessive focus on bottom-line economics – especially through increasing occupant densities and contracts with supplier handcuffs attached.
- Outsourcing of technical and operational skills, with the subsequent loss of in-house knowledge, experience and, in many cases, speed of service.
- Increasing virtualisation of education and design practice and enduring lack of designer engagement with consequences and outcomes.

- Professional judgement trumped by public relations veneering, suppressing feedback and protecting reputations at the expense of learning from admitted mistakes.
- Public-interest professionalism demonised as anti-competitive or elitist.

Notes

1 Versions have also appeared in *Building Services Journal* (June 1998): 41–43; *Facilities Management World*, 1998, September–October; *Building Research and Information*, 1999, Jan; in Clements-Croome, D. (ed.) *Creating the Productive Workplace*, London: E&FN Spon, 2000 (first edition), 2005 (second edition); *Ecolibrium* (5 parts, April–September 2005) and in translation.
2 A memorable response from an Australian building user was 'My productivity is reduced by answering bloody stupid questions like this one'!
3 Our primary sources of data are (a) occupant surveys using the BUS Methodology; and (b) investigative, empirical, building performance surveys using a portfolio of methods pioneered in the Probe series of post-occupancy studies, and subsequently developed *ad hoc*.
4 This sample of n=174 is drawn from the BUS Methodology international database and refers to those buildings which have been studied with this question. The question was added in 2010.
5 Please note: (a) the scale used in Figure 19.2 has been changed from plus and minus 20 per cent to plus and minus 40 per cent. This is a cosmetic change only. The data are directly comparable as the question on the questionnaire remained the same. (b) Benchmarks change over time.
6 See caption to Figure 19.3 for details of significance.
7 For more detail, see: www.usablebuildings.co.uk/Pages/Unprotected/RIBACPDBirminghamPartThree-27Nov14.pdf (accessed Feb. 2016).
8 GreenStar is a feature-based rating system developed by the Green Building Council of Australia. Buildings are rated on a scale from 1–6.
9 The terminology is now less brutal. Sick building syndrome is now known as building-related ill-health.

References

Baird, G. and Dykes, C. (2012) The potential for the use of occupants' comments in the analysis and prediction of building performance. *Buildings*, 2: 33–47.

BBC News (2001) Available at: http://news.bbc.co.uk/1/hi/england/1688081.stm (accessed Feb. 2016).

Bordass, W., Burgon, P., Brough, H. and Vaudin, M. (2014) Trees of knowledge. *CIBSE Journal*, Oct.: 20–26.

Bordass, W. (2000) Cost and value: fact and fiction. *Building Research and Information*, 28(5/6): 338–352.

Bordass, W., Bromley, A. and Leaman, A. (1995) Comfort, control and energy-efficiency in offices. BRE Information Paper 3/95, February.

Bunn, R. (2007) Tales from the Rivergreen, *BSRIA Delta T*, October, pp. 12–16. Available at: www.usablebuildings.co.uk/Pages/Protected/RivergreenCentre.pdf (accessed May 2016).

Bunn, R. (2016a) Making performance visible, Research for EngD thesis, private communication.

Bunn, R. (2016b) Occupation satisfaction signatures: longitudinal studies of changing comfort perceptions in two non-domestic buildings. CIBSE Technical Symposium, Edinburgh, UK, 14–15 April.

Economist Intelligence Unit (2014) *Out of Office: An Overview of Workplace Absenteeism in Europe*. London: EIU.

Flyvbjerg, B. (2006) Five misunderstandings about case-study research, *Qualitative Inquiry*, 12(2): 219–245.

Leaman, A. and Bordass, W. (1997) Productivity in buildings: the killer variables. Workplace Comfort Forum, London, October 29–30.

Lorch, R. (2016) See www.usablebuildings.co.uk/Pages/BRIArticlesForUBTFeb2016.pdf (accessed May 2016).

Nevill, G. (2007) So, how are you doing?, *CIBSE Journal*, November: 32–37.

Norman, D. (2013) *The Design of Everyday Things*, 2nd edn. New York: Basic Books.

Oseland, N. (1999) Environmental factors affecting workplace performance: a review of the evidence. Chartered Institution of Building Services Engineers (CIBSE), Technical memoranda TM24.

Robson, C. (2011) *Real World Research: A Resource for Users of Social Research Methods in Applied Settings*. Chichester: John Wiley & Sons, Ltd.

Way, M., Bordass, W., Leaman, A. and Bunn, R, (2009) The Soft Landings Framework. BSRIA BG 4/2009, Building Services Research and Information Association (BSRIA) and Usable Buildings Trust (UBT) July.

Chapter 20

Enjoy Work

A case study on Chiswick Park

Jason Margrave, Ron German and Kay Chaston

Introduction

Try to imagine a world without Google. When Stanhope began outlining its plans for Chiswick Park in the late 1990s, the world was on the verge of the online revolution. And just as the arrival of WiFi, MacBooks and coffee-shop brainstorms was about to shake up people's working lives, Stanhope realised people's expectations of the workplace would change radically, too. So they created an environment where a modern mobile workforce could thrive. This article explores what they achieved, and shows how property management can have a big impact on productivity at work – by focussing on people.

Question: how to get people to Chiswick?

Chiswick Park is a fantastic example of innovative thinking. However, as is often the way, it all started with a simple question: how could you tempt the best businesses in the world to a business park in Chiswick?

The answer lay partly in timing: Stanhope was developing the Chiswick Park site in the late 1990s, just as the technology revolution was taking off: email and mobiles were changing how we worked, new businesses were prioritising teamwork, interaction and informality over cubicles and reserved parking spaces. Meanwhile the Millennial generation was joining the workforce, and they no longer aspired to work in traditional corporate environments.

In short, ambitious businesses and the younger workforce were beginning to expect more from their workspace. They wanted it to be an experience. Stanhope realised if they could provide this experience – a place where people genuinely enjoyed coming to work, where they were more engaged and therefore more productive – they could entice businesses out of Central London and to Chiswick Park.

Box 20.1   Background to Chiswick Park

For nearly 100 years, the 33-acre Chiswick Park site had served as a London Transport bus garage and works, until it was shut down in the 1980s. The site was put on the market and Stanhope started looking into its potential.

Urbanisation was becoming an important theme in the way in which cities were changing. The out-of-town, car-reliant, greenfield business park was starting to look dated. The time was right for an urban workplace that took the best of the business park and town-centre office models and merged them into a new product. It was this concept that inspired Stanhope, the design team and the investors to create this new offering in Chiswick.

Building a sense of place

How did Stanhope go about creating this experience? Heading up the project for Stanhope was experienced property developer, Ron German. He explains the first thing they did was think about the physical environment *beyond* the buildings themselves:

> We thought to ourselves, how do you get to a position where you've got a grade A property that people love? If you're relying on the fabric of the building, that's pretty challenging. What we learnt from Broadgate was property becomes grade A when it has a coherent sense of place.

People not cars

To develop this sense of place, Stanhope appointed architect Richard Rogers, a recognised visionary in the growth of cities. Lord Rogers' response to Stanhope's brief was to create a people-centric park where individuals and businesses could exchange ideas and embrace new ways of working (Figure 20.1). The park would consist of a family of 12 office buildings situated around a central pedestrian space made up of a lake, landscaping and open-air performance area. Vehicles and servicing would be kept to the perimeter with parking tucked discreetly under the buildings and to the edges of the site. All employees would approach the buildings on foot. To make it easy for people to arrive by public transport, new links to Chiswick High Road and local stations would be upgraded and new bus routes would be set up to service the park.

This master plan implemented ideas that seem unremarkable today. But as Sir Stuart Lipton, former CEO of Stanhope pointed out, at the time they broke many of the established rules of business park design and have helped alter the concept of what a workplace should be:

> We asked Richard Rogers to re-create in a modern way the Georgian vernacular of a villa. His concept was brilliant and produced a series of identical buildings led by a pedestrian-only five-acre central park where all the businesses would have identical status and access.

A place to share

From a productivity point of view, what was most significant about cars being pushed out of the centre was that it made way for a green shared space. This space included coffee shops and quiet areas where people from different companies could take their laptops and work – catering to the growing desire for more informal work spaces and creating a real sense of community linked to the place rather than employers. It's funny to believe now, but this was way ahead of its time.

> If you want to improve productivity, I don't think it's about the buildings any more. It's about responding to what people value.
>
> (Ron German)

Enjoy Work

Even with this physical environment, persuading world-class businesses to move their offices and employees from Central London to Chiswick was not going to be an easy task. The park needed something more.

Figure 20.1 Chiswick Park was designed to create a sense of place beyond individual buildings, and a business community beyond individual organisations

This in itself was not a new thought at the time: developers everywhere were starting to realise that just cutting the grass and collecting rent were not enough to entice occupiers any more. As a result, concierge services were emerging. But often these were a dry cleaner, a gym and perhaps a florist.

The Stanhope team agreed Chiswick Park would have to go much further. Stanhope director, Henry Williams, turned to brand consultants Wolff Olins to help create a new hospitality-based concept for Chiswick Park. The 'Enjoy Work' concept was born.

'If you enjoy work, you do better work. Better work = better business'

It was at this point that Stanhope also brought in premium-hotel industry expert Kay Chaston to bring this new hospitality-based concept to life. Kay explains Enjoy Work was actually based on the very simple fact that if you enjoy where you work, you're going to be more productive, and, in turn, a more productive workforce gives businesses a commercial benefit: 'In its simplest form, the vision was to create a place where people enjoy work. If you enjoy work, you do better work. Better work = better business.'

Enjoy Work is still the proposition that defines Chiswick Park today. However, as Kay points out, 'It's easy to forget that, at the time, it was an industry revolution. The vision and operational ethos of Enjoy Work were the differentiator between just another business park and the creation of a ground-breaking workplace.'

From tenants to guests

Enjoy Work was a bold vision and required different thinking. In developing the Enjoy Work concept, it was not enough to bolt on a menu of concierge facilities and programmes. Kay explains:

> We needed to challenge convention and we did at every level – our structure, operating culture, customer interface, right through to our language – calling our tenants 'guests' – was a mind-set shift. Our mission was to impact the quality of life for thousands of people. Enjoy Work became an additional element in the toolkit of every company on the park, to enable them to attract and retain the best talent and to enhance productivity.

Appealing to the individual

At the time, most events plans for business parks had a strong commercialised element to them. Kay Chaston told us Enjoy Work went out to do the opposite:

> It was about ensuring every aspect of our brand was congruent, relevant and valued by our guests. This wasn't going to be a stage-set for car brands to hand out raffle tickets. Instead our intent was that the overall programme would engage every single individual at some level. So everyone at Chiswick Park would at some point go home and talk enthusiastically about what they did at work today, whether they were a 55-year-old accountant or a 20-year-old trainee.

We looked at the extremes of the demographic and mixed up the events and activities so there was at least one thing that held particular appeal to every individual on site. It meant activities were hugely diverse – from upwards bungee jumping to polo to performances by the English

Philharmonic Orchestra, and a full-on sports programme. We had many measures of what an event should be able to achieve.

Box 20.2   The Enjoy Work Sports Programme

The Sports Programme is a great example of how Enjoy Work helped build a community outside individual organisations. The programme was designed with multiple facets: there was a competitive sports league for five-a-side football and netball. There were also 'rock up and play' sports engaged for people who couldn't commit time regularly (Figure 20.2). These more spontaneous elements engaged people who wouldn't otherwise know each other. It was a successful community-building technique.

Figure 20.2 Enjoy Work's 'Rock Up and Play' Sports Programme has proved a hugely effective way to build a sense of community at Chiswick Park – bringing people together from different businesses for an hour of fun, fresh air and new friendships

Well-being through self-improvement

Kay explains the events plan also placed a specific focus on self-improvement:

> We ran a range of sessions like guitar lessons, golf lessons and language courses. This was really a new level of service that no-one had done. All business environments cater for people's basic needs like comfort and warmth. Many provide convenience in terms of amenities

and transport. However, giving people the opportunity for self-improvement really spurs on people's sense of well-being and purpose.

Stepping out of the employee mind-set

> Creating an environment that 8,000 people take ownership of comes by doing hundreds of different things consistently well and on message. It's not easy, but the result is something precious and rare and real.
>
> (Kay Chaston)

On the face of it, Enjoy Work was a social proposition, but strategically it was much more. Kay says, 'Enjoy Work was about creating a human community in place of a business park and that has been the magic.'

Enjoy Work offered a completely new way of mixing people up that was different to what could be achieved within a single organisation. As Kay points out:

> Enjoy Work events happened over lunch. People from different organisations with shared likes and interests came together for an hour. The next time they were in line in Starbucks, they knew each other. These simple human connectors created a community dynamic that was distinctively new in a business environment.

The other significant thing was that people were stepping out of their 'employee' mind-set:

> Forward-thinking companies like Google, Microsoft … they'd created a culture where some of this stuff was starting to happen. However, Chiswick Park was looking forward to initiating this dynamic within a business community of 40+ organisations. It enabled an economy of a grander scale for all companies. But most importantly, it wasn't in the context of the company. You're stepping out of the 'I'm an employee' mind-set. That's hugely empowering for people's sense of autonomy and individuality.

Box 20.3   A view from Orange Labs

Orange has been a guest at Chiswick Park right from the start, and the benefits of the park were immediately felt. When Carolina Costa, CEO of Orange Labs took charge, she asked her staff what changes they'd like to see in their workplace. The response was a resounding 'Do not move from the Park!' Here she gives her views on the Chiswick Park experience.

> Chiswick Park was visionary. It was seeing a trend where workspace is no longer a place where you just come and do your work; it's a place where you have an experience.
>   I can't imagine what it was like to set it up and think it through and I think it's brilliant at matching the demographics to the various offerings for entertainment and

fun. It's always very easy to settle for the minimum common denominator and instead Chiswick Park had the courage to break those rules.

I always had a sense that the park cares. What a clever way to create loyalty. The work environment becomes the loyalty!

Part of the wider community

Stanhope's vision for Enjoy Work wasn't just to build a community within Chiswick Park, but also to integrate Chiswick Park into the existing community around it (Figure 20.3). From the beginning, the park was open seven days a week. Mums with prams and dog walkers could access freely. Local people were encouraged to use the Fitness Centre. Charity walks, runs and fireworks were organised. The park also engaged early on with schools in Chiswick, offering opportunities for younger children to come and learn about the environment and sustainability, and older students to get involved with more formal NVQ training. This was all part of making it a normal environment, which sounds simple and obvious now, but was unusual and ground-breaking among the traditionally more insular business parks of the time.

Figure 20.3 Chiswick Park was one of the first business parks to have the heart of the park completely car-free, making way for shared green space open to everyone, whether working in the park or visiting.

How do these community ties improve the experience and productivity of people working on the park? Kay says that when you see the impact in person it's abundantly clear:

> Imagine you're working in a five-storey glass building. During your day you're looking down and there are twelve 6-year-olds holding onto a rope going across the bridge, and an Enjoy Work person explaining the different ducks and fish to them. This natural environment brings such a human, soulful component to work. We had mums coming to the Park with their strollers and dads would come out of the office at lunch to kick a football around with their 3-year-old. I remember seeing four suited execs coming back from Starbucks and they suddenly stopped by the lake. They stood there for two minutes watching the ducklings, then went back to work. On what scale would you like to measure that?

100 per cent retention for the first 10 years

Of course, there are metrics that can measure how engaged people are at work, and how this has improved their productivity – and by every measure Chiswick Park's holistic vision of a new type of workplace has been a success.

A fundamental part of the Enjoy Work approach has been regular feedback and continuous improvement to keep the concept fresh and relevant. In the 2011 Guest Survey, for example, 98 per cent of guests said they would recommend working at Chiswick Park to a friend. And 94 per cent said the environment enhanced their productivity.

In the process, a real sense of love and loyalty to the park has developed. Kay explains,

> We've had people leaving one company on the park come right to the Enjoy Work office and ask, 'I'm moving on, who's hiring on the park? I don't want to leave here.' Some of these people were commuting from two hours away.

The strong commercial success story of Chiswick Park includes tenant company retention over the first ten years at 100 per cent, excluding mergers and acquisitions. It is now on the 'must-see' list for companies looking for new space in West London. Over forty companies are currently based at Chiswick Park, including 24 UK head offices, three global headquarters and three European headquarters, among them some of the most dynamic and creative UK and global brands. It has won numerous awards, including the *Financial Times*' 'Best Workplaces' six years running.

Stanhope ripped up the rulebook at Chiswick Park, and many of the ideas implemented are now more common. They all add to our collective understanding of how to create a productive workplace in the future – and how big a part property developers and managers can play, simply by focusing on people.

Chapter 21

The need for a wellness integrator to ensure healthy buildings and businesses

Victoria Lockhart, Mallory Taub and Ann Marie Aguilar

Introduction

While some may be sceptical of the corporate world's interest in health and well-being, there is a mounting movement of research demonstrating the value in strategies that deliver healthy buildings and businesses. With the cost of staff salaries and benefits typically accounting for around 90 per cent of business operating costs (World Green Building Council, 2014), organisations are keen to leverage insights of what they can do to foster a high-performing workforce. Further, innovative products, apps and wearables are transforming how people track their health and building performance. Technology is enabling a citizen-science movement that empowers individuals with the data to start demanding healthier environments, and the duty of care is falling on building owners, designers, and operators to deliver.

The World Health Organization and the Centers for Disease Control define health and well-being as follows:

> *Health* is a state of complete physical, mental and social well-being and not merely the absence of disease or infirmity.
>
> *Well-being* is an active process through which people become aware of, and make choices toward, a more successful existence, including the presence of positive emotions and moods, the absence of negative emotions, satisfaction with life, fulfilment and positive functioning.

In the current world of work, well-being generally resides with the HR and Health and Safety teams. Managers of the 'people environment' typically craft programmes and benefits around drivers of personal health and well-being, raising health awareness, mental health support and improved muscular skeletal management. Progressive firms are prioritising proactive health-care spend to keep their workforce healthy (Figure 21.1), and developing comprehensive corporate wellness 'perks' that boost employee engagement, as well as attract and retain top talent.

Workplace wellness programmes represent a $6 billion-a-year industry, but the success of these has proved variable (Spicer and Cederström, 2015). Smart businesses want to ensure investments in benefits and healthcare provision are delivering maximum value to the widest audience possible. There have been some high-profile failures: a comprehensive study into the efficacy of PepsiCo's Healthy Living programme over seven-years found that lifestyle management interventions delivered no statistically significant effect on healthcare costs (Begley, 2014). There are also some great success stories: at Arup, their HR team has developed a comprehensive wellness programme in collaboration with a healthcare provider that has achieved record levels of employee engagement. By promoting awareness, proactive health screening and

Figure 21.1 Designers at work in Hong Kong
Source: Cheung Tsun.

check-ups, and targeted lifestyle advice and support, within two years Arup is already seeing a drop in absenteeism that includes a significant reduction in long-term sickness. Head of the programme, Evan Davidge, describes how the people management discourse around health and well-being is entering a new era:

> It is no longer a 'one-size-fits-all' approach looking to enforce healthy options and dictate lifestyles, but about being true to our humanitarian company ethos and assuming a more passive, nurturing role. The key is enablement: providing the tools, resources and culture for people to thrive.

The opportunity now is to extend the breadth and ambition of well-being initiatives beyond the realm of people management and into the totality of the workplace environment and employee experience. For a holistic, authentic message, organisations need to include our surroundings and move beyond simply ensuring their legal duties for safe and fit-for-purpose workspaces are met as part of fundamental health and safety. Our environments impact not only our physical health, but also our mental state and emotions: our spaces need to support the tasks at hand, reinforce the company brand and values, as well as facilitate healthier behaviours, ensuring the option that is best for us is also the easiest. There is an emergent need for a *Wellness Integrator* to champion well-being across traditional company silos, uniting HR, Facilities Management,

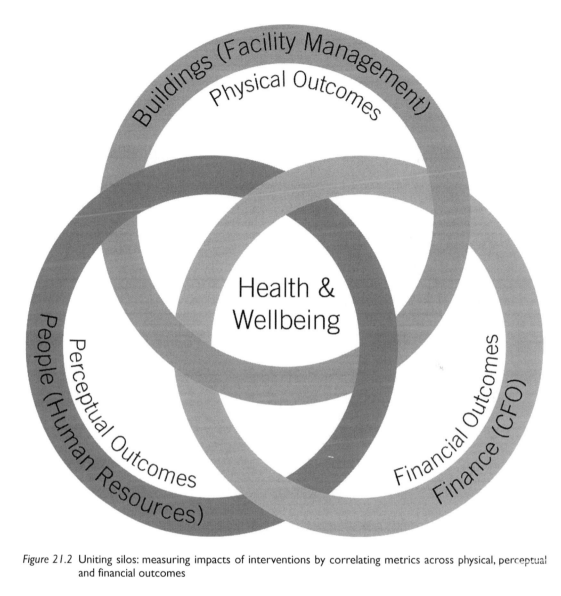

Figure 21.2 Uniting silos: measuring impacts of interventions by correlating metrics across physical, perceptual and financial outcomes

technology and business in a holistic drive towards health and well-being that infuses all aspects of the organisation (Figure 21.2). As well as coordinate, this role will manage the tools and data insights to be able to measure and monitor success and drive improvements over time.

The role of CRE in health and well-being

The question facing Real Estate teams and portfolio managers needs to focus specifically at the asset level: how is *this* building supporting the needs of *these* people? There are a number of intersecting issues across the design, operations and organisational policies in place within a workplace that collectively shape individual experience and personal health and well-being.

Within *design*, there needs to be a proactive approach to improving indoor air quality by minimising airborne viruses and germs, particulate matter, material off-gassing, and mould. Engineering and design can minimise exposure to factors that negatively impact health and hydration such as chlorine, dissolved minerals, sediment, bacteria, and unfavourable taste properties. Focusing on light quality can help avoid disruption to the body's circadian rhythm and visual discomfort. Valuing active design features can lead to spaces and programmes that promote regular physical activity, reducing the negative impacts of sedentary lifestyles. Improving thermal, acoustic, ergonomic, and olfactory comfort can help occupants avoid musculoskeletal disorders, factors inhibiting ability to focus, and chronic stress.

The way in which facilities *operate* also plays a key role. Ongoing programmes of air and water quality testing, together with careful design and monitoring of maintenance and cleaning protocols, ensure assets continue to deliver the exemplary design conditions post-occupancy, and are successfully adapting to the needs of evolving user populations over time. Food options should include convenient healthy, nutritious options, with positive messaging and a balanced, well-labelled selection from which individuals can choose.

Organisations themselves can also support mental and emotional health through policies and procedures, championing ethical procurement and social equity, open information and transparency, offering choice and influence over work setting through family-friendly flexible working practices, and encouraging altruism and community outreach through paid time for voluntary work (Figure 21.3). With stress, anxiety and depression reported as the leading causes of long-term absence (CBI/Pfizer, 2013), we all stand to benefit from conscious design elements and policies that supporting better relaxation, connection to nature and community, and stress management.

As the breadth of these topics demonstrates, this is no longer a topic that HR can address in isolation. While this may be fresh thinking in the commercial sector, there are precedents and lessons to be learned from others. Hoteliers have always placed heavy emphasis on the customer experience, and are extending beyond designated spa facilities and treatments to infuse well-being holistically across communal areas, individual rooms, and restaurants. The residential sector is also responding; in the UK, the Building Research Establishment has identified health and well-being as such a core determinant of housing quality that it forms a prominent overlay to the development of their newest rating tool, the Home Quality Mark (BRE, 2015), which will ultimately summarise a home's performance in terms that are of most relevance to the residents: cost, health and well-being, and environmental footprint.

Real estate teams have the opportunity to reinforce corporate branding messages through healthy design and operations. LYFE Kitchens, an American chain with a mission statement to 'Eat Good, Feel Good and Do Good' have matched their nutritious menu with healthy interiors, publicly committing to WELL Building Certification of all facilities in their five-year development pipeline. UK-developer British Land are looking to integrate the latest research and built-environment recommendations around health and well-being in the evolution of their design briefs, operational practices, estate management and services for customers and tenants to truly deliver 'places people prefer'. For commercial property and real estate services adviser, CBRE, their Workplace360 programme is transforming how employees work and how space is designed and allocated, and includes a strong commitment to employee health and wellness (CBRE, 2015). This is proving a powerful strategy in positioning it as an innovator with first-hand experience and demonstrating industry leadership to current and future clients. Organisations fighting to attract and retain top talent are also choosing to adopt wellness within their real estate strategies: this is the opportunity recognised by Macquarie and Deloitte (Deloitte Australia, 2016), and something being championed at Arup.

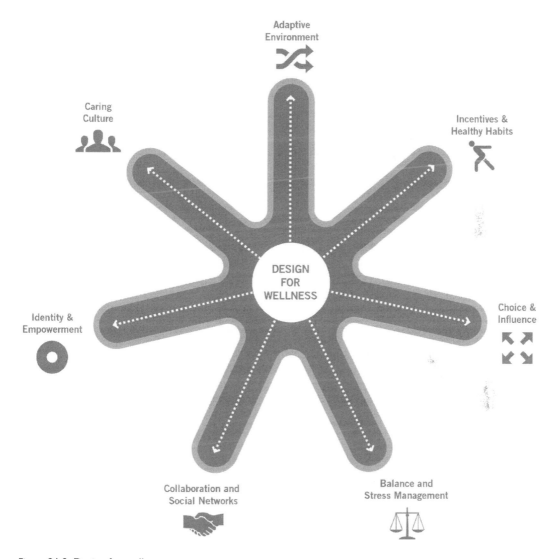

Figure 21.3 Design for wellness

What are metrics for measurement and management?

The question then arises of how to measure 'well-being': what exactly can be tracked, and how can performance be benchmarked? Dovetailing neatly with existing green building rating tools, the WELL Building Standard is one early response from the International WELL Building Institute. Designed to work in tandem with environmental schemes such as LEED or the Living Building Challenge, this framework is the product of seven years of medical research into built environment health impacts, and defines a range of design criteria, operational performance requirements and organisational procedures to support human health and well-being.

The framework advocated by the World Green Building Council proposes that financial, perceptual, and physical metrics are best tracked and cross-referenced through perception surveys, measurements of the physical office environment, and datasets on absenteeism, staff turnover/ retention, revenue breakdown per building, medical costs, medical complaint, and building complaints (WGBC, 2014). In this way, each organisation can identify the key priorities for intervention for each applicable place and time, and build their own specific business cases to track and monitor value delivered.

What is the value to business?

Technology is both a facilitator and agitator within this movement. The reality that both CRE and companies will have to face is that technology enables and enforces transparency. A fundamental sign of a healthy building will be its speed and willingness to openly disclose and display actual performance.

Arup has been researching a smarter approach to office design and the application of emerging digital technologies in buildings, seeing the direct benefits to end-user clients to be improved staff productivity and well-being, and reduced operating costs and costs. Increasingly, developer and landlord clients are keen to differentiate their product in the market and demonstrate these benefits to prospective occupiers.

Box 21.1   An Arup case study: The Internet of Things desk

Michael Stych, Michael Trousdell, Francesco Anselmo, James Richards, Adam Jaworski and Richard Reid

What is it?

The focus of this research in Arup is the development of our Internet of Things or IoT desk project. This is a six-person workplace and meeting space which uses and tests emerging technologies and user-centred design. The desk examines the use of common data and power distribution, open source controls and sensing, data collection and analysis, and direct user interfaces with their environment.

Context

The workplace has undergone significant change with open plan, high occupancy densities, and hot desking the norm. There is also the emergence of both activity-based working and project-based working, which often require people to move much more regularly within what would normally be a 2–5-year fit-out cycle.

The technology in our buildings struggles to keep up with this rate of change and often by necessity has to be ignored. Systems such as lighting, power, air conditioning or data infrastructure remain in their original configurations while the space has changed. We also know from years of occupant feedback that for people to be happy and productive in their environment, they want the ability to choose a quick response to 'I'm too hot or too cold' (e.g., to open or shut a window), and that an increased understanding also increases their ability to adapt to the building.

So what would give us this high performing, user-centric design that is also extremely flexible to change? Words and phrasing such as Big Data, Smart, Connectivity, BIM and most recently the Internet of Things all promise this future of optimised building performance and user experience, but what do these really mean in practice?

With our IoT desk project we are putting these theories and initiatives to the test by exploring web-based technologies, monitoring and personalising our environment hand-in-hand with an appropriate and flexible electrical and data infrastructure.

Power and data

It begins with questioning the way we provide this power in our buildings. Nearly all devices within a modern building use Direct Current (DC), such as a laptop, a smartphone, or the lighting. However, we still use AC power throughout buildings which requires conversion at each connection (your laptop brick) and it is disruptive and expensive to change. DC power, on the other hand, is easier and safer to reconfigure.

DC power also means we can put power and data on a single cable. On our IoT desks, we are using this idea to power all equipment and provide a data connection through a single cable (Figure 21.4). This means each device can have an IP address, making it a functional part of the internet. Hence the reference to the Internet of Things. As addressable devices, they can communicate over the internet directly with each other, or as part of a wider system.

With common power and data infrastructure using internet protocols, devices or 'things' can now exchange data which can be monitored and programmed to do what we like. As with the internet, we can also do something today and change it again tomorrow without disrupting entire building systems or relying on the original system provider.

Figure 21.4 IoT desk cable connection

User-centric approach

Energy use is being monitored from all devices and experimenting with different low cost sensors to measure temperature, air quality, noise and light. This makes it possible to personalise our environments quickly and easily. It also allows us direct access to devices in much the same way as a smart phone would work. So when desks move or a person moves, their preferences move with them or conversely when another user is at the same desk, their preferences follow. Different methods of tracking people movement are also being trialled, thus making it possible to optimise system performance based on actual occupancy.

Open standards

Systems that provide all this functionality do exist in the market but they tend to take the business-as-usual approach to Building Management Systems. This approach is based on well-developed proprietary systems which are segregated from other systems in the building and typically use 'closed' protocol-based applications.

Fundamental to our IoT project is the use of open standards and protocols. As with the internet, using internet protocols, open standards are used that allows all the devices to communicate with each other regardless of source. It can still allow more traditional controls for equipment which require open gateways with the difference being they sit on a common open building operating system.

Figure 21.5 The IoT desk in use

The open approach has been used in building the furniture itself, using open 3-D design software and rapid prototype manufacturing techniques. The desk is designed, printed and assembled locally and is entirely customised to our needs. A service zone has been incorporated within our desks as an accessible route for all the cabling and to allow users to make provision for installing many types of sensors and gadgets and well as the traditional laptop docking station, IP phone and chargers (Figure 21.5).

Summary

Digital technology is set to transform the interaction people have with their buildings and their performance. Today, technology enables clients to actually see and sense what is possible themselves, rather than designers telling them so. IT change is fast, making investment in the right infrastructure that can support and adapt to change critical. This working laboratory is allowing designers to do the practical tests to help us improve knowledge, challenge the existing norms and answer the questions clients are asking about digital technology. Read more at https://allaboutthedesk.arup.com/

A message of proactive disclosure is a far more positive statement than being called out through public online benchmarking sites using widely available consumer items. And as powerfully demonstrated with energy performance across portfolios and markets, underperforming assets will most likely be subject to brown discounts of reduced rental receipts and diminishing market value.

McGraw-Hill (2014) reports that while the benefits of greater productivity, lower absenteeism, reduced healthcare cost and improved employee satisfaction and engagement are generally acknowledged as fundamental benefits of healthy buildings, there is no fixed equation for the precise degree or a guaranteed rate of investment (ROI) for each measure. The industry now needs to leverage existing information and tools to explore this question for each specific building, and each specific organisation. As one example: the CBRE Global Corporate Headquarters in Los Angeles found through a post-occupancy survey that an amazing 82 per cent of staff feel more productive in their new WELL Certified space, and 92 per cent said the new space has had a positive effect on their health and well-being (CBRE, 2016).

As the role of built environment professionals expands to include designing full occupant experience, we will see more and more new, interdisciplinary teams mobilising to successfully address both physical and non-physical aspects. Led by specialists versed in built-environment health impacts, well-being consulting teams will be able to develop bespoke framework to lift existing sustainability guidelines, or guide individual project certification through schemes such as the WELL Building Standard. At a strategic level, organisations may reach out for guidance in embedding well-being principles and approaches into development briefs, fit-out guides and operational policies, and in the formulation of long-sighted workplace strategies that fundamentally combine stakeholder engagement and change-management within wider programmes of real-estate management and renewal.

Corporate organisations will also increasingly discover the need for an internal point of contact for well-being. Echoing the development of the interdisciplinary Sustainability Executive position over the past twenty years, this Well-being Integrator, or Chief Wellness Officer, will develop and champion integrated health and wellness approaches to ensure buildings, employees, and businesses are – and remain – healthy and well.

References

Begley, S. (2014) PepsiCo's workplace wellness program fails the bottom line: study. *Reuters*, 6 Jan. 2014. Available at: www.reuters.com/article/2014/01/06/us-wellness-workplace-idUSBREA0510R20140106 (accessed Aug. 2016).

BRE (Building Research Establishment) (2015) Home Quality Mark: Ratings and Stars. Available at: www.homequalitymark.com/ratings-and-stars (accessed Aug. 2016).

CBI/Pfizer (2013) Fit for purpose – Absence and Workplace Health Survey 2013. Available at: www.cbi.org.uk/media-centre/press-releases/2013/07/work-absence-at-record-low-but-still-costs-economy-%C2%A314bn-a-year-cbi-pfizer-survey/ (accessed March 2015).

CBRE (2015) The Workplace Wire: What you should know about Workplace360. Available at: www.cbre.us/services/brokerage/AssetLibrary/Issue%204_WorkplaceWire_What%20You%20Should%20Know%20About%20Workplace360.pdf (accessed: March 2015).

CBRE (2016) MIPIM 2016: Case study: CBRE WELL Certification. Available at: www.cbre.com/about/mipim-2016#whatWeSee (accessed: March 2015).

Deloitte Australia (2016) Deloitte anchor tenant for 477 Collins Street. Available at: www2.deloitte.com/au/en/pages/media-releases/articles/deloitte-anchor-tenant-for-477-collins-street-040516.html (accessed: Aug. 2016).

McGraw-Hill (2014) *The Drive Toward Healthier Buildings: The Market Drivers and Impact of Building Design and Construction on Occupant Health, Wellbeing and Productivity*. Smart Market Report. Available at: MHC_Analytics@mcgraw-hill.com

Spicer, A. and Cederström, C. (2015) Under the whip of wellness. *New Scientist*, 21 Feb.

World Green Building Council (WGBC) (2014) *Health, Wellbeing & Productivity in Offices*. Available at: www.ukgbc.org/content/health-wellbeing-and-productivity-offices (accessed Sept. 2014).

Chapter 22

Achieving holistic sustainability

Considering wellness alongside resource use in buildings

Jenn McArthur

Introduction

There are significant interactions between the built environment and the wellness and productivity of building occupants, many of which have been discussed in detail in the preceding chapters. This chapter looks ahead to the next generation of buildings, which must be designed to consider both wellness and sustainability. This chapter will: (1) present a brief history of both the sustainability and building wellness movements; (2) discuss perceived conflicts and recent moves to bridge the gap between the two; (3) discuss the key building environmental factors affecting occupant wellness, productivity, and their impact on resource use; and (4) present a recently published assessment framework to guide decision-making to consider both building occupant wellness and sustainability in new building designs and retrofits.

Wellness and sustainability in the built environment

Wellness in the built environment context refers to the promotion of occupant health, both physically and psychologically. Sustainability within the same context tends to instead focus on the environmental impact of the building. While discussions of sustainability typically include elements of wellness related to indoor air quality, comfort, and reduced toxins, performance in categories of energy efficiency, and to a lesser extent, water consumption, material life cycle impact, and site issues dominates.

Since the initial publication of BREEAM in 1990, improving occupant health and wellness has been a priority of the Green Building movement and has been reflected in nearly every building rating system developed. Table 22.1 shows the evolution of credits in major global sustainability rating systems (applicable to offices) targeted to improving occupant health. Table 22.1 demonstrates both the consistent consideration of health and wellness indicators as well as a trend towards increased focused on occupant health, notably in the increasing weight of credits in the LEED® and Green Mark rating systems, and the introduction of a rating system focused primarily on occupant health (the WELL® building standard).

While encouraging building designs to improve occupant health and wellness, apparent conflicts also began to emerge between the energy and occupant health credits within these sustainability ratings systems. The most notable example is the penalty for "excess outdoor air" when compared with a code baseline; significant research. e.g. (Wargocki, *et al.* 2000; Wyon, 2004) has found that increasing outdoor air has a significant benefit to occupant health and productivity, yet systems such as BREEAM and Green Star rank buildings relative to total energy/CO_2 emissions for comparable buildings thus indirectly penalizing the provision of "extra" fresh air. As stated in the Green Star office manual: "There is a balance to be struck

Table 22.1 International sustainability rating system credits related to occupant health

System and version	Year	Origin	Credit allocation
BREEAM v1	1990	UK	10 credits in the 'Health and Wellbeing' category allowing for 15% of available points
HQE	1996	France	7 targets; 4 in the 'Confort' (comfort) and 3 in the 'Santé' (health) category allowing for 50% of total target areas; note that the health category is mandatory
LEED 1.0	2000	USA	15 credits + 2 prerequisites in the 'Indoor Environmental Quality' category allowing for 21.4% of available points
CASBEE	2001	Japan	4 categories of credits in the 'Indoor Environment' score account for 30% of the 'Building Environmental Quality and Performance' score[1]
Green Star (Office, v3)	2002	Australia	27 credits in the 'Indoor Environmental Quality' category allowing for 20% of available points
Green Globes	2002	Canada	5 credits in the 'Indoor Environment' category allowing for 20% of available points
Green Mark	2005	Singapore	6 prerequisites and 8 credits related to occupant health in the 'Smart and Healthy Buildings' category allowing for 19% of available points.
DGNB	2006	Germany	7 credits in the 'Health, Comfort and User Satisfaction' category allowing for 13.9% of available points
LEED 2009	2009	USA	15 credits in the 'Indoor Environmental Quality' category allowing for 13% of available points
BEAM PLUS	2012	Hong Kong	23 credits in the 'Indoor Environmental Quality' category allowing for 20% of available points
LEED v4 (BD+C)	2014	USA	16 credits in the 'Indoor Environmental' category allowing for 14.5% of available points
BREEAM 2014	2014	UK	6 credits in the 'Health and Wellbeing' category allowing for 15% of available credits
WELL Building Standard	2014	USA	102 credits and prerequisites for wellness enablers, accounting for 100% of available credits
Green Mark 2015	2015	Singapore	33 prerequisites and credits related to occupant health in the 'Smart and Healthy Buildings' category allowing for 25% of available points

Note: [1] In CASBEE, this is the y-axis and the environmental impact is plotted on the x-axis. The ratio of these values gives the Building Energy Efficiency (BEE) score.

between providing adequate outside air in recirculation systems to dilute contaminants and the loss/gain of heat with the resulting increased energy consumption needed to maintain comfort levels." The LEED® rating system attempts to balance both needs by allowing up to 25 percent additional fresh air beyond the ASHRAE 62.1 'Standards for Acceptable Indoor Air Quality' requirements to be included in the energy modeling baseline without penalty. Green Mark (Singapore) and BEAM Plus (Hong Kong) avoid such penalties – the former considers the equipment efficiency per ton of cooling load (thus omitting a baseline fresh air rate in the energy model), while the latter explicitly allows the designer to define a baseline fresh air rate at the desired level in design, and provides a credit for exceeding those minimum fresh air requirements at least 30 percent. Table 22.2 summarizes the scope of credits in each of the major systems (latest version).

Table 22.2 Credit comparisons across most widely used international sustainability rating systems

System	Tobacco smoke control	Minimum ventilation	Increased ventilation	Filtration	Thermal comfort	Minimum illuminance	Artificial lighting	Daylighting	Daylighting glare control	CO monitoring	External views	Individual comfort control	Pollution source control	Air change effectiveness	Internal noise levels	Exhaust/ air purging	wellness-focused (e.g. Biophilic design)
BREEAM		O			O	O	O	O	O				O		O		O
LEED	•	•	O	O	O		O	O	O		O	O	O	O	O	O	
Green Star		O	O		O	O		O	O		O	O	O	O	O	O	
BEAM Plus		•	O	O	O	O	O	O		O			O		O		
Green Mark		•		•	•	•	•	O	O				O		O	O	O

Note: (• = prerequisite; O = credit)

Defining wellness in the workplace

"Wellness" has no universally accepted definition when applied to the workplace, however, workplace health promotion has been clearly defined by the European Network for Workplace Health Promotion as "a modern corporate strategy which aims at preventing ill-health at work (including work-related diseases, accidents, injuries, occupational diseases and stress) and enhancing health-promoting potentials and well-being in the workforce" (Union). This term is gaining recognition throughout the buildings industry due to increased attention to new standards and the prioritization of building wellness enablers through sustainability rating systems. The concept of building wellness is not new, the concept of designing buildings to improve occupant health was well understood centuries ago by the architects of the Greek temples to Asclepius, which maximized fresh air, access to clean water, and natural daylight (Shraiky, 2011). Similar strategies were used by architects of early twentieth-century sanatoriums, such as Alvar Aalto, who prioritized views, natural ventilation, and daylight (Anderson, 2010). In the 1970s, the emergence of an office illness, later named "Sick Building Syndrome" by the WHO in 1986, raised this issue to the public consciousness as many office workers began suffering from respiratory illness due to poor air quality in office buildings. In response to this, the American Society for Heating, Refrigeration and Air-Conditioning Engineers (ASHRAE) increased office ventilation rates in the Standard for Acceptable Indoor Air Quality (ASHRAE, 1989). The European Committee for Standardization created a similar document, CR 1752, which has been widely adopted in Europe.

Within the context of the workplace, wellness begins to take on commercial as well as social importance. Lost time due to illness affects productivity significantly, with losses due to workplace accidents and ill-health ranging from 1 percent to 5 percent of GDP across G20 countries, and with a global cost on the order of US$2.8 trillion (ILO, 2014). Studies have shown a correlation between productivity and a number of wellness indicators, many of which have been discussed in detail in previous chapters of this book.

The building wellness movement

Building upon this research, the first international standard aimed specifically at increasing occupant health in buildings – the WELL® Building Standard – was created by the International Well Building Institute and launched at Greenbuild in 2014. This standard consists of 102 credits designed to encourage the inclusion of "wellness enablers" in new and existing buildings. These are grouped into seven categories (Air, Water, Nourishment, Light, Fitness, Comfort, and Mind) and consist of both physical building and policy measures. In 2015, the WELL® building standard was adopted formally by the Green Business Certification Inc. (the entity who certifies LEED® practitioners globally) and the Canadian Green Building Council (USGBC, 2015). In Asia, a similar shift towards increased focus on occupant health and well-being in buildings is evident in the Green Mark 2015 Pilot scheme.

Wellness and the triple bottom line

The "triple bottom line" is a term used to describe a holistic business focus: the financial performance is no longer the only factor considered, social and environmental impacts and outcomes become important factors in measuring organizational performance. Within this context, workplaces must be considered from multiple perspectives: economic productivity, environmental impact in both the short term (construction) and long term (building operation and disposal), occupant health (both physical and psychological, and the social implications of poor health.

Impact of wellness enablers on sustainability

Much has been presented in the preceding chapters of this book on the relationship between building and system characteristics and how they affect productivity. The following sections summarize the key wellness and productivity enablers from the literature, with quantified productivity impacts where available, and indicate how the implementation of these enablers may affect the energy consumption of the building, including potential mitigation measures for increased energy consumption.

Air

The identification of Sick Building Syndrome raised public awareness of the impact of air quality on health, and there has been significant research on this relationship and productivity impacts since that time. Two key elements – the amount of outdoor air and the overall air quality, have been directly related to productivity impacts, as summarized in Table 22.3.

Table 22.3 Measured productivity impacts related to air

Element	Impact on productivity	Context	Reference
Increased Outdoor Air	1.75% increase on office worker productivity per doubling of outdoor air rate	Commercial office	(Wargocki et al., 2000)
Indoor Air Quality	6–9% decreased productivity in poor indoor air quality environments	Commercial office	(Wyon, 2004)
	2% average productivity loss associated with Sick Building Syndrome	Office	(Fisk and Rosenfeld, 1997)

Source: adapted from McArthur et al. (2015).

Increased outdoor air

Minimum outdoor air standards vary significantly across regions. In the USA and its sphere of influence, the ASHRAE 62.1 standard calculated is widely cited by codes as the minimum allowable provision, and has been adopted in several international jurisdictions. In the UK, CIBSE KS17 – Indoor Air Quality and Ventilation, is a guide used for design and allows much higher outdoor air rates than ASHRAE 62.1. This is significant as research has found that for each doubling of ventilation rates, there is a 1.75 percent increase in productivity, defined as the performance of "normal office work" tasks (Wargocki, et al. 2000).

The challenge with increasing outdoor air arises from the energy required to temper and distribute this additional air. In cold climates, all outdoor air must be pre-heated to achieve the desired space temperature and the additional outdoor air increases the building energy required. Similarly in hot or humid climates, additional outdoor air must be cooled and/or dehumidified. Depending on the severity of the climate and occupancy type, the extent of the increased energy required for outdoor air tempering can range significantly. In contrast, in temperate climates where the outdoor condition is within the thermal comfort range for all or part of the year, natural ventilation can decrease the overall building energy consumption for part of the year by reducing fan energy requirements.

Two approaches can limit or even reverse the increased energy required in winter and summer for increasing the outdoor air quantity in temperate climates: (1) economizers on all-air systems; and (2) dedicated outdoor air systems with heat recovery. Economizers modulate the outdoor air flow to meet the desired mixed air temperature; in the shoulder/winter seasons, building cooling loads can be met by increasing outdoor air above the minimum set-point, thus avoiding mechanical cooling for a significant fraction of the year. Dedicated outdoor air systems provide 100 percent fresh (outdoor) air at room temperature and the desired flowrate to all spaces and use local heating and cooling equipment to achieve thermal comfort conditions. Such systems use substantially less energy than "typical" VAV systems by reducing the amount of fan power required to circulate air through the building and avoiding re-heating of pre-cooled air.

Indoor air quality

Poor indoor air quality (or alternately, the presence of indoor air pollution) has been demonstrated to decrease cognitive function and negatively affect occupant health, resulting in increased absenteeism (Feige et al., 2013; Finnegan et al., 1984; Singh, 1996; Wargocki et al., 2000; Wyon, 2004). Several factors influence indoor air quality, including the presence of volatile organic compounds (VOCs), other airborne toxins, and the level of filtration. There are several strategies that can be used to reduce contaminants from external sources. Vestibules reduce infiltration of potentially polluted air while also decreasing heating and cooling loads, entry mats reduce contaminants entering the building on footwear, with no impact on energy, UV treatment in air handling units is an effective way of decreasing airborne microbes and has negligible energy use, and increased levels of filtration removes airborne particles. This inclusion of additional and/or higher effectiveness filters will impact energy use due to the increased static pressure required to blow air through the filter media, and thus increasing the overall fan energy. The final intervention does not affect air quality directly but provides the necessary information to react quickly to poor system performance: air quality monitoring. This is recommended in WELL® buildings and provides a potential benefit to energy management in that it provides real-time information that can be used by the building automation system to optimize system operation and facilitates early detection of equipment malfunction, thus decreasing energy losses associated with de-rated performance.

Water

The reduction of potable water consumption is the primary focus of most sustainability systems and the replacement of low-efficiency with high-efficiency fixtures also provides opportunities for wellness improvements to offices. One such opportunity includes improving water quality through the installation of centralized or point-of-use treatment such as carbon filters, which improve taste and remove toxins, encouraging water consumption. Drinking water is further promoted through the installation of water fountains or bottle-filling stations, although there is a slight impact on energy when these systems have integrated water chilling.

Nourishment

Similar to water, nourishment is not directly tied to energy consumption, but has a significant impact on health and well-being. Several design elements promote the consumption of fresh foods in the workplace: on-site food production, fresh food storage, and the provision of an eating/break area. If located on a roof, on-site food production offers several potential sustainability benefits, including storm-water reclamation (by the garden), opportunities for improved roof insulation as part of the green roof installation, and decreased solar gains, which reduce heating and cooling loads, respectively. Fresh food storage adds a marginal plug load for the provision of refrigerators, while the provision of a break area has no direct effect on energy consumption.

Light

People have consistently indicated preference for daylight, windows, and a good quality view (Hraska, 2015), and the body of research demonstrates that light colour, correct illumination level, and glare control have a measurable effect on human health and productivity as summarized in Table 22.4.

Table 22.4 Measured productivity impacts related to light

Element	Impact on productivity	Context	Reference
Illumination level control	4.5% increase in productivity at workstations with lighting control	Manufacturing	(Juslén et al., 2007)
Daylighting	Learning progress showed 7–26% improvement in highly day-lit rooms compared with low levels of daylight	Schools	(Heschong, 1999)
	Learning progress showed 19–20% improvement when skylight providing additional access to daylight compared with non-day-lit rooms	Schools	(Heschong, 1999)
	Average length of stay (hospitalization) decreased from 16% to 41% in highly day-lit rooms	Hospitals (patients)	(Choi et al., 2012)
Access to views	Learning progress showed 15–23% improvement in classrooms with largest windows	Schools	(Heschong, 1999)

Source: adapted from McArthur et al. (2015).

Daylighting

Daylighting, defined as the use of natural light to achieve all or part of the illumination of a space, has been demonstrated to improve outcomes in both the healthcare (Choi *et al.* 2012) and educational (Heschong, 1999; Samani and Samani, 2012) contexts. Unlike most artificial light, natural light contains a broad spectrum, which varies with the sun's position in the sky, thus providing circadian cues to those exposed to natural light, as well as the mood benefits of full-spectrum lighting (see summary by Hawes *et al.*, 2012) and better sleep quality, resulting in improved wakefulness and decreased fatigue (Boubekri *et al.*, 2014).

Access to views

Access to daylight typically also provides access to views of the outdoors, which also correlate strongly with learning progress (Heschong, 1999), and by extension is understood to improve mental productivity. Providing this access indirectly affects the energy consumption of a building when increased glazing is used to facilitate these views. Due to the low thermal resistance of glass for both conduction and radiation, increased glazing results in increased solar gains (summer cooling load) and envelope heat losses (winter heating load). Several other strategies can be implemented to improve access to views without increasing glazing: open layouts for workplaces, limiting partition heights, increasing transparency of internal walls (i.e. glazed walls rather than opaque), and preferentially locating the glazing in highly-occupied spaces.

Circadian lighting and colour quality

The quality of natural light varies over each day – dominated by blue at dawn, while the blue is preferentially scattered and orange and red begins to dominate in the late afternoon and into the evening – this is the primary stimulus for the human circadian rhythm (Hraska, 2015). Mimicking the characteristics (color and brightness) of natural light can improve occupant wellness by reducing the symptoms of seasonal affective disorder and increasing alertness (Figueiro, 2013). Conversely, a deficiency of daylight or daylight-like ambient lighting is related to health concerns such as hormonal imbalance, depression, and sleep disorders (Hraska, 2015). Evidence further suggests that high circadian stimulation during daytime waking hours can probably be achieved by about 600 lux at the cornea of a 6500 K light source, while bright light (above 2500 lux) has been shown to increase alertness (Figueiro, 2013).

When daylight hours align with working hours, access to natural light is a simple way to achieve circadian lighting conditions. In geographic locations with short winter days, typical artificial lighting is inadequate to trigger melatonin metabolism (Hraska, 2015) but specially-designed artificial circadian lighting can be effectively used to stimulate alertness and increase worker productivity. Tunable white LEDs are able to change the amount of blue 460–480nm spectrum, which triggers melatonin suppression, and controls the wake-sleep cycle in the morning hours. This allows tuning of the circadian rhythm, which benefits health and wellness (Trivellin *et al.* 2015). Energy-conserving LED luminaires that match diurnal daylight patterns have also been developed and tested in the healthcare context (Ellis *et al.*, 2014). Because a link between melatonin disruption (affecting circadian rhythms) and certain cancers has been suggested, the use of long-wave (red) light to stimulate alertness without this risk has been recommended (Figueiro, 2013).

Fitness

There are several elements within the larger office environment that can encourage active behavior of workers, increasing fitness levels and improving overall health, as summarized in the following sections.

Encouraging use of stairs

When designed or adapted to make the experience of using them as pleasant as possible, stairs both promote fitness and reduce electricity usage associated with elevators and escalators. The location of stairs in a day-lit and potentially naturally ventilated atrium further promotes both energy-reduction and occupant wellness.

Enabling active commuting

The presence of two or more physical supports (secure bike storage, showers, lockers) have been demonstrated to encourage active commuting (Kaczynski *et al.*, 2010), with known health benefits. The decreased commute carbon footprint of active transportation rather than single vehicle use is well recognized in a number of sustainability systems (e.g. LEED®). In retrofit scenarios, it is often possible to repurpose a small number of car parking spaces to create a secured bicycle storage area, fitting up to 12 bikes in the space allocated for one car. The provision of showers increases on-site hot water usage but this is mitigated through the use of low-flow fixtures and high-efficiency hot water heaters.

Alternative furnishings

Sit-stand (flexible) workstations and active workstations (e.g. treadmills, which incur a small electricity cost) both have recognized health benefits such as improved cardiovascular health and reduced stress. While sit-stand workstations appear to neither improve nor decrease productivity (Dutta *et al.*, 2014), treadmills have been shown to have variable impacts on performance, improving some creative thinking and problem solving tasks (Ben-Ner *et al.*, 2014; Straker *et al.*, 2009) but decreasing effectiveness when fine motor skills are required (e.g. typing and using a mouse).

Exterior active design

Developing outdoor space suitable for physical activity benefits workers by promoting non-sedentary behavior and providing access to views and biophilic elements. At the same time, this design element promotes green space and seasonal shading, complementing passive design strategies such as natural/mixed-mode ventilation, which reduce overall building energy consumption.

Comfort

Discomfort in the workplace has been demonstrated to negatively affect worker productivity and is associated with four of the five senses. Odor discomfort typically results from poor indoor air quality and has been discussed above. Thermal (related to touch), aural, and visual discomfort effects are summarized in Table 22.5.

Table 22.5 Measured productivity impacts related to comfort

Element	Impact on productivity	Context	Reference
Thermal Comfort	Average of 2% decrease in work performance per degree above 25°C.	Call centres	(Seppänen et al., 2004)
	Manual dexterity deteriorates below 20–22 °C	—	(Seppänen et al., 2004)
	Manual dexterity decreased 5–15% at 18°C compared with 24°C	Factory	(Meese et al., 1984)
Acoustic distraction	Performance loss up to 8% due to lack of acoustic privacy	Office	(Roelofsen, 2008)
Operable windows	Ranges from 7% to 8% improvement in classrooms with operable vs. not operable windows	Schools	(Heschong, 1999)

Source: adapted from McArthur et al. (2015).

Thermal comfort

Several studies summarized by Seppänen et al. (2004) have shown minimal temperature impact on productivity in the 21–25°C temperature range, but measurable decreases in productivity both above and below these values. Standards such as BS EN ISO 7730:2005 – "Ergonomics of the Thermal Environment" and ASHRAE 55–2013 – "Thermal Environmental Conditions for Human Occupancy" (ASHRAE, 1992) were developed to quantify appropriate thermal comfort design conditions. Both consider wet-bulb and dry-bulb temperatures, relative humidity, air speed, and radiant heat and are considered best practice in multiple countries. Radiant heating and cooling, particularly in large spaces, provide improved thermal comfort when compared with all-air (e.g. VAV) systems, and have significantly reduced fan energy costs as the only centrally supplied air is 100 percent fresh air to achieve the desired outdoor air rate. This approach provides an energy-efficient approach to achieve both increased fresh air and enhanced thermal comfort, and is particularly well-suited to retrofit due to the low ceiling service space requirements for this system type.

User control – thermal

Within a reasonable temperature range, the provision of even the illusion of user control has been demonstrated to enhance thermal comfort in occupants (Plous, 1993), although if temperatures become extreme and it is apparent that the user "controls" are non-functional, this benefit ceases. Because perceived comfort is higher with less heating and cooling when user control is installed, it can reduce heating and cooling loads, complementing building controls upgrades. Where building operators want to retain a measure of control over the temperature set-point, limited control thermostats (allowing +/– 2°C adjustment) may be installed.

Operable windows

The ability to open a window has been correlated with improved concentration and health benefits (Heschong, 1999). This is in many ways because it provides the occupant with a degree of control over their surroundings, which is in and of itself a factor increasing occupant satisfaction, and facilitates the increased outdoor air discussed previously. Similar energy impacts exist with operable windows as with increased outdoor air, and the use of limit switches to detect when windows have been opened and shut off the heating and cooling to a room in that condition is a widely used strategy to minimize the energy impact of this element.

Illumination control

Because of the range of tasks undertaken over the course of a working day, there is no single illumination level that can be considered ideal for all working conditions (Rea, 2000). Providing building occupants control over local task lighting allows each individual to adjust their local light levels based on the task at hand. This has been demonstrated to increase productivity in both manufacturing (Juslén et al., 2007) and office (Boyce et al., 2006) contexts. Because task lighting can allow decreased general lighting levels, this intervention has the potential to decrease lighting energy and thus the overall building energy consumption, particularly when integrated with a lighting controls upgrade to install occupancy sensors and photocells for lighting control.

Acoustic comfort

Several acoustic elements must be controlled to avoid aural discomfort: internally generated and exterior noise, reverberation time and sound-reducing surfaces, and sound masking. Walls with higher noise insulation class typically have improved seals, but care must be taken to ensure fresh air supply to avoid Sick Building Syndrome. The introduction of soft elements (e.g. carpeting) reduces reverberation within the space but care must be taken to avoid materials with VOCs and other toxins as discussed in the Indoor Air Quality section. For internally generated noise, silencers and acoustic duct treatment can significantly reduce noise transmission with minimal impact on fan energy.

Mind

Two key elements of the building environment with significant impact on mental health and well-being are design aesthetics and biophilic design. The benefits of the former are in many ways obvious and are of significant focus in architectural and interior design and will not be discussed here. Biophilic, or "nature-loving" design is a significant new focus within both sustainability and architecture and warrants specific discussion.

Since the beginning of the "green building" movement, the relationship between access to nature and occupant health has been recognized. Roger Ulrich (1993) found that views of natural stimuli have consistently correlated with decreased stress and frustration and increased patience and improved mood (Grinde and Patil, 2009; Kaplan, 1995; Söderlund and Newman, 2015; Ulrich, 1993). This has been demonstrated even for indoor plants (Dravigne et al., 2008). At a larger scale, green walls, indoor parkettes within atria, and accessible green roofs provide additional access to nature within workplaces. From a sustainability perspective, green elements have great benefits from an indoor air quality perspective but larger plants or water features also release significant moisture to the indoor environment, producing a latent load that increases cooling requirements in hot or humid weather but is beneficial in dry climates. When installed on the building exterior, these elements have been shown to improve thermal performance, local air quality, and site drainage (Manso and Castro-Gomes, 2015; Natarajan *et al.*, 2015).

Framework for improving sustainability and wellness in existing buildings

> [R]esearch in environmental psychology has tended to focus on the negative impacts of buildings – noise, heat, glare, crowding, poor indoor air quality – with the unstated assumption that high performance and well-being will be achieved if problems are eliminated [but] performance and wellbeing appear to depend *not only on the absence of significant problems, but also on the presence of particular kinds of features and attributes* in buildings.
>
> (Heerwagen, 1998, emphasis added)

The question arises, how should buildings or renovations be designed not only to avoid the bad, but promote the good? A mathematical model to evaluate potential retrofit options has been developed and published (McArthur *et al.*, 2015) to guide this process, shown schematically in Figure 22.1.

In this framework, potential bundle renovations are scored in five categories: financial performance, greenhouse gas emissions, incorporation of wellness and productivity enablers (discussed in previous sections), qualitative elements (e.g. reputation or branding), and risk exposure. Once each category score is assigned, it is normalized based on the best-performing option and then multiplied by a category weighting factor determined with stakeholders early in the design process. The sum of the weighted and normalized category scores is then calculated for each option to identify the preferred design.

In retrofits, even when the over-arching goal is to optimize energy performance or reduce cost, several wellness-enabling elements may be implemented without compromising this goal, as discussed earlier in this chapter. Even for those elements with energy penalties, the improvement in equipment efficiency will often more than offset these penalties. Where cost is a driver, the high staff to energy cost ratio (typically 100:1) incentivizes the inclusion of productivity-enhancing design elements.

The way forward

There is an increasing public awareness of "healthy buildings," which is driving a need within the commercial real estate industry to consider wellness enablers alongside sustainability

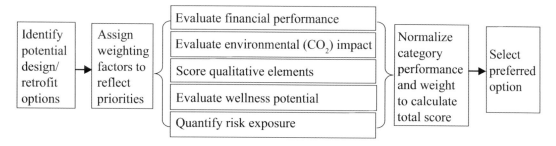

Figure 22.1 Framework for evaluating wellness and sustainability with other factors in building design and retrofit

measures in retrofits and new building construction. As research continues to demonstrate measureable improvements in productivity associated with access to daylight, views of the outdoors, controllability over task lighting and increased fresh air, we can expect to see more emphasis on wellness certifications (e.g. WELL®) and prioritization in sustainable building standards (e.g. Green Mark 2015 and HQE). These standards provide insight on how to design new buildings and renovations to improve occupant health to achieve higher productivity and raise the public consciousness of this issue, reinforcing the need to address these issues in both renovations and new construction. At the same time, increasingly high carbon reduction goals arising from COP21 will continue to make resource conservation – particularly energy efficiency – a top priority, requiring both wellness and sustainability to be considered in the design of new and retrofit of existing buildings. The framework presented above – supplemented by the individual health and productivity benefits as well as energy impacts of various interventions – has been provided to guide the creation of the next generation of both productive and sustainable workplaces.

References

Anderson, D. (2010) Humanizing the hospital: design lessons from a Finnish sanatorium. *Canadian Medical Association Journal*, 182(11): E535–E537.

ASHRAE (1989) *ASHRAE 62.1–1989 Ventilation for Acceptable Air Quality*. Atlanta: American Society for Heating, Cooling, Refrigeration and Air-Conditioning Engineers.

ASHRAE (1992) *ANSI/ASHRAE Standard 55–1992 Thermal Environmental Conditions for Human Occupancy*. Atlanta, GA: American Society of Heating, Refrigerating and Air-Conditioning Engineers, Inc.

Ben-Ner, A. *et al.* (2014) Treadmill workstations: the effects of walking while working on physical activity and work performance. *PloS one*, 9(2): e88620.

Boubekri, M. *et al.* (2014) Impact of windows and daylight exposure on overall health and sleep quality of office workers: a case-control pilot study. *Journal of Clinical Sleep Medicine: JCSM*, 10(6): 603.

Boyce, P.R. *et al.* (2006) Lighting quality and office work: two field simulation experiments. *Lighting Research and Technology*, 38(3): 191–223.

Choi, J.-H., Beltran, L.O. and Kim, H.-S. (2012) Impacts of indoor daylight environments on patient average length of stay (ALOS) in a healthcare facility. *Building and Environment*, 50: 65–75.

Dravigne, A., Waliczek, T.M., Lineberger, R.D. and Zajicek, J.M. (2008) The effect of live plants and window views of green spaces on employee perceptions of job satisfaction. *HortScience*, 43(1): 183–187.

Dutta, N. *et al.* (2014) Using sit-stand workstations to decrease sedentary time in office workers: a randomized crossover trial. *International Journal of Environmental Research and Public Health*, 11(7): 6653–6665.

Ellis, E.V. *et al.* (2014) Auto-tuning daylight with LEDs: sustainable lighting for health and wellbeing. In Proceedings of the 2013 Spring ARCC Conference.

European Committee for Standardization (1998) *Technical Report CR1752: Ventilation for Buildings: Design Criteria for the Indoor Environment*. Brussels: EU.

European Union *Luxembourg Declaration*. Available at: www.enwhp.org/fileadmin/rs-dokumente/dateien/Luxembourg_Declaration.pdf (accessed 25 Jan. 2016).

Feige, A., Wallbaum, H., Janser, M. and Windlinger, L. (2013) Impact of sustainable office buildings on occupants' comfort and productivity. *Journal of Corporate Real Estate*, 15(1): 7–34.

Figueiro, M.G. (2013) An overview of the effects of light on human circadian rhythms: implications for new light sources and lighting systems design. *Journal of Light and Visual Environment*, 37(2–3): 51–61.

Finnegan, M.J., Pickering, C.A. and Burge, P.S. (1984) The sick building syndrome: prevalence studies. *British Medical Journal*, 289(6458): 1573–1575.

Fisk, W. J. and Rosenfeld, A. H. (1997) Estimates of improved productivity and health from better indoor environments. *Indoor Air*, 7(3): 158–172.

Grinde, B. and Patil, G.G. (2009) Biophilia: does visual contact with nature impact on health and well-being? *International Journal of Environmental Research and Public Health*, 6(9): 2332–2343.

Hawes, B.K. *et al.* (2012) Effects of four workplace lighting technologies on perception, cognition and affective state. *International Journal of Industrial Ergonomics*, 42(1): 122–128.

Heerwagen, J.H. (1998) *Design. Productivity and Well-Being: What Are the Links?* Cincinnati, OH: AIA.

Heschong, L. (1999) Daylighting in schools: an investigation into the relationship between daylighting and human performance. Available at: http://eric.ed.gov/?id=ED444337 (accessed 4 September 2015).

Hirning, M.B. *et al.* (2013) Post occupancy evaluations relating to discomfort glare: study of green buildings in Brisbane. *Building and Environment*, 59: 349–357.

Hraska, J. (2015) Chronobiological aspects of green buildings daylighting. *Renewable Energy*, 73: 109–114.

ILO (2014) *Creating Safe and Healthy Workplaces for All.* Melbourne: International Labour Organization.

Juslén, H.T., Wouters, M.C.H.M. and Tenner, A.D. (2007) Lighting level and productivity: a field study in the electronics industry. *Ergonomics*, 50(4): 615–624.

Kaczynski, A.T., Bopp, M.J. and Wittman, P. (2010) Association of workplace supports with active commuting. *Preventing Chronic Disease*, 7(6).

Kaplan, S. (1995) The restorative benefits of nature: toward an integrative framework. *Journal of Environmental Psychology*, 15(3): 169–182.

Manso, M. and Castro-Gomes, J. (2015) Green wall systems: a review of their characteristics. *Renewable and Sustainable Energy Reviews*, 41: 863–871.

McArthur, J.J., Jofeh, C. and Aguilar, A.-M. (2015) Improving occupant wellness in commercial office buildings through energy conservation retrofits. *Buildings*, 5(4): 1171–1186.

Meese, G.B., Kok, R., Lewis, M.I. and Wyon, D.P. (1984.) A laboratory study of the effects of moderate thermal stress on the performance of factory workers. *Ergonomics*, 27(1): 19–43.

Natarajan, M. *et al.* (2015) Living wall systems: evaluating life-cycle energy, water and carbon impacts. *Urban Ecosystems*, 18(1): 1–11.

Plous, S. (1993) *The Psychology of Judgment and Decision Making.* New York: McGraw-Hill.

Rea, M.S. (2000) *The IESNA Lighting Handbook: Reference and Application.* IESNA.

Roelofsen, P. (2008) Performance loss in open-plan offices due to noise by speech. *Journal of Facilities Management*, 6(3): 202–211.

Samani, S.A. and Samani, S.A. (2012) The impact of indoor lighting on students' learning performance in learning environments: a knowledge internalization perspective. *International Journal of Business Social Science*, 3(24): P12.

Seppänen, O., Fisk, W.J. and Faulkner, D. (2004) *Control of Temperature for Health and Productivity in Offices.* San Francisco: Lawrence Berkeley National Laboratory.

Shraiky, J. (2011) Prescribing architecture: a critical evaluation of how design impacts health and wellness. *Journal of Healthcare, Science and the Humanities*, 1(1): 201189.

Singh, J. (1996) Impact of indoor air pollution on health, comfort and productivity of the occupants. *Aerobiologia*, 12(1): 121–127.

Söderlund, J. and Newman, P. (2015) Biophilic architecture: a review of the rationale and outcomes. *AIMS Environmental Science*, 2(4): 950–969.

Straker, L., Levine, J. and Campbell, A. (2009) The effects of walking and cycling computer workstations on keyboard and mouse performance. *Human Factors: The Journal of the Human Factors and Ergonomics Society*, 51(6): 831–844.

Trivellin, N. *et al.* (2015) Effects and exploitation of tunable white light for circadian rhythm and human-centric lighting. IEEE, pp. 154–156.

Ulrich, R.S. (1993) The biophilia hypothesis. In Kellert, S.R. and Wilson, E.O. (eds) *Biophilia, Biophobia, and Natural Landscapes.* New York: Island Press.

USGBC (2015) GBCI and CaGBC join together to advance the WELL Building Standard. Available at: www.usgbc.org/articles/gbci-and-cagbc-join-together-advance-well-building-standard (accessed 14 September 2015).

Wargocki, P. *et al.* (2000) The effects of outdoor air supply rate in an office on perceived air quality, sick building syndrome (SBS) symptoms and productivity. *Indoor Air*, 10(4): 222–236.

Wyon, D.P. (2004) The effects of indoor air quality on performance and productivity. *Indoor Air*, 14(s7): 92–101.

Chapter 23

Making the economic case for good design of workplaces

Sarah Daly

Introduction

Since sustainability, and specifically the low-carbon agenda, have become a headline topic, it has emerged there are some key facets of high energy and high carbon buildings which are also responsible for low performance in people. This chapter explores those specific aspects in order to identify in what way they might affect productivity and to assist in the quantification of 'human capital' paybacks into building performance metrics, thereby making gains for both the sustainability and health and well-being agendas. By proving the links between internal environment and productivity with associated metrics, it should be possible to create a more compelling case for the creation of low carbon, high performance offices, than might be possible by only using carbon or energy use as a driver.

History and context

Certification of green buildings started in the UK in 1990 with the formation of BRE (Buildings Research Establishment), which introduced the BRE Environmental Assessment Method (BREEAM). This was followed three years later by the US Green Building Council, which developed the Leadership in Energy and Environmental Design (LEED) model.

In the UK, the commercial property sector has taken a leadership role, beyond legislation, to increase the sustainability of the building stock. Organisations like British Land, Grosvenor, Hammerson, Hermes and Land Securities are some of the largest property owners in London. Together they have formed the Better Buildings Partnership which seeks to work with tenants and supply chains to reduce the CO_2 impacts in London.

While the focus may seem to be on the glamour of new eco-buildings and state-of-the-art 'statement' buildings, the key issue is predominantly with existing building stock. The market has been polarised over the past decade, primarily in the absence of a clear consensus on the benefits of greener buildings. Early adopters and those in the ground-breaking organisations like the Better Buildings Partnership and the 94 countries represented by the World Green Building Council (WGBC) are now part of a completely new paradigm in construction. As Rick Fedrizzi attests in his introduction to the *Business Case for Green Building*, green construction is no longer viewed as the exception, but is seen more as the driver for a massive transformation in a key global sector where green building is a half-trillion dollar industry in the United States, and more than a trillion dollar industry worldwide (World Green Building Council, 2013).

Laggards in the construction sector and on the client side are finding it increasingly difficult to play catch up – both on a technological/know-how basis and in transforming the language of their business. Where they were previously making excuses for not mitigating their environmental impacts, usually because of 'economic constraints', it was often suspected that it was more to do with lack of corporate 'will' or a comprehension of the real issues and benefits. However, the evidence is now clear that, far from being the meat of upbeat economic times, lean construction has driven a host of savings which have created significant value:

> Going green can produce economic values for both clients and contractors. Early studies reported that green commercial buildings use 26% less energy, save 13% on maintenance costs, generate 33% less greenhouse gas emissions, increase occupancy ratio by 3.5%, raise return on investment by 6.6%, create 7.5% more building value, and improve 27% higher occupant satisfaction (Fowler and Rauch 2008; McGraw-Hill 2006; United States Green Building Council (USGBC) 2010; Lee et al. 2012; Oates and Sullivan 2012).
>
> (Hathaway, 2013)

So is the position any clearer now that we have had a decade of increasing evidence not just on the reality of climate change but on performance metrics which show the unequivocal benefit of 'green' buildings? In the past five years there has certainly been a plethora of publications, reports, books and conferences advocating the benefits with detailed peer-reviewed research and case studies. The key has been moving away from the technical fixation with features of green buildings and moving the conversation to 'the business case' in order to clarify the specific benefits to investors/developers, owners or tenants. For many years the market was batting the arguments to and fro: investors said customers needed to specifically demand green investment; while investors/lenders needed to see the return and not feel they were paying a premium for upgrading specifications just to be 'seen' to be green. Even so, there is still a need for substantial partnership and collaboration between all the stakeholders of buildings to ensure that the right decisions are made and the rewards are reaped directly by the partners, and by reduced environmental and social impacts.

The WGBC's illustration of the benefits to each key stakeholder (Figure 23.1) is a very important guide to how everyone gains in a collaborative approach to investing in better buildings. Indeed, it is essential for all partners to be fully engaged. These buildings require very specific occupier behaviours in order to ensure modelled performance can be delivered. For this reason, 'soft landings' are essential client training and handover sessions, which ensure that new technologies are managed correctly and that staff understand how to adapt to their new environment.

Much of the slowness of uptake of greener buildings has been due to the continuing assumption that 'green costs significantly more' upfront, even if there are paybacks in use or whole life. However, this has now been proven to be a very misleading market myth. Certainly in the early days there were some cost premiums due to the newness of technologies and the high market entry costs (Morris, 2007; Kaplow, 2010).

So we have clear evidence that there is no significant additional cost to building better buildings. Indeed, the benefits are so extensive that one might question why new methodologies are not mandated for zero carbon non-domestic buildings in the UK. Kaplow (2010) cites further reports which also substantiate the paybacks in terms of increased rental yield and sales value on LEED-rated buildings.

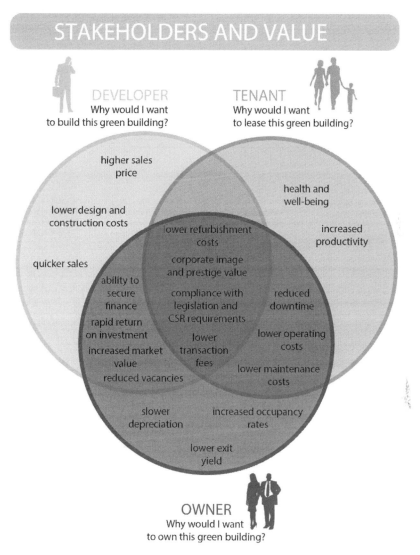

Figure 23.1 Stakeholders and value
Source: WGBC (2013).

Clearly the market advantage will be a short-term supply and demand benefit – but in a sector that has traditionally been driven by short-term gain, the evidence is irrefutable that environmentally-compliant buildings present no financial risk to investors or owners. However, this also means that tenants will be paying a substantial rise in rent to occupy these better buildings. The question has remained as to how these clients will justify higher rates when the investors/landlords will be getting the immediate payback (Figure 23.2).

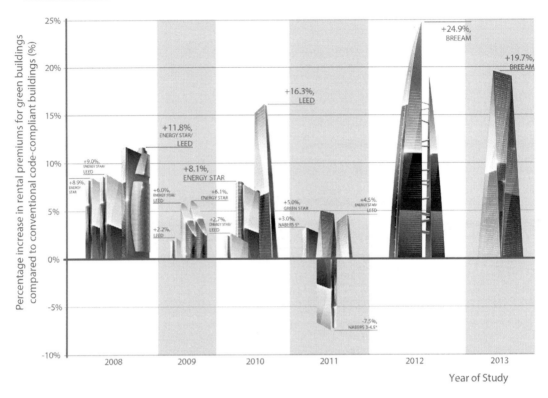

Figure 23.2 Rental premiums for office buildings
Source: WGBC (2013).

Again the evidence shows that tenants have started to identify and seek a range of paybacks from occupying certified green premises. This leads Clements-Croome (Clements-Croome, 2010) to propose the following ratio:

Construction cost	1
Maintenance & building operating costs	5–10
Business operating costs	200

Indeed, Evans (1998) concludes that there is a good deal of evidence that the building itself, if properly designed and managed, can lead to productivity gains of as much as 17 per cent. BREEAM sets critical standards for the environmental impacts as seen in this illustration of the assessment categories (Figure 23.3).

The most significant categories are energy and health and well-being with 15 per cent. Despite this, there has been a lack of understanding in the market place that the greatest returns do not come from energy efficiency but from increased health, well-being and productivity in better workplaces.

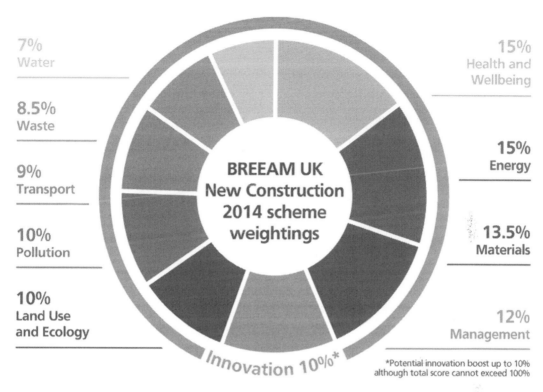

Figure 23.3 BREEAM new construction 2014 scheme weightings
Source: BRE.

While in no way wishing to demean the other 85 per cent of environmental benefits of greener buildings, it is clear that the Human Resources departments should be taking a keener interest in the features of workplaces that impact on people as the correlation between investment and payback is so much more compelling than the factors relating to the traditional custodians in the Estates or Facilities Management departments.

The reason this is significant is that, if presented appropriately, to the C-Suite decision-makers, with identified productivity returns, we should see a significant acceleration in demand for the retrofitting of existing buildings. This would help achieve the building-related carbon reduction targets considerably sooner than 80 per cent by 2050; indeed, given the potential scale of the paybacks notwithstanding the demise of government-backed schemes like Green Deal (DECC, 2010), industry could easily justify reaching its share of that figure by 2025. This would not only significantly reduce carbon outputs and energy demands, thereby affording less justification for controversial fuel supplies like nuclear and shale gas fracturing, it would create substantial employment in the green building sector and associated trades. This is a great example of a triple economic, environmental and social gain in sustainable development.

Which factors create a healthy and productive workplace?

Clearly there are many factors which contribute to a happy, healthy and productive workplace. Frequently people cite poor management or other organisational issues as the main problem and this can indeed be the case, or one of the contributory factors. However, this section seeks to identify and quantify specifically the physical environmental factors. This is not to say that culture, job satisfaction or relationship issues will not still feature in a well-designed, high performance workplace; indeed, many high-performing teams can emerge from poor working conditions. What is clear is that, to optimise performance, an organisation needs to holistically address cultural, personal satisfaction *and* environmental factors.

Derek Clements-Croome is one of the pre-eminent world authorities on the relationship between the built environment sector and improving workplaces. In his (2010) book, *Intelligent Buildings*, he makes a strong case for prioritising the key facets which contribute to a high performance workplace:

> The quality of the environment can affect work performance and there is a need to take this into account when bringing in new technology for the purpose of improving the performance of business organisations. Loftness *et al.* (1997) list seven basic infrastructures to achieve workplace needs:

> - fresh air and temperature control;
> - lighting control;
> - daylight and view, including reduced direct solar gain;
> - privacy and working in quiet conditions;
> - network access;
> - multiple data, power and voice connected systems;
> - ergonomic furniture with environmentally sensitive finishes.

Clements-Croome goes on to describe how lack of productivity can manifest itself in the workplace if employees are unhappy or dissatisfied. Lack of productivity shows up in many ways such as absenteeism, arriving late and leaving early, taking longer breaks, careless mistakes, overwork, boredom and frustration with the management and environment. Townsend (1997) believes that 25 per cent of us enjoy our work and the rest do not. This shows the importance of doing everything possible to engage the majority of employees in respecting and enjoying their workplace; if only because most of us spend more of our lives at work than anywhere else.

Relating this back to the cost of buildings and the focus that goes into designing (both new and retrofitted workspace), it is critical to perceive the building almost entirely from the perspective of its occupants. While construction projects frequently cite 'customer engagement', this is rarely taken to the level required to achieve the optimum working environments as the competing demands of design, cost and the multiple stakeholders often impede this process. It is therefore essential that very clear workspace performance criteria are written into the brief from day one by the design team. Often employees will not necessarily recognise the importance of these factors. For example, clients may mandate air conditioning rather than considering the healthier and more environmentally beneficial solution of natural ventilation or mixed mode (mechanical and non-mechanical ventilation), simply because they do not know about or understand it; or because they associate air conditioning with 'luxury'.

Figures 23.4 and 23.5 again provide some useful quantification of relative additional cost measured against specific paybacks in 'green' office or school buildings over a 20-year period of data collection.

Taking this a step further, we can see that CoStar's analysis of value clearly indicates substantial uplift in greener offices (Figure 23.6).

Costs and Benefits of Green Buildings: Present value of 20 years of estimated impacts based on study data set collected from recent green buildings

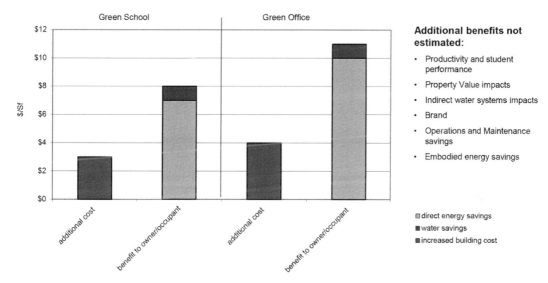

Figure 23.4 Costs and benefits of green building 1
Source: Kats (2009).

Costs and Benefits of Green Buildings: Present value of 20 years of estimated impacts based on study data set and synthesis of relevant research*

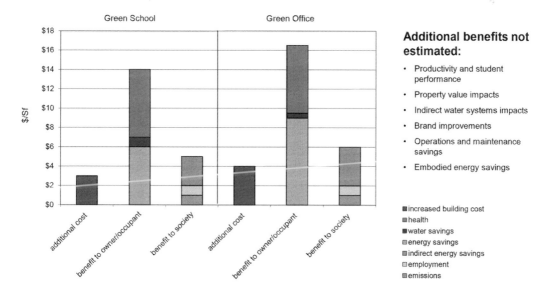

*There is significantly greater uncertainty, and less consensus around methodologies for estimating health and societal benefits.

Figure 23.5 Costs and benefits of green building 2
Source: Kats (2009).

Increased rent, sales, occupancy in green buildings

1st quarter 2008	Non-LEED	LEED certified offices	Difference	% Change
Occupancy rates	88%	92%	4%	5%
Rent ($/SF)	$31	$42	$11	35%
Property value ($/SF)	$267	$438	$171	64%

1st quarter 2008	Non-Energy star	Energy Star Offices	Difference	% Change
Occupancy rates	88%	92%	4%	5%
Rent ($/SF)	$28	$31	$3	11%
Sale price ($/SF)	$227	$288	$61	27%

Source: CoStar analysis, 2008

Figure 23.6 Increased rent, sales, occupancy in green buildings
Source: Muldavin (2008).

Another interesting perspective comes from Gensler's (2013) US workplace survey which identified that while 77 per cent of employees prefer quiet when they need to focus, 69 per cent are dissatisfied with noise levels at their primary workspace. This demonstrates the conflict between open plan offices and the need for concentration and private space. Like the air conditioning 'myth', open plan is often positively associated with 'good' workplaces, simply because there was a dramatic move away from poor cellular spaces. However, there can be a host of performance indicators which contribute to low performance in cellular or open plan offices and they are more to do with comfort and space utilisation than whether they are open or closed *per se*.

Simplified metrics to quantify paybacks from a proposed green building

While there is substantial evidence to show that positive health, well-being and productivity can be linked, among other factors, to optimum working environments, there still appears to be a gap in how this can be simply communicated to a commercial audience to facilitate the payback analysis required to present the business case to the board.

Sustainability Investment Modelling (SIM)

There is no simple yet accurately scientific way of doing this. However, I have developed a pragmatic methodology which creates a self-analysis proforma which is entirely scalable, so it is appropriate for an SME (small to medium-sized enterprise) in one building, or can be applied by department, building or estate to a large corporation.

The purpose of Sustainable Investment Modelling (SIM) is to encourage organisations to take a more holistic view of the paybacks and to understand the factors which will deliver best value, in terms of carbon/energy reduction and organisational performance.

The following structure can be used, with appropriately qualified internal or external experts, to conduct visual audits of the core working areas to identify if the factors listed are conforming to regulation, of concern or below compliance. This can be done easily by using a traffic light system of red, amber, and green to give a clear and immediate indication of how appropriate the current workplace is for health, well-being and productivity (Figure 23.7) (see Appendix, the SIM Framework).

In the example in Figure 23.7, the zones have been identified to include working areas for all grades of employee, with zones 7 and 8 representing the C-suite offices. Clearly, whatever the visual appearance of this building, it is not a good working environment for the majority of employees and presents significant issues that may be difficult to remedy without deep refurbishment, which would probably require phased or whole-scale decanting of employees from the workspaces. In this instance it may be preferable, if possible, to justify the move to an entirely new building which can meet all the performance requirements of the business, sustainably. Figures 23.8 and 23.9 show examples of a poor and an unproductive workplace, with inadequate space, light and ventilation, noise and glare issues.

The People Payback Calculator

In order to provide the financial case, it is important to attribute value to the people cost on this sample HQ building with data provided by the company. The *People Payback Calculator* (Figure 23.10) has been designed to provide a method of identifying investment returns based on three key targets: reducing staff turnover and sickness absence; and increasing employee productivity. In order to identify these values, the client and consultant need to use existing company data (or estimates) on these performance attributes to see if the company is performing above or below industry norms. As shown in the notes for the sample calculator above, high

Sustainability Information Modelling

Sample SIM Report - HQ Building

	Zone 1	Zone 2	Zone 3	Zone 4	Zone 5	Zone 6	Zone 7	Zone 8
Thermal Comfort								
Draughts								
Damp/Condensation/Mould								
Solar Gain								
Glare								
Lux Levels								
Lighting Efficiency and Control								
Natural Light Availability								
Indoor Air Quality								
Ventilation Rates								
Ambient Noise								
External Noise								
Quiet/Focus Space								
Meeting/Collaborative Space								

Source: Sarah Daly

Figure 23.7 Sample SIM report

Figure 23.8 Poor workspace with inadequate space, light and ventilation, noise and glare issues

Figure 23.9 Unproductive workplace with problems

performing companies would expect to have staff churn rates of less than 5 per cent per annum. In this example the company is performing slightly below average in terms of staff turnover at 6 per cent. The average replacement cost of an employee is conservatively estimated at £15,000, which is the figure used in this example; though some reports (Bliss, 2013) estimate the real cost to be around 150 per cent of the person's salary once all the direct and indirect impacts are

Data Entry

Current	
Sector	Office
Number of Employees	117
Average Cost per Employee, per annum (£)	50,000
Company Profit (£)	4,650,000
Staff Turnover (%)	6
Working Days	231
Average Company Earnings per Employee (£)	39,743
Average Employee Replacement Cost (CIPD) (£)	15,000
Average Sickness Absence per Person (days)	8.3

Target	
Target Reduced Staff Turnover (%)	4
Target Reduced Sickness Absence per Person (days)	6
Target Increase in Employee Productivity	10

ROSI calculates savings on staff costs due to sustainable redevelopment of an existing building. This case study is based on turnover £155m at 3% profit. High performing companies have staff churn of >5% and sickness absence of >4 days. 25-30% of sickness absence can be attributed to workplace-related issues. Productivity rises up to 20% in high performing buildings. For direct comparison purposes the employee numbers are kept the same. This calculator is purely indicative however the base numbers and assumptions were verified by the client.

Savings

Sickness Absence	Current	Target
Employees	117	117
Average Cost	£50,000	£50,000
Average Work Days	231	231
Average Sickness Day Absence per Person	8.3	6
Sickness Absence Cost per Person	£1,796	£1,298
Total Sickness Absence Cost	£210,132	£151,866
Total Sickness Saving		£58,266

Productivity	Current	Target
Profit	£4,650,000	£5,115,000
Average Company Earnings per Person	£39,743	£43,718
Increase in Productivity %		10
Add Profit per Person		£3,975
Additional Productivity Profit		£465,069

Staff Retention	Current	Target
Staff Turnover/Churn %	6	4
Average Replacement Cost	£15,000	£15,000
Attrition Cost	£85,500	£57,000
Additional Staff Turnover Saving		£28,500

| Net Benefit per Annum | | £551,835 |

Figure 23.10 Return on Sustainable Investment (ROSI): People Payback Calculator

Source: Sarah Daly/IAHAA/DesignBuilder

considered. Had this higher figure been used, the annual saving to this firm could be considerably higher. The calculator is designed to allow the client to use absolute figures or to flex the options to find a justifiable outcome and attainable targets.

In terms of sickness absence, this example shows the company is averaging 8.3 days per employee per annum; and has set a conservative target reduction of six days. High performing companies would expect to see an average of less than four days per employee per annum. If a proportion of sickness is attributed to poor working environment, then it is clear that improving the workplace could save this business in excess of £58,000 per year. Taking the frequently cited findings of Preller (1990), as cited by Heerwagen, sickness absence could be reduced by up to 34 per cent by improving environmental conditions/control.

However, the most significant contribution comes in productivity increases. A very poor workspace with most or all of the environmental issues outlined could see substantial and immediate double-figure productivity increases. In this instance the client chose 10 per cent as a conservative estimate of the benefit they would expect from eliminating all the environmental detractions in their workplace; even though as explained earlier, Evans (1998) found that cumulative benefits can be up to 17 per cent. Clearly this figure equating to over £465,000 contribution is a considerable sum, with the overall potential annual recurring benefit of their optimised workplace estimated at over £550,000.

While this is not a scientific figure, it gives a very clear indication of the correlation of the cash value to the bottom line of the business, of a high performance workplace. If the client is motivated to think in terms of specific paybacks, they can then decide how long they would expect a reasonable payback to be and flex this figure with the cost of the refurbishment or proposed move. Many organisations are very surprised to see that if they implement the recommendations, they could see paybacks in less than one year. Over time, and often as a shock to the board, sustainability returns are often far greater than any other business improvement options. They may not deliver immediate 'growth' but can substantially increase profitability and enhance reputation – which does indeed lay foundations for sustainable growth in the medium to long term, not least as working capital is released for further investment, if the additional profits are not taken in dividends.

In addition to the identified people gains, the company should calculate into their whole business case:

- the proposed energy savings;
- the benefits in carbon accounting (if the organisation falls in a Mandatory Carbon Reporting (MCR) category);
- the reduced operating costs in terms of maintenance;
- that the business may also benefit from Enhanced Capital Allowances;
- the 'added value' in their ability to retain and attract clients with the additional motivation of their people and the added credibility which goes with perceptions of cutting-edge businesses

The latter point is substantiated by Harvard Business School in *The Impact of a Corporate Culture of Sustainability on Corporate Behavior and Performance* (Eccles, 2011) which shows that, tracked over 18 years, highly sustainable businesses out-perform their low sustainability peers in both stock market and accounting performance.

Conclusion

In the early days of green building design, the preoccupation was with technological advances and energy-saving performance rather than substantive occupier benefits, despite their vastly more significant direct and indirect paybacks. This skewed approach, which frankly missed all the most marketable facets of return on investment for greener buildings, has meant that uptake has been much slower than might otherwise have been the case. Today the culmination of a greater understanding of the benefits of the physical attributes of greener buildings, together with more empirical evidence, means that there are not only justifications but imperatives for businesses to reduce their impacts and reap the multifarious rewards.

Sector leadership, through organisations like BRE, WGBC and Better Buildings Partnership are creating greater acceptance and collaboration between the stakeholders within investment, construction and occupier groups, which is accelerating the shift as each feeds from the other. Indeed, the results are estimated to have created a trillion dollar global sector for green building and refurbishment. Shared value for the partners, and especially focusing on the needs of the occupiers, for whom the building exists in the first place, is therefore key.

One of the most damaging myths, which has also hampered speedier take-up of greener buildings, has been that 'green costs more'. Not only is this clearly proven to be untrue, the cost premium, where it does exist, is deemed to be 'statistically insignificant'. Indeed, even if there were to be cost differentials, these are completely offset by substantially greater sales and rental values, where customer demand is completely outstripping availability, especially of higher BREEAM and LEED-rated buildings.

There is also capacity for further savings in the delivery of greener buildings as Building Information Modelling (BIM) became mandatory for UK public buildings in 2016 (BIM Task Group, 2013). This policy will drive its use throughout the built environment sector. BIM aids design and construction phases by creating real-time collaboration which increases the effectiveness of solutions. Benefits also include detailed cost control, which negates second-stage 'value engineering'; it also detects clashes, which often cause costly delays on-site. Overall, BIM makes a major contribution to the effectiveness of design and delivery on-site where complex performance is required across professional teams. It is also useful for the entire life of the building as all the design and maintenance information can be kept up-to-date and managed more effectively; which yields further savings for the building-in-use.

Understanding the good and poor features in the current workplace, and benchmarking against best practice, offer the most thorough way for employers to ensure that they do not replace one set of environmental issues with another. The SIM tool, which I developed in conjunction with the design team, while Managing Director of Heath Avery Architects, is ideal if properly executed, in systematically identifying all the factors which need the greatest attention in a deep refurbishment. SIM, coupled with the People Payback Calculator and the other paybacks, can create the compelling financial case which will be key to stakeholders accepting that investment in low carbon, high performance workplaces makes sense on every level.

Creating high performance workplaces will only succeed if a completely holistic approach is taken to all the contributing elements – this cannot be done selectively or even sequentially. This chapter has focused on the paybacks from high carbon impacts on human performance such as heat, light and ventilation. However, there are other non-carbon/energy-related issues such as toxicity, which can have a major effect on employee health, well-being and hence, productivity.

Over time, greener buildings are becoming simpler to use. Building Management Systems (BMS) are becoming more intuitive to operate and are often linked to centralised control systems which mean that they can be pre-programmed for variable working patterns, can respond to sensors or receive data on occupancy levels and changing external conditions and modify aspects such as thermal comfort in advance.

Emerging technologies in personal control will typify the high performance workplaces of the future; where individual preferences for temperature, ventilation and light will be controlled within the employee's 'pod' and linked to sensors which will ensure equipment is switched into hibernate mode or powered-down if the space is unoccupied; thus reducing energy while increasing productivity.

While this chapter has concentrated on the organisational benefits of high performance workplaces, there is a significant societal benefit to reducing workplace-related sickness. The collective culpability of UK employers to act should therefore be recognised and this should perhaps be reflected in more direct relief for those investing in healthier working environments. One such stimulus and incentive could be reducing or removing VAT on BREEAM Excellent/ Outstanding or LEED Gold/Platinum buildings; or on approved 'healthy' products within refurbishment programmes as an extension of Enhanced Capital Allowances (DECC, 2013), which currently only includes selected equipment.

In conclusion, it is clear that there is a vast plethora of direct and indirect benefits from all elements of the construction industry – from design teams through the entire supply-chain, in partnership with employers, to drive through solutions which deliver lower carbon; energy, water and waste reduction, while creating happier, healthier and more productive workplaces.

The triple gains, economic, social and environmental, have been well documented in this chapter, thereby substantiating the promotion of the built environment as one of the most influential sectors in global sustainable development.

Appendix

Table 23.1 Sustainability Investment Modelling (SIM) sample template

Information gathering	☐	*The Client*
		Client details
		Lines of communication
		Access
		Maintenance regime and backlog
		Available drawings
	☐	Understanding the Issues
		Target outcomes
		Energy
		Emissions, CO_2
		Performance
		Environmental
	☐	Questionnaire
		People Payback Calculator
		User canvassed issues
	☐	Site Inspection
		Site visit for fact finding:-
		Broad identification of target issues
		Assessing probability of target outcomes
		Defining areas for the Sustainable Review

Information gathering	☐	*The Client*
Sustainable Review	☐	Site survey
		Central plant and systems
		Metering
		Heating controls
		Lighting efficiency and controls
		equipment in use
		Occupancy and use
		Natural ventilation and air quality
		Mechanical ventilation and control
		Condensation, mould
		Temperature
		Solar gain, glare
		Water use
		Building fabric and insulants:-
		Walls
		Floors
		Roof
		Windows and glazing
	☐	Traffic light matrix
		Simple visual indicator, showing survey results using colour coding:
		Red – Non-compliant: requires immediate intervention
		Amber – Borderline: requires further investigation
		Green – Compliant
	☐	Summary Report and Recommendations
		Summary report on the Review findings, clarifying and making recommendations for further investigation and improvement.
		This forms the basis for the scope of the detailed studies to follow.
Energy Evaluation	☐	Energy Use Audit
		Meter checking – ID and function Tariffs
		Historical use and cost analysis
		Benchmarking
		Reduction targets
	☐	Central plant and installed system appraisal
		Age and efficiency
		Pumps
		Heat emitters/rads. etc. and circuits
		Operation
		Size and duties
		Lifespan
		Maintenance

(Continued)

Table 23.1 (Continued)

Information gathering	☐	*The Client*
	☐	Metering and Sub-metering
		Opportunities for zoned metering and monitoring
		Identification of energy use anomalies
		Continued monitoring
	☐	Heating – main and secondary controls
		Central controls
		Timers
		Outside temperature compensation
		Thermostatic controls
		User controls
	☐	Hot water heating and controls
		Central plant and storage
		Age and efficiency
		Controls and temperature
		Timers
		Distribution and System appraisal
		Isolated appliances and systems
	☐	Voltage optimisation study
		Matching supply with usage and requirement
	☐	Lighting installations – control and efficiency
		Light fittings
		Efficiency, frequency
		Efficacy
		Lighting levels
		Controls, timers etc.
	☐	Equipment in use.
		Efficiency and power usage of:–
		Copiers
		Computers
		Printers
		Audio
		Catering equipment
		White goods
Building Fabric Evaluation	☐	Thermographic survey
		Infra-red camera external survey showing heat losses, leakage and temperature variations
	☐	Insulation
		Current levels of insulation
		Exploratory investigations of walls and roof.
		Opportunities for improvement
		Heat loss calculations
		Energy saving analysis
		Specification

Information gathering	☐	*The Client*
	☐	Condensation and mould growth
		Location, cause and rectification
	☐	Glazing/window efficiency
		Window specification
		Heat and energy losses
		Glazing specification
		Orientation characteristics
		Air leakage/draughts
	☐	Air leakage
		General fabric leakage paths
		Heat losses
		Improvements
	☐	Water Use
		Water saving devices
		Fixtures and fittings
		Metering
Occupancy Evaluation	☐	Overheating – solar and internal gains
		Orientation
		Improvements, glass, blinds etc.
	☐	Ventilation – passive
		Availability
		Effectiveness
		Extent
		User operability
		Occupational assessment
	☐	Ventilation – mechanical
		Effectiveness
		Need
		Maintenance
		Control
		Noise
	☐	Daylighting adequacy
		Extent and amount
		Orientation
		Shading devices
		Full radiance contour mapping if required.
	☐	Lighting adequacy
		In use characteristics
		Colour rendering, mood, ambience
		Distribution and design/function -v- use of space
	☐	Glare
		Incidence of glare
		Improvements

(Continued)

Table 23.1 (Continued)

Information gathering	☐	The Client
	☐	Glare
		Orientation
		Devices
	☐	Acoustics – internal and external to the space
		In space assessment
		Reverberation characteristics
		Undesirable external intrusions
		Plant noise, traffic noiseImprovements
	☐	Occupancy levels
		Estate-wide occupancy
		Building stock and use
		Development planning
	☐	Functionality and space planning
		Internal space planning, layout
		Use and function
	☐	Airborne pollutants
		Radon gas detection
		CO_2 levels
		Body odour
		VOCs
		Off-gassing
Sustainable Masterplan		Findings
		Improvements
		Benefits
		Cost estimates
		Programme and sequencing.
		Recommendations and Conclusions

Source: IAHAA.com

References

BIM Task Group (2013) *BIM* . Retrieved from BIM Task Group. Available at: www.bimtaskgroup.org/
Bliss, W.G. (2013) *Cost of Employee Turnover*. August 2. Available at: www.isquare.com: www.isquare.com/turnover.cfm
Clements-Croome, D. (2010) Building environment, architecture and people. In D.J. Clements-Croome, *Intelligent Buildings: Design, Management and Operation*. London: Thomas Telford Limited.
DECC (2010) *The Green Deal: A Summary of the Government's Proposals*. Available at: www.gov.uk/government/uploads/system/uploads/attachment_data/file/47978/1010-green-deal-summary-proposals.pdf
DECC (2013) *ECA*. Available at: Energy Technology List: ECA Scheme: https://etl.decc.gov.uk/etl/site.html
Eccles, R.G. II. (2011) *The Impact of a Corporate Culture of Sustainability on Corporate Behavior and Performance*. Boston: Harvard Business School. Available at: http://hbswk.hbs.edu/item/6865.html

Evans, R.H. (1998) *The Long Term Costs of Owning and Using Buildings*. London: Royal Academy of Engineering.

Gensler (2013) *2013 Workplace Survey*. Los Angeles: Gensler.

Hathaway, H. (2013) *Turning Green to Gold in the Construction Industry: Fable or Fact?* Washington, DC: American Society of Civil Engineers.

Heerwagen, J. (2000) Green buildings, organizational success and occupant productivity. *Building Research and Information*, 28(5): 353–367.

Kaplow, S. (2010) Green building costs less than conventional building. Available at: www.stuartkaplow.com/library3.cfm?article_id=173

Kats, G.J.B. (2009) *Greening Our Built World: Costs, Benefits, and Strategies*. New York: Island Press.

Morris, P. (2007) What does green really cost? *PREA Quarterly*, Summer.

Muldavin, S. (2008) *Quantifying "Green" Value: Assessing the Applicability of the CoStar Studies*. London: Green Building Finance Consortium.

Preller, L.E. (1990) Sick leave due to work-related health complaints among office workers in the Netherlands. *Indoor Air 90*, 1: 227–230.

Townsend, J. (1997) How to draw out all the talents. *Independent*, July 24.

World Green Building Council. (2013) *The Business Case for Green Building*. Geneva: World Green Building Council.

Further reading

BBC News (2012) Average earnings rise by 1.4% to £26,500, says ONS. November 22. Available at: www.bbc.co.uk/news/business-20442666

Black, D.C (2008) *Working for a Healthier Tomorrow: Review of the Health of the Working Age Population*. London: TSO.

Centers for Disease Control and Prevention (CDCP) (2013) *Indoor Environmental Quality: Chemical Contaminant Sources*. Available at: www.cdc.gov/niosh/topics/indoorenv/chemicalsodors.html

Chegut, A.E. (2011) *The Value of Green Buildings*. Maastricht: Maastricht University.

Edwards, B. (2003) *Green Buildings Pay*. London: Spon Press.

Hinkin, P. (2013) Do you want a productive workplace? Then let there be light. Available at: www.2degreesnetwork.com/groups/built-environment/resources/do-you-want-productive-workplace-then-let-there-be-light/

Kats, G.H. (2003) *Green Building Costs and Financial Benefits*. Boston: Massachusetts Technology Collaboration.

Leonardo Meeus, P.K.-M. (2012) *How to Refurbish All Buildings by 2050*. Florence: European University Institute.

Parker, J. (2012) *The Value of BREEAM*. London: BSRIA.

Philips Lighting (2011) Offices: feel what light can do for office life. December. Available at: www.lighting.philips.com/pwc_li/gb_en/connect/tools_literature/offices_2011.pdf>. Netherlands: Philips Electronics NV.

RICS (2013) *Sustainability: Improving Performance in Existing Buildings*. London: RICS Books.

Savills & BCO (2013) *What Workers Want*. London: BCO.

Singh, A. (2009) *Life Cycle Cost Analysis of Occupant Well-being and Productivity Impacts in LEED Offices*. Available at: http://books.google.co.uk/books?id=sjvhMjXV4jMC&printsec=frontcover&source=gbs_ge_summary_r&cad=0#v=onepage&q&f=false: Michigan State University.

Wargocki, P.S.C. (2007) *Indoor Climate and Productivity in Offices: How to Integrate Productivity in Life-Cycle Cost Analysis of Building Services*. Brussels: REHVA.

Chapter 24

Building performance
The value management approach

Bernard Williams

> All groups, as I recall, felt that the more the building offered visually and physically, the better the quality of workspace and quality of educational opportunity. Similarly ownership in the designs, finishes, colours, furniture, etc. played a huge role.
>
> (Headmaster involved in the planning of his new primary school)

Introduction

The preceding chapters have made a very powerful case for the proposition that commercial buildings can have a significant impact upon the performance of those who use them. This chapter accepts the view attributed to Lord Kelvin that if you cannot measure something, you cannot understand it, and if you cannot understand it, you cannot improve it. So it examines some of the ways in which people have tried to measure the performance of buildings in an attempt to understand and improve them, and it shows how this process fits into the more formal process of value management.

Building performance and the premises policy

The premises policy

'Premises' means 'place of business' and that has connotations which are much wider than 'buildings'. The premises policy has three strategic centres:

* location
* size
* quality (performance).

The premises policy should articulate the organisation's premises performance requirements but, more importantly, it should state with equal clarity the reasons why the performance levels are needed, i.e. the risks to the business to be avoided.

So the risk management policy (for this is what it is in effect) needs to specify the ongoing premises management functions, the service levels identified as being appropriate to contain the risks and any service-level resource drivers, for example, local environmental conditions, densities of occupation, etc., which may control the actual levels of service needed.

On this basis the premises should be 'cost-effective', provided procurement is efficient. The Intelligent Client Function (ICF) must take responsibility for continuous monitoring of the quality achieved and its continuing relevance to the business requirements. An important issue to consider at this point is that quality and risk are reciprocal.

Building performance

Performance, in business terms, means 'the manner or quality of functioning' which, of course, includes buildings; the ability to understand building performance and thence control it, and, if necessary, improve it, is on the critical path towards increasing productivity and improving sustainability.

Of course, it is one thing to understand what is meant by performance and another to be able to measure it. What Lord Kelvin is actually arguing for is the need to make sense of complexity, not necessarily by fully calculating costs and benefits but by recognising and evaluating patterns of relationships.

Building performance is conventionally considered primarily in terms of physical integrity and durability and the associated capital and revenue costs, but the reality is that it goes infinitely deeper than that. Buildings are simply a means to an end.

A building's response to accommodating the users' demands represents its performance, i.e.

the contribution made by a building or estate to the functional and financial requirements of the occupiers and/or owners, the associated physical and financial characteristics of the fabric, services and finishes over time and the overall sustainability of that contribution.

(Williams, 2008)

Sustainability of buildings

It is now commonly accepted that there are in fact three facets of sustainability (Figure 24.1):

- environmental
- social
- economic

and the Venn diagram in Figure 24.1 depicts their interrelationship. The following is a brief resume of the key issues addressed by each facet.

- *Environmental sustainability.* In brief, environmental sustainability relates to the way that the building as constructed and used impacts upon the environment and its ecology.
- *Social sustainability.* It is generally accepted that social sustainability is concerned with social equity, liveability, and other socially desirable outputs from community development and occupation.
- *Economic sustainability.* This has been defined as 'the ability of an economy to support a defined level of economic production indefinitely' (www.thwink.org).

In the case of 'building sustainability' these three domains have to be considered at the 'micro' level although of course the sustainability of each building must inevitably have a macro-impact.

The original version (1989) of the 'Performance of Buildings' diagram in Figure 24.2 has now been updated to incorporate the concept that overall sustainability is indeed at the heart of all aspects of building performance while at the same time deferring to the fact that individual aspects of sustainable performance have to be addressed within the building's performance itself.

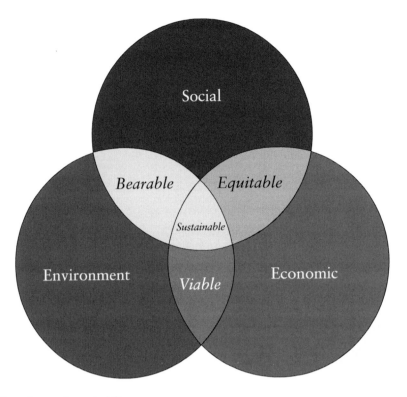

Figure 24.1 Three facets of sustainability

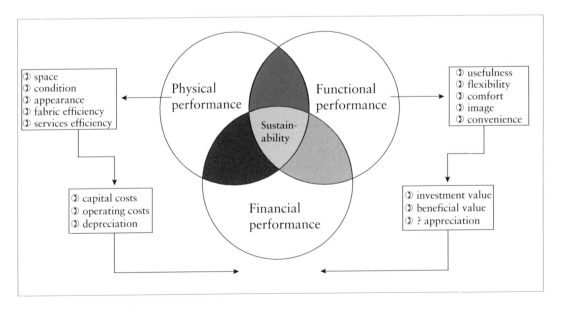

Figure 24.2 The three facets of building performance
Source: Williams (2008).

There are three components of building performance: (1) physical; (2) functional; and (3) financial.

- *Physical performance* relates to the behaviour of the fabric, services and finishes embracing physical properties such as structural integrity, internal environment (heating, lighting, etc.), cleanability, maintainability, durability, inherent energy efficiency and carbon emissions in use: it also impacts upon the sustainability of a building in terms of the materials and systems used in its construction
- *Functional performance* is the term used to describe the properties afforded by the building to the benefit (or otherwise) of the occupier. Examples are space (quantity and quality), layout, ergonomics, image, ambience, amenity, movement/communications, security, health and safety and flexibility. Other chapters deal with the *social* sustainability (human relationships, physical well-being and the like) generated by buildings – implicitly if not expressly so. Here the impact of the building's functions in respect of environmental (e.g. energy consumption) and economic sustainability are considered further below.
- *Financial performance* is a combination of capital and revenue expenditure, rate of depreciation, investment value and contribution to profitability/efficiency. It springs from the physical and functional performance of the building and the way in which it is used. A building should be economically sustainable in terms of its cost in use and its value as an asset; a wasting or unaffordable asset is definitely NOT economically sustainable.

These three facets are inextricably linked, although the significance of this relationship is frequently missed by those whose preoccupation is with one particular facet only, oblivious to the fact that their contribution forms only a part of the total solution in the overall scheme of things.

Life-expectancy of components and life-cycle costs

Life-cycle cost appraisal is an important discipline encouraging designers to justify their decisions to the future occupier. The concept of 'soft landings' addresses the links between initial and lifetime expenditure, and a web-enabled design team tool for controlling that link (the CombiCycle Comparator) is described below; this tool also measures the environmental sustainability related to the building's physical performance.

The costs of physical performance are normally minuscule relative to the costs of the functions they accommodate. However, the consumption of energy-in-use over the life of the building will continue to be a major source of concern to designers and their more philanthropic clients.

Nevertheless more and more attention is now being paid to the effects of the built form upon the environment and its ecological centres. New methods of measuring, valuing and controlling the environmental and economic impact of physical performance of buildings are considered later in the chapter.

Cost/benefit analysis

Many decisions to spend money on buildings in the name of higher quality or performance are not formally justified in terms of return on investment because the 'benefits' are difficult to quantify. One pragmatic but effective method (the return on sustainable investment) is described in Chapter 23 in this volume.

Benefits may come in the performance of the spaces provided or the 'scenery' surrounding them. Thus, natural stone facing is perceived as higher quality than the reconstituted variety: we know the cost differential in both capital and life-cycle terms but what value does natural stone add to bottom-line profit (assuming that the options are both permissible)?

Similar question marks may hang over investments in faster, bigger lifts, comfort ventilation and so on right through the full range of building elements. Anecdotes abound but, this present volume excepted, good hard data is difficult, if not impossible, to find.

One quite simple pragmatic method of investigating the costs/benefits involves Functional Analysis which can form a useful part of the formal value management process discussed below. A typical proforma for use in this process is illustrated in Table 24.1. In this technique the client and the design team together test all the key options against an absolute minimum (zero-base) option. No attempt is made to calculate costs or an investment return; the panel is merely asked to say whether they think the proposal impacts upon either the functional or physical facets in terms of the risks and benefits ('life-cycle' and 'environmental' impact are both aspects of physical performance). It is important to note that the physical side *alone* (excluding energy costs) rarely gives a large enough return to justify investment in levels of physical performance above zero base.

Table 24.1 Cost/benefit option appraisal: 'first-strike' analysis

Subject:	Partitions	Estimated Costs
Location:	Cellular Offices	
Zero-base specification:	Metal stud and plasterboard	£ 10,000
Proposal:	Proprietary demountable	£ 25,000
Benefits analysis — subjective evaluation		
Effect of proposal on functional performance	Perceived quality	better
	Visual ambience	better
	Comfort	-
	Ergonomics	-
	Flexibility	better
	Safety	-
Effect of proposal on life-cycle costs	Cleaning	-
	Energy	-
	Maintenance and repairs	better
	Security	-
	Insurance	-
	Replacement	worse
	Management	better
Effect of proposal on environment	Energy consumption	N/A
	Embodied energy	worse
	Sustainability	better

Source: Williams, Facilities Economics, IFPI Ltd.

The concept whereby *all* design decisions are made on the basis of justification of expenditure over and above a zero-base is at the heart of modern thinking on value-management. The problem here again is one of measurement and valuation: you can measure the payback on energy-efficiency measures but how do you value the comfort implications of the sound reduction qualities of triple glazing?

An answer to that could, in the first instance, be tested across all the range of probability by the use of sensitivity analysis; over time, the constant use of such calculations and demands for better information by the users will encourage the necessary research to take place in order that the quantification process should become more scientific and valid.

This brings us to the consideration of how the functional efficiency of the building influences the overall productivity of an organisation by the way it accommodates its activities. In fact, the level of performance of premises should extend from the business requirement and the cost of achieving such performance should be tested for return on investment within the context of the business plan. However, to achieve such mathematical correlation requires a level of understanding of the concept of the functional value of buildings which is rarely found in current techniques of cost estimating and investment valuation.

Performance and value management

Performance is of course a key to the ability to value-manage building solutions. In its simplest but most profound definition, value management, and its key component activity 'value engineering' both entail the 'elimination of redundant performance, i.e. the avoidance of expenditure on any item of construction which does not add value to the product or which makes the product achieve more than is required' (Williams, 2008).

Value management must look beyond the cost consequences of physical performance if the building design process is to have a real impact on the organisation's efficiency and hence profitability. Unfortunately real estate appraisal in this context is restricted merely to the issue of 'functional obsolescence'. Generally speaking, market valuation is made by reference to 'comparative valuation', which may well result in the blind leading the blind. That may get by in the world of real estate but it is not good enough in a business productivity context.

What we therefore need is methods of appraising a property which reflect its performance in terms of the business requirement – one of which features may well be the location and asset value; however, in spite of the old assumption, propounded by real estate agents, that the three most important features of a property are 'location, location and location', a case study later illustrates the fact that this may not be the principal determining factor in terms of value to the user. However, we must not run ahead of ourselves, for we first need to consider what value means to the user and how to measure it.

Value management of the premises policy

Value management

This ability to see a strategy in the wider context of value to the business is fundamental to the discipline of 'value management'. BS EN 12973:200 covers this whole area. Although not all the definitions below are taken directly from the BS, they all fit well within the process it describes and advocates.

The concept of value

An appropriate definition of the value of facilities is 'the usefulness of the facilities provided in the context of the activities they support' (ibid.). This definition is drawn widely enough to encompass both economic activities (e.g. retail) and social activities (e.g. education).

'Value' is used sometimes to qualify a 'price' or 'cost'; in these circumstances it is usual for adjectives such as 'good' or 'best' to be used in the qualifying process, i.e. 'good value' or 'best value' which then expresses not only 'usefulness' but also the reasonableness of the price paid, i.e. the 'value for money'.

BS EN 12973:2000: Value Management states that 'the concept of value relies on the relationship between the satisfaction of many differing needs and the resources used in doing so'. It offers the formula: Value = Satisfaction of Needs/Use of Resources.

The document further goes on to state that 'the fewer resources used or the greater the satisfaction of needs, the greater is the value'. This latter part of the definition seems to ignore the economic concept of diminishing returns and needs to be examined carefully in the context of facilities management – and, indeed, with respect to any business case founded upon a calculation of return on investment (ROI) – see section, 'Value for money'.

The BS goes on to define 'value management' as 'a style of management particularly dedicated to motivate people, develop skills and promote synergies and innovation, with the main purpose of maximising the overall performance of an organisation'. Clearly the value management of the organisation's facilities is an important sub-set of this management process.

Value for money

The common definition of 'value for money' is 'something well worth the money spent'; from this it becomes clear that the usefulness of a commodity (a building in this context) has to be set against the price paid for it. Value is of course discrete to the beneficiary of the offering.

In all but the most affluent micro-economic environments people and companies can normally make do perfectly well with simple-functioning offerings – *real* needs, not wish-lists, are the order of the day.

Providing 'greater satisfaction of needs' may represent value but, on the other hand, may not represent optimum value for money – a point which the more or less universally adopted cost/value equation reinforces. The economic law of diminishing returns always comes into play when enhancements to an offering cost more than the added value created, so the offering no longer provides 'best value' (see below).

In simple terms, nothing is cheap if it is not what you need. So, more quality for proportionately less cost does not necessarily deliver a 'best value' solution; nor does getting more out of the budget available.

Best value

The term 'best value' may therefore be defined as: 'the offering which provides the beneficiary with the highest return on investment (ROI)'. Whether that investment and return are measurable in tangible (actual) or intangible (hypothesized) terms does not matter, provided that in the latter case a diligent and meaningful analysis of costs and benefits is carried out.

In the case of buildings, most functional performance benefits are 'soft'. i.e. difficult to quantify, for example, comfort, cleanliness, ergonomic efficiency, whereas the costs of construction and service provision are 'hard' and tangible. This means that calculation of a hypothetical return on the tangible investment may have to rely on financial or social gains assessed through observations, experience or judgements of the beneficial effects of the offering, rather than on actual recorded income.

Affordability

The ability to *afford* to buy something relates to having the money or access to funds rather than the desire to make an optimum investment. Most organisations have what is known as the 'criterion rate of return' on their investments, i.e. the minimum return they must be sure of if the investment is to be sanctioned. In practice, the rate often varies depending on the object of investment and the risks attached; in times of cash-flow difficulties, firms will often seek a far greater return on projects or services involving capital up-front than they will seek when payment can be deferred or provided by others, for example, new build owner-occupation as opposed to rental. This is a form of 'cash-rationing'.

However, any proposal which does not achieve the criterion ROI is de facto *not* affordable, regardless of the actual availability of funds because the available funds should be reserved for offerings which *do* meet the required ROI.

According to Kelly *et al.* (2010), value management of projects is 'a service which maximises the functional value (of a project) by managing its evolution and development from concept to completion, through the comparison and audit of all decisions against a value system determined by the client or customer'. The term 'value system' here is critical. Organisations need to know what is worth investing in and to have established systems and tools to help them in those investment decisions.

Value management of facilities

Facilities can account for as much as 20 per cent of an organisation's outgoings and premises are often its principal asset after its staff. They should therefore clearly be part of the overall business value management process and not dealt with off-line. In a facilities management context, 'value management is the process whereby facilities which are useful to the business are provided at a price which is both fair and affordable' (Williams, 2008). A 'fair' price is one which represents a good bargain in the relevant market place; an 'affordable' price is, as discussed above, one that meets the organisation's criteria for return on investment (ROI).

The value management process

A state-of-the-art approach to value management promotes the concept of a formal value management regime supported by clearly specified procedures involving appropriate tools and techniques. There are three inter-related facets of value management: identification/appraisal, implementation and monitoring (Figure 24.3).

In essence, facilities come in the form of:

- provision of buildings, equipment and supplies;
- operations;
- maintenance.

The principles to be applied are the same in each case. A policy must be developed relating to the business plan, testing for and eliminating any 'redundant performance' in the high level

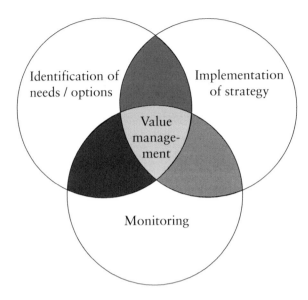

Figure 24.3 The three facets of value management
Source: Williams (2008).

brief. All stages of specification implementation and monitoring will then need to be carried out in tune with the original facilities policy and the value plan it underwrites.

Value management procedures

Whether we are considering buildings or facilities services, the process of value management is in principle the same. Figure 24.4 illustrates the consecutive and cyclical order of the three facets of value management and the activities within each one. How these activities are structured within a Work or Job Plan is up to the people who have to deliver the result.

An overview of the value management process

Stage 1 represents the formal process of identifying, say, a facilities requirement and evaluating the optimum level of quality and cost to be adopted in the facilities policy in order to deliver a 'best value' solution.

The policy having been settled, Stage 2 begins with the procurement of the facility which must be accompanied by strategies for measuring input and output performance.

Stage 3 is the measurement process which includes the ongoing requirement to make sure that changed circumstances are always detected and reflected in changed strategies where necessary – thereby completing the cyclical nature of the whole process.

The pre-briefing issues can be addressed formally using what is known as a 'value tree'. A value tree is a diagram that describes the business driver (mission) for a project or service and the criteria that need to be satisfied in order to achieve it. A value tree should be developed at the earliest stage in order to inform the brief. It should ideally be carried out by the Intelligent

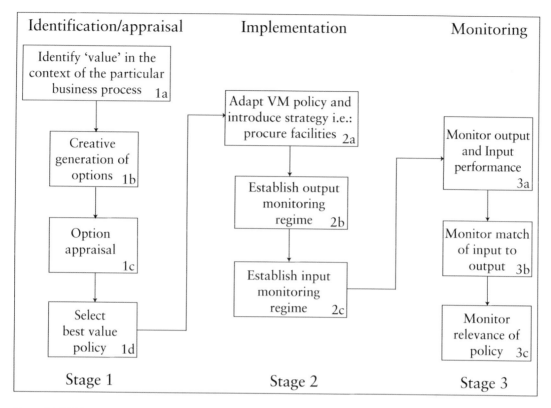

Figure 24.4 Value management processes

Client Function although, unfortunately, key facilities decisions are too often taken with little or no input from facilities professionals.

Value management of the premises policy

The premises policy has three strategic centres:

- location
- size
- quality.

Figure 24.5 shows how one organisation used a value tree to identify the *raison d'être* behind the accommodation solutions and express them in terms the business could understand. In the example, both 'size' and 'quality' constitute components of 'performance' and the value-managed premises policy looked at each strategic centre in turn, testing and scoring a number of costed options against an agreed list of weighted 'business impact drivers'.

The requirements for size should be determined by a competent space planner. However, the location and quality requirements can be assessed in-house; examples of techniques for carrying out such studies are given in Table 24.2.

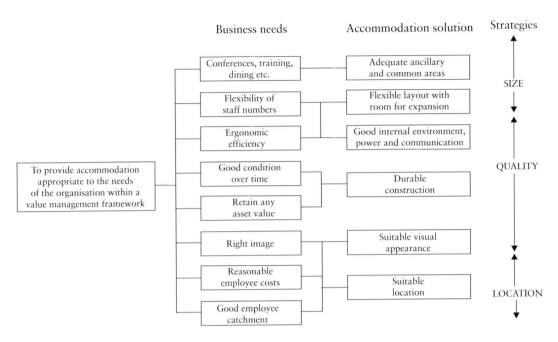

Figure 24.5 Value tree accommodation strategy

Table 24.2 shows how 'quality' was tested and scored out of 10 in the existing (zero-base) options; the 'strategy drivers' used here are higher-level versions of the 'quality centres' in some of the more formal measurement systems considered below, but they address the same issues.

In the final analysis, all three strategy centres were scored and costed for six alternative options (see Table 24.3). It is interesting to note that building performance, expressed in terms of 'size' and 'quality', scored very much higher than location in all the options although the importance of having an adequate supply of space (size) accounted for most of the points in every option. This was not indicative of a generic trend, but it reflected the aspirations of a fairly low-profile organisation with dedicated staff unlikely to be 'fazed' by a less than ideal working environment.

It should, however, be noted that their scoring was not assisted by any formal quality measurement system – it was just intuitive and guided by the future project architect. Nevertheless, the fact that a 'weighted points' total relating to the impact of performance on the business emerged from the value management process is more than just of passing interest. The bespoke refurbishment of their old premises in options (e) and (f) scored 30 per cent higher than the fitted-out spec-built alternatives, showing that the users not only could see the benefits in business impact terms accruing from a higher building performance but also were reasonably confident of their measurement of them.

The BQA system considered later holds back from making the connection between building performance and organisation-specific user requirements in direct business terms when measuring relative performance of buildings. Nevertheless the system can be used in that way by changing the weightings built into the system to weightings deduced from the business policy as portrayed in Figure 24.6 later.

Table 24.2 Evaluation of the building quality – existing (zero-base) option

Strategy drivers	Image – external	Image –internal	Ergonomics	Asset value	Statutory obligations	Recruitment of staff/volunteers	Weighted score	
							Total	Av per driver
Visual impact	4	4	n/a	4	n/a	3		
Physical impact	4	4	3	3	8	4		
Communications	5	5	5	6	n/a	5		
Depreciation	n/a	n/a	6	6	n/a	n/a		
Weight of importance	6	4	7	2	8	8		
Weighted Score	78	52	98	38	64	104	434	109

Table 24.3 Cost/benefit analysis of accommodation strategy options

Strategy options	Weighted scores					
	Location	+ Size	+ Quality	Total	Average Annual Costs £K	£ per Point
(a) Existing	142	100	109	342	840	2.46
(b) London suburban High St	133	363	188	684	1026	1.50
(c) SE provincial town centre	123	363	188	674	1010	1.50
(d) SE Provincial secondary	117	363	188	668	950	1.42
(e) City fringe front (existing) and suburban back office*	138	363	238	739	1121**	1.52
(f) City fringe front (existing)/ back - office*	141	363	238	742	1173**	1.58

Notes:
* Split locations.
** Figures subsequently reduced as a result of rentalising the refurbishment costs in a modernised lease.
+ ideal requirement (except for existing).

Measuring functional performance

Methodologies available

Several methodologies of performance evaluation are already available at home and overseas, one example being the Building Quality Assessment (BQA) procedure, which originated in Australia and New Zealand and was validated by the Building Research Establishment for UK and mainland European application. It consists of a sophisticated software program with market weighting for various performance characteristics established by reference to consultants, users and property owners. The output is an Index of Performance which can be used on a comparative basis to assess the relative usefulness of one building to another.

The concept of 'serviceability', developed by Gerald Davis in Canada, is also helping users to measure the usefulness of a building's capacity in the context of their own specific needs.

In studies of 'intelligent buildings' (Duffy, 1987) and 'the responsible workplace' (Duffy, 1993), Frank Duffy *et al.* have also shown a way forward in understanding the true worth of well-designed premises and facilities and Frank Becker and Robertson Ward Jnr in the USA are among others who have helped to enlighten the conventional wisdom.

As more data is made available, the appraisal of buildings will have to cover performance in all its aspects: functional efficiency, physical efficiency and financial efficiency and, of course, sustainability.

In search of better methods of building performance evaluation, the interaction between the building, its occupants and the activities they carry out within it must become a critical area for consideration. Equally importantly, however, the relationships between building-related costs and other expenditure by organisations must be examined to identify the likely scope for added value, or savings in general costs, and the factors that may influence such benefits.

Case study 24.1 Selecting the right building

This case study demonstrates how one Quality Measurement System – the Building Quality Assessment (BQA) program developed originally at the University of Victoria, Wellington, New Zealand – was used to help a company develop and implement an accommodation strategy for its Headquarters estate.

Commco plc (the pseudonym for one of the UK's largest firms in the communications sector) were running short of space in their three headquarters office buildings and needed to crystallise their accommodation strategy to avoid acquiring unsatisfactory premises. They also did not want to have to rely upon any estate agent's opinion as to good or bad quality, or features/ characteristics to be sought or avoided. Further, they knew intuitively that one of the three buildings was not up to scratch but they could not prove it in hard terms.

The BQA system

The system sets out to give an objective view and comparison of the designed quality of buildings, which it considers under nine main categories:

- Presentation
- Space Functionality
- Access and Circulation
- Amenities
- Business Services
- Working Environment
- Health and Safety
- Structural Considerations
- Building Manageability.

Within these categories, the system embraces some 130 factors identified as having a major influence on the overall perceived and operational quality of a building. These factors are grouped under sections within each category.

By a process of scoring and weighting, BQA provides category scores and total BQA scores that represent the conventional wisdom with regard to the comparative usefulness of different levels of specification and designed features. As such, it provides an opportunity for facilities managers to benchmark the quality of their stock to internal and (potentially) external peer groups.

The Commco plc headquarters estate

The estate comprised three office buildings – we shall call them Sterling Gate, Hampton Tower and Kings Place. Hampton Tower and Kings Place were the original headquarters buildings and Sterling Gate, a later development nearby, was acquired in a hurry when sudden dramatic growth left the company desperate for additional space.

The footprints for the three buildings are given in Figure 24.6. All three buildings would be described by the estate agents as 'prestige air-conditioned offices suitable for headquarters use'; but, as the BQA survey illustrated, such statements cannot be relied upon to describe a building's quality with any degree of accuracy.

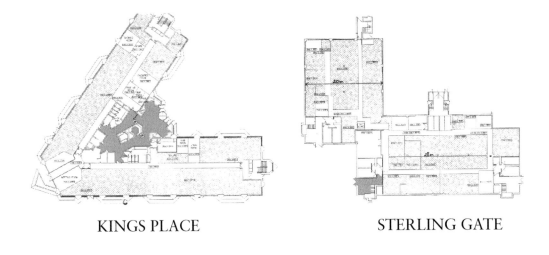

KINGS PLACE   STERLING GATE

HAMPTON TOWER

Figure 24.6 Building plans for CommCo headquarters estate

The overall BQA results

Figure 24.7 shows the results of the survey; the total scores, the top set of bars of the figure, illustrate the fact that Sterling Gate was indeed a comparatively poor building – whatever the estate agent said! Hampton Tower and Kings Place are pretty close in total, although inspection of the category scores identifies some fairly considerable differentials in individual cases. This is an interesting feature of BQA, in that it is interrogable, i.e. users can check that the quality centres, from which the total scores derive, have scored levels which coincide with their own aspirations or requirements. For example, the scores for 'presentation' show Kings Place on a pinnacle – in fact this building's score for presentation would be comparable to, or better than, that in most headquarters buildings in Commco's peer group. On the other hand, Hampton Tower is not up to 'flagship' standards in terms of presentation and Sterling Gate is clearly 'naff'.

The first and immediate benefit from the appraisal was the subjective vilification of Sterling Gate being substantiated by hard-nosed, objective measurement. The facilities managers took the report to Board level and got approval in principle to off-load the building at the earliest appropriate opportunity.

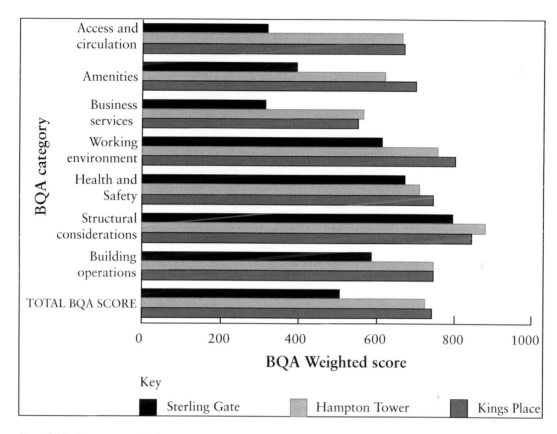

Figure 24.7 Comparison of BQA scores for Commco buildings

At the same time, the FM team were developing their accommodation strategy. They were able to demonstrate to their Board the usefulness and practicality of using BQA to specify minimum quality levels both in terms of overall totals and totals for individual categories. Indeed, they also used external BQA comparators (not illustrated here) to benchmark appropriate scores for different types of external user, thereby demonstrating that their aspirations were normal and not unduly ambitious. Should a new-build feature at some time in the future, the BQA program could provide benchmarked target costs to match overall total scores and elemental cost targets to match the scores required in each category encouraging development of innovative and value-engineered solutions.

There is no doubt that measurement systems like BQA, not necessarily as complex but used intelligently, can be of enormous benefit to facilities managers in setting an accommodation policy in terms which can be quantified, compared and vindicated. Some examples of such pragmatism are described below.

Case study 24.2 Functional performance and business growth

The example in Figure 24.8 derives first-hand from a professional practice which in 1989 still occupied the original premises originally leased in 1972, a couple of years after start-up. By

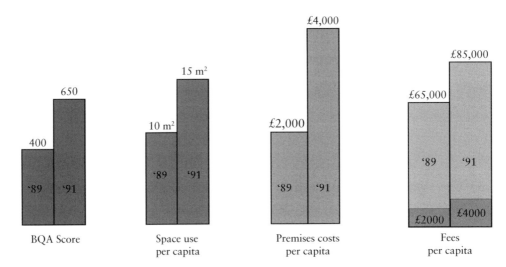

Figure 24.8 Premises and the core business growth

1989, they had outgrown the premises in terms of space and also the quality was clearly inadequate both for the job to be carried out and for the status the practice had by then attained.

The Building Quality Assessment score of the old building in 1989 was briefly assessed to have been around 400 and the new building that the practice moved into in 1991 was much higher at around 650.

They also increased the usable space per capita from 10m² to 15m² per person and that doubled the premises costs because they had moved up-market into a higher rental location. Fee earnings per capita in the period following the move increased by one-third whereas the premises costs (shaded at the bottom of the histograms in Figure 24.8) rose from around 2.75 per cent of turnover to 5 per cent of turnover – the latter being, as it happens, exactly the appropriate benchmarked level for maximum benefit in offices according to a well-established premises costs and performance database.

It is safe to say that everyone responded tremendously well to having far better facilities and they encouraged their clients to come to see them (and dine in their new conference rooms), whereas previously they had desperately tried to keep them away!

Had they not made the change, they would undoubtedly have missed a lot of the new business which did eventually come their way. So they could prove the return on investment — to their own satisfaction – by the avoidance of risk of adverse consequences, regardless of any positive gains.

Case study 24.3 Effects of building quality on educational achievement

Perhaps the most startling real-life illustration of the effects of building quality on performance is shown in the results of a case study carried out by a local authority, which looked at the relationship between building quality and educational achievement (Figure 24.9).

Using a fairly coarse high-level adaptation of the BQA system for the purpose of appraising primary school buildings, 12 sample buildings were analysed and given a quality score

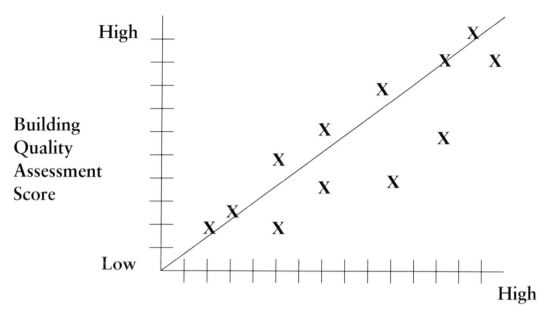

Figure 24.9 Benchmarking quality of buildings and educational achievements: a primary school study

(as shown on the vertical axis) and the educational achievements on the horizontal axis were taken from the OFSTED results. It is quite amazing to find that there is an almost straight line correlation between higher quality and better educational achievement – and, in case you are wondering about the small sample size, the statistical program which was used eliminated the possibility of the size of the sample being a distorting factor.

The other principal factors in this equation, i.e. the socio-economic grouping in the school catchment areas and the teacher assessments, were eliminated in the selection of buildings for this study. Therefore, this correlation is so strong in isolation that it must be seen that enormous benefits could be derived from taking this benchmarking study forward to understand the reasons why the educational achievement varied with different aspects of the quality of buildings.

Measuring the physical and financial performance of buildings

Measuring physical sustainability

The primary objective of this book is to review the performance of buildings in so far as it affects productivity in the workplace. However, given the evident pollution of our ecological environment, much of which is down to the way that buildings are designed, specified and constructed, it does seem important that we should review the ways in which the physical sustainability of buildings is currently measured and controlled. After all, the delivery of productivity through building performance must surely have regard to the impact of the resources consumed in that delivery on the safety and inhabitability of our planet.

There is a generally accepted and well-documented argument (e.g. the Kyoto Protocol) that carbon dioxide emitted in the generation of sources of energy (e.g. gas, electricity), in the mining and processing of raw materials for manufactured products, in transporting the latter to site and in the construction process, has a significant impact on climate change. Other ecological issues such as water pollution, eutrophication, ozone depletion, mineral extraction, etc. are also attributable to the provision of resources for building construction.

It is not appropriate here to investigate and report on the plethora of research underlying current theories on the sustainability of building materials, most of which is generally accepted by scientists as being irrefutable. However, it is appropriate that we consider ways in which the impact of various materials and processes on the physical environment is measured and review the validity of incorporating them in the design process.

Sustainability measurement systems

Measurement of the sustainability of new buildings in the Western world is predominantly carried out using the LEED and BREEAM rating systems. Both BREEAM and LEED are certification systems; each produces a rating which takes on board social and economic sustainability as well as the more familiar built environment issues. In both cases the scores are based on the provision of sustainable facilities and building specifications;

The BREEAM rating system

There are BREEAM rating systems for 'New UK Construction and International Construction' and also for buildings in use, refurbishment and masterplanning of whole communities.

BREEAM provides credits according to the performance of a building in respect of:

Management – How sustainability is managed from start to finish.

Energy use – Consumption and carbon emissions.

Health and well-being – How the internal and external environmental conditions impact upon people's health and general well-being.

Pollution – Effect of the building as designed and specified on water and air pollution.

Transport – Consideration of the effect of location in respect of demands on transport and consequent carbon emissions; provision of facilities for cyclists.

Land use – Brownfield and greenfield site usage and treatment of contaminated land.

Ecology – Conservation of the ecological value of the site and its environs and improvement where possible.

Materials – The environmental impact of the building materials used in construction and over time, including sources and recycling.

Water – Efficiency of consumption and provision including use of water from alternative sources.

The building is rated (by licensed assessors) as Pass, Good, Very Good, Excellent or Outstanding depending on the total score gained. An overall BREEAM rating of Excellent is generally a prerequisite for obtaining planning consent for non-residential development in the UK.

The Green Guide to Specification

In terms of the BREEAM Environmental rating, *The Green Guide to Specification* (Anderson *et al.*, 2009) is adopted by the BREEAM System. It is a bible for designers and manufacturers seeking to secure a favourable rating for product and system solutions, especially if seeking a BREEAM certification.

The Green Guide to Specification considers 13 'environmental impact categories', all of which represent a measure of risk to the environment. These 13 categories are weighted against each other in terms of their perceived significance resulting in module ratings from A + to E (Low: High relative environmental impact) depending on the ratings for the individual components in a design solution. The A+ to E ratings generate 'Ecopoints' which are used in the overall BREEAM rating. The ratings are only comparable as between similar building types and groups of similar items within elements, so do not have absolute universal values which can be transferred by the user across other building types and elements.

Component life expectancy

The *Green Guide* ratings take into account the impact of each component on each of the 13 listed environmental risk centres and also embrace the life-cycle replacement required in respect of the component over a 60-year period. The *Green Guide* authors say they have regard to the effects of commercial requirements on the actual life expectancy of components, for example, frequent refurbishment and re-fitting – often at 5-yearly intervals as in stores and offices; however, there is no apparent means for modifying the ratings in the event of any declared intention to shorten or extend the life of a component or element.

The life-cycle of a component has four main implications:

1   replacement cost
2   maintenance cost
3   sustainability
4   productivity disruption.

Replacement cost

Having just one all-embracing rating taking some kind of 'typical service' life may quite reasonably favour a durable material being used in a long-life (say, 30 years) replacement scenario but will unfairly prejudice a short-life component (say, 10 years) in a short-life replacement regime. For example, a component's life expectancy under normal conditions may be 30 years but if it gets replaced every 5 years in some commercial scenarios, that durability characteristic counts for nothing. The construction of the Green Guide algorithm is not declared.

The component life-expectancy model published in *Facilities Economics* has been adopted by the 'CombiCycle Comparator' Whole-life Cost and Sustainability Prediction program (described briefly below).

Maintenance cost

The *Green Guide* builds in predicted planned and reactive maintenance cost over a 60-year period according to building category. However, in excessive 'churn' and other short building life-cycle scenarios, such as in commercial stores, maintenance is reduced or omitted toward the end of the expected life-cycle so the actual figure over time is difficult to accommodate in one factor.

Sustainability

Almost without exception the environmental impact of building materials and components is overwhelmingly related to the extraction and processing functions rather than the on-site construction activities; the latter makes up less than about 5 per cent of the embodied carbon emitted during the whole cradle-to-grave construction process. Recycling will of course impact on the quantum of damage but the fact remains that a sustainable component replaced every 5 years will probably do more harm than one which is less eco-friendly which is going to be there for the medium or long term. Therefore, the ratings are rather more reliable in long-life component scenarios than in those where replacement intervals are more frequent.

Productivity disruption

The ability to identify short-life components at the feasibility stage and design them out reduces the risks to productivity, replacement costs and sustainability. A longer-life product will score well in this department although it may of course suffer from curtailed life expectancy due to business change.

Overall implications

The BREEAM ratings, of which the building's sustainability profile is a significant proportion, do not extend to an overall discrete rating for a building based simply on its built form; rather it awards 'Ecopoints' for the use of a particular specification which are added to the overall sustainability rating for the building as designed.

The basic system has been developed into specialist models such as the Code for Sustainable Homes assessment tool.

The LEED System

The LEED System originated in the USA, and was developed by the US Green Building Council (www.usgbc.org/). Like BREEAM, LEED is a certification system based on the award of credits for properties and design characteristics appropriate to the particular project you have in mind. There is an option for multiple-building estates.

It deals with 'all buildings everywhere regardless of where they are in their life-cycle' and there are versions for new build (including major renovation) and interiors as well as discrete versions for BOM, Neighbourhood Development and Homes.

LEED focuses on four aspects of building provision:

- materials
- energy
- indoor comfort/health
- water efficiency.

It takes a whole-building life-cycle approach to project certification and offers advice to designers on how to optimise the whole-life cost and sustainability performance of their buildings.

The process encourages Environmental Product Declarations concerning how products are made, material ingredients and who makes them. This is a fundamentally important requirement for the accurate appraisal of the sustainability of manufactured products if they are to be brought seamlessly into the sustainability evaluation process and one which requires substantial encouragement and development in the UK.

Also like BREEAM, the LEED system avoids scoring the building as a whole from first principles but does includes a building assessment alongside a rather more simple range of environmental sustainability factors. On the whole, it is rather more pragmatic than BREEAM and simpler to use and administer, which probably explains why it has developed so successfully around the globe.

Holistic processes of measuring whole-life cost and sustainability

BREEAM and LEED fill a void in current application of measurement to sustainable building performance. However, here we are focusing mainly on the more specific and holistic state-of-the-art approaches to measuring physical building performance rather than those that are currently best established. As well as the systems described below, there are other rating systems available and in development around the world – in particular those concerned with the energy performance of buildings – which tend to be more detailed and comprehensive in dealing with their more focused topics.

IMPACT

The Integrated Material Profile and Costing Tool (IMPACT), developed by Integrated Environmental Solutions (IES), allows users to measure the life-cycle cost and embodied carbon performance of buildings. Using real design data and relevant quantities, it integrates life-cycle assessment, life-cycle costing and BIM and permits the development of sustainable whole-life building solutions by an incremental development of specifications against a default template for a particular building type. It can be integrated into the BREEAM ratings system helping users to obtain the requisite credits.

CombiCycle Comparator

A newcomer to the physical performance measurement scene is the 'CombiCycle Comparator'; this is a web-enabled model which predicts the whole-life costs and sustainability of individual building components and then aggregates them to provide a whole-life cost and sustainability prediction for the complete building. It is designed to offer in-depth analysis in respect of every aspect of physical performance and to produce finite scores in all topics.

Like IMPACT, the CombiCycle Comparator is a planning tool intended to be used in the design process from the feasibility stage onwards. Based on the proposed shape and size of the building, the model produces a whole-life cost and sustainability plan for the type and quality of building the client has in mind. This 'default' analysis is fully interrogable, enabling the user to test alternative design and specification options against the default which can then be modified to produce a bespoke project cost and sustainability plan.

Output from the model includes:

- capital cost
- life-cycle replacement costs
- maintenance costs
- cleaning costs
- energy consumption and costs
- U-values of the elements
- energy management predictions

- embodied carbon
- project programme
- project cash-flow
- life-time cash flow
- component sustainability ratings
- total building sustainability score
- priced bill of approximate quantities
- building weight.

With the help of funding from UKCES, the model is now also able to predict the whole-life cost and sustainability consequences of offsite construction processes, such as modular and volumetric production. The model also links into data held in BIM libraries and on manufacturers' web-sites and is set to be able to derive all the data it needs from the future Environmental Product Declarations referred to above.

A typical output from the model at the Feasibility stage is shown in Figure 24.10.

Unlike BREEAM and LEED, the CombiCycle is not a certification system although it is both simple and comprehensive enough to aspire to that status before long. The sustainability scores per component are calculated by reference to the topics established in the *Green Guide* and

Project: Retail - Building: Retail Outlet Case Study	
GIA: 1000 M² - Location: Greater London	
Cost Center	**Default**
Viewing Result Totals ▼	
Quality	Average
Cost Analysis Period	30 Years
Capital	£ 1,252,939
Life-cycle replacement	£ 371,143
Maintenance	£ 447,991
Cleaning	£ 201,174
Energy (in occpation)	£ 1,359,748
Waste Disposal	
Demolition	
Whole Life Total	£ 3,632,996
Whole Life sustainability factors (Show/hide)	
Sustainability rating	
Initial sustainability	5.5
Sustainability Rating	B
Replacement sustainability	
Time on Site	
Time on Site (weeks)	38.2

Figure 24.10 The CombiCycle Comparator result at the Feasibility stage prior to bespoke modifications

generally adopt their weightings; they are calibrated so as to closely reflect the *Green Guide* scores which is useful for designers and manufacturers where no *Green Guide* rating is available for a particular component.

However, the CombiCycle's scoring goes further than either BREEAM or LEED in that the weighted scores for individual components are again weighted in order of their quantitative significance within the building; the totals are then aggregated to provide a sustainability score for the whole building, see Figure 24.10, and a quantification of the energy (energy-in-use and embodied) with their respective carbon emissions.

The model allows the user to inspect the scores given for each component against the environmental impact factors and also the coefficients of component mass used to compute the amount of embodied carbon in each component. There is also the facility to adjust the scores and coefficients according to the proportion of the component's materials which are recycled.

Importantly, and like IMPACT, the CombiCycle Comparator is able to take into account the shape and size of a building when making the Feasibility stage predictions. This is of particular significance when benchmarking costs and sustainability, where the results are directly influenced by the building's configuration, e.g. the carbon emissions (embodied and in use) from a small building will be much higher per sqm of the floor area than in a larger building – for a variety of reasons which the model identifies and takes on board. It is therefore possible for an organisation to set targets for energy consumption and embodied carbon at this early stage by reference to best performance results from the model related to comparable building uses and configurations.

IMPACT and the CombiCycle Comparator are there for users who wish to take a more proactive approach to controlling the sustainability of their buildings in the widest sense of the term.

Conclusion

Sometimes people in construction get carried away with the idea that the building is everything, whereas it is really only a part of the premises strategy which again is part of the Business Policy.

Nevertheless, in its own right, 'building performance' has been shown here and throughout this book not only to have a definite impact on productivity but also to be capable of being measured and valued in all its aspects. The day must be close when the premises policy identifies the required building performance relative to a weighted score that everyone accepts as true and valid. Till then, the enlightened few will stay ahead of the game while the rest remain slaves to the conventional wisdom.

References

Adams, W.M. (2006) Report of the IUCN Renowned Thinkers Meeting, 29–31 January 2006. Retrieved on: 2009–02–16.

Anderson, J., Shiers, D., and Steele, K. (2009) *The Green Guide to Specification*. Bracknell: IHS BRE Press.

Duffy, F. (1987) Intelligent office buildings on three continents. *Facilities* 5(3): 7–10.

Duffy, F. (1993) *The Responsible Workplace: The Redesign of Work and Offices*. Oxford: Butterworth Architecture.

Kelly, J., Male, S. and Graham, D. (2010) *Value Management of Construction Projects* Chichester: John Wiley & Sons, Ltd. Available at: http://onlinelibrary.wiley.com/book/10.1002/9780470773642

Williams, B. (2008) *Facilities Economics*. IFPI Ltd. Available at: www.int-fpi.com

Part IV

Future horizons

Stranger than we can imagine

The future of work and place in the twenty-first century

Mark Eltringham

Introduction

Predicting the future is a game for fools, some say. However much we know about the forces we expect to come into play in our time and however much we understand the various social, commercial, legislative, cultural and economic parameters we expect to direct them, most predictions of the future tend to come out as refractions or extrapolations of the present. This is a fact tacitly acknowledged by George Orwell's title for his book, *1984*, written in 1948, and is always the pinch of salt we can apply to science fiction and most of the predictions we come across.

This is the fundamental reason why a typical report or feature looking to explore the office of the future invariably produces a hyped-up office of the present. This has sufficed to some degree up till now because the major driving force of change – technology – has developed in linear ways. Its major driver since Gordon Moore produced his eponymous law in 1965 has been miniaturisation. If we can expect computing power to double every 18 months, as Moore predicted, we at least have a degree of certainty about technological disruption. Of course, this has already had a profound effect on the way we work and the way we use buildings. So too has the secondary prime technological driver of the early twenty-first century: the digitisation of the past and present.

Disruptive though these forces are, they have developed in ways and within a context that we can readily understand and forecast. That is all about to change and in ways we have no way of knowing with any certainty. There's a good chance we cannot imagine what is about to happen with some of the technologies now being developed and which may soon start to feed back into themselves in a positive feedback loop. As the biologist J.B.S. Haldane once remarked:

> I have no doubt that in reality the future will be vastly more surprising than anything I can imagine. Now my own suspicion is that the Universe is not only queerer than we suppose, but queerer than we *can* suppose.
>
> (Haldane, [1927] 2001)

We are no longer faced with an era of linear miniaturisation and digitisation, but one in which a number of technological forces coalesce to create a perfect storm of uncertainty. For each of these, there has yet to emerge a consensus about the nature of the technology itself and its implications for the world, so the idea that we can predict with any certainty what will happen in the eye of the hurricane is fanciful at best.

Even if there were a general consensus about the implications of specific new technologies, it would likely be out of date before this book had a chance to garner even the thinnest layer of dust. But we must be aware of them and gauge their implications for commerce, society, philosophy and the economy. Eternal vigilance is not just the price of freedom but is now the price of living in the twenty-first century.

Challenges

There are a number of specific challenges that this creates for those who work in the fields of office design, architecture, commercial real estate, facilities management, human resources and IT and all the myriad disciplines and professions involved in the chimera we now call 'the workplace'. The most important is one that has been around for a very long time and it is how to resolve the tensions created by the different speeds and life cycles we might attribute to the facets of the workplace. In particular, because the way we work changes so quickly, buildings need to have flexibility built into them so that they meet our needs today but anticipate what we will need tomorrow.

In his (1994) book, *How Buildings Learn*, Stewart Brand outlines the process whereby buildings evolve over time to meet the changing needs of their occupants. He describes each building as consisting of six layers, each of which functions on a different timescale. These range from the site itself which has a life cycle measured in centuries, through to the building (decades), interior fit-out (years), technology (months), to stuff (days). The effectiveness of a workplace design will depend on how well it resolves the tensions that exist between these layers of the building.

The principles behind this complex situation have been known to us for a long time, at least since the 1970s when Frank Duffy first introduced the world to his ideas about the physical and temporal layers of the building – in his terminology, the 'shell, services, scenery and sets'. The balance between these layers may have shifted significantly in recent years, but the tensions between them continue to determine how well we design and manage our workplaces.

Consequently, the ability to respond to change is perhaps the most important facet of an effective design. Creating this level of responsiveness is described in the *Facility Design and Management Handbook* by its author Eric Teicholz as 'the basic driver of the facilities management workload' (Teicholz, 2001).

While the nature of work has already changed in many ways, the pace of change has increased even more dramatically over recent years and we still have not seen anything yet. So the challenge is how best to manage change, keep costs down and provide a flexible home for the organisation so that whatever happens in the future, we can at least meet it with a degree of confidence. Successful management of change is a good thing, an agent of growth and commercial success. Change handled badly can hamstring an organisation.

The standard answer to the challenge is to build flexibility into the building. At the property management level, this may mean a change in contractual terms, notably in the length of leases, and the provision of lease breaks. Varying levels of flexibility must also be apparent through the rest of the building in terms of its design and management. If we take an idealised view of the modern office as a flexible, social space for a peripatetic, democratised and technologically literate workforce, the solution lies in an increased use of desk sharing, drop-in zones, break-out space, space as a service and other forms of multi-functional workspaces. In many offices, individual workspace is already being rapidly replaced by other types of space, quiet rooms and collaborative areas.

Flexibility must be hardwired into the building at a macro-level. Not only must floorplates be capable of accepting a wide range of work styles and planning models, servicing must be appropriate and anticipate change. That does not mean just in terms of technology and telecoms but also basic human needs such as having enough toilets to deal with changing occupational densities. It also means having a HVAC specification that can deal with the changing needs associated with different numbers of people and different types of equipment.

Elements of the interior that once were considered static are also having to offer far greater degrees of flexibility, including furniture, lighting, storage and partitions. This issue of flexibility has become more important in interior design. Interior elements should now define space, portray corporate identity, comply with legislation and act as an aid in wayfinding. They must do all this and be able to adapt as the organisation changes.

Yet all of this is still only scratching the surface of the issue. It's not exactly cosmetic and it will apply to a far larger proportion of the office market than many workplace futurists would lead you to believe, but it is not exactly game-changing. That will happen elsewhere and will involve a complete rethink of the way we view work and workplaces.

This presents a particular challenge for the various workplace disciplines because they are still clinging on to both their own established ideas and the demarcations they think still apply. At some level, they are aware that the gig is up, which is why you will see trade associations toying with allegiances with others who have overlapping interests. It is why commercial property firms are moving into the fit-out market. It is why the major technology firms are moving into new realms in the physical world such as the Internet of Things and driverless vehicles. It is why coworking spaces are coming to dominate the commercial property markets in the world's major cities. It's all a sign of an upcoming great reckoning which will see the creation of a new order for the workplace.

There will be casualties, especially among those organisations who cannot grasp the enormity of what is about to happen and so will drown in the imminent technological immersion. Trade associations are still hankering for a place at the boardroom table unaware of or unwilling to admit to the fact that their immediate priority should not be status, but survival. They still view Big Data as a way to build their case, not as part of the wave of technology that is about to fall over their heads.

One of the UK's best writers on the potential for this to fall around the ears of the property industry in particular is Antony Slumbers. Writing in August 2016, he said:

> All around us companies are offering us what we want, when we want it. We might pay more for something pro rata, but we don't care as we are only buying what we need. And will property remain aloof from all this? Long leases, upwards only rent reviews, fixed space? Not a chance is the answer. And therein lies the biggest change to the real estate market since the first skyscraper was made possible by the invention of the 'personal elevator'. Tech is all around us, has consequences.

We can already see the first signs of how this may play out. The way we work has changed profoundly in a very short space of time. In the UK, more than half of employers now offer some form of flexible working, according to The Work Foundation (2016), and there are calls for it to become the norm for everybody in employment.

It already is the norm for the 18 per cent of the UK population who work in the gig economy, a catch-all term that does not do justice to the range of working types it incorporates, ranging from the pickers and packers of the precariat to freelancers and the self-employed, including the rapidly growing number of those who make a good living on their own terms in the creative and digital industries who are almost certainly the main agents of change. The government appears to have little grasp of the people who work in this world, often confusing them with traditional small business and aggressively wary of their tax arrangements.

This is the group of people who are doing the most to drive the uptake of space as a service, which is almost certainly the key office phenomenon of this decade. They understand the need to be around other people, but only at certain times and for certain tasks. They have no need for a corporate office, a commute and a routine day. They certainly do not need to pay the huge rates now demanded for the best office locations next to the larger firms with which they would like to work and they don't want or need a lease that will outlive their next business relationship and possibly their business.

This is a fundamentally different mindset in which offices are consumed and experienced, not owned or leased and we need to get used to it, especially because the ideal experiential office will soon follow in the wake of coworking and cross into mainstream thinking. The office is not about to die, as we have been hearing for way too long now. But it is going to transform into something else entirely.

What will happen beyond the next few years is anybody's guess and we would be foolish to predict it. What we can say is that we are set to address some key questions about how we relate to the world and to work and we are going to have to make some very difficult decisions. For example, some time in the near future we're going to have to address the issue of how we introduce a basic income for people in response to a changing world in which many of the current tasks we do will be carried out by robots, freeing us to do other things and work in new ways. This will happen sooner than you might think. Earlier in 2016, the World Economic Forum said that the so-called Fourth Industrial Revolution would result in 5 million job losses in the 15 countries it surveyed by 2020 and that this was merely a pre-shock for the seismic changes to follow.

Meanwhile the government still appears to think that the past is a guide to the future. In the Spring of 2016, the newly formed Infrastructure and Projects Authority published its construction strategy paper for the period up to 2020. By definition, the department is responsible for planning and creating the UK's infrastructure for decades beyond that time and yet the document only uses the word technology three times and, even then, only with regard to the application of BIM as a way of improving the construction process. Perhaps more worryingly, the very short section at the end of the document on whole life approaches only deals with the issue of sustainability. It makes no mention of creating the physical infrastructure capable of dealing with a rapidly changing world.

What we must also be wary of is an idea that seems to inform the endlessly rolling debate about the 'office of the future'. This supposes that just around the corner there is an idealised end point for office design which will resolve all of the issues we have with work and the workplace. What this fails to account for is that the office is always out of date and always in a state of transition.

We make the same mistake when we consider our own place in the world. We humans assume that we are somehow at the apex of the evolutionary tree when the truth is that we are transitional forms in exactly the same way as all other creatures. We do not need to seek the missing link, because we are it, and always have been.

As for the far future, we can leave the final word on what that holds to the astrophysicist, Martin Rees, in a lecture in 2006:

> Most educated people are aware that we're the outcome of nearly 4bn years of Darwinian selection, but many tend to think that humans are somehow the culmination. Our sun, however, is less than halfway through its lifespan. It will not be humans who watch the sun's demise, 6bn years from now. Any creatures that then exist will be as different from us as we are from bacteria or amoebae.

References

Brand, S. (1994) *How Buildings Learn*. New York: Viking Press.

Haldane, J.B.S. ([1927] 2001) *Possible Worlds*. New York: Transaction,

Infrastructure and Projects Authority. *Government and Construction Strategy, 2016–2020*. Available at: www.gov.uk/. . ./infrastructure-and-projects-authority

Slumbers, A. (2016) What is Tech? *Estates Gazette*, August 30.

Teicholz, E. (2001) *Facility Design and Management Handbook*. New York: McGraw-Hill.

Work Foundation (2016) *Working Anywhere*. The Work Foundation.

Chapter 26

How to prevent today's ergonomic office problems in the future?

Veerle Hermans

The classic office workstation and environment

In almost all the classic ergonomic textbooks of the 1980s and 1990s, a description of an optimal computer working posture is presented, with emphasis on adjustments of the office chair and the position of the computer screen and keyboard (and a few years later, also the computer mouse). For an example of a classic workstation set-up, see Figure 26.1. This somewhat ideal posture was supposed to minimise the musculoskeletal load on the upper limbs and back and consequently reduce possible musculoskeletal complaints in the neck and arm (for a review, see Wahlström, 2005). In 1990, the European Council Directive 90/270/EEC on the minimum safety and health requirements for work with display screen equipment was published and translated in the European countries into specific guidelines. Also the ISO standard 9241 followed, with 14 chapters regarding the set-up of a workstation, but also discussing the hardware and software requirements. As well as emphasis on the set-up and analysis of the workstation, also emphasis on increasing workers' knowledge regarding prevention of musculoskeletal disorders when working at a computer workplace is given. For an example of a workstation analysis, see: www.osha.gov/SLTC/etools/computerworkstations/checklist.html.

The set-up of a computer workstation could be seen in rooms occupied by one person (what is called a cell-office) or two or three people (a shared-room office) (Danielsson *et al.*, 2014). In these rooms, it was quite easy to set up the workstations, taking into account the environmental circumstances that influence the well-being of a person:

- *lighting conditions* (e.g. no direct discomfort of daylight or artificial light or no indirect discomfort by reflections on the computer screen);
- *climate issues* (e.g. too hot/too cold, too much ventilation could be individually arranged);
- *noise disturbances* (e.g. sounds from colleagues in other offices could easily be removed by closing your door).

Besides cell-offices, also open plan environments were created, where people with comparable jobs were put together, sometimes divided by screens, walls and plants to create differentiation and privacy. The primary driver of this was an economic strategy: higher profitability due to less necessary office space. But also a social objective was mentioned: open plan offices would increase the well-being of the workers (Hermans and Pullen, 2006).

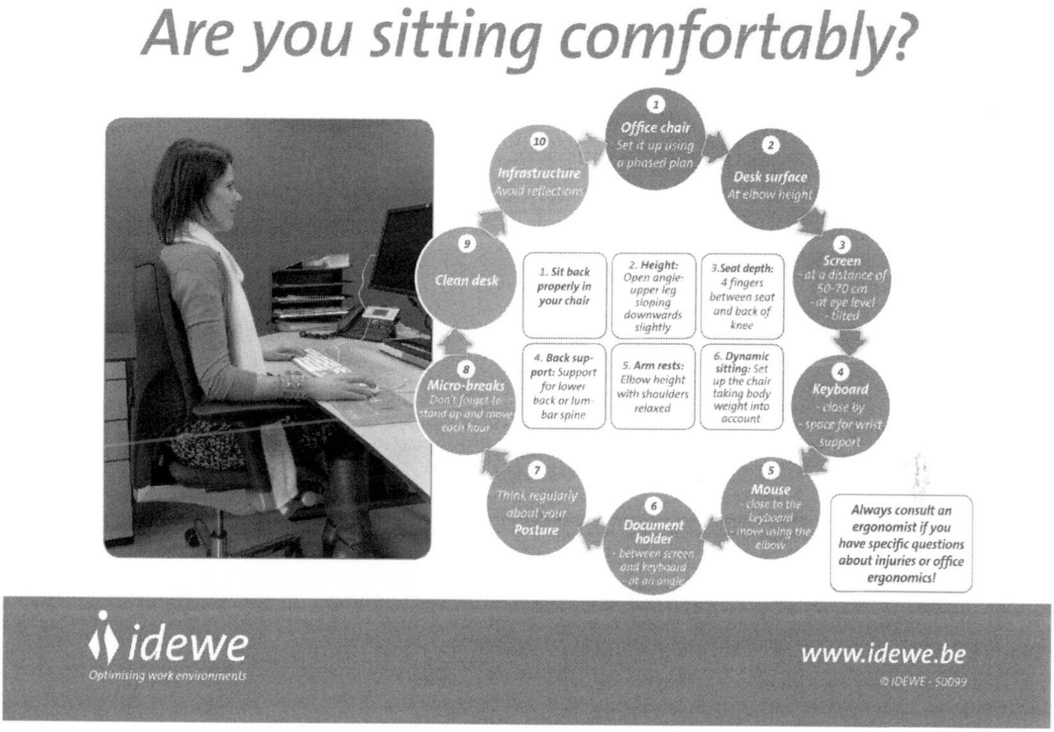

Figure 26.1 Set-up of a traditional workstation
Source: IDEWE.

Today's offices

The revolutionary increase in mobile technologies and communication media, created an increase in open plan offices. The open layout is often combined with a flexible work organisation, a work practice that allows employees a certain amount of flexibility in respect of time, place and duration of work (Bakker Elkhuizen, 2013). So flex-offices or shared offices are often seen in an open plan layout (Danielsson *et al.*, 2014). The development of mobile technologies has an important impact on this, since mobiles have helped create a 'place out of place', or interspace, that allows users to be physically in one location but mentally elsewhere (Rutledge, 2013).

The optimal balance between organisation and accommodation was supposed to promote efficient work, higher job satisfaction, more productivity and a reduction in facility costs. But, as mentioned in Chapter 11 in this volume by Stephen Bowden, the current focus on collaborative forms of open plan offices has taken hold. There is evidence from the scientific literature that open plan office design can be counterproductive in terms of impact on employee well-being and productivity. Now, let us look at the type of problems we are facing today and how to overcome them in the future.

Environmental problems

First of all, the noise paradox of communication versus concentration. High satisfaction levels can be found regarding communication between workers in a shared office environment, and this occurs for formal and informal meetings, and for small chats between colleagues (Hermans and Pullen, 2006). This is positive, since it stimulates creativity and the productivity of the workers. However, when tasks requiring concentration have to be performed, the noise of the communication disturbs the work of the other office workers (Pullen and Bradley, 2004) and increased distraction, reduced privacy and increased concentration difficulties are found (Kaarela-Tuomaala *et al.*, 2009).

Second, it is very difficult to create optimal visual conditions when many people have to work together in the one space. Increased visual discomfort when moving from single unit offices to an office landscape has been reported. This is often attributed to increased glare, reflections on the screen due to large window areas in an office landscape or having no gaze line parallel to the windows (Helland *et al.*, 2011).

Creating ideal indoor climate circumstances is also very challenging in open plan layouts. Research mentions that workers in open plan offices are more likely to perceive thermal discomfort, poor air quality and more frequently complain about mucous membrane symptoms than occupants in multi-person and cellular offices (Pejtersen *et al.*, 2006). Consequently, the workers in open plan offices took significantly more days of sickness absence than workers in cellular offices (Pejtersen *et al.*, 2011). More specifically, more occurrences of short sick leave in traditional open plan offices occurred (Danielsson *et al.*, 2014).

But, by careful design and construction of an office landscape with regard to, for example, lighting and visual conditions, transfer from individual units to an open plan layout may be acceptable (Helland and Horgen, 2012). Furthermore, nowadays organisations offer a wider range of casual open and enclosed collaborative spaces for smaller groups of people, and mobility between work spaces is promoted depending on the type of task that you do (more concentration: more enclosed space; more teamwork: casual open space).

Fancy furniture

Together with the range of casual open and enclosed collaborative spaces, casual, lounge furniture and fancy lighting are increasingly being seen in offices. Also trendy coloured walls, art objects and products with an ecological touch can be found. It is suggested that these work environments boost creativity that strengthens product and process innovation and consequently the competitiveness of companies. Dul and Ceylan (2011) describe work environments in two dimensions: (1) the social-organisational work environment (e.g. the organisation's culture, its HRM policies, autonomy, support); and (2) the physical work environment (the architecture/indoor design, environmental aspects, workplace). From their experiences, it is clear that the work environment can enhance employee creativity, also creating, for example, a positive mood, which will have an impact on employee comfort and health. But how can you be creative if your office suffers from poor ergonomics? Often lounge furniture is not suitable for providing good posture positions, so it is not the correct kind of place to spend hours each day. A trendy chair is acceptable in reception, in a coffee corner or in a short brainstorming meeting room, rather than at an office desk. A desk bench where everybody has to sit at the same table height rather belongs in the work cafeteria. And what about the home office? Often the employer does not plan for ergonomic tools and accessories to create a suitable work posture (Bakker Elkhuizen, 2013). So, even in these fancy environments, we should still promote the classic ergonomic workstation set-up (as explained in ISO 9241). Of course, we have to take into account new

developments in technology. For example, the introduction of multiple screens and large monitors requires the use of adjustable monitor arms and a proper set-up so a comfortable head
and neck position can be maintained and correct visual conditions are created. And laptop
computers or tablets require the use of supporting devices, although an ideal situation will not
be created (Hermans *et al.*, 2016).

Is sitting a disease?

But then we have the comfort-paradox: people tend to sit too long in their comfortable chairs . . .
In the 1990s, ergonomics already mentioned the importance of a dynamic sitting behaviour to
reduce static load, but nowadays, even more emphasis is put on the negative effects of sedentary
behaviour: 'Sitting is the new smoking; sitting makes you sick; the more you sit, the sooner you
die, etc.' The reason for these slogans is that scientific research now demonstrates the relation
between sitting and obesity, diabetes, cardiovascular disease and even earlier mortality (e.g.
Biswas *et al.*, 2015). So, besides the musculoskeletal importance to varying postures, there is the
added value of a general health improvement if sedentary behaviour is reduced, both at home
and in the office. The best way to do this at work is to replace sitting with light to moderate
intensity physical activity. There are several possible ways to do this:

1   *Changes in the workplace environment and design.* With the creation of an office building
    or a renovation, mobility between spaces should be promoted. For instance, the creation of
    a separate printing room, a centralised coffee corner, an attractive and central staircase, a
    greater diversity of spaces for alternating between sitting and standing, etc. The integration
    of more sport elements could also be considered (e.g. a ping-pong table near the cafeteria,
    a (safe) darts board in the coffee corner). Restructuring office layouts by providing greater
    physical activity opportunities (e.g. manipulating distances to destinations) might nudge
    workers to increase step counts and interrupt extended periods of sitting time (Smith *et al.*,
    2014). There does not always have to be a fitness room in the office, although of course this
    would also help to improve more movement during lunch or before/after working hours.
    With this, you would stimulate workers to reach the WHO guideline of daily moderate
    exercise of at least 30 minutes for general health improvement, but that does not really
    change the sedentary behaviour during work.
2   *Changes in the design of office desks.* Sit-stand tables are found in office environments to
    reduce sedentary behaviour. A recent review study (Shrestha *et al.* 2016) revealed that sit-
    stand desks can reduce sitting between a half to two hours per day. Also people will reduce
    their sitting periods lasting longer than 30 minutes. However, one study analysed the effects
    after 6 months and found that sitting was reduced by less than one hour. This is consider-
    ably less than the 2–4 hours that is promoted by an expert guideline (Buckley *et al.*, 2015).
    Also, standing alone is not enough to have sufficient change in your energy expenditure
    during the day, therefore it is recommended not only to break sitting with standing peri-
    ods, but also to move more during work. A lot of new devices are coming onto the market
    to promote movement, such as an office bike or a treadmill workstation. At the moment,
    sufficient research has not been done regarding the effectiveness of these workstations. It
    is clear that an optimal balance has to be found between the amount of movement and the
    task that has to be performed since the multi-tasking of a dynamic body movement may
    interfere with cognitive thinking.
3   *Counselling and information.* Even if people are aware of the adverse effects of sitting, and
    have access to facilities and programmes to decrease sitting, they will still find it difficult

to adapt to the new behaviour. It requires a conscious effort for a person to interrupt their normal sitting behaviour and engage briefly in some physical activity of light to moderate intensity while at work (Shrestha *et al.*, 2016). One possible way to help people with this is the installation of prompting software so that a 1-minute reminder to take a break appears on their screen every 30 minutes (Evans *et al.*, 2012). Other nudging possibilities are the use of signs, emails, text messages or counselling by consultants or peers. So far, mixed results regarding the effectiveness of these interventions have been reported (ibid.).

4   *Global company policy.* It is expected that most effects could be found when all these intervention types are combined in a multilevel organizational policy approach towards the reduction of sedentary behaviour in the office. For now, the evidence for reduced sitting due to multiple categories of interventions was found at follow-up at 12 weeks and at 6 months, but not at follow-up at 12 months. This again stresses the importance of changing behaviour techniques in the long term.

Mental and psychosocial issues

As mentioned when discussing the noise paradox, communication by colleagues could increase the distraction of workers. But besides colleagues, digital confounders could also interfere with concentration and the possibilities that new technology offers become pressure (Popma, 2013). The drive to be continuously online and to be contactable by phone, computer, tablet, even within seconds, causes a lot of multi-tasking, which has proven to decrease efficient work (Compernolle, 2014). Apart from lower productivity, also health problems may arise: overwork, overtiredness, chronic fatigue, burn-out, etc. Furthermore, due to the flexiwork possibilities, a loss of social cohesion and a disturbed work-life balance could occur (Popma, 2013). Some companies, such as Yahoo, have even decided to ban home work again, since they equate workplace productivity with real time in the office. Other companies are trying to solve the problems by using, ironically, digital tools to reduce digital behaviour, or by creating no-digital-zones in the office.

Bad ergonomics, but also bad economics

The economic advantage of creating open offices (higher profitability due to less office space) is not always reached. The benefit in space reduction often created the need for other investments. There is a need for more information and communication technology, renovation costs, more expense on furniture (not only in the office, but also at home and/or at satellite offices, more meeting rooms), costs for external and internal project developers, mobile security management, etc. (van der Voordt *et al.*, 2001). This should be kept in mind.

Conclusion

The father of occupational medicine, Bernardino Ramazzini, was the first to describe in 1713 the risks associated with office work:

> First, constant sitting, secondly the incessant movement of the hand and always in the same direction, thirdly the strain on the mind from the effort not to disfigure the books by errors or cause loss to their employers when they add, subtract, or do other sums in arithmetic.
>
> (Ramazzini, 2001)

Figure 26.2 Example of a dynamic working environment
Source: www.kraaijvanger.nl/nl/projecten/1491/rabobank-gouwestreek/

Although office workplaces have changed considerably over time (for a short overview, see Hermans *et al.*, 2016), sustained seated work, mental overload and physical problems still appear today. It is a challenge for project developers and architects to integrate ergonomics knowledge in their future developments. Doing so, ergonomics could indeed foster the creativity of all workers (Dul and Ceylan, 2011). An example of such an inspiring environment with the integration of ergonomics, a diversity of sit-stand possibilities etc., can be seen in Figure 26.2.

References

Bakker Elkhuizen (2013) International Flexible Working Survey. Available at: www.bakkerelkhuizen.com/international-flexible-working-survey/

Biswas, A. *et al.* (2015) Sedentary time and its associations with risk for disease incidence, mortality and hospitalization in adults. *Annals of Internal Medicine* 162: 123–132.

Buckley, J.P. *et al.* (2015) The sedentary office: an expert statement on the growing case for change towards better health and productivity. *British Journal of Sports Medicine* 49(21): 1357–1362.

Compernolle, T. (2014) Brain-hostile open offices. Available at: www.brainchains.org

Danielsson, C.B., Chungkham, H.S., Wulff, C. and Westerlund, H. (2014) Office design's impact on sick leave rates. Ergonomics 57(2): 139–147.

Dul, J. and Ceylan, C. (2011) Work environments for employee creativity. *Ergonomics* 54(1): 12–20.

Evans, R.E., Eawole, H.O., Sheriff, S.A., Dall, P.M. and Grant, P.M. (2012) Point-of-choice prompts to reduce sitting time at work: a randomised trial. *American Journal of Preventive Medicine*, 43(3): 293–297.

Helland, M. and Horgen, G. (2012) Visual challenges using Video Display Units (VDU) in office landscapes, *Work*, 41: 3575–3576.

Helland, M., Horgen, G., Kvikstad, T.M., Garthus, T. and Aaras, A. (2011) Will musculoskeletal and visual stress change when Visual Display Unit (VDU) operators move from small offices to an ergonomically optimized office landscape? *Applied Ergonomics*, 42: 839–845.

Hermans, V., De Vriendt, L. and de Kyser, A. (2016) Improving neck postures during tablet use. PREMUS 2016.

Hermans V. and Pullen W.R. (2006) Werkbeleving in innovatieve kantooromgevingen. *Psychologos*, 21(4): 20–25.

Kaarela-Tuomelaa, A., Helenius, R., Keskinen, E. and Hongisto, V. (2009) Effects of acoustic environment on work in private office rooms and open-plan offices: longitudinal study during relocation. *Ergonomics*, 52(11): 1423–1444.

Pejtersen, J., Allemann, L., Kristensen, T.S. and Poulsen, O.M. (2006) Indoor climate, psychosocial work environment and symptoms in open-plan offices. *Indoor Air*, 16(5): 394–401.

Pejtersen, J.H., Feveile, H., Christensen, K.B. and Burr, H. (2011) Sickness absence associated with shared and open-plan offices: a national cross sectional questionnaire survey. *Scandinavian Journal of Work, Environment and Health*, 37(5): 376–382.

Popma, J. (2013) The Janus face of the 'New Ways of Work': rise, risks and regulation of nomadic work. Brussels: ETUI.

Pullen, W. and Bradley, S. (2004) Modernising government workplaces: towards evidence, as well as experience. *Facilities*, 22(3/4) 70–73.

Ramazzini, B. (2001) De morbis artificum diatriba (diseases of workers). *American Journal of Public Health* 91(9): 1380–1382.

Rutledge, P.B. (2013) The psychology of mobile technologies. In P.A. Bruck and M. Rao (eds) *Global Mobile: Applications and Innovations for the Worldwide Mobile Ecosystem*. Medford, NJ: Information Today Inc., pp. 47–92.

Shrestha, N., Kukkonen-Harjula, K.T., Verbeek, J.H., Ijaz, S., Hermans, V. and Bhaumik, S. (2016) Workplace interventions for reducing sitting at work. *Cochrane Database of Systematic Reviews*, Issue 3. Art. No. CD010912. DOI: 10.1002/14651858.CD010912.pub3

Smith, L., Ucci, M., Marmot, A. *et al.* (2014) Active buildings: modelling physical activity and movement in office buildings; an observational protocol. *BMJ Open*, 3:e004103. DOI: 10.1136/bmjopen-2013-004103.

Van der Voordt, D.J.M. and Negen, M. (2001) Meer- en minderkosten van werkplekinnovatie. *Facility Management Magazine*, 20–6.

Wahlström, J. (2005) Ergonomics, musculoskeletal disorders and computer work (in-depth review). *Occupational Medicine* 55: 168–176.

Chapter 27

Future landscapes

Despina Katsikakis

Flexibility, choice and engagement

Over the last 10 years, technology has given us the choice of where and how to access information. Being connected anywhere has enabled a shift from work as 'somewhere you go' to work as 'something you do' anytime, anyplace.

While this new approach to work increases flexibility, it also brings increased working hours and information overload as people are lost in their devices, 24/7, with little awareness of their surrounding environment. The results in the workplace are people who are both disengaged and distracted. Gallup (2015) reports that 70 per cent of American workers, are 'not engaged', and are just going through the motions of working or are 'actively disengaged', hate going to their work and undermine their companies with their attitude. These figures are consistent with data from the UK and even more extreme figures in the developing world.

While not yet effectively implemented as the norm, the arguments in favour of more flexible working practices are powerful and are here to stay. In the UK, Thompson and Truch (2013) estimate the value of productive hours gained to be at least £6.9 billion and workstation savings of at least £1.1 billion, as flexible ways of working enable office buildings to be used more intensively with workspace being used on a shared, as-needed basis. Findings consistently suggest that workers also gain a better work-life balance, are more productive, can concentrate better and experience reduced stress and commuting times, when they have choice of where and when to work.

One of the usual arguments against offering people greater autonomy over where and how they work is a lack of control and consequent lack of effort from employees. New evidence by the German Institute for Economic Research (Beckmann *et al.*, 2015) suggests what actually happens is the opposite. When employers relinquish control, people actually work more. People who enjoy autonomy on average put in an extra seven hours each week and are more committed to their employer.

In this new, increasingly paradoxical world, helping companies to design the infrastructure to support and enable engagement in the workplace is at the core of helping them to be productive. The current focus of work is on supporting knowledge workers. The core of knowledge work is non-routine problem-solving which requires an integrated approach that includes spatial, technological and managerial issues. *Even though technology enables a great deal of knowledge work to be performed anywhere and anytime, the role of the office is still very relevant but it needs to be redefined.*

New ways of supplying, leasing and servicing the workplace are needed. Assuming an overall reduction in space requirements for office users, given intermittent patterns of occupancy and increased sharing of space over time, landlords can plan for less real estate to be better used.

This densification approach can be used as part of a wider strategy to make workspaces more valuable and command higher rents by finding new ways of adding value for tenants by providing shared spaces beyond the office that they lease to be used as alternative places to work. This allows the landlord to make more of the real estate asset. By providing flexibility to tenants and activating the shared spaces to create a vibrant community that people want to be a part of, the building itself becomes a destination. Such an offer will both attract new tenants and also retain them beyond the normal lease period as it can support their changing business requirements and offer them access to a unique ecosystem of talent.

What we design today will be our future heritage. It must be a sustainable and resilient resource that stands the test of time. 'Long life, loose fit, low energy' should be the guiding principle. A minimum life expectancy of 60 years is not unreasonable for new buildings but they should be flexible to accommodate a variety of uses over that time. The dynamic changes enabled by technology add another dimension to time, that of the day-to-day and hour-by-hour change of settings for work. People regularly report that freedom and choice matter most; they feel better when they are in a flexible space that they can change to meet their work needs, mood, or inspiration at the moment.

- What if space could be adapted for business shifts in 'real time', to be continually re-aligned with the core business objectives.
- What if space was able to be continually informed with real-time metrics.
- What if true sustainability in terms of workspace was able to be directly measured not only as environmental, but also financial, productive, cultural and market competitive.

All these scenarios have a consistent theme; they are dynamic and fluid, much like the use of space in cities. Recent models of the workplace, such as distributed working, hoteling, teleworking, agile working, etc., are dynamic in principle but primarily are intended to maximise efficiency and cannot deliver real flexibility unless they embrace a wider real estate context. Developers and landlords need to start thinking of their buildings as vibrant communities and create a new approach to provide optimum (and timeless) versatility and adaptability for new ways of working by shifting traditional ownership and lease constraints to pay as you go, and providing the workplace as a service.

The working environment can either stimulate and sustain people's engagement and energy or dampen and drain it. For it to be a positive experience that adds value, it must meet a series of basic human needs:

- our need to renew our physical energy;
- our need to feel valued;
- our need to focus and be creative;
- our need to connect with others in a range of meaningful ways.

We perform at our best when we move, spend time outside getting daylight, and alternate between different physical, emotional, mental and spiritual states.

The combination of open plan office design and email has shattered people's capacity to focus on deep work due to constant interruption, distraction and lack of freedom and choice. We have come to see multitasking as an essential skill when in fact it destroys our productivity. The lack of places to work without interruption means that we further reinforce a culture of intermittent thinking that tends toward the narrow, short-term and superficial. As we work more continuously, the natural breaks we took in the past have been replaced with constant access to mobile email, increasing our need for intentional high quality renewal.

Technology-induced stress and a lack of meaning in everyday work creep into most workplaces. Brigid Schulte (2014) states that, on average, initial enthusiasm for the job fades after six months when the majority of employees feel overwhelmed and disconnected from their management team and its vision. In her book, *How to Work, Love and Play When No One Has the Time*, she looks at the stress caused by a culture that glorifies constant busy-ness and encourages organisations to implement policies that promote a 'digital detox' and true vacations in order to liberate people from the 'ideal worker' paradigm.

To cope with the intensity of work today we need more access to quiet spaces to concentrate, think and recharge, as well as access to flexible spaces for meeting, collaborating and socialising. We should change positions and spaces and stand up more often and ask ourselves if it's really necessary to do all of our tasks sitting in a chair.

The World Green Building Council (2014) reports overwhelming evidence that a range of office design factors – from air quality and lighting, to views of nature and interior layout – can significantly impact the well-being and productivity of staff.

Attracting the best and brightest staff to your organisation and fostering a happy and healthy workforce can be significantly impacted by the quality of the working environment. The workplace can affect the physiological and psychological performance of people, so it is necessary to work with the users to co-design places that energise, encourage social interaction and collaboration, enhance personal control and provide services and events to manage the blurring of working and living to improve the quality of life.

Work is inherently a social endeavour. The focus of large companies is centred on people, so creating places that provide for the well-being of people at work is critical for business success. David Rock (2009) says, 'social interactions are delicious things to the brain' and that is why we are drawn to them, but he also stresses that:

> Productivity is ultimately about choice and autonomy and if we give people the opportunity to move between different spaces to focus when they need, to collaborate when they need and to have great social interactions, we are giving them what they really need at work.

These elements of community and mutual support are inherent in the shared workplace culture. Co-working spaces can provide an extremely nurturing context for start-up companies, and while initially were much more prevalent in technology companies, they have now spread across all sectors of economic activity. Successful co-working environments curate authentic experiences; ubiquitous Wi-Fi, great coffee, healthy food and services, alongside networking events, and demand for them is exploding. In 2011, there were only 1000 coworking spaces worldwide, with a dominant presence in Europe and the USA. The latest survey by CoWorking Europe Conference (2015) demonstrates that four years later, there are almost 7,800 coworking spaces.

The forecasts suggest that their growth is unstoppable: by 2018 there will be 37,000 coworking spaces spread across all continents and there will be over 2.5 million professionals who buy membership in a coworking space.

In the City of London, Ramidus (2014) found that around 70 per cent of serviced office space is occupied by SMEs and predicted that the market for serviced offices could grow by 77 per cent by 2025. Potential for growth exists, based on three principal sources of demand. First, there is strong and sustained growth in the number of small, often technology-enabled, knowledge-based, businesses in London. Second, corporate occupiers are becoming accustomed to supporting their core property needs with flexible on-demand space. Third, small businesses that are occupying secondary properties in conventional leases will likely opt for a different approach, spurred by a diminishing supply of small and short-term office space in the conventional leasing market and by the need for better employee engagement.

In New York City, there have been almost 500 tech start-ups in coworking spaces, incubators and accelerator sites (Bowles and Giles, 2012) but the value of the phenomenon has now been recognised in many finance and media businesses worldwide, with many of the defining characteristics of coworking spaces being adopted in corporate environments, such as an emphasis on collaborative rather than individual working and a range of spaces to support innovation. These internationally established, 'third-space' workplaces vary in terms of scale, variety of settings and even where they lie on the leisure-work continuum, but they share certain layout characteristics, including zones dedicated to concentrated working, touchdown work areas for collaborative working and short duration visits, formal and informal meeting rooms and areas, a café and other social spaces and business support spaces, including reprographics and technology support. Such is the dominance of this new work style that it can now be met in a range of forms. Some coworking spaces have leisure and social activities at their core, much like private members' clubs such as Soho House, the Hospital and the SocietyM business club in CitizenM hotels. Others have workspace at their core but also offer social and leisure facilities, such as Dryland Business Members' Club in London's Kensington High Street.

The workspace-as-service model means that there is no economic bar to blurring the boundaries, allowing us to rethink space, work and the city. This new blurring of boundaries of space, time and use has served to increase rather than relax the pressure on work settings to perform. The only constant is dynamic change. *We can safely say that the office environment will no longer be made up of rows of desks but of a rich variety of settings and curated events which will blur the boundary between personal, shared and public spaces to support organisational innovation.*

AI, talent, knowledge and community

The nature of corporations is changing so they will be more agile and reliant on dispersed talent networks and open source innovation and, as such, the nature of employment is changing and less likely to provide lifelong careers and job security. Intuit (2008) reckon that more than 80 per cent of corporations are planning to increase their use of flexible workforce in the coming years. In the USA, 45 per cent of workers are already described as contingent, and 33 per cent of the UK workforce is currently described as independent or freelance and this proportion is projected to be 40 per cent by 2020. This trend is now spreading to other regions as it aligns with the desire of new workers not to work for a company, but instead to be a part of a community.

We live in an economic context that is constantly and rapidly changing and the way we work is central to that change. Economic growth used to mean more jobs but that is no longer the case. Rotman (2013) estimates that output can now grow overall, with no increase in employment. Since 2000, output in the USA has grown faster than employment, suggesting that technology already is destroying more jobs than it creates. Schiller (2014) estimates that the robotics and 3D printing revolutions could accelerate this trend still further, as the comparatively low entry costs for these disruptive technologies make them widely accessible to everyone, including developing economies. Losing occupations does not necessarily mean losing jobs in the conventional sense – just changing what people do. *A growing proportion of jobs in the future will require creative intelligence, social intelligence and the ability to leverage artificial intelligence.*

The Future of Work Conference (Birnbaum *et al.*, 2014) proposed that physical and reasoning tasks are increasingly being done by machines alongside people, enabling people to work on more strategic things rather than look at spreadsheets. Through the 'creative destruction' of technology, a lot of jobs will disappear (particularly for middle management) and a lot of new jobs we cannot yet imagine will be created. The growth in new jobs will occur as much through crowdsourced freelancers as within the bounds of the corporation.

Birnbaum *et al.* (2014) state:

> As machine learning progresses at a rapid pace, top executives will be called on to create the innovative new organisational forms needed to crowdsource the far-flung human talent that's coming online around the globe. Those executives will have to emphasise their creative abilities, their leadership skills and their strategic thinking.

As the war for talent increasingly happens outside the traditional organisational boundaries, the implications are huge. New organisational forms will develop that overlay the responsiveness of start-ups through the nimbleness of network structures with the execution efficiency of a traditional hierarchy.

PWC (2014) forecasts that organisations will avoid hierarchy and opt for flexible, flat and fluid organisational structures. They will have a network of relationships with third-party research centres, innovation firms and universities through which they will fund and source new products and process ideas. They will use mechanisms such as idea-sourcing platforms, challenge contests and seeding of venture funds and incubators to bring a constant flow of opportunities on stream. This is validated by Ramidus's (2015) research in the City of London, where differences between sectors are now seen to be eroding as corporations focus on technology work and become reliant on dispersed talent networks and open source innovation.

To facilitate this transformation, the employee-employer relationship is changing from how much value can be extracted from workers to how much can be instilled in them. The benefits of tapping the full range of people's knowledge and talents may be obvious, yet it is surprising that so few companies have done so. Elite universities and hospitals, Goldman Sachs and McKinsey have all been adding value to valuable people for a very long time. Google and Apple are more recent examples. They do this in myriad ways – by providing networks, creative interaction with peers, stretch assignments, training and association with a brand that confers elite status on employees and collaborators.

Connections can lead to new learning. Companies should create environments – both physical and virtual – that help employees to develop new connections and also to strengthen their existing relationships, as it is now well proven that traditional work environments of rows of desks are obsolete for this kind of working. To support effective connections it is essential to create workplace environments that foster serendipitous encounters. Many firms already build their workplace environments with the common areas strategically positioned to allow workers to 'bump into each other'. These types of environments should also be developed in virtual settings. While some companies try to ban access to social media to manage distractions, Waber *et al.* (2014) estimate that social media has the potential to save companies \$1.3 trillion, largely owing to improvements in intra-office collaboration. It is clear that the experience of work needs to be understood and curated inside and outside corporate office space, in both the physical and virtual realms.

The office workplace evolved to support the uninterrupted flow of paper processing, where the main aim was efficiency. As the process of work has changed to focus more on the value of knowledge and the production of ideas, we have become confused about the purpose of the office. In order to successfully create and share knowledge and to innovate, we need to bring the focus of the workplace back to people.

Corporate management teams are increasingly recognising the importance of putting people's needs at the core of their workplace strategy. Piet van Schijndel, a member of the Board of Directors of Rabobank Nederland, says:

> I predict that over the next ten years, one of the biggest problems we will face is how to get good people to join our company. If you have something to offer where people can balance their work and their home life in a modern way which suits those people, then that would naturally be a way for our company to attract people.

After several years of development Rabobank Nederland, the banking arm of the largest financial services provider in the Netherlands, Rabobank Group, rolled out an organisational and technical infrastructure that allows employees to connect to one another from practically anywhere while still meeting the stringent encryption standards that banking systems require. With no fixed offices or rigid job descriptions, Rabobank's employees are responsible for the results of their work, but they are free to choose how, where, when and with whom to carry it out. This approach requires managers to place an extraordinary amount of trust in their people, and it demands that employees become more entrepreneurial and collaborative.

The business environment of the future needs to trust people and technology and provide flexibility and choice for employees to connect with complementary skills across a network, to work together on challenges, to learn fast, unlock their passion and improve performance. Such an environment helps people feel energised and connected to the organisation and attracts, inspires and retains talent as well as redefines our definition of places for work.

In Duffy's (2008) 'networked office', complexity underpins the next stage of real estate evolution; the moment when knowledge work, supported by promiscuous networked information technology, has eroded all the spatial and temporal conventions of twentieth-century work of all kinds.

The speed of technological progress, such as the popularity of the 'Internet of Things', will have a huge impact on the way we work over the next ten years. Information technology helps us to reimagine space as well as connectivity – it seems to minimise the significance of the synchronicity and colocation of conventional office buildings, while it augments the importance of other aspects of place: physical transport and access, virtual and social connectivity.

Flexible working is therefore not placeless: virtual work and physical place are transforming each other and reinforcing the value of certain places as the hubs of both physical and virtual networks. This apparently counter-intuitive view is widely proposed by economists and theorists: Edward Glaeser, for example, in *The Triumph of the City* (2011), argues that the role of the city as the most effective way of transferring knowledge has in fact been reinforced by the rise in technological connectivity – 'urban proximity' being a key factor in concentrating, clustering and incubating talent.

- What if – our workplace actively supported our life at work?
- What if – we had a say in the way we work and could make a difference?
- What if – we felt a genuine connection to our community of colleagues?

Connectivity and access to knowledge are the defining features of contemporary business and society and are helping to redefine how and where work is accomplished. By embracing the sociability of where work happens, we can enable people to connect with other like-minded people at inspiring spaces and events – to collide, collaborate and co-create value for themselves, their business and their community.

Culture, purpose and well-being

Healthy employees are significant factors in a healthy bottom line but our entire approach to the workplace requires transformation. Our current well-being paradigm is stuck measuring the cost of various degrees of illness rather than calculating the value of higher levels of wellness and proactively enabling us to thrive. It is not a simple solution; a gym, or a standing desk, but it is an ongoing process that requires an integrated approach by leadership, space, technology and policies to deliver change. Huffington (2014) introduced well-being as the much-needed Third Metric of Success. She makes the point, that there is no work-life balance. We have only one life and a company culture that does not expect employees to be wired and responsive 24/7 needs to become the norm to make our workplaces truly sustainable.

BCO's (2014) research estimates that more than a third of participants accuse their employer of not valuing their well-being at all. The report comes up with three starting points to help employers create a culture of well-being: care; control; and collaboration. The study found that nine out of ten workers feel their well-being diminishes if they do not have control over their day-to-day activities. In addition, they want the flexibility and control to mix collaboration with colleagues with quiet moments of concentration to help them get 'in the zone'. Nine out of ten workers claim that working 'in the zone' helps them perform better as well as feel better. However, currently over three-quarters of people feel they are hampered by a noisy open-plan environment and a further quarter are frustrated by a lack of privacy, while more than two-thirds would like to see relaxation areas in their workplace. Companies can meet this need for control by offering employees flexibility and choice in how and where they work and trusting them to decide their own working patterns.

Our places of work are always communicating corporate values, brand and culture as well as enabling certain behaviours. It is clear that the office environment can play a key role in supporting our well-being goals by mediating the way we undertake the daily required tasks and activities. People work best when they can move freely between quiet and more social spaces and have choices.

In addition, nine out of ten employees believe that support from colleagues enhances their well-being and makes them more productive. However, building a collaborative environment as flexible, and as remote working grows, means companies need to embrace connectivity to ensure that employees have the tools to work, discuss and innovate together no matter where they are. Contrary to many schools of thought, the survey reveals that virtual connectivity actually contributes to well-being according to more than half of the workers surveyed.

When deciding on the most appropriate space – including physical and virtual 'places' – in which to carry out a work activity, a variety of factors must be taken into account but it all starts with personal awareness of what you need to do, how you feel and having the choice of where to do it. *When space is designed with people and purpose in mind and has a clear narrative, it can make our life at work more meaningful.* It can help make us more aware of what we are doing and who we are 'being' at work; to more meaningfully connect with others, to share knowledge and ideas, to concentrate and focus, to activate our mind and body, to connect with nature, to recharge our energy and to inspire ourselves and others to thrive.

As the war for talent intensifies, employees are behaving more like customers; being choosy about who they work for and looking for organisations that convey authentic culture and values in their workplace. Everywhere we look there is now a demand for genuine, authentic experiences. From craft beer, artisan cheeses and locally sourced products, to mindfulness meditation, we are constantly looking for ways to increase our awareness and to reconnect with our humanity, with nature and with a sense of purpose.

We need to bring more humanity into the workplace and provide environments with a new purpose – environments that delight, stimulate, energise and connect us with each other.

Disconnection from community and limited time with family are common stress factors for people in many large cities, that currently rely on commuting, forcing people to travel to the centre every day to work. In London, the 'average' commute time is 74 minutes and the population of the city of London increases by 56 per cent during a normal working day. Leveraging work delocalisation, changes to transport methods and business structures to generate diversified multi-centres, in which coworking spaces become neighbourhood services, thus reducing commute times and car usage will improve not only the work-life balance of millions of people but also will improve local communities and the growth of local economies. Corporations are starting to embrace this by using coworking spaces close to where people live to cut down commute times, access innovative talent through the coworking ecosystem and benefit from 'spaceless growth' – maximising flexibility while minimising fixed costs.

The workplace is now a hub for bringing colleagues together. It has become a 'high-tech coffee shop', where networked individuals meet, share, collaborate and develop ideas, strategies and solutions. As such, the workplace is increasingly being designed and managed less as a static backdrop to routine solitary work, and more as a 'flexible', 'hotel-style' facility that provides a high level of service and experience to its demanding 'guests'.

While we now have four generations at work they are all aligned on their expectations of choice and flexibility, greater transparency, more teamwork and more amenities to support authentic sociability, knowledge, convenience and well-being (Ramidus, 2015).

Puybaraud and Kristensen (2015), looking to 2040, propose a compelling future:

- choice-based restructured patterns of work; personal choice dictates working patterns;
- access to wide range of coworking facilities less than 20 miles away from home;
- mixed facilities in one single location creating a community environment;
- access to a workplace is a reward and provides outstanding experience for users;
- all facilities are multipurpose, mixing different activities (work, leisure, entertainment, sport, medical centres . . .);
- wellness is at the core of our way of living, moving from wearable to implantable;
- service delivery is people-centric and technology-focused to enhance the user experience.

It is easy to see this unfold and how real estate portfolios will increasingly become a dispersed network of workplaces; social and adaptive working environments, empowering users and teams across different work contexts and collaboration modes. Our own workplace will be a menu of coworking environments that leverage our social networks and support our personal needs and aspirations day to day and hour by hour.

This context poses some clear directives for the design, leasing and servicing of buildings:

- *Space* is used as a key medium for expressing corporate culture, brand and values.
- *Design and leasing* for continuous adaptability and diverse usage and patterns.
- *Interiors* are loose-fit and focused on activity-based settings for collaboration, creativity and contemplation.
- *Shared spaces* are used as a means to facilitate collaboration and community.
- *Amenities and service provision*, to support life at work (food, well-being, learning, convenience, etc.).
- *Technology interfaces*, that are intuitive and seamless to improve the user experience.
- *Events* are curated and managed to create memorable experiences and to attract talent.
- The public realm is permeable and designed to reinforce a sense of community and connection to the city.

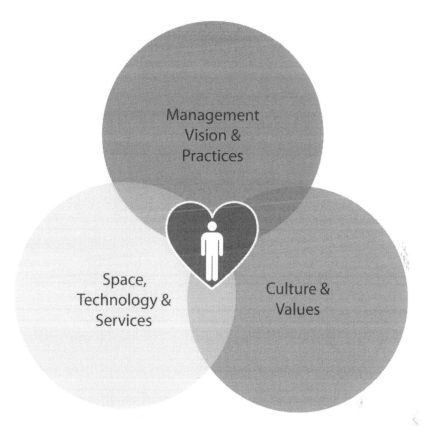

Figure 27.1 Integrate the Corporate Mind (leadership and vision), Body (space and technology) and Spirit (policies and culture) to create people-centric experiences

The design and management of buildings are much less about the 'hardware' of work – the desks, the partitions, technology, electricity, and so on, and much more about the 'software' of work – the cultural, social and value systems of the organisations. A focus on the 'aspirational' aspects of the workplace: empowering workers to do their best work.

The challenge will be breaking down the corporate services silos to integrate workplace and resource planning and focus on creating people-centric experiences (Figure 27.1).

References

BCO (2014) Making the business case for wellbeing. British Council of Offices Research. Available at: www.bco.org.uk/Research/Publications/Making_the_Business_Case_for_Wellbeing.aspx

Beckmann, M., Comelissen, T. and Krakel, M. (2015) *Self Managed Working Time and Employee Effort: Theory and Evidence*. Berlin: Deutsches Institut für Wirtschaftsforschung [German Institute for Economic Research].

Birnbaum, L., Hammond, K. *et al.* (2014) How technology will change the way we work. Paper presented at The Future of Work Conference, Northwestern University, Illinois.

Bowles, J. and Giles, D. (2012) *New Tech City*. New York: Center for an Urban Future.

Coworking Europe Conference (2015) Available at: http://coworking.nexudus.com/en/blog/read/93724634/cw-europe-conference-2015-together-you-go-further

Duffy, F. (2008) *Work and the City*. New York: Black Dog.

Gallup (2015) *State of the American Workplace: Employee Engagement Insights for U.S. Business Leaders*. Gallup. Available at: www.gallup.com/services/178514/state-american-workplace.aspx

Glaeser, E. (2011) *The Triumph of the City*. Harmondsworth: Penguin.

Huffington A. (2014) *Thrive*. New York: Random House.

Intuit (2008) *The Intuit 2020 Report*. Available at: http://about.intuit.com/futureofsmallbusiness

Puybaraud, M. and Kristensen, K. (2015) *Smart Workplace 2040: The Rise of the Workspace Consumer*. Johnson Controls Global Workplace Solutions.

PWC (2014) *Future of Work: A Journey to 2022*. PWC. Available at: www.pwc.com

Ramidus (2014) *Serviced Offices and Agile Occupiers in the City of London*. London: The City of London Corporation.

Ramidus (2015) *Future Workplaces and Future Workstyles in the City of London*. London: The City of London Corporation and The City Property Association.

Rock, D. (2009) *Your Brain at Work*. London: HarperCollins.

Rotman, D. (2013) How technology is destroying jobs. *MIT Technology Review*, June 12.

Schiller, B. (2014) 10 ways the world will get worse in 2015. Fast Company. Available at: www.fastcoexist.com/3038263/10-ways-the-world-will-be-worse-off-in-2015

Schulte, B. (2014) *Overwhelmed: How to Work, Love and Play When No One Has the Time*. New York: Picador.

Thompson, J. and Truch, E. (2013) *The Flex Factor*. RSA Action & Research Center.

Waber, B., Magnolfi, J. and Lindsay, G. (2014) Workspaces that move people. *Harvard Business Review*, 92(10): 68–77.

World Green Building Council (2014) *Health, Wellbeing and Productivity in Offices*. Available at: www.worldgbc.org/activities/health-wellbeing-productivity-offices

Chapter 28

Coda

Derek Clements-Croome

> The major problems in the world are the result of the difference between how nature works and the way people think.
>
> (Gregory Bateson, *An Ecology of Mind*, video, 2012)

In a way, this book is about change. Every generation has new outlooks and attitudes reflected in enormous steps of social change. Think back two generations to one's grandparents and if they returned to the world today how baffling they would find the whole field of human relationships, fashion and technology. In contrast, look forward to our grown-up grandchildren and what they will have witnessed and partaken in across the maelstrom of life and it is difficult to predict. Are there any constants we can foresee?

People want more and more to express their individuality rather than just be absorbed into a seething amorphous mass. Personalisation has become the norm with the advent of the wearable technologies and digital devices embedded in the world around us. Our basic sensory systems have been augmented in so many ways and data collection from our minds, bodies and objects is enhancing our knowledge, eased by the many sophisticated software analytic platforms that have been developed. This is likely to result in a deeper understanding of our interaction with the built environment which is the focus of this book. The WELL Standard and the Flourish models are examples of this and show that holistic thinking, by including medical evidence and absenteeism data, for example, can aid in making good decisions that can increase the probability of achieving good human performance. The Danish word *hygge* (pronounced *hue-gah*) has recently been adopted into our language and means contentment through simple pleasures which can be social or environmental ones.

We know that many building occupants' surveys consistently show that a lack of personal control of the environment is a frequent complaint, and this can be significant in accounting for losses in productivity. However, the main drivers for productivity are health and well-being. The workplace or the place where you work plays a very significant role not only in productivity but also in creativity because the sense of place is an innate ingredient of the everyday human experience. Where we are and what is around us all make our day and imprint our memories. Of course, other factors such as management, organisation, social ambience and personal matters are part of this story too. Increasingly people are choosing the places where they can work most effectively and creatively.

We are living in a more digitally connected world. That can be good but there can be downsides if human interactions are deleted. Take shopping, where a smile between customer and assistant can lift the mood in a way an automatic machine cannot. The argument about replacing people's jobs with robots continues and extends all the way to humanoids. Again, some value can be gained but not always. We speak of artificial intelligence but do we really want artificial emotions too?

Connectivity works in another way too. Developments occur at different paces in various sectors. It is worthwhile to study across sectors to see how ideas might permeate others. We rarely, if ever, have medics at our seminars on the built environment and yet they have a profound understanding and carry out peer-reviewed research on how the body reacts to various environmental stimuli. A similar argument could be made for ergonomists, occupational psychologists and others who could make valuable contributions to building planning and design.

In our work we often need to interact with colleagues but also we need quiet space and time to think and contemplate. The daily onslaught of emails can tire the mind and suck up creative energies. Every week we can read a little more about how the brain and mind work even though an understanding of consciousness eludes us as yet. People can often choose where to work but not always. Multinational organisations still use the traditional office set-up although the newer ones have modern technologies installed. Smaller companies or consultancies may mix working from home or local venues so they are more mobile in choosing places to work. There is nowadays much more interplay between our personal and work lives.

Another aspect that has come to the fore and will last is our connectedness with Nature. With the Industrial Revolution we began to lose it but now we are regaining it. Whether in cities or towns, Nature can be with us outside and inside the building. The medical evidence of its effects on health, mood and well-being is overwhelming. We must never lose this connection again and let biophilic design remain with us and incorporate it into all our city and building plans.

Biophilic design can offer technical as well as health and well-being advantages. The Bio-Intelligent Quotient Building in Hamburg has algae-growing tanks built into part of its façade. The algae can be harvested to make a bio-fuel and this makes a significant contribution to the remaining energy generated by renewable sources. The artificial leaf is another development by Nocera at Harvard University which could feature in façades in the future. Both of these bio-façades depend on photosynthesis which is the very basis of the plant world but they also point to another way that Nature can interplay with architecture.

As our world becomes ever more complex socially and technologically, it is easy to forget simplicity which often has hidden depths, besides giving relief from the rivers of chaos in which we can so easily drown. Over-complex systems can be unreliable, and need constant maintenance and updating. The Jean-Marie Tjibaou Cultural Centre near Noumea in New Caledonia, designed by Renzo Piano, is an example of an intelligent building which is simple in operation using the vernacular Kanak culture as an inspiration, and yet is appealing to the visiting public and copes in an elegant way with the moods of the nearby Pacific Ocean using elegant wooden louvred shields made from the iroko wood.

It is hoped that this book, the product of many contributors based in many diverse disciplines, will be useful and even inspiring or at least will make the reader stop and think.

Index

Page numbers in italics refer to figures. Page numbers in bold refer to tables.